P9-CQO-915

EXPLORING HUMAN BEHAVIOR AND THE SOCIAL ENVIRONMENT

L. ALLEN FURR

University of Louisville

ALLYN AND BACON

Boston   London   Toronto   Sydney   Tokyo   Singapore

For Abby Shapiro and Anna Furr,
my family

Series Editor, Social Work: Judy Fifer
Editor in Chief, Social Sciences: Karen Hanson
Editorial Assistant: Jennifer Jacobson
Marketing Manager: Quinn Perkson
Editorial Production Service: Chestnut Hill Enterprises, Inc.
Manufacturing Buyer: Megan Cochran
Cover Administrator: Suzanne Harbison

Copyright © 1997 by Allyn & Bacon
A Pearson Education Company
Needham Heights, MA 02194

All rights reserved. No part of the material protected by this copyright notice may be reproduced or utilized in any form or by any means, electronic or mechanical, including photocopying, recording, or by any information storage and retrieval system, without written permission from the copyright holder.

Library of Congress Cataloging-in-Publication Data
Furr, LeRoy Allen,
    Exploring human behavior and the social environment / L. Allen Furr.
      p. cm.
    Includes bibliographical references and index.
    ISBN 0-13-148727-2 (hardcover)
    1. Social service.   2. Human behavior.   3. Social role.
  4. Context effects (Psychology)   I. Title.
  HV40.F87   1996
302—dc20   96-14465
                                                     CIP

Printed in the United States of America
10 9 8 7 6 5 4 3 2   01 00 99 98 97 96

Photo Credits:

Photo credits are found on page 417, which should be considered an extension of the copyright page.

CONTENTS

Exploring the Issues

PREFACE

I introduce the course called "Human Behavior and Social Environment" to social work students by offering the following metaphor. I ask them how they would study the behavior of a particular species of fish that lives in the ocean. Students quickly agree that catching a specimen of the species and putting it on the deck of the boat would tell us little about its behavior. Students further concede that placing the fish in an artificial aquarium setting would tell us a little more, but would not give us the whole picture of the fish's lifestyle.

I then ask, "What is missing?" And they all say, "The ocean!" "What is it about the ocean that makes it such a key ingredient in understanding the fish's behavior?" I ask. The students then proceed to tell me about the fish's role in the food chain as well as its mating habits and survival strategies. We also talk about the water itself and humans' influences on the sea: pollution, global warming, overfishing, and so forth. In other words, they neatly explain the fish's systematic relationships with its environment.

Then I ask them how my "fish story" concerns human behavior and their futures as social workers? We discuss that humans, too, live in a metaphoric "ocean." If we were to try to understand people's behavior out of their natural context of relationships with other people, memberships in communities, involvements with institutions, and relationships with the natural environment, would we have an accurate picture of human behavior? We conclude by agreeing that, to be a competent social work practitioner, a student must master the notion that, to understand the fish, one must understand the ocean.

This book is about the human "ocean." Its goal is to introduce students to the notion that individuals' behaviors are a function of their interactions with the bio-psycho-social contexts in which they are situated. Consequently, considerable attention is paid to the various aspects of those environments. Topics such as the effects of social class and community on behavior are given considerable attention. How individuals and groups relate to political and economic systems and bureaucracies are important themes as well.

The book focuses strongly on diversity. It has five chapters devoted to human diversity: communities, social class, ethnicity, gender, and sexual orientation. Furthermore, the family and life cycle chapters include important discussions related to gender, ethnicity, and sexual orientation. Pertaining to diversity, discussions on physical health, mental well-being, family patterns, involvement with groups, and relations with institutions are stressed.

Chapter 1 introduces the framework used in this book. This chapter divides the environment into six domains, or influences on human development and well-being, and then argues that deficits in those domains are the sources of human problems. Chapters 2 through 6 discuss individual development over the life cycle. Chapters 7 through 11 discuss the characteristics of a number of communities and social groups. Finally, Chapters 12 through 14 examine family organization, diversity, and problems.

From a pedagogical standpoint, the book has one main objective. It argues that students must look beyond the personal characteristics of clients when conducting assessments and planning and executing interventions. It is assumed here that assessment accuracy lies in relating clients to the web of systems to which they are undoubtedly connected. Systems, both large and small, influence people's emotions, thinking, and behavior. The pedagogical goal, therefore, is to train students to think in terms of transactions with systems and to avoid solely individualistic perceptions of behavior.

Each chapter begins with a case study from the author's practice files. All cases portray accurate accounts of clients' situations, although names and other identifying information have been changed to protect their confidentiality and privacy. General questions pertaining to the cases are found at the end of each chapter. These questions connect the case to each chapter's content.

My wish is that in some way this book facilitates your growth as a social work professional. Social workers have one agenda, and that is to help their clients free themselves from oppression, pain, and unhappiness. If this book contributes to that honorable goal, then my labors are rewarded.

There are a number of people who deserve recognition for their contributions to the production of this book. I am fortunate to be surrounded by many wonderful friends, colleagues, and family members, and, over the course of the two years required to write this text, many were asked either to read something or to listen to some idea. I also appreciate everyone's tolerance of my being so preoccupied and absentminded for those same two years.

I am particularly indebted to Dr. S. Abby Shapiro, my wife, best friend, and favorite editor. She helped organize the basic framework of the book and contributed considerable insight on several topics. I also want to recognize the contributions of Dr. Barbara Grissett of East Texas State University. Not only did she write one of the chapters of the text, she also provided a valuable critique of the original plan of the book and the chapters once they were written. Thanks also go to Drs. Ara Lewellen and Linda Kraus for commenting on the manuscript. I would like to acknowledge two student assistants who made my job easier. Leah Davis contributed her excellent library skills and Ruhiyyih Henderson helped research several topics and made special contributions on the section dealing with minority women and AIDS. Special thanks go to Dr. Jon Rieger, of the University of Louisville, and to Ms. Sarah Kovich, who practices in Dallas, Texas.

I also want to thank Dr. Willie Edwards, Dr. Bill Thompson, both of East Texas State University, and Dr. Tom Keil of the University of Louisville for their friendship, encouragement, and support.

The following reviewers are acknowledged for their contribution: Sharon Eisen, Mott Community College; Charles W. Mueller, University of Hawaii; Brett Seabury, University of Michigan; Rose Marie Penzerro, Our Lady of the Lake University; Woo Sik Chung, Boston College; Katherine M. Dunlap, University of North Carolina–Chapel Hill; Steven R. Rose, Louisiana State University; Patricia W. Ivry, Western Connecticut State University; Joseph Steiner, Syracuse University; and Larry W. Sheffield, La Sierra University.

Finally, I want to give special mention to Judy Fifer and Karen Hanson of Allyn and Bacon. Their support and expertise were indispensable. A writer could not ask for better editorial guidance.

L. Allen Furr

CHAPTER 1

THE CONTEXT OF
HUMAN LIFE

OBJECTIVES

After reading this chapter, you should be able to answer the following questions:

1. Why is studying human behavior in the social environment important for social work practice?
2. What do social workers mean by "the person-in-environment" framework and what is its relationship to social work knowledge and skill?
3. What are the components of the environment that impinge upon human development?
4. How is performing social roles significant for understanding human development?
5. What is systems theory? How does a systems approach facilitate assessment?
6. What is structural social work practice theory?

CASE STUDY

John is a fourteen-year-old European American who had been ordered by a judge to see a social worker after being arrested for theft. John and three friends were caught by police officers breaking into automobiles, stealing radios and the cars' contents. A few days after being processed by the court, John's mother, Martha, made an appointment to see the social worker at a sliding scale counseling agency.

John arrived at the agency with his mother and his father, Bill. John was polite, clean, and dressed as one would expect from a teenager. Martha and Bill were cordial and dressed casually. During the first interview, Martha did most of the talking. She often answered for her son and made it hard for the others to express their views. Bill's body language was very closed throughout the interview. He contributed little information and seemed put off by the entire process. When he did speak, he gave short answers that revealed little useful information. Bill and Martha agreed that John's behavior was wrong and that they would not tolerate it. They also agreed that "something was wrong with him." Thus their expectation of social work intervention was to "fix" their son.

Bill was a forty-one-year-old mechanic. He had graduated from high school and had learned his trade in vocational school. He served two years as a private in the military before marrying Martha. He indicated no aspirations for doing anything different with his life. His annual income was about $22,000.

Martha was forty years of age. She also was a high school graduate and worked as a secretary for a small business. She earned about $17,000 a year. She and Bill dated during high school and they were married as soon as he returned from his military duty. She became pregnant with her first son, Thomas, within the first year of their marriage.

Thomas, who never attended any of the meetings with the social worker, was eighteen years old and was about to graduate from high school.

He did well in school and, according to his parents, had never had any problems. Thomas kept to himself and had few friends.

John's marks in school were barely passing. He showed little interest in school and did not participate in extracurricular activities. He had no real plans for the future and did not show any motivation or drive. John sat passively through the interview, allowing his parents to talk for him. John had no explanation for his behavior. He denied having any problems and never revealed any of his own feelings or ideas about his situation.

THE SOCIAL WORK FRAME OF MIND

What frame of mind do we need to understand John's behavior? One way would be to isolate John and think of him as completely autonomous, as if his behavior happened in a social vacuum. This way of thinking, however, neglects the influences that other people and relationships in his social surroundings have on his "symptoms." To cut off John from his social environment, and then try to understand him, would be like trying to study a fish's behavior without also knowing about the ocean in which the fish lives.

The social worker working with this family knew to avoid this mental trap. In the following interviews, he began to assess the dynamics of John's family life, the neighborhood he lived in, and his family's relationship to the community. After further probing, the social worker learned that John was "lost." John was not a bad child; he was a desperate child seeking to find ways to cope with a world that frustrated him.

On broadening the scope of the assessment, the social worker learned a great deal more about this family. John's family had many troubles, though his mother and father worked hard to conceal them. Bill and Martha actually fought a great deal. Tension escalated quickly in their marriage and they shared little affection or commitment. Bill went out every Friday and Saturday to dance halls and drank heavily. He worked long hours during the week and, when he came home, he rarely interacted with his family.

Martha eventually admitted that she coped with this tension and his absences by abusing prescription drugs. The drugs gave her a sensation of detachment and euphoria; they "removed" her problems. Another way she responded to the marital conflict was by keeping her sons very close to her, elevating them to become her peers. Thomas's leaving for college made her turn toward John for emotional comfort and solace. In many ways, she was desperate for attention from John.

The family also had financial problems. Their incomes barely made ends meet, especially considering that Bill spent a great deal of money on his weekend adventures. Bill was very frustrated in his work because he knew he would never make a high salary and he had no chances for advancement. Both Bill and Martha found their work meaningless and boring. They often argued over money and worried about layoffs. Neither had health insurance.

With this new information, how might we understand John's behavior? As a fourteen-year-old, John is in the early stages of adolescence and thus has strong desires to pull away from his family. Doing so in this family is difficult because his mother is trying to pull him closer to her and his father largely ignores him and has failed to give him guidance or a structure for handling the pressures of adolescence. Bill and Martha are frequently absent, both physically and emotionally, as is his big brother who is a loner and emotionally detached. So John is often alone without supervision or anything meaningful to do.

In response to the lack of strong family relationships and the lack of accessible resources due to the family's low income, John turns to peers who offer him excitement and, most importantly, acceptance. They give him the kind of structure and attention he craves from his parents. These peers, unfortunately, also value nonconformity and deviant behavior. To get his acceptance and belongingness needs met, John committed his crime and was arrested.

If the social worker had not explored John's situation more deeply, he would have missed the context and meaning of the undesired behavior.

Otherwise, the worker's interventions would have essentially had a blaming and judgmental flavor to them and would have added to John's frustrations about not being understood. By opening up the social context of the behavior for assessment, the worker began to see John's behavior as a function, or consequence, of that environment, hence expanding the likelihood of planning an intervention that would help John *and* his family deal with their problems.

This book is about the social work frame of mind. This way of thinking enables a social work practitioner to understand individual behavior within the scope of the larger social scene in which individuals live their lives. The social work frame of mind rejects the notion that individuals are autonomous and self-standing. Instead it holds that the social systems in which people live profoundly affect individual development and behavior. Resolving problems by assessing the meaning of behaviors amid their context is the key to successful social work practice. The social work quality of mind allows practitioners to grasp the relationship between individual behavior and the social world that envelopes it. It is a consciousness, a way of understanding why people do the things they do. It is how social workers see the world, a world where everything is interrelated.

THE PERSON-IN-ENVIRONMENT

Fortunately, human behavior is not random. People act with orderly and predictable regularity. Because people are social beings, they are required to organize their experiences and expectations so that they can live together, reach their goals, and survive. Organized living is indeed indispensable to human existence. If human actions were random, the species would not endure.

Human beings are born into organized social, psychological, and natural contexts that, combined, constitute the human environment. Specifically, the *environment* consists of the recurrent and organized experiences and conditions repeatedly encountered by an individual or group over the course of time. The environment provides a set of circumstances that govern individuals' basic orientations to life and includes the characteristics of the social and psychological worlds around them.

The environment is preexisting; that is, it is in place before a person enters the world, and continues after the person is gone. The environment prescribes the ranges of acceptable behavior and regulates human experiences. How external conditions encroach on people and how they respond to them determines in large part the kind of people they become and the lives they will lead. Life is predictable and systematic because the environment is stable. People incorporate the environment into their sense of self.

Social work knowledge is grounded in the philosophical assumption that human development and problems are the result of how individuals and groups are rooted ecologically in their environment. Without studying the context in which a person or group exists, social workers cannot fully comprehend the complexities of human experiences. The focal point of social work research and practice, and indeed the benchmark of the profession, is to develop a body of knowledge and skills that (1) illuminates the interrelatedness of individuals and their surroundings, and (2) improves the interactions between people and their social environment.

The Nature of the Environment

It is a mistake to think of the environment as a solitary concept. To the contrary, the environment is complex and multifaceted. In social work practice it is useful to divide the environment into six *domains* or spheres that impact human functioning. Each of these domains has important implications for understanding human behavior. The domains of the environment are: (1) culture; (2) the social environment; (3) the psychological domain; (4) biology; (5) physical and spatial settings; and (6) nature. All six spheres interact with each other. They influence and are influenced by human actions. Taken in sum, they constitute the environment of human existence (See Figure 1.1).

The Cultural Domain

Think of yourself as a newcomer to your hometown. Even if you have lived there your entire life, imagine yourself as an immigrant to that place.

FIGURE 1.1 Six Domains of the Environment

DOMAIN	EXPRESSIONS	MECHANISMS OF INFLUENCE
Culture	Material and nonmaterial creations; patterns of lifestyle	Norms, values
Social Domain	Organized relationships; status-positions; categorical identity	Wealth & power; roles; institutional practices
Psychological Domain	Psychological impact of social forces; psychic dynamics among people within milieu	Security; emotions; intellectual stimulation; response to life cycle
Biological Domain	Physiological makeup of organisms	Provides limits; genetics, illness & injury; life cycle
Natural Domain	The natural world	Climate; topography; resources
Physical & Spatial Setting	The "built" world	Density; arrangement & quality of spaces & buildings; security; familiarity

You don't know the language or customs of the people there and everything seems foreign. You soon realize that people are acting in coordination with each other: they understand each other, share symbolic meanings, and hold similar values. The rules of appropriate conduct that govern this behavior were established prior to your arrival, so one of your primary tasks as an outsider is to adjust yourself to conform to those rules so that you can live successfully in that environment.

Now come back to being a native. As with the immigrant, even as a native your home culture was foreign to you until you learned it. In other words, people are born into, or immigrate to, preexisting cultural conditions that specify how things are done. Culture largely determines which behaviors the group will tolerate and which it will not.

Human beings, unlike other animals, are born without rigid biological determinants of appropriate behavior. There are no instincts, behavioral mandates that appear in all normal members of a species. The human neurological system (brain and spinal cord) is too complex for such a relatively simple organic construct. Rather than having biological directives that override volition, humans produce cultures that serve as blueprints for social living.

The *cultural environment* consists of all the material and nonmaterial creations of a social group. In essence, culture is a design for living and consists not only of the physical objects that people use and assign meaning, but of abstractions such as language, beliefs, ideas, customs, skills, and family patterns. Furthermore, culture determines the individual's philosophical understanding of life. As people grow up, they unconsciously make conforming to cultural abstractions a part of themselves, rarely questioning their correctness. This process, called *internalization,* leads people to conform automatically to cultural expectations (Robertson 1987).

Societies have dominant cultural patterns that a majority of people and groups share. Practices and sentiments, such as a common language, political philosophy, and religion, provide a cultural core that serves as a framework within which people organize their daily lives. Within most populations, however, there are groups that maintain preferences, styles, and modes of thought that are distinct in various degrees from the dominant culture. Within populations, cultural differences may arise among those who differ in wealth, national origin, race, religion, and sexual orientation. People in these groups have a way of life that contradicts the dominant culture, often leaving them in conflict with the mainstream culture.

Mechanisms of Influence. Culture influences behavior through shared rules and symbolic meanings.

Norms are standards and guidelines for appropriate behavior in particular situations. Norms specify how people ought to act and insure that social life proceeds smoothly (Robertson 1987). The pressure to conform to norms is so intense that we often forget that norms are relative to time and place.

As the classical American sociologist, William Sumner, discovered, there are two types of norms that differ according to the degree the rule is considered important by the social group. First, folkways are the ordinary customs and habits of a group or community. Eating with a knife and fork and wearing gender-appropriate clothing are examples of folkways. The punishment for breaking a folkway is usually not severe. The violator may be labeled eccentric or odd, but typically is not treated as a criminal.

Second, *mores* (pronounced "mor-ays") designate ways of acting to which people attach a moral significance. Mores are behaviors and thoughts that groups consider essential for public welfare. People who violate mores often elicit strong emotional reactions, and punishments for such violations, therefore, are more grave. Examples of mores include childraising practices, covering genitals in public, and honoring the property of others. Some mores are written into law. In these cases, the punishments are also codified and are applied somewhat objectively.

Values are a group's ideas of right and wrong, good and bad, and acceptable and unacceptable.

Values represent a group's projection of worth. Norms are expressions of values; groups expect behavior that is consistent with the abstractions of worth. Respect for sacred artifacts, such as the national flag, capitalism, individualism, and materialism are examples of core values. People and rhetoric that challenge these values are branded as abhorrent and as violating "our way of life." Social groups that advocate values that dramatically differ from the mainstream are often resisted, expelled, or written off as eccentric.

Within heterogeneous populations, values often conflict. While groups may hold values that oppose those considered "official," compliance to these "official" values is still expected. For example, the family life of racial and ethnic minorities is often judged according to European American middle-class family standards. Because many groups in American society have different cultural traditions, parenting and marital styles may not match those customs of Anglo Americans. Sometimes dominant values are passed along as neutral or as desirable, without considering the relative nature or inherent qualities of the values.

Social workers need to be aware of the cultural practices of their clients. Assessing the meanings of clients' norms and values is essential in planning a successful intervention. Sensitivity to cultural features works within clients' cultural framework and makes social work intervention less threatening.

The Social Environment

Whereas culture represents the styles of life shared by a people, the social environment is active life itself. The social environment refers to patterns of behavior. The social environment has three levels: repeated relationships, arrangements of social positions, and categorical identity.

At the first level, the social environment refers to institutionalized practices shared by a group of people. Specifically, the term represents the interactions between people. The repetitive actions of people have structure; that is, these patterns have an organization of predictability (Blau 1977).

Second, the social environment defines the patterns of *status-positions,* which are placements in a social organization or population. Group members relate to each other based on the statuses within it. For example, on first meeting someone most people notice the other's major indicators of

Roles in families are no longer as rigid as they were in times past. Social and cultural changes have blurred the traditional household division of labor. Men are more involved in the everyday tasks of parenting as the sociocultural environment becomes more supportive of their changing identity. Women, however, continue to perform more household chores than men.

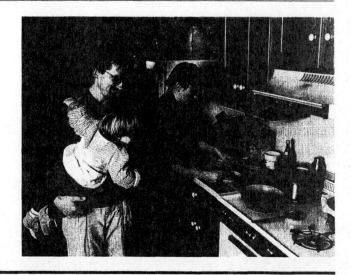

status such as sex and age. Their behavior is likely to be based to some degree on the meanings the person attaches to those qualities. Many people act differently toward men than they do around women, for example.

Each status-position has roles, behaviors attached to and expected of the position. Assessing families, for example, includes having family members express their interpretations of their place in that family. How are family members treated because of the positions they hold? What is expected of the mother, father, wife and husband positions? Do expectations for these statuses differ by gender?

Finally, social environments provide meaningful categorical identities that affect, channel, or constrain behavior (Warriner 1970). There are two types of social categories. First, people respond to *ascribed statuses* (those which are assigned to them) in fairly predictable ways. What does it mean to be a woman or a homosexual in society at large and in interpersonal interactions? Why is it that African Americans and Hispanics are overrepresented in poverty?

People respond to *achieved statuses* as well (those positions gained through effort and choice). People often defer and acquiesce to persons holding positions perceived as having greater social import. Physicians, lawyers, and wealthy businesspersons generally control interpersonal communication with people who hold positions considered lower in status.

Social Institutions.   *Social institutions* are expansive social systems designed to meet societal needs. An institution is not a specific organization like a corporation, school, or family, but represents the system that links similar organizations together. Accordingly, there are six social institutions. One, the economic system functions to meet a society's subsistence needs. It regulates the production and distribution of goods and services and distributes wealth. Two, the polity functions to provide law and order. It represents society's need to govern itself, maintain group security, settle disputes, and regulate enterprise. Three, education

is the system of transmitting a culture's knowledge, skills, and heritage to newcomers. It prepares children and adults for adult status-positions and socializes them into important norms, values, and personal characteristics. Four, the institution of religion takes care of spiritual needs and provides a code of morality. Important for social cohesion, religion unites groups and contributes to personal and group identity. Five, the family institution is society's strategy for regulating sexual behavior, reproducing, providing emotional security for children, and meeting the emotional and intimacy needs of adults. Although the composition and functions of the family have changed more than other institutions in the last half century, the family persists as the primary source of emotional attachment and affection. Finally, the media function to meet communication needs.

Mechanisms of Influence.   The social environment affects behavior and development institutionally and interpersonally. Decisions by those people who control social institutions exert tremendous, though sometimes covert, influence over what people do, what their preferences and desires are, and even how they respond emotionally to certain situations. Global trade and financial practices affect Mexican immigration to the United States; political strife in Haiti and Cuba, among other places, pushes many people, especially the poor and disenfranchised, to leave their homes and move to a foreign country. The media affect people's tastes, values, and to a certain extent, their behavior.

Those people who control wealth and power in a society or smaller group are in a position to shape the policies that command conformity from the group's members. These dictates range from quality of life issues such as the salaries, wages, and benefits paid to employees to mundane everyday behaviors. An example of the latter occurred when social workers and other staff members in a hospital's psychiatric unit were instructed by administrators how to end telephone conversations. Staff members were ordered to say "good-bye" rather than "bye" or "bye-bye," which are common expressions. Management actually conducted covert, bogus phone calls to monitor the policy. Violators were given demerits.

The social environment directly influences behavior as individuals play out their *roles*, which are the behaviors assigned to status-positions. Throughout the course of people's lives they move in and out of numerous status-positions, each commanding countless behavioral expectations. Daily pressure not to deviate from role expectations means that they must adjust their impulses and desires to maximize role performance. Conforming to roles has practical implications. Individuals could not hold jobs, for example, if they didn't conform to the demands of occupational positions.

Roles instill in people acceptable patterns of responsible behavior. They learn what being a good boy or girl is and what someone does by discovering and playing out the roles attached to social labels. Norms and values validate roles, giving them legitimation and objective definitions. Because social roles are firmly rooted in cultural standards, it difficult to violate a role's expectations.

Many roles are identified in relation to a broader societal context. Behaviors are often grouped together in discrete contexts "as a way of making sense of disparate behaviors in different contexts" (Turner 1982: 375). There are father and mother roles, male and female gender roles, and child and adult age roles (Turner 1982). Roles that have particular value in the social world elicit social reactions from others, and help us adapt effectively and anchor our self-conceptions. Major status-positions become important indicators of self and public identity and gauges of social competence. Most people, for example, identify with and place significance on their racial or ethnic category, gender, age, family position, or occupation as often if not more than personality traits. The more people identify with roles, the more committed they are to the group or system in which that role is based.

In some circumstances, the status-positions people hold create difficulties for them. Intrapersonal stress and interpersonal troubles often arise when the performance of roles is impeded by the demands of the structured expectation. *Role strain* occurs when a person has difficulty meeting the demands of the status-position. For example, single mothers who earn a low income may feel stress and depressive symptoms when they are unable to provide basic housing and medical care for their families. Low wages do not allow single parents to buy basic necessities, which is expected as part of the role attached to the mother position. Thus single mothers often experience intrapersonal stress. *Role conflict* occurs when the performance of one role violates or contradicts another role. Let's say that a single mother is offered a better paying job, one that would allow her to improve her quality of life. This job, however, requires her to work nights, which would take her away from her children. The two roles, mother and employee, are incompatible, unless the children's father or some other support can be found to help.

Social workers need to assess clients' relationship to their social environment. Concerning institutions and roles, for example, it is important to learn the following: How do clients interact with social institutions? Are clients economically successful? Are they members of social groups that lack political strength? How do they feel about what is expected of them? Did they choose their roles or were they imposed on them? Are roles stressful? How do they respond to that stress?

The Psychological Domain

The *psychological domain* refers to the psychological aspects of the social systems in which people live (Tajfel 1981). The psychological realm involves the patterns of emotions and behaviors of others that are open to direct experience. The psychological domain constitutes events that impact the behavioral, emotional, and cognitive maturation of individuals and families. It involves those interpersonal processes that affect intrapersonal qualities such as motivation, perception, intelligence, and emotional responsiveness. The psychological sphere is composed of: (1) the psychological impact of social forces, and (2) the set of repetitive psychological dynamics of nearby individuals: their emotions, personality traits, cognitive styles and abilities, and behaviors.

Mechanisms of Influence. Features of the psychological environment are as much fixtures in the developmental landscape as are economic and social realities. In general, the psychological environment affects personality development, role performance, emotional expressions, and intellectual functioning through four mechanisms: security, the emotional climate, intellectual stimulation, and responses to life-cycle development.

To raise healthy children, the environment must provide physical and emotional security. Children need to feel protected from danger and uncertainty. Living in a familiar, stable place and having parents who act predictably and protectively help children feel comfortable in their surroundings. Should the immediate environment expose children to violence, abuse, and other physical and emotional risks, they are more likely to become anxious and have a harder time adjusting to other people and feeling good about themselves.

The emotional tone of one's environment has a strong effect on human development. While some emotions, such as fear and sadness, are innate for infant survival (Izard 1991), other emotions, such as guilt, shame, and grief, are known as social emotions and develop through social interactions. Individuals share feelings, imitate the emotions of people around them, and infect others with their feelings (Denzin 1984). They interpret the emotions of others, learning to anticipate the emotional conditions of objects and people in the environment. For example, even before seeing an exam, you might feel anxious and worry about your performance and being evaluated. People do the same with other individuals: They learn to have certain emotions in anticipation of their predictable emotional state with which they have become accustomed.

The recurrent emotional atmosphere leads people toward important conclusions about themselves. They interpret others' emotions, especially those of family members, as indicative of their judgments of them. If the interpretations are sufficiently reinforced, they will be incorporated as emotions about self-worth and desirability (Denzin 1984). For example, people are likely to translate loving, supportive, and nurturing emotional surroundings into positive feelings about themselves. "I am a good person," so one might think, "because others treat me with respect, listen to my thoughts, and accept me as I am." Conversely, a tense, negative, and abusive emotional climate may be interpreted as people's response to a bad, worthless person. Hostility may be read as negative feedback to one's own character, which might foster feelings of worthlessness, self-doubt, and helplessness.

Intelligence, long a controversial topic in both sociology and psychology, is a function of the interplay between genetic makeup and environmental stimulation. Children whose minds are invigorated by creative and challenging activities and, perhaps most importantly, are rewarded for being "smart," maximize their innate biological capabilities. Intellectual stimulation comes from learning toys, being read to, and having intellectual activities such as reading and writing modeled by parents. Children's learning abilities improve if the environment defines education and academic skills as having value and a real payoff. Cognitive abilities vary by social class, for example, because poor children are not exposed to environmental cues that challenge them intellectually. Parents who are well-meaning may not be able to afford books and other learning toys for young children. If they are not well-educated themselves, parents might have difficulty assisting children with their studies or finding enjoyment in reading. For children to learn, they need an environment that poses academic challenges that make sense to them and reward them for doing well.

Each stage of the life cycle involves unique needs, goals, and relationships to the environment. How the environment reacts to developmental stages affects an individual's transition from one stage to the next. If people in the environment respond appropriately to a child's age and intellectual ability, then children are more likely to engage in behaviors suitable to their developmental level. If, however, parents and other significant people are out of sync with a child's developmental level, then the child will have great difficulty moving to the next level. For example, some parents insist upon turning their children into "little gentlemen" and "little ladies" long before they are capable of adult behaviors. Forcing children to grow up ahead of their intellectual and emotional abilities may lead to angry and rebellious behavior. Similarly, denying a child's maturation, for instance treating a teenager like an elementary-aged child, also can create conflict and emotional disturbance. As developmental needs change, the environment must adjust itself to accommodate those changing needs.

Assessing the emotional atmosphere of clients' environment is critical. The failure of the psychological domain to provide a sense of emotional security can have far-reaching affects on behavior. The same is true for intellectual stimulation. Social workers should assess how environments promote and encourage learning. It is often the case that barriers to emotional and cognitive fulfillment are found in the social environment. A key to a successful assessment is to point out those linkages when they appear.

The Biological Domain

The *biological domain* refers to the physiological makeup of a human organism. Social workers are inclined to overlook the biological components of behavior, emotions, and cognitive ability, yet there is no question that physiology influences personality and psychological development. To say that biological qualities are singular determining factors in behavior and emotions, however, is as far-fetched as disregarding them altogether. The long-standing contest between "nature" and "nurture" as discrete causes of human behavior and personality is moot. The character and content of behaviors, thoughts, and emotions are the by-products of the interaction between one's social, psychological, and biological resources. Any attempt to understand human dynamics must in-

clude an assessment of biological functioning and possible impairments.

Mechanisms of Influence.   Symbolic thinking, consciousness, and creativity are qualities that distinguish humans from other animals and they are functions of sophisticated neurological and muscular–skeletal processes. How chemistry affects people's social and psychological selves, and vice versa, is largely unknown. Nevertheless there are four general ways in which biology is important to human behavior (Longres 1990).

First, biophysical states and processes provide the outer limits of human development. One cannot exceed biological capabilities. Age, for example, not only signifies social status, but enables, or disables individuals from engaging in certain behaviors. Several examples illustrate this point. A ten-year-old, for example, has neither the strength nor stamina to keep up physically with a young adult. Once they reach middle adulthood, individuals' reaction time to stimuli declines with age. One individual may be more vulnerable to certain diseases than another person may be. For example, a survivor of scarlet fever is more vulnerable to heart disease. In sum, people must all live within their biological boundaries.

Second, genetic inheritance has a profound impact on human development. People are not biogenetic copies of each other; they have a unique genetic endowment that defines their capacities. Individual tastes and predispositions probably stem from genes that set limits for what people can and cannot do. While geneticists are learning more about the influence of genes on personality, their knowledge of genes remains primitive. It is likely, however, that genetic blueprints are contributing factors in certain types of mental illness, such as schizophrenia and major depression. Recent research has found an increasing number of genetic links to physical illnesses as well, including many neurological disorders, disorders of the endocrine system, and possibly cancer.

Third, illness, injury, or disability may lead to modified behavior, affect, and mental adeptness.

From your own experience, you know that having a cold or the flu alters your mood and ability to concentrate for a relatively short duration. A long-term illness, especially one that restricts ordinary functions, can negatively affect psychological well-being. Stroke, AIDS, kidney disease, among many other disorders, impair the sufferer's psychological functioning.

Fourth, biology affects individuals differently throughout the life cycle. As they mature physically, people are capable of different, more complicated tasks. Women are capable of bearing children only during the years between menarche and menopause, for example. At some point in time, however, individuals' bodies betray them and they experience a decline in physical prowess and, possibly, in mental competence as well. As people age, their bodies slow down, stiffen, and perform with less reliability than during younger ages. Consequently, activities requiring physical stamina and quick reflexes are not performed with the same keenness as before.

Social workers should assess clients' current physical condition, medical history, and the age-related effects on behavior.

The Natural Environment

The *natural environment* is comprised of the natural world inherited by humans. It represents the geographical conditions influencing a community of people and includes climate conditions, the topographical structure of the region, and the availability and scarcity of valuable natural resources.

Mechanisms of Influence.   Geography is the study of the relationship between Earth and human organizations. The forms of many cultural characteristics and social practices, such as economic systems, products and inventions, clothing styles, and habitats, emanate from the challenges and resources of the physical environment.

It is especially important to weigh the impact of geographical changes on people who have immigrated from one place to another. For example, a great deal of social life in tropical Haiti is organized around the front porch, a traditional meeting place for informal gatherings. On porches, friends and relatives exchange news and gossip, make business deals, and solidify relationships. This important feature of Haitian life is disrupted following immigration to New York and New Jersey, where winters are long and cold. This change in climate has resulted in greater isolation of Haitian families and individuals and has made immigration a more difficult ordeal than it might otherwise have been.

Physical and Spatial Environment

The *physical environment,* the last of the six spheres, is comprised of the built world constructed by human beings (Germain & Gitterman 1986). It is comprised of treasured objects, buildings, streets, places, and spatial patterns. The quality of a community's infrastructure affects its ability to achieve goals and emotional security. One component of infrastructure, transportation for example, provides means for getting to work, participating in leisure activities, and acquiring necessary services.

Mechanisms of Influence.   Physical surroundings create a terrain in which people live their lives. This human-constructed topography affects people's efforts to meet basic needs, most important of which is safety. Inferior physical surroundings have been linked to stress for individuals, families, and communities. Inadequate housing, costly transportation, and poorly maintained buildings jeopardize a person's feelings of security and attachment. The quality of one's material surroundings can have a profound impact on self-esteem, attitudes, social opportunities, and physical health as well.

Emotional security is connected to loyalty, comfort, and familiarity with places. Identity is closely tied to a sense of place in broad terms—a city, region, or country—and in specific terms—a particular house, a room, or a special spot (Germain & Gitterman 1986). People are so attached to physical spaces that they exhibit "territorial" behaviors: sitting in the same seat in class and having a "place" at the dinner table, for example.

Attachments to spaces become clear when people lose them; they are likely to feel uncomfortably out of place or even anxious and depressed.

The density of a population influences behavior, attitudes, and social arrangements. Overcrowded conditions affect the amount of space available to each person. In large families and densely populated urban areas where many people share a limited amount of personal and public space, respectively, the degree of interpersonal coordination required often creates considerable stress (Germain & Gitterman 1986).

When several people have to share a limited space, conflicts over using the space are inevitable. Families become overloaded when they have one bathroom, one television, and few drawers. Family members possess less personal space and do not fully control what they do have. Satisfactory levels of privacy are difficult to attain in overcrowded conditions. Every person needs some time alone to relax, reflect on thoughts and feelings, and temporarily disengage from stress. Privacy is necessary for personal autonomy (Germain & Gitterman 1986). Teenagers especially need time alone to observe their changing bodies and experiment with styles of fashion.

Finally, the arrangement of immovable objects, such as hallways and elevators, has an impact on quality of life (Germain & Gitterman 1986). Many housing projects designed during the Urban Renewal movement of the 1960s were later destroyed because they were built for architectural efficiency rather than the living needs of tenants. Residents complained of poorly lit and unprotected stairways, numerous "hiding places," places where children could easily go unsupervised and where criminal behavior was hidden, and many other problems. These kinds of conditions made coming home burdensome and unsafe. Assessments of client conditions should include an analysis of their spatial relationships.

Conclusion

For the social worker's purposes, the cultural, social, and psychological spheres are the most im-portant because they constitute the subject matter of social work and related helping professions. This does not suggest that the other three make no less a contribution to human development and that social workers should not be aware of their dynamics. Social workers, for the most part, specialize in interventions within the psychosocial realms of client systems and consider the influence that the biophysical and geographic domains have on psychosocial functioning. Other professions selectively concentrate on other dimensions of human development. Medicine, for example, focuses on the physiological needs of clients with a secondary priority placed on their psychosocial development.

The psychosocial environment often acts on people coercively. On many occasions they follow the expectations of norms, values, roles, and ideologies when they would prefer not to do so, when they might be better off having not done so, or when they have no choice. For example, public expressions of affection are regulated by heterosexual norms. Consequently, many gays and lesbians are pressured into refraining from simple displays of intimacy such as holding hands in public, a behavior that heterosexuals take for granted. In a related example, ideologies often exclude gays and lesbians from participating in mainstream religions because many religious dogmas forbid homosexual behavior.

CREATING SOCIAL ENVIRONMENTS

Up to this point, I have described the relationship between the environment and human behavior as a deterministic process in which environmental conditions appear to "cause" behavior. It is important to remember, however, that causality goes both ways. Environments are created by human behavior. Just as environments shape who people become—by conforming to role expectations, norms, and values for example—they simultaneously create their environments as well.

As you can see in Figure 1.2, as people act out their roles, they consciously or unconsciously decide between two choices as to how they will engage the role. They can either change themselves to conform to the expectations of the status-position, or they can change the role to meet their own needs and expectations. Both decisions result in the ongoing construction of the psychosocial environment. Accepting and conforming to norms, roles, and values that were already there reinforces and, hence, perpetuates them. Thus the environment continues.

The second choice is to modify the expectations of a status-position to accommodate values and preferences that vary from the preexisting ones. How people play out roles is based on their subjective interpretation of what is expected. Whereas some roles are clearly described, others, such as husband, wife, father, and mother, are not. Individuals will act those out according to what they believe is expected and what they bring to the role in terms of needs, desires, and previous exposure to the role.

When a person rejects part or all of a role, other people have to adjust to the new role performance. When this occurs, an alternative environment has been created.

People conform to or resist role expectations for a number of reasons. Some conform because a particular system works to their advantage. Their self-interest is vested in conforming to the role. Others conform to role expectations for survival. For example, the poor and members of the working class rarely rebel against an economic system that pays them low wages or fails to provide sufficient work because to do so would likely ruin them economically.

People will change the environment in order to rectify problems or enhance their own status. Some resist the social expectations when their social and psychological needs are not met. For example, ethnic groups, women, and gays and lesbians have formed organizations that are dedicated to altering the psychosocial environment that negatively affects them.

Environments can change simply from the addition of new members. Family roles are profoundly altered when the first baby arrives. Adults must change individually as well as their interpersonal relationships to accommodate the new child. The disposition of that baby adds a further dynamic. Should the child be a "difficult baby," one with colic or in later months prone to tantrums, parents may tire of the baby or become frustrated, and then they become more troubled themselves. If the child is a "good baby," then it helps create a more loving environment.

SYSTEMS

If human behavior is not random, then it must be organized. The environment is a complex web of interacting phenomena organized into systemic processes (Meyer 1983). In simple terms, the en-

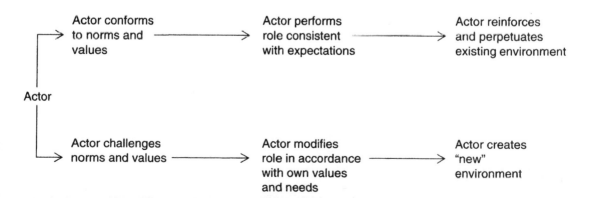

FIGURE 1.2   Individuals Create Psychosocial Environments

vironment actually consists of the systematic linkages of all phenomena. The task before social workers is to understand the basic nature of that organization in terms of understanding human development and assessing the onset and perpetuation of problems. Perhaps the most successful framework for conceptualizing the broad spectrum of human behavior is an approach known as systems theory.

Systems theory is actually less a theory than it is a descriptive framework for organizing the pieces of the complex human puzzle. Rather than attempting to specify causal relationships, systems theory describes interactive patterns between people, groups, and institutions. The systems approach sees all the elements of life as an interrelated entity. An individual, therefore, is embedded in this whole. The systems approach focuses on individuals as they interact within a context, which refers to a person's unique situational intersection with the six spheres of the environment. The situational context of a person's life is dynamic. It is constantly changing, evolving to some new state or condition. A person's relationship within that context is thus a dynamic process as well, adapting and adjusting to changing environmental demands.

A *system* may be defined as a set of objects (which includes people) and the relationships among them and among their attributes (Rodway 1986). Each part of a system functions interdependently with the other parts. Therefore, no part of a system acts independently. Since no person exists outside of some biological or psychosocial context, each individual is functionally related to everyone else in varying degrees. If one part of a system changes its course or function, then the other parts must adjust to that change. In sum, systems theory focuses on the mutual and orderly interdependence among people and the domains of their environment. It investigates how the behaviors and emotions of people are systematically functions of each other.

The "dance" metaphor provides a good illustration of how systems theory approaches human behavior and makes the systematic organization of interrelated behavior less abstract. As one part-

ner "steps," the other partner follows with a coordinated response that continues the dance. If one partner does not know the steps in the dance, both dancers stumble over one another and do not complete the dance as it was intended. Systems function the same way. When the parts of the system are functionally coordinated, it runs smoothly.

The "dance" of systems is comprised of several elements and processes. The discussion that follows looks at the dynamics that define, regulate, and enhance the effectiveness of social systems.

Goals.   Systems are goal-oriented mechanisms. They are arranged and driven to accomplish some task, including survival. Goals are reached more efficiently if they are clearly specified and agreed on by members of the system. Goals provide a sense of direction for members of a system and give the system a unified purpose.

In many cases, a system's goals are ambiguous. When this happens, the processes that govern system behavior and outcomes are scrambled, perhaps even chaotic. For example, family systems have several goals, such as providing a satisfying emotional life for parents and children, providing a safe environment for children, and reaching economic self-sufficiency, among others. When the system does not have the internal or external resources to attain one or more of these goals, the family is likely to experience some degree of trouble.

As a system's context changes, so must its goals. The goals of a young family, for example, are very different from those of a family whose children are about to leave home. Not changing the goals to accommodate the natural evolution of systems is typical of rigid, inflexible systems. Goals need to be fluid and ever-evolving to meet the contextual demands of the environment.

Subsystems

Subsystems are the internal divisions within a more complex system. A nuclear family system composed of two adults and children, for example, is subdivided into three interactive subsystems:

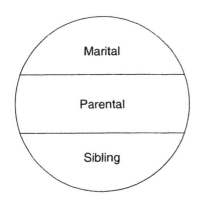

FIGURE 1.3   Family Subsystems

the marital subsystem, parental subsystem, and the sibling subsystem (see Figure 1.3). The marital subsystem involves the adults' interactions with each other as a couple. Interactive patterns of this subsystem include a sexual relationship, provision of an income, mutual emotional comfort and satisfaction, and adult companionship. In this subsystem, the adults do things to maintain an adult relationship; therefore, the children are not included in the marital subsystem.

The parental subsystem involves the same people, the adults, but now their behavior is oriented to the children. The parental subsystem is the set of transactions between the adults and the children. Behavioral goals of the parental subsystem include disciplining children, providing their material needs, and creating a stable emotional climate for them. Although the marital and parental subsystems involve the same people, there are clear distinctions in the patterns of behavior.

The sibling subsystem involves the behavioral patterns of the children. This subsystem includes such tasks as participating in school activities, learning the norms and values of the culture, and learning to curb impulses in order to live harmoniously with other people. This subsystem is the children's world and incorporates a child's privacy, activities, interests, and emotional reactions to various stimuli.

All three subsystems have internal processes unique to themselves, yet they are meticulously in-

tertwined. Behavior in one subsystem forces the others to respond. The following example illustrates the "ripple" effect of how a disruption in one subsystem can affect the other two. Let's say that the parents in a family have a terrible argument concerning family finances that lasts well into the night (marital subsystem). The next morning, the parents, still angry over their dispute and deprived of sleep, yelled and cursed at the children, ages eleven and six, during breakfast (parental subsystem). The children, who responded to their parents' arguments and outbursts with anxiety and fear, were uncharacteristically despondent at school, performed poorly on exams, and got into arguments with classmates (sibling subsystem).

The parents' argument regarding marital-level issues (finances) spilled over into their parental roles (yelling at the kids) and affected the children's emotional and behavioral functioning (poor performance at school). One of the many things a social worker would want to know about this situation is the frequency of the parents' fights. If this were an isolated incident, the likelihood of the children being chronically affected is slim. If this were a common feature of the marriage, which it would likely be if a social worker were involved with this family, then the sibling subsystem is likely to develop repetitive and perhaps destructive responses designed to cope with the constant tension the children feel at home. They may routinely underachieve and "act out" their home troubles by engaging in conflict with their peers at school. The systems framework guides the social worker toward completing a picture of this family by assessing the repetitive exchanges between the subsystems. In simplistic terms, assessing a system in terms of its transactions between its subsystems can be accomplished by asking: "When _____ happens, what do you do and how do you feel?"

Boundaries

Boundaries are the perimeters of a system's transactions. Boundaries specify the distinctiveness of the system as separate from others and define rules for how people should participate within the system. Boundaries also identify who is a member of the group and who is not. Many boundaries are unquestionable: membership in your class and your family, for example.

A system typically has three sets of boundaries. The first boundary separates the system from the general environment. This boundary divides that which is contained within the system from everything else. This boundary is represented by the circle that surrounds the family in Figure 1.3. What is inside the circle is the family and what is outside is not. The second type of boundary in a system separates the subsystems within the larger system. Finally, there are those boundaries that mark the "personal space" of each individual within the system.

Boundaries vary in their degree of permeability. Healthy systems maintain semipermeable boundaries; they allow transactions with outside forces, yet keep appropriate control over the system's internal structure. A system has functional boundaries if it allows the free flow of energy yet maintains the integrity of the system and its subsystems.

Return to the example of the arguing couple above. In the best possible scenario, the parents should have kept the conflict completely inside the marital boundaries and not have allowed it to encroach into the parental subsystem. In this case, the boundary separating the marital and parental subsystems is too open; there is no separation between them. If this is a repeated episode in this family, then the social worker would certainly explore the nature of this boundary problem and try to determine what might be behind the pervasive conflict. If, for example, the target of the intervention was the children's behavior, one strategy in helping this family would be to explore ways to shore up its internal boundaries to reduce the impact of the marital stress on the children.

Let's add to the story of this troubled family. After the parents argue, the mother detaches herself from the household and is uninvolved with the family. The father similarly abandons his parental role and begins to abuse alcohol. When this happens, the eleven-year-old child assumes parental responsibilities and takes the role of a parent. The older child insures that the younger sibling is clean, receives meals, and gets to school. This change illustrates another boundary "violation." The older child is "promoted" from the sibling subsystem to the parental subsystem in an attempt to restore family functioning and reach family goals, such as surviving and caring for the younger, more dependent child.

Adding to the scenario: After the parents explode, the father not only turns to the oldest child for parental assistance, but he also makes incestuous demands on the child. Again a boundary has been inappropriately bridged. Here the oldest child is promoted to the marital subsystem by being forced to engage in behaviors that are the "territory" of that subsystem. Furthermore, the father violates the child's personal boundary regarding sexual privacy. To conceal and protect his abusive behavior, the father doesn't allow the children or his wife to have friends over for visits or permit them to visit anyone else. No one is allowed to talk about family problems and everyone must present themselves as if nothing is wrong. The boundary setting the family apart from the outside environment is rigid and minimizes the exchanges between them.

Assessing boundaries is an important task within the systems approach. Doing so helps in understanding system rules and processes and can point to trouble spots in the system's functioning.

Open versus Closed Systems

Feedback is an important process in the goal-seeking action of systems. This process, sometimes called the feedback loop, is the response to stimuli, a continuous process of action/reaction. There are two types of feedback, positive and negative. Positive feedback maintains the equilibrium of the system and sends the signal that it is on a steady course towards its goals. Negative feedback disrupts the system and indicates the system has deviated from its goals and requires correction (Greif & Lynch 1983). Feedback in a system is regulated by the degree to which its boundaries are open or closed.

Systems vary by their permeability, which is the amount of access system members have to other systems. *Closed systems* are self-contained and have little outside contact, thereby incorporating few external ideas or resources into their own processes.

Systems with open boundaries are the opposite phenomenon. *Open systems* are characterized by an active exchange relationship with the environment, with which members freely interact. Open systems allow so much involvement from external systems that they lack any internal structure. The system with wide open boundaries is governed solely by external forces.

No system is completely closed or completely open; all fall somewhere in between these extremes. Systems unusually closed or open usually fail to reach maximum performance or develop the flexibility to resolve problems and accomplish goals. As Rodway (1986) states, systems function best when they reach an optimal degree of openness.

My earlier example of the family illustrates a system with open internal boundaries, but a rigidly closed boundary that sets it apart from the outside environment. The closed boundary does not allow many transactions with the environment, a defining feature of closed systems.

Here's another example of a family with a boundary problem. While working with families, I notice on occasion that when I ask a child a question, I get the answer from a parent. I typically let the first incident go, storing the information for future reference. As I continue the interview, I see that this communication pattern is in fact a characteristic of the family system, and it becomes clear that the family has problems with boundaries. When children are not allowed to respond with their own thoughts or are not permitted to interact with another system, in this case social services, family boundaries are most likely rigid.

Self-Regulation

Systems are thought to *self-regulate*. This means that they function to maintain themselves, a state referred to as *homeostasis*. Systems develop mechanisms for self-adjustment in order to persist and reach goals. Couples who talk through their problems or seek outside help, for example, are adjusting their marital system to cope with a system-threatening problem. According to systems theory, a system is in a constant state of dynamic tension and continuously adjusts to internal and environmental feedback and obstacles. People usually think of self-correcting attempts as positive actions, but systems can regulate themselves using negative strategies as well. A violent husband may strike his wife to keep her under his control, for example. Unfortunately, this strategy is too often effective in maintaining the family system. Or, to illustrate negative self-correction in a larger system, a corporation may adjust its financial position through extensive layoffs.

LEVELS OF SYSTEMS

Human behavior is embedded in four levels of systems, each intertwined with the other, that organize human experiences. Using Bronfenbrenner's (1979; 1986) typology, these levels are macrosystems, mesosystems, exosystems, and microsystems (see Figure 1.4).

Macrosystems are the organized social and cultural patterns that envelope human behavior. Macrosystems represent broad, repetitive phenomena that exist at a scale greater than the individuals participating in it. The economic and governmental systems are two examples of macrosystems. Macrosystems typically have indirect influence on human behavior.

Microsystems are immediate small-scale social, psychological, and biological systems. Families, peer groups, day care centers, and schools, for example, are psychosocial systems that have direct influence on development. Each individual is a microsystem as well. *Mesosystems* are the links that connect one microsystem with another. For example, the effects of day care on parent–child attachment constitute a mesosystem linkage. The influence of peers on adolescents connects teenagers and their families to groups outside the family. A conference between a parent and a child's teacher is yet another example. Mesosystem links

FIGURE 1.4 Four Levels of Systems

SYSTEM	FORM	INFLUENCE ON BEHAVIOR	EXAMPLE
Macrosystem	Organized social & cultural patterns	Indirect	The economy
Microsystem	Immediate social & psychological dynamics	Direct	Family, peer group
Mesosystem	Links multiple microsystems	Direct	Day care
Exosystem	External community forces that link microsystems to macrosystems	Direct	Parents' workplace

Adapted from Bronfenbrenner (1979; 1986)

have important implications for understanding external influences on intrafamily processes (Bronfenbrenner 1986).

Exosystems are external forces in communities that have a direct effect on development and microsystems. These include parents' workplaces, parents' social networks, and community influences such as the media and social service agencies. Exosystems are often direct links between individuals and families to macrosystems.

The position taken in this book is that systems theory provides a framework for organizing the dynamic processes of the exchanges within and among systems. It is the broadest grid by which to conceptualize human phenomena. From this base, social workers begin to narrow their focus, using theories of human behavior derived from social work, sociology, and psychology to explain the content of those transactions. These substantive theories will help you to understand three important and interrelated phenomena necessary for the successful practice of social work: (1) the "normal" development of human beings as a function of environmental systems; (2) the effects of macrosystems on individual development; and (3) the quality of social systems as sources of social and personal troubles. To begin this quest, let's first look at the structural theory of social work practice. This theory posits that the extent to which individuals (and larger systems as well)

reach their goals is an outcome of (1) the quality of their transactions with the environment, and (2) the environment's ability to provide the resources required to meet their needs.

THE STRUCTURAL MODEL OF SOCIAL WORK PRACTICE

In social work, both research and intervention involve the interaction between individuals and groups and their environment. One of the major paradigms that addresses this dilemma, and serves as the guiding framework of this book, is the structural model of social work practice.

The *structural model of social work practice* asserts that humans are needs-oriented beings who engage in purposeful, goal-directed behavior. The degree to which human needs and goals are met is determined by the quality of the surrounding environment. People are driven to satisfy three broad categories of needs: tissue, social, and psychological. All three require successful transactions with the environment for gratification. For their fulfillment, tissue needs (e.g., food, water, shelter) and social needs (jobs, adequate income, health care) involve interaction with social institutions, such as the economic and political systems. Psychological needs are what people require from the environment to create a healthy personality, e.g., affection, trust, security,

Two Stories in the History of Treating the Mentally Ill

Conditions are publicly defined as social problems when a powerful and influential group perceives them as such. How these groups label and comprehend negative conditions determines in large part public interest in the problem and society's response to it. The following example taken from the Middle Ages demonstrates how a powerful institution, religion, creates the social definition of a problem and affects the public's reaction.

In Europe in the thirteenth and fourteenth centuries, most scholars and theologians believed that mental illness was caused by demon possession and being in league with the devil. Insanity, in virtually all forms, was "known" to be the fruit of supernatural powers, evil spirits, and satanic associations. These "scientific" conclusions were not without empirical evidence, such as it was, for any odd or nonconformist behavior was perceived to be possible only if inspired or controlled by heinous creatures in service to Beelzebub.

Consequently, most Christians of the day believed that "curing" mental illness meant driving out evil spirits, reforming the soul, or forcing compliance with behaviors prescribed by the community. Typical "treatment plans" for the insane in Europe of this day included exorcisms, bondage in chains and stocks, and solitary confinement in underground dungeons. In some towns, mentally ill persons were placed in iron cages or boxes and placed near the town gates where they were humiliated, taunted, and abused. Franciscan monks who treated the insane compelled their patients to become more Christlike by means of daily whippings. They attempted to expel the demons causing the afflictions by burning their patients (Zilboorg & Henry 1941).

Bethlehem Hospital in London, one of the oldest hospitals in Europe, was founded in 1247, but did not begin admitting "lunatics" until 1377. Treatment of these patients involved little more than locking them in chains and manacles and whipping them for even the most insignificant violation of hospital norms. Over time, the name Bethlehem Hospital was corrupted to "Bedlam," a term that came to mean chaos and confusion.

The Muslim world of the 1200s and 1300s approached the treatment of mental illness in a far more rational and humane way. The insane were not possessed by evil malevolent demons, but were believed to have a special gift from God. Because the insane were thought to be forever childlike, they were free of human failings and weaknesses and completely honest and genuine. Only people singled out by Allah himself could have qualities of such purity. Insanity, to the Muslims, was divinely inspired.

Islamic cultures treated the insane very differently than did the Christian contemporaries. Hospitals, which were actually uncommon in Europe, flourished throughout the Middle East and North Africa. There were over sixty hospitals in Baghdad alone. In Damascus, the hospital did not charge for health services rendered to the insane. In Baghdad's House of Grace, one of the first hospitals to have a mental illness ward, patients with mental disorders were brought in from all regions of Persia. Patients received medical care until they recovered, and were visited and examined by a magistrate monthly. After being discharged by the magistrate, patients received medical care for months to prevent relapses (Zilboorg & Henry 1941).

In the hospital in Cairo, each patient had two attendees and well-paid physicians directed their treatment. Patients were entertained with dancing and light comedy. If they were unable to sleep, patients were carried to a separate room where staff members played soft music and told stories. When discharged, each patient received five gold coins.

Islamic scholars and physicians believed that a relationship existed between physical afflictions and emotions. They combined crude psychological methods and medical explanations for the symptoms of mental illness (Alexander & Selesnick 1966). Though there is evidence that some Muslim hospitals placed mentally ill patients in shackles, these practices were uncommon and inconsistent with dominant cultural views on the origins of insanity.

and discipline. Gratification of these needs hinges largely on the quality of the immediate psychosocial surroundings.

The well-known humanist psychologist, Abraham Maslow (1968; 1970), helped to clarify how individuals are motivated to act. He believed people are moved to fulfill a hierarchy of needs (see Figure 1.5). In Maslow's scheme, needs at the first level must be satisfied before those at the next, and so forth. The most basic level of needs is physiological or tissue needs, such as food, water, and shelter. These needs are necessary to sustain the organism. Unquestionably, these motives must be satisfied before others can be gratified. Many people erroneously believe that no one wants for tissue needs in western societies, but this is far from the truth. Countless homeless people, low-income families, and elderly persons lack proper nutrition, housing, and health care. It is not difficult to understand why people in these

situations experience high rates of psychosocial problems.

Once basic physiological needs are resolved, individuals can move to the next level of motives—safety needs. These include safety from crime, the weather, and financial disaster. Love needs are the next level of motivation, according to Maslow. Love needs include affection, intimacy, and feeling a sense of belongingness to meaningful social groups. The fourth level is the need for esteem. This refers to making positive self-evaluations and involves the need for success, recognition, achievement, and power. The final level of needs is the quest for self-actualization. Self-fulfillment is possible only when the other four levels of needs have been satisfactorily resolved. Self-actualization refers to reaching one's fullest human potential.

The categories of needs are not discrete; there is considerable interdependence between them. For example, if a family is homeless, its main concern is finding a secure, affordable place to live. Emotional issues may temporarily become less urgent until the housing problem is resolved. The lack of housing, however, does not preclude the existence of psychological needs, whose satisfaction remains necessary for the well-being of family members. The deprivation in housing is likely to lead to deprivation in psychological needs such as empowerment, security, and privacy. Family members, in this case, suffer from interrelated social and psychological losses.

According to the structural model, this family does not cause its homelessness. Its "symptoms," including being homeless, are outcomes of the social system's failure to provide adequate housing and income. In this way of thinking, environmental systems impede people from accessing the resources and opportunities they require to flourish.

At the heart of the structural model lies the assumption that human problems are expressions of deficiencies in the environment (Wood & Middleman 1989). The manner in which environmental domains are organized may facilitate or impair functioning and the attainment of goals. Barriers

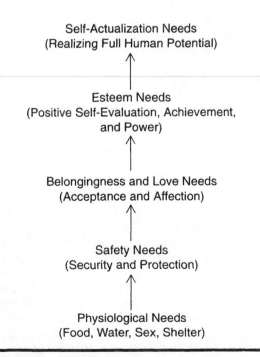

Self-Actualization Needs
(Realizing Full Human Potential)

↑

Esteem Needs
(Positive Self-Evaluation, Achievement, and Power)

↑

Belongingness and Love Needs
(Acceptance and Affection)

↑

Safety Needs
(Security and Protection)

↑

Physiological Needs
(Food, Water, Sex, Shelter)

FIGURE 1.5   Maslow's Heirarchy of Needs

such as discrimination, lack of opportunities, oppression, and abuse limit the emotional and tangible resources individuals need to maximize their fullest potential and increase the chances that they will lose control over their lives and futures.

The structural view avoids *blaming the victim,* which is the belief that holds sufferers responsible for their plight when the actual causes of their condition can be found in the social environment. Many people presume that behaviors, emotions, and cognitive skills are completely volitional. In this way of thinking, for example, if someone is mentally ill then that person chooses to engage in dysfunctional behavior. Or, if someone is poor, then poverty was a freely selected lifestyle. The same thinking holds true for homosexuality: gays and lesbians choose to engage in same-sex contact over heterosexual sex. If all problems were reduced to psychological choices based on free will, then to make interventions social workers would have to look no further than the individual who, for some reason, makes immoral and injudicious decisions.

Avoiding assessment of the impact of the psychosocial environment on behavior has serious political implications. To say that individuals are totally responsible for their problems avoids a more likely explanation for those problems. Look-

ing at systems as possible causes for people's ills means to tamper with the status quo. This can be very threatening to those who have strong interests in maintaining things as they are. It is difficult, for instance, to get businesspeople to understand poverty in terms of low wages and inadequate job opportunities when creating large numbers of jobs at good rates of pay cuts into their share of the wealth.

At the micro level, alcohol-abusing parents, whose children are underachieving and isolating themselves at school, may prefer to say that the children are "defective" and reject family interventions for fear of exposing their addictions. It is more convenient and self-serving for parents to blame children for their own problems (and the parents' problems, too) rather than take responsibility for the strained family system they have created.

The intention of the structural model is to uncloak the injurious arrangements of social and psychological systems that deny people the opportunities to enjoy a prosperous and satisfying life. Rather than aiming to help individuals adjust to their situations, understand their motivations, or change their ways of thinking and acting, the structural model strives to modify the environ-

Interactions within day care centers represent both microsystems and mesosystems. Dynamics within the day care constitute a microsystem, though the ways in which day care influences children and affects their behavior in other systems links those systems together as a mesosystem.

ment to meet the needs of individuals and groups (Wood & Middleman 1989).

The Nature of Macrosystems

Let's turn to the structural approach's image of macrosystems. Society is seen as a competitive arena where different groups vie for control of scarce resources, particularly wealth, power, and prestige. Social groups, sometimes referred to as communities, are formed around interests, which are goals and needs common to community members. People generally act to maximize their own interests or gratification, whether as individuals or as members of larger groups. Under these circumstances, the attempt to maximize interests results in conflict and patterns of economic and political disparity (Sanderson 1988). The poor and working class, for example, strive for more jobs, higher wages, and better benefits, commodities controlled by corporate elites who aim to hold onto wealth by reducing labor costs and minimizing benefits. Racial and ethnic groups compete with European Americans and each other for jobs, housing, and educational resources. Gays and lesbians compete with heterosexuals for civil rights.

As in any competition, there are winners and losers. Society's institutions provide the "playing field" for the contest, but the field is not always level for all contestants. The objective of the structural model, therefore, is to resolve two questions: Who benefits from social arrangements? Who is disadvantaged by social arrangements?

Some groups in society are in a stronger position to realize their goals because they have control over the social institutions that produce the resources for which groups compete. The privileged, those who reap more benefits from the way society is organized, gain many of their advantages at the expense of other people. Having control of social institutions, especially the economy and polity, ensures that those in power will maintain their position. As examples, business owners and senior managers determine wages and working conditions for workers. Government leaders, who are mostly European American,

Christian, middle-class males, have direct access to the legislative system to promote their values and interests.

Human problems, in this perspective, are the result of social systems that produce inequality. When a society systematically oppresses and disadvantages specific groups, it follows that "losing" groups will suffer disproportionately, while the "winners" fare well. The disparity between resources and needs is not due to the lack of resources per se, but to the system of distributing resources and the unavailability of resources to disadvantaged people. This book will discuss many problems common to disadvantaged groups and how these problems affect their members throughout their lives.

As I have said, all behavior and emotional states are purposeful and goal-oriented. People act because some end is desired. These goals are learned, legitimated, and reinforced through cultural, social, and psychological processes. Because goals are organized by environmental factors, rather than individual volition alone, behavior differs among individuals within sociocultural groupings.

The Nature of Microsystems

Now let's look at the structural perspective's model of microlevel behavior. This model suggests that individuals seek out objects in the environment that help meet emotional, behavioral, and developmental needs. These objects include other people, such as parents, peers, and spouses, pets, or inanimate objects, such as drugs, alcohol, or a child's teddy bear. The relationship a person has with these objects is usually repetitive and somewhat predictable. The availability and attributes of those objects, the resources they provide, and the feedback individuals receive as they strive to meet their needs determine the degree to which those needs are met.

Personalities are constructed through the processes of *conditioning* and *internalization*. As a behavior or emotion is rewarded or punished by the environment (conditioning), individuals learn to regulate their behavior themselves by transforming outside controlling forces into self-direction (internalization). For example, if parents approach children with firm yet flexible discipline that does not humiliate or physically hurt and demonstrate affection and nurturance, children will internalize this positive feedback as good feelings about themselves. If the environment is not threatening, frightening, or vengeful, but loving and protective, a child's personality will be a reenactment of those positive qualities. When individuals' needs are met in a positive way, they are likely to exhibit minimal psychological distress.

A hostile, rejecting, or nonresponsive environment, on the other hand, conditions a person to feel angry, threatened or depressed. People who are chronically exposed to negative psychosocial surroundings come to personalize the unreliability of others. Anticipating all-too-familiar negative feedback, they are likely to avoid relationships, exhibit anxiety when relating to others, or try for control in situations and of other people. Trust doesn't come easily for a person socialized in an insecure and dangerous environment. As negative traits and expectations are reinforced, they are incorporated as characteristics of personality, which (1) reduces one's effectiveness in coping with problems, and (2) makes one vulnerable to destructive behaviors, such as harmful relationships, drugs, or isolation, to cope with personal troubles. Poor coping skills often leave a person frustrated and usually more symptomatic.

On some occasions, behavior that may seem irrational may indeed be a rational response to internal distress, previous psychological injury, or social inequality. A fear of water, for instance, a common phobia, appears idiotic to swim enthusiasts and even casual swimmers. Within the psychic world of the phobic person, however, there is a rational explanation for the anxiety experienced when around bodies of water. A childhood trauma or repeated messages from a phobic parent planted the fear response, so that when the person enters a swimming pool, anxiety symptoms such as increased heartrate and a strong sense of dread appear.

The concept of internalization does not imply a direct correspondence between the environment as it is and the environment that gets internalized. Individuals internalize what they perceive the environment to be like. How individuals interpret and make sense of the environment is critical for understanding how they make the environment part of themselves.

The antecedents of many behaviors and mood states are grounded in the unconscious, where rationality may be obscured. The following case illustrates this idea. A bright, attractive thirty-three-year-old woman complained that her long-time boyfriend inappropriately teased her in public. Both the woman, whose earlier marriage ended in divorce and who had later been in a four-year cohabiting relationship, and her boyfriend were college graduates and held professional positions. At dinner with two other couples one evening, the boyfriend twice joked, "Gee, it's 8:00 and you haven't been divorced lately!" Rather than fighting back or assertively telling him that that kind of teasing was not appropriate, she crumpled, sitting quietly and taking the verbal assault.

From later discussions, it was learned that the woman, whom one would think would not stay with such a tormentor, held herself in low esteem. As a child, her family did not support her desire to excel academically. Instead of providing her the assistance she needed to achieve, her family undercut her and offered little praise. As an adult, she had accepted those messages from childhood that implied her lack of worth. Her staying with an emotional abuser then made sense: she believed someone like him was the "best I can get" (author's notes). In other words, he sent messages that were consistent with how she felt about herself.

CONCLUSION

The social work frame of mind conceptualizes individual and group behavior as taking place within a larger ecological context. For social work interventions to be successful, accurate qualitative and quantitative assessments of the transactions between individuals and their environment are necessary.

The environment is a complex web of interacting domains and is responsible for providing the resources people need to meet their needs. Human problems, both at the macro- and micro-levels, are assumed to be caused by insufficiencies in environmental resources. Conversely, when "things go right," that is, when one is able to pursue an appropriate life course without impairing distress, then it is assumed that the environment is providing adequate resources to cope with problems and reach developmental goals.

CASE STUDY REVIEW QUESTIONS

Respond to the following questions about John, the case described at the beginning of the chapter.

1. How would you describe John's family using systems theory? Describe the family's goals and boundaries.
2. What do family members do to maintain the family system?
3. What macrosystems influences affect John and his family? How might the family's income affect family life?
4. In what ways does John's psychosocial environment fail to provide the resources he needs to meet his needs?
5. What kinds of resources are needed for John and his family? What referrals might you make?

KEY TERMS

Achieved status: Those positions gained through effort and choice.

Ascribed status: Those status positions assigned by social processes.

Biological domain: The physiological makeup of a human organism.

Blaming the victim: Holding victims responsible for their plight when the actual causes of their condition can be found in the social environment.

Boundaries: The perimeters of a system's transactions; boundaries define rules for how people should participate within the system.

Closed systems: Systems that are relatively self-contained within rigid boundaries and have little outside contact.

Conditioning: The process of repetitive rewarding or punishing a behavior or emotion.

Culture: All the material and nonmaterial creations of a social group.

Environment: The recurrent and organized experiences and conditions repeatedly encountered by an individual or group over the course of time.

Environmental domains: The six separate but interconnected aspects of the environment that affect human functioning.

Exosystems: External forces in communities that have a direct effect on development and microsystems; exosystems are often direct links between individuals and families to macrosystems; parents' workplace and community influences, such as social service agencies, are examples.

Feedback: A response to a communicated message or other stimuli.

Homeostasis: The state of self-regulation in a system.

Internalization: Making cultural and social rules and expectations a part of one's personality; learning to regulate one's behavior by transforming outside controlling forces into self-direction.

Macrosystems: The organized social and cultural patterns that envelope human behavior; broad, repetitive phenomena that exist at a scale greater than the individuals participating in them, the economy, for example.

Mesosystems: The links that connect one microsystem with another: for example, the effects of day care on parent–child attachment constitutes a mesosystem linkage.

Microsystems: Immediate social and psychological systems directly open to the individual's experience, the family, for example.

Mores: Ways of acting to which people attach a moral significance.

Norms: Standards and guidelines for appropriate behavior in a particular situation.

Open systems: Systems with loose boundaries and an active exchange relationship with the environment; open systems usually lack any internal structure; the system with wide open boundaries is governed solely by external forces.

Physical and spatial setting: The aspect of the environment that is comprised of the built world constructed by human beings.

Psychological domain: The aspect of the environment that designates the psychological aspects of the social systems in which we live; this domain involves the patterns of recurrent emotions and behaviors of others that are open to direct experience.

Role conflict: Anxiety or tension that occurs when the performance of one role violates or contradicts another role.

Role strain: Anxiety or tension that occurs when a person has difficulty meeting the demands of a status-position.

Roles: The behaviors assigned to status-positions.

Self-Regulation: The processes systems utilize to maintain themselves.

Social institutions: Large-scale social systems designed to meet societal needs.

Status-position: Placements in a social organization or population.

Structural Model of Social Work Practice: A theory of social work practice that contends that people engage in purposeful, goal-oriented behavior and that the degree to which human needs and goals are met is determined by the quality of the surrounding environment.

Subsystem: The internal divisions within a more complex system.

System: A set of objects and the relationships among them and among their attributes.

Systems theory: A descriptive framework that focuses on the mutual and orderly interdependence among people and their environments; systems theory describes interactive patterns among people, groups, and institutions and sees all the elements of life as an interrelated entity; the systems approach focuses on individuals as they interact within a context.

Values: A group's ideas of right and wrong, good and bad, and acceptable and unacceptable.

PREGNANCY AND
EARLY CHILDHOOD

OBJECTIVES

After reading this chapter, you should be able to answer the following questions:

1. How does conception occur and what is the role of prenatal care in maintaining a healthy pregnancy and fetus?
2. How can an expectant mother's lifestyle affect her developing fetus?
3. What emotional and developmental tasks face expectant mothers and fathers?
4. What causes severe postpartum depression?
5. How do attachment relationships form and what patterns can attachment take?
6. What are the major points of the theories of Erikson, Mahler, and Stern? How do they differ?
7. How do young children affect family life?
8. How does community membership affect child development?

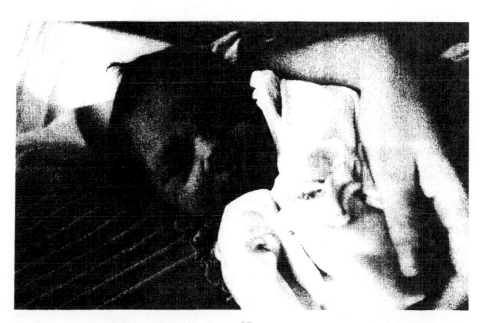

CASE STUDY

Catherine was a European American five-year-old kindergartener who was referred to social work services by her teacher and principal. Catherine was having significant behavioral and learning troubles in school. She was getting into fights with classmates, speaking too loud and out of turn, having difficulty staying focused, and often refusing to do her work or participate in group activities. She was standoffish and seemed unable to join other children's play groups during recess.

Catherine had lived a full life by the time she started kindergarten. She was being raised by her paternal grandmother, Mary, and stepgrandfather, Paul, whom she called mother and father. Her natural mother, Beth, was a poly-drug abuser who had a long history of drug abuse, criminal arrests, and emotional instability. According to Mary, Beth used an assortment of illegal substances as well as alcohol while pregnant with Catherine.

Her natural father abandoned Catherine in infancy. He, too, had a history of drug abuse. Though he still lived in the same city as Catherine and his mother, he rarely visited. When he was around, Catherine called him "uncle."

At six months of age, Catherine was taken from Beth by child protective services. CPS placed Catherine in the care of Mary and Paul. Catherine showed evidence of extensive physical abuse and neglect. She was covered in welts, burns, and open sores, and was clearly malnourished. Under close medical supervision, she eventually recovered from her injuries and gained weight. Within a few months, Beth's parental rights were terminated. Her natural father, Alex, relinquished his paternal rights. It was then that Mary and Paul became her legal parents.

About three years later, near Catherine's fourth birthday, Beth pleaded with Mary and Paul to give her a "second chance" to mother Catherine. Eventually Mary and Paul decided to let her have that opportunity. Within the first few days that Catherine lived with Beth, Catherine experienced another episode of traumatic abuse. Beth wanted to go on a trip of a few hours duration

without Catherine. Unable to find a baby-sitter, Beth locked Catherine in a closet where she stayed several hours until she was released by one of Beth's friends who happened by. She was immediately returned to Mary and Paul who never heard from Beth again.

INTRODUCTION

The Western world generally celebrates birth as the beginning of life. Between conception and birth, however, newborns have already amassed considerable experiences. As a product of the interaction between biology and the psychosocial conditions of their environment, newborns and young children are very different and the paths they will take depend largely upon the quality of the psychosocial world around them. The first part of this chapter describes conception and prenatal development. Having a working knowledge of "where babies come from" is important for social work practice. Many adolescents, and adults for that matter, who are pregnant or at risk for becoming pregnant, often have an immature understanding of conception, pregnancy, and fetal and child development. Learning what happens to them and their offspring gives people more control over their bodies and the decisions they will make.

After a child is born, a wide range of profound environmental factors start the baby on its way to taking on its own personality and character. The second part of this chapter looks at how developmental issues of early childhood are more easily accomplished when young children's interactions with their environment are positive.

CONCEPTION

The potential for a human organism begins at *conception,* the instant a sperm cell and an ovum unite. Females are born with about 400,000 *ova,* or eggs, all that they will ever have. Most eggs never mature and eventually dissipate. Once a girl reaches puberty, menstruation begins and her ovaries will release a single mature egg or ovum. The egg is carried by cilia, fine hairlike projectiles that line the *fallopian tubes,* through the fallopian tubes and into the uterus or womb. The trip takes about five to seven days. At the same time, the lining of the uterus, the *endometrium,* collects a large supply of blood vessels in anticipation of providing nutrients to a fertilized egg. If the egg is not fertilized, blood and the built-up uterine lining are discharged during the menstrual flow. Each egg carries twenty-three, or one-half, of the woman's chromosomes, the material that carries an individual's genes.

Sperm are produced by a male's testes and carry his genetic coding. Sperm consist of three parts: the head that contains the twenty-three chromosomes and is capped with an enzyme called hyaluronidase which allows the sperm to penetrate the ovum; the midsection that supports and provides energy to the tail; and the tail, a whiplike feature that propels the sperm. Some three hundred million sperm are contained in a normal ejaculate. During ejaculation, sperm are transported in seminal fluid produced by the cowper's gland, the seminal vesicles, and the prostate gland. Seminal fluid provides a supportive environment for sperm to live and reach the ovum. Semen has an alkaline base to protect sperm from the acidic environment of the male urethra and the female vagina and contains nutrients to "feed" the sperm. Semen also contains a hormone that dilates the uterus to provide more room for the sperm to swim.

Virtually all sperm die within the first few minutes following ejaculation. They are destroyed by the acidic environment of the vagina or they lack the proper tail structure to make the journey to fallopian tubes. Many others swim to the wrong fallopian tube, the one that does not contain the discharged egg. Within about forty-five minutes to an hour, only about 300 sperm will have reached the egg and only one will penetrate the wall of the egg cell. The egg and the sperm unite to form a cell with all forty-six human chromosomes and, therefore, traits from both the mother and the father. At that moment the potential for human life begins (Rosenblith 1992).

Once fertilized, the egg, now called a *zygote,* continues its travels through the fallopian tubes to the uterus. By the end of the three to four day journey to the uterus, the zygote has divided into twelve to eighteen cells and can consume external nutrients. By the fifth day, the zygote may contain as many as sixty-four cells, which are beginning to differentiate in size and function. As the cells divide, they move away from the center of the cell mass to form a cavity and separate into two layers, the small inner layer that will become the embryo and the flat layer of cells on the outside that will form the placenta. The placenta is the organ through which food, oxygen, and wastes are exchanged between the mother and the baby. The outer layer of cells also develops into the amniotic sac that surrounds the fetus and other supportive structures.

The embryo is still floating in the uterine lining. Once the outer layer of cells has matured, the egg mass begins to implant itself in the wall of the uterus. This process begins about eight days after conception and takes seven to ten days to complete. The location of the implantation is critical for the success of the pregnancy and for minimizing complications in fetal growth and delivery. If the zygote settles to the bottom of the uterus, for example, the placenta may detach too early or block delivery. The blood supply to the uterus is not evenly distributed, so if the zygote attaches in an area lacking in adequate blood vessels, it might receive inadequate nutrition. In about 15 of every 1,000 reported pregnancies, the fertilized ovum implants in one of the fallopian tubes or somewhere else outside the uterus. Known as *ectopic pregnancies,* they usually terminate within two to three months, either by severe bleeding when the placenta becomes detached or by rupture of the tube, or both. Abdominal pain and vomiting are the most common symptoms (Rosenblith 1992).

Once implanted firmly in the wall of the uterus, the zygote develops structures to receive nutrients from the mother and expel its own wastes. The mass of inner cells begins to specialize in function and the process of forming organs and body structure begins.

Figure 2.1 shows a timetable of fetal development over the course of a full-term pregnancy. Gestation is divided into three trimesters. In general, each trimester has a particular developmental function. The first trimester is characterized by the formation of organs. Because of this, the fetus is very vulnerable to environmental influences that may cause abnormalities in organ growth. For example, drugs, alcohol, viruses, and x-ray radiation are particularly harmful to the embryo and fetus.

In the second trimester, the tissues and organs formed in the first trimester mature. Few physical deformities occur at this time, but the death of cells in the brain or spinal cord could result in postnatal behavioral disturbances (Langman 1981). The eyes of the fetus open at the end of the second trimester and the fetus is sensitive to sounds and light. Should the fetus be born during the second trimester, the likelihood of survival is slim. Key systems for independent survival, e.g., respiratory and nervous systems, are not yet fully functional.

The third is one of growth and maturation. The fetus gains most of its length and weight during the last few weeks of the pregnancy. By twenty-eight weeks, the fetus is capable of survival outside the uterus, though medical assistance is required.

Prenatal Care

Having regular medical examinations during pregnancy is the best predictor of a smooth pregnancy and delivery and giving birth to a healthy baby. After the initial visit to a physician to confirm the pregnancy, women should see their doctor or nurse midwife at least once a month until they are thirty-six weeks pregnant. At that point weekly visits are indicated. It is critical for expectant mothers to follow the health and behavioral regimen their health professional plans for them.

During the first follow-up visit, women are given an internal exam. Vital signs, blood analysis, and other routine lab tests are conducted. The uterus and fetus will be felt by abdominal palpation. The health professional will instruct the expectant mother on diet and nutrition, issues of

FIGURE 2.1 A Timetable of Pregnancy and Fetal Development

MONTH 1

Pregnancy
- Conception and period is missed
- Body produces hormones necessary for fetal development
- Breasts become bigger and slightly sore
- Morning sickness and nausea are common
- Need to urinate more often
- Smoking, drinking, and using drugs are dangerous activities because embryo's organs are forming

Fetus
- Fetus is called an embryo during the first eight weeks
- Limb buds that will become arms and legs first appear
- Heart and lungs begin to form; heart starts to beat by twenty-fifth day
- Neural tube, which becomes the brain and spinal cord, begins to form

MONTH 2

Pregnancy
- Early symptoms, such as sore breasts and morning sickness, may continue
- Fatigue is common as the body is using energy to fuel the pregnancy
- Expectant mothers should drink more fluids, take prescribed vitamins, and eat a well-balanced diet

Fetus
- All major organs and systems are formed but are not completely developed
- Ears, wrists, ankles, fingers, and toes are developed
- Eyelides form, but are closed
- By end of the second month, embryo resembles a human form
- Embryo is about one inch long and weighs less than one ounce

MONTH 3

Pregnancy
- Symptoms of early pregnancy may continue
- Headaches and dizziness are possible
- Clothing may feel tight as the new mother may have gained up to four pounds by now

FIGURE 2.1   Continued

Mothers experience considerable weight gain
during this month

Fetus

Fetus freely opens its eyes and rigorously kicks
and stretches

Fetus responds to light and sound

The head is about in proportion with the rest of
the body

The lanugo begins to shed

Hair on the head begins to grow longer

Could survive if born by the end of the seventh
month, though it lacks the important heat-
insulating layer of fat; now considered
legally viable

Fetus now is about fifteen inches long and
weighs about three pounds

MONTH 8

Pregnancy

Stronger contractions are likely

Colostrum, the fluid that nourishes the baby
until the milk comes in, may leak through the
breasts as they begin to produce milk

The uterus begins to crowd the lungs and so the
mother will likely feel a shortness in breath

The top of the uterus is just under the rib cage

Fetus

The fetus is probably too large to make
swooping turns now

Bones in the head are soft for easier passage
through the birth canal

Fetus usually moves into the head down
position where it will stay until delivery

Fetus is almost fully mature

Fetus's lungs are still immature, but chances for
survival outside the mother are very high

The fetus reaches about eighteen inches in
length and weighs up to five-and-a-half
pounds

MONTH 9

Pregnancy

Breathing becomes easier after the baby drops
into the pelvis area ready for birth

Swelling in the ankles and feet worsens

Cervix begins to dilate (open up) and efface
(thin out)

Mothers usually feel uncomfortable because of
the pressure and weight of the baby

Strong Braxton Hicks are frequent

Fetus

Baby moves less now because there is less room

Lungs are finally mature and ready to function
on their own

Baby weighs six to nine pounds and is nineteen
to twenty-two inches long

Baby's bowel is filled with meconium, a mixture
of excretions from the baby's alimentary
glands, bile pigment, lanugo, and cells from
the bowel wall

---

personal care, and how to deal with common discomforts associated with being pregnant.

Later visits involve less invasive testing. The fetal heart tones will be analyzed and other issues are discussed. When weekly exams commence, toward the end of the pregnancy, pelvic exams are conducted to check for dilation and indications of a possible premature birth.

An adequate diet during pregnancy is essential for maternal and fetal health. Research has found that a diet deficient in protein, key vitamins, and minerals is associated with low fetal weight, length, and condition at birth (Cefalo & Moos 1988). Prescription-strength vitamins are usually given to expectant mothers as well as information to help families plan meals that maximize nutritional intake.

Prenatal Screening

How can prospective parents know if their baby is developing normally and on schedule? For many parents, early knowledge of their baby's physical condition may help them plan, both emotionally and logistically, for the needs their offspring will require. Several diagnostic tests can identify a wide range of disorders, impairments, and other information about the baby. These tools reveal different kinds of information and are used in specific situations.

Who should be tested? Mothers and fathers who are at high risk for the problems the tests de-

In the first trimester of pregnancy, most of a fetus' internal organs are formed. Harmful substances that are consumed by the mother pass through the umbilical cord and are ingested by the fetus.

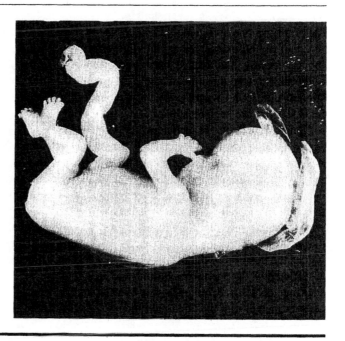

tect should have their babies tested prenatally. For example: *amniocentesis* and *chorionic villi sampling* can identify various genetic disorders; birth defects in the limbs are often visible in the images produced by ultrasound examinations; and pregnant women who are at least forty years of age are at risk for giving birth to a baby with Down's Syndrome, a condition recognized by amniocentesis.

Cultural expectations of physical appearance and capabilities are often powerful environmental messages. To have a baby that fails to live up to those demands may leave new parents humiliated, saddened, or frightened. Many parents may feel guilty or that they are being punished for something they did wrong. Consequently they may reject the child or deny its limitations (Masters, Johnson, & Kolodny 1992). Others may respond with extra love, nurturance, and acceptance. Early detection of fetal impairment may lead parents to terminate the pregnancy, if abortion is within their value system. Abortion may be an alternative if the problem could endan-

ger the life of the mother or if the parents feel incapable of rendering appropriate care for the baby once it is born.

The following section describes the three prenatal tests most widely used. The uses, timing, and procedures of each diagnostic are reviewed.

Ultrasound. *Ultrasound* examinations create images, called, *sonograms,* of the developing fetus. The technique transmits high-frequency sound waves through a quartz crystal. The waves are reflected off dense tissue back through the crystal to create pictures of the fetus. The moving image of the fetus can be viewed on a television monitor. Obstetricians often invite new parents to bring a videotape with them to record the first "home movies" of their new child.

Sonograms allow measurement of fetal length, cranial circumference, and age. Skeletal structure, fetal heart rate, and the position of the placenta can be determined from sonograms. If the baby is positioned correctly, its sex can be determined visually as well. In addition, numerous birth defects, such as hydrocephalus (a buildup of fluid in the brain), can be ascertained with ultrasound.

Ultrasound exams are commonly performed, though recently there have been suggestions of overutilization. At this time, there is no evidence to suggest ultrasound waves pose any danger to the fetus. There have been no studies, however, testing for long-term effects the technique may cause.

Amniocentesis.   *Amniocentesis* is the most invasive of the three prenatal examinations. After deadening the abdominal wall with a local anesthetic, a long needle is inserted into the uterus to withdraw amniotic fluid, the liquid which engulfs the fetus. In most cases, an ultrasound image guides the position of the needle in order to locate a sufficiently deep pocket of fluid and to avoid sticking the fetus. Cultures are grown from the cells extracted from the amniotic fluid.

Amniocentesis is performed at sixteen weeks into the pregnancy and requires about four weeks to yield results. Earlier use of the test is not possible because there is not enough amniotic fluid to allow safe insertion of the needle. The method can detect the presence of about 200 metabolic defects, congenital disorders, and chromosomal disorders, including spina bifida, anencephaly, Tay–Sachs disease, cystic fibrosis, and Down's syndrome. The technique can determine whether the virus that causes German measles (rubella) has reached the placenta. Positive identification of the fetus's sex is possible. Amniocentesis carries a small probability of risk to the fetus; there is about a one percent chance amniocentesis may cause the death of a fetus.

Chorionic Villi Sampling.   A technique more recently developed for identifying fetal abnormalities is *chorionic villi sampling* (CVS). Less invasive than amniocentesis, this method involves inserting a thin catheter through the vagina and cervix into the uterus and removing a small sample of tissue from the chorionic villi. Chorionic villi are small threadlike protrusions of the membrane that surrounds the fetus.

CVS has several advantages compared to amniocentesis. First, it can be performed at about eight weeks; second, the results are available in two days. Earlier detection of a serious abnormality would reduce the psychological trauma and the physical risks of an abortion, which during the first trimester is far safer than an abortion at twenty weeks. CVS has detractions, too. First, it does not detect as many disorders as amniocentesis. Second, some research indicates there is a higher risk of spontaneous abortion (just under four percent) (Hogge, Schonberg, & Golbus 1986). Third, CVS technology is not widely available. Only a few medical centers perform the test. Consequently, new parents needing a prenatal test might have to travel a far distance to a facility that offers the test and commit finances and time not required of amniocentesis.

THE MATERNAL ENVIRONMENT

The physical and mental health of an infant, and certainly for the years to come, is influenced by the mother's lifestyle. All that she eats, drinks, and inhales is likely to be consumed by her baby. Prenatal education includes instruction on which substances the mother may ingest are harmful or beneficial to the developing fetus. Not only must parents be aware of the dangers of certain drugs, both legal and illegal, on the baby, but maternal diseases can also affect fetal development and lead to serious birth defects. The following section reviews the effects of maternal diet, disease, and drug ingestion on the growth and development of a baby. Social workers working with pregnant women must be aware of basic environmental effects on fetal development, be able to educate their clients on appropriate lifestyle choices, and make knowledgeable referrals.

Influence of Maternal Diseases on Fetal Development

Both infectious and chronic noninfectious maternal diseases may affect the developing fetus and the newborn child. Some of the disorders act on the fetus while others affect the baby at birth.

Let's first look at infectious diseases that may spread to the fetus and lead to serious congenital birth defects. The likelihood of a mother contracting one of these illnesses and subsequently passing it on to the baby is not evenly distributed throughout the population. Disadvantaged groups experience higher rates of these problems and receive fewer of the social and medical services that would control maternal and fetal morbidity.

Rubella. Rubella, commonly known as German measles, has a profound effect on the fetus, especially if the mother contracts the disease during the first trimester of pregnancy, when fetal organs are forming. Infection during the month prior to the pregnancy may damage the fetus as well. The effects diminish, but do not disappear, if the mother is infected during the second and third trimesters.

Exposure to rubella affects the young fetus differently according to the timing of the exposure (McIntosh 1984). Deafness and heart defects, for example, are common outcomes to maternal rubella, but are most pronounced if the exposure occurs during the first trimester. Cataracts form on the eyes if infection occurred prior to day sixty, and stunted growth is likely if infection was in the first eight weeks of the pregnancy.

The incidence of chronic birth defects resulting from maternal rubella infection has diminished greatly in the last thirty years. Screening and detection techniques and the control of measles in the general community have reduced the number of rubella syndrome cases to under 1.5 per 100,000 births (Rosenblith 1992). This progress has not benefited all groups equally (Kaplan et al. 1990). African American and Hispanic newborns have a significantly greater risk of rubella syndrome than Anglo Americans because they are less likely to be protected from German measles through immunization.

AIDS. The mother can transmit the human immunodeficiency virus to the baby in utero or through breast milk, and need not have developed AIDS symptoms to pass the virus to the child. The infant AIDS rate is steadily increasing and it is estimated that over 3,000 HIV-positive children are born each year. AIDS births are twelve times higher among African Americans than European Americans (Rosenblith 1992).

About 30 percent of babies born to mothers with HIV become HIV-positive themselves (Gwinn et al. 1991). It is not clear why some babies become infected and others do not. According to reports commissioned by the federal government, the following variables may influence the chances of a baby becoming infected (U.S. Dept. of Health & Human Services 1988, 1987; National Commission to Prevent Infant Mortality 1987):

- The presence of other maternal infections
- The mother shows symptoms of HIV infection during pregnancy
- The stage of pregnancy the mother became infected
- The number of pregnancies the mother has had while infected with HIV
- Repeated maternal exposure to HIV

Many infected babies, however, will not test positive for HIV because they are screened too early. As with older children and adults, there is a window of time in which an HIV screen may reveal a false negative. Most physicians consider HIV tests unreliable until the child reaches fifteen months of age. If a mother is HIV-infected and has developed HIV antibodies, one of three things could happen to the baby during the pregnancy: (1) the baby could receive HIV and HIV antibodies, (2) the baby could receive HIV antibodies but not the virus itself, and (3) the baby could receive neither HIV nor HIV antibodies. If the baby receives HIV from its mother, it will produce antibodies of its own. The HIV tests, however, can not distinguish the baby's antibodies from the mother's. The mother's antibodies can stay in the baby's blood for up to fifteen months. If the baby tests positive for HIV antibodies after that time, physicians know that the antibodies were likely produced by the baby's immune system (Centers for Disease Control 1987).

AIDS in babies and young children differs from adult AIDS in several ways. Babies are more likely than adults to (U.S. Dept. of Health & Human Services 1988, 1987; DeVita et al. 1988; Iannetti et al. 1989):

- Get bacterial infections
- Have malnutrition and failure to thrive
- Be anemic
- Have pneumonia not caused by Pneumocystis carinii
- Develop AIDS in a shorter amount of time
- Die more quickly
- Fail to develop Kaposi's sarcoma
- Have ear, liver, kidney, skin, and nervous system disorders
- Become developmentally disabled

The onset of AIDS in HIV positive babies may be any time between two months and five years. Children live only about fourteen months after being diagnosed with AIDS. About 30 percent of babies who develop AIDS within the first year of life live longer than a year, although almost 90 percent of older children who develop AIDS live more than a year (Centers for Disease Control 1989).

AIDS in children, for the most part, is similar to AIDS in adults. Symptoms of AIDS in children includes weight loss, diarrhea, recurrent fever, swollen lymph glands, severe thrush, and pneumonia. There is one difference between early childhood and adult AIDS, however. Unlike in adults, AIDS in children destroys the body's ability to fight off bacterial infections.

Herpes.   With the public's focus aimed at AIDS, other sexually transmitted diseases have received less notice than they deserve. Herpes virus, particularly herpes virus hominis (HVH), has been at serious epidemic levels for a number of years, affecting about 300,000 new cases per year. In women, the virus usually affects the vagina or cervix and, if active at the time of birth, may infect the fetus (Rosenblith 1992). HVH lies dormant most of the time and causes no symptoms, the most important of which are lesions or open sores.

When the herpes virus is not active, the level of contagion is low to nil.

An infant can contract the virus during the delivery process by coming into contact with a lesion in the birth canal. About half of exposed babies will contract the virus and of these, 15 percent will have localized infections that are not serious. For the remaining 85 percent, the morbidity and mortality rates vary according to the type of infection. Localized infections result in a lower death rate than whole-body infections. For example, a localized infection in the central nervous system results in infant death in about 50 percent of the cases. The mortality rate for whole-body infections is 90 percent. Treatment results in lower mortality, though survivors will develop microcephaly, spasticity, paralysis, seizures, deafness, or blindness (Whitley et al. 1980).

Herpes infection has no cure. For infected pregnant women, the best course of action is to take medications that reduce the probability of active lesions during late pregnancy and planning a cesarean section to protect the baby from contact with any unknown lesions.

Syphilis.   Unlike viruses, most bacteria are too large to pass through the placental barrier. The syphilis bacteria, however, readily crosses the placental tissue and enters the body of the fetus. Syphilis affects the baby only if the venereal disease is contracted after week sixteen of the pregnancy, when most of the baby's organic structure is already formed. Syphilis creates lesions on organs and threatens the life of the fetus. About 34 percent will die before birth and more will die early in life. Survivors are likely to suffer retarded growth, peritonitis, anemia, central nervous system problems, poor vision, and irregular teeth (Ricci et al. 1989).

The introduction of antibiotics in the late 1940s and 1950s almost swept syphilis out of the American population. Recent government cutbacks in programs that delivered these drugs to low-income persons have allowed syphilis to reappear and become again a critical public health problem. Women with low incomes who are sexually active are most likely to contract syphilis and not receive treatment. Routine prenatal care and assistance in distributing antibiotics could eliminate the effects of syphilis on fetuses.

Gonorrhea.   Gonococci is another infectious bacterium transmitted to an infant primarily at the time of delivery. Many women may not realize they are infected because the symptoms of this disease are often mild. Before the advent of penicillin and other antibiotics, gonorrhea was among the leading causes of congenital blindness in newborns. Most states now require that penicillin drops be placed in the eyes of newborns as a prophylaxis.

Group B Streptococcus.   This group of bacteria infects about 11,000 babies during delivery each year. Infection is life-threatening: about 55 percent of premature infected babies and 15 percent of full-term babies who are infected will die. Treating the mother with antibiotics reduces the infant death rate significantly, but treating infected babies usually results in unfavorable consequences (Enkin et al. 1989).

Let's turn now to several chronic conditions of the mother that may affect fetal growth and the neonate: diabetes, hypothyroidism, and hyperthyroidism.

Diabetes.   Diabetes can affect fetal development and is associated with spontaneous abortions and stillbirths. At 30 percent, the miscarriage rate is twice the nondiabetic rate (Miodovnik et al. 1990).

Babies that live are much more likely to develop a long list of congenital health problems, such as heart, neural tube, skeletal, and kidney troubles, defects that occur during the first trimester (Klitzmiller et al. 1981). Babies born to diabetic mothers are often macrosomic, which means maturationally retarded. They are often large, weighing over ten pounds. Babies at this weight are usually delivered by c-section and automatically tested for diabetes.

Mothers who control their diabetes with medical treatment and diet greatly reduce the

probability of giving birth to a baby with these problems (Rosenblith 1992). Among diabetic mothers who do not control their disease, about 40 percent of live births suffer some serious defect. That rate is reduced to four to five percent among controlled diabetics. The rate of birth defects for nondiabetics is about three percent.

Hypothyroidism.   Hypothyroidism is a condition in which the thyroid fails to produce enough thyroid hormone. Treatment includes hormone replacement or supplement. If the mother receives no or insufficient treatment, effects on the fetus can be severe. Maternal hypothyroidism can lead to spontaneous abortion, premature delivery, stillbirths, and defective infants (Jones & Man 1969). For those infants who survive, deficits in motor and cognitive abilities are expected. Researchers have recorded lower IQs for these children as late as age seven (Man, Holden, & Jones 1971).

Hyperthyroidism.   An overactive thyroid gland negatively affects the fetus, but far less than hypothyroidism. In addition to the harm brought on by the disease, the drugs used to treat hyperthyroidism can cross the placental barrier and damage a developing fetus. Hyperthyroidism is associated with the following fetal conditions: fetal death, goiter, thyroid disorder, Down's syndrome, undescended testes, and heart problems.

Influence of Drugs on Fetal Development and Delivery

A large number of drugs, both legal and illegal, have adverse effects on the developing fetus and the pregnancy. Drugs have different consequences based on the chemical agents in the drug, how much was consumed, and when the drug was taken. For many women, stopping drug use after they confirm their pregnancy may not be enough to avoid harmful outcomes as many serious drug effects occur before a pregnancy is verified. It is also important to know if a pregnant woman is a polydrug user, because the interactions among drugs can have a potent effect on the pregnancy and fetus. This section reviews the relationships between many commonly taken drugs and pregnancy.

Illegal Mood Altering Drugs.   Drug and alcohol abuse have a major impact on families, especially women and children (Finkelstein 1994). Maternal drug abuse causes several medical conditions and complications during pregnancy and delivery. Many of these conditions extend well into the life of the child and produce serious psychosocial implications. Maternal drug use often results in the *boarder baby* phenomenon. A "boarder baby" is one who remains at the hospital longer than medically necessary because its parents are unable or unwilling to assume responsibility for its care. Many parents involved with drugs simply abandon their infants at the hospital. Most boarder babies end up in substitute care with foster families or other family members (Marcenko et al. 1994).

When they do go home, children born to drug-abusing women are more likely to be maltreated and neglected. Consequently, they are placed out of the home more than other children (Marcenko et al. 1994).

Women who abuse drugs during pregnancy are likely to share several psychosocial characteristics. According to Finkelstein (1994) and Marcenko et al. (1994), maternal drug abusers have the following problems:

- Poor informal social supports
- Periodic homelessness
- Emotional instability
- Deprivation of basic needs such as clothing and food

In addition, when compared to women who do not abuse drugs, maternal drug abusers are more likely to:

- Delay seeking prenatal health care
- Live on their own
- Do not know how their family feels about their pregnancy
- Do not know how their family will be helpful to them

- Have another family member with a drug or alcohol problem
- Have been abused as a child
- Have another child already in foster care
- Smoke cigarettes
- Lack marketable job skills
- Have inadequate financial resources

For women with emotional and financial deficits and highly stressful living conditions, the demands of day-to-day infant care are particularly burdensome (Johnson & Rosen 1990). Their general quality of life is low and they are often depressed. Cut off from meaningful relationships, many maternal drug abusers feel disconnected and lack the pleasure, satisfaction, and sense of worth many women receive from relationships (Finkelstein 1994). Abusing drugs and alcohol may relieve those feelings of disconnectedness, while pushing the women further away from valuable and needed relationships that might provide emotional and tangible support and affiliation.

Attachment between mothers and their infants can be impaired if the mother has a drug or alcohol problem (Mundal et al. 1991). Mundal identified three factors associated with poor attachment between a drug abusing mother and her infant. First, in comparing maternal users and nonusers, Mundal found that users: (1) have less overall contact with their infants; (2) have poor eye-to-eye contact; (3) are less attentive to their baby's needs; and (4) touch them less affectionately. Second, maternal drug users are likely to be guilt-ridden individuals with poor self-image and self-confidence, qualities that restrict early mother–infant interaction. Points one and two are associated. Low levels of interaction with their infants reflect maternal self-consciousness and uncertainty. As one woman in Johnson and Rosen's study remarked: "People will think I'm crazy if they see me talking to a baby" (1990:286). Third, babies born to drug addicted mothers tend to have passive dispositions. Therefore, their feedback to the mother is diminished and may lead the mother to feel ineffectual and powerless. Even as babies become more vocal over time, mothers involved with drugs do not show greater levels of vocalization or interaction (Johnson & Rosen 1990).

Mothers under intense stress, especially drug abusers, have difficulty differentiating internal from external, and maintaining coherent and stable relationships. As Johnson and Rosen point out, such a mother is quite likely to attribute her distress and feelings of inadequacy to her infant. Thus it is not surprising that mothers who abuse drugs see their infants as "difficult babies," rather than as "easy babies."

In general, children born to maternal drug users suffer several short-term and long-term effects. Although many children are surprisingly resilient to the effects of maternal drug abuse, most do not get off to a good start in life. They are more likely to be born immature, have lower Apgar scores, and require longer stays in the hospital. In the long run, they run risks for chronic health problems, personality disturbances, mood disorders, and learning difficulties (Mundal et al. 1991). With these general effects in mind, let's turn now to the effects of specific drugs on infant and child development with a focus on both the medical and psychosocial consequences.

Cocaine.   Taking cocaine during pregnancy has both direct and indirect effects. Direct effects are those caused by the actual chemical properties of cocaine on the fetus. As a potent stimulant of the central nervous system, cocaine has a profound effect on physiology. Cocaine use during pregnancy is associated with other independent, or indirect, factors adversely affecting pregnancy outcomes: poor nutrition, higher incidences of sexually transmitted diseases, and multiple drug abuse with marijuana, cigarettes, opiates, and alcohol (Frank et al. 1988). Cocaine, therefore, affects virtually all aspects of reproduction: fetal growth, pregnancy, and infant development. In fact, the effects of maternal cocaine use last throughout the child's life.

Cocaine use during pregnancy is linked to several development delays in the fetus. These babies have higher rates of urinary tract infections and other malformations and low birth weight. They are more likely to be born prematurely than nonexposed babies. In their report on maternal cocaine use, Chasnoff et al. found a 38 percent miscarriage rate (1987). Stillbirths and spontaneous abortions within a short time span following a cocaine injection (Berger et al. 1990).

Within five to twenty minutes after injecting cocaine, pregnant women may develop headaches, labor pain, back pain, and vaginal bleeding (Berger et al. 1990). Snorting cocaine slows the effects, but does not eliminate them.

Cocaine babies have depressed interactive abilities. They are irritable, have difficulty focusing attention, and are less aroused by visual stimulation than normal babies (Berger et al. 1990). They experience problems in motor and visual–motor development, muscle hypertonicity, and poor sleep–wake organization. Several studies report a greater incidence of Sudden Infant Death Syndrome (SIDS) among cocaine babies (Lester & Tronick 1994). SIDS strikes about two to five percent of all births. Among cocaine babies, however, the rate of SIDS may be five to ten times higher (Pitts & Weinstein 1990).

As a result of these cognitive and motor-skill deficits, cocaine babies are usually less affected by stressors (Karmel et al. 1990). When stressed to the point of crying, however, normal weight cocaine babies have higher-pitched, longer-lasting, and more variable cries (Lester et al. 1991). Low birth weight coke babies, on the other hand, take longer to cry, have fewer cries, and cry less loudly. Compared to normal babies, differences in crying styles may interfere with a mother's ability to form an attachment with her newborn.

Follow-up research reported by Howard et al. (1989), Beckwith (1988), and Berger et al. (1990) indicates that the effects of maternal cocaine use continue into childhood. Emotions, social behaviors, and cognition are either directly affected or affected because of other problems, such as emotionality and the inability to concentrate. In a study of two-year-olds, Berger found cocaine children less articulate and more likely to experience perinatal strokes; many had respiratory problems.

Heroin and Methadone.   Opiates, such as heroin and methadone, pass through the placenta and enter the bloodstream of the fetus. The newborns of addicted mothers, therefore, are born addicted themselves. The severe withdrawal symptoms kill many addicted neonates. Heroin exposure retards physical development; exposed babies are shorter and have smaller head circumferences than other newborns. Those who survive will have several behavioral difficulties in setting sleep cycles, soothability, and motor skills (Rosenblith 1992).

If taken during pregnancy, methadone, a legal narcotic used to substitute for heroin in weaning addicts off the drug, similarly results in chemically addicted newborns. Though withdrawal from methadone is not as life-threatening as heroin, it is still very dangerous for the weakened infant. Methadone babies have high rates of perinatal mortality. Tremors, agitation, restlessness, and sleep disturbances persist for four to six months (Hans 1989).

Regardless of prenatal attention and the quality of parental care, babies exposed to opiates in utero have long-lasting injuries and deficits. For these babies, motor incoordination is about three times more frequent and mental retardation is about ten times more prevalent than among non-exposed children (Hans 1989).

Marijuana.   Despite animal studies which connect maternal marijuana use with impaired offspring, marijuana use among pregnant women has not been linked to any major fetal or infant defect or anomaly. Occasional marijuana smoking does not correlate with premature births, low birth weights, miscarriage rates, Apgar scores, or congenital anomalies (Fried 1989; Hatch & Bracken 1986).

Fried and Makin (1986) found signs of neurobehavioral consequences in the first few days of life for babies prenatally exposed to marijuana. Among the symptoms were increased tremors, exaggerated startles, and affected sleep.

Long-term effects of maternal marijuana use on child development depend on the quantity consumed. Fried (1989) found a negative relationship between the amount used and offspring cognitive ability at age four. The greater the exposure, the lower the child's intellectual performance.

Legal Drugs.   In recent years, public outcry against maternal drug use has resulted in prosecution of new mothers who used dangerous drugs while pregnant. Hostile public sentiment, however, is selective and has not been as concerned for children born to mothers who abused alcohol, smoked cigarettes, or took other legal drugs while pregnant, even though these agents can have significant harmful affects on children. Physicians take care not to prescribe certain medications to pregnant women, providing they know their patient is indeed pregnant. The abuse and simple misuse of legally prescribed drugs, however, occur. The section that follows reviews the effects of legal drugs on fetal and child development.

Alcohol.   Research has proved alcohol to be a particularly harmful *teratogen,* which is any drug or substance that causes fetal defects and malformations. As the number of alcoholic women continues to rise, the number of offspring exposed to fetal alcohol syndrome (FAS) has increased to the point that FAS, the most severe form of prenatal alcohol exposure, is now the leading cause of mental retardation, ahead of Down's Syndrome and neural tube defects (Jacobson et al. 1993). Only FAS, of course, is preventable. The average incidence of FAS ranges from 1.1 to 1.9 per 1,000 live births. Among women who abuse alcohol, 59 out of 1,000 births will result in "full-blown" FAS.

Since the effects of maternal alcohol consumption depend upon the amount the mother drinks, many questions regarding the relationship between alcohol and fetal and child development remain unanswered. FAS, the most dramatic consequence of maternal alcohol abuse, is associated with heavy drinking. Most medical research and obstetrical clinical wisdom indicate that very light drinking of alcohol has no effect on the fetus or the pregnancy. However, the danger line between safe and dangerous drinking is not yet determined. The best way to avoid any negative outcomes of drinking alcohol is to avoid it altogether.

FAS is identified by a variety of physical, intellectual, and behavioral symptoms. Physical symptoms commonly include:

- Pre- and postnatal growth deficiency (below tenth percentile)
- Dysmorphic facial features, such as narrow eye width, thin upper lip, short upturned nose and underdeveloped groove between base of nose to top of upper lip, and hypoplasia of midfacial area
- Slight build
- Small head
- Joint and limb defects
- Cardiac defects
- Dental defects
- Vision and hearing impairment

Common intellectual and behavioral symptoms include (Warren & Bast 1988; Giunta & Streissguth 1988):

- IQ range between 16 and 105, the average is 65
- Sixty percent are below the mean for their age-group
- As infants, poor sucking reflex
- Poor sleep
- Intrusive and overly talkative
- Unaware of social cues
- Strong attention-seeking behavior and hyperactive
- Social immaturity
- Difficulty forming peer relationships
- Attention deficits

The incidence of FAS is not evenly distributed among social groups. Native Americans experience a higher rate of FAS than European Americans. On the whole, Native Americans' FAS rate is 1.3 times higher than European Americans, but for some tribes the rate can reach thirty times that of European Americans (Davis et al. 1992; Duimstra et al. 1993). For high incidence tribes the FAS rate reaches 10.3 per 1,000 births (Duimstra et al. 1993). Lower educational attainment and less adequate prenatal health care con-

tribute to Native Americans' high FAS rates. Among Southwestern Indians, 23 percent of the mothers of FAS children die by the time their children are screened for FAS (Masis & May 1991).

Smoking. Nicotine from smoking tobacco is one of the most injurious teratogens. Maternal smoking is associated with serious neonatal and long-term outcomes and indicates a woman's disregard for her baby's health.

Infants are more likely to die both before and around birth if their mothers smoke while pregnant. Smoking during pregnancy results in an estimated 50,000 spontaneous abortions and between 4,000 and 14,000 infant deaths *per year* (Feldman 1985; Lincoln 1986). Racial minorities, especially African Americans and Native Americans, are at higher risk of infant mortality related to maternal smoking (Singleton et al. 1986; Davis et al. 1992; Bulterys 1990). For babies that survive, many have long-lasting disadvantages. Women who smoke tobacco run a higher risk of a troubled pregnancy and having a damaged child. Figure 2.2 lists outcomes associated with maternal smoking.

The effects of maternal smoking are not limited to medical conditions. The emotional, cognitive, and behavioral development of children are affected as well. At age three, children of mothers who smoked during pregnancy demonstrate lower cognitive and language abilities. Children of heavy

FIGURE 2.2 Physical Effects of Maternal Smoking

EFFECTS ON PREGNANCY	FETUS–INFANT– CHILD QUALITIES
Premature Birth	Reduced Birth Weight
Spontaneous Abortion	Heart Defects
Shortened Pregnancy	Respiratory Problems
Ectopic Pregnancy	Malformations
Placental Irregularity	Neurological Symptoms
Vaginal Bleeding	Higher Risk of Illness
Delayed Conception	More Hospitalizations

Source: Ceffalo & Moos (1988)

smokers also suffered motor development lags (Cefalo & Moos 1988).

Not all smoking effects are caused by the mother's smoking during pregnancy. Secondary smoke inhalation can also damage infants and young children. After the baby is born, both new mother and father should stop smoking, or at least smoke where the baby's air will not be contaminated.

Prescription and Over-the-Counter Drugs. Pregnant women should always inform their physicians of their pregnancy and not take any prescription or over-the-counter drugs without their physician's approval. Many of these drugs can affect the pregnancy and harm the developing fetus.

PREGNANCY AS DEVELOPMENTAL PROCESS

Pregnancy is usually regarded as a biological process, therefore most interest is on how the fetus develops and how the mother's body changes over the course of the pregnancy. Less attention is paid to the developmental implications of pregnancy. As most research indicates, pregnancy also involves relatively predictable emotional and social processes for both expectant mothers and fathers (Valentine 1982).

At the beginning of pregnancy, many expectant mothers and fathers feel ambivalent. They may have doubts about the pregnancy and their abilities to parent, especially in the first pregnancy. Many prospective parents may worry about finances, their careers, their relationship, and the availability of support. These anxieties are more pernicious if the pregnancy is unexpected. Early ambivalence may contribute to even more anxiety: "If I'm ambivalent about having a baby, does that mean I will be a bad parent?" In actuality, mixed feelings are common and do not necessarily predict how good or bad a parent a person will become.

The first few weeks of pregnancy can create significant tension for couples. It is a key developmental milestone and can bring up unpleasant family of origin issues. For example, the initial experience of domestic violence for many battering couples occurs within a few weeks of first becoming aware of the pregnancy.

By the twelfth week of the pregnancy, most couples will have accepted the pregnancy and have adjusted their lives to accommodate it. On hearing fetal heart tones (at ten to twelve weeks), the expectant mother and father realize that a baby is actually there and they will begin to treat it as an individual. This realization is an important motivator for changing habits such as smoking, drinking, and eating poorly.

At twenty-four weeks, expectant mothers often retreat to their own worlds. Becoming more introverted gives them "space" to prepare for approaching motherhood. In a sense, they are "getting ready." They think about their new roles and how their old ones may change. They talk about the baby incessantly. Though this may bore their friends, it is actually important preparatory behavior. It is a time when women seek out their own mothers, even if their relationship has been conflictual. Partners become more self-focused as well, though they may feel left out during the woman's introversion. In dealing with these emotional changes, men must realize the function of the woman's behavior, and women should attempt to include them in their plans and concerns.

The last few weeks of pregnancy, thirty-six to forty, can be volatile emotionally. The expectant mother may experience mood swings, going from states of emotional lability to exaggerated excitement. These swings are due to hormones and the excitement of the impending birth. Usually the emotional shifts are worse if medical or relationship problems are present. Partners are often alienated during this time and describe themselves as "walking on eggshells" to avoid "setting off" the other.

Women and men have several developmental tasks associated with the experience of pregnancy. Mastery of these tasks predicts subsequent task accomplishment and adaptation to future adult and parental roles. Valentine (1982) summarizes the principal tasks of expectant mothers and fathers in Figure 2.3.

FIGURE 2.3 Developmental Tasks for Expectant Parents

TASKS OF EXPECTANT MOTHER

- Development of an emotional attachment to the fetus
- Differentiation of the self from the fetus
- Acceptance and resolution of the relationship with her own mother
- Resolution of dependency issues
- Evaluation of practical issues, such as financial responsibilities

---

TASKS OF EXPECTANT FATHER

- Acceptance of the pregnancy and attachment to the fetus
- Evaluation of practical issues, such as financial responsibilities
- Resolution of dependency issues
- Accepting and resolving relationship with his own father

The overriding themes for prospective mothers and fathers are similar. Both need to plan financially and also evaluate their relationships with their own parents. Dependencies and unresolved issues with their parents are likely to interfere with their ability to parent effectively. Men and women need to develop some kind of coherent role structure that now accommodates not only their own changing needs, but also the needs of the infant (Valentine 1982).

POSTPARTUM DEPRESSION

Childbirth and the passage from singlehood or couplehood to parenthood are stressful developmental transitions. For a large group of women, about 50 to 80 percent, the transition to parenting is marked by depressive symptoms, a condition known as *postpartum depression* or the maternity blues (Millis & Kornblith 1992). Beginning three to four days after delivery, the blues usually peak between five to seven days after the onset of the symptoms and are fully resolved within two weeks. Postpartum depression results from drastic drops in progesterone and estrogen levels immediately following delivery. The rapid loss of these hormones, accompanied by the stress of labor and delivery, fatigue, mourning the loss of the pregnancy, and losing the attention that being pregnant gives, leaves sufferers tearful, labile, irritable, sad, guilty, and lonely. Symptoms may also include nightmares, depressive thoughts, mood swings, and feelings of detachment.

For some women, about 7 to 10 percent, symptoms will persist beyond the initial postpartum period (Millis & Kornblith 1992). What distinguishes these women from those whose symptoms abate? The answer lies in the quality of the mother's relationship with her psycho–social environment. The main factors in mother–environment exchanges that affect whether postpartum depression will persist are: (1) the quality of the support the mother receives, (2) the source of the support, and (3) the early relationship with the baby.

In regards to the mother, meeting the mother's needs is the most important task for her immediate psychosocial environment. When material support is provided by family members, post-delivery stress and depressive symptoms are relaxed. Providing adequate care of the newborn and older children is critical in giving the new mother sufficient time to recover from the stress and exhilaration of giving birth. Most women expect to receive assistance from their partners and other family members. Those who are disappointed in the help they actually receive are more likely to develop persistent and troublesome depressive symptoms. On the other hand, women who are particularly close to their partners and have partners who provide the support they need experience a shorter duration of symptoms (Logsdon 1990). Support reduces the extent to which circumstances are evaluated as stressful, promotes a positive frame of mind by enhancing self-esteem and self-efficacy, and reduces strenuous activity (Collins et al. 1993). Satisfaction with support from others, especially the spouse or partner, improves the probability that difficult maternal blues will be avoided.

The early relationship with a new baby is a secondary source of stress that may contribute to extended depression (Millis & Kornblith 1992). If the pregnancy was not planned or if the mother has second thoughts about becoming a parent, she may feel guilty and/or estranged from the infant. Infants vary in the degree to which they are irritable or responsive. The more temperamentally difficult a baby is, the fewer positive feedback messages the mother receives. In this situation, mothers may not feel as close to the baby as they would otherwise. Finally, unrealistic expectations of infants may disappoint mothers. Thinking that newborns are capable of behaviors advanced for their actual age, adults who demand compliance from their children may become frustrated. Similarly, parents may have unrealistic expectations about themselves. Some women have internalized cultural attitudes about mothering to the point that they create a mother role that is beyond reach. The more women accept cultural expectations of the mothering role, the more likely they may feel that their personal worth and value rests ultimately on their success as a mother. When something goes wrong, such as the baby crying at an inconvenient time, and their baby is not "perfect," anxiety, guilt, inadequacy, and depression are probable outcomes.

Postpartum depression impacts the family system in three ways: effects on the father, older children, and the development of the neonate itself. Many fathers are confused and sometimes irritated by the new mother's depressive and sometimes hostile affect. The father sees everyone, including himself, as excited about the new baby and becomes puzzled at the mother's seeming lack of interest or willingness to share his level of enthusiasm. Behaviorally, the father may vent his fear or anger on the mother, which will probably heighten her emotional burden and detachment. Social workers can help prepare new parents by explaining and normalizing postpartum depressive symptoms in new mothers and helping them discuss their feelings. Social workers can help fathers find ways to express themselves without further injuring the mother.

Mothers with postpartum depression who have other children may neglect their emotional and physical needs. The mother's physical or emotional absence may disturb older children and create abandonment and rejection guilt. Social work intervention should include reassuring them that they are not to blame for their mother's illness and behavior and teaching the father to listen to his children's complaints and fears.

The absence of the mother from the newborn may affect the emotional and physical well-being of the baby itself. Early maternal absence can have a profound impact on the psychosocial development of the baby. Rotnem (1989) found that infants whose mothers were unavailable due to postpartum depression were more likely to exhibit developmental problems as late as age eight. Having a depressed mother or father is stressful for the baby, who does not understand why its calls for needs fulfillment are not answered in a swift and nurturing manner. Infant anxiety is a common outcome and the longer the parent's depression lasts, the more severe the anxiety.

Hospital practices can help reduce postpartum depression. Rooming-in, having the baby and mother share recovery rooms, and other mechanisms for increasing mother–infant contact improve mothering behavior such as eye contact, fondling, tactile stimulation, and verbal interactions. The more contact the mother has with the baby, the more self-confidence and competence she has and the fewer feeding troubles she encounters (Winkelstein & Carson 1987). The more positive the mother's postpartum experience is, the more the likelihood of severe postpartum emotional disturbance is reduced.

ATTACHMENT

According to Erikson (1963), the main psychosocial development task of infants is establishing a sense of basic trust in people and institutions. Children learn to trust the world through consistent and gratifying caretaking. If the environment adequately and supportively meets their needs through regular and appropriate attention and affection, children will learn that the world is a safe place and that they are in harmony and sync with

Male and Female Circumcision: Two Different Stories

Circumcision is usually associated with boys, yet, in some cultures, girls, too, are circumcised. Male and female circumcision, however, have very little in common. Why the surgery is performed and the aftermath of the procedures are markedly dissimilar, as the following comparison indicates.

Circumcising boys involves surgically removing the skin called the prepuce, or foreskin, that covers the head of the penis. The practice is thousands of years old. Egyptian mummies dating back to 6000 B.C. reveal evidence of circumcision. Circumcision is largely associated with religious ceremonies. Jews, for example, have long used circumcision as a means of identification and showing a commitment to Abraham's convenant with God to circumcise all of his male descendants. Other reasons for circumcising boys include hygiene and making a more attractive penis.

There may be evidence that male circumcision provides certain health benefits as well. Uncircumcised male children are much more likely to develop urinary tract and kidney infections than circumcised males (Wiswell 1990). Critics of the practice argue, however, that most of these infections are caused by poor hygiene and washing habits, rather than the presence of the foreskin.

Others condemn circumcision on humanistic grounds. They are concerned that forcing pain on males so early in life can have long-term implications on personality development. Does circumcision affect males' ability to trust others? Does it cause males to withdraw socially? Most likely it does not; too many uncircumcised males are withdrawn and have trouble with intimacy. Humanistic concerns, however, do raise interesting points about the exchange aspects of circumcision. Is the low risk of future health problems worth the acute pain, trauma, and the risk of surgical error associated with circumcision? Does it take circumcised infants longer to form attachment bonds than uncircumcised males?

The reasons for circumcising males during the first days of life are connected mostly to group identification and hygiene. Female circumcision, on the other hand, is about behavior control.

When applied to girls, the term circumcision is really a misnomer, for the prepuce of the clitoris is not necessarily removed. In female circumcision, the clitoris itself, as well as other tissues in the vulva, are cut or burned off. In some cultures, such as in the Sudan, the vaginal opening may be stitched nearly closed during the ritual.

Female circumcision does not take place necessarily during infancy as it does with boys. It is performed on girls anywhere from age four to thirteen. This is not an insignificant difference in the rituals because having girls remember their clitoridectomies is important in achieving the ritual's goal.

On some occasions, female circumcision takes place in a medical facility with trained medical personnel. Most, however, are performed in the child's home, and often by untrained persons. In one common technique, girls are tied to their beds and a family elder cuts the clitoris and the labia with a knife, which is rarely disinfected. The room is hardly sterile either, and the bandages are usually nothing more than cotton cloth. Anesthesia and antiseptics are not often used. In Egypt, after the ritual is over, the clitoris is wrapped to the girl's wrist for several days.

Many girls who are circumcised in this way exhibit a wide range of negative outcomes. Infections are common and the pain is severe. Short-term psychosocial consequences include anger, humiliation, and shock. Long-term consequences include high divorce rates, loss of sexual interests, and feelings of reduced femininity (Mahran 1981). Due to high rates of vaginismus, sexual intercourse is painful to many circumcised women. Husbands of these women frequently take mistresses.

Why do cultures practice female circumcision? The practice is found mostly in African and Islamic societies where women's social status is low. By definition, female circumcision denies females sexual sensation. In so doing, it is assumed that women will lose sexual interest and develop loyalties to their husbands that can not be destroyed by sexual attraction to another man. In this way, women can be counted on to perform labors for men who need not fear sexual competitors. Mutilating women's genitals helps keep women "in their place" by destroying their sexuality and making them fearful of the patriarchal system in which they live.

Adapted form Gordon (1980:19–25).

it. If caretaking is inadequate, inconsistent, or painful, children come to understand that life is unpredictable and that people are not trustworthy.

Trust is established and maintained through the vehicle of attachment. Attachment, according to Anselmo (1987), refers to strong bonds of affection directed toward particular people. Humans have an innate desire to be close to preferred individuals and will attach to a person considered stronger and wiser. When a child is separated from or unwillingly loses a special person, emotional distress and personality disturbance usually follow.

Bowlby (1969), one of the first researchers to pose a theory of parent–infant attachment, maintained that infants form attachments by having personalized contacts with caretakers; being fed and having other physical needs met are insufficient to form attachments. Bowlby recognized certain infant behaviors, such as crying, smiling, calling, and clinging, as a behavioral system designed to insure the close proximity of the primary caregiver, usually the mother. Consequently, infants will form the strongest attachments with those persons who respond consistently and readily to those signals.

From the experiences infants have with their primary caregivers, infants develop a representational model (the "internal working model") of their attachment figure. Babies who recognize their attachment figures as accommodating and responsive to their calls for help will anticipate the figure's future helpful behavior and internalize beliefs that the self is worthy of support and protection. Therefore attachment relationships are important in the infant's developing perceptions of self-worth (Schachere 1990).

Bowlby delineated four phases in the development of attachment in infants. The phases are not discrete and will vary from person to person.

In attachment phase one, infants cannot identify their mothers directly, but show what is called undiscriminating social responsiveness, certain behaviors that orient them to other people. During this period, which lasts from birth to about eight to twelve weeks, infants turn their attention to people in the room, follow them visually, smile, vocalize needs, listen, make position adjustments when held, and often stop crying when others attend to them. As Bowlby notes, these behaviors attract adults and enable them to spend time with the infant. By the end of this phase, babies can recognize their mother's voice and face and therefore are positioned to begin attachment (Anselmo 1987).

Attachment phase two, discriminating social responsiveness, lasts until about six months of age and is a time when infants begin to differentiate people's responses. Babies usually show an amiable interest in others, but are clearly more enthusiastic when interacting with the person with whom they have a primary attachment. Infants are clearly familiar with their caregiver's caretaking and social behaviors, a fact that indicates that infants learn from birth and are aware of interpersonal differences in responsiveness.

Attachment phase three, active initiative in seeking proximity and contact, continues through age two. In this phase, children use the attachment figure as a base to explore the world around them. Children's behavior becomes increasingly differentiated as they alter their behavior according to the persons with whom they are interacting. Interactions with strangers become sources of anxiety and concern, especially in the absence of the primary caregiver.

In attachment phase four, which Bowlby called goal-corrected partnership, behavior becomes more flexible. By their third birthday, children have a better understanding of the goals and expectations of the attachment figure. They can alter their behavior to accommodate the caregiver's demands and enter into more complex relationships. At the same time, they have a greater understanding of the factors that influence the caregiver's behavior and can therefore be more sophisticated in their efforts to modify the caregiver's behavior to meet their own needs (Rosenblith 1992).

On some occasions, problems occur in the attachment process and the strength and quality of the attachment relationship are weak and distressing. Ainsworth's landmark studies of infants exposed to increasingly stressful separations and reunions with caregivers and strangers identified different patterns of reunion behavior (1969; 1974; 1978). How the baby responded to the caregiver following the distressful period was hypothesized to represent the baby's level of attachment and expectations of the caregiver to reduce the heightened tension. From this research, Ainsworth and her colleagues identified three major patterns of attachment, two of which represent troubled and insecure attachment.

Securely attached infants (Type B) seek contact with the primary caregiver and have the expectation that he or she will appropriately respond and attend to their needs. They are easily soothed by bodily contact following a period of brief separation. The internal working models of secure infants reflect the integration of attachment affect and the expectation of caregiver sensitivity to this affect (Fish & Condon 1994). Most babies, about 70 percent, are securely attached, according to Ainsworth.

Anxious–avoidant infants, Type A attachment, appear to avoid caretakers following separation. Infants with avoidant internal working models of attachment "have deactivated their attachment needs and affects" (Fish & Condon 1994:96). Caretakers of avoidant infants are physically or psychologically unavailable and often reject the infant's initiatives for attachment (Main & Weston 1982). About 20 percent of infants are Type A.

Type C attachment, anxious–resistant infants, is characterized by ambivalent behavior. These infants will both cling to and push away the attachment figure. At separation, ambivalently attached infants show intense anger and fear. Parents of anxious–resistant infants respond inconsistently to the infant's needs and signals for attachment affect. Caretakers of Type C infants, for example, might pick up their infants when they are exploring contentedly and then put the infant down when the infant is signaling attachment needs. Ainsworth suggested that about 10 percent of all young children are Type C.

More recently, Main and Hesse (1990) proposed a fourth attachment relationship, Type D insecure–disorganized/disoriented. On reunion, these infants display contradictory behavior, such as approaching with head averted or strong avoidance following intense attempts to gain proximity to the caregiver. The Type D infant may appear dazed and confused and will wander aimlessly approaching the caregiver and then look away, seemingly in a state of fear. Mothers of Type D infants have a history of abusive behavior and/or having experienced an unresolved traumatic loss in their life. Already frightened by a separation, responding to a frightening or frightened caregiver leaves the child confused and disorganized (Main & Hesse 1990). The internal working model in Type D infants is chaotic; they own no coherent strategy for meeting attachment needs because they are in an unresolvable predicament (Fish & Condon 1994).

Attachment relationships can change over time. Although most infants remain in the same attachment category as they get older, the range of those children who change categories varies widely. One study found substantial stability in attachment style (Waters 1978), whereas another found only 53 percent remained in the same attachment pattern from twelve to nineteen months of age (Thompson et al. 1982). Changes in attachment reflect changes in family circumstances or in the behavior of the attachment figure. For example, most children who change from secure to insecure attachment are those whose families are under extremely high stress or whose mothers take employment outside the home. These conditions do not guarantee change in attachment, however. How the caregiver mediates environmental stress and changes can reduce the chances of the child developing insecure attachments.

Quality of attachment is an important predictor of later preschool functioning. Sroufe's (1985) review of attachment literature found that secure attachment is related to enthusiasm, positive affect, and persistence in a problem-solving situation at age two. By age three-and-a-half, securely attached children are more peer oriented, socially competent, happy, curious, and actively engaged in their environment. Securely attached infants tend to become children who interact with teachers in friendly and appropriate ways, whereas insecurely attached infants become overly dependent on teachers, demanding their attention unnecessarily and clinging to them instead of playing with other children or exploring the environment (Sroufe et al. 1983). At age four, boys who are insecurely attached are more aggressive, while insecurely attached girls are excessively dependent (Berger 1994).

A common question about attachment concerns its relationship to maternal employment. As more women have entered the paid labor force during the last twenty years, a greater number of children are placed in substitute care while their mothers work. Does maternal employment change or alter attachment? Does the mother's employment damage children's psychosocial development? Barglow, Vaughn, and Molitor (1987) discovered that attachment and maternal employment were indeed connected. These researchers found that the babies of full-time employed mothers were more insecurely attached (Type A) than those whose mothers were not employed. The fact that this study only included those families in which the infant remained at home with a babysitter and the care was judged as satisfactory adds merit to these findings.

Employment per se does not negatively affect attachment relationships, however. For example, the number of hours spent at work has differential influences on attachment. Infants whose mothers work about twenty hours per week are more likely to be securely attached than infants whose mothers work fewer hours or who work full-time. This is due to the likelihood that the mother who works half-time is with her child more and for regular, predictable periods. Furthermore, a mother working half-time can arrange more regular, stable childcare services than women who work fewer hours per week. Working ten to twenty hours per week is most detrimental in terms of cognitive and emotional outcomes (Baydar & Brooks–Gunn 1991).

The timing of the mother's return to employment is critical in attachment formation as well. The longer the reentry into the paid labor force is delayed, the fewer the negative effects of maternal employment. Postponing employment fosters attachment by allowing more maternal contact and later easing the transition to maternal employment because the child's emotional and developmental maturity enables him or her to handle the separation. Early return to employment correlates with lower preschool cognitive scores and interrupts constancy and consistency in terms of establishing a firm maternal representation. Boys are more vulnerable than girls to disruptions in mother–infant relationships, less quality care, and poorly attentive or attached caregivers. If the mother returns to full-time work two to three years after the child's birth, the effects of her employment are virtually nil (Baydar & Brooks–Gunn 1991).

The type of attachment relationship is closely associated with maternal characteristics. Ainsworth contended that maternal responsiveness to the infant's communications and signals was the primary predictor of strong attachment formation. Subsequent researchers have revealed several specific maternal qualities that correlate with securely attached infants. These mothers:

- Are sensitive to their infant's needs
- Respond quickly to their infant's cries of hunger and discomfort
- Maintain appropriate levels of stimulation
- Are more sensitive, warm, and communicative
- Have less anger and frustration with the maternal role
- Hold high self-esteem
- Have positive recollections of their own childhood

Furthermore, infants with more involved and responsive fathers are more attached and competent (Lamb 1977).

Mothers of insecurely attached infants share common traits as well. Mothers of anxiously attached infants feel less accepted by their own parents and understimulate their infants. Avoidant attached infants are subject to overstimulation and maternal depression. The psychologically unavailable mother is less affectionate, abrupt, and more interfering (Benn 1986; Belsky et al. 1984; Cicchetti & Aber 1986; Main & Weston 1982; Ricks 1985; Sroufe et al. 1983).

Many attachment theorists believe that attachment is a property of the caregivers' marital subsystem, rather than the particular traits of the individual caregiver (Schachere 1990). Parents whose relationship is mutually supportive, flexible, and less stressful provide an environment that facilitates attachment and trust. High marital adjustment, identified by parents who work together, communicate well, and have sound problem-solving and coping skills, fosters secure attachments as well.

Some researchers contend that infant temperamental features predict the quality of attachment at later ages (Izard et al. 1991). Irritability at three months, for example, is predictive of resistant behavior at one year of age. Izard also learned that children with significant heartrate variability are more behaviorally reactive to distressing situations as well. There is no question that physiology affects the ways in which children regulate emotions or respond to autonomic activity. The degree to which temperament, and hence attachment, is a function of endowed biological attributes, however, is unknown.

THEORIES OF CHILD DEVELOPMENT

Stage Theories

Traditional theory holds that child development occurs in linear, discrete stages, each of which requires certain tasks to be fulfilled before advancing to the next stage. Accomplishment of the tasks at a lower stage prepares the individual for what is to come next. Failure to master the physiological and psychological requirements of one stage not only prevents successful advancement, but may lead to pathological self-development and psychopathology as an adult. As a child matures, previous stages are left behind and the focus turns to the current developmental stage. Three important stage theories of development are presented here.

Freud's Psychosexual Theory. Freud believed that personality is the product of innate sexual and aggressive drives which move from one point of the body to another as the child matures. During the first years of life, according to Freud, children go through several stages. The boundaries of each stage are marked by shifts in energy to different parts of the body. As the center of energy shifts, the child supposedly enters a new life stage and new developmental needs emerge. The environment reacts to these drives and either frustrates them or assists in their normal and appropriate expression.

Satisfaction of the needs generated by each stage requires assistance from significant others, especially parents. Conflicts that arise from the failure of the environment to satisfy or control instinctual urges, if left unresolved, can persist throughout adulthood. This is Freud's classic discovery: The "past is alive in the present." Freud argued that unresolved conflicts usually remained in a person's unconscious mind, that is, are not directly knowable, but had tremendous influence on personality development. For example, Freud hypothesized that if parents are too strict and demanding during toilet training, then the child may become anxious and habitually retain feces and later develop personality qualities collectively known as anal retention. Examples of these traits include orderliness, selfishness, and being obsessive about neatness. The individual may not realize that these traits are derived from anxiety caused by parents not appropriately allowing the expression of their natural instinctive urges during early childhood.

Freud further hypothesized that individuals regress to the stage in which they are developmentally "stuck." Being stuck refers to the stage in which the individual failed to satisfy and control instinctual urges. For example, adults who as three-year-olds learned to get what they want by throwing tantrums may act in infantile ways when angry because they never learned to control their aggressive impulses as a child.

From birth to about twelve months of age, the center of instinctual energy and the main source of physical pleasure is the mouth (the *oral stage*). Therefore infants and toddlers seek gratification by sucking, eating, and biting. They are quick to put objects, large or small, into their mouths. To Freud, this behavior satisfied the young child's stage-specific sexual impulses. If children are overindulged or frustrated during this period, they might become orally fixated, which includes such qualities as being gullible (will "swallow anything"), sarcastic, and seeking oral gratification by smoking or drinking heavily.

The *anal stage* begins at about age two, the time Freud believed the anus becomes the focus of pleasurable sensations. Toilet training and learning to control feces are the most important activities of this period. A child gains pleasure through self-control and being rewarded for the appropriate expulsion of feces. Referring back to the earlier example, if toilet training is particularly stressful, then the children may not resolve their needs to gratify their anal urges.

From three to six, Freud believed that children are in the *phallic stage* of development. The genitals are now the center of psychic energy. The phallic stage is one of the most controversial concepts in the social and behavioral sciences because Freud argued that during this period, children fall in love with their parents and then become excessively anxious about their attachment. Successful completion of the phallic stage requires resolving their "love affair" with their parent.

This process differs for boys and girls. In traditional psychoanalytic thought, boys are said to have sexual desires for their mothers, on whom they have been totally dependent, and want to possess them totally. They figure out they are no match for their fathers, however, whom they see as rivals for their mother's attention. Sons then come to fear that their fathers will punish them for having sexual desires by castrating them. This fear, known as castration anxiety, is relieved by identifying with the father and trying to become like him.

Girls resolve the phallic stage in very different ways. Girls also love their mothers, but when they realize that they do not have a penis, they blame their mothers for their apparent castration

(Why else would they not have the organ that is the center of their psychic energy?) and desire a penis. Girls then want to do away with their mothers and make themselves sexually desirable so that someone with a penis, preferably their father, will fall in love with them.

Freud's stage theory has been successfully criticized over the years for possessing several faults. First, the theory is unidimensional. The argument that sexual gratification is the sole developmental task of each stage is overly simplistic and excludes other tasks that are equally necessary. Second, the theory lacks empirical verification. There is little evidence to support the hypothesis that unresolved sucking needs lead to alcoholism, for example. Third, the theory is inherently sexist. What Freud saw as penis envy was probably status envy. Freud lived during a time when the status of girls and women was much lower than that enjoyed by males. Perhaps Freud encountered girls who wanted to be like boys, not because they coveted a penis, but because they wanted the privileges that males had.

Freud argued that, as children progress through these stages, three bio–psycho qualities, or components of the mind, were developing as well. The terms id, ego, and superego are metaphors representing clusters of personality functions and traits.

The *id* is the original energy present at birth that is the source of unconscious impulses that require gratification. In short, the id includes the impulsive, needs-seeking, aggressive qualities that are driven by the pleasure principle. The id is satisfied by the release of energy and relieving tension. Individuals must learn to release this tension in socially appropriate and gratifying ways. When people do not learn to do this, they become anxious and will attempt any strategy to lessen the stress. For example, when some people become depressed they feel hungry and will eat to excess.

The *ego* includes those psychological functions that control impulses. Eventually children learn that certain desires must be delayed. The ego, which is driven by the reality principle, is the rational and executive aspect of personality and mediates between needs for satisfaction (the id) and the demands of the world. In some situations, as parents teach their children, one does not get what is wanted, and gratification has to wait. In practice settings, you may hear jargon such as: "My client needs to improve ego functioning." This implies that this client has poor judgment, thinks unclearly, and copes poorly. Weak ego functioning is further demonstrated by poor decision-making, failing to deal effectively with reality, and spending a lot of time daydreaming and wishing.

The *superego* component of personality deals with morality. At about four or five years of age, children begin to internalize their parents' moral standards. Parents' transmission of the community's values and ethical codes is one way that families link individuals and the society at large. The superego is one's conscience. When a moral standard is violated, guilt usually becomes the dominant emotion. The qualities of the superego compel people to tell themselves that certain desires and impulses are bad or undesirable.

Freud's contribution to understanding human development should not be obscured by the errors of his stage theory. Freud was the first scholar to present a serious scientific theory of human development and define the questions that future researchers would ask. His insights into the force of the unconscious mind were revolutionary, and making linkages between a person's childhood and present behavior and personality remains a powerful therapeutic technique. Finally, Freud's concept of ego functioning helps social workers understand how clients relate to the demands of the real world and control sexual and aggressive impulses.

Erikson's Psychosocial Theory. Erik Erikson argued that individuals experience eight psychosocial crises during the course of the life cycle. Each stage represents a major adjustment people must make to the biological and psychosocial environments. The stages may be thought of as a struggle between two opposite or conflicting personality characteristics that arise from the individual's efforts to meet their needs. For example, the trait of trust competes with mistrust in an infant's personality (Thomas 1985). To Erikson, the term *crisis* refers to tensions between an individual's developmental needs and environmental responses to attempts to satisfy those needs. Psychological growth, in Erikson's thinking, is the development of individual capacities for mastering the social environment and reaching psychological maturity. Successful resolution of each developmental challenge is an outcome of the degree that the environment supports or restrains the child's attempts to complete the tasks and the child's own competencies. Although the issues of each stage are experienced throughout life, Erikson believed that each issue ascended at particular points in the life cycle.

Erikson's eight developmental crises are trust, autonomy, initiative, industry, identity, intimacy, generativity, and integrity. The stages trust, autonomy, and initiative occur in early childhood.

The first, *trust vs. mistrust,* begins at birth and continues to about one year of age. Through this crisis, the infant learns if the world is a safe and dependable place in which its basic needs will be met. From good caregiving, children form the general impression that their environment is trustworthy. If the quality of affectional relationships is poor, with the parent emotionally rejecting the baby, the baby becomes frustrated and its sense of trust is damaged. This repeated frustration convinces the infant that life is unpredictable and that people are not trustworthy.

From the ages of about one to three, the primary ascending psychosocial tension is between *autonomy and shame and doubt.* This phase corresponds to the young child's physical maturation and ensuing sense of power. Children build self-confidence by gaining control of their own bodies. As children discover they can do things for themselves, the environment should respond with praise and facilitate appropriate autonomous behavior. At the same time, parental firmness is required to keep children from overstepping their bounds and hurting themselves. In some cases, however, parents and other agents may punish a child for asserting normal autonomy. Not only is self-confidence not established, but the child may

FIGURE 2.1 Continued

Exercise is desirable

Fetus

Embryo now called a fetus

About twenty tooth buds are formed in the mouth

Fingernails and toenails are formed, though they are soft

Fetal heart beat can be heard from ten to twelve weeks

Fetus is about four inches in length and weighs just over one ounce

MONTH 4

Pregnancy

Morning sickness should have disappeared by now

The new mother begins "to show" and feel more active

Fetus's first movements may be felt

Mother and fetus have separate blood systems, but all of baby's nutrients come from the parent

Substances in the mother's blood stream enter the fetus within one to two hours

The placenta becomes the main source of hormones necessary to the mother during pregnancy and for the production of milk

A dark line (the linea nigra) down the center of the mother's abdomen may form; it usually fades shortly after birth

The mother's nipples and the area around them darken

Fetus

Placenta is formed

Fine hair called lanugo begins to form

The fetus moves, swallows, and hears sounds

Hair on the fetus's head and brows becomes coarser

By the end of the fourth month, the fetus is six to seven inches long and weighs about five ounces

MONTH 5

Pregnancy

The uterus has grown to the height of the mother's belly button which the growing uterus begins to push out

Mother's heart rate increases and she is easily tired

Muscle cramps may occur if calcium intake is insufficient

Mother may feel fetus hiccuping

The mother may have any of several pregnancy related symptoms, such as heartburn and indigestion, sore gums, and side stitches

Fetus

As the fetus is more active, it begins to sleep at regular intervals

Fingernails have grown to ends of fingers

Eyelashes begin to grow

Taste buds form in large numbers; many disappear before birth

Organs and systems continue to mature

Month five is a period of rapid growth; by the end of the month, the fetus is between eight and twelve inches in length and weighs from eight ounces to one pound

MONTH 6

Pregnancy

Mother feels the fetus kicking strongly and turning over

Back pain from carrying the extra weight occurs

The skin covering the belly may begin to itch

Fetus

Eyelids begin to open

Finger and toe prints are visible

Skin has color, is wrinkled, and is now covered with lanugo; skin is changing from being paper-thin and transparent to being opaque

Buds for permanent teeth come in

Hands are capable of gripping

At the end of the sixth month, the fetus is too small and its lungs too immature to survive outside the womb; if born now, the fetus might survive with intensive care

Rapid growth continues; length is between eleven and fourteen inches and weight is one to one-and-a-half pounds

MONTH 7

Pregnancy

Ankles and feet may swell from standing

Stretch marks may appear

Braxton Hicks, false labor contractions, may be felt

Mothers often have trouble maintaining their balance

continued

feel ashamed for attempting to be assertive and doubt its abilities.

Initiative vs. guilt, Erikson's third psychosocial crisis, occurs between the ages of four and five. During these years, the child gains more skill in using language. Communicating desires, interests, and fantasies speaks of initiative, ambition, and independence. Children now have knowledge of their independence and are consciously aware of their bodies. Punitive, shaming parents, who are overly critical of children's expressions and creativity, stymie children's initiative, leaving them to feel guilty for having ideas and for acting out their own inventiveness. Children should form a sense of pride in their activities during this stage.

Separation–Individuation Theory.   Margaret Mahler's classic theory of separation and individuation is one of the most utilized in social work practice. Whereas Erikson's theory traverses the whole life span, Mahler and her associates concentrate solely on early childhood. According to Mahler, the development of the self requires the awareness of being a separate and individual entity, a process known as self-constancy. Mahler referred to the gradual unfolding of becoming an individual as "psychological birth" (Mahler 1974; Mahler, Pine, & Bergman 1975).

To Mahler, personality begins in a state of *psychological fusion* or "oneness" with the primary caregiver and then works through a gradual process of separation. This approach assumes that newborns cannot distinguish themselves from their environment. They are undifferentiated. The caregiver serves as an auxiliary ego for the infant by satisfying needs and preventing excessive frustrations. Over time, the infant begins to trust others and rely on the self to satisfy needs rather than be dependent upon others. This process occurs in three developmental stages (Mahler, Pine, & Bergman 1975).

The first stage Mahler called *normal autism.* From birth to about one month of age, infants spend most of their time sleeping. They are, in human functioning terms, disoriented. The basic task of this stage therefore is to achieve a balance of the organism outside the womb. Mahler contended that newborns cannot differentiate between their own attempts to reduce tension (urinating, regurgitating, squirming) and the actions of the caretaker to reduce hunger and other tensions and needs (St. Claire 1986). The infant gradually attains a dim awareness that satisfaction of needs cannot be accomplished by itself, but comes from outside the self.

Stage two, *normal symbiosis,* begins when the infant becomes aware of the need-satisfying object which is usually the mother. The infant, according to Mahler, acts as if infant and mother were an "omnipotent system" or a "dual unity." This omnipotent fusion with the primary caregiver suggests that infants do not perceive a boundary that separates them from their mothers. During symbiosis, the infant–parent dyad enters a rhythmic pattern of need-tension-relief. The "good parent" meets the infant's needs consistently and with soothing verbal and nonverbal stimulation. The "bad parent" makes the pattern irregular and unpredictable and forces the child to separate too quickly and rely upon its own resources to satisfy needs. The lack of nurturance leads the child to respond to needs and tension with anxiety. Many researchers and clinicians contend that infants with the "bad parent" grow up looking for the fusion that was unavailable to them at the developmentally appropriate time. According to this perspective, older children, and adults for that matter, who are severely disturbed often regress to this mental state of fusion in an attempt to soothe the anxiety and losses they feel. If the symbiotic union with the caregiver is positive, however, the infant begins to make positive evaluations of the self while simultaneously expanding the self as separate from the caregiver. The child learns that it is safe to separate from the caregiver because the responses of the parent to tension are predictably comforting.

Stage three is separation and individuation, the two "paths" of development. *Separation* involves the emotional distancing and disengagement from the parent. *Individuation* refers to emotional autonomy, the ability to stand on one's own feet. This stage involves the child learning to function separately in the presence of the parents, without needing to be emotionally dependent on them. There are four subphases in this stage. (1) *Differentiation* is the time infants increase their awareness of being separate. By seven to eight months, children are usually competent crawlers and begin to distance themselves from the caregiver. While children are on their own, they begin *"checking back,"* looking for verbal and nonverbal (e.g., smiling) behavior that tells them that their separation behavior is safe and that the parent is monitoring them. Mahler believed that checking behavior signals the recognition of differentiation and understanding of what is mother's body and what is not. If the symbiotic period was uncomfortable, the resulting stress may show at this time in the form of insecure attachment behaviors. The child may push away and create distance from the parent, trying to be independent too early.

(2) *Practicing.* This subphase commences as the child's motor skills become more sophisticated. Faster, more ambitious crawling and standing signify greater autonomy and interest in their own activities. Children often return to parents for reassurance and comfort, but if a child is overly clinging, he or she may perceive the environment outside the comfort of the caregiver as threatening and hostile.

By twelve to fourteen months, developmentally on-track children begin walking. Walking represents the single greatest step in individuation (St. Clair 1986). Once children become capable walkers, they will play running away games in which they entice the parent to chase them. This game is important to the child's developing autonomy. As long as the parent pursues them, the child practices being away under the safety of the loving parent.

Also during the practicing subphase, toddlers begin to say a defiant "No!" According to Mahler's approach, this behavior is further indication of the child's blooming autonomy and differentiation. "No" becomes boundary-setting in children's minds and expresses the need to have some control over decisions and experiences.

(3) *Rapprochement,* the third subphase, begins at around eighteen months. Children at this

Comforting distressed children tells them that they deserve having their pain attended to and eased. As children learn to feel safe in trusting others when they are distressed, they are less likely to feel uncertain and anxious about their place in their social world. By learning to trust others, children feel good about themselves and to have faith in their own perceptions. In turn, the more they trust their own feelings, the more they can pursue their own initiatives without feeling guilty or ashamed.

age are becoming more aware of physical separation. Their improved cognitive skills allow them to think in a more sophisticated fashion. Similarly their mobility is continually advancing. These two processes often cause frustration in children. As they feel the need to separate, they also feel the need to stay near the parent. Mahler referred to this conflict as the rapprochement crisis. They want the parent to share in their new skills and experiences and typically delight in bringing products of their new skills to the parents for approval. Still they often fight with the parents, an autonomous behavior, while simultaneously not letting them stray too far away.

(4) Finally, *object constancy,* which occurs at three years of age, is the final stage in differentiation. The child should have worked through fusion and separation and now be able to relate to the parent as a distinct object in the environment. Children should see their parents as having both good and bad qualities without fearing rejection and abandonment when acknowledging the bad characteristics. Children begin to form what Freud called the superego, the conscience. They now should understand that their behavior has consequences and demonstrate rudimentary social emotions such as embarrassment and guilt. By this age, children should have internalized basic parental controls and tell themselves "no."

Enlarging Self Theory

More recently, researchers have criticized the validity of traditional stage theories. One approach, Stern's *theory of the enlarging self,* has surfaced as a legitimate alternative to the traditional view that children develop and progress through discrete, linear stages.

Stern (1985) rejects the notion that development is marked by phases. Almost from birth, the young infant has a clearly differentiated capacity for relatedness that enlarges and becomes increasingly more elaborate as the child matures. This capacity advances in organized "quantum mental leaps," which are organized subjective perspectives about how infants understand themselves and objects in the environment (1985: 34).

According to Stern, the infant's sense of self expands its ability to process information and relate to the environment. With maturity, the infant enters a new, and more mature, form of social experience. Previous experiences, however, are not left behind, but merge with the new, more advanced relatedness ability. These advances are not stages, but additive abilities of self- and other-relatedness. In enlarging self theory, the baby begins life not fused with the mother, but already separated. Developmental issues are never left behind. They are always present and can appear at any time.

YOUNG CHILDREN AND FAMILY LIFE

Perhaps the most profound developmental change in family life is the birth of a baby. When a baby enters a family, virtually all aspects of the parents' world take a dramatic turn. Family systems undergo three general developmental challenges when children are born: (1) reorganizing the family and marriage to deal with new tasks; (2) encouraging the child's growth while maintaining safety and parental authority; and (3) deciding how to implement personal and family goals. These tasks will be mastered only if the couple has resolved certain developmental issues of its own, e.g., separation from their families of origin, establishment of clear and appropriate boundaries between friends and relatives, and the resolution of conflict between individual's and couple's needs (Brown & Christensen 1986).

The advent of a new baby changes the role structure of the family. New parents must negotiate the additional responsibilities the baby requires. Despite fathers' increasing involvement, most of the responsibility of childcare falls to the mother, regardless of her employment status. Even among dual income, highly androgynous couples, women remain the primary caretakers. Problems occur when parents cannot make this shift and struggle with each other about taking responsibility, or otherwise indicate their refusal or inability to behave as parents to their children

(McGoldrick et al. 1993). Parenthood can raise family of origin and other emotional issues, and lead to conflicts for new parents. Insight into unresolved problems concerning one's own parents can minimize these new conflicts. Parents must also understand the roles of children. Many parents have unrealistic expectations of their children's capabilities. Some may erroneously believe that two-year-olds should have the competencies of much older children, or say that a two-year-old is "out of control" for acting within the developmental limits of a child that age.

Parents must establish rules that maintain safety and parental authority and still encourage growth. As children become more mobile, they are expressing their need to be inquisitive. Toddlers need parents' support in their quest for autonomy and their investigation of their newly discovered environment. Parents should encourage toddlers to make certain age-specific choices and, for example, take responsibility for feeding and dressing themselves. As a toddler gets older, gradual separation from parents is healthy. Time away from them allows children to explore and make mistakes. At the same time, however, parents must set appropriate limits and boundaries for their young children with authoritative, rather than authoritarian, discipline.

Families with young children must reorient their family and personal goals to accommodate the presence and needs of children. Parents need to know why they decided to have a baby and how parenthood fits with or disrupts their personal plans and their lives together as a couple. New family goals and rules must be negotiated and personal interests may have to be compromised to some degree. Commitment to parenting is important for new parents to assess within themselves.

DIVERSITY AND INFANCY

Divisions within the social world are apparent as soon as life begins. Newborns, who have no knowledge of the world they have entered, are already subject to social forces that affect their immediate quality of life and expectations for the future. Babies are completely dependent on caregivers for meeting all their physical, cognitive, and emotional needs. Social and cultural factors affect the ways in which adults respond to a baby. Although in most instances the differences are not great, ethnic groups often maintain separate practices of relating to infants.

Community membership exercises two general influences on infants. First, community membership can affect babies' physical well-being; second, it will influence how others will interact with them.

Diversity and Infant Health

Minority infants are at risk for a number of health problems that can lead to negative outcomes. As I discuss in a later chapter, infant mortality among minority groups, especially African Americans and Native Americans, is extremely high. Higher rates of prematurity and low birth weight, which can have negative long-lasting effects, also are found in minority communities.

A host of other health problems disproportionately clusters among minority infants. For example, African American infants have a greater prevalence of iron deficiency without overt anemia than European Americans (Carter 1983), and Asian Americans show a high prevalence of short stature, which is likely due to a combination of genetic factors and nutritional deficits. Low iron stores are associated with decreased attentiveness, fatigue, impaired performance on intellectual tests, and longer latency and associative reaction time. Iron deficiency, therefore, can impair transactions between the infant and the environment (Garcia Coll 1990).

Health problems, such as low birth weight, per se might not predict future outcomes. The stress these problems may add to already taxed families, however, may place infants at risk for neurodevelopmental problems and subtle behavioral deficits (Sameroff 1986). Garcia Coll (1990) offers the following example. Most premature infants do not show major long-term developmental outcomes. When raised in impoverished, stressful environments, however, these infants start to show a higher incidence of neurodevelopmental deviations. For instance, they are less synchronous, or responsive, in interactions with caregivers. In this case, biological conditions interact with psychosocial environmental factors to predict developmental outcomes.

In another example of biological and social interaction, preterm infants born to teenage mothers exhibit different developmental outcomes than premature babies born to adult mothers. In a study of low-income African American mothers, Field and associates (1980) found that those premies born to adults had achieved superior mental developmental accomplishments at eight months of age than those born to teenagers.

Some of the infant health risks associated with minority status is a function of genetics. African American children have higher rates of sickle cell anemia, and cystic fibrosis is prevalent among Pueblo Indians of the American southwest. Nevertheless, the bulk of health problems among minority children can be explained by their poverty status and the underutilization of health care. Cultural and economic factors interfere with accessing the health system for many groups. The Hmong living in California, for example, experience significantly lower birth weights than European Americans. Though almost all Hmong pregnant women receive prenatal care before delivery, they begin prenatal care much later in their pregnancies than European Americans (Helsel et al. 1992). Cultural and economic barriers are the main causes of their late entry into health care.

Other health problems are caused by inferior conditions in physical and spatial settings. Disadvantaged children living in old, dilapidated housing are at high risk for ingesting chemicals that result in acute or chronic health problems. One problem that has captured a great amount of attention is poor children eating lead-based paints. Despite the removal of these products from the market decades ago, slum housing that landlords fail to maintain is still covered with leaded paints, which have a sweet taste pleasurable to children. Because of their metabolic rates, young children

are highly vulnerable to lead poisoning. Furthermore, poor children are often deficient in iron, calcium, and zinc, which predisposes them to absorb lead at higher rates. High lead levels affect the neurological functioning of children and limit their learning capacity.

Diversity and Beliefs about Babies and Child-Rearing

Part of any cultural system is a set of beliefs and values concerning the nature of babies and interactions with them. Minority parents often share ideas about children that differ from other cultures. Minority infants, therefore, are exposed to caregiving environments differentiated by unique cultural beliefs and caretaking practices that might vary from Anglo American patterns (Garcia Coll 1990). Care must be taken, however, to avoid creating ethnicity-based typologies of beliefs and parent–infant interactions, for there is more overlap among groups than variation. For example, with their young children, poor and working-class Mexican American parents tend to be somewhat less authoritarian, less achievement oriented, more protective, and individualistic than African American and European American parents of the same social class position (Durrett et al. 1975). Durrett goes on to explain, however, that these groups are quite similar in terms of their child-rearing styles. Although their parental goals differ, their actual child-rearing behaviors are about the same.

Other cross-cultural studies of parenting styles report several differences between groups. Bartz and Levine (1978) compared African American, Chicano, and Anglo parents of similar socioeconomic status. These researchers learned that African American and Chicano parents expect responsibility and autonomy from their children earlier than Anglo parents. In short, they expect children to overcome the dependency of infancy as soon as possible. As a consequence of these values, African American and Chicano parents encourage the accomplishments of walking, weaning, and toilet skills early when compared to Anglos.

Parental perceptions of crying appear to vary by ethnicity. Anglo-American mothers hear infant crying as more distressing and "sick sounding" than African American mothers (Zeskind 1983; Garcia Coll 1990). Consequently, responses to infant crying vary as well. Because they label their babies' cries as more urgent, European American mothers pick up and cuddle their crying infants more than Cuban Americans and African Americans.

On a similar theme, Haitians hold traditional beliefs that infants have little potential for cognition (Widmayer et al. 1990). Therefore they engage in less play and talk with their babies. It must be understood that this belief does not mitigate the amount of affection Haitian parents show their infants.

The degree to which parents talk to their infants varies by ethnicity. Beckwith and Cohen (1984) found that Spanish-speaking Mexican Americans talk less to their infants at ages one month and eight months than English-speaking mothers. This finding cannot be generalized to all Hispanic groups, however. Cuban mothers interact with their babies more than African Americans and other Latino groups. They also talk to their babies longer and play more teaching games. As a result perhaps, Cuban infants are more facially expressive, but also engage in the most fussing and are more easily distracted. African Americans talk less to their infants and play fewer games with them perhaps because of African American traditions of not wanting to "spoil" children (Field & Widmayer 1981).

Many differences between ethnic groups, however, can be explained by social class and other environmental factors. A study comparing highly acculturated Mexican American mothers and low-income Anglo and Mexican American mothers found that the degree to which a mother is integrated into the dominant social structure, either by way of assimilation or economic status, predicts mothers' conceptions of child development (Gutierrez & Sameroff 1990). Unacculturated Mexican Americans and low-income mothers of both ethnicities tend to think of child develop-

ment in categorical rather than perspectivistic terms. Categorical beliefs are those in which single causes are associated with single outcomes. *Categorical thinking* is more rigid and reduces a person's ability to adapt their child-rearing practices for children who differ from parents' expectations. *Perspectivistic thinking,* on the other hand, allows a parent flexibility. Not only can outcomes have multiple causes, but there may be multiple outcomes as well. These parents adapt their behavior to a variety of outcomes. In short, the greater the cultural flexibility of parents, the more likely they are to have cognitive flexibility and the ability to transcend the modal patterns of accepted behavior and explanations of that behavior found in a more traditional cultural setting (Gutierrez & Sameroff 1990).

In a study of Haitian American children living in Florida, Widmayer et al. (1990) found that socioeconomic conditions affected parenting styles and children's developmental outcomes. This research compared rural and urban Haitian Americans. Rural Haitians suffered greater social and economic disadvantages than urban Haitians. Rural Haitians' housing is more dilapidated with poor ventilation and plumbing. They are not likely to have a telephone or air conditioning and their households are usually overcrowded.

Overcrowding creates a more restrictive environment for infants and young children to develop. There is less play time, fewer toys, a smaller number of safe areas to play, and less private time for parents and children to interact. Overcrowding either deprives young children of opportunities for stimulation or overstimulates them and is associated with delayed psychomotor development and lower cognitive performance at age one.

These conditions add stress to an already distressed Haitian community. Many rural Haitian mothers feel unable to provide infants with adequate care. They are preoccupied with the challenges of daily survival and avoiding deportation. They receive little assistance from an unwelcoming social and political environment in the United States. This research shows that even within the disadvantaged Haitian community, environmental differences within it create differences in infant development.

CONCLUSION

To a large degree, young children's experiences before birth can affect whether they will accomplish their developmental tasks. The structural model of social work practice requires the identification of what provisions are supplied by the environment to facilitate children's attempts to meet their developmental expectations. By analyzing the conditions of clients' conception, birth, and early childhood, social workers can study the history of clients' developmental history and look for patterns in client–environment exchanges.

Using the structural model as a framework for assessing parent–child attachments is particularly strategic. When parents, representing the main force in the social environment, work to build trust and reinforce appropriate autonomy, children are able to advance to the next levels of developmental expectations.

CASE STUDY REVIEW QUESTIONS

Refer to the case of Catherine that introduces this chapter. Given what you have learned, please respond to the following questions.

1. Catherine is clearly off-track developmentally. What should she be doing at her age?
2. How is Catherine doing using Erikson's developmental theory as a guideline? How would you explain Catherine's behavior in Eriksonian terms?
3. What might be the role of Catherine's prenatal environment on her psychosocial development?
4. In what ways do you think that Catherine's present anger is related to her early traumas?
5. What kind of attachment relationships has Catherine developed? Explain your response.
6. Place Catherine's life experiences in the context of Mahler's developmental scheme. How might Mahler see Catherine's experiences?

KEY TERMS

Amniocentesis: A prenatal examination in which amniotic fluid is taken from the uterus and studied for fetal abnormalities.

Autonomy vs. shame and doubt: Developmental stage when children build self-confidence by gaining control of their own bodies.

"Boarder baby": A baby that remains at the hospital longer than medically necessary because its parents are unable or unwilling to assume responsibility for the baby's care.

Categorical thinking: A cognitive sytle in which single causes are associated with single outcomes; categorical thinking is rigid and reduces parents' ability to adapt their child-rearing practices to children who differ from their expectations.

"Checking back": Verbal and nonverbal (e.g., smiling) behavior that tells children that their separation behavior is safe; when first learning to crawl and walk, children frequently look back to see that the parent is monitoring them.

Chorionic Villi Sampling: A prenatal examination in which tissues from the membrane that surrounds the fetus are removed and studied for fetal abnormalities.

Conception: The instant a sperm cell and an ovum unite.

Crisis: Erikson's term that refers to tensions between an individual's developmental needs and environmental responses to attempt to satisfy those needs.

Ectopic pregnancy: Pregnancy in which the fertilized ovum implants in one of the fallopian tubes or somewhere else outside the uterus.

Endometrium: The lining of the uterus where a fertilized egg will implant several days after conception.

Enlarging self theory: A theory of child development that contends that young infants have a clear capacity for relatedness which enlarges and becomes increasingly more elaborate as the child matures; this capacity advances in organized "quantum mental leaps"; the sense of self expands with maturity and is additive rather than growing in stages.

Fallopian tubes: Short tubes that connect the ovaries with the uterus.

Initiative vs. guilt: Developmental stage in which children begin to show initiative in their own activities and ideas; confidence and pride in the child's activities should be demonstrated during this stage.

Normal autism: Early infant stage of being disoriented; the basic task of this stage is to achieve a balance of the organism outside the womb.

Normal symbiosis: Stage of infant development when the infant becomes aware of the need-satisfying object; the infant is symbiotically fused with the caregiver.

Object constancy: The ability to remember and visualize an object when it is out of sight; Mahler's final stage in differentiation in which the child should have worked through fusion and separation and be able to relate to the parent as a distinct object in the environment.

Ovum: A human egg.

Perspectivistic thinking: A cognitive style that allows a parent flexibility; in this style it is understood that outcomes have multiple causes; this style allows parents to be more adaptive and flexible.

Postpartum depression: A period of depressive symptoms that often follows childbirth.

Practicing: A phase of development in which children's motor skills become more sophisticated and they "practice" being separated from parents; though they are able to crawl and walk, young children often return to parents for reassurance and comfort.

Psychological fusion: The first stage of infant development, when it is assumed that newborns are undifferentiated and cannot distinguish themselves from their environment.

Rapprochement: A phase of child development when children are becoming more aware of physical separation; a crisis occurs as the child feels both the need to separate and the need to stay near the parent.

Separation and individuation: The time infants increase their awareness of being separate from their caregivers.

Sonogram: Reflected images of a fetus used for prenatal diagnostics.

Teratogen: Any drug or substance that causes fetal defects and malformations.

Trust vs. mistrust: Developmental stage when infants learn if the world is a safe and dependable place.

Ultrasound: Prenatal examination that creates images, called sonograms, of the developing fetus.

Zygote: The first stage of the fertilized ovum.

CHAPTER 3

PRE-ADOLESCENCE

OBJECTIVES

After reading this chapter, you should be able to answer the following questions:

1. What physiological changes occur between early childhood and adolescence?
2. In the past, theorists have referred to this period as latency because it was believed that little happened developmentally. Now we know that this period is critically important psychosocially. What developmental tasks confront pre-pubescent children?
3. How is the family affected by a child in the pre-adolescent stage?
4. What is the role of peers during this stage?
5. What are the different types of child maltreatment? What factors are associated with each and what are their effects?
6. What are the main mental health issues of pre-adolescent children?
7. How do community influences affect the lives of children?

CASE STUDY

Rico, a ten-year-old fifth-grader who was having trouble at home and school, was brought to a social worker by his parents. He was the oldest of three children: his brother was eight, and his sister was three. His parents, Gloria and Stefan, have been married for thirteen years and claimed to have the "perfect" marriage. Stefan was a self-employed engineer and Gloria was a teacher before quitting to stay at home with the children. Although Stefan's business was going well at the time, that had not been the case earlier in the marriage when he and Gloria struggled financially. It was not until Rico was about seven that the family was able to buy its first home and have some financial "breathing room."

Rico was a very intelligent boy. He showed a great deal of initiative in science projects; he liked to build things and displayed an interest and aptitude for electronics. Stefan and Gloria agreed Rico was bright and was a "born engineer." Rico, however, did not do well in school. His grades were average at best, but were not indicative of his apparent potential. Furthermore, he was very hostile in his relationships at school. He surrounded himself with a small group of other boys whom he dominated and engaged in not so innocent mischief.

Rico was in his third school in less than a year. His parents had withdrawn him from public school a year before, because of poor grades and behavioral problems, and placed him in a private school. Rico's parents hoped that the private school's smaller classes would stimulate him intellectually and keep his behavior in check. However, after only a few months in this school, Rico's behavior was out of control and he was falling further behind in his studies.

His parents next tried a private school that specialized in emotionally distressed children. The student–teacher ratio was very small and all teachers had specialized training in behavior modification and anger management. The teachers were sensitive to the emotional needs of their students and were trained to postpone school work to tend to psychosocial needs when the children were feeling stressed. Rico seemed to feel even more threatened in this environment than at the other two schools and his behavior became less restrained. A few weeks after registering for school, he assaulted his teacher.

At home, Rico was hostile and distant. He refused to perform any age-appropriate household chores such as picking up his belongings and clothes. When his parents tried to enforce these kinds of rules, he would become belligerent and throw tantrums.

He and his father argued constantly; most arguments were over Rico's perceived laziness, failure to follow rules, and his sarcasm. Stefan showed little patience with Rico, especially compared to the other children with whom he showed much less anger. Almost every time Stefan and Rico attempted an activity together, it would erupt into a fight and end in chaos. Sometimes the arguments ended with Stefan striking Rico with his hand or a belt. He often locked Rico in his room for as long as an hour without access to food, water, or the toilet.

Whenever Rico and Stefan escalated their arguments into battles, Gloria played the role of peacemaker. She most often took Rico's side and protected him from Stefan's attempts to discipline him. This dynamic had considerable implications for the family, for it highly increased Rico's power. To placate Rico, Gloria would cater to almost every whim he had. She rarely set or enforced limits for him. For example, she would not finish her own meal to prepare something different for Rico if he did not like what was being served, which was frequent. In one interview, the social worker asked Gloria to tell Rico that she wanted him to start picking up his clothes up off the floor of his room. She was unable to do this without laughing.

After meeting with the family for several months, often without the children, it was learned that the marriage was not the perfect, no-problem union Stefan and Gloria maintained. In fact, the marriage had more than its share of conflict and tension. A great amount of the distress remained repressed and unconscious, however.

The conflict began when Rico was two. Called "The General" by his father, Rico had not been an easy youngster. He was an active and temperamental child. Nonetheless, Rico was not an unusual or pathological child; he was simply full of energy and inquisitive.

Furthermore, Rico's birth placed considerable economic strain on the family. Stefan actually left the family and relocated in another state without his family for a few months to earn an income when Rico was a baby. Life in those days for Stefan was hard, uncertain, and frightening.

To Stefan, Rico was a threat to the stability of his marriage. Though Stefan tried to blame his anger problems on his precocious son, he was actually afraid that Rico was coming between him and his wife.

Stefan's background helps us understand this better. His parents divorced when he was two. He did not see his father much after the divorce and he died when Stefan was nine years of age. Stefan's mother remarried when he was seven to a gruff, uncharitable man named George. George terrorized Stefan and his younger brother. He had very exact expectations for his step-sons and he enforced his will with physical violence. Stefan remembers many times that he and his brother would have to hide to avoid George's rampages. George also hit the boys' mother as well.

Stefan worshipped his wife. Gloria was a kind-hearted, loving woman who always managed to right all the family's problems. Stefan was also terrified that Gloria would someday leave him. Insecure in his marriage, Stefan deferred to Gloria on issues pertaining to Rico, as well as other differences. Though Stefan felt that Gloria was "too easy" with the children, he rarely argued with her about childraising issues, preferring to repress all marital conflicts. Keeping his problems inside, of course, fueled his rage and made him passive–aggressive.

Gloria and Stefan decided to bring Rico to the social worker when Rico started having repetitive nightmares about seeing devils and being burned alive. They had taken him out of school and were at a loss for what to do next.

INTRODUCTION

Middle childhood, a life cycle stage also called preadolescence, is often believed to be a time of carefree play and blissful nonresponsibility. This idyllic portrayal neglects the very real stresses and developmental tasks that affect children of this age.

Pre-adolescence is an important stage in the unfolding of one's life. Children must learn to succeed in school, become more independent and resourceful, and curb their emotions and behaviors in order to get along with others. This chapter explores middle childhood with the intent of dispelling the myth that little developmental progress is made between the ages six to twelve.

PHYSIOLOGY AND GROWTH

Unlike early childhood and adolescence, which are characterized by rapid physical maturation, growth during middle childhood is slow. During this time children become slimmer and taller and their muscles stronger, but the rate of this growth is relatively slight compared to the stages just before and after. Nonetheless, the growth that does occur during this period is vitally important. Increased muscular and skeletal maturity, paired with enlarging lung capacity, which occurs during middle childhood, allows pre-pubescent children to engage in more complex physical activities such as organized sports and dancing.

Perhaps the most significant factor of physical growth during middle childhood is the refinement of motor skills. School-age children can perform almost any motor skill activity, as long as it does not require power or judgment of speed and distance (Berger 1994). Boys and girls are about the same during these years, with boys having slightly more arm strength and girls having more flexibility. Motor skills are related to other abilities such as body size, brain maturation, and genetics, as well as practice. For example, as the brain, muscles, and skeleton mature with age, reaction time decreases, thus quickening the child's response to stimuli. Therefore, the older individuals become, the faster and quicker they are.

Not all children physically mature at the same pace; some are ahead of their peers. Genetic factors and nutrition affect the size and rate of maturation. For example, children of African descent tend to mature somewhat more quickly than children of European ancestry. African Americans have slightly accelerated bone growth and lose their baby teeth sooner when compared to European Americans. In turn, European-descended children tend to be maturationally ahead of Asian American children (Berger 1994).

Differences in maturation size and pace hold subjective importance for children. Those who physically mature more slowly than their peers may find themselves at a social disadvantage. Hartup (1983) found that differences in size negatively affect friendships and adjustment. Shorter children, for example, may face peer rejection. Being rejected for something out of the child's control can in turn affect the child's own feelings of adequacy and value. Research that shows that smaller children are more likely to be shy, anxious, or depressed supports this view.

A more recent study, however, found that height deficiency does not predict behavioral problems, though older boys who are shorter describe themselves as less socially active and having a few more problems than boys of average height (Sandburg, Brook, & Campos 1994). They were, however, significantly more competent than a psychiatric referred sample of boys of comparable age and do not report more behavior disturbances than a normative sample. Based on height, girls' behavior and affect are indistinguishable. In fact, smaller girls, ages eight to twelve, describe their athletic promise and social skills more positively than normal-size girls. The authors suggest that this is due to greater social acceptance of "petite" girls than "petite" boys.

DEVELOPMENTAL TASKS
OF PRE-ADOLESCENCE

Early developmental theorists, most notably Freud, described pre-adolescence as a time in which little significant development occurs. During these years, often called the *latency* period, children's emotional and sexual drives are relatively calm and repressed, especially when compared to early childhood and adolescence.

Other theorists, however, note that development during the latency period is not so dormant. Pre-adolescent children are very active thinkers and builders. They are beginning to enter relationships free from parental control and learn the tools necessary to survive in the adult world. Patricia Miller (1983) contends that, as pre-adolescents expand their world to include teachers, neighbors, and peers, they are acquiring cognitive skills and learning to adjust to cultural values.

Cognitive maturity has a profound impact on how children develop emotionally, behaviorially, and socially. As children's ability to think becomes more complex, their relationship to the environment becomes more sophisticated as well. Young children, ages two to seven, lack the ability for consistent logical thought. Children of these ages, which Piaget called *preoperational,* have great difficulty with direct cause and effect relationships and have mental representations that are limited to their concrete and immediate experiences. What is real and what is imagined are routinely confused. Preoperational children are easily fooled by appearances. For example, young children often believe that a man literally becomes a woman if he has long hair. According to Piaget, young children often focus their attention on single aspects of objects, a process he labeled *centration.*

By age seven or so, children's cognitive skills have progressed to *concrete operations,* which is the ability to think symbolically and rationally. Children are no longer misled by men with long hair (they are still males) and can now process information in terms of cause and effect. Children's level of cognitive maturity allows them to refine their ability for *classification,* the ability to shift attention from overt, visible qualities to abstract or conceptual categories. For example, a pre-operational four-year-old may sort pictures of animals by color, whereas a ten-year-old child may sort the pictures by animal families: mammals, birds, reptiles, and so forth.

A second cognitive development that occurs in concrete operational thinking, according to Piaget, is *conservation.* When a child realizes that an underlying physical quality of a substance does not change despite its shape, that child has mastered the cognitive task of conservation. For example, when four-year-old children see a tall and a short glass containing the same amount of water, they will usually say that the tall glass has more water in it because the glass is taller. Pre-operational children follow the same thinking patterns concerning length, area, and number.

The primary developmental tasks of pre-adolescence concern learning to become productive. Erikson (1963) saw this period as children's "entrance into life," in which youth of all cultures begin the process of learning to be productive. During this time, children learn to win recognition by learning the skills and tasks necessary for producing things. In Erikson's terms, children develop a sense of industry and show keen interest in mastering the tools and skills demonstrated in school and by peers and relatives.

The tension of this stage lies in the possibility of the child developing a sense of inadequacy or inferiority. Inadequate instruction and failed attempts to master skills may lead children to despair and may discourage them from identifying with those skills. One conclusion consistently drawn in the social and behavioral sciences is that early school failure predicts future adjustment difficulties. When a sense of industry is not instilled in children, they run the risk of losing hope and confidence in their own abilities to solve problems and become successful in their endeavors. To avoid these negative outcomes, programs such as Head Start try to enhance children's skills and compensate for families holding fewer resources to prepare children for school life.

As children begin school, they must resolve the anxiety that ensues when separating from parents. Children who have been in institutional day care before kindergarten may not have as large an adjustment to make, but for children who are leaving their homes for the first time, school may be a frightening experience. What is at stake is the child feeling that the omnipotent security that parents offer is threatened. Children may feel abandoned, undermined, or vulnerable when first going to school. Most children require a few days to adjust to the changes of attending school, to become accustomed to another adult authority in the teacher and principal, and to adapt to the structure and demands of schooling. When adjustment takes longer than usual, it may be an indication of attachment difficulties or some other tension at home. The child having difficulty adjusting to school may feel a need to stay home to protect a parent or may fear leaving home for dread that something disastrous will happen.

PRE-ADOLESCENCE AND THE FAMILY

Most theorists do not consider families with school-age children as a separate developmental stage in the life cycle of the family. This period in the family's development is believed to be a continuation of the tasks of families with younger children. These theoretical constructs fail to consider the family's role in the child's developmental tasks of industry and accomplishment.

When children begin their formal education, many aspects of their lives change. From a life cycle perspective, therefore, the developmental tasks of the family should change to accommodate the child. Families have four tasks for school age children which differ from the needs of pre-school, younger children.

One, parents need to help children learn to relate to a bureaucracy. Schools have formal organizational rules to which children must adjust their behavior or suffer some consequence. Punctuality, classroom demeanor, and completing assignments are but a few of the many expectations children must satisfy. Children must learn the "ropes" of the bureaucratic hierarchy as well. Knowing the functions of different offices and positions is vital for survival in the organization.

Two, parents must support their children as they learn to relate to adults on their own. Applying proper respect and etiquette to teachers, principals, and other school officials is now expected from children without the immediate intervention of the parents. Helping children express themselves and solve problems with adults who are not family members is an important step toward individuation and self-confidence.

Third, parents must accommodate the child's work assignments and foster a commitment to learning. Teaching solid work and study habits, stimulating learning, and helping children with homework require changes in the family's routines. Supporting extracurricular activities such as dance, music lessons, and athletics may mean extra efforts on the part of parents to transport children, buy the necessary supplies, and encourage participation.

Finally, parents of pre-adolescent children must support them as they begin to relate to peers in ways different than early childhood. Now peer relationships include educational and extracurricular activities that may invoke issues of competition and possible failure. Children are now interacting more without immediate parental intervention, therefore they should have support developing sound problem-solving and relational skills.

The concept of family also distinguishes pre-adolescent children from other developmental stages. Unlike adolescents, who understand their families as biological connections and tasks, school-aged children, whose cognitive abilities have progressed from early childhood, ascribe affective, or emotional meanings to their families. Girls in middle childhood in particular stress specific family roles and the importance of doing things together in their definition of family (Newman, Roberts, & Syre 1993). This finding is consistent with Gilligan's (1982) idea that interpersonal orientation has greater moral, developmental, and identification importance among women.

PRE-ADOLESCENCE AND PEER GROUPS

As children reach school age, peers rival the family for influence. Middle childhood is a child's first exposure to a social world that the children themselves have created. Children make up their own culture, with their own language, customs, values, and rules. Conforming to the social environment of middle childhood is demanding and somewhat stressful. Rules are strictly enforced and failing to follow the rituals set forth by peers can be devastating to a young child. Children form clubs, making lifelong pledges to abide by the rules set forth by their "charters." Being accepted or rejected by peers may affect how children feel about themselves.

Peer relationships satisfy important needs for children: (1) Peers provide social contacts and opportunities for children to have fun and express themselves with others having similar experiences; (2) Relationships with peers provide arenas for practicing for future adolescent and adult relationships. Through interactions with each other, young children practice expressing their opinions, learn to respect others' feelings, share, and learn to curb their behavior to accommodate the needs of others and the rules of social groups. Children, furthermore, learn the responsibilities of maintaining friendships; (3) Peer groups fulfill children's needs to form relationships outside the family. With peers, children assign importance to things, behavior, people, and events independently of parents' definitions of significance. Peer conformity provides the security of acceptance and fulfills belongingness needs; (4) Peer groups allow children to evaluate themselves relative to reference groups. In making evaluations and competing with peers, children learn about desirable traits and qualities and to adjust their behavior while away from their families.

Children do not fare equally with their peers; some are popular while others are not. Popularity is based on several factors. Individuals who are most popular rank high in overall adjustment. They enthusiastically participate and cooperate in group activities and are sensitive to group overtures. Their good adjustment is reinforced by their popularity (Specht & Craig 1987). In addition, IQ predicts peer approval: Those scoring higher on IQ tests tend to be among the most popular in school. Children who are athletic are also more popular among their peers. The ability to form close relationships with peers is indicative of social competence. Successful peer relationships also predict adjustment in later life (Cassidy & Ashur 1992).

Problems with Peers

Not all children, however, are equally integrated into the "children's society." About 10 percent of five to twelve-year-olds feel lonely or are dissatisfied with relationships at schools (Cassidy & Ashur 1992). Children rejected by their peers tend to be shy and less prosocial, which are behaviors that benefit others more than the one who performs the behavior. Difficulty forming peer relationships may be indicative of underlying emotional problems.

One study of ten- and eleven-year-olds found three subgroups of unpopular children (Hymel, Bowker, & Woody 1993). Each group exhibits distinct profiles according to peer perceptions, school performance, and relations with adults. The first subgroup, the *aggressive–withdrawns,* has the most problems and is most disliked by peers. They are perceived as socially incompetent and deficient. They are the most left-out. Furthermore, these children have the most academic difficulties and have more negative encounters with adults.

The second subgroup, the *aggressives,* are rated less negatively than the other unpopular groups. This group exhibits some qualities that facilitate integration into peers. Although members

Peer rejection and exclusion can be devastating to a child. A social worker might approach this problem in two ways. First, help children adjust to the peer culture in which they desire to join. Second, and most important, treat the child's social problems with peers as potentially symptomatic of other problems within the child's constellation of social systems. Family problems, for example, may interfere with a child's ability to relate to age-mates.

of this group are usually academically incompetent, they are often athletically adroit and may display a sense of humor. They tend to overestimate their competencies and have poor relations with adults. They are not as left out of peer activities, having their own networks of friends.

Withdrawns, the final unpopular group, are frequently competent academically, but athletically inept. Peers perceive them as socially incompetent and often leave them out of peer activities. Members of this group are often unattractive physically and think of themselves in the poorest light. They are usually more lonely and depressive than those in the other groups (Cassidy & Ashur 1992). As a rule, they present few behavioral problems at school and maintain good relationships with adults.

Other research has associated peer relation problems to abuse and insecure parental attachment. Salzinger and associates (1993) found that abused children have lower peer status and less positive reciprocity with peers than children who are not abused. Other children perceive them as more aggressive and disturbed and less cooperative. Abused children tend to form social networks that are negative and atypical. Poor peer relations have also been linked to insecure maternal attachment (Howes, Hamilton, & Matheson 1994). Children who are highly dependent on teachers for social contact and feeling safe have distressed peer relationships. Rather than socially interacting with friends, these children attach themselves to teachers whom they perceive perhaps as parent replacements to compensate for the absence of a secure parental relationship.

Similarly, some children become highly dependent on peer approval for validation. Hartup (1970) found that children who place great importance on conforming to peer demands have low self-confidence and high social sensitivity compared to children who are less dependent on peers.

CHILD MALTREATMENT

The social problem of child abuse portrays best the *raison d'être* of the social work profession. Histori-

cally, social work's greatest contributions have been made in the service of children abused by hostile economic systems and physically and sexually assaulted by adults. Social awareness of child maltreatment began during the late 1800s and early 1900s with the passage of child labor laws that prevented the economic exploitation of children. Only since the 1970s, however, has American society been responsive to abuse within families.

Child maltreatment refers to deliberately harming or endangering someone under the age of eighteen. Abuse occurs during all ages of childhood, including infancy and adolescence. It is during middle childhood, however, when abuse often increases, especially sexual abuse. Within the general category of child maltreatment are two types of problems: *abuse,* which includes all actions against children that are intentionally harmful to their physical and psychological well-being, and *neglect,* which is the intentional failure to protect children and meet their basic needs.

How much abuse is there? This is a more difficult question to answer than it appears. Conclusive figures on the frequency and prevalence of child abuse are elusive for two reasons: (1) the technical means of counting abuse cases, and (2) definitional differences among studies.

There are essentially four ways to collect data on the actual occurrence of child abuse. First, there are official crime reports that tally calls to police and child protective services and the number of abuse cases actually adjudicated. The primary problem associated with these data is that they exclude unreported cases. Consequently all that is measured are police and court activities. A second means of measuring the incidence of child abuse is to interview or survey a representative sample of adults and ask if they were abused or neglected. Victim surveys usually render the highest abuse and neglect rates. Numerous researchers have attempted to estimate the actual prevalence of abuse by drawing random samples from the society-at-large and asking a series of questions designed to reveal incidences of abuse. These studies, although probably more accurate than official data, are limited. Because of the emotional and

Exploring the Issues **3.1**

Psychosocial Characteristics of Homeless Children

Children are among the fastest growing groups of homeless people in America. When children lose their homes, the outcomes extend far beyond the uncertainty of shelter life and the fear of not knowing what tomorrow brings. Homeless children are at serious risk for long-term physical, social, and psychological impairment (Hausman & Hammen 1993).

The loss of their home uproots everything meaningful and dependable in children's lives. There is no sense of stability or safety and nothing is familiar to them once they are homeless. Relationships with parents are typically distressed and support diminishes. It is no surprise that homeless children experience several developmental, emotional, behavioral, and educational problems.

About half of homeless children experience at least one developmental delay, compared to 16 percent of children in permanent housing (Rafferty & Rollins 1989). They lag behind in gross motor skills, fine motor coordinations, and personal and social development (Bassuk 1990). Homeless children also have severe language disabilities and impaired cognitive skills (Hausman & Hammen 1993).

Emotional and behavioral problems are far more prevalent among homeless children than housed youths. The former group suffers higher levels of anxiety and depression and about half are be-

lieved to require psychiatric evaluation (Bassuk 1993). Research has found that homeless children have four times more behavioral problems than the general population of children.

Homelessness is associated with school failure as well. Enrollment and attendance are low and many homeless children do not perform well when they do attend. Consider these statistics about homeless children's educational record (Hausman & Hammen 1993):

- over 40 percent have repeated a grade
- 25 percent are in special education classes
- 50 percent are failing or doing below average work

Life in school is not easy for homeless children. "School is a living purgatory for homeless kids. Deeply ashamed of their circumstances, they invent addresses. If their homelessness becomes known, they are bullied, taunted and often beaten up by other children. Teachers treat them harshly ...,either because no one has warned them that these children may express their insecurities by being too aggressive or withdrawn, or because the homeless child, having become the target of playmates' abuse, turns into the teacher's scapegoat as well" (Hirsch 1986: 10, cited in Bassuk 1990).

---

legal nature of child abuse, many adults and children are reluctant to admit having been victims. On the other hand, many adults may feel self-conscious about admitting abuse or want to protect the offender. One shortcoming of these studies is that they use different operationalizations of abuse. As a result, there is little consistency among them.

A third method for estimating the prevalence of abuse is to interview those trained professionals who are likely to contact abused or neglected children. This technique asks professionals such as teachers, child-welfare workers, nurses, physicians, staff at day-care centers, probation officers,

and police officers, among others, to name all the children they known to have been abused. Then the results are extrapolated to the nation as a whole (Berger 1994).

A fourth measure is to ask adults about their own neglectful and abusive behavior. This technique is widely used, most prominently by Gelles and Straus (1986; 1988). The data gained from this method is believed to be the most limited because of adults' desires to protect themselves, the likelihood that sexual abuse is underreported, and because parents may not know when and if they are neglecting their children.

Prevalence studies of child sexual abuse best illustrate researchers' lack of agreement in operationalizing abuse. You may have heard a statistic that claims one in three girls and one in nine boys have been sexually abused. Despite the popularity of these "findings," they have no scholarly basis to them. Prevalence studies report ranges from six percent to 62 percent for females and from three percent to 31 percent for males. Concerning these prevalence findings, Finkelhor says that "although even the lowest rates indicate that child sexual abuse is far from an uncommon experience, the higher reported rates would point to a problem of epidemic proportions" (1986: 19).

Many studies that reported extremely high rates of sexual abuse included noncontact abuse such as being a victim of an exhibitionist. Still, with noncontact abuse excluded, these studies conclude that abuse is a greater problem than commonly thought. The wide diversity of prevalence rates can also be explained by the method used to gather data. Finkelhor (1986) found that studies that collect data through face-to-face contact yield higher prevalence results than questionnaires and telephone surveys. He believes that rapport with sympathetic, non-judgmental interviewers conveys the message that discussing abuse experiences is acceptable and important.

In sum, there is no "official" rate of sexual abuse prevalence. Although the one in three and one in nine measures are popularly believed to be factual, they are not supported in the scholarly literature. Nonetheless, it may not be appropriate to discard them altogether. These figures fall about midway between the ends of the ranges of estimated prevalence, so they are perhaps suitable compromise numbers. Second, regardless of the exact figures, all prevalence studies suggest that sexual abuse of children is a serious problem. Having a public that believes that a third of females and 11 percent of males are abused in this fashion keeps attention drawn to the seriousness of sexual abuse.

Neglect is the most common form of child maltreatment. As many as 14.6 in every 1,000 children in the United States are victims of child neglect, which makes neglect almost three times as prevalent as physical abuse and almost seven times as prevalent as sexual abuse (Wolock & Horowitz 1984). About 65 percent of all reported maltreatment cases are neglect (American Humane Association 1985).

Physical Abuse

The effects of physical abuse are numerous and serious. It affects both medical health and psychosocial well-being. At the extreme, children can suffer death, disfigurement, or a permanent handicap as a result of abuse (Walker, Bonner, & Kaufman 1988).

Physical abuse is often detected when the child is presented for medical attention. Nurses and physicians are trained to identify particular bruises, fractures, and other problems that are likely to be the result of a trauma, blow, fall, or strong yank. Certain bruises are apt to be indicative of abuse. Bruises to infants not yet ambulatory are one example. On older children, bruises on various parts of the body may indicate that a child has been hit from several directions. Bruises on the back of the legs, upper arms, chest, neck, head, or genitals are often the marks of abuse. Bruises hidden by clothing or imprints of objects such as a clothes hanger or belt buckle or a palm print often indicate abuse. Marks that go around the body may indicate the use of ropes or cords against the child (Davis 1982). Medical and social work professionals should learn to identify bite, choke, grab, or pinch marks as well.

Burns are common in child abuse. Burns inflicted by hot water, cigarettes, ropes, or electricity manifest distinctive patterns, though are often hard to evaluate. They are easily concealed and can be "explained away" by the offending parents.

Physical abuse can have serious behavioral, cognitive, and emotional consequences. Abused children, like all youths, respond to their environments. Their behavior reflects the unpredictability and instability of their surroundings. Abused children often exhibit behavioral problems and tend to be developmentally delayed, hyperactive, and continually irritable. They are difficult to manage for the most part and may be unresponsive to parents' routine attempts to manage them (Kelly 1983). Their behavioral problems, which are linked to past abuse, add to the burden of parents who are already ill-prepared to tolerate and cope with stress.

Specifically, abused children experience an increased incidence of antisocial behavior, aggressiveness, and delinquency. Adult criminal behavior has been related to abuse during childhood, one of the long-lasting results of childhood abuse (Walker, Bonner, & Kaufman 1988). Maltreated children often develop poor peer relationships as well. They have not learned to give and take and are hesitant to share with others. Their aggressive or extremely shy behavior and fear of rejection make forming friendships very difficult (Tower 1993).

Maltreated children are at heightened risk for impaired intellectual functioning. They perform poorly in school and on cognitive tests when compared with nonabused, demographically matched peers. Cognitive impairment is likely the result of neurological damage from assaults to the head, poor nutrition, or insufficient stimulation (Vondra, Barnett, & Cicchetti 1990). Abused children may demonstrate verbal inhibitions as well. Talking too much at home may have dangerous consequences. Abused children are less expressive and less able to describe their feelings and ideas. The lack of expressiveness may stem from parental disapproval of the expression of affect or needs. "In effect, these children may become 'overcontrolled' in efforts to meet parental demands" and lose their ability to communicate their needs (Cicchetti 1989: 396).

The emotional impact of physical abuse is overwhelming. Abused children are a collage of passivity, anger, and fear, emotions that impede any positive experience they may have. They use several defense mechanisms to avoid further punishment or rejection. For example, withdrawal, regression, and hypervigilance are common characteristics of abused children (Tower 1993). Regression is a particularly strategic defense. Through baby talk, thumb-sucking, and other "babyish" behavior, children unconsciously return to earlier stages of development when they felt nurtured and loved. Hypervigilance is also markedly telling in this population. Martin and Beezley (1976) use the term to describe the quality of passive watchfulness. Fearing that an attack can come at any time or place, abused children learn quickly to be on their guard at all times. They are sensitive to motion and may respond to physical actions with a defensive posture.

Abused children have an impaired capacity to enjoy life. Life for them is unrewarding and they respond to it with low self-esteem, temper tantrums, bizarre behaviors, enuresis, and encapresis. They are not confident in their own abilities at home or school, yet they have a strong fear of failure. The combination of wishing not to displease someone in authority or one from whom a positive evaluation is desired for fear of harsh punishment, and not receiving support and encouragement, injure the child's ability to follow directions, stay on task, and complete assignments (Tower 1993). In short, life for abused children is a series of anxious moments.

Causes of Physical Abuse. The causes of abuse can be approached at the macro and micro levels of analysis. The causes of the physical abuse of children are not solely rooted within the pathology of the offender. To the contrary, family violence against children has sociocultural antecedents that (1) distress caregivers beyond their ability to cope, (2) legitimate violence against children, and (3) provide limited resources to support both families and children. As we shall see, parents who physically abuse their children have personality traits that distinguish them from nonabusers. Yet putting these traits into an ecological milieu reframes them as functions of powerlessness and distress whose etiologies stem from environmental dynamics.

Poverty is significantly linked to child abuse. Although abuse occurs within all socio-economic groups, adults under economic distress are the most likely to abuse their children physically. Poverty prevents adults from acquiring certain resources, such as education, recreation, and day care, that mitigate everyday stress and enhance personal strengths. Parents in poverty are frequently frustrated and feel out of control of their lives. Their plight pushes them beyond their ability to cope and their children are the misplaced targets of their anxieties.

In this culture, children are perceived as economic liabilities. No longer producers, children consume a share of the adults' earnings. When a family has severe economic distress, children may be scapegoated or blamed for the adults' misfortune. They are seen as taking away assets and resources.

Other sociocultural factors, such as individualism, affect poor and nonpoor families alike. In an individualistic culture, a dehumanized child is perceived as an impediment to personal gratification. The narcissistic need to maximize stimulation, gratification, and self-aggrandizement may exclude consideration of children's needs or the parental responsibility to nurture and protect children.

A final sociocultural aspect of child abuse is the failure of society to provide substantive social support for children and their families. Society does not provide any tangible, formal assistance to bolster families. The community refuses to participate in child-rearing except to step in reactively after damage has already occurred. Modern family structures often do include extended kin, who could help with childcare and other services. Because adults are mobile in this society, most do not reside near their own parents or other sources of informal support. As a consequence, the parental role is more isolated than it ever has been in history.

Much has been made of the legitimization and acceptance of violence in western culture. There is no doubt that media images of violence as means to solving problems, the glorification of violent sports, and the violent content of everyday language (e.g. "I got murdered on that exam!") desensitize us to have high levels of tolerance regarding violence. Keep in mind, however, that violence has been a part of the American character throughout its history. Interpersonal violence in families and on the street and institutional violence have always been a part of history, perhaps in greater extremes than today. Children have historically been the victims of violence, and often with the support of the law, religion, and other institutions. It is only recently that people have become aware of the damaging affects abuse has on young people and taken steps to prevent it.

Within the social and cultural context described above, families and personalities develop that heighten the probability of child abuse. Looking at families first, there are two categories of variables that predict abuse: (1) demographic and structural factors, and (2) family dynamics.

Among demographic variables, family size and composition predict abuse. Large families, particularly those with four or more children, are most likely to be abusive. Large families mean less money is available per family member; there is less space per person, and less attention can be spent on each member of the family. These conflicts breed tension, jealousies, and resentment (Wiehe 1992).

Family composition, especially in concert with variations in income, is associated with physical abuse. Single mothers and fathers are more likely to abuse than parents in relationships. For mothers, abuse declines as income increases. Money is spent for baby-sitting and other services and goods that relieve or prevent stress. Increases in income may improve self-esteem for women and raise their levels of self-efficacy, thus making them less prone to physical violence with their children. For fathers, however, the story is quite different. For single fathers, income is irrelevant. Money simply does not matter; single fathers in all income categories are about equally likely to be abusive (Straus & Gelles 1986).

Many studies have researched the interactional dynamic patterns of families that are abusive. Most conclude that abusive families generally are one of two types: They are either extremely intractable in terms of roles and expectations or they are chaotic and unorganized. In the former, children never satisfy their parents' unaltering, rigid demands and constantly, yet unknowingly, frustrate and disappoint them. Strict family rules and parents' hostile responses usually appear irrational to the children who do not understand the inflexibility and the family system. Since children never fulfill their parents' unreasonable expectations of them, they are often labeled as "bad kids" who need to be punished and controlled. The rules are so strict and unreachable that the children are practically "in trouble" all the time.

In the latter family type, the chaotic, children are uncertain about family rules. No one knows what is expected. There are no patterns to predict which behaviors bring praise and encouragement or which bring on punishment. In some families, even receiving meals may be unclear from day to day. Chaotic families similarly produce anxiety and apprehension in children. Not knowing what to expect forces children to walk on "eggshells" while fearing that any behavior, whether good or bad, could illicit a hostile response from a parent. When the adults in the household are in conflict, which is usually the case when abuse is present, the effects of these family types are exacerbated.

Two other family dynamics factors have been identified in abusive families. The first concerns the degree to which the child is wanted. When a child is the product of an unwanted pregnancy or if the child is not wanted, abuse is more likely to occur. Furthermore, if the child is the "wrong" sex, abuse is more probable. With this in mind, it is perhaps no coincidence that girls are abused more than boys (Wiehe 1992). Second, parent–child role reversals are common in abusive families. Offending parents often hold expectations that children are supposed to be responsible for the happiness and emotional well-being of the parents (Bavolek 1984). Parents who exchange roles with their children are perhaps responding to having been parentified themselves as children and are now playing out the child role as adults.

Finally, let's turn to the traits of the abusive parents. Despite public opinion, parents who physically abuse their children are not significantly different from nonabusers. Perhaps one in ten are pathological; that is, they are so deluded or emotionally and cognitively dysfunctional that they never recognize the basic needs and vulnerabilities of their children (Berger 1994). Those parents who are abusive, however, do have certain personality traits and thinking patterns that, when combined with stressful environmental conditions, distinguish them from nonabusing parents. Abusers tend to be less trusting, self-assured,

Child neglect is not always the consequence of misguided or pathological parents. Neglect due to homelessness is a good example of neglect caused by the failure of macrosystems to provide adequate housing and employment for all people to maintain their families. Being without a home often has long-term consequences for children. Most experience some sort of developmental lag, do poorly in school, and have psychological problems such as depression, anxiety, or psychosomatic complaints.

adaptable, and patient than nonabusers. They are more concerned with their own needs than the needs of their children (Belsky & Vondra 1989).

Abusers' threshold for pain is short; they are easily enraged. This quick rage is perhaps due to their feelings of powerlessness. Many researchers believe that physical abuse is an expression of the parent's need to gain control or some degree of balance (Patterson 1982). They are unable to discipline their children without losing control. This theory is consistent with abusers' own testimonies that they love their children and only want the best for them. Many abusers claim that the maltreatment was intended as punishment, but that they lost control of their efforts to discipline their child appropriately.

Two factors may help explain why parents lose control so easily. One is the lack of empathy. Abusers are unable to imagine the feelings of being abused or identify with the child's discomfort, even though many were abused as children themselves. Nonabusing parents, on the other hand, demonstrate a high degree of empathy, which presumably enables them to avoid hurting their children.

Two, abusers are easily provoked. They are threatened by innocent glances, facial expressions, or words, and often believe that their children are vindictive, revenge seekers who are challenging them for power and control. Feelings of insolence are projected onto the children, whom abusing parents may perceive as sarcastic insubordinates.

The intergenerational cycle of physical abuse has been widely discussed by scholars, clinicians, and laypersons as well. On the surface, a theory that purports to be a model of abuse based solely on imitation is concise and easy to understand. However, abuse is more complicated than this. Indeed, about 30 percent of abusers are victims themselves (Kaufman & Zigler 1987), yet whether the transmission of abuse is explained by simple imitation is doubtful. Many victims do not grow up to become abusers and many nonvictims are engaging in first generation abuse. In fact, according to Gelles and Straus (1988), the rate of first generation offenders is increasing.

The relationship between childhood victimization and adult offending is not deterministic. Several factors can mitigate against this happening (Wiehe 1992). For example, loving and caring alternative caregivers can provide a positive environment that help children deal with the abuse experience. As adults, abuse victims may have the influence of a spouse or partner who did not experience abuse and this may prevent the former victim from abusing. Parents may make a commitment not to treat their children as they were treated themselves. Parents may gain new knowledge and skills about parenting that exclude abuse. Learning new skills and gaining insight into the emotional sensitivies of abuse are important barriers to continuing hostile behavior.

Neglect

Despite its prevalence, neglect has failed to receive proportionate attention from researchers and practitioners. Perhaps one reason for the failure to address the issue of neglect is the ambiguity of the concept. There is considerable disagreement on how neglect should be defined. Some definitions are broad, while others are narrower. For my purposes, the definition of neglect provided by Dubonitz et al. will suffice: "neglect occurs when the basic needs of children are not met, regardless of cause" (1993: 12). The "basic needs" of this definition of child neglect include food, shelter, clothing, health care, education, nurturance, and protection. It focuses on the failure of those in the child's immediate environment to provide those requisites that are expected in this culture.

A second reason that neglect has not received appropriate attention is the belief that neglect is not as damaging to victims as physical and sexual assaults. As shall be seen shortly, neglecting a child's basic needs can be particularly injurious. In some cases, the results can cause more harm than physical and sexual abuse.

Child neglect is heterogeneous; there are many different types, each functioning on a continuum of severity and frequency. Zuravin (1991) has described twelve types of child neglect:

1. refusal or delay of medical care
2. refusal or delay of mental health care
3. absence of supervision
4. refusal of custody
5. custody related neglect
6. abandonment/desertion
7. failure to provide a stable home
8. neglect of personal hygiene
9. housing hazards
10. inadequate housing sanitation
11. nutritional neglect
12. educational neglect

Dubowitz suggests that each basic need and type of neglect should be rated along a continuum that ranges from optimal to grossly inadequate care. The estimation of severity of neglect is based on the amount or degree of harm that results from the neglect.

The effects of neglect depend on its severity and the developmental stage of the victim. Crouch and Milner (1993) identify four types of effects: physical effects, intellectual consequences, social and behavioral outcomes, and effects on affective development and psychological adjustment.

Zuravin and Grief (1989) found that about 25 percent of neglected children suffer a physical injury. Examples of physical effects include failure-to-thrive syndrome in infants, illness or death resulting from malnutrition, illness or death as a result of withholding needed medical care.

Neglected children demonstrate deficits in both cognitive and linguistic functioning (Dietrich, Starr, & Weisfeld 1983). Cognitive outcomes are largely functions of severe neglect. Fox, Long, and Langlois (1988) found that, when compared to physically abused and generally neglected children, the severely neglected have the lowest language comprehension abilities. Neglect is associated with low IQ scores (Rogeness et al. 1986) and poor academic performance (Wodarski et al. 1990).

Victims of neglect display more avoidant and resistant attachments to their primary caregivers than non-maltreated children. They tend to be more aggressive with peers and their parents, show less

affection, and initiate play less frequently (Lamb et al. 1985; Crittenden 1992; Bousha & Twentyman 1984). Widom (1989) found that neglected children are more likely to engage in criminal and other antisocial behavior than non-neglected youths.

In a longitudinal study of victims of neglect, Egeland and Sroufe (1981) learned that these children show less positive and more negative affect than non-maltreated children. Furthermore, these children exhibit less effective coping skills. Other research has found that neglect during early and middle childhood is associated with adolescent psychiatric disorders, especially conduct disorders (Williamson et al. 1991).

Causes of Child Neglect. Not all people and conditions that produce child neglect are the same. For example, Nelson, Saunders, and Landsman (1993) found that newly neglecting parents differ from chronic neglecters. Newly neglecting caregivers are likely to have faced a crisis in the family because of illness, injury, or family dissolution. They show more confused thinking and dread, are more isolated from family and friends, and live in dangerous, drug-ridden environments. Chronic neglecters have multiple problems in addition to the challenges of child-rearing. Problems that chronic neglecters face include: poor hygiene, poor money management, unemployment, a child's mental retardation or mental illness, inadequate medical care, inadequate housing, parent–child conflicts, truancy, and adult mental illness. As a rule, these families are larger and have lower incomes than newly neglecting families.

Neglecting mothers differ from non-maltreating mothers in several regards. In comparison, neglecting mothers are more bored, depressed, restless, lonely, and less pleased with and interested in life. In fact, neglecting mothers may show more pathology than abusive mothers. One study found that neglecters are more hostile and impulsive, the least socialized, and under the most stress, when compared to abusive and non-maltreating control mothers (Fredrich, Tyler, & Clark 1985). Other studies characterize neglecting mothers as apathetic, emotionally numb, incompetent, and dependent. Alcohol and drug abuse are significant problems as well (Nelson, Saunders, & Landsman 1993).

Neglecting parents' interaction with their children is less positive when compared to non-neglecting parents. Those who neglect interact less often with their children, and are more controlling with them. In addition, they make more requests of their offspring while not responding to their children's requests from them. Neglectful mothers have unreasonably high expectations of their children and have an unsophisticated knowledge of their children's needs (Nelson, Saunders, & Landsman 1993).

But as Wiehe (1992) argues, findings from such studies inappropriately blame and label the mothers. He contends that analyzing such data from an ecological perspective would reveal that many of the mothers function in powerless, gender-related roles within the family. They receive little if any support from their partners and have a limited social network. Neglecting mothers are often caught in an intergenerational cycle of neglect. The deprivations from the neglect that they experienced themselves as children provide few psychosocial resources to avoid repeating their own experience and maltreating their own children.

Research that emphasizes the attributes of mothers fails to account for the environments in which these women live (Wiehe 1992). Poverty is a significant factor in child neglect. As family income declines, the likelihood of neglect increases. Many families are caught in no-win dilemmas in which they may have to choose between taking a job, paying rent and utilities, and providing proper supervision for their children. In many cases, the actual neglect may be society's neglect of the family (DiLeonardi 1993).

Sexual Abuse

Prohibitions against incestuous sexual contact and other sexual acts with children are universal cultural artifacts. Throughout history, all societies have maintained and enforced taboos sanctioning sex with children. Although history shows peri-odic normative exceptions to incest restrictions (e.g., marriages within aristocratic families in Europe and ancient Egypt), all societies have developed rules against incest. Humans learned early that incestuous relations disrupted family life, causing competition over sexual partners to interfere with the cooperativeness required for economic stability and survival. The belief that incestuous sex produced ill-formed and unstable children is found in most cultures throughout history as well.

Before the 1970s, sexual abuse was largely ignored by scientists. Many dismissed sexual abuse as an uncommon phenomenon; others actually believed that sex with adults was benign at worst and beneficial at best. Beginning in the early 1970s, however, social and behavioral scientists began to understand sexual abuse as aggressive behavior which damages the normative development of the child–victim. As more knowledge was gained and prevalence studies showed that sexual abuse was not only not rare, but widespread, abuse was redefined as an extension of dysfunctional social and psychopathological conditions that disinhibit the abuser from integrating and adhering to the ascribed taboos.

Who is at Risk of Sexual Abuse? Identifying which children are at a higher risk of sexual abuse is not an easy task. Since much sexual abuse is hidden, many victims and their offenders escape detection and study. From those victims and offenders who have been available for research, however, several risk patterns have surfaced. David Finkelhor, one of the foremost researchers in the area of sexual abuse, reviewed the risk literature (1986). In doing so, he synthesized the extant research to determine those factors that increase the probability of sexual abuse. These factors will be briefly discussed in this section.

Girls are at a much higher risk of sexual victimization than boys. Victim studies have found different sex ratios of victims—the range varies from about 3:1 to 9:1. Though it stands to reason that females are the likely targets of sexual assaults in a culture that continues to sexualize females of all ages, it is believed that the abuse of boys is greatly underreported. This may occur for several reasons according to Finkelhor. First, boys are reluctant to admit victimization because it threatens their masculinity. Second, the homosexual nature of many abuse cases may inhibit disclosure. Third, since girls are at a higher risk, public stereotypes have made parents and professionals less likely to identify boys as victims.

Children are more vulnerable to abuse starting in pre-adolescence. There is an increase in vulnerability at ages six to seven and another dramatic increase at age ten. Ages ten to twelve are years of particularly acute risk when children are victimized at more than two times the average rate (Finkelhor 1986).

It would seem common sense to assume that sexual abuse, like physical abuse, is more prevalent among the poorer socioeconomic strata. Research consistently finds no relationship between social class and sexual abuse, however. Neither mother's nor father's level of education or income correlates with a child's risk for sexual abuse.

Similarly, research has failed to identify any differences in sexual abuse among European Americans and African Americans. Rates for Asian Americans and Jews are significantly lower than the national victimization rates. Sexual abuse among Hispanic women, however, is the highest among American ethnic groups. Kercher and McShane (1984) found that 21.7 percent of Hispanic women reported being sexually abused as children compared to 9.8 percent of European Americans and 10.4 percent of African Americans.

Children who are socially isolated have a high probability of sexual abuse. Contrary to the stereotype, sexual abuse is not more prevalent among rural residents. Research has found that children who have no or few friends and are estranged from peers are at high risk regardless of place of residence. The cause and effect relationship is not clear with this variable, however. An abused child's isolation may easily be the *result* of sexual victimization rather than a risk factor. To protect the "secret," the boundaries of abusive families are often closed in order to minimize macro- and mesosystems interactions. The children and the parents have few friends and contact with social institutions is minimal.

Girls who live without their natural fathers or mothers at some time during childhood are at a high risk of sexual abuse. Girls who live apart from their natural mothers are almost three times more likely to be abused than girls living with their mothers. Girls whose parents are less available due to chronic illness (including substance abuse and depression), disability, or employment report more sexual abuse.

Having a conflicted relationship with parents is one of the most common correlates of sexual abuse, according to Finkelhor's review. Abused women report a more distant relationship with their mothers, who are often described by their daughters as harsh, punitive, and emotionally cold.

Sexual abuse victims not only report conflict with their parents, but conflict between their parents as well. Poor marital relations among victims' parents is a particularly strong risk variable. Victims routinely describe their parents' marriages as unhappy, troubled, and unaffectionate.

Many studies, though not all, have found the presence of a stepfather to increase the risk of sexual abuse. Wilson and Daly (1987), for example, conclude that stepparent households are especially at risk for all kinds of abuse because stepfathers are less knowledgeable about their role in the family and form less secure attachment bonds with their stepdaughters than natural fathers are likely to have. Consequently, taboos against stepfather–stepdaughter sexual contact are less stringent and have less deterrent effect. Furthermore, stepfathers may be less protective of stepdaughters when friends or relatives make sexual advances to them (Finkelhor 1986).

Effects of Sexual Abuse on Children. Though all children are negatively affected by the experience, not all are affected the same way or to the same degree. The intensity of the effects of sexual abuse depend on several variables. The psychosocial effects of sexual abuse are more severe:

1. if the offender is someone inside the family or a very close family friend
2. if the abuse is sadistic or violent
3. as the duration of the abuse increases
4. if the sexual contact includes genital contact, bringing the offender to orgasm, and intercourse
5. if the victim is physically hurt
6. if the abuse affects the accomplishment of developmental milestones and tasks
7. if the victim's report of the abuse is not believed
8. the longer the victim delays disclosure

Degree of Trauma.   Sexual abuse affects all aspects of an individual's psychosocial functioning and can be divided into four categories (Finkelhor 1986). The first, traumatic sexualization, refers to distortions in sexuality. Victims typically act in ways that are inappropriate for their age, e.g., sexualizing nonsexual relationships. There is a distortion in the perception of sexual norms and a confusion between sex and affection. They usually feel strong shame and guilt attached to their abuse specifically as well as to generalized sexuality.

Second is stigmatization. Negative messages are communicated to the abused individual and are often incorporated into the victim's self-image. Many victims believe their body is "damaged goods" and feel very uncomfortable with themselves (Segroi 1982). Body image is distorted and somatic complaints, eating disorders, self-destructive behaviors, including suicide, are common outcomes.

Powerlessness is the third category of effects. Sexual abuse victims feel out of control of their lives. They are chronically fearful and anxious. Self-efficacy and feelings of confidence are low. Many victims socially withdraw and nightmares and phobias are common indications of their apprehension and dread.

Finally, betrayal is an important consequence of sexual abuse. The inability to trust is a common outcome because they are deceived by someone whom they trust. Betrayal is further rooted in the anger held at the nonprotecting parent. Mistrust and anger are often generalized onto all people of the same sex or age as the offender, which leads to difficulty forming and maintaining relationships.

Causes of Sexual Abuse.   Studying sex offenders is one of the most engaging enterprises in the social and behavioral sciences. Sexual abuse is more complicated than other forms of child maltreatment because of the cultural taboos prohibiting the behavior and the existence of different types of sexual aggression. Finkelhor's (1984) comprehensive model of abuse integrates micro-, meso-, and macro-level phenomena into a coherent ecological theory that strives to account for that complexity. He contends that several preconditions must be met before sexual abuse will occur. These are: (1) motivation to sexually abuse a child, (2) overcoming internal inhibitions against sexual abuse, (3) overcoming external impediments to abuse, and (4) overcoming the child's resistance to abuse.

First, perpetrators must have some motivation to abuse children sexually. Finkelhor identifies three motivating factors: emotional congruence, sexual arousal, and blockage of normal sexual outlets. Offenders often find relating to children emotionally gratifying. Due to their own low self-esteem, arrested emotional development, and feelings of inadequacy and powerlessness, relationships with children provide a sense of power and fulfill social expectations of male dominance.

By definition, adults who have sex with children are aroused by children. This arousal is reinforced by child pornography, erotic images of children in legal advertising, and the male tendency to sexualize all emotional needs. Sexual arousal is not, however, unequivocally characteristic of sexual aggressors against children. In other words, arousal is not sufficient to produce sexual aggression in all cases (Hall & Hirschman 1992). What separates adults who are and are not aroused by children is a complicated question. Finkelhor suggests arousal is a result of conditioning experiences in which children were strongly paired with sexual stimuli. Another possible explanation is that perpetrators experienced a traumatic childhood sexual episode that caused sexual interests to "get stuck" at earlier stages of development.

Blockage refers to the offender's inability to have emotional and sexual needs met by other adults. Humiliating, rejecting, or unsuccessful previous attempts to gratify sexual needs with age-mates may cause the offender to shy away from future attempts. Such traumatic sexual experiences with appropriately aged persons are common antecedents to attempting sex with children. Inadequate social skills and marital discord are typical of child offenders. Because of these problems, offenders are often impotent when attempting sex with other adults.

Finkelhor's second precondition for sexual abuse includes those factors that predispose an adult to overcome internal inhibitors. Alcohol abuse, psychosis, impulse disorders, and a failure of the family system to protect children are common among child molesters. Several social and cultural forces reduce inhibition as well. For example, weak criminal sanctions against offenders, patriarchal prerogatives for fathers, child pornography, and males' lessened ability to identify and empathize with the needs of children facilitate overcoming inhibitions (Finkelhor 1984).

Precondition three includes factors that predispose adults to overcome external inhibitors. These conditions include: an absent, ill, or unprotective mother; a mother who is dominated or abused by the father; social isolation; unusual opportunities to be alone with the child without supervision; and unusual sleeping or rooming conditions. These variables may be associated with a lack of social supports and economic equality for women.

The fourth set of predisposing factors are those that help perpetrators overcome the child's resistance to the abuse. Children who are emotionally insecure or deprived, uninformed about sexual abuse, are unusually trusting of the offender, or are easily coerced are most likely to suffer sexual maltreatment. It is possible that raising the social power of children and making sex educa-

tion more readily available could negate some of these conditions.

Psychological Abuse

Of the different types of maltreatment, psychological abuse is the most difficult to define and identify. As Tower (1993) notes, most parents have been guilty of committing emotional abuse at least once in their parenting careers. Admonitions made too loudly or sharply hurt the feelings of the child and may have long-lasting effects on self-esteem and confidence. Though the behavior may be uncomfortably common, there are means to separate isolated occurrences from abusive behavioral patterns.

Psychological abuse refers to a behavioral pattern in which an adult attacks a child's self-esteem and social competence. This form of maltreatment includes such behavior as verbal comments with the intent of ridiculing, insulting, threatening, or belittling the child (Wiehe 1992). According to Garbarino, Guttmann, & Seeley (1986: 8), psychological maltreatment takes five forms:

- *Rejecting:* The adult refuses to acknowledge the child's worth and the legitimacy of the child's needs.
- *Isolating:* The adult cuts the child off from normal social experiences, prevents the child from forming friendships, and makes the child believe that he or she is alone in the world.
- *Terrorizing:* The adult verbally assaults the child, creates a climate of fear, bullies and frightens the child, and makes the child believe that the world is capricious and hostile.
- *Ignoring:* The adult deprives the child of essential stimulation and responsiveness, stifling emotional growth and intellectual development.
- *Corrupting:* The adult "mis-socializes" the child, stimulates the child to engage in destructive antisocial behavior, reinforces that deviance, and makes the child unfit for normal social experience.

These parental behaviors are basic threats to human development and are the underlying, unifying themes of all child maltreatment.

Effects of Psychological Maltreatment. According to Tower's (1993) review of the literature, children who are emotionally maltreated suffer feelings of being inadequate, isolated, unwanted, or unloved. Their self-esteem is low and they consider themselves worthless. Children's response to abusive messages is twofold: They either engage in aggressive, hostile behavior or they turn their anger inward and develop depressive, self-destructive, and withdrawn characteristics. Many of these children develop somatic complaints such as headaches, asthma, and colitis. Disturbances in sleeping habits are common. Emotionally maltreated children are usually negative in their communication and interaction with others and are active attention-seekers. Delinquency becomes an avenue to act out their negativity and anger and to call attention to their problems.

Causes of Psychological Maltreatment. Wiehe (1992) identifies two sociocultural factors (macro) associated with psychological maltreatment—stress and sex-role stereotyping. Parents may feel so overwhelmed with their problems that they are unable to empathize with their children's emotional needs. Psychological maltreatment is most likely to be found in distressed communities where unemployment and pervasive poverty create a sense of powerlessness and frustration. When formal and informal resources for family support are inadequate, families are overwhelmed by child care responsibilities and lose whatever positive coping skills they may have and fall into an escalating pattern of abuse (Garbarino, Guttmann, & Seeley 1986).

Psychological abuse occurs in middle- and upper-class families as well as those in poverty, although to a lesser degree. These families live in alienating, rejecting neighborhoods or engage in destructive practices. These maltreating families usually lack social networks and are isolated from others. Thus they are left to cope with their own stresses alone.

A second social factor underlying psychological maltreatment is sex-role stereotyping. Parental expectations about gender-appropriate behavior may influence the way parents understand their children. Religious and cultural values may define sex-role expectations that do not allow children to develop their full potential (Wiehe 1992). Parents who subscribe to traditional sex-role expectations may use humiliating or abrasive tactics to reinforce them.

A number of family factors (micro) are associated with psychological maltreatment. There is often a tense and aggressive atmosphere in these families, and the whole family environment conveys psychic threat (Herrenkohl & Herrenkohl 1981). Marital discord, chronic mental or physical illness, or substance abuse are examples of problems that erode the emotional meanings and ties of the family and lead family members to disrespect each other. In these situations, family members find being together aversive (Garbarino, Guttmann, & Seeley 1986).

In psychologically maltreating families, communication consists primarily of angry, negative interchanges that emphasize what the children are doing wrong. There is a noticeable absence of prosocial interaction, communication that rewards children for good behavior. Aversive communication may reinforce negative behaviors such as whining and misbehavior as attention-seeking strategies, even though the parents' response may be abusive (Wiehe 1992).

Another characteristic of maltreating families is the adults' lack of parenting skills. Their knowledge about child development limits their capacity to cope with the demands created by the child's needs and behaviors (Herrenkohl & Herrenkohl 1981). The parents may not understand the importance of supervision, regular eating and sleeping habits, or their role in stimulating and encouraging the child (Whiting 1976). They may doubt the adequacy of their parenting skills and vary the methods they use to handle their children, thereby communicating an atmosphere of doubt for the children (Garbarino, Guttmann, & Seeley 1986). The parents likely disagree on parenting issues and style and have frequent disagreements about the correct parenting methods to use (Herrenkohl, Herrenkohl, & Egolf 1983).

Emotionally maltreating parents are unavailable to meet their children's psychological needs. They tend to ignore, isolate, and reject their child. There is little physical or verbal closeness between parents and their children and parents are unaware of the child's need for warmth, support, and love. They lack respect for and discount the child's personality, thoughts, feelings, and behaviors and undervalue the child's accomplishments. In many ways, children are bothersome to the parents (Garbarino, Guttmann, & Seeley 1986).

Psychologically abusive parents were psychologically maltreated themselves as children. They received inadequate nurturance, support, and encouragement from their parents and have become emotionally needy, disturbed, and unstable adults. They are dependent on their children to satisfy their own dependency needs and so parentify their children, frequently asking for comfort and support from them (Garbarino, Guttmann, & Seeley 1986). Parents who emotionally abuse their children share many qualities with physical and sexual abusers, given that many of these abusive behaviors overlap.

CHILDREN'S MENTAL HEALTH

Thinking of young children as mentally distressed is a recent phenomenon (Early & Poertner 1993). Once thought to be a time of bliss and carefree play, psychopathology in middle childhood is now the focus of research and clinical interest. From these investigations, social and behavioral scientists are becoming increasingly aware of the range and the depth of psychiatric distress among pre-adolescent children. Estimating the prevalence of disturbed children is perhaps as much art as it is science. Though estimates of mental illness among children range considerably, most suggest that about 11 to 14 million, or 17–22 percent, are in need of mental health services (LeCroy & Ashford 1992). One government study further concluded that about 8 percent of all children have a

severe mental disorder (U.S. Department of Health and Human Services 1990).

Estimates of middle childhood problems may be conservative for two reasons. First, many childhood disorders, especially depression and anxiety, may be camouflaged. Problems of conduct, hyperactivity, refusal to attend school, and developmental transitions all may conceal underlying emotional, cognitive, and identity distress (Allen–Mears 1987). Second, many adolescent and adult disorders have their roots in negative, stressful experiences of early and middle childhood. The disorders, however, may not manifest themselves during the pre-adolescent years, leaving them unnoticed at that time. Middle childhood psychological distress can have serious consequences. These disorders frequently preclude children from functioning effectively at home, in school, and with social relationships.

During pre-adolescence, boys are more likely than girls to develop a diagnosable disorder. Between the ages of five and nine, males have a higher rate of psychiatric disorder than females in all treatment settings (Gove & Herb 1974). For example, of children ten years of age and younger, boys constitute two thirds of the admissions to inpatient psychiatric programs (National Institute of Mental Health 1986). Gove and Herb's theory of sex-role socialization perhaps best explains why this time is more stressful for boys. The theory can be summarized in three points. First, these authors contend that boys are under more stress than girls because girls develop intellectually and physically faster. Boys, however, are expected to perform as well, if not better, than girls. Second, Gove and Herb suggest that boys have a lower frustration threshold than girls. Boys are more impulsive, competitive, and aggressive, thus placing them in more stressful social situations and under more stressful evaluations.

Third, sex-role guidelines for boys are less flexible than traditional rules for girls. Girls are allowed to engage in traditionally masculine activities, whereas boys are encouraged to "act like men" and develop a masculine identity. Girls are not usually punished for acting like boys; young boys, on the other hand, are not awarded such tolerance. Young boys who receive traditionally masculine messages and opportunities spend a great amount of their time in day care centers, preschools, schools, and homes where they are largely exposed to adult women. Boys may experience more obstacles in expressing their masculinity and adopting a masculine identity in these environments. The lack of congruence between pressures to adopt features of a masculine identity and a social context predominantly supervised by women may leave young boys frustrated as to how they should behave (Cockerham 1989).

Gender alone, of course, is not the sole explanatory factor for psychiatric problems among pre-adolescents. Research has revealed two sets of factors, intrinsic and extrinsic, that strongly correlate with the increased incidence of diagnosable disorders among children.

Extrinsic Factors

Most studies associate environmental factors with childhood psychopathology. Table 3.1 lists those factors that are associated with mental disorders among children. Of these factors, parents' marital discord, parental divorce, parents' own psychological distress, and poverty are the strongest predictors of childhood disorders and deserve further discussion.

Severe parental marital discord is a significant precursor of psychological problems, especially conduct disorders, in children. Marital distress and conflict are associated with a wide range of deleterious childhood outcomes, such as depression, poor academic performance, and conduct problems. The more parents show hostility toward each other when resolving their marital disputes, the greater the likelihood that children will exhibit some form of antisocial behavior (Katz & Gottman 1993). Katz and Gottman (1993) conjecture that the purpose of children's behavior problems may be attempts to distract parents from their marital problems.

One important clarification should be made at this point. Marital discord in the form of chronic

TABLE 3.1 Extrinsic Factors Associated with Mental Disorders among Children

Parents' marital discord and instability of family Environment

Parents who are mentally ill

Parents who abuse drugs and alcohol

Paternal criminality

Foster care

Poverty

Homelessness

Prolonged parent–child separation

Lack of consistent caretakers

Crowded, inner-city neighborhoods

Catastrophic events

Bereavement

Source: U.S. Department of Health and Human Services, 1990.

arguing and bickering, violence, and game-playing, and not divorce per se, are the destructive forces that are harmful to children. Open marital conflict displayed in front of children leaves them feeling tense, angry, confused, and fearful of an impending separation and divorce. For children of conflicted parents, the future is frightening; each day could mean the loss of a parent and the loss of some semblance of security and normalcy.

As marital conflict mounts, antagonisms spread throughout the entire family system. Generational boundaries may become diluted and parental feelings may be projected onto the children. Roles may be reversed and accomplishing developmental tasks is affected. Chronic persistent marital discord scares children, and they often experience sensations of being lost and ungrounded.

Parents' divorce is the second factor. School-age children commonly react to their parents' divorce with depression, withdrawal, anger, grieving, fear, and shame. As they deal with the losses they incur from their parents' separation, academic performance suffers and peer relations are strained. Pre-adolescent children dwell on fantasies of reconciliation and are confused over issues of parental loyalty. As students, children whose parents divorce become less productive, more dependent, and have more failure anxiety (Guidubaldi et al. 1983). The effects of parental divorce appear to vary by sex. Pre-adolescent girls show fewer negative effects following divorce than boys, who manifest difficulties in a variety of adjustment areas, such as aggressive behavior problems and depression (Kalter et al. 1989).

Third, children of depressed parents are at a much higher risk for developing psychopathological symptoms themselves. These children are two to five times more likely to develop behavioral problems than children of nondepressed parents. What accounts for this pattern? Cummings and Davies (1994) contend that emotionally distressed parents transfer symptoms through poor parenting and interaction skills. Depressed parents are often emotionally unavailable to their children when their children need them. At the same time, however, depressed parents are more critical and intrusive with their children than nondepressed parents. Depressed and anxious parents further experience greater marital discord as well.

In response, children will externalize and internalize their parents' lack of engagement and emotional insensitivity. Externalized behaviors include aggressive and "acting out" behaviors such as running away and drug abuse. Internalized responses to parents' depression include social withdrawal, anxiety, and passivity. These symptoms have been detected as early as the first year of life. However, Hops and associates (1990) found that symptoms increase at about age eleven.

Ecological factors in family functioning contribute to the elevated occurrence of psychological distress in children of depressed parents (Cummings & Davies 1994; Early & Poertner 1993). Interactive dynamics are the primary links between parents with emotional problems themselves and the transgenerational qualities of psychopathology. In fact, these same interactional factors that are found between depressed parents and their children are also found in families that include parents who show no signs of psychological problems but have children with diagnosable disorders (Cummings & Davies 1994).

Fourth, poverty is indirectly linked to child psychopathology, but powerfully so (Comer 1985; U.S. Department of Health & Human Services 1990). Family processes and relationships are directly influenced by severe economic hardships, which in turn can influence the socioemotional functioning of the child. For example, children's risk of developmental impairment increases with parental rejection, and parental rejection increases during times of economic distress.

Economic hardship is associated with three sets of factors which are connected to higher rates of child psychopathology (see Table 3.2). Poverty negatively affects family dynamics, interferes with the provision of basic care, and distorts parents' beliefs about their own efficacy as parents. Poverty diminishes parents' sense of effectiveness as parents and reduces the extent to which they reward children's mastery over skills and encourage trust. Children in poverty are trapped in a double bind. On the one hand, they live in a culture that defines success in materialistic terms, yet they are

TABLE 3.2 Links between Economic Hardships, Family Dynamics, and Child Psychopathology

---

Poverty and Family Dynamics
  Reduced parental supervision
  More single parenting
  More adverse child-rearing patterns

Poverty and Basic Care
  Inadequate nutrition
  Poor health care
  Inadequate housing
  Fewer child care resources

Poverty and Parenting Beliefs
  Diminished belief that parents' actions can be
    instrumental in improving the environment
  Diminished belief in parents' sense of
    effectiveness
  Less receptivity to change
  Less flexibility

Source: U.S. Department of Health and Human Resources, 1990.

not afforded the resources to gain that success on their own. Added to this burden, the psychosocial toll of poverty on parents prevents many poor children from receiving the emotional and physical attention and resources they need to escape impoverishment and flourish in all areas of life.

Because of their overrepresentation in poverty, minority children experience higher rates of psychiatric and developmental disorders. Poor minority youths are more likely to experience (1) the stress of living on the socioeconomic fringes of society, (2) problems of accessing health care, and (3) institutional, cultural, and language barriers and discrimination.

Intrinsic Factors

Research has also identified intrinsic factors that are empirically correlated with psychological problems during middle childhood. Children who are developmentally delayed or have certain medical conditions are at higher risk for psychopathology. For example, low birth weight, brain damage, epilepsy, and mental retardation are factors that markedly increase the risk of psychopathology in children. Caution should be used in drawing inferences about the importance of any single intrinsic indicator of risk, however. Many of these factors occur in combination with each other and interact with environmental factors. Research has not yet clarified the specific influences of these variables on mental health outcomes.

Potential Protective Factors

As with virtually all social and behavioral phenomena, relationships between variables are not deterministic. Cause and effect relationships are believed to be probabilistic. That is, given a sufficient number of trials, what is the probability of a particular outcome occurring? Children exposed to the environmental and medical conditions discussed above have a *higher probability* or risk of experiencing psychological distress.

Some, if not many, children are exposed to ecological "hazards" that impede mental health but escape without impairment. How is this so? What factors reduce the probability of negative outcomes for children living in unhealthy and threatening environments?

There are three potential protective factors that reduce the risk of psychopathology and limit the occurrence of disorders in children exposed to persistent or traumatic adversity (U.S. Department of Health & Human Services 1990). First, certain intrinsic personality qualities of children foster adaptation to a hostile environment. Good problem-solving and social skills, for example, enable children to negotiate their problems, reconcile differences, and cope with difficulties beyond their control. Second, a supportive family milieu provides tangible protection. Warm, caring relationships with adult family members furnish structure, meaning, acceptance, and feelings of safety and security in an otherwise threatening setting. Finally, a support system outside the family can provide positive compensatory experiences for stress within the family and neighborhood. Positive relationships with adults and peers encourage and reinforce children's coping efforts and strengthen them by inculcating positive values. Those relationships also serve as positive models of functional, prosocial behavior.

PRE-ADOLESCENCE AND HUMAN DIVERSITY

Differences in ethnicity appear in middle childhood. How children play out their developmental tasks, have access to life chances, and engage their environments is based on the meanings of their memberships in certain groups.

Personality differences are noticeable during the pre-adolescent years. In a study of eight- and eleven-year-old children, Rotheram–Borus and Phinney (1990) identified personality patterns associated with ethnicity. These authors discovered that Mexican American children are more group-oriented and reliant on authority figures for solving problems than African Americans and European Americans. Mexican American youths are more focused on sharing, affiliation, and cooperation. Rather than trying to change a difficult situation, Mexican American children are more likely to change their behavior to adapt to an interpersonal challenge, and they are less assertive expressing themselves to peers and adults than European Americans and African Americans.

Such qualities have important implications as children interact with social institutions. For example, the cooperative nature of Chicano children suggests that school performance would be enhanced in cooperative learning settings (Kagan 1983). School social workers should be mindful that the social arrangements of traditional classrooms are often competitive and individualistic, factors that are biased against Mexican American children.

African American children demonstrate different characteristics. They are more action oriented, assertive, and expressive, and more verbal in dealing with peers and adults than Mexican American children. Both groups show deference to authority, but in different ways. African American children apologize more, whereas Mexican American children tend to "feel bad" (Rotheram–Borus & Phinney 1990).

In a comparison of European American and African American children, Last and Perrin (1993) actually found more commonalities than differences regarding personality and clinical features. Only a handful of attributes differs between the two groups. European American children exhibit more school refusal than African American children. Even when socioeconomic status is controlled, African Americans refuse to attend school less often than European Americans. Last and Perrin suggest this may be due to the lower levels of performance anxiety around school-related tasks and greater comfort in school demonstrated by the African American children they studied. Of the two groups of mainly poor children, European American children experienced more severe anxiety. On the other hand, African American children have a somewhat increased rate of post-traumatic stress disorder. The high African American PTSD rate is due to the greater intensity of the stressors they face; particularly crime and violence. Poor European American children exhibit higher rates of PTSD than middle-class European Americans as well.

Research consistently identifies lower income, inner-city African American children as running a disproportionately high risk for negative psychosocial and educational outcomes compared to affluent African Americans and to European Americans (Myers et al. 1992). These ecological stressors, with their incumbent injurious affects on parenting, e.g., higher rates of parental substance abuse and psychopathology, facilitate excess vulnerability to a wide scope of negative outcomes among pre-adolescent children. Several environmental factors disproportionately produce a higher risk for negative psychosocial outcomes in African American children. These include: disruptions in family structure due to economic downturns and regressive social policies, ineffective parental coping, hostile-rejection parental practices, and substance abuse among parents and peers (Myers et al. 1992).

On the other hand, several factors mitigate the deleterious effects of socioeconomic adversity within the African American community. Family resourcefulness and adaptability, cohesive family structure, reliable and effective social ties, protective parenting styles, and the maintenance of a positive outlook on life (rather than dwelling on the negative) are associated with reduced negative behavioral and emotional outcomes in children (Myers et al. 1992).

Another factor has been shown to improve self-esteem and reduce drug and alcohol abuse among African American children. Holding an *Africentric worldview,* a set of beliefs and assumptions that reflect basic African values, negates many of the harmful influences of poverty, discrimination, and stress (Belgrave et al. 1994). A study of African American eleven-year-olds revealed that those children whose value system and overarching orientation to life was centered on African psychocultural attributes engaged in fewer delinquent acts and felt better about themselves than African American children who did not hold such an orientation. An Africentric worldview includes: a high degree of spirituality, an emphasis on expressive communication and oral tradition, an interpersonal collective orientation, use of rhythmic movements and stylistic expressions, a perception of time as fluid, and a preference for multimodal perceptions and learning. These Africentric qualities enhance community attachments and social integration and serve as protective forces to offset the stresses and challenges of poverty and discrimination.

Hispanic children are also at risk for behavioral and emotional problems due to their disproportionate rates of impoverishment. As with Africentrism, culturally relevant means of relating to troubled children improve psychosocial functioning. For example, a study found that when compared with traditional western-based therapies and no interventions, *cuento* treatment significantly reduces anxiety in Puerto Rican pre-adolescents (Constantino, Malgady, & Rogler 1986). The benefits are long-term as well. *Cuento* refers to telling traditional Puerto Rican folktales that convey knowledge, values, and skills useful for coping with stresses commonly experienced by Puerto Rican children. Characters in *cuentos* are culturally similar and model values and behaviors with which the children can identify. The examples of Africentric orientation and *cuentos* as having beneficial mental health implications emphasize the importance of cultural sensitivities and community-based interventions in social work practice.

Asian children exhibit a different orientation to family, social life, and to themselves as well. For most Asian groups, filial piety is especially important among children. They learn very early to save face and avoid behavior that would bring shame and disgrace to the family and the community. For the most part, most Asian children are oriented toward the needs of the family, which puts them at odds with the dominant individualistic culture (Redick & Wood 1982).

For example, Hmong children are torn between the cultural expectations of their neighborhoods and schools and the traditional customs that guide children's lives within the Hmong family (McInnis 1991). Traditionally, Hmong families are very strict and corporal punishment is a normative and unquestioned practice. When paired with the Hmong's high poverty rate, stoic family life leaves many Hmong children on the margins of social life outside the boundaries of the community. As the children become acculturated, however, they not only become links to the outside world, they come under its influence. As a result of this cultural tension, many Hmong children feel rejected, confused, and angry about their social isolation, feelings that push many toward depression and social withdrawal. In school, depressed Hmong children are often mistakenly identified as good, nondisruptive students (McInnis 1991).

Health

The social environment, especially poverty and other social deprivations associated with ethnicity, is related to the quality of childhood health (McGauhey & Starfield 1993). Among European Americans, low income is a consistent risk factor for poor health, but among African American children, low income is not a lone risk factor. Other social risks, such as low maternal education and a mother's negative perception of her own health, increase the risk for poorer health among African American children.

There are several protective mechanisms for European American children's health that offset the effects of the environment. Parents' high school education and a mother's positive self-perception of her own health enhance the health of children. For African Americans, however, there are no comparable protective factors (McGauhey & Starfield 1993).

African American and Hispanic children experience particularly detrimental health consequences. Poverty is associated with higher rates of infectious diseases, more chronic conditions, dental problems, and injuries for minority children. Poor children have more days of restricted activity, miss more school days due to illness, and have more days of bed confinement. Homicide rates are very high for African American children, and murder rates for Hispanic children are higher than for European Americans. Asthma is also a serious problem for minority children because of their overrepresentation in poverty (Sorenson et al. 1993).

Poverty has particularly negative effects on the health of Hispanic children. They are more likely to die from infectious diseases, drowning, motor vehicle accidents, poisoning, burning, and choking, all conditions associated with social deprivation. In addition, they have very high rates of obesity. These outcomes are attributed to low incomes and less knowledge about nutritional matters (Olvera–Ezzell, Power, & Cousins 1994).

National origin is an important differentiating factor in the health of Latino children. The health of Hispanic children varies by community. Among Latino groups, Puerto Ricans are at the highest risk of serious poverty; consequently, Puerto Rican children suffer far more health problems than either Cuban American or Mexican American children. Puerto Ricans are concentrated in the highly urbanized northeastern United States where they are exposed to both environmental decay and pollution and the increasing social disorganization characteristic of industrialized urban areas. Their socioeconomic profile is seriously depressed and the economic prognosis offers little hope of improvement (Angel & Worobey 1991).

CONCLUSION

This chapter shows how the psychosocial environment has a strong impact on children's lives. The structural model of social work practice contends that improving children's well-being is best served by altering the environment to provide more resources and opportunities for them to be safe, nurtured, and properly nourished.

As demonstrated in this chapter, the causes of children's troubles are the social relationships around them. These relationships inhibit productivity, emotional growth, and self-empowerment. Intervention plans that solely focus on teaching

adaptive skills to children fail to consider the source of their problems. For example, poor children who see no advantage in learning in school do so not because they lack motivation, but because they see no tangible and meaningful outcome to formal education.

Many children have difficulty taking advantage of social opportunities because their immediate psychological environment does not encourage emotional and intellectual maturation. They are emotionally stymied because of abuse or their parents' marital discord or emotional problems. Children will carry these problems with them into adolescence and most likely have difficulty in that stage as well.

The structural model encourages social workers to plan interventions that change the organization of the social systems in which children are embedded. This means working on behalf of children at all levels of systems: macro, meso, and micro. It is only through changing the ecological relationships of children and their families that the needless hardships of children's lives will ever abate.

CASE STUDY REVIEW QUESTIONS

Given what you have learned, how would you respond to the following questions concerning Rico, about whom you read at the beginning of the chapter?

1. What developmental tasks should Rico be focusing on? How might you assess Rico using Erikson's terms?
2. How might Rico's problems be connected to his parents' own distress?
3. Describe how you think Rico interacts with age-mates. How should Rico be relating to peers?
4. Do you think Rico is a scapegoat? Explain your answer.
5. From what you know, what are the effects of Stefan's rage and violence on Rico's psychosocial development?

6. What do you think Stefan really meant by referring to Rico as "the general"?
7. How did Rico gain power in the family?
8. What type of "unpopular child" would you consider Rico? Why?

KEY TERMS

Abuse: All actions against children that are intentionally harmful to their physical and psychological well-being.

Africentric worldview: A set of beliefs and assumptions that reflect basic African values.

Aggressive–withdrawns: One subgroup of unpopular children; this group has the most problems and is most disliked by peers. These children have the most academic difficulties, are most left out by peers, and have more negative encounters with adults.

Aggressives: One subgroup of unpopular children who are rated less negatively than other unpopular groups. This group exhibits some qualities that facilitate integration with peers; although members of this group are usually academically incompetent, they are often athletically adroit and may display a sense of humor.

Blockage: The inability of sexual offenders to have emotional and sexual needs met by other adults.

Centration: The ability to focus one's attention on single aspects of objects.

Child maltreatment: Deliberately harming or endangering someone under the age of eighteen.

Classification: The ability to shift attention from overt, visible qualities to abstract or conceptual categories.

Concrete operations: The ability to think symbolically and logically; the ability to process information in terms of cause and effect.

Conservation: When a child realizes that an underlying physical quality of substance does not change despite its shape.

Corrupting: A form of psychological abuse in which the adult "missocializes" the child, stimulates the child to engage in destructive antisocial behavior, reinforces that deviance, and makes the child unfit for normal social experience.

Cuento: Telling traditional Puerto Rican folktales that convey knowledge, values, and skills useful for coping with stress commonly experienced by Puerto Rican children.

Ignoring: A type of psychological abuse in which the adult deprives the child of essential stimulation and responsiveness, stifling emotional growth and intellectual development.

Isolating: A type of psychological abuse in which the adult cuts the child off from normal social experiences, prevents the child from forming friendships, and makes the child believe that he or she is alone in the world.

Latency: Freud's developmental stage that begins at age seven and lasts to age eleven. Freud believed that children's emotional and sexual drives are relatively calm and repressed during this time.

Neglect: The intentional failure to protect children and meet their basic needs.

Preoperational: Phase of cognitive development in which the child has yet to develop the ability for consistent logical thought.

Rejecting: A type of psychological abuse in which the adult refuses to acknowledge the child's worth and the legitimacy of the child's needs.

Terrorizing: A form of psychological abuse in which the adult verbally assaults the child, creates a climate of fear, bullies and frightens the child, and makes the child believe that the world is capricious and hostile.

Withdrawns: A subgroup of unpopular children who are frequently competent academically, but athletically inept; peers perceive them as socially incompetent and often leave them out of peer activities. Members of this group are often unattractive physically and think of themselves in the poorest light; they are usually more lonely and depressive than those in the other subgroups.

CHAPTER 4

ADOLESCENCE

OBJECTIVES

After reading this chapter, you will be able to answer the following questions:

1. What are the physiological changes that signal the beginning of adulthood?
2. What is meant by the search for identity? What are the emotional, cognitive, sexual, and social aspects of adolescent development?
3. How do adolescents affect family life?
4. What is the importance of peer groups among adolescents?
5. What are some of the more significant problems teenagers often experience?
6. What is the influence of human diversity on adolescent development?

CASE STUDY

Nathaniel was a seventeen-year-old European American who was about to begin his senior in high school. He was referred to social work services for exposing himself sexually in his neighborhood. He lived with his mother, Caroline, his father, David, and his twelve-year-old brother, Jerry. Both of Nathaniel's parents were employed. Caroline was a secretary and worked for a large corporation and David was a mechanic.

Nathaniel denied any intentional wrongdoing in the sexual exposure incident. He claimed to have been accidentally locked out of his house trying to get something quickly off the front porch.

Nathaniel was a tall, lanky youth. He played trumpet in the high school band and by his own admission was "pretty good." Nathaniel's most glaring quality was his speech—he had a strong stammer and had trouble delivering two consecutive sentences without getting stuck. He was clearly very anxious during his first meetings with the social worker.

Nathaniel's father worked a part-time job in addition to his regular one. As a consequence he was often absent from the family. Caroline, on the other hand, overfunctioned in the family. She was the primary decision-maker and seemed to control everything that went on in the family. In working with another social worker in the same agency, Caroline admitted to feeling out of control emotionally unless she exerted herself throughout the family system.

The overfunctioning, underfunctioning imbalance within the parental subsystem of this family created considerable distress for Nathaniel. Caroline had trouble letting go. That is, she continued to relate to Nathaniel as if he were a pre-adolescent rather than a teenager. She vetoed his getting a driver's license, would not let him get a part-time job, and spanked him.

Nathaniel had trouble relating to peers. He felt embarrassed around girls, so he rarely dated. Though he had friends his own age, Jerry was his "best friend" and they spent a great deal of leisure time together.

Nathaniel had no plans for his future. Despite nearing graduation from high school, he did not know if he would attend college and in what field he would study if he did. He did not have a clear picture of his interests outside music, which seemed to be the foundation of his identity.

After working with the social worker for a few weeks, Nathaniel and his family went on vacation. One evening while his parents and Jerry were at the motel swimming pool, Nathaniel watched pay-for-view soft-porn movies on the motel's television system. The charges could have gone unnoticed except that he ran up a large bill flipping from one movie to another.

Nathaniel and the social worker worked together for eight months. In that time, Nathaniel learned to be more assertive about getting his developmental needs met. He also learned to express anger at his mother and father. In her own work, Caroline learned to let Nathaniel be a teenager without fearing overwhelming emotional loss. As they made these changes, Nathaniel was allowed to drive and get a job. The more he expressed his anger and was allowed some degree of autonomy, the less he stammered.

INTRODUCTION

Adolescence is a very important time in people's lives. It is the period of transition from childhood to adulthood and is marked by contradictions and paradoxes. Adolescence is when individuals become self-aware and move toward independence, yet they remain dependent on their parents. It is both exciting and stress-inducing, blissful and tumultuous.

This chapter discusses the biological, psychological, and social development of adolescence and explores the difficulties many youths face in their journey to discover themselves and the nature of the world around them.

PHYSIOLOGICAL MATURATION

Puberty

Puberty (from the Latin *pubescere,* to be covered with hair) is the period of rapid growth and sexual maturation that marks the end of childhood and the beginning of physical adulthood. The pubescent period involves the most physiological changes a person undergoes, with the exception of the first two years of life, and transforms virtually all human biological systems to adult size, shape, and sexual capability.

The physiological mechanism that triggers puberty is unknown. Some theories suggest that body weight or a ratio between height and weight initiates the process—puberty often commences when a child reaches about 100 pounds. However triggered, puberty begins internally with a series of hormonal changes in the brain. Hormones are chemical substances that stimulate and regulate organ functioning and the production of other hormones.

The *hypothalamus* is the part of the brain that regulates certain metabolic activities such as water balance and sugar and fat metabolism as well as temperature control and hormone production. At the onset of puberty, the hypothalamus enlarges and secretes neurochemicals that instruct the pituitary, a gland located at the base of the brain, to discharge greater amounts of gonadotropins into the bloodstream. The *gonadotropins,* which are identical in males and females, are hormones that stimulate the gonads. The consequences of gonadotropins, of course, vary by gender: In males they cause the testes to increase testosterone output, and in females they bring about elevated estrogen levels in the ovaries. Puberty begins anywhere from ages nine to sixteen, and it may take three to four years to complete the process. The onset of puberty is usually earlier for girls, from age nine to thirteen. For boys, puberty typically begins at age thirteen. The growth spurt that accompanies puberty also occurs earlier in girls than boys, typically at about ages twelve and fourteen, respectively; this results in girls often being taller than boys during early adolescence. The onset of puberty before age eight is called precocious puberty and is usually not an indication of a serious medical problem. When this occurs, however, a physical examination is warranted.

Female Puberty.   For girls, puberty includes physical growth in height and weight, the first *menstrual period,* and the development of *secondary sex characteristics.* Menstruation is the monthly vaginal discharge of blood and the lining of the uterus. Secondary sex characteristics are physical traits that distinguish males and females but are not essential for reproduction. In women, secondary sex characteristics include the emergence of breasts, underarm and pubic hair, and widening of the hips. External genitals, the labia, enlarge, and internal sex organs change as well. The walls of the vaginal cavity become thicker and the uterus enlarges and becomes more muscular. Within one to two years after the appearance of secondary sex characteristics, the PH value of the vaginal environment changes from alkaline to acidic as the vagina and cervix begin to secrete fluids characteristic of adult women. Within a few months of this development, the first menstrual cycle, known as *menarche,* occurs.

Menarche is the most definitive marker indicating the transition to adulthood. Most girls reach menarche by twelve or thirteen, although athletic girls who engage in vigorous physical activities and those with weight-related health problems, such as anorexia nervosa, may have delayed menarche and irregular menstrual cycles.

The ovaries of newborn girls already hold all the eggs they will ever produce, though the eggs are merely immature cells at birth. Once menstruation begins, about every 28 to 30 days, the pituitary gland signals the ovaries to produce a mature egg, called an ovum. Several eggs mature, though only one eventually emerges. As the ovum develops, it "tells" the pituitary, through the hormone estrogen, of its progress. When the egg is ready, the pituitary secretes the hormone *LH* (*luteinizing hormone*) into the bloodstream.

LH stimulates the *egg follicle* (tiny sacs within the ovaries, each containing an ovum) and causes its eventual rupture. Many follicles are stimulated, but usually only one matures. The ovaries, through the production of the hormones estrogen and progesterone, cause the endometrium (the lining of the uterus) to thicken in preparation for receiving a fertilized egg. These events mark the first phase of the menstrual cycle, called the *follicular phase.*

The second phase of the menstrual cycle is the *ovulatory phase.* A few hours, normally twelve to twenty-four, after LH reaches its highest level, the follicle ruptures and the mature egg is released. This is termed *ovulation.*

The third phase of menstruation is called the *luteal* or secretory phase during which the endometrium is ready for the implantation of a fertilized egg. High levels of LH continue to affect the follicle vacated by the released egg. Follicular cells multiply and fill the now empty space. The new growth (*corpus luteum*) is yellow in color and secretes progesterone and renews the manufacture of estrogen. If the egg is not fertilized, the corpus luteum shrinks, decays, and is replaced by other tissue. As the activity of the corpus luteum declines, progesterone and estrogen levels decrease, signalling the pituitary to stop releasing LH.

If the egg is fertilized and attaches to the endometrium, the corpus luteum continues to produce progesterone, which maintains the uterine wall for fetal development, stimulates mammary glands, and prevents premature contractions.

If there is no fertilization, small patches of the endometrium break off and constricted arteries open up. The beginning of menstruation, the fourth phase, is the flow of menstrual fluid, menstrual bleeding, and shedding the excess tissues of the endometrium.

Menarche does not necessarily mean that a girl is fertile. The first menstrual cycle is usually anovulatory; it occurs without ovulation. In fact, most girls are unable to conceive within the first year of menarche; during this time, ovulation is irregular. Should an egg become fertilized, spontaneous abortion is likely because the uterus is not fully formed. Pregnancy is possible following menarche, simply less probable.

Male Puberty.   For boys, puberty is indicated by a fairly rapid increase in height and weight, broadening of the shoulders, and increase in size of the penis and testes. About a year before the visible signs of puberty appear, the maturing testes increase production of testosterone. The heightened levels of testosterone elicit physiological changes in boys: the testes and scrotum become noticeably larger, pubic hair begins to grow, the penis grows, the body's growth spurt begins (broadened shoulders, hardening of muscle tissue, increased height), the voice lowers, and facial and underarm hair appear.

Boys' equivalent of menarche is *spermarche,* the first ejaculation to contain sperm and the indicator that boys possess reproductive potential. This often occurs during sleep in a nocturnal emission or through the first full ejaculation, usually by masturbation. Just as girls are not usually capable of reproduction immediately following menarche, boys' first ejaculation does not signify their fullest reproductive potential. Several months to more than a year can pass before the seminal fluid may contain a sufficient concentration of sperm to fertilize a mature egg.

Pubescent males are also likely to experience temporary cases of severe acne and *gynecomastia.* During puberty, the skin begins to secrete an excessive amount of oil that clogs the pores, especially on the face. Since teenagers are often intensely aware of their appearance and sexual maturity, acne can lead to self-consciousness and shyness in relating to peers. Acne occurs in females as well, but it is more common among teenage boys. Gynecomastia is the temporary enlargement of the breasts that occurs in most pubescent boys. As hormone production stabilizes and the body adjusts to the changes of puberty, gynecomastia typically disappears.

Psychological Responses to Puberty.   Puberty is a time when the so-called mind–body connection is apparent. Concurrent with the sexual maturity of the body is the sexualizing of relationships, beginnings of sexual fantasies, and a self-consciousness that now includes sexualizing the self. Adolescents become increasingly aware of their appearance and spend a great deal of time in front of the mirror, fretting over their hair, facial and body features, and clothing styles. For girls, body weight and breast development become significant measures of self-evaluation. For boys, a broad chest, wide shoulders and strong arms are important for ranking each other. Boys also worry about the size of their penises, equating size with masculinity. Another source of discomfort and embarrassment for teenage boys is inability to control the erection reflex, which leads to erections at inopportune times, such as in class, on the bus, or while dancing. Boys need to know that these occurrences are normal and happen to most youngsters their age.

DEVELOPMENTAL TASKS
OF ADOLESCENCE

Adolescence is essentially a cultural creation, rather than a true biological stage, and did not exist as a cultural artifact until the early years of western industrialization. Before that time, there were essentially two stages of life: children were children until puberty, at which time they became adults. In many cultures, complex ceremonies and rituals "delivered" children into the adult world and proved to the community that they possessed the wherewithal to perform adult roles. In Jewish tradition, for example, the Bat Mitzvah or Bar Mitzvah, usually at age thirteen, is an important religious and cultural event that tells both the child and the public that the child is entitled to adult standing within the religious community. Other than the Bar or Bat Mitzvah in Judaism and confirmation among some Christian groups, there are few normative ceremonies that are accepted throughout western culture.

Perhaps the closest practice adolescents have that signifies the transition to adulthood in the U.S. is obtaining a driver's license, at age sixteen in most states. This is done, however, with little fanfare or recognition, but does carry with it adult rewards, most noticeably the freedom of mobility. Able to drive, the adolescent can go places without adult supervision and more freely experiment with and explore behaviors, values, and ethics. Other adult activities, such as voting and serving in the military are extended to older teenagers as well. Other than these privileges, adolescents are typically left to invent their own rites of passage into adulthood. Unfortunately, these rituals may include alcohol and drug use and uncomfortable or degrading sex.

The essential problem during this stage is that adolescents lack a frame of reference to guide and give meaning to their behavior and emotions. During childhood, children depend on parents and other adults to provide stability and a framework for solving problems. The environment is protective and children benefit from the familiarity of social contexts. Adolescence, on the other hand, is a time children become marginal persons; puberty separates them from younger children, but social practices and opportunities deny them adult status. The happiness and security of childhood are replaced by the need to develop self-control, values, adult goals, and self-esteem—usually without any guiding framework.

Seltzer (1989) describes adolescence as living in "no man's land," where children are on unfamiliar, unsteady ground. They have outgrown the roles of early childhood, but adult roles are not yet attainable. Seltzer describes the psychosocial condition of adolescence as *frameworklessness*. Having reached their sexual maturity, teenagers are physiological adults; society, however, has extended the emotional and psychological dependency of early childhood well beyond the time of physiological maturity. The emphasis placed on a minimum of a high school education by the job market and laws that define children as "minors" until age eighteen set the limits of adolescence. For many, going to college and perhaps on to graduate school perpetuates dependency on the family of origin well into the child's twenties. In such cases, the end of adolescence is hard to determine. Such situations typify the ambiguity most teenagers experience during these transition years.

Developing an Identity

The search for identity, i.e., individuals' attempts to define themselves as unique people (Erikson 1968), begins in adolescence. For Freud, the quest for identity centers on genital and sexual pleasure. He referred to adolescence as the *genital stage* because sexual stimulation is sought. Because energy is focused on the genitals, Freud believed that people are motivated to express their sexual needs, marry, and raise a family.

As in the other life stages, a great deal more is happening than concentration on sexual energy. Adolescents are expected to enter adulthood with a clear understanding of their values, goals, abilities, talents, and limitations. According to Erikson, the psychosocial conflict of this period, *identity versus identity confusion,* represents the struggle of teenagers to integrate all the components of the self into a unified whole. Optimally, youths should have an idea of the kind of job they would like to hold and be prepared to enter adult social relationships.

Identity confusion results in individuals, according to Erikson, if social and psychological pressures prohibit the person from incorporating the various streams of their lives into an integrated totality. Troubled adolescents become fragmented, alienated from themselves and their community. They are not sure who they are or where they are going. They are usually ineffective in most, if not all, aspects of life. Erikson understood that the metamorphosis into adulthood is not solely a matter of awareness or control of internal psychological drives and motivations, as Freud hypothesized. Becoming a "healthy" adult requires the environment to provide secure emotional attachments. These bonds are the foundation of a mature integrated sense of self.

Developmental Tasks

If the general goal of adolescence is to form an identity with sound moral grounding, what specific tasks must occur for this to happen? As Figure 4.1 shows, there are four sets of developmental tasks for teenagers to master in order to

move on to adulthood with minimal difficulty. These tasks, as the arrows on the left side of the figure indicate, do not function independently of each other, but are interactive. Each task requires the other for its own completion. Despite the apparent turmoil of adolescence and the rising rates of serious problems experienced by youths today, most teens adjust to puberty's biological changes and the socially marginal adolescent status without disturbing or overly disruptive consequences. This is not to say that teenagers and their families do not experience occasional stress and tension, but that most individuals and families have the adaptive resources and flexibility to complete these developmental tasks and produce a "healthy" self-concept within the context of mature and productive relationships.

Independence and Self-Direction. The prolonged adolescence society has created is not without its functionality. Having several years to prepare for adulthood under the legal and emotional auspices of parents allows the child more time to disengage from childhood dependencies. Independence means more than task independence in terms of making a living, though that is an important quality of living self-sufficiently. Independence requires the ability to detach emotionally from the people and objects that provided childhood security, i.e., parents. The existential reality of life in a culture that glorifies the individual is that individuals must possess the quality of

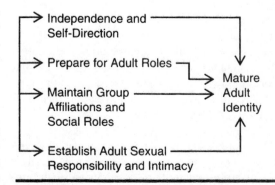

FIGURE 4.1 Adolescent Developmental Tasks

mind necessary to confront the challenges and barriers that society and relationships will present. Individuals best prepare for these conflicts by developing an autonomous self, one that is engaged in meaningful relationships, but is capable of setting its own limits, knows appropriate personal and social boundaries, and aspires to reasonable goals. Teenagers should begin to separate from parents and be able to perform basic tasks of self-sufficiency without excessive dependency on parents or others. The self-directed autonomous self validates its own existence and is comfortable being alone. Furthermore, the highly individuated person can distinguish needs that others fulfill from needs that must be self-furnished. For example, by late adolescence, young people should be able reaffirm the self and feel good about who they are and are becoming. Those who are less differentiated from their families and peers need others to provide validation of their identities.

Prepare for Adult Roles. Developing and practicing cognitive, moral, and emotional maturity are prerequisites for success in the adult world. Teens,

then, need to formulate a sense of personal propriety and soberness, and exhibit sufficient flexibility to conform to the demands of social structures. As students, teens should work to learn the symbols and cognitive skills of the culture necessary to function literately and work productively. Their morality code should emphasize social and personal responsibility so that they can interact effectively with others. The teen should also learn to attribute the socially appropriate emotion to a given situation and learn to control impulses and express them in appropriate and mature ways.

Maintain Group Affiliations and Social Roles. During adolescence, several lessons about living and working with others should be learned. An important task for teenagers is to sublimate their impulses to conform to social roles within groups. Most adult roles, such as employment, require individuals to adjust personal wants and desires to satisfy the demands of the employer as well as colleagues. As adults, people are expected to listen to others and consider their opinions, feelings, and needs in making decisions about their own be-

Teenagers are caught in sometimes confusing and often conflicting roles. They are thought of and treated like children, while having experienced the biological maturation that signifies adulthood. Since society and the culture-at-large do not provide social expectations that are in sync with their developmental status, teenagers are often without meaningful social roles. Giving adolescents worthwhile responsibilities leads to more life and self satisfaction and lowers the risk of getting into trouble.

havior. Teenagers must also incorporate the social and psychological factors of the social groups to which they belong into their sense of self. They must consider race, ethnicity, gender, and social class memberships in developing a sense of identity. The egocentricity of childhood must be replaced by an understanding that humans function in conjunction with others.

Establish Sexual Responsibility and Intimacy. Finally, adolescents must prepare for intimate adult commitments. Testing sexual values and ethics and becoming aware of what is sexually comfortable are among the most difficult challenges facing young people. Teenagers soon realize that the hormonal changes that vaulted them into sexual beings did not prepare them for fulfilling intimacy needs. Adolescent relationships, both those that include sex and those that do not, are essentially practice sessions for young people to learn to relate to others in gratifying and nonthreatening ways. For teenagers, this means learning to express their own needs appropriately without infringing on the feelings of others while listening to the needs of others and adjusting their own behavior accordingly. In short, adolescents are expected to develop a sense of adult etiquette and a presentation of self that is desirable to other people. Adjusting behavior to others' is accomplished by incorporating social rules into one's repertoire of behaviors and emotions.

These developmental tasks of adolescence occur in large measure while adolescents are still living at home. Parents have the task of preparing their adolescent children for what family therapists often call "launching," leaving home to pursue adult roles. This involves allowing increasing independence and freedom while still providing guidance and coaching if a mistake is made. Adolescence, then, is paradoxical. On the one hand, the teenager is working to detach from the once protecting family; on the other hand, the teen, not yet self-sufficient, needs the family for emotional support, guidance, and economic security.

While parents are striving to provide appropriate freedoms and limits for their teenagers, peer groups begin to rival the family as primary sources of influence. Young people turn to each other for leadership and guidance to steer them through what many adults recall as the most tumultuous period of their lives.

ADOLESCENCE AND THE FAMILY

Having a teenager in a household radically changes the dynamics of family interactions. Once parents were the center of their child's life and provided a sense of meaning in the world. When the child reaches adolescence, parents must begin the process of letting go of that control and allow the child greater autonomy and a more substantial role in family decision-making. For many parents, adjusting parental roles and styles is an arduous transition. Most parents relate well to their adolescents, but many continue the traditional parental role appropriate to younger children. Many parent/teen conflicts emerge when parents fail to adapt to the changing developmental needs of their son or daughter.

It is important to remember that parents' influence on their adolescent children diminishes, not disappears. Hendrey (1992) found that influence becomes domain-specific: young people listen to parents in some areas of life, and listen to peers in others. For instance, teenagers were influenced by parents on such issues as career plans and schooling. Peers' ideas and examples carried more weight on fashion, choice of companions, use of leisure time, drinking, sex, and drugs.

The point at which peers' influence surpasses parents' is often the fodder of parent–teen conflicts. Most battles are fought over rather mundane topics like hair and clothing styles, household chores, sleeping late, and musical tastes (Hill & Holmbeck 1987). The content of these arguments may be trivial, but the issues underlying them, such as the child's need for independence, are considerable. Most parent–teen conflicts take place in early adolescence and with mothers rather than fathers (Steinberg 1990).

Parents often initially respond to their child's newly acquired assertiveness with their own assertiveness. Early adolescent children, in parents' view, have clearly forgotten the rules of conduct and respect they seemed to have previously understood. Thus, slow to realize the psychological and social changes accompanying puberty, parents may initially bear down on their children and insist upon compliance with family rules and principles. Firstborn children, understandably, usually have more conflicts with parents than younger siblings do (Small et al. 1988); older children "teach" their parents how to recognize puberty and the social and psychological differences it implies. In doing so, firstborns prepare the way for siblings to have an easier time with experienced parents.

Compared to families in which the parents are married, recently divorced, cohabiting, or remarried, stable, single-parent households experience less parent–adolescent conflict (Smetana et al. 1991). In stable single–parent homes, autonomy is not an issue; many single parents have already dealt with their child's independence and have negotiated family rules awarding adolescent children more freedom and power in family decision-making.

Parenting style also has an effect on conflict with teenage children. Parents who are more authoritative—that is, they demonstrate acceptance, allow appropriate autonomy, and exert reasonable control over their child's behavior—facilitate healthy orientations toward schooling and work. Adolescents whose parents treat them warmly, democratically, and firmly, express more positive attitudes and stronger beliefs in achievement, and demonstrate psychosocial maturity. (Steinberg et al. 1989; Parish 1987).

Permissive and overly strict parenting styles, however, correlate with dysfunctional adolescent outcomes such as rebelling against parents by leaving home too soon, abusing alcohol and drugs, and being sexually active before age eighteen. Those parents who exercise moderate discipline tend not to have children who resort to these behaviors to have their needs met.

The quality of parent–child interaction affects adolescent development as well. Children who perceive their parents as hostile and uncaring, and

their families as generally unhappy, are likely to experience chronic life problems and underachieve (Parish & Wigle 1985). Shinn (1978) and Parish (1987) learned that the reverse is true also. Parents, particularly fathers, who are encouraging and supportive tend to have children who perform well in school, get along well with peers and adults, and avoid deviant behaviors.

As children are thrust into pseudo-adulthood following puberty, they can now create adultlike relationships, acting them out in ways consistent with their own feelings of themselves. If their environment is not stable and supportive, teenagers are likely to look for emotional satisfaction through the newly available adolescent culture. For these kids, drugs, alcohol, and sex, other than what might be labelled normative experimentation, become tools to facilitate the quest for identity. The failure of the social environment to foster proper attachments leads them to search for other objects in the external world to meet developmental and social needs: acceptance, gratification, and separation from the environment that was ineffectual in providing those needs.

ADOLESCENTS AND PEER GROUPS

Adolescents need each other to provide the raw materials of psychosocial development (Seltzer 1989). Teenagers are closely intertwined with one another and provide a code of "do's" and "dont's" in the face of adolescent frameworklessness. As young people deal with deeper levels of self-awareness, they compare themselves to others of the same age to see if they measure up. Teenagers depend on acceptance by peers to get them through the transitional period to adulthood.

Teenage relationships, according to Seltzer, can be thought of as "peerships" rather than friendships, because teens use each other as counselors, sounding boards, and confidants to cope with the turmoil of adolescence. A large proportion of teenagers' self-image is determined by what their peers think of them. There is a social hierarchy within teen culture. Teenagers' positions in that hierarchy are determined by the degree to which they meet the teen culture's norms and values. These social rankings translate into real value. For those in the highest ranks, rewards are usually forthcoming. It's usually the football star, not the math whiz, who has school and community notoriety; and it's the cheerleader, not the best artist, who becomes homecoming "queen."

Status divisions within teenage culture can affect self-esteem. Adolescents who may not be athletically inclined or attractive are likely to be taunted and shunned by the popular "in" groups in school. Many of these youths turn to intellectual activities, which may be labeled "nerdy," thus reinforcing differences among the students. Others, especially those with poor social skills or emotional problems, may be rejected by almost everyone. Like all adolescents, these "outcasts" form their own peer group within which they can obtain acceptance and feedback. Such peer groups are comprised of teens who are similarly distressed or disadvantaged, and it is these youths who are at the highest risk for deviant and dysfunctional behavior.

While teens in the most favored groups have more ready sources of positive feedback, they are not free of any risk of problem behavior. In fact, these teens may be better at concealing their family and emotional problems because they appear to be getting along so well in school and with peers. For example, many children of alcoholic parents overachieve to compensate for the powerlessness and instability they experience at home.

Conforming with peers' expectations grounds the teen's experience and search for identity. Young people cannot accomplish the tasks laid out for them without the foundation of peer group acceptance. This important social grouping safely allows youths to experiment with adult behaviors. The peer group in many ways is a family substitute in which children embrace one another, for they realize they are sharing the same experience.

Seltzer contends that not until late adolescence are teenagers able to form true, authentic friendships, because until then they are self-focused in their mission to gain a stable identity and sense of purpose. Teens psychologically borrow

from each other and are eager to try out new experiences together. They feel good when they are needed, which counters sensations of instability and irrelevance. Their need for each other, however, is more about satisfying developmental challenges than about forming genuine and deeply involved attachments. Seltzer identifies five conditions that adolescents share that lead them to form peership groups rather than intimate friendships. First, each adolescent child is in transition between childhood and adulthood. Therefore children of this age are not thinking about permanency in relationships. Second, teenagers are experiencing biological, intellectual, and emotional changes, all of which give rise to changes in personality, social interests, and overt actions. Third, due to the quantity and frequency of these changes, each child is unpredictable and subject to ups and downs of moods that accompany their daily experiences. Fourth, norms of fluctuation and excitement, rather than stability, govern adolescent behavior. Immediate gratification supersedes delaying gratification and thinking of the future. And fifth, identity and self-image are in the process of formation. Thus, teens need each other not so much for genuine intimacy, but as tools with which to experiment with different behaviors in the journey towards an integrated sense of self.

The kinds of friends that youth make, of course, predict the specific behaviors likely to be reinforced. How are adolescent peer groups formed? I talked earlier of how outcasts turn to each other and how athletic or attractive teens are more likely to be in the "in crowd." Even within these divisions, however, young people with common social identities and social-psychological backgrounds cluster together. Children are first sorted out by class, race, and ethnic categories. Research has widely documented that friendship groups remain strongly segregated on these variables. Simultaneously, the psychological needs of youth begin to channel them towards those with similar needs. Children who are abused and begin to act out their abuse in deviant ways, for example, are attracted to agemates with similar emotional needs. Not only do they provide a framework for each other, but they jointly reinforce the behavior that functions to assuage the needs. Those children whose emotional needs do not complement group members', and neither approve of nor are willing to act according to the norms of the group, are not likely to be accepted by it. In other words, groups will form among adolescents who share a worldview and who gratify important needs. In the search for meaning and identity, teenagers are only going to select peers who will facilitate that process, and that selection of friends is filtered by emotional and social needs and limitations.

PROBLEMS AMONG ADOLESCENTS

To some extent, the dilemmas and questions teenagers face today are the same ones that youths have confronted for generations. Teens still say that they will not make the same mistakes their parents made and that when they are adults, the world will be a better place. Youthful idealism and vitality, however, are being eroded by such serious problems as pregnancy, drug abuse, and poverty. The very will to live even escapes many young people. The section that follows reviews four problems that are affecting youth in contemporary society: depression and suicide, pregnancy, drugs and alcohol, and deviance.

Depression and Suicide

Depression.   Moodiness in teenagers has long been a complaint among parents. Most youngsters will undergo irritable and rapidly changing moods; this is a normative expectation of this stage of development and is usually short-lived. Not all "bad moods" can be written off as adolescent quirks. Full-blown depressive symptoms are becoming increasingly prevalent and are having more life-threatening consequences than ever before.

Adolescent depression closely resembles adult depression. The most common symptoms of depression include:

- negative or antisocial behavior in boys
- substance abuse
- failure to attend to personal appearance
- increased emotionality
- school difficulties
- withdrawal from social activities
- sulkiness
- restlessness
- grouchiness
- aggression
- reluctance to participate in family activities
- desire to leave home with accompanying feelings of being misunderstood (Petti & Larsen 1987)

There are several types of mood disorders found among adolescents. Anthony (1970) found that some instances of depressive symptoms—the normal moodiness of teenagers and "depressive equivalents," e.g., boredom, restlessness, and "acting out"—did not represent clinical depression, but should not be dismissed as trivial behavior and affect. Adolescent mood disturbances that warrant an assessment of full depression include: acute depressive episodes in which there is a crisis in self-esteem, strong personality themes of shame, and identity problems; chronic depression that begins in puberty and is characterized by a predominance of guilt; and depression associated with borderline and psychotic attributes.

Depression in adolescence can be a function of a reaction to a past or current loss, especially if the loss has not been satisfactorily resolved (Malmquist 1971). This loss can take the form of an absent parent—from death, unexplained separation, or divorce—or the loss of normative activities due to bad health, disability, or abuse.

Because of inconsistent sampling methods and disagreement with regards to measuring depression, it is difficult to determine the frequency and prevalence of depression in the teenage population. Research has found that 15 to 28 percent of all teens exhibit full-blown clinical depression. Researchers do agree that whatever the percentages, they are probably conservative estimates. Teens are adept at denying and projecting depressive symptoms, thus concealing their emotional state from clinicians and investigators. Furthermore, other disorders, such as school phobias, anorexia nervosa, a conduct disorder, and psychosomatic complaints like stomachaches, may mask depression (Petti & Larson 1987).

Sociodemographic variables do not correlate with depression, with the exception of gender. Because girls experience more challenges in early adolescence than boys, girls present with more depression than boys and are more likely to attempt suicide (Peterson et al. 1991). There are no apparent social class or ethnic differences in depression among adolescents; however, children from extremely poor families have higher rates of depression.

The causes of depression among adolescents are often the same as adult depression. Curry et al. (1992) found an inverse relationship between coping resources and responses and depressive symptoms; those teens with greater coping skills experience less depression. Coping skills that help to avoid depressive symptoms include: seeing the positive side of stressful situations, keeping one's mind off problems, and using respite or exercise to reduce tension. Capable problem-solving, the ability to develop a plan of action and approach a stressful situation in a reflective or systematic manner, also protects young people against depression and suicidality.

On the other hand, what Curry and associates term *emotional discharge* is related to social maladjustment. Emotional discharge refers to dysfunctional tension-reducing efforts such as overeating, smoking, drinking, or displacement of negative affect onto others.

Environmental stressors, which increase during adolescence, are also frequent precursors of depression (Rubin et al. 1992). Teens face an increase in the number of negative life events, life changes, and responsibilities, which, in turn, may lead to psychological distress. If the distress is not properly resolved and managed, depression is likely.

Adolescents appear to be more vulnerable to certain stressors. For example, teens, whose families impose high expectations of achievement on them, often experience chronic stress and feelings of insecurity. In attempting to carry out the parents' agenda, these teens may develop an overwhelming fear of failure rooted in shame-based emotions and a false sense of self (Rubin et al. 1992).

The most significant predictor of teenage depression is the family environment. Children who present with depressive symptoms usually live in a family atmosphere in which parents neglect their emotional and physical needs. Tension or grief may be the dominant emotional themes of these families. Overly permissive and authoritarian parenting styles are also associated with depression in children. Having a depressed parent is a further predictor of this disorder.

In addition to poor family cohesion, depressive affect is also connected with stress around sexuality and attractiveness, especially for girls (Rubin et al. 1992; Hawkins et al. 1992).

Suicide.   Teenage suicide is one of the most alarming problems parents, educators, and social workers face. There is a macabre irony in young people taking their own lives. It is disturbing that a child, who would seem to adults as living in an exciting and exhilarating time, can also have the quality of mind to end it all. The frequency of teens killing themselves has trebled since the early 1960s.

What leads one in every 10,000 adolescents to terminate his or her life? Research has shown that no one factor or event gives rise to a suicide attempt. Shafii et al. (1985) found that teenagers who attempted suicide differed from nonattempters on four variables. Attempters are more likely to engage in antisocial behavior, to have received prior psychiatric treatment, to have made prior suicide attempts, and to have been exposed to parents' emotional problems, parental absence, and abuse. Another study found similar characteristics among teens who attempt suicide. Garfinkle et al. (1982) found high rates of mental illness in the families of attempters; about 8 percent of their sample had a family member who had also attempted suicide. Furthermore, this research found that about a third of adolescents who try to kill themselves have a drug or alcohol abuse problem. Curran (1987) concluded that suicide attempts occur within the context of long-standing problems, especially chronic family problems characterized by anger, ambivalence, and rejection.

Although suicide attempts are often impulsive, most teenagers who attempt to injure themselves have warned others of their plans in more or less subtle ways. Troubled youths who feel trapped in an inescapable crisis may first hint to friends, teachers, or family members that they are desperate and have run out of ways to cope with their problems. Positive as well as dysfunctional coping mechanisms, such as drugs and alcohol, have failed to resolve the pain.

Warnings of suicidal intentions are usually well disguised behaviors and messages that indirectly communicate the emotional crisis and the confusion the youngster is experiencing. Figure 4.2 lists examples of the warning signals adolescents may give to alert others to rescue them.

The research of Rubin et al. (1992) identified several factors that protect teenagers from depression and suicide. First, family cohesion and close friendships mitigate against vulnerability to depression. These social supports protect against maladaptive outcomes by providing instrumental help and emotional support during the developmental tasks of adolescence. Furthermore, family and friends offer alternative sources of gratification that counteract the negative impact of life's changes and disappointments.

Teenage Sexuality and Pregnancy

Sexuality. The ability to achieve mature, sexually intimate, and responsible relationships is expected by late adolescence. However, perhaps nothing causes as much anxiety during adolescence as sexual decisions and changes. Adolescents may be capable of fully engaging in sex acts, but they generally lack the knowledge, judgment, and emotional development for mature sexual relationships. There are many pressures and motivators for youngsters to be sexually active,

FIGURE 4.2 Suicidal Clues

VERBAL MESSAGES INDICATING HOPELESSNESS

- "I just want to give up."
- "I don't feel like trying anymore."
- "I want to sleep forever."
- "I can't go on this way."
- "Things are going to be different soon."
- "My family would be better off without me."

BEHAVIOR CHANGES

- Giving away prized possessions
- Sudden decline in achievement and participation in school
- Withdrawal from relationships
- Difficulty concentrating, apathy, and hopelessness
- Abrupt mood and behavioral changes
- Changes in sleep and eating habits
- Running away, promiscuity, and other delinquent behavior
- Sudden improvement in mood and behavior after long period of depression
- Preoccupation with death

such as a desire for acceptance and conformity, proof of love, proof of desirability and popularity, curiosity, need of intimacy and passion, and adult status. Other teenagers may sexually act out because of a strong need to rebel against a family that has forsaken their emotional and developmental needs (Sebald 1977; Weinstein & Rosen 1991).

Irresponsible sexual behavior is often symptomatic of family changes during adolescence and a lack of family cohesiveness. Adolescent intercourse has been linked to inconsistent, rigid, and maladaptive family dynamics as a means of coping with the loss of familial affection. When families abandon children emotionally, children will search for compensatory love objects to gain the nurturance and affection that is missing at home (Fox 1980; Grotevant & Cooper 1986). Young people who long for emotional comfort are vulnerable to exploitation, disease, and pregnancy, because their psychological motivation is to feel loved and accepted rather than emotional and behavioral responsibility. Teenage intercourse is a good example of the behaviorist concept of negative reinforcement. Sex is conditioned, and thus repeated, because it terminates a negative condition or emotional state, which in this case is the lack of affection in the family of origin.

Strong family bonds protect youngsters from sexual behaviors whose consequences they are not ready to confront. Parents who appropriately supervise their teenagers, maintain flexible discipline, and have open and direct communication with their children, lower the chances that their adolescents will have an active sex life (Barnet, Papini, & Gbur 1991).

Teenagers, despite their intentions to live differently than their parents, tend to recreate adult sexual practices. Rarely is adolescent sexuality random. Rather, it usually occurs in the context of an ongoing relationship. Boys still are expected to initiate sexual advances, while girls fear being labeled promiscuous and aggressive.

Adolescent sexual encounters, especially early ones, are often disappointing. Expectations of passion and "bells ringing" are seldom fulfilled. What are more common for adolescents are sexual dysfunctions, such as premature ejaculation and inorgasmia. Sometimes intercourse may be painful, particularly for girls. Teenage sex is often rushed and clouded by feelings of guilt and shame. Many are left feeling used and exploited.

Most adolescents engage in autoerotic sexual practices. Virtually all boys and about 75 percent of girls masturbate. Sexual fantasies, which usually accompany masturbation, are common to most youths. Autoerotic behavior has many advantages: it provides a release to sexual tension, gives an opportunity to learn about one's own sexual functioning, and is a rehearsal for sexual contact with a partner. Masturbation has a number of negative aspects, however. Adolescents often believe the various myths attached to masturbation and have irrational fears. Guilt and shame are prevalent feelings adolescents attach to their autoerotic behavior.

Pregnancy.   In recent years there has been an increase in the rate of intercourse among high school students, and the average age of first intercourse has steadily gone down. As a result, it is not surprising that the United States has the highest teenage pregnancy rate in the industrialized world. Over the last decade or so, the teen pregnancy rate has remained fairly steady, though teenagers' access to abortions has been substantially reduced. About two-thirds of all teen pregnancies are terminated. Still, about a half million teenagers give birth each year. Girls who become pregnant as teenagers are likely to become pregnant again before they reach twenty years of age.

Teenage pregnancy has many undesirable social and psychological costs.

1. *Economic.* Teenage parents are forced to enter the labor market before they are ready. This means schooling is interrupted and they will earn a lower income than their peers who delay parenthood. Furthermore, teenage pregnancy drains public resources. Since many young mothers are poor, or become poor, they must rely on public assistance for their economic survival.

2. *Depression and suicide.* Smith (1988) reports that the suicide rate for adolescent mothers is ten times the national average. Depression is common for both the young mother and father. The emotional turmoil attached to pregnancy and parenthood can easily overwhelm a young person's coping skills. From a developmental perspective, the adult responsibilities of pregnancy and parenting end adolescence. The loss of childhood can lead to depression as well.

3. *Abuse.* Smith also shows that young parents hold unrealistic expectations of their infants. Teenage parents may expect their babies to meet their dependency and intimacy needs. When the baby does not respond to these expectations, a young parent, who is perhaps depressed and inexperienced in child development, is at high risk for abusing that infant.

4. *Health.* Infants of adolescents are exposed to a number of health risks. Adolescent mothers have high probabilities for giving birth to babies with low birth weights, general health problems, and who are born prematurely. The mothers themselves are at risk for spontaneous abortion, difficult pregnancies, and hard deliveries. The infant mortality rate for teen mothers is high as well.

One solution to the adolescent birthrate problem is to consider children's motivations to become pregnant. For many teenagers, having a child is a rational means to goals such as emancipation from their family of origin and/or having someone to love them. Giving teenagers meaningful outlets for feeling accepted and loved and providing opportunities to belong to groups that award them with status may help deter many teens from becoming pregnant. Self-esteem and assertiveness training for teenage boys and girls would help prevent them from using a pregnancy to compensate for problems in their lives. A final possibility for reducing teenage pregnancy is to help teenagers sort through all the mixed messages about sex and parenthood they receive in the social environment. Teenagers are bombarded with contradictory messages from the media, family, peers, religion, and elsewhere. Appropriate sex education would help teens sort through all these messages and establish their own code of sexual values. Sex education in many communities, however, is either nonexistent or insufficient.

Drugs and Alcohol

For many generations, drug and alcohol abuse among adolescents has served as a rite of passage ritual, a protest against parental authority, and as a vehicle for conforming to peer group demands. The National Institute on Drug Abuse (NIDA) has actually reported a gradual decrease in the overall use of illegal drugs (Johnston et al. 1991). For example, among high school seniors, lifetime prevalence rates (defined as rates for having ever used) for abusing marijuana, crack, cocaine, stimulants, tranquilizers, PCP, and other drugs have declined. The fact remains, however, that overall rates of drug use by teens in the United States exceed those of all industrialized nations. Just under half

of all high school seniors have used an illicit drug; 29 percent have used an illicit drug other than marijuana. About one in thirty seniors has tried crack, a particularly dangerous form of cocaine, and 2.2 percent smoke marijuana daily.

Alcohol remains the most dangerous and most abused drug among adolescents. Despite the fact that it is illegal for virtually all high school students and most college students to purchase and possess alcoholic beverages, experience with alcohol is almost universal among them (Johnston et al. 1991). About 90 percent of high school seniors have tried alcohol and about one-third are active drinkers. The NIDA learned that 32 percent of seniors had had five or more drinks in a row at least once in the two weeks prior to the survey. Not all the news is disheartening, however. The overall alcohol consumption rate among teens, though high, has been been declining for several years.

Many adolescents' drug career begins with cigarettes (Brook et al. 1992). By late adolescence, sizeable proportions of young people have established cigarette habits. Since NIDA studies began in 1975, cigarettes have consistently been the substance most frequently used on a daily basis by high school students. While the daily smoking rate for seniors dropped considerably between 1977 and 1981, from 29 percent to 20 percent, it has remained somewhat constant since that year at about 18.8 percent.

Smoking and other initial drug use rarely begins without a social context in which there is some social reward to be gained. The most important of these rewards are looking like an adult and being accepted by a circle of peers who value smoking, drinking, and taking other drugs.

Adolescents who continue smoking, consuming beer and wine, and perhaps advance to more sophisticated and expensive drugs, have many characteristics in common. Most come from emotionally or economically stressed families. The adolescent who experiences chronic family disruptions due to abuse, neglect, divorce, and discord, learns quickly the medicinal qualities of alcohol and drugs. Abusing drugs, thus, has two significant advantages. First, drugs assuage the effects of emotional pain derived from the failure of the family of origin to meet developmental needs. Second, the drug culture offers the youngster an alternative set of people with whom to share intimacies, common experiences, and meanings of life.

Teens who are socially isolated and not well accepted by peers may also find it hard to resist experimenting with the forbidden. They are marginal in the world-at-large. Abusing elevates them to a status that is new and exciting and it eases the pain of their marginality.

Drug abuse contributes to other problems for adolescents. Expensive drug addictions may require criminal conduct for income. Drugs affect a student's concentration, learning skills, motivation, and interconnectedness with school activities. Relationships suffer, as nonusing friends no longer hold any social interest or worth. As a result, many teenage abusers are socially isolated, cutoff from significant networks of support and attachments.

In sum, drug abuse often fills a vacuum created by society in general and families in particular. Society, which provides no formal transition to adulthood, often encourages drug abuse, equating it with being an adult. Beer and cigarette advertisements are very seductive and tantalizing to young people in search of an identity and acceptance. Being "cool" implies presenting oneself in an acceptable package, and using drugs is a key part of many adolescent styles.

Deviance

Simply put, deviance is the violation of norms; it means breaking the rules. Everyone, at some point, is deviant: driving just over the speed limit, arriving late to class, slightly fudging on taxes. These acts are harmless, more or less, and do not usually draw the attention of social control agents or require social work or psychological intervention.

In decades past, adolescent mischief was relatively benign compared to the activities of many of today's youths. The reaches of adolescent deviance now extend to behaviors that are insidiously destructive and life-threatening. Crimes such as vandalism, theft, bodily harm are prevalent; about 80 percent of all adolescents commit one of these offenses. Nationally adolescents account for a third of all arrests (Binder et al. 1988).

High schools and junior high schools have become dangerous places in many areas. Weapons, drugs, and violence are as much fixtures at schools as are books and desks. Campuses across the country have installed metal detectors in entryways to control guns and knives among students. Police routinely patrol schools because of the violence that has become part of the educational curriculum. Violence is the leading cause of death among African American adolescents and thousands of youths are wounded in drive-by shootings and muggings. Wearing trendy clothing and traveling to and from school are dangerous activities for many students. Living in such a fearful setting undermines their ability to concentrate and study, and adds needless anxiety to their already stressful lives.

There are two complimentary approaches with which to understand juvenile violence; both are useful in assessing teenagers engaged in deviant behavior. One, the macro perspective, portrays deviance not as a function of individual volition or choice, but as the reasonable, understandable product of individuals constrained by external social forces (Bortner 1988).

What are those social forces that act so heavily on adolescents that cause them to violate the rules? Some sociologists associate adolescent delinquency with the economic and political marginality of teenagers. Adolescents' economic status, which depends on the status of their parents, renders youths powerless and dependent. Opportunities for employment are scant, especially for minorities, and are low in the social hierarchy. Adolescents' contributions to economic endeavors are not highly valued. Their relative lack of power, the reality of "having little to lose," and their creation of a tightly knit peer subculture make them less responsive to formal mechanisms of control (Christie 1978). According to Christie, age is used to maintain the social preferences awarded to adults and to exclude young people from all the benefits of citizenship. This is especially true for poor and minority adolescents, who are most likely to be labeled deviant by an authority agent. High delinquency rates occur when the acute lack of power and the low social status of adolescents coincide with cultural values of social mobility and desires for material wealth. Deviance among adolescents is a function of being developmentally out of sync with a social environment that presses them into dependence and excludes them from important social functions.

Adolescent deviance correlates to several socioeconomic variables. For example, teenagers from marginal, powerless groups are more likely to commit certain crimes, especially vandalism and crimes against persons. African American and low-income youths are found disproportionately among high frequency or chronic offenders (Elliot & Ageton 1980).

According to Chambliss (1973), the differential response of society to delinquent behavior contributes to delinquency. In his famous study, "Saints and Roughnecks," Chambliss shows how social control agents in society, such as the police and schools, selectively label some persons and groups as deviant. Chambliss studied two groups of adolescent boys from different social class backgrounds. The delinquent behavior of the middle-class group was largely ignored by authorities, while the delinquency of working-class youths was condemned by the community. Chambliss concluded that deviant, "outsider" status is produced by societal labeling, whereas nondelinquent, "insider" status is maintained by avoiding punitive labeling. Those youths who were labeled deviant were more likely to engage in a deviant "career." They developed an image of themselves as deviants and selected friends who affirmed that self-image. Similarly, youths who develop a law-abiding self-image form a commitment to resisting deviance.

The second approach to understanding adolescent deviance is the micro perspective, in which the focus is on the ways individuals relate to their immediate social environment. Hirschi's (1969) *social bond theory* explores the attachments between individuals and conventional society. Delinquency is a consequence of the weakening bonds between an adolescent and society. When an adolescent has a bond of affection with conventional others, those who conform to social norms and values, there is less motivation to deviate from socially approved standards of behavior. Delinquency is deterred by attachments to family, conventional peers, and institutions such as schools. When an adolescent's connection to others does not provide a satisfactory outcome, on the other hand, the youngsters are left to their own devices to compensate for what is missed. This may mean substituting normative attachments for bonds with people that may approve of and reinforce deviant behavior.

Hirschi identified four types of bonds that connect people to other people and to social forces:

1. *attachment:* caring about others and their opinions and expectations
2. *commitment:* time, energy, and investment of self in conventional behavior
3. *involvement:* engrossment in conventional activities
4. *belief:* attribution of moral validity to conventional norms

Recent research shows that teenage deviance is associated with the degree of involvement in family life and family stability. Children from disrupted homes are likely to "act out" family stress through aggressive behavior, drug abuse, truancy, and other troublesome behaviors (Frost & Pakiz 1990). Attachment to parents controls deviance in children because parents reinforce and support conventional behavior. Children who spend more time with their parents are likely to incorporate positive messages about what is right and wrong and are better equipped to resist deviant impulses. Children with healthy self-esteems, which are usually the consequence of positive interactions and attachments with parents, are less attracted to the gratifications of deviance. They know the consequences of violating social rules and have the constitution not to be attracted to people who act against those rules.

Hirschi makes similar points regarding commitment, involvement, and beliefs. If children actively commit to and participate in legitimate social activities, such as schooling, then deviance is controlled because they develop a loyalty to conventional practices and have neither the time nor the energy to become involved in deviant activities. Beliefs play an important role in protecting children from deviance. A belief in the legitimacy of rules and institutions that forbid delinquency commits the child to normative behavior and binds his or her conduct to societal norms.

ADOLESCENCE AND DIVERSITY

Gender

The timing of puberty influences how boys and girls feel about themselves. Children who mature significantly earlier or later than their agemates find themselves having different experiences. For girls, early maturation is at first a trying time. Since their growth spurt and secondary sex characteristics are ahead of others', they are often teased for their big feet and budding breasts. They may be taunted by their girlfriends for being "boy crazy" and soon realize that they have no peers to share their new interests and problems. Some girls may try to hide their out-of-place physical features by slouching to appear shorter and wearing baggy clothes to conceal their breasts. Compared to girls who mature on time and later, girls who mature before their agemates have been shown to have a poorer body image, to commit more acts of social deviancy, to participate less in family activities, to be less influenced by their families and less accepting of them (Brooks–Gunn 1987).

As Simmons and her associates (1983) found, girls who mature early and begin dating often have low self-esteem. Early maturing girls may feel constantly evaluated by their parents, criticized by their friends for not spending enough

time with them, and pressured by older boys into sexual activities. Age at menarche, in fact, is a stronger predictor of age of first intercourse than race, religion, and socioeconomic status (Bingham et al. 1990). Most early developing girls, of course, do not have sexual intercourse at very young ages. Just as there are pressures to have sex, there are pressures to abstain as well.

The first period of early maturation is often painful for young girls. Many report, however, that they benefited more than suffered from developing before their peers. Faust's (1983) study found that girls who experience early puberty gain more status, respect, and popularity than later developing girls. These girls had learned successful coping skills, having been teased and pressured by others at a young age. Furthermore, the experienced early maturers could coach younger girls when they were learning to wear a bra, attending to menstruation needs, learning to kiss, and so forth. For the most part late maturers have more difficulty coping than early maturers. Whatever troubles early maturers have disappear by adulthood (Brooks–Gunn 1987).

Whereas early maturing girls are stressed, it is the late maturers among the boys who have a harder time during adolescence. Boys who mature late may have psychosocial problems lasting into adulthood (Brooks–Gunn 1987). First they are overtaken by girls who have begun the growth spurt and are developing secondary sex characteristics, then they are passed over by boys who develop early and at the average age. Late maturing boys have been shown to be less poised and relaxed and more restless and talkative than early maturing boys, who are more likely to be selected leaders. Late maturers also are more playful, creative, and flexible than other boys, but these traits are not always admired by other adolescents (Berger 1994). Not all late maturing boys feel inferior, nor are the problems associated with late maturation necessarily long-term. In fact, the most significant developmental factors that correlate with low self-esteem among adolescent boys are personal features that are most unlike the traditional masculine stereotype: short in stature, not

EXPLORING THE ISSUES 4.1

Recognizing Gang Communication

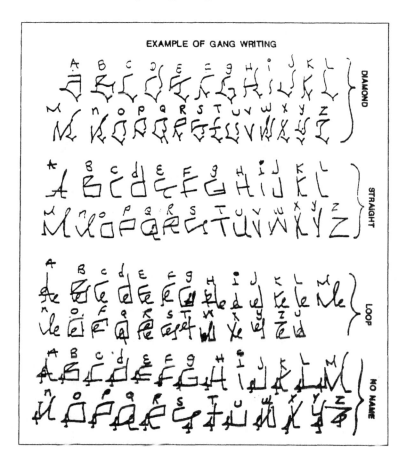

EXAMPLE OF GANG WRITING

Gangs have developed their own styles of communication to express themselves and promote group solidarity. Using their own words helps them to identify each other and their gang affiliations and enables them to communicate without being understood completely by outsiders. Gang slang and writing style may be a clue that a teenager is associating with gang members. A rudimentary knowledge of "gang speak" may help identify an adolescent as a "gangster."

GANG TERM	DEFINITION
ace kool, main man, tight	best friend, backup
bo	marijuana

GANG TERM	DEFINITION
book, break	run, get away
bullet	one year in custody
busting	involved in violence, fighting
chotas	police
claim	to identify one's gang affiliation
cluckhead	crack addict
cuz	crips
dime speed	10-speed bicycle
dis	show disrespect
drop a dime	inform on someone

(continued)

GANG TERM	DEFINITION	GANG TERM	DEFINITION
double duece	.22 caliber gun	kicking back	relaxing
down	tough, loyal, ready to fight	O. G.	"original gangster"; a respectful term for someone who has "been around"
durag	handkerchief wrapped around head		
dusted	under influence of PCP		
essay	anyone of Hispanic heritage	packing	carrying a gun
		placa	graffiti on structures that identifies a particular gang or person
four five	.45 caliber		
gangbanger	gang member		
gangbanging	being in a gang	ride	a vehicle or car
gat	gun	righteous	true or correct
get down	to fight	roscoe	gun
head up	to start a fight	set	any particular gang clique
holding down	controlling turf or area	slippin'	being careless
homeboy, homey, homes	a comrade or associate	slobs	derogatory term for bloods
		tiny	young gang member
hood, varrio, barrio	neighborhood	transformer	a spy
hook	phony or imitation	tray eight	.38 caliber
jack	to commit a holdup	what set you from?	asking what gang one belongs to
jiving	attempting to fool or con someone		
		vatos	Spanish slang for "guys"
jumped in	initiated into group by being beaten		

athletic, appearing physically weak or unattractive, and not sexually experienced. These factors are more important considerations than onset of puberty in predicting self-image problems for boys.

Gay and Lesbian Adolescents

As teenagers' bodies mature sexually, how young people understand themselves as sexual beings matures as well. Youths receive countless messages from their social environment directing them toward the mainstream heterosexual orientation. Parents' expectations of their children growing up, getting married, and having children of their own are communicated often in direct ways. The media typically portrays homosexuals as anomalies, at best, and as deviants at worst.

For many teenagers, expectations of heterosexuality and the traditional life script feel "wrong." As some youths' sexual selves mature, many recognize that their fantasies and sexual attractions do not fit normative social expectations. Rather, their attractions are oriented toward people of the same sex. Because prevailing social forces reinforce heterosexual values and behaviors, realizing and accepting homosexual desires may be a disturbing and traumatic process.

In many cases, homosexual fantasies during adolescence are fleeting phenomena. Not all youths will act out the attraction, and for many, homosexual desires are temporary occurrences. Consequently, adolescent same-sex passions and cognitions are not necessarily predictive of adolescent or adult homosexual orientation. Of those teenagers who engage in homosexual voyeurism, exhibitionism, touching, mutual masturbation, and other behaviors, many do so experimentally.

For others, these early feelings and contacts do indeed foreshadow adult sexual orientation.

Gay men often report that they were aware of their homosexuality in adolescence, sometimes as early as age thirteen. Many lesbian women, however, recount that their sexual orientation during adolescence was more ambiguous. They were not certain of their orientation until late adolescence or early adulthood. Many gays and lesbians do not realize their orientation until middle or even late adulthood.

For adolescents who recognize that their sexual orientation is different from the mainstream culture, the teenage years can be particularly painful. When the teenager is engaged in the paradox of needing parental support and guidance to become separate from them, the gay or lesbian teen might face three further dilemmas that heterosexual youths do not: (1) sudden rejection by parents and friends over something not of their choosing, (2) greater difficulty forming a sexual identity, and (3) absence of a normative homosexual framework by which to evaluate their behavior.

When adolescents reveal their homosexuality to parents and friends, outright rejection is risked. Because of the hostile prejudice and discrimination directed to gays and lesbians in American society, it is only normal for parents, even the most liberal individuals, not to want their children to be homosexual. The range of parental response varies from complete support to ostracism and rejection. Those parents who support their child understand the turmoil he or she is experiencing and demonstrate their support by listening to their child's emotions and concerns. They accept their child's differences because they genuinely and unconditionally accept her or him; they are not worried about their public image.

Parents reject their homosexual children for several reasons. Some feel personally responsible for their children's homosexuality and project their "failure" onto the child. Thus the child represents parental irresponsibility and rejecting the child protects the parent's personal sense of well-being and self-efficacy. Furthermore, by rejecting the child, the parent's social identity is preserved as well. The parent is seen as "doing the right thing" by important reference groups such as religious congregations, extended family members, or friends. The social stigma of having a homosexual child and the parent's own homophobia may be more powerful than the emotional bond the parent may have with the child.

When a family excludes a child for being homosexual, the consequences may be severe. Many of these children develop strong feelings of abandonment, guilt over causing family conflict, and self-disgust and shame that result from society's disapproval of homosexuality. Many rejected teenagers may become clinically depressed and have suicidal ideas and/or turn to destructive coping devices such as alcohol and drug abuse. Some homosexual children are kicked out of their homes. At best, many of these children can live with friends, relatives, or other homosexuals. Others, who may not have such support, are left to live on the streets and forced to drug dealing and prostitution for survival.

Friends of a gay or lesbian adolescent often respond similarly. They may become distressed acknowledging a friend's homosexuality and terminate the relationship. These friends may fear becoming homosexual through association, worry over the friend "hitting on" them, or perceive a loss of social status by having a gay or lesbian friend. Peers may ostracize gay or lesbian teens and deprive them of important social contacts at a time when they are desperately needed. Friends' behavior may reinforce feelings of self-hatred and drive the youth further into depression. Feeling alone and abandoned, depressed adolescents may turn to older homosexuals for safety, support, and nurturance but find themselves trapped in an abusive or exploitative relationship, leaving them feeling hurt, used, and scared.

Forming a sexual identity and sexual intimacy are more difficult for gay and lesbian teenagers. Unlike their heterosexual peers, they have the added complications of finding romantic partners and confidants with whom they feel safe talking about their desires and urges. The process of forming a sexual identity is delayed. As Bell and his associates (1981) have learned, becoming comfortable with a homosexual sexual identity takes longer, in part because finding an accepting peer network is harder.

The adolescent period can be traumatic for gay and lesbian youths. With little guidance or support to organize their experiences, lesbian and gay teenagers have a more pronounced sense of frameworklessness. Their homosexual orientation makes them more marginal in the community and among their peers. Unlike straight adolescents, whose teenage years mark the transition from childhood to a normative adulthood, adolescence for lesbian and gay youths transfers the youngster to an adulthood of uncertainty and the prospect of becoming an outcast. Lacking structure and a frame of reference, therefore, can deepen the detachment and depression that gay and lesbian youths often feel.

Hispanic Adolescents

The psychosocial development of Hispanic adolescents has been virtually ignored in the social and behavioral sciences. Research on this group has focused on negative, deviant, or pathological dimensions, rather than their achievements, self-esteem, and adolescent roles and status in families (Mirande 1986). Much of what is written on Hispanic youths reinforces the stereotypes that Latinos and Latinas are knife-wielding fighters who drink and take drugs heavily and are intellectually inferior. The overwhelming majority of Hispanic adolescents do not conform to this deviant stereotype and all face the same developmental tasks and conflicts as other teenagers. How Hispanic adolescents differ from mainstream teenagers is due to cultural differences, migration patterns and family history, and adapting to poverty.

Hispanic culture influences adolescents' psychosocial experiences. One of the most important cultural features common to Hispanic groups is the strength of family relationships. Expected loyalties to the family, however, may create tensions between Hispanic parents and their teenage sons and daughters. Many Hispanic parents are still living in the culture of their homeland, for example, and expect their children to adopt their norms, values, and customs (Carrasquillo 1991). Adolescent children who have been exposed to the material enticements of American culture, and have seen the more liberal relationships allowed to boys and girls, may resist the traditional expectations of parents. Parents may not understand their children and their children do not understand their parents. As Fitzpatrick (1982) stated:

> Puerto Rican families have frequently lamented the patterns of behavior of even good boys in the United States. Puerto Rican parents consider them disrespectful. American children are taught to be self-reliant, aggressive and competitive, to ask why, and to stand on their own two feet. A Puerto Rican child is much more submissive. When the children begin to behave according to the American pattern, the parent cannot understand it (p. 53; quoted in Carrasquillo 1991).

One cultural trait that is more stereotypical than reality is that Hispanic adolescent boys demonstrate machismo. Though there may be some reality to this, it is also true that teenage boys from all ethnic groups act with greater bravado than they do before puberty. Why the macho label is reserved for Hispanic boys is a function of negative labeling by those in dominant groups who do not understand the cultural traits of Hispanics and seek to denigrate that culture.

Hispanic teens differ from Anglo youths in other regards. Research shows, for example, that Hispanic youths are less accepting of suicide and are less likely to commit suicide (Mirande 1986). Hispanic adolescents tend to believe that suicide is sacrilegious and is a serious moral transgression that should not be condoned. They do not see suicide as an acceptable, legitimate alternative to dealing with life's problems (Domino 1981).

How Hispanic adolescents handle psychosocial tasks not only varies by their culture/country of origin, but by generation as well. In a study of Mexican American youths, Virgil (1979) identified three groups of Hispanic adolescents, based on their cultural and time proximity to their homeland. The first, Mexican-oriented youths, are those that are least acculturated. They are primarily urban, but were born in Mexico in rural areas or small towns. With strong parental support, these youths identify with Mexican culture and see themselves as Mexican. Anglo-oriented adolescents are third (or more) generation American. These adolescents are more economically secure and have higher aspirations for success. They are more mobile and identify themselves as American and perhaps as European American. Chicano-oriented teens are caught in the middle of two cultures. These adolescents, whose parents or grandparents were born outside of the United States, may feel ambivalence in terms of their ethnic, social, and personal identity. They reject Anglo-centered culture, but recognize that they are neither Mexican nor American. These youths are indeed marginal to both worlds. Chicano-oriented teens, because of their cultural marginality, are more likely to perform poorly in school and participate in gang activities (Virgil 1979).

Hispanic youths have high aspirations, but hold lower expectations of achieving them (Lauver & Jones 1991). Realizing the limitations, prejudice, and discrimination imposed on them by virtue of their membership in a minority group, poor Hispanic adolescents, just as others who are poor, are at risk for acting out their disadvantaged position in society in deviant ways. A number of studies show that, despite no differences in self-esteem (Mirande 1986), Hispanic youths have high rates of early drug use and criminal behavior, and are overrepresented in mental health centers.

Like African Americans, Hispanic youths are overrepresented in the juvenile and criminal justice system. Inadequate recreation facilities, overcrowded and poor housing conditions, low educational attainment, unemployment, and lack of opportunities in the urban environment are forces associated with Hispanic juvenile delinquency. These forces define the experiences of many Hispanic youths and interrupt their attempts to achieve the measures of success valued in American culture (Carrasquillo 1991).

Hispanic youngsters, because of their poverty, are at risk of other disadvantages. They have high chances for contracting HIV, being victims of crimes, dropping out of school, and becoming teenage parents.

African American Adolescents

African American adolescents face some of the most stressful conditions in this society. A large number are poor, and the opportunities for economic advancement are meager at best. Unemployment among African American youths is extremely high. The jobs offered them tend to be unattractive, providing few chances for mobility or the acquisition of salable skills (Thornberg 1982). The economic plight of African American youths, many of whom are concentrated in inner city urban neighborhoods, is worsening. The job markets near their communities are declining as factories and other businesses leave and investors ignore the inner cities. What remains are unskilled jobs or service jobs, such as hairstyling, that cater to the specific needs of African Americans.

Adolescent unemployment stresses families and provides less income for education, which would improve the odds for escaping poverty (Leigh & Peterson 1986). Poverty and adolescent unemployment undermine the accomplishment of developmental tasks, especially autonomy and the need to separate. Financial dependence does not allow African American teens the opportunities to explore all their talents and test their independence in normative ways. Poverty frustrates African American youths and fails to provide meaningful roles in the community.

Two social and psychological conditions stand out as important for African American adolescents and will be discussed here: high out-of-wedlock birthrates and finding meaningful reference group identification.

African American adolescents have extremely high birthrates. The out-of-wedlock birthrate for African American adolescents and young adults is six times that of European Americans. Having a child during teenage years in the African American community does not carry the long-term guilt common among European Americans (Leigh & Peterson 1986). It does, however, force young men and women into adult responsibilities before they are ready. As with girls from other ethnicities, teenage parenthood dampens the likelihood of finishing school and gaining meaningful work experience.

Recent research has shown that teenage parenting has long-term effects on the child of the adolescent parent, too. In a study of poor African American mothers, Zahn and colleagues (1992) found that the birth of an adolescent's child was often part of a cycle of dependency that resulted in long-term deficits within the child.

When teenagers have a child, they essentially have two options, according to Zahn. First, they can become dependent on their family of origin for support, which is common when jobs are scarce. Household dependency is both distressing and functional for the young mother. Extended family networks provide many important services, such as day care, for unmarried mothers in the African American community. Research shows that support from family and a male partner decreases psychological distress for African American adolescent mothers (Thompson & Peebles–Wilkins 1992). Being dependent upon their families, however, makes teenage mothers marginal in their own home—they are both a child and a parent, but not comfortable in either role. A young mother's second option is to continue with schooling and work. Either way the baby is deprived. If the mother is household dependent, no long-term investment in the child's future is made; if the mother is absent while attending school and working, there may be long-term emotional deficits due to parental deprivation during the child's early years of emotional growth. These children are, in effect, in double jeopardy.

Fatherhood may be one of the few viable and legal options to achieve adulthood status and a sense of accomplishment for African American boys (Smith 1988). The failure of the environment to provide purposeful education and professional opportunities to youths leaves boys at high risk, as evidenced by their shorter life span and high homicide rates. The suicide rate for African American adolescent boys is rising as well. Restricted social opportunities mean that boys must find alternative means to attain adulthood and that they must form an identity without the benefits of education and occupational achievement (Smith 1988). Fathering a child may serve as an alternative to the normative adolescent activities of dating, planning for the future, and delaying gratification, because the future looks no different than the present.

African American teens have two tasks in addition to those European American adolescents face. First, they must develop a healthy racial and

Though some may see adolescent smoking and drinking as simply "normal" teenage experimentation and rebelliousness, these activities are not so harmless. Any use of tobacco and alcohol by an underage person is substance abuse because it is illegal. Much of the public's concern about teenage drug abuse is with so-called "hard drugs"; however, tobacco and alcohol are very often "gateway" drugs. This means that adolescents who use marijuana, cocaine, and other illicit substances, first smoked tobacco and drank alcohol.

ethnic identity in which they feel secure about themselves as members of their group. Second, African American adolescents have to reconcile their feelings about belonging to a group that is socially and economically subordinate to a more favored group. Not only must African American teens ask "Who am I?" but must also ask "Who am I as an African American?" These questions reflect a "double consciousness" that most African Americans struggle with over the course of their lives. This struggle usually begins during adolescence. In American society, race, along with class and gender, are taken as measures of an individual's worth and identity. African American families have the formidable task of preparing their children for the social world, where attempts to get ahead are frustrated by continued prejudice and discrimination (Leigh & Peterson 1986).

Native Americans

Native Americans are perhaps the most disadvantaged adolescent population in the United States. Indian teens rank among the highest in virtually all categories of social problems: unemployment, suicide, alcohol and drug abuse, truancy, and dropping out of school. These conditions are not surprising. The neglect of Native Americans' social needs by the economic and political institutions has "trickled down" to the daily lives of Native American teenagers who have one of the lowest life expectancies of any social group in America. Many Native American youths live in desperate social conditions in which there is little hope for success. Jobs beyond government and tribal positions are few, and education has negligible payoffs.

In recent years, Native Americans have promoted a renaissance in Indian identity, culture, and heritage. For Indian adolescents, identity formation may mean rebelling against western culture. Still there is a lure, however, to many aspects of mainstream European life, especially the material items important to adolescents everywhere— "fad" clothing, CDs, and cars. Desire for Anglo conformity, even in minimal terms, may place

Native American teens at odds with parents and tribal leaders, and create identity issues regarding who they are and are going to be.

Asian Americans

Because of the diversity of Asian American adolescents, their experience in Anglo-centered culture varies. Japanese American youth, for example, achieve high levels of acculturation, whereas the children of recent Southeast Asian immigrants have greater difficulty adjusting to western life.

Two processes may cause Asian American adolescents' problems to go unnoticed. One, Asian children are often stereotyped as model citizens and two, traditional values in Asian communities tend to minimize conflict and maintain dignity (Land & Levy 1992). These values, along with cultural differences, may lead to a reluctance of these children and their families to seek help. In addition, recent racist attacks have further isolated Asian families from mainstream society.

Asian American teenagers, whose parents were born in Asia, or were born overseas themselves, are often caught between two very different worlds. Marginality, for Asian American youngsters, leads to several specific kinds of conflict. One such conflict is that which occurs between home values and public, Anglo values. Their parents maintain old world values and expectations of behavior. At the same time, the host culture and peers exert demands to blend into the mainstream adolescent world. This cultural "tug-of-war" divides adolescents' loyalties between family and peers. Pressures to conform to American lifestyles and developmental expectations force Asian teenagers to be at odds with parents and other elders over the basic rules that govern social life. Conforming to traditional Asian expectations may mean rejection from the youth's new reference groups, i.e., other teenagers.

A second conflict Asian American youths face is role conflict within the family. These adolescents are often the only members of the Asian immigrant family that speak English. Knowledge of English places these children in a position of some authority in the family. They become gatekeepers in the flow of information between the family and the English-speaking community, and, in a sense, speak for the family, guiding parents through the unknown society to which they have moved. Such power for a young person is foreign to traditional Asian families and may be the source of family tension (Land & Levy 1992). Playing the role of intermediary can lead to role ambiguity and the violation of strong traditional values such as respect for elders and parents.

Another problem expressed by Chinese American leaders is the increasing rebelliousness, criminality, and radicalism of many Chinese youths, especially among those living in Chinatowns (Huang 1976). The formation of delinquent gangs has become a serious problem in Chinatowns in California and New York. Huang contends that the growing delinquency among Chinese youths reflects the frustration and adjustment problems they experience in America. Recent arrivals from Hong Kong or Cambodia, for example, are unfamiliar with American language and culture and are usually unemployed or in the lowliest of jobs. They typically live in overcrowded, slumlike quarters with inadequate recreation and education facilities. For alienated Asian youths, gang behavior serves as an alternative means of filling status and identity needs (Huang 1976).

Foreign-born Asian adolescents, or those whose families maintain strict traditional practices and values, tend to be more conservative than American-born youths. Traditional Asians are less sexually active than European American, African American, American-born Asian, and Hispanic teenagers (Cochran et al. 1991). Furthermore, Asian youths who are born in the United States tend to be more individualistic, rather than collectivistic and communal. When compared to European American adolescents, Chinese Americans are more group oriented, especially in regards to the family. As Chinese Americans become more acculturated to western lifestyles, they come to value self-realization and focus on individual growth (Leong & Tata 1991).

Adolescents in Rural Areas

Since 1950, there has been a convergence in lifestyles between urban and rural families. Advances in technology, the media, and transportation have exposed rural teenagers to urban lifestyles, leaving them little different from their urban peers. The rural population, despite public perceptions, is not homogeneous; it varies by geography, ethnicity, social class, and history. Consequently, the experiences of rural teenagers are as likely to differ as much, if not more, as those of rural and urban youths. Nevertheless, teenagers in rural environments experience special problems unique to their geographic setting.

One of the main problems rural adolescents face is loneliness. Rural teens experience high rates of loneliness when compared to other teenage groups (Woodward and Frank 1988). Isolated from the recreational, cultural, and social facilities that cities offer, many rural teens, particularly those in remote places, spend a great deal of time alone and with their immediate families. Friends and schoolmates may live several miles away. Most rural adolescents cope successfully with isolation by entertaining themselves in various ways, such as listening to music, watching television, calling friends and relatives on the telephone, playing sports, or using the resources available to them, such as church activities, social organizations and clubs like 4H, and organized sports (Woodward and Frank 1988).

Loneliness for rural teenagers may be situational or chronic. Woodward and Kalyan–Masih (1990) found that rural teens feel more lonely when rejected, when feeling out of control of a situation, or when alienated from positive persons, places, or things. Chronic loneliness, on the other hand, is associated with adolescents who have low self-esteem and less personal involvement in positive social and family activities. This study also found that negative coping strategies, such as drug and alcohol abuse, were not common among rural teenagers who felt isolated. Programs to help these teenagers include developing a variety of positive adapting mechanisms and resources to relieve negative feelings and improve self-esteem.

In the context of the main tasks of adolescence—separation, exploration, and identity formation—rural teens have fewer opportunities than urban youths to try out new behaviors. As a rule, rural communities are less diverse, and in many cases, less tolerant of psychological and social differences. The pressures to conform to prevailing social mores and lifestyles are strong and deviating from these expectations may be socially and emotionally costly.

One social control mechanism that enforces conformity is the family. In many rural areas, especially Appalachia, adolescents maintain strong commitments to their family networks and obligations. Demands to maintain family bonds and live up to family expectations conflict with developmental needs to become independent and may lead to intrapersonal and relational problems. Nevertheless, the press to fulfill family obligations is effective: research shows rural youths remain closer to their places of births than urban adolescents (Peters, Wilson, & Peterson 1986).

CONCLUSION

The main developmental tasks of adolescence are to separate from parents and establish a stable identity. In accomplishing these tasks, adolescents begin learning what is necessary for surviving in the adult world they are likely to enter. Therefore, the quality of their psychosocial environment is the best predictor of their mastering those tasks. The structural model of social work practice examines adolescents' transactions with their environment and asks several questions: Does the environment provide the emotional, cognitive, and tangible resources the adolescent needs to separate appropriately? Or do the social systems in which the adolescent lives fail to encourage appropriate independence? What kind of value system is presented to the teenager? What are the rules that govern the youth's behavior? Do these rules and values lead to stable identity formation or create anxiety, self-doubt, and dependency?

The quality of the environment is important for adolescent development for two reasons. First, it must be remembered that adolescence is a culturally contrived stage of life. By creating adolescence, the social environment by definition also creates problems by not timing social adulthood with biological adulthood. Second, the psychosocial environment affects the degree that youths feel frameworkless. In the absence of meaningful opportunities, teenagers will create their own world that often involves behaviors that get them into trouble and interfere with future development. Assessing teenagers' interactions with the environment will reveal the kind of structure teens live in. If that structure maintains a sense of orderliness, love, and age-appropriate discipline, then teenage children will handle the period of social marginality with fewer difficulties.

CASE STUDY REVIEW QUESTIONS

Refer to the case of Nathaniel, presented at the beginning of this chapter. Think about the psychosocial development of adolescents and respond to the following questions.

1. How would you describe Nathaniel in Erikson's terms? Describe his progression in terms of Erikson's developmental crisis.
2. Nathaniel seems to lack a clear sense of identity. Given what you know about him, how would you relate his family experiences with his lack of personal "mission"?
3. Developmentally speaking, what should Nathaniel be doing? What emotional and behavioral consequences of failing to be developmentally on schedule do you see in this youth?
4. What do you think about Nathaniel's problems with inappropriate sexual expressions? How might shame be a factor in his sense of self?
5. How is Nathaniel expressing his anger at the overinvolvement of his mother and the underinvolvement of his father? What is he missing from his father's emotional abandonment?
6. How does the concept "frameworklessness" apply to Nathaniel? From a structural social

work perspective, what needs to happen for him to improve his sense of structure?

KEY TERMS

Corpus luteum: Tissue that forms in the ovaries and secretes progesterone.

Egg follicle: Tiny sacs within the ovaries that contain an ovum.

Emotional discharge: Dysfunctional tension-reducing efforts.

Follicular phase: The first phase of the menstrual cycle during which the follicles develop.

Frameworklessness: A concept that describes the transitory nature of adolescence; teenagers are caught between childhood and adult roles and expectations without a suitable, coherent set of role demands.

Genital stage: Freud's final stage of development that begins in adolescence; during this stage, the genitals are the center of pleasure and individuals seek out sexual stimulation and form love relationships.

Gonadotropins: Hormones that stimulate the gonads.

Gynecomastia: The temporary enlargement of the breasts that occurs in most pubescent boys.

Hypothalamus: The part of the brain that regulates certain metabolic activities such as water balance and sugar and fat metabolism as well as temperature control and hormone production; it is thought to play a role in the onset of puberty.

Identity vs. identity confusion: According to Erikson, the psychosocial conflict of adolescence; it represents the struggle of teenagers to integrate all the components of the self into a unified whole.

Luteal phase: The third phase of the menstrual cycle during which the endometrium is ready for the implantation of a fertilized egg.

Luteinizing hormone (LH):   Hormone secreted by the pituitary that stimulates ovulation.

Menarche: The first menstrual cycle.

Menstruation: The monthly vaginal discharge of blood and the lining of the uterus; the final stage of the menstrual cycle.

Ovulation: The release of a mature egg into the ovary.

Ovulatory phase: The second phase of menstruation during which the follicle ruptures and the mature egg is released.

Puberty: The period of rapid growth and sexual maturation that marks the end of childhood and the beginning of physical adulthood.

Secondary sex characteristics: Physical traits that distinguish males and females but are not essential for reproduction.

Social bond theory: Theory that contends juvenile delinquency is a consequence of the weakening bonds between an adolescent and the social environment.

Spermarche: The first ejaculation to contain sperm.

CHAPTER 5

EARLY AND
MIDDLE ADULTHOOD

OBJECTIVES

After reading this chapter, you should be able to answer the following questions:

1. What are the biological changes that occur during early and middle adulthood?
2. How do reproduction and sexuality change during early and middle adulthood?
3. Is there one experience of adult living or do adults experience transitions from one period of adulthood to another?
4. What are the developmental tasks of early and middle adulthood?
5. What factors affect the psychological well-being of adults?

CASE STUDY

Daniel is a forty-two-year-old man who sought social work services after experiencing major stress and disruptions in his life. Within a period of a few months, he lost both his job and his marriage of twenty-three years. He lost his job because his employer sold the business to a corporation that immediately cut about a third of the firm's jobs. Shortly thereafter, his wife, feeling trapped, left him. Daniel felt that he had "lost everything" and that his life was ruined and a "disgrace."

Daniel considered himself an "old-fashioned" person. He came from a very traditional, conservative, and religious family. He tried to recreate that family with his own wife and children. Daniel's idea of success was having a home, stability, and a devoted family. Until his problems, Daniel occupied an important lay position in the Catholic community. He held key positions in fund-raising activities and served on boards of local religious social and charitable groups.

Daniel and his wife, Elizabeth, had three children. Their ages ranged from ten to twenty-one. He had believed that his marriage was "perfect," until, of course, Elizabeth left him. He seemed not to understand her unhappiness and was surprised that she felt so strongly about leaving.

Before the divorce, Daniel was the "master of his castle." He held complete authority at home. Elizabeth, on the other hand, felt powerless at home. She did not work outside the home and assumed almost all the responsibility for housework and childcare. Daniel and the children routinely discounted her opinions and contributions to the family. Eventually she tired of being a "junior partner" in the marriage and at age forty, with only a high school education and a limited work history, she and the youngest child moved out.

Before everything fell apart for him, Daniel felt on top the world. He believed that he had reached a point in his life that all he needed to do was maintain. He had reached all his goals and was living out a life that was very comfortable for him. Now he felt bewildered, lost, and ashamed.

These emotions were interfering with his ability to find a job and keep his place in the religious community. In short, Daniel had fallen apart.

INTRODUCTION

The quality of a person's life during adulthood is a consequence of the combined effects of pre-adult experiences and the resources available to adults to function independently. Being a competent adult means to be economically and emotionally independent, to engage in mature love relationships, and to raise healthy, secure children. Things go wrong with these goals when the psychosocial environment contradicts individual efforts to be autonomous.

As a result of increased longevity and the size of the baby boom cohort, more individuals are reaching midlife than during any time in history. Consequently, social and behavioral scientists are showing more interest in the quality of life at this stage (Julian, McKenry, & Arnold 1990). Of special concern is how changes in roles and physical abilities affect how people feel about themselves and how they behave.

This chapter examines the health and developmental tasks of early and middle adulthood. Particular attention is given to showing how adulthood is not a unitary experience, but instead is marked by many transitions and phases.

PHYSIOLOGICAL CHANGES

As people grow older, their bodies gradually change in ways that not only affect their health and well-being, but their sense of selfhood as well. At some point, they begin to receive messages that life is different than it was when they were younger. They can no longer run as fast or lift as much. They find that they have more injuries and ailments that linger longer than in years past. They also notice that they no longer appear the same. Looking into the mirror has new meanings when they see wrinkles, gray (or no) hair, and two chins. For many individuals, growing old simply requires an adjustment to their body's slowing down. For others, however, the signs of aging are troublesome and even a little frightening. For this latter group, aging is a threatening experience that conjures up images of regrets, frustrations, and remorse over how they have spent their lives.

Early adulthood is a time of good health and low disability. Morbidity and mortality due to disease are low during this stage of the life cycle. Health problems and disability that do arise occur from personal actions rather than aging itself (Sinclair 1989). As the body ages, however, it becomes increasingly vulnerable to disease, wear and tear, and injury. By age thirty, the efficiency of virtually all body functions has started to decline, albeit very gradually. What's more, most men and women engage in less physical activity after age thirty-nine. Less exercise in midlife accelerates skeletal loss, especially among women, and decreases in heart and lung fitness (Dan, Wilbur, & Hedricks 1990). The following section reviews the age-related changes in the various biological systems.

Appearance and Strength

For the most part, people stop growing in early adulthood. Height caps at about age twenty-one and physical strength peaks at age thirty, as connecting tissues, muscles, and bones weaken. As soon as growth stops, the first physical appearances of aging are apparent. By the late twenties and early thirties, facial skin begins losing its elasticity and the first wrinkles appear.

During middle adulthood, changes in body appearance and functioning are more obvious. By age forty, people take on an appearance unlike any they have had before. Individuals start to see a resemblance between themselves and photographs and memories of their own parents, whom they remember at the ages they are now. For men, and less frequently women, hair loss in varying degrees is common. For many men and women, gray hairs seem to be taking over. Skin loses more of its elasticity and gains more fatty tissues so that the face sags and looks more full.

The size and shape of the body changes in midlife. As fat settles in various parts of the body, many people experience the "middle-age spread" and gain weight. As people age, they are usually more sedentary, and so burn off fewer excess fat calories. While people tend to get "broader" with age, they also tend to get shorter. By age sixty, individuals can lose as much as an inch of height due to collapsing vertebrae (Whitbourne 1985).

Age-related changes in appearance have a differential effect on individuals. People who assign great importance to personal appearance find that diminishing facial and body appearance threatens their self-esteem and social status. The more individuals are externally controlled, that is, they allow other people to define who they are and provide their self-esteem, the more they are likely to have anxiety over age-related changes in appearance. They may work hard to maintain a youthful look and deny their natural appearance. Most people, however, accept their appearance comfortably and without despair.

You are probably familiar with the expression "Men age gracefully, women just age." Sexual stereotypes are a key ingredient in perceptions of aging. Because this culture persists in sexualizing women, youthfulness and "good looks" are highly valued commodities. How middle-aged women look is considered less attractive and desirable. Men, on the other hand, are awarded more grace as they age. Middle-aged men look "distinguished," as the stereotype goes. In the last several years, many "older" women, especially those working in the media, have fought legal battles to keep their jobs when employers have attempted to remove them because they were no longer youthful looking. Because of the women's movement and the demographic shift to an older population, values denigrating the appearance of middle-aged women seem to be abating. Nevertheless, sexist differences in judging men's and women's appearance persist.

Cardiovascular System

The function of the cardiovascular system is to pump blood throughout the circulatory system. Blood, of course, carries oxygen, nutrients, cells of the immune system, and other cells necessary for life. As individuals reach middle adulthood, significant limitations in this function are apparent. The walls of the heart gradually become more rigid with age, so the heart loses its efficacy as a pump. As the heart slows down, it moves less blood through the body, which in turn transfers less oxygen to cells. These cardiovascular changes reduce enjoyment of and participation in a wide array of activities that were formerly gratifying. After many years of stress, a high fat diet, and little exercise, adults in midlife are vulnerable to heart disease. Regular exercise and a low-fat diet reduce the probability of heart disease and may actually retard the effects of aging on the heart (Whitbourne 1985).

Respiratory System

The function of the respiratory system is to exchange oxygen and carbon dioxide. In the lungs, oxygen is transported to the blood and carbon dioxide is extracted. In midlife, the efficiency of the exchange process lowers, limiting a person's ability to perform muscular work. Studies of adults in their forties show that regular exercise increases lung capacity, which allows individuals to maintain a higher level of oxygen in the bloodstream. The cumulative effects of long-term smoking and exposure to environmental pollutants begin to appear in the form of emphysema, lung cancer, and other respiratory disorders during the midlife years.

Vision

Vision problems are common markers of entering mid-life. People who have worn corrective eyewear since childhood often find that their vision does not change significantly until they reach their late 30s and early 40s. From about age 30 to the middle 60s the eye becomes gradually more hypermetropic, or farsighted. This is due to the lens increasing in size and flattening.

Aging affects visual acuity as well, especially in low light and for seeing moving objects. After age 40, people are more susceptible to glares and bright lights, experience a decline in depth perception, and adapt to darkness more slowly. Developing an astigmatism, a problem in the eye's ability to focus appropriately and which leads to bifocal wear, is common in midlife. The rate of glaucoma, especially among African Americans, goes up during middle adulthood as well (Wilson 1989). These vision changes increase the risk of accidents, such as misjudging stairs and falling or being unable to walk through a dark room without tripping.

Auditory System

Hearing problems are common complaints among those in middle age, especially among men. Beginning at age forty, men's hearing typically worsens at the higher frequencies. Hearing loss is more pronounced in men than women perhaps because throughout their lives men have encountered more occupational noise hazards or listened to loud music (Fisch 1978).

Digestive and Excretory Systems

For the most part, age-related effects on the digestive and excretory systems are nominal in early and middle adulthood. Age, however, may play an indirect role in numerous gastrointestinal diseases that impair the efficiency of digestion. Lifetime habits of alcohol ingestion and poor nutrition may begin to take their toll on various organs. Numerous diseases of the colon, liver, and stomach, for example, are directly related to lifestyle and social environmental conditions.

Sleep Patterns

How people sleep changes with age. As age increases, the amount of time spent lying awake in bed at night goes up. Sleep interruptions begin for men at about age thirty, but not until age fifty for women. Periods of wakefulness gradually increase in frequency to the point that by late adulthood, 20 percent of the night may consist of periods of wakefulness, including the time spent falling asleep, intervals of awakening during the night, and in lying awake before arising in the morning (Whitbourne 1985).

REPRODUCTION AND SEXUALITY

Early adulthood is considered the prime period of fertility. Women who give birth in their twenties have fewer complications and give birth to healthier babies than new mothers in their teens, late thirties, or forties. Sexual response peaks in the twenties and early thirties and few people of these ages report difficulties with sexual activities.

One of the most important markers for women entering midlife is the *climacteric,* the gradual but persistent decrease in ovarian activity that precedes the cessation of menstruation. The term *menopause,* which is often confused with *climacteric,* refers to the last menstrual period and lasts about one week. The climacteric may take as long as fifteen years to complete (Notelovitz 1987). The climacteric is the transition period during which a woman's reproductive capacity diminishes. Menopause signals that the climacteric is complete (Whitbourne 1985).

Unlike men, who remain fertile throughout their lives, women gradually lose their ability to bear children. By age 55, virtually all women have stopped ovulating and can no longer conceive. During the period of transition leading up to menopause, women's menstrual cycle shortens from about thirty days at age thirty, to twenty-five days at forty, and to twenty-three days by the late forties. As women approach menopause, the last menstrual cycles are irregular and the reproductive organs become gradually less capable of sustaining a pregnancy. Beginning at age thirty-five, the eggs released each month are increasingly more likely to have a defect. If such an ovum were fertilized, it would result in an abnormal fetus (Whitbourne 1985).

There are three stages in the climacteric transition: the *early climacteric* (35–45), the *perimenopause* (45–55), and the *late climacteric* (55–65).

Each period is characterized by specific changes that affect the immediate and eventual health of women (Notelovitz 1987).

Early Climacteric

The first sign of the beginning of the climacteric is the shortening of the menstrual cycle, which is associated with a decrease in estradiol production. Periods are irregular with intermittent and prolonged spotting or prolonged periods of amenorrhea with sudden and profuse bleeding. This signals women that their ovaries are beginning their functional descent. Pregnancy is still possible during this time; 75 percent of women between forty and forty-five years of age ovulate regularly. Should women become pregnant, health risks for them and the fetus are extremely high, however. Because of the changes in the ovaries and in hormone secretion, women age thirty-five and over and who are physically active should not use oral contraceptives except in very low dosages. Women who smoke should avoid oral contraceptives altogether (Notelovitz 1987).

Premenstrual syndrome (PMS) is common among women in the early climacteric. Symptoms such as irritability, depression, insomnia, alterations in sex drive, and fatigue can be part of the climacteric experience.

Perimenopause

During the second stage of the climacteric, ovarian functioning continues to diminish. At some point, the last natural menstrual period, or menopause, occurs (Notelovitz 1987). As estradiol secretion by the ovaries diminishes, stimulation of the endometrium is reduced. Eventually stimulation is reduced to nil and no endometrium tissue is discharged. Menstruation has ended.

The actual menopause is accompanied by several symptoms, such as hot flashes, perspiration, palpitations, and specific tissue changes, such as vaginal dryness. About 75 percent of menopausal women experience hot flashes, which are temporary (lasting about thirty minutes), increases in body temperature, and a sudden increase in blood flow.

Other changes that occur during the perimenopausal period result from declines in estrogen production. Drops in hormone levels are believed responsible for the depression, impaired memory, insomnia, and irritability that some postmenopausal women experience. Women on estrogen therapy often report an improvement in general well-being, cognitive functioning, and sleep patterns (Notelovitz 1987).

Late Climacteric

The late climacteric stage includes other changes that result from the drop in hormone levels. Women experience changes in their secondary sexual characteristics. Breasts sag because mammary glands atrophy and are replaced with fat, which is less firm than the original glandular tissue. The alveoli become smaller, and sometimes disappear in late adulthood. Nipples decrease in size and become less erect when stimulated. Stretchmarks darken and become more wrinkled. In the vulva area, pubic hair thins and gets coarser and the labia majora and minora become thinner and wrinkled. Due to estrogen loss, the biochemical climate changes in the vagina, which becomes subject to more infections. The vagina becomes less elastic and loses its ability to change size and shape to accommodate an inserted penis. During sexual response, the uterus does not elevate as it does in earlier stages of life. Hence, there is less room for the vagina to expand. Pain, irritation, and other discomforts are often associated with coitus as a result of these physiological changes. Other changes include a distribution of fat that alters body shape and facial hair growth.

The third stage of the climacteric transition involves a postmenopause period in which age-related conditions, most notably osteoporosis and atherogenic disease, are possible. *Osteoporosis* is a condition in which bone mass decreases to a point where structural failure may occur. Though the exact cause of osteoporosis is unknown, many factors contribute to its development. These

factors include: estrogen deficiency, increasing age, smoking, high alcohol, caffeine, or high protein intake (which depletes calcium), and lean body mass. Bone mass can be increased, thereby reducing the probability of osteoporosis, by estrogen replacement after menopause, adequate dietary calcium, and moderate exercise (Steinberg 1987).

Heart disease is three times greater among postmenopausal women than in premenopausal women. Exercise, diet, and other lifestyle factors can reduce the likelihood of heart disease and hypertension.

Other health problems related to midlife changes in women include urinary incontinence and certain cancers, especially cancers of the breasts, lungs, and colon/rectum. Preventive measures, such as stopping smoking, regular medical examinations, and proper diets, are effective in managing women's midlife health.

For the most part, however, menopausal women do not report more symptoms or poorer health, and do not increase their use of medical services. According to McKinlay and McKinlay, "The 'typical' menopausal woman is neither sick nor a high user of medical care" (1986: 244).

Climacteric in Men

Men also experience a climacteric period, though men do not lose their ability to reproduce. Going through "the change of life" is less pronounced for men. The primary effect of hormone decline is the reduction in the number of viable sperm. Also the motility, or movement, of sperm, which peaks between the ages of twenty-six and thiry-five years of age, decreases at age fifty. Before age fifty among healthy men, there is virtually no change in sperm count or semen volume. The male climacteric simply involves a reduction in the delivery of active sperm.

At about forty years of age, changes in the prostate gland are seen in many men. By forty-five, men's risk of prostate disease, especially cancer, increases as the gland atrophies more quickly. Changes in the prostate gradually reduce the volume of seminal fluid; hence the pressure of ejaculate wanes.

Sexual and Emotional Responses to the "Change of Life"

The climacteric period produces few real sexual and emotional changes for most middle-aged women and men. The majority of middle-aged women view menopause as benign, nonstressful, and uneventful (Reinke et al. 1985).

For some women, menopause does cause significant emotional stress. The cessation of menses, for example, may force them to recognize their aging body and the reality that they are moving closer to death (Whitbourne 1985). Anxiety over aging may indicate previously unresolved conflicts, fading dreams, and other unfinished business. In addition, if women feel discomfort from the symptoms of the climacteric, such as mood changes, the transition may be more difficult.

For most women, the symptoms of menopause pale in comparison to the symptoms of monthly menstruation. In actuality, many feel relief that menses is over. Since most women, and men for that matter, in their fifties are not likely to want additional children, the loss of reproductive capability is not all that important.

Despite physiological changes in sexual anatomy and functioning, most middle-aged men and women do not experience any noticeable differences in sexual performance. Few report difficulty reaching orgasm and multiple orgasms are still possible for many older women. For some women, menopause marks the beginning of some degree of sexual freedom. Freed from the possibility of becoming pregnant and the expense and hassle of birth control techniques, women often become more spontaneous and carefree in their sexual behavior.

Sexual capability is somewhat affected by aging, however. In general, the overall sexual response of middle-aged men and women is less intense, less strong, and requires more stimulation to achieve arousal (Fordney 1986). Because age affects the penis by hardening penile tissues,

veins, and arteries, men are more likely to experience higher incidences of impotence. Full erections gradually decline with age, though healthy men rarely lose their ability to sustain an erection sufficiently for sexual intercourse. Retarded ejaculation is common during middle age as well. These dysfunctions, which are frequently situational, do not necessarily mean that sexual intimacy is not possible. Hormonal changes, such as women's loss of estrogen during the climacteric, do not affect sexual desire. The sexual desires, passions, and needs of middle-aged men and women vary little from their needs at younger ages. Sexual performance hardly changes, especially if the couple enjoys sexual activity, has no limiting health problems, and values their relationship with each other.

Childbirth in Midlife

Fertility (as measured by actual live births) is traditionally highest for women in their twenties. Although women remain fecund through their thirties and into their forties, most women give birth in early adulthood. As the "Baby Boomer" generation reaches midlife, unprecedented demographic changes have occurred. More and more women, who had delayed marriage and childbirth to attend to other needs such as educational and occupational attainment, are giving birth beyond the ages considered to be the "prime" for childbearing. It is not uncommon to see women past thirty-five having their first child now.

Many older new mothers may feel a social stigma for being "out of step" with younger mothers. As Mansfield (1988) notes, midlife pregnancy is frowned upon by many medical professionals who hold pessimistic attitudes against bearing children past thirty-five years of age. Traditional medical advice indicates that late pregnancies carry high risks for both the mother and the baby and should thus be avoided. Newer evidence suggests that the risks of a difficult pregnancy or delivery for older mothers may be somewhat overblown. Beliefs that older women are at higher risk during pregnancy may actually give rise to added feelings of worry over childbearing complications (Mansfield 1988).

Nonetheless late childbirth is not without certain risks. As I stated earlier, increased maternal age is associated with a higher incidence of certain types of birth defects, especially chromosomal disorders, and other problems. Down's Syndrome is perhaps the best known example. Table 5.1 shows the relationship between maternal age and the incidence of this disorder. With advanced maternal age, comes a rapidly increasing rate of birth defects. As noted in Chapter 2, prenatal testing can diagnose many of these disorders.

Older mothers have higher rates of other complications as well. For example, new mothers aged thirty-five and over experience high rates of hypertension, toxemia, and myoma. New mothers who are forty and older suffer higher rates of hypertension, postpartum hemorrhage, preeclampsia, and abruptio placentae (Resnik 1986). About 31 percent of mothers thirty-five and over have cesarean deliveries. The rate soars to 63 percent for women in that age group having their first child (Resnik 1986). It is not clear, however, if these cesarean deliveries are due to actual complications or reflect a bias of physicians because the patient is older. Elective abdominal deliveries may be more common among mid-aged women because their physicians anticipated complications, not because complications were actually present (Mansfield 1988).

The children of older mothers have certain developmental disadvantages compared to children of younger women. The frequency of fine motor

TABLE 5.1 The Relationship between Maternal Age and Down's Syndrome

MATERNAL AGE	RATE
30	1:885 Births
35	1:365
40	1:109
45	1:32

Source: Resnik 1986

skills problems is five times greater among children of older mothers and these children have more visual–perceptual dysfunctions and attentional deficit signs as well (Gillberg et al. 1982). On the positive side, IQs have been shown to improve with advancing maternal age (Lobl et al. 1971).

TRANSITIONS IN ADULTHOOD

Daniel Levinson (1978; 1986) views adulthood as alternating periods of stability and transition (see Figure 5.1). To Levinson, what remains stable and what changes is a person's *life structure,* which he defines as the pattern or design of a person's life at a given time. Life structure represents one's relationships, involvements with groups and institutions, roles, activities, and physical settings. Life structure is the bridge between a person's inner self and the demands of society. As one study describes them, life structures are the connections between self and circumstances (Wolfe, O'Connor, & Crary 1990). The meaning of life structure is described by Levinson as the answer to the question, "What is my life like now?" (1986: 6).

> *As we begin reflecting on this question, many others come to mind. What are the most important parts of my life and how are they interrelated? Where do I invest most of my time and energy? Are there some relationships—to spouse, lover, family, occupation, religion, leisure, or whatever—that I would like to make more satisfying or meaningful? Are there some things not in my life that I would like to include? (Levinson 1986:6)*

Each period of life creates its own life structure and people have to make different decisions based on "where they are in life." In doing so, it is important to consider what resources are available and what kinds of relationships are desirable. The important choices in adult life concern work, family, friendships, love relationships, where to live, recreation, religious values and practices, involvement with the community, and short- and long-term goals. Therefore, differences between the periods of adulthood reflect a shift from one set of decisions, resources, and relationships to another.

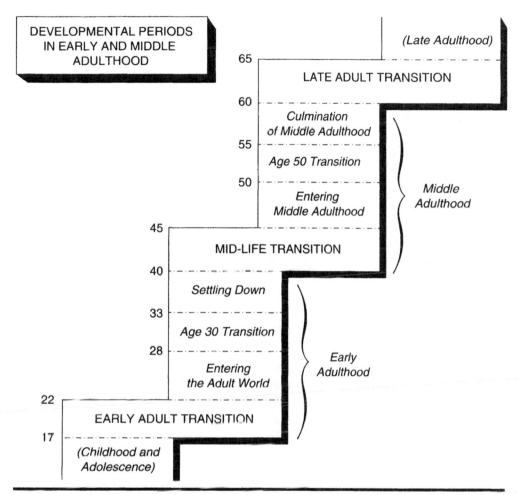

FIGURE 5.1 Levinson's Stages of Adult Life (From *The Seasons of a Man's Life,* Daniel J. Levinson et al. Copyright © 1978 by Daniel J. Levinson. Reprinted by permission of Alfred A. Knopf, Inc.)

As life structures change, different aspects of one's life take on importance.

Levinson's periods are formed around developmental tasks, which he believes are the main goals, objectives, or problems a person faces during a particular time of life. A period ends when its tasks or key elements lose their significance and new tasks or issues emerge. Therefore, life structures are not permanent. Whether tasks are completed well or poorly does not affect moving on to the next period, as is the case in other stage theories. To Levinson, problems in completing life tasks affect the *quality* of future decisions and the options a person may have in reaching future goals.

In sum, adult stages of development involve sets of choices and how people build their lives around their decisions. Adults try to build life structures that are satisfactory to them and to the social world in which they live. In time, the existing life structure confronts new questions or problems and so new choices are required. Thus, a new life structure will eventually form.

What are Levinson's alternating periods of adult development? First, *structure-building* periods are stages of stability. The primary task in a structure-building period is to form a life structure and enhance life within it. Stable periods last six to eight years and involve making certain crucial choices and working to attain particular goals derived from those choices.

Second, *structure-changing* periods are transition stages, times when people reappraise their current life structure. They rethink earlier decisions and present relationships and respond to new challenges in the environment. In addition, adults explore possibilities for change in themselves and the world around them. Changing the general pattern of their lives requires people to question "where they are in life" and the direction in which their lives are headed. Transition periods last about five years. As a transition comes to an end, individuals start making important choices that give them meaning and commitment. Once these decisions are made, a new life structure is created around them. The primary tasks of structure-changing periods, therefore, are to terminate the existing life structure and initiate a new one.

According to Levinson, choices are the major products of transitions. For example, individuals may wrestle with improving their work or their marriages. Perhaps they desire to explore alternative lifestyles or to come to terms with themselves. Choices must be made: "This is what I will settle for." Once individuals decide what they want to do about their work or marriage, they start building the relationships and changing themselves to play out those decisions. At some point, according to his theory, those choices and decisions are replaced by new questions or desires. A person evaluates previous choices as either favorable or unsatisfactory.

Levinson identifies several periods of structure-building and structure-transition during early and middle adulthood (see Figure 5.2). Each is discussed below.

Early Adult Transition (from age 17 to 22)

The *early adult transition* period is a developmental bridge between preadulthood and early adulthood. This transition involves two major tasks.

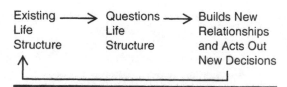

FIGURE 5.2   Process of Adult Changes

The first is to terminate the adolescent life structure by modifying relationships within the family and with other people to allow independence and autonomy. The second task is to take a preliminary step into the adult world. This involves exploring and making choices about how early adult life will be lived. Major life events within this transition may include graduating from school, moving out of the family home, entering college, or going to work. The transition ends when individuals create a stable life within the adult world (Levinson 1978).

Entry Life Structure for Early Adulthood (from 22 to 28)

The *entry life structure for early adulthood* is the time for building and maintaining an initial style of adult living. During this time, young adults explore and make commitments to adult roles and responsibilities. Young adults need to create a stable life structure by becoming responsible and "making something" of themselves. At the same time, young adults must keep their options open and avoid making strong commitments that they are not prepared for or that can limit their futures. Examples of important life events that often occur during this period include making an occupational choice, marriage, and the birth of children (Hultsch & Deutsch 1981).

The Age 30 Transition (from 28 to 33)

The *age 30 transition* is an opportunity to reappraise and make changes in the entry to early adulthood life structure. The goal of this transition period is to create the basis for the next life structure. Many important new choices are made, or old decisions are reaffirmed. Individuals during this time often balance their decisions with their talents, dreams, and opportunities.

Adult life is now becoming more serious and the focus is on adjustment and enrichment. As Levinson says, many people hear a voice inside them that says: "If I am to change my life...I must now make a start, for soon it will be too late" (1978: 58). For many, this transition is particularly difficult. Divorce and occupational change are common during these years.

The Culminating Life Structure for Early Adulthood (from 33 to 40)

The *culminating life structure for early adulthood* period is the time when people realize their youthful aspirations. Levinson originally referred to this period as "settling down" because it emphasizes stability and security. Individuals are deeply absorbed in their commitments to their occupations, families, and other significant relationships and activities. Individuals act on long-term goals and make plans for success. The task in this period is to become a successful, competent adult. Doing so involves asserting one's own independence and authority within the context of their roles and relationships.

The Midlife Transition (from 40 to 45)

The *midlife transition* terminates early adulthood and begins the shift into middle adulthood. For some, the transition is a relatively smooth one, but for others it can be intensely stressful. Often called the "midlife crisis," people during this time may ask questions such as "What have I done with my life? What do I really get from and give to my spouse, children, friends, work, community, and self? What is it I truly want for myself and others?" (Levinson 1978: 60). A task of the midlife transition is to work on and partially resolve the discrepancy between what is and what will be (Hultsch & Deutsch 1981).

The midlife transition can be a period of great struggle. Adults in their early forties question nearly every aspect of their lives and feel that they cannot go on as before (Levinson 1978). During the midlife transition, old decisions about adult tasks are reappraised and neglected interests and desires seek expression and attention. Life seems to take on a new urgency for adults in the midlife transition. This is perhaps a consequence of realizing their own mortality.

Life Structure for Middle Adulthood (from 45 to 50)

The tasks of the midlife transition should be completed by age 45 or so. A new *life structure for middle adulthood* develops to accommodate the decisions made from questioning the life structure of early adulthood. In other words, what life changes have been made as a result of reappraising earlier life decisions?

For many, the transition to middle adulthood involves a drastic life change such as a divorce, an extramarital affair, a serious illness or death of loved one, or an occupational change. For most others, changes in life structures are subtle and may include little more than changing their approach to work. In this case, perhaps an individual feels that work is oppressive and boring. Seemingly small changes in approaching work, such as marking time to retirement, make that work more tolerable (Levinson 1978).

Some individuals are unable to reach the goals they set during the midlife transition. Emotional deprivations in childhood, poor outcomes to earlier decisions, the absence of a supportive environment, or a lack of opportunities are common barriers to a satisfactory life structure during middle adulthood. When this happens, people often feel trapped by their ambitions and desires.

Fulfilling transition choices is highly satisfying and exciting for adults who have the resources and opportunities that enable them to act on their choices. These adults are more deeply attached to others, yet are able to realize their own ambitions. Many adults feel that this period of life is the most satisfying and enriching time of their lives.

The Age 50 Transition (from 50 to 55)

Though Levinson stopped collecting data on subjects when they were 45 years of age, he hypothesized that the shifting between periods of transition and stability continues into later adulthood. He proposed a period called the *age 50 transition,* which offers a chance to modify and perhaps improve the middle adulthood life structure. This period would be analogous to the age 30 transition. During this period, adults would work to further the tasks of the midlife transition and alter the life structure formed in the mid-forties. The age 50 transition could be a time of crisis for adults who made unsatisfactory choices in earlier transitions and are having trouble realizing their own aging. This transition period is followed by another structure-building period similar to the settling-down period but involves the issues of later adulthood.

Criticisms of Levinson's Theory

According to Levinson, adults strive toward stability and the realization of dreams and develop through shifting periods of stability and change. He identified these periods of transition and stability from empirical data collected from interviews of forty men. Herein lies one important problem. Does the theory apply to women as well as men? Levinson contends that there is marked similarity between men and women, though it is probable that the patterns of the transitions vary. Wrightsman (1994), however, questions the applicability of Levinson's theory in explaining the lives of women. He argues that the genders differ in their perception of what the valued developmental milestones are and that, as a rule, women reflect greater diversity in lifestyles than do men.

Other studies on adult women's development reveal patterns that differ from those described by Levinson. Though the timing of developmental periods and tasks for women are similar to those of men, the content may be different (Wrightsman 1994). Women may increase the complexity of their lifestyles over the course of adulthood and experience more stress as a result. For women

who make marriage and family commitments rather than pursue a career in early adulthood, the family-related aspects of life structure remain fairly stable. By age thirty, however, these women frequently become more dissatisfied with family life, experience considerable personal disruption, and express a desire for a more egalitarian relationship with their husbands (Reinke et al. 1985; Stewart 1977, cited in Wrightsman 1994).

A high percentage of women experience dramatic changes in the way they live their lives or the way they think about themselves that differ in content from Levinson's theory (Reinke, Holmes, & Harris 1985; Harris, Ellicott, & Homes 1986). These changes manifest themselves in different ways by different women, but appear to have three common phases.

The first phase usually begins between ages twenty-six and thirty and is characterized by a feeling of personal disruption. Women reassess their lives and seek some unknown change. Life and personality changes are common during these years (Wrightsman 1994).

The second phase, which usually begins between the ages of twenty-eight and thirty-one, involves a focus on the self and self-development. Women see themselves as less oriented to others and seeking something for themselves. Many set personal goals for perhaps the first time. Satisfaction with traditional women's activities often wanes during these years. The third period begins at age thirty and lasts about five years. This period reflects a new sense of well-being. Women often have a heightened sense of self-satisfaction and are increasingly self-confident. In summary, heterosexual women experience changes similar to those Levinson saw in his sample of adult men; however, the content of those transitions is likely to differ.

A second criticism involves social class issues and midlife development. Levinson studied men in four occupational groups: novelists, biologists, business executives, and factory workers. Little emphasis, however, is placed on macrosystem issues. Tamir (1989) reports social class differences in perceptions of the onset of midlife. Men in the working class are likely to consider themselves middle-aged by forty, whereas middle-class men often consider themselves middle-aged in their early fifties (Hunter & Sundel 1989).

A final criticism is Levinson's reliance on age as boundaries between periods. Other theories of adult development focus on significant events such as marriage, birth of children, and retirement. This criticism appears relevant. For example, does a twenty-year-old with a new baby experience the same developmental options in the same way as a twenty-year-old without a child? The kinds of

---

EXPLORING THE ISSUES 5.1 _____

Defense Mechanisms

Anxiety is an unpleasant feeling. Freud believed that people use "defense mechanisms" to ward off anxiety, maintain their integrity, and preserve their peace of mind. Defense mechanisms, which are often unconscious, are normal responses to stress and help people meet the demands of daily life. Although they may distort reality and involve self-deception, the defenses are usually effective for relieving anxious feelings.

Defenses are not always used functionally, however. When defenses interfere with self-esteem, meeting needs, and relationships with other people, then the defenses are believed to be too strong and individuals are shielded from effectively dealing with their problems. The jargon description of people as "well defended" refers to those individuals who have their guards up and are constantly working to protect themselves from pain. Defenses help people cope with problems that they may not be able to tackle directly, but should not be used to substitute for direct resolution of problems.

Below is a list and brief description of eight of the most common defenses: displacement, sublimation, reaction formation, denial, projection, rationalization, repression, and regression.

Displacement: Freud considered displacement one of the healthiest defense mechanisms. This defense displaces unacceptable desires and energies into more acceptable forms.

Example: A student who is angry with a professor, then goes home and exercises. Displacement involves channeling "negative energy" into positive activities.

Sublimation: This is the second healthy defense, according to Freud. This defense is believed to be associated with relieving the guilt produced from sexual and aggressive drives. Sublimation allows a person to turn these drives into a higher order goal or achievement.

Examples: A particularly aggressive person who uses that energy to become a star athlete; the redirection of maternal drive into teaching, nursing, and social work practice.

Reaction formation: Reaction formation refers to deliberately forming emotions, ideas, and behavior patterns that are opposite to what the person really feels and wants to do.

Example: Acting macho and fearless when on the inside the person feels insecure and threatened.

Denial: Denial takes the form of ignoring or refusing to recognize certain facts.

Example: People with drug and alcohol problems typically deny that their abuse is serious or that it causes any problems in their relationships.

Projection: Projection involves attributing to others one's own unacceptable thoughts and desires.

Example: People who feel uncomfortable about their own sexuality may "see" sexual irresponsibility in others.

Rationalization: Rationalization refers to inventing excuses for doing something wrong, though it was something the individual wanted to do anyway.

Example: A student who fails a social work course may rationalize the failure by claiming a lack of desire for ever wanting to become a professional social worker.

Repression: Repression is a form of denial in which particularly unpleasant thoughts are pushed into the unconscious.

Example: Many victims of child abuse use repression to avoid remembering and confronting the abuse.

Regression: Regression is behavior drawn from an earlier stage of development.

Example: When stressed out, a person using this defense may resort to infantile behavior such as throwing a tantrum.

choices they make are likely to be influenced more by the event of childbirth rather than the fact that they are twenty years of age.

Despite these criticisms, the dynamic process of alternating periods of change and stability has merit in understanding adult development. Most adults do undergo changes in the basic emphases of their lives, though many of these changes may be small.

Gender and Transition to Midlife

Several developmental changes signal the transition to midlife. Most apply to both men and women, but in different ways. For example, as I noted earlier in this chapter, physiological changes in appearance, functioning, and health mark the transition to middle age in both sexes, though the process differs greatly. Both sexes realize the finiteness of life, another transitional marker, at about the same time. Changes in family roles also indicate middle age for both men and women, but because parenting roles differ, how people change when their children are preparing to leave home varies according to gender.

There are also noticeable differences in transitional markers to midlife, however. Men's transition to midlife is largely marked by employment patterns and achievement. Most men reach their peaks in productivity and influence by middle age. Women's transition to midlife, however, is not as clearly defined in this regard. As a transitional marker, employment status is not as useful for women because they are more likely to make occupational shifts than men over the course of the life cycle. Women in the middle years are about equally likely to either reenter the paid labor force or terminate full-time employment. These changes are frequently based on marital stability. Middle-aged men are less likely to change their employment status when their children leave home (Smith & Moen 1988).

Given women's orientation toward relationships (Gilligan 1982), it seems particularly useful to examine transitions in women's lives within the context of their families' development (Ellicott

1985). Psychosocial changes in women are frequently paired with phases in the family life cycle. Most of the women in Ellicott's study experienced major psychosocial transitions during three phases of family life: (1) the starting a family–preschool stage, (2) the launching phase, and (3) the postparental phase.

About 80 percent of adult women, according to Ellicott, undergo a major transition at the start of a family–preschool phase. Role changes associated with the birth and rearing of children are particularly disruptive for women, often involving role strain and role conflict. This phase is often characterized by leaving the workforce, marital dissatisfaction, and frustrations with childrearing, all of which have a harmful impact on self-esteem and identity.

Many women experience psychosocial disruptions during the launching phase when children are leaving home. About 40 percent of Ellicott's sample were more dissatisfied with their marriages and perceived decreases in their personal development at this stage in life.

Finally, the postparental phase, the stage of family life when the last child leaves home, is the last period in which women make significant psychosocial transitions. Many women report increased life satisfaction, personal stability, and general personality changes such as increased confidence, assertiveness, and expressiveness of opinions (Ellicott 1985). Her findings indicate that the so-called *empty-nest syndrome* is not as universal as previously believed.

According to the empty-nest hypothesis, women suffer a lack of definition and a loss of organized activities that provide meaning and purpose when the maternal role is redefined or lost because the last child has left home. Most of the evidence discounts the prevalence of the empty-nest syndrome. Women typically see the empty-nest period as a positive experience. They have more time to spend with their husbands and to work toward achieving personal goals. The postparenting period is characterized by increased marital satisfaction, an increased acceptance of life, and a more mellow outlook (Ellicott 1985).

DEVELOPMENTAL TASKS OF ADULTHOOD

The four main tasks for adults involve meeting intimacy and family needs, satisfying achievement needs, taking care of elderly parents, and coping with end of life issues. The first two needs are met as young adults leave home and form their own families and by making sound occupational choices. For most theorists, adult maturity is defined by the ability to form secure intimate relationships with others and become emotionally and economically self-sufficient. Intimacy and achievement needs are not always accomplished by individual initiative alone, however. The social environment has a major impact on persons' accomplishing these needs. Finally, as adults reach middle age, they begin confronting their own mortality and the finiteness of life. Roles change as their children leave home and their own parents' well-being declines. As middle-aged adults are helping their own children begin adulthood and their elderly parents are becoming dependent, the middle or "sandwich" generation is beginning to think about freedom from parenting responsibilities and preparing for their own retirement. Let's review these four general developmental tasks by looking at intimacy and family formation.

The Tasks of Intimacy and Forming Families

Intimacy. To Erikson (1963), the developmental crisis *intimacy vs. isolation* concerns the need to share one's life with someone else. Intimacy involves a sense of connectedness and mutual trust with other adults. Mature intimacy, to Erikson, includes individuals' willingness to change their cycles of work, procreation, and recreation to meet the needs of their partner.

Genuine intimacy, as opposed to intimacy based on narcissism or excessive dependency, involves being faithful and committed to another person. Making sacrifices and denying certain self-serving needs allows the mature person to maintain mutually satisfactory relationships. The key to successful intimacy is to fuse identity without losing sight of individuality. Intimacy "in-cludes the ability to experience an open, supportive, tender relationship with another person, without fear of losing one's own identity in the process of growing close" (Newman & Newman 1975: 270). Intimacy is about authentic understanding and reciprocal giving and receiving. Intimacy makes gratifying relationships possible.

The antithesis to intimacy is isolation. Remaining alone and unrecognized are the threats to well-being during this stage of life. The key to establishing intimate relationships is the degree to which a successful identity was formed during adolescence. Young adults who have not resolved that earlier crisis will likely remain focused on identity issues and be less able to form truly intimate ties to another person.

For example, let me describe the situation of a young adult, John, who came to me seeking social work services. He was a young man, age twenty-seven, who complained of being depressed. John showed less interest in hobbies and activities that used to interest him and he had just separated from his wife of five years. He had a stable work history, but admitted that lately he was slacking at work and not putting forth much effort. He did not particularly like his job and believed that he was an underachiever. His wife had moved out of their house, but took most of the furniture and other possessions with her.

John's parents divorced when he was thirteen. After that he saw his father infrequently. His mother became emotionally abusive. She often berated him, putting him down in front of other people. She was very critical and gave him little encouragement or useful guidance.

High school was a difficult time in John's life. He exerted minimal effort in the classroom and rarely participated in extracurricular activities. He did not date much, feeling unattractive and uncomfortable around girls. He had close male friends in school, but, for the most part, his friends had similar kinds of problems as he.

While in college, he first met his future wife, Mary. He was immediately attracted to her strong will and decisive manner. They were married about a year after meeting and John dropped out of college to work. After a short time, John said, the marriage began having difficulties. His major complaint was that his marriage lacked mutual affection. He believed that his wife was not highly involved in their relationship and that he was overly attached. He had few friends and little contact with family members.

After a few interviews, we began to explore the possibility that John's trouble in his marriage and his depressed mood were in large part consequences of having not resolved the developmental tasks of adolescence. John had little sense of personal organization or direction in his life. His emotional dependency on his wife was perhaps connected to his need to have the parental attachments he lost when his parents divorced. "Drifting" through adolescence without an emotionally stable social environment, John was unable to plan goals for himself and discover the kind of person he wanted to be. Instead, adolescence was focused on his parents' conflicts, his father's rejection and abandonment, and his mother's harshness.

John carried these problems with him into young adulthood. Consequently, his marriage was based on his needing his wife to be his "good parent" and to provide emotional comfort. Similarly, work was something he did simply to survive rather than an activity that was interesting or stimulating for him.

Forming mutually satisfying relationships is hard when individuals do not have a handle on who or what they want to be. Game-playing, one-sided love, excessive dependency, and social withdrawal are typical outcomes when one or both partners has failed to resolve the identity crisis of adolescence. These outcomes most likely lead to unrewarding, conflicted relationships that have a good chance of collapse. When they do last, individuals may feel alone and disengaged from their partners.

Individuals should have established a sense of autonomy by the time they reach early adulthood. That is, they should be able to relate to parents more equally, see themselves as persons distinct from their families of origin, and have mastered

self-sufficiency. Dependency on parents, however, sometimes continues longer than in times past. Attending college and graduate school or having trouble landing a job that pays a decent wage may prevent young adults from overcoming their dependency on their parents. When this happens, intergenerational conflict is common. Tension between adult children who still require parental support and their parents is the consequence of a developmental lag for both the child and the parents. The child, of course, desires autonomy, but is unprepared or unable to attain it. Parents may be at a developmental stage in which they want to be freed from parenting responsibilities. Their attention turns to their own developmental tasks, which may not include dependent children.

The larger psychosocial environment can have a major impact on this problem. At one level, for example, this developmental conflict is not of families' own choosing. The failure of the economic institution to provide enough jobs that pay well enough for self-sufficiency keeps many young adults in a continued state of dependency. When opportunities for adult success are limited, fewer people can take advantage of and enjoy their rewards.

At another level, the psychological domain of children's environment may have encouraged dependent behavior. Parents who fail to promote confidence, initiative, and tangible skills in their children run the risk of creating adults who do not know how to take care of themselves.

Forming Intimate Relationships and Families. How do people form relationships? Affairs of the heart have been the topic of discussion throughout human history. Only in the last few decades, however, have social and behavioral scientists researched the way people are attracted to others and why.

People form different types of love or intimate relationships to meet different kinds of needs. Some romances are not intended to escalate to deeper attraction, while other relationships seem destined from the start to progress to marriage. What are the differences?

Most intimate relationships begin as *infatuation*. Early attraction to another person is based on superficial qualities such as appearance, age, clothing style, and presenting behavior. None of these attributes tells much about deeper qualities— such as values, attitudes, empathy, and behavioral styles—that are more important when actually choosing a partner. In the absence of knowing the "true" personality of the other person, people typically fill in the holes with their projections of what their ideal love interest would look like. Many theorists suggest that people project qualities that they wish they had onto desired others. Other theorists contend that individuals project qualities based on the intrapsychic needs they need fulfilled by the relationship. For example, if a person is very dependent and passive, then that person might project qualities of strength and power onto another. During the first few encounters with another person people are working through the differences between their fantasy of what that person is like and the way the person really is. The more two people are together, the more they disclose about themselves and the more this gap should narrow.

Exchange theory is one of the best approaches for understanding the beginnings of an intimate relationship. Exchange theory assumes that people are rational and that relationships are formed following a calculated cost–benefit analysis. This approach suggests that people weigh the benefits and the costs of being with another person. General rewards for entering and/or maintaining a specific relationship include belongingness, companionship, acceptance, sex, and support. Costs that people may encounter in relationships, on the other hand, include such things as unequal roles, power imbalances, status differences, abuse, exploitation, uncomfortable sexual expressions, and a loss of personal freedom. According to the theory, as long as individuals believe that the benefits of a relationship outweigh the costs, the relationship will continue.

The more self-disclosure there is in a relationship, the more information the couple has to "bargain." This means that each person has more information about the other to weigh as a cost or a reward. Differences between the two people have to be negotiated in order to resolve the conflicts that arise from the differences. When individuals choose a person to form an intimate relationship, they are actually accepting that person's negative qualities, because they see them as less costly in light of the benefits that person has to offer.

Individual attributes are not the only ones being exchanged. The social environment strongly influences the kinds of attributes people are likely to consider acceptable. The environment restricts choices in dating and mate selection by making members of certain groups off limits. Resistance to interracial dating, for example, remains very strong. Couples with great differences in age, religion, or social class often catch the attention of others who may respond in a negative way. In short, people rarely, if ever, exhibit free will in choosing their partners for intimate relationships. Though people experience intimacy as a private individual act, they often forget that the social environment is very intrusive in instilling values of what is attractive and desirable.

Another concept that shows the environment's intrusion into personal life is the *marriage gradient*, which suggests that in heterosexual relationships men should have slightly higher status than women in virtually all aspects of life. According to this rule, husbands should be older and taller, have more education, make more money, and have a more prestigious occupation than wives. In times past, the marriage gradient forced women into powerless roles in order to achieve marriage, which was about their only avenue to status in traditional culture. Today women have more opportunities for success without being dependent upon a man, yet the marriage gradient is still strong. Conforming to the marriage gradient protects a man's sense of self. Insecure with powerful or highly skilled women, some men exclude these women from the "marriage market."

In the early stages of a relationship, one individual may decide that the other has qualities that cannot be negotiated or exchanged. If a quality is judged to be unacceptable and therefore costly for some reason, then the relationship does not go very far. Relationships also do not become established if one or both of the persons has no interest in forming such a relationship. In this case, the idea of a relationship is presumed to be costly.

Relationships proceed if the couple desires a relationship and continues to find each other rewarding. This early stage of relationships is called the *passionate stage* (Walster & Walster 1978). The passionate stage is a period of peak emotional excitement. The loved partner is idealized and faults are overlooked. Everything is seen as sexually exciting, even qualities seen later as undesirable, and there is a strong feeling of excitement in being together.

Thus far in the relationship exchanges have gone well—perceived differences and negative attributes are not too great to handle. Therefore there is little conflict during the passionate stage.

Over time, however, the passion begins to fade. There are several reasons why people cannot keep the passion stage alive for very long. Eventually individuals must return to normal life. Concentrating on school, work, and other activities becomes important again and there is less time and energy for romantic excitement. Similarly the more time people spend together, the more significant everyday details become. No longer finding socks on the floor "cute," there is more conflict as couples try to integrate the relationship into the totality of their lives. As couples spend more time together and adapt to one another, the more important mundane, routine experiences become. In other words, life goes on.

Another reason the passionate stage ends is that several needs, especially security, predictability, acceptance, and understanding, are better met the more people know each other. If the interest is there, most people eventually want to deepen their relationship in order to satisfy other, more important needs.

Finally the passionate stage ends because eventually it becomes tiresome and boring. People have a difficult time maintaining that level of intensity and will eventually tire. The effect of the stimulation gradually wears off as well, leaving the couple to find other ways of entertaining and relating to each other. There is less excitement in a relationship when the lovers become adapted to one another.

Shortly after the passionate stage peaks, some people begin to feel insecure about themselves and their relationships. They miss the allure of the passionate "hunt" and feel confused when passion wanes. Often these people have an *external locus of control,* which means that their self-esteem and sense of self are based on external relationships rather than internal qualities. They require the excitement of a new relationship to feel important, needed, and loved. Sensing rejection by the end of the passionate stage, these individuals may lash out at the partner in anger and pick fights. In these cases, relationships will end because the individual needs to search for another person in order to receive the intense emotional feedback required to buffer fears of rejection. Settling down into a comfortable, calm relationship is unthinkable to the person with these needs and fears.

If relationships continue past the passionate stage, they enter the *companionate stage.* This stage is described as quiet affection. The relationship is less emotionally intense, though the attachment to each other is deeper. The couple's lives are more integrated now as they have shared considerable experiences together and have woven a new life for themselves. There is less urgency about sex, but more conflict than earlier in the relationship.

Getting Married. Marriage no longer holds the same significance it once did. Though almost all adults will marry at least once, there is an increasing pool of people who remain voluntarily single. Furthermore, many young people mistrust marriage and believe it to be inconsistent with modern realities.

Nonetheless, most adults will marry and will do so for many reasons, only one of which is love. Though most people say they are in love with the person they marry, there are many personality and social factors that push people toward marriage. Some of the reasons people marry include:

- to offset loneliness
- to feel like a "whole person"
- for money
- for sex
- to enhance social identity
- for security
- to have dependency needs met
- to rebel against or escape from families of origin

Consider the following example of a woman, Bonnie, who married to escape her family of origin. Bonnie's parents adhered to a strict fundamentalist religion and denied her the opportunity to engage in mainstream adolescent culture. She was not allowed to wear makeup or stylish clothes, date without a chaperone, stay out late, or attend parties unless they were sponsored by her church. Bonnie felt angry and embarrassed by her parents and the teachings of her religion.

Bonnie lived next door to Frank, a rebellious fellow who was "hip" to all the trends of teenage life. On the sly, Bonnie would see Frank romantically and would eventually envision him as a way out of her family. Bonnie was ignorant of sex, but allowed Frank to make advances. She found sex very exciting, plus it allowed her to get away with something her parents frowned upon. Getting this kind of passive revenge on her parents helped her cope with their rigidity. Bonnie and Frank married the summer they graduated from high school.

Frank was a fairly heavy drinker in high school and after the wedding began to drink more and more. What intimacy they had began to break down within a year of their marriage. At about that time, Frank became violent and started hitting Bonnie. Bonnie bore two sons in the next eighteen months. When the youngest, Tommy, was about six months old, Frank threw a soft drink bottle at Bonnie, but missed and hit Tommy in the chest. That night she took her sons and left Frank, never to return.

Bonnie realized that her marriage did not live up to her romantic idealizations. She believed she loved Frank when she was eighteen. She probably did love him, but what she apparently did not realize at the time was the likelihood that her love for Frank was perhaps more connected to the need she felt to escape her parents' inflexibility than true love. Her haste to leave home impaired her ability to learn more about Frank. From an exchange theory point of view, the benefits of leaving home outweighed Frank's characteristics of alcohol abuse and rebelliousness.

Having Children.   In times past, having children was an expectation that few people voluntarily ignored. Then as now in preindustrial, tra-

The large majority of interracial couples marry for love and compatibility, just like intraracial couples. Despite this similarity, interracial couples may have more adjustment problems to handle. Cultural differences and stress derived from negative evaluations by others may create problems that are difficult to negotiate and bargain.

ditional societies, children were economic assets who worked, brought in income, and produced food for the whole family. In industrial societies, however, children are economic burdens.

In industrial societies adults work for a wage outside of the home in a factory or other business. Having more people in the family means that each member's share of those wages is smaller. Children in these families are not producers, they are consumers. In a wage economy, large families are economically dysfunctional.

Not only are children an economic burden in today's world, but being a parent contradicts cultural values of individualism. Successful parenting involves a certain amount of self-sacrifice and self-denial. Finding the time to play with children, offer guidance, and provide for material needs requires adults to abandon some activities that perhaps are more fun or self-serving. Unless a parent avoids sleeping altogether, there is not enough time in the day to spend with children and to fulfill other personal goals.

People who become parents before resolving identity and intimacy issues are not likely to make good mothers and fathers. Much of their energies are dedicated to resolving, or at least buffering, the anxiety and dread that come with having trouble knowing who they are and feeling comfortable living with another person. The motivation to relieve intrapersonal distress takes a great deal of energy, leaving little to give to children. Many adults concentrate on careers and other interests and do not attend to children's needs for attention, affection, and stability.

As a consequence of the economic burden of children and the obstructions they pose to individual gratification, people now ask "Why have children?" More adults are delaying childbirth or avoiding it altogether now than in any time in history.

People have children for several reasons, depending on their own psychosocial situations. One, people become parents to gain adult status. In many traditional families and communities, becoming a parent represents a transition into adulthood. Two, people have babies to share unconditional love. Forming families helps to promote affection, bonding, and emotional security. Three, some people may choose to have children because they feel powerless. Parents have unquestionable power over their children. For people who are powerless at work and have limited resources for self-empowerment, children become a legitimate audience for the expression of power and control. Four, some people have children as a misdirected means for resolving marital problems. Believing that a baby will bring them closer together, new parents are often disappointed and frustrated when they realize that children require a great deal of work. Romanticizing parenthood usually is followed by a letdown when the realities of parenthood set in and actually cause more distress than was present before the pregnancy. A final reason for having children seems to be more important for men than women. Many families and communities stress the importance of maintaining a family line and leaving a legacy. For many people, children are men's mark on the world and reassure them that something of them will continue after they are gone.

Achievement Needs

People work for a variety of different reasons, such as money, prestige, companionship, personal recognition, and satisfaction (Terkel 1972). The occupational role provides an identity for an individual that holds both social and personal significance. One of the first questions a person is asked by a new acquaintance is "What do you do?" From the response, stereotypical conclusions are drawn that help "understand the person better." The jobs people do are important for evaluating the self as well. Individuals who feel good about what they do and receive a sense of accomplishment and meaning from their work see their occupation as an integral part of the self. In this case, occupational identity is a source of growth, pride, and fulfillment. Therefore an important development task of young adulthood involves progress toward finding stable, meaningful employment and adjusting oneself to meet the demands of working: punctuality, conforming to employer expectations, and competency.

The importance of work satisfaction should not be minimized. Working is a core component of an individual's life and identity. People who are frustrated by their occupational positions or experience stress on their jobs carry those tensions home with them. Conversely, men and women who possess satisfying and stable occupational identities are more likely to experience secure intimate relationships and psychological well-being (Merriam & Clark 1993).

Why are some people satisfied with their work and others unhappy? Job satisfaction is more complex than a particular feature of a job that is liked or disliked. Instead, job satisfaction is related to more intrinsic and dynamic factors of a job, activity, or workplace. Rogers' (1986) summary of the literature found that several factors predict job satisfaction among adults. These factors include:

- a belief that one's talents are appropriately utilized
- progressing up the promotional ladder
- holding jobs with meaning, purpose, and dignity
- controlling the pace of work and making independent judgments
- assigning work, rather than following orders

Pay is not necessarily a factor unless a worker is making less than others with similar skills, abilities, and seniority. For example, middle-aged workers may hit a promotion plateau and will see their pay level off and not rise as fast as junior colleagues who are moving up the hierarchy. When this happens, wages may affect satisfaction.

The Meaning of Work at Midlife. Erikson's second developmental task for adulthood focuses on the need for achievement during midlife. Erikson realized that adults need to feel successful at something in order to give their lives meaning. The conflict between *generativity vs. stagnation* addresses those needs. Erikson contends that those needs are met through work and childrearing.

Success in adulthood is achieved by feeling connected, being willing to take care of others, and wanting to share what they have learned. In midlife, people often become concerned about the legacy they will leave behind. Finding ways to share their wisdom and learning with younger generations becomes a task central to satisfaction with life. Middle-aged adults are driven to take their place in society and to help others find theirs.

Emotional and intellectual stagnation is the opposing force to generativity. Stagnated adults are those who show an unwillingness or reluctance to include other people in their concerns. Rather than sharing their wisdom and using their creativity to serve the well-being of others, stagnated people either hoard the knowledge and wealth they have accumulated or they stagnate in the despair of never having gained the tools or skills needed to have positive life experiences. Stagnation is the outcome of being alone or emotionally cutoff from other people.

Generativity is the gratification of enjoying positive relationships with family and friends and producing something to leave behind that will improve the lot of someone's life. Stagnation, on the other hand, results from failing to accomplish earlier tasks. It is the continuation of mistrust, shame and doubt, guilt, inferiority, and isolation.

The Interaction between Love and Work

Most people think of work and intimacy as separate domains of life. However, Merriam and Clark (1993) found that love and work are closely related.

The first was the *parallel pattern* in which patterns of love and work were congruent. In this pattern, when people feel satisfied with their relationships they are more likely to feel good about their work, and vice versa. Declines in one area are paired with less satisfaction in the other. In the parallel pattern, there is a conscious effort to achieve a balance between the two domains. Work and love change together.

The parallel pattern is characterized by a high degree of stability and resistance to change. Marriages are durable and job changes are infrequent. The lives of people with this pattern are marked by continuity and stability. An example of the parallel pattern is a person whose satisfaction with work improves once children have left home and home life has calmed down.

The second pattern Merriam and Clark called the *steady/fluctuating pattern* in which either work or love remains largely steady while the other domain changes freely. Unlike the parallel pattern, changes in one area do not cause changes in the other. An example of this pattern is individuals whose family remains loving and supportive when they lose their job.

In the third pattern, the *divergent pattern,* love and work satisfaction are oppositional. That is, when one domain is going well, the other is faring poorly. Change in work and relationships among these individuals is frequent and there is a need for a sense of control in at least one of the areas. Usually work plays a dominant role, providing a source of stability in an environment of turmoil.

Change in work and love are not random events in the divergent pattern. Events in one domain often compensate for events in the other. An example of the divergent pattern is a person who invests more energy into work when feeling down over an intimate relationship that is not going well.

The marital relationship and the spousal role are very important in the lives of both men and women during midlife. Contrary to popular beliefs that middle-aged men are career-oriented and that the family is only secondarily significant to them, men's social self and self-experience tend to be focused increasingly on their families. In fact, men's relationship with their wives is the primary predictor of life satisfaction for men at midlife (Julian, McKenry, & Arnold 1990).

The "Sandwich Generation"

Adult children of the elderly, particularly those adults who are roughly between forty-five and sixty-five years of age, are sometimes called the "sandwich generation" because they are under pressure from the needs of both their own maturing children and their elderly parents who are living longer. This position of adult children exposes them to a unique set of stresses in which the giving of resources and service far outweighs receiving or exchanging them (Miller 1981).

> *This imbalance occurs when the middle-aged adults are themselves confronting major personal developments such as loss of youth and concomitant recognition of their own incipient aging.... They are ready for relaxation and self-indulgence, only to find that their grown children are not quite independent and their parents have moved from autonomy to a degree of dependence (Miller 1981: 419).*

The "sandwich" position produces considerable stress for the middle generation. The adult children run the risk of becoming the overburdened serving unit in the three-generational family (Schlesinger 1989). Stress results from situations such as the following:

- Too many crises involving several members of the family from one or more generation that can occur at the same time;
- Issues regarding autonomy versus dependence are constantly a source of conflict;
- An elderly parent suffers an accident or acute illness resulting in institutionalization;
- A pressing decision about institutionalizing an elderly parent;
- Already stretched financial resources are acutely strained (Miller 1981).

Institutionalizing parents is perhaps the most painful and stressful decision adult children have to make regarding the care of their parents. Seeing parents lose their autonomy and independence and fearing maltreatment in substandard homes add to the burden of making this decision.

Adult caregivers of elderly parents often experience several severe emotional effects when the parents are in a nursing care facility (Brody, Dempsey, & Pruchno 1990). How they cope with the burden of caring for their infirm parent(s) depends largely on the personal and social resources they possess. For adults with fewer time constraints, support within their own families, suffi-cient financial resources, and minimal unresolved emotional conflicts, caring for elderly parents is less stressful. If, on the other hand, caring for an elderly parent creates time pressures or financial problems or conjures up old emotional tensions, then caregiving is likely to be perceived as a bur-den. When parents are placed in nursing homes, adult children who provide care often see a de-cline in their own health as well.

Daughters and younger children of elderly parents in nursing homes are most likely to experi-ence depression while rendering care. Some care-givers, especially women, leave the work force to care for their parents, which can affect retirement benefits for their own old age (U.S. Bureau of the Census 1992).

Group interventions have been shown to be effective in helping "sandwich" generation adults cope with their stresses (Miller 1981; Dobson & Dobson 1985). Figure 5.3 illustrates some of the tasks and solutions of such groups.

The actual number of families bearing the double burden of supporting adult children while supporting frail elderly persons at the same time is not large. In 1989, only 16 percent of families had at least one child aged eighteen to twenty-four; of these families, only 39 percent had at least one child attending college. Furthermore, most middle-aged persons do not have elderly parents in poor health. It is not until after age eighty that severe mental and physical ailments become common and economic resources are more reduced (U.S. Bureau of the Census 1992).

End of Life Issues

The classical psychologist Carl Jung (1933) be-lieved that the primary goal of the second half of life is to confront death. The gradual decline in health, the death of parents and other loved ones, and the loss of roles, such as parenting, force middle-aged adults to recognize their own mortal-ity. During midlife, adults must cope with the loss of other people as well as begin to plan for their own retirement and old age.

FIGURE 5.3   Group Intervention with "Sandwich Generation" Adults

---

ISSUES

- Fear of one's own aging, dependency, and death
- Fear of parents' dependency
- Lack of preparation for taking care of parents
- Interference of caretaking with the freedom anticipated with middle age
- Sibling rivalry over sharing the responsibility for parents
- Helping aging parents through situations involving grief and loss
- The increasing self-centeredness of aging parents and their lack of interest in others
- The need to communicate feelings of anger, sadness, and grief
- Ambivalence about the conflicts between duty to parents and duty to children

---

GROUP TASKS

- Allow group members to express emotions and experiences
- Provide information about community resources and the aging process
- Discuss the various aspects of institutionalization of parents
- Focus on parent–child relationships and the implications of role reversal
- Learning to set boundaries with elderly parents and avoiding passive–aggressive behavior
- Learning to preserve their marriage while caring for parents and their own children

---

Coping with the death of one's parents has become a normative developmental task of midlife (Scharlach & Fredrikson 1993). Over 50 percent of adults between the ages of forty and sixty will experience the death(s) of one or both parents. This is a relatively modern phenomenon. In earlier times, when life expectancy was much shorter, people lost their parents at a younger age.

Many middle-aged adults experience a num-ber of emotional and somatic reactions to the loss of their parents. For example, Scharlach and

Fredrikson (1993) found that adults experience grief reactions such as sadness, crying, anxiety, fear, and a decline in health as long as five years after the loss of their mothers and fathers. As many as two-thirds of their sample had crying "spells" one to five years after the death of their mothers. About half had similar experiences after their fathers died. The majority of adults in this study, however, emerged from their parents' deaths feeling more mature and autonomous. From their parents' deaths, they learned to accept the finiteness of life and turned their attention to personal goals previously ignored. Many adults improved their own health and exercise habits ("I don't want to end up like Dad") or became more religious.

Middle-aged adults also have to start planning for their own retirement. As life expectancy increases, people are living longer without steady employment. Ensuring that retirement is affordable takes place in middle life. Creating investments and savings, paying off mortgages, taking care of insurance needs, and writing a will, among other related tasks, are important steps to take. Middle-aged adults start to think about where they want to live and what kind of lifestyle they want to pursue after they retire.

Economic resources affect the way adults think about and plan for their retirement. Lower income adults have fewer resources to carry with them into retirement. For them, thoughts of retirement or poor health that restricts working are anxiety-producing. Social security was never intended to replace wages for the elderly; it was designed to supplement income derived from savings and investments. Many people have insufficient discretionary income to set aside for old age, and so are forced to live solely from low social security benefits. Therefore, the prospects of ending employment are not necessarily enticing.

MENTAL WELL-BEING

Many factors contribute to the psychological well-being of adults. Psychological health during earlier developmental stages, how middle-aged adults deal with their impending old age, voca-

tional stability and satisfaction, and health create stress and affect adults' ability to cope with problems. Let's look at these four areas and see how they relate to adult's mental health.

Prior Functioning

Research shows that adult psychological well-being largely depends upon the quality of psychosocial environments and well-being during earlier stages of life. Franz, McClelland, and Weinberger (1991) found that parental warmth and affection at age five is significantly associated with the child's social accomplishment at age forty-one. Adults whose parents were more nurturing sustained long and relatively happy marriages, raised secure and competent children, and had more stable relationships outside the marriage. On the other hand, families of origin that were cold, unaffectionate, and emotionally unstable lead to diminished social accomplishment among adult children.

An earlier study by Roff and Wirt (1984) uncovered similar patterns. They learned that young adult adjustment is associated with secure adjustment during adolescence. Adolescents with low peer status and low participation in school activities had more mental health problems in early adulthood than young adults who were securely attached as adolescents.

Specifically, four adolescent qualities improve adult psychological well-being (Hightower 1990).

1. Emotionally positive interpersonal skills: Adolescents who have emotionally supportive peers and who have bonded appropriately with age-mates will likely have fewer mental health problems by midlife.
2. Forming social bonds with adults: Adolescents who form close, mutually supportive relationships with adults other than parents, e.g., teachers and neighbors, will have fewer mental health problems at mid-life.
3. Authoritative parents: Adults whose parents allowed them to explore their independence within an environment that included appro-

priate guidance, discipline, and love will have fewer emotional problems.

4. Respect for parents: Adolescents who maintained respect for their parents, rather than relying heavily on peer influence for social identity and counsel, will become more emotionally stable as adults.

These qualities help adolescents learn to create responsible, caring, committed relationships with others and to have positive evaluations of themselves. Because their parents taught them to manage their lives with practicality and sensitivity, they reaped the emotional benefits of close friendships and harmonious interpersonal ties with the community (Hightower 1990).

Impending Old Age

As mentioned earlier in this chapter, realizing and accepting the finiteness of life is an important developmental task and is a marker for the transition into middle-age. Physical changes in appearance, stamina, and strength send the signal that the body does not retain its youthfulness forever. How individuals adjust to these changes affects psychological health.

Some people deny the natural changes in their bodies. If self-esteem is closely tied to physi-

cal qualities, then physical decline can be extremely distressful. Rather than learn to accept the normalcy of aging, many individuals seek out cosmetic surgery or buy products that promise the "fountain of youth"; for them, there is an almost desperate obsession with looking young.

Those individuals whose self-concepts are based on nonphysical characteristics, such as intelligence or vocational competence, may feel young until relatively late in life. This is not to say that this group is nonchalant about their appearance and loss of physical strength, but they accept themselves and what they are becoming (Rogers 1986).

Impending old age can have very tangible implications for members of certain groups. Among middle-age lesbians, for example, fearing isolation during old age is particularly strong. Worries over becoming unattractive and unable to find a partner in midlife or being unable to care for oneself financially or physically during old age can be sources of intense distress (Sang, Warshow, & Smith 1991).

Though coming out at midlife is considered a healthy step for lesbians, there are many costs that intensify with age (Bradford & Ryan 1991). Harassment and losses of familiar and supportive relationships are common among middle-aged lesbians. Lesbians are twice as likely to live alone than women of the same age in the general popu-

The "Sandwich Generation": When middle-aged adults' parents are in a position to care for their aging parents as well as their own children, role conflict is a frequent outcome. Taking time, energy, and resources to tend to the needs of their parents may interfere with their own parenting responsibilities.

lation. They are five times more likely to have financial problems as well. Many do not seek health care for fear that being a lesbian compromises their relationship with their health care professional (Bradford & Ryan 1991).

Lesbians in middle age have to create their own developmental guideposts and markers. They live by their own improvisations since no social norms or timetables are defined. According to Sang (1991), those lesbians making the best adjustments are those who find a sense of fulfillment in their lives and have a high degree of self-confidence.

Occupational Stability

In Western culture, the kind of work people do and how and where they do it are integral aspects of self-esteem and social definition. In a competitive society that highly values material success, prestige, and occupational power, people are often judged less by personal attributes and traits than by the kind of work they do and the resources they control. The nearly absolute adherence to philosophies such as the Horatio Alger story, social Darwinism, and the protestant work ethic exert a great deal of pressure on adults to be successful economically. For example, the dean of the business college at a large university told me that he did not understand getting a degree in social work because the earning power of the degree would never pay off economically. Clearly, in his mind, education had to maximize return on the investment of getting it and a social work education would never carry someone to success as he defined it.

People who find their niche in the work world enjoy many psychosocial benefits. They are comfortable with themselves and the contributions they are making to the world. Contented adults satisfactorily integrate their productive selves into their overall sense of identity.

Employment status is particularly important for women's mental well-being. During midlife, employment is more important than changes in maternal roles for understanding women's mental

health. If women are involved in achievement-oriented activities, especially employment, they are more likely to feel greater self-satisfaction in midlife than full-time homemakers (Adelmann, Antonucci, & Crohan 1989).

Men at midlife often reevaluate their work role. Research finds that overall life satisfaction for men is more closely related to interpersonal job satisfaction than external success (Julian, McKenry, & Arnold 1990). The degree to which men realize their dreams, which usually focus on occupation, is significantly related to mental health: Men who are fulfilling their dreams manifest less depression and anxiety (Drebing & Gooden 1991).

On the other hand, people who feel incongruent with their work are more likely to question themselves and previous life decisions. These individuals are more likely to have a more serious midlife crisis and to feel that their lives have been wasted. How they feel about themselves ebbs and flows along with their work. Their productive selves, they feel, are failures and work brings great psychic pain. So central is work, that individuals who experience high job stress and feel underutilized, unappreciated, or undercompensated often feel that nothing else in life is really important or worthwhile. Middle-aged adults, who upon introspection realize that their occupational choices have not worked out, may develop strong feelings of resignation, resentment, or anger, and depression is possible. Dealing with these emotions can lead to alcohol abuse and other self-destructive behavior.

Health

Ill health is another threat to happiness, particularly in middle age. The potential for more chronic disorders increases with age (Rogers 1986). By this time in life, family members and friends begin to experience more health problems, so adults have more anxiety about changes in their own physical condition. Those who are particularly sensitive to changes in health may jump to conclusions whenever a lump is felt or there is pain in the chest.

When declines in health are real, depressive responses are possible. Losing functions, abilities, and roles due to health problems may cause adults to suffer inordinate sadness and the loss of otherwise interesting activities.

The Midlife Crisis

Several markers such as recognition of mortality, changes in family roles, and limits in vocational potentials indicate the transition to midlife. These changes represent a transition to a different style and orientation to life. As Levinson (1986) suggested, these changes require adults to make new decisions about what is to happen next and how time is to be spent. The question that many people ask is whether these markers constitute the proverbial midlife crisis?

The idea of a midlife crisis has almost become a cliché explanation of adult behavior. Whenever an adult makes a change in some aspect of life, others attribute it to the "crisis" of midlife. Midlife crises do exist, though perhaps not as universally as lay thought would have it.

The midlife crisis is a crisis of identity. As individuals realize their mortality and experience changes in roles that symbolically represent the passage of time, they engage in extensive introspection and soul-searching. They question the correctness of their previous decisions and evaluate the meaning of their lives (Koski & Steinberg 1990). Men are believed to experience midlife identity issues more than women (Julian, McKenry, & Arnold 1990).

Some adults dwell on the loss of their youth and fear growing old without reaching certain goals. They feel that life is passing them by and they have little to show for it. These reactions can be particularly intense. Therefore many try to recapture their youth by having sexual relationships with younger people, buying a "toy" such as a sports car, or wearing clothes in the style of younger people. Though intense self-focus and being overwhelmed with one's own concerns may disrupt parenting and other relationships, midlife crises usually pass without doing great harm.

Not all middle-aged persons will experience a midlife crisis of identity. Though all have to accept the finiteness of life, most work through this "reality" without difficulty. Accepting mortality can actually renew the vigor in one's approach to life. Realizing that time is relatively short helps many adults live each day to its fullest and stay focused on unmet life goals.

Several studies have sought to distinguish adults who experience a crisis in midlife from those who do not. Braverman and Paris (1993) concluded that one source of a midlife crisis among men can be neglectful parenting during childhood. As you saw in earlier chapters, children whose parents did not attend to their needs grow up with emotional deficits. When these children reach adulthood, they often use work or some other activity as a defense against emotional needs. By midlife, however, work is less successful as a coping strategy and the problems of childhood can reemerge (Braverman & Paris 1993). Another study found that how men adjust to changes in roles predicts midlife distress. Men who have stressful, conflicted relationships with adolescent children are more likely to have midlife stress (Julian, McKenry, & Arnold 1990).

Several factors may mediate the effects of the midlife transition. Stable and satisfying marriages have been shown to offset to some degree the distress of intense midlife transitions (Julian, McKenry, & Arnold 1990; Koski & Steinberg 1990). Other factors associated with minimizing midlife distress include inner directedness, a commitment to learning, and a positive emotional tone (O'Connor & Wolfe 1991).

CONCLUSION

Adulthood is the longest developmental stage in a person's life. It is usually the time of greatest productivity and fulfillment. Adulthood is not a solitary experience for people; individuals undergo different phases or periods in which they are asking different things from life or have changing issues with which they must deal.

Furthermore, adult experiences vary because of diversity in environmental resources and opportunities. The structural model of social work practice examines how adults' attempts to accomplish their developmental tasks are affected by differential resources and opportunities in the environment. How adults' intimacy and achievement needs are satisfied is largely a consequence of the psychological and social domains of preadulthood. Did their family of origin provide them the emotional and intellectual skills necessary to engage in mature, gratifying relationships free from game-playing and hidden agendas? Did their psychological domain foster secure attachments so that they have the confidence and self-contentment to engage another person in a mutually satisfying, nonthreatening way? Finally, did their social environment provide the necessary resources and opportunities for them to realize their dreams, become self-sufficient, and avoid dependencies?

If one's environment fosters emotional and instrumental self-confidence, and provides opportunities to succeed, then adulthood is likely to have fewer problems. If the environment, on the other hand, denies opportunities for self-enrichment and self-empowerment, then adulthood can be filled with economic and relational instability. In these cases, stress, physical and mental health problems, and economic deprivation are likely consequences. Rather than focusing just on individuals' adaptation to environmental conditions, social workers should concentrate on mobilizing resources in the six spheres of the environment that could relieve adult problems. Using the structural social work model gives workers a conceptual framework for not only understanding clients' problems, but for planning interventions to alleviate those problems.

Social workers should be aware of the markers that signal the transition into middle age. Physical changes in the body and changes in roles lead adults to approach life differently. The degree to which individuals have control over these changes, rather than the reverse, improves how adults feel about themselves and their overall feelings of satisfaction with life.

CASE STUDY REVIEW QUESTIONS

Given what you have learned from reading this chapter, respond to the following questions about the case of Daniel, presented at the beginning of this chapter.

1. From what you know about Daniel, describe his life in terms of Levinson's theory of structure-building and transitions. What are some other concerns that Daniel may be having as he makes the transition into midlife?
2. Given Daniel's description of his marriage, how would you describe his ability to establish genuine intimate relationships? What seem to be his expectations of intimacy?
3. Achievement needs are very important to Daniel. Because of losing his job and marriage, he has suffered significant blows to his self-esteem and social prestige. Furthermore, being a devout Catholic, divorcing carries a particularly important stigma for him. In your thinking, what might be the sources of his emotions of shame and humiliation?

KEY TERMS

Age 30 transition: The period when adults reappraise and make changes in the entry to early adulthood life structure; the goal of this transition period is to create the basis for the next life structure.

Age 50 transition: The period of development in which adults modify and try to improve the middle adulthood life structure.

Climacteric: The gradual but persistent decrease in ovarian activity that precedes the cessation of menstruation.

Companionate stage: Stage of intimate relationships that follows the passionate stage; a period described as quietly affectionate and less emotionally intense, though the attachment to each other is deeper; the couple's lives are more integrated.

Culminating life structure for early adulthood: The period of adult development when people realize their youthful aspirations; Levinson originally referred to this period as "settling down" because it emphasizes stability and security; individuals are deeply absorbed in their occupations, families, and other significant relationships and activities.

Divergent pattern: A pattern in which love and work satisfaction are oppositional; that is, when one domain is going well, the other is faring poorly.

Early adult transition: The developmental bridge between preadulthood and early adulthood; during this transition young adults terminate the adolescent life structure and take a preliminary step into the adult world.

Early climacteric: The first stage of the climacteric.

Empty-nest syndrome: The notion that women suffer a lack of definition and a loss of organized activities that provide meaning and purpose when the maternal role is redefined or lost because the last child has left home.

Entry life structure for early adulthood: The time in young adulthood for building and maintaining an initial style of adult living.

Exchange theory: Exchange theory assumes that people are rational and that relationships are formed following a calculated cost–benefit analysis; this approach suggests that people weigh the benefits and the costs of being with another person.

External locus of control: A state of mind in which self-esteem and sense of self are based on external relationships rather than internal qualities.

Generativity vs. stagnation: Erikson's psychosocial crisis based on adults' needs to feel successful at something in order to give their lives meaning; Erikson contends that those needs are met through work and child-rearing; success in adulthood is achieved by feeling connected, a willingness to take care of others, and a desire to share what one has learned.

Infatuation: Early attraction to another person based on superficial qualities.

Intimacy vs. isolation: Erikson's psychosocial stage that concerns the need to share one's life with someone else; it involves developing a sense of connectedness and mutual trust with other adults; to Erikson, mature intimacy includes the willingness to change patterns of work, procreation, and recreation to meet the needs of a partner.

Late climacteric: The third stage of the climacteric.

Life structure: The pattern or design of a person's life at a given time; life structure represents one's relationships, involvements with groups and institutions, roles, activities, and physical settings.

Life structure for middle adulthood: A stable life structure that develops to accommodate the decisions made after questioning the life structure of early adulthood; this period results from the reappraisal of life that occurred during the midlife transition.

Marriage gradient: The notion that in heterosexual relationships men should have higher status than women in virtually all aspects of life.

Menopause: The last menstrual period.

Midlife transition: The period of adult development that terminates early adulthood and begins the shift into middle adulthood.

Osteoporosis: A condition in which bone mass decreases to a point where structural failure may occur.

Parallel pattern: A pattern in which satisfaction with love and work are congruent; when people feel satisfied with their relationships they are more likely to feel good about their work, and vice versa.

Passionate stage: The early stage of a love relationship; a period of peak emotional excitement.

Perimenopause: The second stage of the climacteric.

Sandwich generation: Adults under pressure from the needs of both their own maturing children and their elderly parents.

Steady/fluctuating pattern: A pattern in which satisfaction with either work or love remains largely steady while the other domain changes freely; changes in one area do not cause changes in the other.

Structure-building: Periods of stability; the primary task in a structure-building period is to form a life structure and enhance life within it.

Structure-changing: Periods of transition; times when people reappraise their current life structure.

CHAPTER 6

LATE ADULTHOOD

OBJECTIVES

After reading this chapter, you should be able to answer the following questions:

1. Why is the population getting older?
2. What happens to the body as it ages? How might these changes affect psychosocial functioning and well-being?

3. What are the developmental tasks of late adulthood? What theories have been devised to understand the experiences of the elderly? How do compensation, selection, and optimization skills improve the condition of older people?

4. How do the elderly typically interact with their families, with peers, and in institutional settings?

5. There is considerable diversity among the elderly population. How do experiences in late adulthood differ by race and ethnicity, gender, sexual orientation, and place of residence?

6. What are the most pressing physical and mental health concerns of the elderly? How are the elderly's mental health problems related to the social and physical aspects of aging?

CASE STUDY

Cynthia, age forty-five, called a geriatric clinic at a hospital and asked for help with her father, Edward, age seventy-two. Edward was recently widowed and had just moved in with Cynthia, her husband, and two children, aged fourteen and twelve. Cynthia and her parents had always had a strong relationship. They were mutually supportive and had become good friends in Cynthia's adulthood. Cynthia's husband, James, had a positive, loving relationship with his in-laws as well. Cynthia's parents had lived in the same city and the families saw each other fairly regularly.

Cynthia's mother died suddenly of a stroke a few weeks prior to her call. Between her mother's death and her father coming to live with her, Cynthia began receiving phone calls from Edward's friends and neighbors concerning his well-being. Cynthia learned that her father had been wandering the neighborhood aimlessly and seemed lost on numerous occasions. The friends also noticed that his appearance was more disheveled and that his house was not well kept. Cynthia noticed that when she drove her father to the supermarket, he could not figure out what he needed to buy and that he had difficulty writing a check. Cynthia and James concluded that these "symptoms," which surprised them, were due to grieving the loss of his wife of fifty years.

Things took a turn for the worse when Cynthia received a call late one night from Edward.

He told her he did not know where he was and was completely disoriented. He moved into his daughter's house that night and never returned to his home to live.

INTRODUCTION

Old age is a stage of the life cycle that also qualifies members as a minority group. Not only must older individuals cope with changes in body functions and the loss of significant social roles, but they also face prejudice and discrimination from the social environment. *Ageism,* the differential and unfair treatment of older people, takes many forms. Examples of institutional discrimination against seniors include forced retirement, expensive and sometimes unavailable health care, and unfair housing policies. At the interpersonal level, discrimination is manifest as dehumanizing and infanticizing the elderly and discounting their value. Without doubt, the elderly meet the criteria of a disadvantaged group.

As people age, their bodies and relationships undergo dramatic changes. Not all of these changes, however, are necessarily unpleasant because people interpret the effects of aging subjectively. Many people, for example, rejoice at retiring from work, while others lament the loss of their productivity. How people respond to aging is a consequence of their feelings about themselves and the quality of the social environment in which they live. This chapter reviews the developmental aspects of aging and discusses aging in its social context.

THE "GRAYING OF AMERICA"

One of the most dramatic and significant changes in the American social landscape is the aging population. During colonial days, half the population was under age sixteen and few people lived to old age. Just over two hundred years later, in 1990, less than one in four was under age sixteen and half were thirty-three or older. During that census year, one in eight Americans was elderly. The aging of the population is expected to accelerate even faster in the next several decades. Demographers predict about 20 percent of the population could be sixty-five and older by the year 2030 and that over half the population will be over forty-three years of age by 2050. The elderly population increased by 22 percent during the 1980s and will expand even faster during the first decades of the twenty-first century (U.S. Bureau of the Census 1992).

Several factors account for the so-called graying of America. First, improved public services, such as sanitation and clean water, have reduced the spread of infectious diseases. Second, medical technologies have controlled many deadly childhood and other infectious diseases such as small pox, diphtheria, polio, and dysentery, among many others. Medical interventions have had a positive impact on other disorders such as heart disease and some cancers that allow people to live longer after diagnosis.

A major change in fertility patterns is another reason the population is older. After World War II, the United States witnessed an unprecedented population expansion. Between 1946 and 1964, about 75,000,000 babies were born. In comparison, this "human tidal wave" totaled 70 percent more people than were born during the preceding two decades. By 1990, the Baby Boomers, as they were called, were about one-third of the population (U.S. Bureau of the Census 1992).

As the Boomers reached traditional childbearing age, sociocultural changes were happening as well. The women's movement and women-controlled birth control techniques enabled women to have more reproductive, social, and economic control over their lives. Moving away from traditional self-concepts and roles has allowed women to make different decisions about having children than their mothers and grandmothers. Consequently, the Boomers' fertility declined greatly, compared to all previous generations, resulting in what is known as the Baby Bust. Paired with increased life expectancy, the boomers' low fertility resulted in an increase in the elderly's percentage of the total population. Therefore, not only are there more older people, but their percentage of the population is higher as well.

Social workers need to develop a greater understanding of aging and its affects on the psychosocial well-being of both elderly persons and their families. The need for gerontological social workers is expanding greatly, not only because there are increasing numbers of older people, but because the elderly will have smaller families to provide care. Therefore, a greater number of younger clients in the future are likely to have gerontological issues in their families. Let's look at aging and the body and then turn to the psychosocial issues of growing older.

AGING AND THE BODY

Why do people age? If there were no deaths from disease or trauma such as accidents and murder, humans would still die as a result of the body's inability to maintain homeostasis over time (Kenney 1989).

Researchers have developed several competing theories of why people and all other animals age. Most likely no one theory fully explains why cells of the body change over time; the probable explanation is that the process of aging varies among the different cells.

Biological theories of aging fall into three categories. One theory, the wear-and-tear theory, suggests that declines and changes in the body's structure and functions are simply due to the depletion of energy, which is inevitably exhaustible. This approach contends that the body is like a machine and that it will eventually wear out from use. Though there is some experimental data to support this perspective, most researchers discount this approach as overly simplistic.

The second set of theories concerns genetic qualities and processes. One genetic approach suggests that aging is caused by one or more harmful genes within each organism that become active only late in life. These genes alter the structure and function of cells and cause cell death. A second gene theory contends that aging is caused by genetic mutations that change the body's physiology. Several studies have shown that older laboratory specimens of mice have more genetic mutations than younger specimens. Among humans, it is known that radiation causes mutations and shortens life span. Therefore natural radiation alone might accelerate the aging process (Spence 1989).

The final group of aging theories concerns cellular function. There are several approaches within this group. Some suggest that errors in protein synthesis cause cells to die out over time, while others theorize that as cells age they accumulate inert substances that interfere with cellular functioning. One important cellular theory is the *free radical theory*. Free radicals are highly unstable atoms that are found in human cells and are by-products of normal cellular processes involving oxygen. Free radicals can damage DNA and interfere with normal cellular processes. Many believe that the accumulation of free radicals may contribute to the aging process.

Let's turn now to how aging affects different biological systems and to the psychosocial implications of those changes.

Skin

Changes in the skin can have an important impact on how elderly people feel about themselves. Sagging skin, wrinkles, and spotting alter elderly individuals' appearance and provide a constant reminder that they are aging. The condition of the skin of the elderly is due both to environmental factors and to the effects of aging. For people whose occupations and recreational activities kept them outdoors, prolonged, unprotected exposure to the sun caused the skin to decline earlier than for those whose activities kept them indoors (Spence 1989).

The aging process affects the skin as well, though most of the changes are not health- or life-threatening. The following changes occur in the skin with age:

- The number of cells that produce the pigment melanin decreases. The remaining pigment cells are larger and move together to form aging spots.
- The skin loses its elasticity and is less smooth; wrinkles and sagging are common.
- There are fewer sweat and oil glands, so older people tend to sweat less and have drier, scalier skin. With less perspiration, they have more difficulty regulating their body temperature and are more likely to suffer heat stroke during hot weather.
- There are fewer hair follicles, resulting in hair loss.
- The elderly's skin is more vulnerable to bruises and skin sores and heals more slowly.
- Nails become thicker and curved and grow more slowly.

Muscular–Skeletal

Declines in muscular functioning can have a disheartening effect on the elderly. Losses in strength, quickness, stamina, coordination, and appearance are ever-present indications of aging and mortality. The main age-related effect of aging on muscles is the reduction in total muscle mass. Muscles atrophy with age, and fat replaces lost muscle fibers. Proper exercise and nutrition can retard this process, however.

Age-related changes in the skeletal system are mostly based on the loss of calcium in the bones, especially among women. Some studies have found that by age seventy, women have lost 30 percent or more of the calcium in their skeletal system (Spence 1989). Men typically do not begin to lose calcium until after age sixty. Calcium loss, paired with reduced bone growth, results in porous, fragile, and breakable bones.

Cartilage, tissue that cushions bones in the joints and prevents bones from rubbing against each other during movement, degenerates with age. Thinning cartilage restricts movement and makes motion uncomfortable. For people whose lifestyles were more active over the years, the cartilage may deteriorate sooner. Less active people, however, are likely to experience cartilage loss as well. Cartilage, especially in the chest, sometimes calcifies, or hardens, reducing flexibility and making breathing difficult. Finally, cartilage between the vertebrae in the spine compresses, causing back pain in some older adults.

Decline in the muscular–skeletal systems results in loss of height and stooped posture. As mobility is lost, routine daily tasks, such as going to the bathroom, bathing, walking, preparing food, and recreation become increasingly difficult. Falling is also associated with age-related declines in muscle functioning and posture (Kaufmann 1994).

The Nervous System

Although numerous changes occur in the nervous system due to aging, each individual responds uniquely. Among some older individuals, profound structural changes occur without inhibiting functional abilities, whereas in others minor changes can result in serious impairments (Kaufmann 1994). Nerve cells, which transmit impulses, are lost over the course of a lifetime. Most of them are not replaced. The effects of the reduction in nerve cells depend on where the losses occur. By age eighty, the brain has lost about seven percent of its maximum weight; men experience a greater loss of brain mass than women (Kenney 1989).

The areas of the brain are not equally affected. Whereas some regions of the brain are essentially untouched by aging, about 25 percent of the specialized cells in the cerebellum, which is responsible for coordinated movements, is lost during aging. Balance and the coordination of fine movements may be seriously impaired as a result (Spence 1989).

The loss of neurons in the brain is believed to account for the loss of older people's ability to

think clearly, learn new skills, maintain verbal abilities, respond quickly, and maintain short-term memory. Certainly not all elderly people experience significant declines in cognitive abilities. In fact, psychosocial factors may have a direct impact on long-term brain functioning. Older people who are better educated and who kept intellectually active retain better memory and cognitive acuity in old age. As Spence says, "it seems as if 'exercising' the brain helps to maintain its normal functioning" (1989: 97).

The Circulation System

Age has two major effects on the circulation system: (1) the heart muscle weakens, and (2) the blood vessels harden and shrink. Both processes restrict the free flow of blood throughout the body. For those with heart disease, however, the heart may actually become enlarged with age.

Age affects the structure of the heart. Heart muscles gradually thin after age fifty and accumulate fat. Heart valves and the lining of the heart thicken due to deposits of fat and other tissues. It is also common for valves to calcify. In short, the heart pumps less effectively with age.

These changes result in less blood being delivered to the body, which means less oxygen is available to cells. For the elderly, simple tasks are increasingly taxing. Because less oxygen is getting to the body, more rest is necessary to complete a physical activity (Dean 1994). Exercise increases the cardiac output, the volume of blood pumped per minute by the heart, and benefits peripheral circulation, blood flow to the body's extremities.

Blood vessels change over time as well. Both arteries and veins lose their elasticity, which is particularly problematic as an older person's blood pressure increases. Furthermore, arteries may also narrow due to the gradual accumulation of lipids in their walls. Regular exercise can reduce cholesterol buildup in the arteries.

Hypertension, high blood pressure, is common among older adults. Because symptoms of hypertension are not always clear, individuals may neither realize they have the condition nor seek medical attention. Heart disease, stroke, and kidney failure are possible outcomes of untreated hypertension (Dean 1994; Kannel 1985).

The Respiratory System

The respiratory system of the elderly is less efficient than that of younger people. Virtually all structures involved in the respiration process are negatively affected with age. The trachea and bronchi harden and the mucous membrane lining them deteriorates. Thus, the breathing and self-cleaning efficiency of the lungs and the respiratory tract is greatly reduced.

Breathing is further complicated by calcifying cartilage in the rib cage and changes in the spinal curvatures. Both processes reduce the volume of the thoracic cavity and require an individual to make an extra effort to expand the stiffening rib cage in order to breathe. This explains why older people have more difficulty breathing while lying on their backs. Most seniors breathe with greater ease if their upper bodies are elevated by pillows or an adjustable bed (Spence 1989).

Because the elderly experience a reduction in pulmonary function, pulmonary diseases, such as bacterial pneumonia, are more likely to produce serious complications for the elderly (Rowe & Minaker 1985).

The Immune System

The immune system changes with age. Nearly all immune functions in the elderly differ when compared to younger populations. Over time, immune responses to foreign antigens decrease and render the elderly more susceptible to infectious diseases. Declines in immunity are linked to genetic and environmental factors. Environmental influences on immunity include disease, nutrition, and exposure to radiation (Hausman & Weksler 1985). Most of the decline in autoimmunity is the result of the degeneration of the thymus gland, which is important in the regulation of antigen-fighting cells.

The Digestive System

The effects of age on the gastrointestinal system can dramatically alter lifestyle. What's worse, the psychosocial conditions of the elderly may impact the digestive system, exacerbating the decline in the structure and functioning of the system. From the mouth to the intestines, the elderly experience a wide range of problems that change their approach to life.

Beginning with the mouth, almost half of all persons sixty-five years of age have or need dentures. By the age of seventy-five, about 75 percent of older people have lost all of their teeth (Spence 1989). What causes tooth loss? For most, gum disease, caused by recession of the gums due to gum atrophy and shrinkage, causes tooth loss. As gums continue to decrease in size, dentures fit more poorly, which affects the ability to chew hard foods. Consequently, many elderly are forced to eat softer, often less nutritious foods. Other changes occur in the mouth of older people as well. Salivary glands, for example, produce less saliva and therefore taste and natural cleaning functions of saliva diminish. Many older people report an increased liking for sweets, however.

The esophagus is affected by age, too. Difficulty swallowing, esophageal pain, "heartburn," and belching are common complaints among the elderly. These problems are usually caused by the weakening of the esophageal sphincter. This muscle, located just above the entrance into the stomach, regulates the movement of food from the esophagus to the stomach. As the sphincter loses its firmness, food, stomach acid, and gas can pass from the stomach into the esophagus.

For most individuals, the lining of the stomach thins with age. Consequently, secretions of stomach fluids that digest foods are reduced. This can cause chronic gastritis and bacterial infections in the large intestine.

The intestines also structurally change in old age. The walls of both the small and large intestines become weaker. This condition is responsible for "bubbles" forming in the intestinal walls, a disorder known as diverticulosis.

Many older persons suffer problems with bowel and bladder movements and may fluctuate between constipation and incontinence. Constipation may not necessarily result from the aging process as much as from lifelong personal practices. For example, constipation may be caused by overuse of laxatives, reduced fluid intake, lack of bulk in the diet, little exercise, irregular bowel habits, and stress (Spence 1989). Constipation is the main cause of hemorrhoids, swollen or ruptured blood vessels located in the lower bowel, which are common complaints among the elderly.

Since eating is a social as well as a biological process, the isolation of the elderly may lead them to fail to prepare and eat the most nutritious foods. Other older persons may compensate for their loneliness and grief responses by overeating, which, as Cox says, may be the "only pleasure they derive from an otherwise dreary existence" (1984: 66).

The Urinary System

The kidneys, bladder, and urethra undergo considerable changes with age. By late adulthood, the kidneys have lost as much as 40 percent of their normal functioning capacity (Rowe & Minaker 1985). The same is true of the bladder and urethra. The walls of these organs weaken and lose elasticity with age. The capacity of the bladder is about half of that of a young adult, and the reflex signaling the need to urinate is frequently delayed in the elderly. Therefore the need to urinate is more urgent and, because of weakened muscles, the ability to hold the bladder is harder as well.

The Senses

Human bodies receive information about the physical world through the specialized senses, a complex part of the nervous system (Hooper 1994). Vision, hearing, taste, smell, and touch are perceived via sensory channels that link the peripheral nervous system to the central nervous system. The sensory process begins with a stimulation, such as a sound or a visual image. People then in-terpret that stimulation in order to recognize and comprehend it. Sensations are "experienced" in the nervous system and any neurological degeneration can affect perception. Consequently, with age-related declines in the nervous system come impaired sensory perception.

Impairments in the special senses can have a profound impact on individuals' quality of life. Declines in the senses can affect an individual's safety, create dependency, and deny access to activities that provide enjoyment, pleasure, and relief. Loss of perceptual abilities can certainly lead to irritability and depressive symptoms in older men and women.

Vision.   Vision declines among virtually all aging adults. Several structural changes occur: loss of fat around the eyes that causes eyes to recess, decreased strength of eye muscles, decreased tissue elasticity and tone, degeneration of sclera, pupil, and iris, increased density and rigidity of lens, and slowing of central nervous system information processing. These age-related changes cause the following functional declines:

- poor eye coordination
- distortion of images
- impaired night vision
- decreased near vision
- loss of color sensitivity
- difficulty with objects that are moving, have a complex figure, or appear in and out of light quickly (Hooper 1994)

Hearing.   A number of anatomical changes occur within the auditory system. In general, two major changes happen: (1) the "hearing" cells in the ear and the nerves that transmit "sound" degenerate, and (2) neurotransmitters are lost. As a result, the elderly have difficulty hearing higher frequencies, can distinguish pitches less efficiently, have trouble understanding the speech of others, and have diminished speech abilities themselves.

Taste and Smell.   Taste changes relatively little with age, although the elderly have fewer taste buds than younger people. Some older adults con-fuse tastes. This problem appears related to the presence of mouth fungus, denture wearing, or other problems (Hooper 1994). For those whose sense of taste is affected by age, the risk of ingesting spoiled foods or other toxic substances is greatly increased.

The sense of smell declines with age, as research shows that older persons have more failures in identifying odors. What's more, for many odors, the elderly require greater volumes of the substance before they are able to detect them. As Kenney (1989) points out, taste and smell have important protective functions. These senses detect foods and other substances that if consumed would bring harm to the organism. When age affects these senses, the individual is endangered.

Touch.   Due to slower nerve impulses, diminished circulation, degeneration of touch cells, and dietary deficiencies, the elderly suffer decreases in their ability to respond to tactile stimuli, or touch. The results of such loss include declines in pain and temperature sensitivity. The elderly are more adversely affected by temperature extremes. Many social service agencies design special programs for them during the very hot or cold times of the year (Hooper 1994).

Sex and Reproduction

The elderly are frequently stereotyped as uninterested in and unable to have sexual relations. In fact, many retirement and nursing homes have policies that prohibit or deny sexual contact among residents. In a youth-oriented culture, the elderly are seen as not only asexual, but *un*sexual. There is so much denial about sex during old age that many older people themselves accept the myth of sexlessness and deny their own sexual urges. Nonetheless, many older adults continue to be sexually active. The two main predictors of sexual activity in old age are (1) the presence of a surviving spouse, and (2) good health (Harman & Talbert 1985).

Like the rest of the body, the reproductive system does change with age. As you learned in

the last chapter, significant reproductive changes occur in middle adulthood. By late adulthood, the climacteric is complete, though reproductive tissues continue to degenerate and atrophy.

All sexual organs function in healthy older men, albeit at lower levels. Unlike women, men maintain their fertility throughout life, though sperm count continues to decrease. Elderly men are capable of erections, but the erections are not as firm, and ejaculations are not as strong, because, by age fifty-five or so, the penis gradually becomes smaller, and erectile tissue becomes more rigid and less elastic.

Older men experience a gradual decline in testosterone production as well. It is interesting to note that the rate of testosterone decline is related to opportunities for sexual expression. The fewer opportunities a man has for sex, the lower his testosterone levels will be (Spence 1989). Another important change in men concerns the prostate gland. By age fifty, this gland begins to atrophy, creating a high risk for cancer and other problems. Regular prostate exams can detect these disorders fairly early.

In postmenopausal women, several changes occur that can affect sexual behavior and health as well. The vagina becomes less elastic, narrower, and shorter, making penile penetration more difficult. Furthermore, the lubricating glands atrophy, causing the vagina to be drier and less acidic. As a result, sexual intercourse can be painful, and older women suffer more bacterial infections. The ovaries degenerate during old age and the uterus becomes half its previous size. Breasts change as well: nipples become smaller and less responsive to touch. Due to these changes, cancers of the uterus, ovaries, and breast are more common among older women.

Health problems frequently have a negative effect on sexual desire and behavior among older people. For example, problems with muscles, joints, and bones affect movement and flexibility. Neurological problems affect sexual responsiveness and prostate cancer can affect ejaculation. A number of medications that are commonly prescribed for the elderly can affect sexual response as well, especially medication for hypertension and cardiovascular disease.

DEVELOPMENTAL TASKS OF LATE ADULTHOOD

Just as there are theories that attempt to explain biological aging, a number of theories address the social and behavioral aspects of individual aging and of the aged in society. This section is divided into two parts. First, five theories of psychosocial aging are discussed: disengagement theory, activity theory, role theory, continuity theory, and Erikson's psychosocial perspective. Then the developmental tasks of late adulthood are reviewed.

Social Theories of Aging

Disengagement Theory.   Disengagement theory was the first major theoretical system to explain how aging affects the relationship between the individual and society (Fry 1992) and was a dominant approach in the 1960s and 1970s. This theory suggests that the elderly disengage or withdraw from society, and that society withdraws from them. Disengagement theory posits that as people age they have less ability and fewer interests in maintaining social connections and performing their roles. The theory further argues that this separation is an inevitable, natural process. According to the theory, the elderly's withdrawal from social life is highly functional because it guarantees the orderly transfer of power from the old to the young. Disengagement from social life is believed to facilitate successful adaptation to aging because it prepares individuals for their impending death.

Disengagement theory no longer carries much influence among scholars and practitioners. Critics contend that most elderly persons, especially those in good health, do not disengage, but maintain fairly high activity levels. To assume that disengagement is inevitable discounts the contributions the elderly make and minimizes the important supportive roles they play and the activities they engage in for self-fulfillment. Some

elderly do disengage from social relationships; however, it is often not clear if this disengagement is voluntary or forced upon them by other people, a decreasing peer group, or bad health.

Activity Theory.   Activity theory was also popular from the 1950s to the early 1970s. It suggests that successful adaptation to aging occurs by staying active. Maintaining middle-age roles and replacing lost roles are the keys to high life satisfaction during old age. If replacing lost roles is not possible, individuals should engage in compensatory behaviors to keep up a steady level of activity.

Although this approach is more positive than disengagement theory, it is not without its shortcomings. Staying active per se is not the panacea to cope with all the stresses and strains of aging. Some activities may not necessarily promote psychosocial well-being during late adulthood. For example, acting out roles that are not socially meaningful or valued may not enhance individual self-concept or lead to higher levels of morale (Markides & Mindel 1987). Keeping active is associated with psychological prosperity during old age for many people, but not necessarily for all. Furthermore, activity theory does not explain those people who do disengage and yet remain in good spirits. In short, activity theory is overly simplistic when attempting to understand the psychosocial complexities of aging.

*Role Theory.   A more useful theoretical perspective in the study of aging is *role theory*. This approach contends that the elderly have to adjust to conditions that are markedly different than other stages of life. First, during late adulthood individuals experience a traumatic relinquishing of roles. Second, the elderly must accept the social relationships of and roles stereotypically or negatively associated with being old (Fry 1992).

Role theorists assume that the loss of important roles such as spouse and work roles affects people's self-concept and personal goals. When key roles are suddenly lost, role theory suggests the possibility that the person's system of rewards and mechanisms for self-definition are disturbed. If people define themselves through the roles they play, then, when roles are lost, life satisfaction and adjustment decline.

Roles for being old are not clearly specified in this culture. Instead, being old in a youth-oriented culture is typically stereotyped and negatively labeled. Many elderly persons may accept the stereotypes and act out an aged role that includes characteristics such as dependency, helplessness, and despair. Playing out a negative "old age" role deprives the elderly of the potential rewards accompanying older adult status (Fry 1992).

Role theory defines successful aging as the ability to enact social roles and behaviors appropriate to this stage of development (Fry 1992). Consequently, role theory stresses the importance of adjusting to lost roles, redefining roles, and establishing an appropriate social identity. Social workers can help the elderly reorganize their social environment so that it can provide satisfying role relationships within the group setting.

Role theory has some empirical support in the academic literature. Using a multivariate analysis, George and Maddox (1977) found that role loss is a significant predictor of psychosocial adaptation to aging. These researchers learned that occupational prestige and education correlate with adjustment to role loss. In other words, higher levels of perceived role loss are associated with lower levels of life satisfaction. The more significant individuals believe their role losses to be, e.g., a high prestige occupation, the greater effect the losses have.

Continuity Theory.   *Continuity theory* suggests that older adults adapt to the changes of later adulthood by preserving and maintaining existing internal and external structures. In short, the elderly are motivated and predisposed to use familiar strategies for dealing with changes associated with aging (Atchley 1989).

The concept implies that there is a continuity in the way people act, think, and relate to others. Continuity can be both internal and external (Atchley 1989). *Internal continuity* refers to the

continuation of psychological qualities such as temperament, affect, preferences, dispositions, and skills. *External continuity* pertains to familiar physical and social environments.

For example, people who kept to themselves and preferred a small social network during earlier stages of the life cycle will tackle the challenges of late adulthood more successfully if they are in an environment that allows them to have a sufficient amount of time to themselves. Conversely, people who previously thrived in a large social network need to maintain a broad circle of friends and activities to be happy in old age.

Research shows that when older adults are able to maintain internal and external continuity, life satisfaction and morale are high (Fry 1992). When people continue to relate to themselves and the world around them in consistent ways, then their approach to life in general is more secure. Life-span continuity promotes predictability and self-esteem and helps older adults meet their needs.

The loss of roles is inevitable in late adulthood. Not all individuals, however, suffer long-term negative consequences from those losses. If individuals can maintain their important interests and activities during this period, then the effects of inevitable losses are reduced. As Fry (1992) notes, continuity theory is a reminder that most individuals occupy several role positions and that the disruption of one may be relatively independent of others in the adaptation to aging. Though a person may lose the spouse role, for example, other roles such as parent and friend persist.

In summary, continuity theory suggests that people cope with age-related changes in much the same way they coped with challenges in earlier stages of the life cycle. Adaptation to aging is predicted, therefore, by persistent patterns that the individual has displayed throughout life. Poor adaptation is caused by a personal history of poor coping skills or disruptions in coping skills due to health problems or environmental forces.

Erikson's Psychosocial Theory.   As people reach the end of their lives, they often look back and review their decisions, relationships, and life's work. Most older people enjoy and seem to thrive upon telling stories about the past. At first, one might think that telling stories is a sign of dementia or senility, and an indication that the elderly person can not stay in the here and now. In actuality, storytelling has an important function for the elderly. Retelling the adventures of their lives serves to validate their existence and justify the decisions that they cannot undo now.

Erikson (1963) recognized the importance of looking back during the final stage of life, and defined the main psychosocial challenge of this age as *integrity vs. despair.* He believed that how older people remember and feel about their lives is the key to successful aging. Individuals who are satisfied with their lives and look back with pride and acceptance will willingly embrace the tasks of old age with less distress and more tolerance. In Erikson's terms, they have achieved a sense of integrity over feelings of despair.

For others, however, growing old can be a time of remorse and despondency. People who have failed in relationships, accomplished less than they expected or desired, or never achieved a strong sense of self are likely to look back on their lives with regret, sadness, or bitterness. They grieve over what may have been and may be bitter that time has run out.

Individuals who approach old age with integrity, according to Erikson, are those who began life in an environment that fostered trust and autonomy. They went on to succeed in school and work and had stable satisfying relationships. Integrity is the fulfillment of the previous seven stages. On the other hand, those whose old age is filled with despair have a different life track. Their psychosocial environment was more confusing and threatening and inhibited integration of a stable sense of self.

Developmental Tasks of Aging

As in other stages of the life cycle, there are certain tasks that are most likely to confront individuals during late adulthood. In this section, re-

tirement, death issues, and aging as a process will be discussed.

Retirement. *Retirement* is often considered a milestone that marks a person's transition into late adulthood. The term refers to separation or withdrawal from work in which the person was employed (Beaver & Miller 1992). Retirement forces changes in virtually all aspects of life: daily activities, community involvement, social roles, and self-perception.

Retirement in today's world is a different experience than it has been in the past. First of all, this society is sufficiently productive to allow older persons to subtract themselves from the economy. Enough wealth is generated to support a largely dependent population. A second difference from times past is that retirement today is a normative rather than unplanned event (Bosse et al. 1993). Now people plan the end of their work lives. In fact, the process of anticipating retirement is already underway within fifteen years of retirement (Evans, Ekerdt, & Bosse 1985).

Older men are retiring sooner than in years past (U.S. Bureau of the Census 1992). In 1950, about 69 percent of men 55 and older, and 46 percent of men 65 and older were in the labor force. In 1990, 40 percent of men 55 and over, and about 16 percent of men 65 and older were working for pay. Labor force participation for older men is expected to continue declining as well. The same pattern does not hold for women. Women in their fifties are more likely to participate in the labor force now than in the past. About 23 percent of women 55 and over are presently working for pay, as compared to 19 percent in 1950. For women 65 and over, 8.7 percent were working in 1990, which is about the same as in 1950 (9.7 percent). With more men retiring earlier, but living longer, pensions, savings, and Social Security are spread over a longer period than in the past (U.S. Bureau of the Census 1992).

Community membership and the social environment have a strong impact on when a person retires (U.S. Bureau of the Census 1992). For example, professionals and managers have a longer work expectancy than laborers and semiskilled workers. Self-employed workers have the longest working life expectancy compared to other groups of workers. Educational attainment also affects work life: the higher one's achievement in education, the longer one can expect to work. Although African Americans and European Americans work about the same number of years, African Americans live for a shorter amount of time and have fewer years of retirement.

Retirement means different things to different people. Some face retirement as a dreaded event and then find life without employment distasteful and stressful. For others, retirement is a blessing of sorts. They replace work with enjoyable activities such as travel, gardening, and other endeavors that they did not have time to do while working and parenting. What distinguishes these two groups?

Research has found that retirement satisfaction is based on several factors. Retirees who have difficulty adjusting to retirement are more likely to have health, financial, or marital problems (Bosse et al. 1991). Many of the marital problems are related to the spouse's declining health. These stressors are intensified during retirement because the retirees can no longer escape their problems by going off to work. Bosse's research also discovered that retirement is stressful for those whose retirement carries negative implications. For example, people who are forced to retire be-

cause of bad health, plant closures, or changes in corporate policy and direction, experience retirement with more adversity. Retirement stress is not related to personality traits.

Retirement can be seen as a process rather than as an abrupt event. Most people plan for their retirement. Long before they stop working, many in middle adulthood begin to plan financially by establishing budgets, savings accounts, pensions, and by paying off mortgages.

Anticipatory planning is important in today's economy because retirement can come at any time in middle or later adulthood because of corporate downsizing or ill health (Evans, Ekerdt, & Bosse 1985). Most preretirees use informal methods for preparing for retirement. For example, they may engage in mental rehearsals of living on a lower income and having more free time. The process is important for acknowledging and negotiating the changes that are to come. Mental rehearsals also help bring one's worklife to closure. Proximity to retirement is a better predictor of preretirement behavior than age (Atchley 1976). People begin planning when they are approaching a planned retirement, regardless of age.

Once retirement occurs, many retirees experience a euphoric, or "honeymoon" phase. During this phase, time seems to pass quickly as retirees keep busy and are enthusiastic about being free from the rigors of work. About thirteen to eigh-

Isolation is a particularly serious problem for older women. Compared to elderly men, they are more likely to live alone and have fewer resources. Isolation may be more critical for European-American women because they are less involved in their families and they have fewer adaptive strategies for survival.

teen months after retirement, however, retirees often experience a letdown as feelings of life satisfaction and physical activity decline. Atchley (1976) referred to this phase as the *disenchantment stage* of retirement. Retirees are less optimistic about the future and are more dysphoric. About nineteen months after retirement, these deficits in life satisfaction and physical activity diminish and retirees enter a *reorientation stage* of retirement (Ekerdt, Bosse, & Levkoff 1985; Atchley 1976). This, the final stage, is when retirees adjust to retirement. By this time, they have settled into predictable and satisfying stable routines.

The amount of stress that retirement is believed to create may be overstated. Bosse and associates (1991) found retirement to be the least stressful of thirty-one different stressful life events. Nonetheless, the loss of one's productive role in a culture that values economic success, self-reliance, and self-sufficiency should not be taken lightly. With the loss of the job may come the loss of important activities such as work-related social activities, union meetings, and interactions with colleagues (Beaver & Miller 1992).

Death.   An important task in old age is coming to terms with one's impending death and the deaths of significant others. Declining health, physical limitations, and deaths of family members and friends signal the elderly that the end of their lives is approaching. Death is more than dying: It includes completing one's affairs, resolving prior conflicts, grieving, and changing everyday life to accommodate the losses.

It is commonly assumed that the elderly have a strong fear of dying. Research shows, however, that they express no more and possibly less fear than younger people (Westman, Canter, & Boitos 1984). Of course, some elderly persons do experience death anxiety and they are distinct from those who do not in several ways. Wagner and Lorion (1984) found that low morale and depression are associated with death anxiety. Older people who experience death anxiety express a diminished sense of purposefulness and feel a lack of direction in their lives. They also experience time differently

than those people who are less worried about death. Anxiety is related to feeling pressured by the passage of time, a tendency to procrastinate and use time inefficiently, and feeling that time is moving forward (Quinn & Reznikoff 1985).

Several social variables correlate with death anxiety as well. Low church attendance, less religiosity, and being married were the strongest social predictors uncovered by Wagner and Lorion's study. Participation in religion is a buffer against death anxiety because it provides both a social support network and a comforting ideology. The married elderly are probably more anxious about death for fear of leaving their spouse behind and concerns about the spouse's well-being. Surprisingly, physical health and social support systems are not related to death anxiety.

Older persons who do not experience death anxiety share traits as well. Worries about death are lower among people who have higher life satisfaction, have more education, have a stronger sense of personal well-being, and accept that their death is imminent (Flint, Gayton, & Ozmon 1983). When people perceive their lives as meaningful and are content with themselves and their life's work, they feel that their time was well spent and that they can die without any regrets.

Coping with the loss of others, especially family members, is particularly stressful for older adults. The loss of spouses leaves survivors without their long-term partners and closest confidant. When a spouse dies, a great deal is lost. In many cases, survivors become isolated from previous friendship groups comprised of couples (Rawlins 1992). Women, however, are often able to establish relationships with other widows. Widowers, on the other hand, may risk more isolation than widows because there are fewer single older men with whom relationships can be formed and because men tend to have smaller social networks than women, especially if they are retired.

It is often the case that after a spouse dies, the health of widows and widowers declines. Within two months after the loss of a spouse, many survivors experience a significant increase in new illnesses and worsening of conditions already present. More medications are used and overall health declines. This effect is more pronounced among women than men, perhaps because men are conditioned to deny symptoms of weakness (Thompson et al. 1984).

On the other hand, men experience significantly higher levels of stress-related responses, such as depressive symptoms, following the death of nonspouse family members (Siegel & Kuykendall 1990). Two social factors, however, reduce the impact of the loss. First, married men show fewer symptoms than widowers. Widowers have smaller social support networks than widows and married men and women, so they have fewer buffers against stress. Second, church or temple membership moderates symptoms among men.

The death of a sibling is probably the death most frequently experienced by the elderly since older persons usually have more than one brother or sister (Moss & Moss 1989). Siblings are one of the few people who can see the entire historical development of a person and therefore are able to review and validate early life experiences. When a sibling dies, a critical void is created.

The impact of a sibling's death varies according to the degree of intimacy the siblings shared. Brothers and sisters who have maintained closeness and minimized sibling rivalries and competitions will feel a greater sense of loss. In addition, the impact of the death of a sibling can be more intense if the deceased played a key role in family dynamics. For example, if the deceased was the family leader or provided family solidarity, then the loss of those roles will be strongly felt throughout the family and may have to be filled by someone else (Moss & Moss 1989).

Over the years, several theories have been devised to describe the process of grieving. Most of these approaches portray grieving as occurring in stages or phases of emotional responses with attending behaviors accompanying them. These theories basically describe the same process, though they may use different labels and definitions. Because of the similarities, it is possible to synthesize these approaches into a general description of the grieving experience. People vary in their responses to the death of someone close and not all

follow the ordering scheme of the stages or even experience all of the stages.

In general, people experience three emotional and cognitive responses to the death of a loved one. First, people often feel shock or a sense of numbness. They may deny the reality that the person is gone and feel an overwhelming sense of disbelief. This is more likely to occur if the death is sudden and unexpected. Eventually the death will be acknowledged. When this happens, the bereaved enter a second emotional–cognitive state in which grief may appear as anger, sadness, or despair. There may be a longing to be with the lost person and thoughts, memories, and fantasies are centered around the deceased. Finally, survivors readjust to life without the deceased. Reorganization may take anywhere from three months to over a year. During this time, the bereaved sever their links with the past and face the future (Rogers 1986). They slowly begin to socialize with friends and relatives and reorganize their home to suit their needs for living alone. In the case of spouses, the bereaved may dispose of some of the deceased's possessions and learn to accept themselves as a widowed person.

Successful Aging as Process. Unlike developmental approaches that concentrate on what people should do to age successfully, Baltes (1994) focuses on how successful aging is achieved. She argues that looking for strategies that facilitate successful aging, and not exclusively for the goals or outcomes that define successful aging, is the best way to understand successful aging in light of the losses and deficits that define late adulthood.

Baltes identifies three interacting processes that facilitate successful aging: *selection, compensation,* and *optimization.* Selection refers to an "increasing restriction of one's life world to fewer domains of functioning as a consequence of or in anticipation of losses in personal and environment resources" (Baltes 1994: 189). Selection may involve avoiding one domain or goal altogether or it may mean limiting goals or tasks within a domain. Baltes gives the example of elderly persons with a chronic illness who avoid or give up sexual behavior and reduce their participation with other people within their social network, but maintain their level of involvement with family members.

The second process of successfully adapting to losses due to aging is compensation. When individuals lose their capacity or skill to perform at optimum or adequate levels, developing compensatory skills will minimize the deficits that follow the loss. Compensation is the process of counterbalancing, or compensating for, a particular functional or behavioral loss. Technological innovations such as hearing aids and the acquisition of new skills help people learn to adjust to unavoidable impairments.

Compensatory behaviors may be planned or they may occur automatically. For example, a social worker saw a retired salesman, Mr. Woods, who was feeling a strong sense of loss on retirement. Making the sale not only was his business, it was a source of self-esteem and self-definition. Mr. Woods also enjoyed gardening and had recently moved to a place with more land available for planting fruits and vegetables. As a way of compensating for loss of the importance of "making the sale," Mr. Woods began selling his vegetables in a roadside stand in front of his home. He took great pride in not only selling, but in selling products he had grown himself. In a short time, Mr. Woods' depressive feelings dissipated.

Baltes' third process of successful aging is known as optimization. Old age is not only a time of engaging losses, it also represents a time of growth, fulfillment, and engagement. The elderly may continue to enrich their lives through optimizing strategies such as practice, training, or other attempts at self-improvement. Optimizing strategies may be applied to existing goals or reflect new goals and expectations. As Baltes contends, the process of optimization is contingent upon the presence of stimulating and enhancing environmental conditions.

AGING AND GROUPS

Family and marital life remain important during late adulthood, another indication that the elderly do not disengage from social networks. Marital satisfaction is often very high during this stage of life. Most elderly couples have been together for many years and have experienced countless changes, struggles, and successes. Most have achieved a level of bonding unavailable to younger couples. For others, however, the transition to old age levies stresses on the marriage and breeds discontent. Long-standing, but unresolved conflicts will persist after parenting and working have ended.

The lack of role continuity is one factor associated with marital unhappiness during late adulthood. How people perceive the losses that accompany old age is affected by prior levels of psychosocial functioning, coping skills, the status of the former roles, and the meaningfulness of their support system. When older persons define their losses as severe and their sense of self as greatly diminished, then they make the transition into late adulthood with more anxiety and a less clear image of what they want to do and what kinds of people they want to become. When people retire to nothing, that is, they have no plans or aspirations after retirement, they have no clear guidelines to give their lives meaning. When this happens, marital satisfaction suffers. The frustrations stemming from the awkward transition to late adulthood are brought to the marriage and tensions ensue. The reverse appears to be true as well. When there is internal and external continuity from midlife to late adulthood, the likelihood of marital satisfaction in old age is high. Previous marital functioning is an important factor as well. If emotional stability, intimacy, and problem-solving skills are characteristic of the marriage prior to retirement, then those qualities are likely to carry forward into late adulthood.

The availability of social support is one of the main factors associated with psychosocial well-being among the elderly. Who provides that support is affected by the marital status of the older individual (Stolar, MacEntee, & Hill 1993). Married people are more likely to turn to their spouses for assistance with emotional comforting and instrumental tasks. Widows also seek help with their families by relying on their children as their main helping resource. Divorced and never-married elders, however, are more likely to call upon friends and seek formal assistance when they are in need.

Unlike those who are currently married, divorced people over sixty-five are less likely to perceive their children as a significant source of support. The divorced and never-married groups are more isolated and are likely to call no one when they feel lonely. Being married brings other benefits to establishing social support networks. Married elderly are better connected to their neighbors and have more contacts with their children than the other three status groups.

In late adulthood, many people rekindle relationships with their brothers and sisters. Many siblings do not maintain close ties during their early and middle adult years because their lives took them in different directions or they live far apart. If, however, they maintained a friendly relationship during that time, siblings often become close friends during late adulthood, especially after their spouses have died. Because siblings share memories of childhood, their parents, and perhaps past support, they have a level of intimacy unattainable with other age-mates. Many older sibling relationships provide both emotional buffers against the losses incurred in late adulthood and instrumental support as well. For example, some may pool their resources and live together.

Not all siblings become close during late adulthood. Lifelong sibling rivalries are likely to continue into the old-age years. In these cases, siblings may become distractions and foster feelings of additional loss as they realize they will never be close.

Peers

Peer relationships take on new meanings during late adulthood and play important supportive roles. During old age, many people renew friendships with "old" friends with whom they have invested the time and effort to sustain their attachment over the years (Rawlins 1992). Although occupational and geographical mobility may have kept them apart during middle adulthood, they easily become close friends again.

Several studies have found that mutually supportive relationships with friends are a better predictor of life satisfaction than relationships with family members and contribute more to an elderly person's psychosocial well-being (Crohan & Antonucci 1989). There may be several factors that explain this. First, friendships are voluntary, not obligatory like family relationships. The voluntary nature of friendships usually includes a high degree of reciprocity in exchanging support and minimizes feelings of dependency. Because the elderly's friends are about the same age and sex, they can help each other deal with the problems of being old. On the other hand, kin provide more instrumental supportive tasks, e.g., long-term sick care and financial assistance, than friends. However, peers supply important compensatory support, which means they replace family members when they are nonexistent or unavailable.

Second, friendships are the primary sources of enjoyment and pleasure for older people. In providing companionship, elderly friends connect each other to the larger community by encouraging participation in social activities such as shopping, going to ball games, and visiting other people (Arling 1976). Relatedly, having close friends as confidants acts as a buffer against the losses common to late adulthood. Age-mates with whom there is a history of mutual support are important outlets for emotional comforting when grieving the loss of a spouse or role. Friendships, in this regard, serve an integrative function by keeping elderly persons connected to social groups and as a buffer to stress.

Because of cultural norms or the financial and physical health of the elderly, family relationships are often based on the formal obligation of adult children to care for their elderly parents (Crohan & Antonucci 1989). Elderly adults who require assistance with daily living may experience role reversal with their children or other family caregivers. Differences due to age, interests, lifestyles, or unresolved conflicts can create tensions between elderly individuals and their kin who are providing instrumental support (Wood & Robertson 1978). Elderly friendships are based more on feelings of egalitarianism rather than dependency or duty.

Institutional Living

A large group of elderly persons opt to relocate after they retire from working. Some migrate to warmer climates where they have more opportunities to be active and they can avoid their heightened sensitivities to cold weather, while others may move closer to their children, grandchildren, or other relatives. When older persons make these moves voluntarily and are not mentally or physically incapacitated, many housing options are available. Condominiums are a popular choice because there are fewer household responsibilities—no lawn mowing and fewer repairs and "chores." Many housing options for the elderly are set within planned communities or buildings that offer a wide range of services and opportunities, as well as restrictions. The decision about what kind of housing to choose is primarily affected by the amount of money one is willing to spend and the kinds of services desired. For the elderly who have health limitations or require some assistance in daily living, several options are available as well. These choices are affected by the level of care that is required.

There are two residential settings in which nurses or other trained caregivers are present: retirement homes and nursing homes. The least restrictive of the two types is a *retirement home,* which ranges from independent living to assisted living. The services provided at independent living centers vary. The more expensive facilities provide more services, while others allow residents to choose which services they want. Most independent living facilities provide one or two meals each day, social activities, a full-time nursing attendant, emergency call systems, security, and transportation.

To qualify for independent living, individuals must be able to provide all their own personal needs such as hygiene and bowel and bladder functions, prepare at least one meal each day, take care of their own medical needs, such as setting appointments, and do their laundry. In general, they have to be alert and oriented enough to care for themselves and live independently in a monitored setting.

Assisted living facilities vary from one center to another. In some, residents can choose the services they need from a "menu." They only pay for the ones selected. For example, residents who require help bathing, taking medication, monitoring vital signs regularly, and preparing meals, contract with the facility for those services. Other facilities do not provide choices in services and offer a "one price fits all" program. To qualify for assisted living, individuals must be able to get around in their apartment or room by themselves, get to and from meals, and not require any ongoing nursing care such as a catheter or feeding tubes.

The second type of residential setting is the nursing home. In nursing homes, two levels of care exist: intermediate care and skilled care. Admission to nursing homes must be ordered by physicians. Therefore, the mode of care changes from a social model to a medical model. In *intermediate care,* there is an expectation that residents are capable to some degree of involvement in the everyday life and events of the nursing home. This means that individuals must be able to cooperate in their treatment. For example, if food is brought to residents, they must be able to eat it without aid. Although they may need assistance in most activities, they are generally able to participate in their own maintenance and can be left alone safely.

Skilled care residents are unable to care for themselves. They are usually bedridden or, if taken from bed, they must be secured because they have lost the ability to control their movements. These residents may have catheters, naso-gastric tubes, or other monitored medical services. Skilled care residents who require intravenous tubes (IVs) or life-support systems receive those services in a hospital.

Most skilled care residents have Alzheimer's and other dementing illnesses. As a result, nursing homes are developing special units to accommodate their needs. Dementia-disordered residents, though cognitively impaired, may be physically quite healthy. Within nursing homes, as well as independent or assisted living facilities, there may be separate units that cater specifically to individuals who suffer from a dementing illness.

Nations in Which Older Men Outnumber Older Women

It is generally accepted that women live longer than men. In most societies, the sex ratio, which is the number of men per 100 women, highly favors women past age 60. In the United States for example, the sex ratio among this age group is about 73 men per 100 women. This relationship holds true in most developing countries as well. There are exceptions, however. In a few countries older men outnumber women.

In twenty-two nations around the world, men outnumber women among those age 60 and older. Most of these countries are in Africa, the Middle East, and Asia, and in almost all of them "traditional" religions or Islam predominate. The societies are poor and highly partriarchal. It would appear that in societies where women's status is low, they do not live as long as men. How can this be? Low status translates into poor nutrition, insufficient health care, violence, and economic disadvantages—all factors that affect life expectancy for women.

Below are the countries in which there are more older men than women. With the exception of Bangladesh, the societies are ranked by sex ratio at age 60 and over. Bangladesh's population data are for those 50 and over. Sex ratios were calculated from census data reported in the United Nations' *Demographic Yearbook* (1995).

RANK	COUNTRY	MALES AGED 60 AND OVER PER 100 FEMALES 60 AND OVER
1	Qatar	168
2	Solomon Islands	149
3	Maldives	146
4	Afghanistan	139
5	Liberia	131
6	Iran	127
7	Jordan	124
7	Bangladesh	124* (Aged 50 and over)
9	Zambia	122
10	Bahrain	120
11	Sudan	119
12	Sri Lanka	114
12	Tunisia	114
12	Ivory Coast	114
15	Niger	113
16	Nepal	112
17	Sabah	109
17	Senegal	109
19	Andorra	106
20	Papua New Guinea	105
21	India	104
22	Central African Republic	101

In Qatar, the sex ratio among those aged 60–64 is 212. This means that there are over twice as many men as women in that age group.

In four countries in Africa and Central America, the sex ratio of older persons was near 100, which represents the same number of men as women: Ethiopia (99.9), Belize (99.8), Mali (99.6), and Uganda (98.6).

The life of residents in nursing homes has been a widely discussed and controversial topic of late. Over the last several years, reports of maltreatment, neglect, and insensitivity have reached the point of national scandal. Many nursing homes, especially those that operate for profit, have horrible records of abusing residents. These violations have been so voluminous that many people are afraid to have a loved one admitted to such a facility.

Aside from the cases of abuse, the main question about institutional living concerns whether nursing homes facilitate successful aging. Nursing home residents, unlike older people who live in neighborhoods or planned communities, must satisfy all their private and social needs within a relatively confined environment (Rogers 1986). The narrowing of the elderly's world may have a profound impact on their quality of life. One study found that after three weeks of institutionalization, residents demonstrated some decline in their ability to care for themselves. After twelve months, about half of the residents demonstrated extreme deterioration, including death. This rate of decline was about 2.5 times that of a control group (Tobin & Liebermann 1976; Rogers 1986).

LATE ADULTHOOD AND DIVERSITY

The aging experience varies across social groups. The social environment affects how the body ages and the quality of life an older person will have. Though most ethnic groups have assimilated to varying degrees, there is considerable diversity in life experiences among them. As I have discussed earlier, these differences are due to cultural features within each group and the relationships each group has with the dominant or core group. These factors affect how each group approaches aging and have led to a heterogeneous elderly population within the United States.

Before modernization, families cared for their elderly members. With industrialization came economic surplus and the ability to retire from being productive. As this happened, the elderly relied less on their family members for support, and more upon formal, institutional resources and programs such as Social Security, pensions, hospitals, in-home social and nursing services, and so forth. Consequently, responsibility for caring for the elderly fell to the government and private bureaucratic systems. A negative outcome of this historical process has been the systematic exclusion of minority group members from the full services and advantages these programs offered (Cox 1984). The minority elderly are underserved because of economic deprivation and discrimination by these programs. This sec-

Retirement requires adjustment. Compensating for losses by establishing new relationships and forming new interests helps assuage losses.

tion examines how the lives of the elderly may differ because of race and ethnicity, gender, sexual orientation, and place of residence.

Race and Ethnicity

Aging patterns differ by race and ethnicity. How groups express their meanings of aging and how they treat old people often differ from the dominant culture. For the most part, these patterns vary because ethnic minorities have suffered lifelong discrimination and prejudice. Today's nonwhite elderly grew up during times when their communities were denied access to formal social institutions that could affect quality and length of life. Let's turn now to see how being old in these groups varies from one to another and from the experiences common to European Americans.

African Americans.   The life expectancy of African Americans is considerably less than that of European Americans. According to Vital Statistics calculations (1992), present life expectancy projections for European Americans exceed those for African Americans in both sexes:

Females
<blockquote>
European Americans   79.2
African Americans   73.5
</blockquote>

Males
<blockquote>
European Americans   72.7
African Americans   64.8
</blockquote>

From these statistics, it is clear that African American men are far less likely to reach old age.

Subdividing groups by age, however, uncovers differences that do not favor the aged of European origins (Gibson 1994). The death rate among people seventy-five years of age and younger is higher for African Americans, but the death rate for people over 75 is *lower* for African Americans. This pattern has been observed by Vital Statistics since 1900, according to Gibson, and has no certain explanation. One possibility is based on a social selection process. Because of race-related health issues, such as high rates of hypertension among people of African descent, and be-

cause overrepresentation in poverty increases the likelihood of premature death, African Americans who live to 75 years of age are perhaps a more select subgroup than elderly European Americans. Schoenfeld et al. (1994) refer to this group as "super survivors." Another possible explanation is that African Americans and European Americans age at different speeds. There is some evidence that supports this notion (Markides & Mindel 1987).

The family of elderly African Americans differs somewhat from European Americans. Research indicates that African American families provide for and help the elderly to a greater extent than European American families do (Markides & Mindel 1987). The reverse has been found as well: that the elderly are more likely to provide more instrumental support for younger family members than European Americans. Two points must be noted in regard to these findings. First, contact between the elderly and their children declines as income increases and that contact does not always improve the morale of the elderly (Wolf, et al. 1983; Arling 1976).

Retirement, as both an economic and psychological period of life, came later historically to African Americans than European Americans. Because of low incomes throughout their lives and the low incomes their children were likely to have as well, African American elderly have been denied the same kind of retirement experiences that many European Americans have enjoyed. Many live solely on Social Security benefits. Because financial resources are a critical predictor of successful adaptation to retirement, African Americans experience more retirement stress and socially fare more poorly than European Americans (Markides & Mindel 1987).

The mental health and life satisfaction studies of African American elderly do not indicate different rates of pathology than that found in other groups. However, African American elderly are overrepresented in psychiatric hospitals. It must also be noted at this point, that African American elderly are *underrepresented* in nursing facilities. A number of writers conclude that these processes are the result of institutional discrimination in which state psychiatric facilities function as nursing homes for minority poor who cannot afford nursing home care (Markson 1979; Markides & Mindel 1987).

Most of the problems encountered by African American elderly are due in large part to economic deprivation. Ethnicity is a factor, too, however. Jackson (1980), a well-known student of minority aging, contends that the experience of the African American elderly differs from that of most other ethnic groups because they have suffered from institutional racism all their lives. Despite reductions in the incidence of poverty among elderly African Africans between 1955 and 1990, older African Americans are about three times more likely to be poor than European Americans. Among elderly European Americans, 10.1 percent are poor, whereas 33.8 percent of African American elderly are beneath the poverty line (U.S. Bureau of the Census 1992).

Hispanics. Hispanics are the fastest growing elderly group in the United States. Census projections indicate that the elderly Hispanic population will more than double from 1990 to 2010 and may be eleven times greater by 2050. About four percent of the country's elderly were Hispanic in 1990; by 2050, over 15 percent of the elderly population will be Hispanic if current demographic trends are maintained (U.S. Bureau of the Census 1992). Therefore the demand for social work services to older Hispanic persons is likely to increase rapidly in the near future.

Much has been written about the strong feelings of allegiance commanded by Hispanic families. Though it is true that members of Hispanic families tend to rely on each other for assistance more than nonHispanics, many writers have distorted the character of Hispanic families to paint an idealistic, but perhaps unrealistic, picture. Hispanics, as a rule, do have a strong sense of familism, however, and of the ethnic communities in the United States, Hispanics are most likely to exchange services and provide mutual aid with kin. Hispanic elderly tend to live in closer proximity to

relatives than the elderly of other groups and have stronger in-family social networks. These qualities, which have been verified in research, should not lead someone to an idealistic image of life in Hispanic families. Older Hispanics have high expectations of support from family, but the actual delivery of that support from kin often does not match those expectations (Markides & Mindel 1987). Another study found that elderly Chicanos' feelings of closeness and affection with their children and grandchildren are associated with emotional well-being. However, actual associations with their children are related to depressive symptoms (Markides & Krause 1985).

The family remains central to the lives of contemporary Hispanics, albeit in different ways. Today's Hispanic elderly are very likely to speak only Spanish and to be less assimilated than younger generations. Though the family may not provide as much support as in the past, the family continues to be the main link between the elderly and formal support systems.

Another traditional value in Hispanic cultures is the age hierarchy. As people age, their status in the family and the community enhances. The young are expected to respect and obey older family members. This value appears to be changing (Maldonado 1979). As the socioeconomic gap between generations increases, younger Hispanics become increasingly more Anglo-like, and extended families are no longer necessary or desired; Hispanic elderly are becoming more isolated and hold less traditional authority within the family (Maldonado 1979).

The poverty rate of Hispanic-surnamed elderly persons is quite high: 22.5 percent (U.S. Bureau of the Census 1992). Mexican Americans and Puerto Ricans are more likely to be poor than Cuban Americans. This fact is not surprising given the conditions under which many Hispanics came to this country and decades of economic discrimination. Consequently, retirement is economically stressful. Hispanics have high rates of seasonal and agricultural employment that are low-paying and provide few benefits. Jobs urban Hispanics hold are likely to be low-paying and without a pension as well. Therefore it is difficult for Hispanics to have a great deal of money available to them when they retire.

Sanchez (1992) and Sena–Rivera (1980) have identified several sources of stress for Hispanic elderly:

- Social problems such as poverty, low education, language barriers, and inadequate housing
- Prejudice and discrimination from institutions
- Anger and disillusionment regarding the behavior of the young
- Feelings of lack of worth because of the lost ability to contribute to the economic well-being of the family
- Anger about being imposed on for child care responsibilities and other needs of the family caused by poverty
- Loneliness from diminishing peer group relationships

These stresses are related to mental health problems among Latinos. Contrary to beliefs that mental health problems are low among Hispanics, depression and anxiety complaints are not uncommon among elderly Cuban Americans, Puerto Ricans, and Chicanos. In fact, mental health is the third most urgent need communicated by elder Latinos after physical health and income (Sanchez 1992).

Native Americans. The problems of Native American elderly are perhaps the most pressing of all elderly groups. The poverty of reservation economies and family resources is such that the large majority of elderly Native Americans must live as wards of the government (Block 1979). One measure of these troubles is life expectancy. Census data (Indian Health Service 1994) reveal that the life expectancy for Native Americans is considerably lower than that of European Americans, despite significant increases since 1940:

	MEN	WOMEN
1990	66.0	74.7
1940	51.3	51.9

These improvements in life expectancy are due primarily to better medical services available to Indians on reservations. The increase in life expectancy for Native Americans possibly has leveled off, because there was no change between 1980 and 1990. In fact, life expectancy declined slightly during the 1980s.

Before the European conquest of the Indian nations, there were variations in the meaning and role of elderly people among the tribes. For example, among nomadic tribes, in which life was more severe, abandonment, neglect, and suicide were the normative responses to a person who had become nonproductive due to age-related physical limitations. In sedentary tribes that had more productive economies, the elderly enjoyed more status because they could perform useful functions despite physical limitations (Block 1979).

In virtually all Native American cultures today, the elderly are highly revered. The status of the old, however, is being eroded by federal programs that emphasize younger Native Americans and younger people who adopt European values such as materialism (Block 1979). Another problem is that the traditional kinship support system breaks down in a modern, capitalist economy. The jobs that younger Native Americans have are low-paying, so they can neither afford to have elderly relatives live with them nor send them cash. In some instances, the only jobs available for younger Native Americans are not near their homes. Geographic relocation forces younger generations to abandon the elderly. The poor economic base of Native Americans leaves most of the elderly without financial resources and socially isolated.

The traditional kinship support system is not completely forsaken, however. Native American elderly provide support for children and grandchildren. About 26 percent of Indian elderly care for at least one grandchild and two-thirds of the elderly live within five miles of their kin, with whom they engage in mutual support activities (National Indian Council on Aging 1981).

The availability of proper medical services is one of the most critical problems for elderly Native Americans. The geographic isolation of many Indians is a significant barrier to medical intervention. When aged Native Americans require nursing home care, for example, they frequently must travel a long distance. Institutional living, therefore, can further isolate the elderly from friends and kin. The absence of sufficient resources of both families and the community limits the choices that the elderly have when they require medical and social services. Poverty prevents construction and operation of programs such as adult day care centers that might allow the elderly to remain near their families and receive the services they need (Block 1979).

Social work services must be consistent with Native American cultures. Red Horse (1982) recommends several important guidelines for conducting assessments and planning services for this population:

- Include tribal history to provide a sense of belonging
- Honor and work with spiritual beliefs
- Minimize culture shock in nursing home services and develop nursing services on reservations
- Discuss and cooperate with tribal and kinship groups
- Define eligibility according to tribal standards
- Provide unmet nutritional needs
- Utilize Native American social workers or provide interpreters
- Support indigenous networks
- Adapt to tribal remoteness
- Eliminate barriers to services

Asian Americans. The stereotype of Asian groups constituting the "model minority" is a misleading representation of Asian Americans, especially when applied to Asian elderly. Thinking of Asian Americans as having few difficulties and being self-sufficient ignores the fact that Asian elderly have the same problems that face other groups. In many ways, their difficulties are more serious.

Several factors magnify the challenges of aging among Asian Americans. One is assimilation. Many older Asians are immigrants to the United

States and chose not to assimilate or were barred from completely joining mainstream American society. One of the resulting problems is the language difference that prevents Asian Americans from communicating with other groups. A second factor that adds stress to aging is a value clash between traditional Asian and Western values. Asian values, such as social politeness, tolerance, and respect for traditions and family, conflict with European values of independence, individualism, competition, and materialism. This incongruence in lifestyle and expectations leaves the elderly frustrated, alienated, and angry (Lee 1986).

Another problem facing elderly Asian Americans is their exclusion from access to professional social services. Lee (1986) discusses five reasons for this population being underserved.

1. Most services targeting older Asian Americans are culturally inappropriate. Non-Asian social workers are frequently perceived as insensitive and unresponsive to Asian needs and priorities, for example failing to ensure that clients' nutrition and personal health care utilize foods and practices consistent with their culture.

2. Asian values often prohibit the elderly from seeking help. Taking one's problems to a stranger may mean losing face, implying that one has failed to be self-reliant and family-centered.

3. The history of prejudice and discrimination makes many elderly Asians distrustful of the government and social agencies. Their suspicions lead to feelings of helplessness and vulnerability.

4. Organizational barriers, such as failure to provide interpreters, publicize programs in Asian neighborhoods, and locate agencies near Asian elderly, limit access.

5. Social alienation limits participation in programs. The more traditional and less assimilated people are, the more they are likely to feel powerless and disenfranchised and hold lower status.

Some researchers have found elderly Asians to have more psychosocial problems than European Americans (Kiefer et al. 1985). Several risk factors are thought to create higher stress for

Asian Americans. For example, Asian Americans who have immigrated are at particular risk on reaching old age (Sakauye 1992; Kiefer et al. 1985). Immigration is associated with depression, anxiety, and post-traumatic stress disorder. Other risks include little or no proficiency in English, low educational achievement, living alone, and the lack of employment.

Gender

Most social gerontologists agree on the existence of the *double standard of aging,* a concept that suggests that being old may be a different and in some ways a more negative experience for women than men (Harris 1994). The double standard of aging can be seen in social attitudes and in differences in quality of living.

Older women are subject to greater stigmatization than are elder men. Several studies have found that people tend to believe the signs of aging are less attractive on women than on men. Since women are more likely to be judged by their age and appearance, more women than men try to conceal their age by coloring their hair and using cosmetics to cover wrinkles. According to Harris, women attempt to hide their age to enhance their self-esteem, which "fits with the idea that physical appearance is an important part of women's self-concept" (1994: 156). Sexism is clearly visible when considering the differing significance of aging for older men and women. In a social climate that sexualizes women, the signs of aging erode women's sexual, and thus social, value.

Because women live longer than men, they are increasingly likely to suffer more losses of important relationships and roles and encounter longer periods of dependency. Longer periods of living alone in late adulthood, and a lifetime of economic discrimination, leave elderly women with fewer economic resources at their disposal.

There is little wonder, therefore, that elderly women are overrepresented in poverty. Although women make up about 58 percent of the elderly population in the United States, they comprise 74 percent of the elderly poor (U.S. Bureau of the Census 1992). Minority women are especially disproportionately poor. For example, African American women constitute about five percent of the elderly population, yet they are 16 percent of the elderly poor. In 1990, about two million elderly women lived alone and of them, half received means-tested assistance through various programs such as Medicaid, food stamps, and subsidized housing. The median income of men in the three largest ethnic groups—European Americans, Hispanics, and African Americans—is higher than women in their respective groups. The income of European American men over age sixty-five is about 75 percent higher than Caucasian women and about double that of African American and Hispanic females. These disparities in income negatively affect all facets of women's lives.

Prolonged dependency also affects elderly women's position in their families. Elderly women often turn to their children for support, but support may not be readily forthcoming:

> *... widows' need for support may strain their relationships with adult children. Both children and the widow fear and resent the possibility of her increased dependency. These dynamics are most pronounced when the child is a white middle-class male (Lewittes 1988: 140).*

As familial relationships become distressed, elderly women often turn to friends for support. Not only do relationships with friends serve a compensatory function for getting needs met, they also relieve family tension. Friends help widows combat loneliness and provide companionship for social activities (Lewittes 1988).

Another economic problem women encounter concerns Medicaid policies and nursing home care. Since husbands tend to be older than wives and have a shorter life expectancy, they usually require advanced nursing care sooner. In most cases, the couple pays for his home and institutional care with their own resources, leaving the surviving wife with fewer assets with which to live out her life. When elderly widows require nursing care, they have less money to acquire better services. Because Medicaid policies place more emphasis on services that replace the family than on services that support the family, some women have been forced to legally separate from their husbands or file suit against their institutionalized spouse for maintenance (Faulkner & Micchelli 1988).

For the most part, the experiences of minority elderly women and European American women are similar. Padgett (1988), however, makes note of two differences. First, minority elderly women play more integral roles in their family networks. As "kintenders," they provide more instrumental and expressive support to their adult children and grandchildren. On the other hand, the interaction patterns of older European American women include both family and non-kin relationships.

Second, minority women have developed more adaptive survival strategies than European American women. In response to poverty and discrimination, Hispanic and African American elderly women, for example, share economic and social resources moreso than European American women, whose needs to develop strategies for survival are far less urgent. Providing and receiving social support from kin networks not only gets needs met, but serves to reduce feelings of alienation caused by living in an often threatening social environment (Padgett 1988).

Sexual Orientation

Most concerns of elderly gays and lesbians are the same as those for heterosexuals: declining health, body changes, physical limitations, isolation, loss of partner, and lower incomes (Berger 1984). Nonetheless, gays and lesbians face additional problems imposed upon them by a hostile social environment.

Today's older gays and lesbians face special problems of invisibility. For most of their lives, they were forced to hide and conceal their sexual orientation (Friend 1987). Since their sexual identity was being formed "pre-movement," which means before the gay liberation movement began, protecting themselves against stigma and open discrimination carried a greater sense of urgency than it does today. It is possible that many more young homosexuals isolated themselves or passed as straight pre-movement and now find themselves socially isolated as older persons.

Economic problems confront older lesbians more than aging gay men. Lesbians have lived on one or two low incomes for their entire lives, owing to sexual inequalities in the workforce. On retirement, there is simply less money.

A third problem concerns interactions with insurance and medical organizations whose policies discriminate against lesbians and gays. For example, most intensive care units exclude everyone except blood relatives and legal spouses from visiting and sitting with patients. Physicians and nurses who hold anti-gay sentiments may keep partners separated and prohibit expressions of affection. Many older homosexuals dread entering nursing homes for fear of not being allowed to show their feelings toward their partners. Insurance companies may not recognize surviving partners as the beneficiary of insurance policies and partners cannot inherit property without a will. Good legal counsel and advanced planning can avoid the latter kind of discrimination, however (Friend 1987).

A final problem unique to gays and lesbians is that they are likely to face aging without family support. Loneliness is a significant problem for aging gays and lesbians because they are often ostracized by their families and by society in general (Kehoe 1990). The stereotype that older homosexuals are alone and cutoff from any meaningful social contact does not hold true, however. Elder lesbians and gay men tend to associate mainly with other older homosexuals and replace family with a "family of friends." As is true for heterosexuals, closed-couple lesbians and gays with a strong commitment to the relationship have been shown to be the happiest and best adjusted older homosexual group (Lipman 1986).

Some writers contend that the coming out process and gender role flexibility better equip gays and lesbians for adjusting to old age. The coming out process helps individuals learn to deal with conflict. *Crisis competence,* the ability to manage difficult problems, is believed to be high among homosexuals who handled their coming out successfully and have high self-acceptance. Crisis competency provides individuals the coping mechanisms to generalize to other crises in later life (Kimmel 1978). Gender role flexibility is believed to facilitate successful aging among homosexuals by helping individuals take care of themselves (Friend 1987). Unlike heterosexuals, who may be used to having or expecting a spouse to take care of them, gays and lesbians may be less traumatized by living alone and performing a wider range of self-care tasks.

The Rural Elderly

More elderly persons live in metropolitan places than in rural areas. The 1990 Census reported that about 26 percent of all persons sixty-five and older live in nonmetropolitan places. However, the elderly accounted for a larger percentage of the nonmetro population—15 percent to 12 percent of the urban population (U.S. Bureau of the Census 1990).

The rural elderly is an at-risk, vulnerable population that experiences high levels of stress due to life events and chronic strains (Johnson, Waldo, & Johnson 1993). Compared to urban elderly, older rural residents have significantly less education, although they are quickly catching up to their urban counterparts, and are more likely to be poor. Poverty rates are higher among nonurban elderly and the gap increases with age; among those aged sixty-five and over, the rural poverty rate is 15.4 compared to 10.0 percent among the urban old. About one-third of rural elderly are considered to be near-poor, whereas 22.3 percent of urban elderly are in relative poverty (McLaughlin & Jensen 1991). The poverty rate for minority elderly is particularly high. For example, 68 percent of rural elderly African American women are poor (Belden 1993).

Because of their geographic isolation and lack of resources, rural residents face aging with additional burdens not encountered in the cities. These problems include housing, transportation, and the availability of health services.

Housing conditions for the rural elderly are often much worse than in the cities and suburbs

(Belden 1993). About 10 percent of the housing units occupied by the aged in rural areas are substandard. This is two percentage points higher than the rate for urban elderly. Of all the substandard housing in nonmetropolitan places, 30 percent are occupied by persons over age sixty-five. Belden (1993) suggests that two factors may explain these differences. One, there is more homeownership outside the cities, so people may stay in their houses longer, but without the resources to maintain them. They may do this to remain independent or because they have few housing alternatives, such as apartments or intermediate care facilities. Two, real estate values in most rural areas are lower than in the cities. Because migration to cities from "the country" continues, the rural elderly are less likely to sell their properties and convert their equity into retirement funds.

As agriculture declines and people leave small towns for opportunities in the cities, the plight of the rural elderly worsens. For those who elect to stay in their homes by choice or because they cannot sell, the ability to attain services is increasingly difficult. Many small towns no longer have supermarkets or a physician or a pharmacy. Traditional gathering places no longer exist. For older people who cannot or should not drive, the lack of transportation becomes an imposing obstacle to meeting basic needs and maintaining a tolerable quality of life. Many older people are forced to drive despite slowed reflexes and vision impairments. Transit programs serve most of the rural elderly, but these trips are usually reserved for medical and nutritional purposes, not discretionary trips (Kihl 1993).

Despite the stresses and strains of rural living for the elderly, their chances of being depressed are no greater than urban aged (Ortega, Metroka, & Johnson 1993). This finding is not surprising because rural elders practice more extensive preventive health behavior, have significantly larger social networks, have greater access to caregivers for assistance in time of need, and engage in more leisure activities (Penning & Chappell 1993). For those elders who experience depression and other mental health problems, services are grossly inadequate and unavailable and are more seriously affected by changes in the economy (Furr 1992).

LATE ADULTHOOD AND HEALTH

Physical Health

Chronic disorders such as cancer, arthritis, heart disease, diabetes, osteoporosis, and senile dementia, among others, rather than acute disease and disability, pose the greatest threat to successful aging. With the exception of respiratory infections, the likelihood of acute illness actually declines with age. As you saw at the beginning of this chapter, the aged suffer numerous functional limitations. These impairments present the most health problems for the elderly (Rose 1991).

These limitations and complaints do not necessarily translate into the need for personal assistance. The need for personal assistance with everyday activities, which is a good indicator of need for health and social services, advances with age. In Table 6.1 below, notice that among noninstitutionalized people, the need for personal assistance in bathing, dressing, moving out of beds and chairs, toileting, and eating, is not a significant factor until the oldest old age groups. Among those people under sixty-five years of age, just over two percent require help and 9.3 percent of adults sixty-five to sixty-nine need assistance. For the oldest two categories, eighty to eighty-four

and eighty-five and over, the percentage jumps to 23.6 and 45.4, respectively. All groups are not equally represented among individuals who are functionally impaired. Elderly women, people who live in households with low incomes, and elderly African Americans have higher rates of functional limitations (U.S. Bureau of the Census 1992).

Most elderly persons have age-related health complaints. Rakowski and Hickey (1992) found, however, that there are potentially aversive consequences of attributing at least some types of health problems to old age as opposed to specific diseases. Asserting that a symptom is a function of aging may direct attention away from some real disease. Social workers and health care professionals should attend to these statements and search for other potential causes of complaints. Rakowski and Hickey fear that a self-fulfilling prophecy may come to pass if people believe their bodies are failing because of age.

Another study addressed the importance of *subjective health*, which refers to how persons perceive their own physical well-being. Most elderly persons rate their health as good or excellent, while few score their health as bad or poor (Schoenfeld et al. 1994). In fact, those who believe their health is poor or bad are nineteen times more likely to die than individuals who perceive their health as excellent. This effect holds even when statistically controlling for race, sex, smoking, marital status, education, alcohol use, and other health-related variables. These findings demonstrate the meaningfulness of subjective health on physical health and longevity (Schoenfeld et al. 1994). While working with the elderly, it is important to explore psychosocial factors that may lead clients to rate their health negatively.

Social stratification is one of the most salient predictors of how health changes with age (House et al. 1994). There is a positive relationship between social class position and health: the higher an elderly person's social class, the better his or her health. As social class declines, older adults suffer more functional limitations. Class exposes individuals to different health risks that accumu-

TABLE 6.1 Percentage of Persons Needing Assistance with Everyday Activities by Age

AGE	PERCENT NEEDING ASSISTANCE
85 and Over	45.4
80 to 84	23.6
75 to 79	18.9
70 to 74	10.9
65 to 69	9.3
Under 65	2.4

Source: U.S. Bureau of the Census, 1992

late over time. Lower social class is associated with more smoking and drinking, greater stress, more physical labor, poor diet, less social and health support, and fewer feelings of efficacy or control over one's own health. Not only are the working class and poor more vulnerable to health risks that shorten life, but the *impact* of those risk factors is also higher (House 1994). For these reasons, working-class and poor men and women are less likely to survive to old age, and, when they do, they have significantly more health problems.

Another study also found that psychosocial factors affect health in late adulthood. This research learned that occupying multiple roles in early adulthood leads to better health in old age (Moen, Dempster–McClain, & Williams 1992). Occupying several active roles augments individuals' social networks, power, prestige, resources, and emotional gratification. Perhaps these benefits from holding multiple roles translate into higher self-esteem, self-efficacy, and rates of subjective health.

Mental Health

A traditional belief about aging is that mental health declines with advancing years. Because of greater stressors, loss of significant people, lost roles, and declining physical abilities, the elderly have been stereotyped as a depressed and senile lot who have little interest in life. More recent findings disagree with the idea that depression is a normal part of aging. While a number of studies do show an increase in mental health problems for many older adults, others report that for many elderly persons mental health actually improves with age (Markides 1986). These studies suggest that economic security, Medicare, and political action on the part of groups, such as the American Association of Retired Persons (AARP) and others, improve happiness, pride, and self-esteem (Markides 1986).

Most studies do not show declines in mental well-being among the elderly (Markides 1986). The majority of older persons fail to develop clinical depression, which is the most common psychiatric syndrome among the elderly, or other psychiatric disorders.

Still, the mental health picture for the elderly is not bright. The incidence of mental illness is higher among the aged than younger populations. The suicide rate for those over sixty-five years of age is disproportionately high as well. Too, the likelihood of psychosis increases after sixty-five years of age, and moreso at seventy-five (Biegel, Shore, & Silverman 1989). It is estimated that 25 percent of persons over age sixty experience some mental health problem. The utilization of mental health services by the elderly is low, however. Older adults receive only 6 to 7 percent of community mental health services.

Several factors affect mental well-being during late adulthood: (1) health, (2) mental health history, (3) income, and (4) interpersonal resources. (1) Physical health has a particularly significant impact on mental health. Physical fitness has been shown to improve cognitive speed and certain memory tasks (Chodzko-Zajko, Schuler, & Solomon 1992). On the other hand, illness and functional disability are associated with depressive symptoms (Fry 1986; Berkman et al. 1986). (2) In an important longitudinal study, Valliant and Valliant (1990) learned that a stable, cohesive childhood and a history of emotional well-being predicted successful aging as defined by self-esteem and better self-care. (3) Having a sufficient income improves mental health. Financial resources allow elderly to purchase suitable housing, nutritious meals, recreational activities, and better health and supportive care. (4) Finally, interpersonal resources affect mental health. Informal, but meaningful activities in ongoing relationships improve overall life satisfaction because such relationships provide role supports necessary for maintaining self-esteem and self-concept. Information networks and interpersonal resources, such as family support, reduce the likelihood of depression (Harel 1988). Living arrangements also affect emotional well-being. Living independently with one's spouse has a positive effect on mental health during old age, whereas living in an institutional setting is believed to cause depressive symptoms

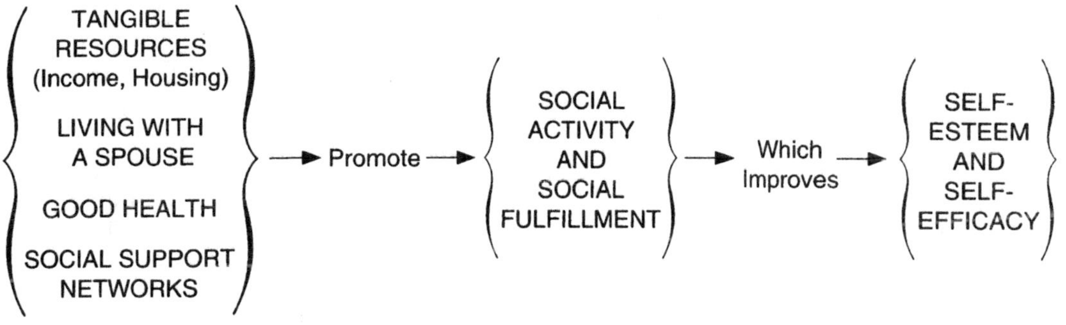

FIGURE 6.1   What Predicts Mental Well-Being among the Elderly?

(Riley 1994). In summary, having resources, living with a spouse, and being in good health promote social activity and social fulfillment, both of which advance self-esteem and self-efficacy (see Figure 6.1). Elderly people who are infirm or isolated, however, live in an environment in which access to rewarding social interaction is limited (Creecy, Berg, & Wright 1985).

Depression in the elderly population often presents similarly to depression in younger groups. Themes of loss and hopelessness are commonly seen in both groups, though these symptoms may be more reality-based among the aged, who have little chance of replacing or restoring lost relationships, homes, and independent living (Riley 1994). Other indicators of depression in an elderly adult are apathy, lack of pleasure and interest in activities, withdrawal, self-depreciating behavior, and psychomotor decline. As Riley notes, it is often difficult to assess when an elderly person is suffering a depressive disorder or is experiencing a reasonable reaction to poor health, poverty, loss of significant others, impending death, and the other losses encountered in late adulthood.

In addition to traditional depression, there are two forms of depression that are typical to older people. First, many depressed older adults mask their depressive symptoms (Riley 1994). In this form of depression, which is called *somatic depression,* older adults will complain of changes in sleep patterns, appetite, weight, energy levels, and

sexual functioning. When discussing these symptoms, the elderly person is not likely to discuss feeling sad, unhappy, or hopeless. Physical complaints will be given instead and the person may seem to be *hypochondriacal,* a condition in which someone is preoccupied with or has an irrational fear of having a serious medical problem when none exists. Somatic depression is more common among individuals who have their first depressive episode after age sixty-five. In working with these individuals, first refer them to a physician for a medical exam to rule out illness. Then explore emotional and relational factors that may underlie the depression. Precipitating events such as the death or illness of a close person, changes in quality of living, or retirement should be investigated, for they can lead to emotional disturbances.

The second form depression may take in older adults is called *pseudodementia,* which describes depressed older adults who do not complain of melancholia, hopelessness, or physical symptoms, but who present with cognitive and memory deficits. Most often these individuals, as will those with the somatic type, are likely to go first to their family physician, rather than a mental health professional, thinking that their problem is medical, not psychiatric. Doing so can lead to inaccurate diagnoses of a dementia disorder such as Alzheimer's disease (Riley 1994).

In terms of cognitive impairment, depression and dementia differ in several ways (Riley 1994). Dementia has a gradual onset of cognitive dysfunctions about which the individual has little awareness. Depression, on the other hand, has a relatively sudden onset. The depressed person exhibits a high level of complaints of memory loss. Dementia symptoms will eventually appear in neuropsychological testing and will become significantly worse over time. The intellectual abilities of depressed persons are typically not detectable in testing results and complaints of memory loss do not become severe and will cease when depression is successfully treated.

Gender and Depression.   Common sense might suggest that older women have more psychiatric problems than aged men. After all, elderly women have higher rates of widowhood (half of elderly women are widowed compared to one in eight men), lower incomes (elderly women have higher rates of poverty than men), and are likely to live alone (most older men live in families). These three factors—widowhood, low income, and isolation—are usually associated with mental disorders. Research shows, however, that elderly women are no more likely to report more psychological impairment than older men, despite their higher vulnerability (Feinson 1987). How might this be explained? Feinson suggests three possibilities. First, men's and women's roles converge during later years. There are fewer differences between gender roles during late adulthood than during young and middle adulthood. When younger, women have more role overload than men, but in late adulthood their encounters with role strain and role conflict abate. Second, older women and men are more similar than different in terms of control and power. And third, women may have different and more successful ways of coping with stress.

Suicide.   The suicide rate for the elderly is about three times greater than the risk in younger persons. In fact, older men of European descent have the highest rates of suicide among social groups. By age eighty-five, the suicide rate for white males is triple that of all others (Beaver &

Miller 1992; Fry 1986). The rates of elderly suicide are likely conservative figures because older adults are at risk for "hidden" suicide as well. Depressed elderly who want to end their lives may ignore their physician's orders, fail to take medications, eat improperly, and abuse alcohol and prescription drugs (Beaver & Miller 1992). Therefore, many suicides may be mislabeled as deaths due to other causes such as auto accidents or disorders related to malnutrition.

Riley (1994) has listed eleven clues and risk factors that may identify an individual as a higher risk for attempting suicide. Most elderly persons who try to kill themselves are depressed, although some are reacting to a diagnosis of a terminal illness or the death of a spouse. All indicators or verbal cues of suicidal thinking must be taken seriously. Effective intervention can prevent many suicides. The eleven risk factors are as follows:

1. depression
2. feeling hopeless
3. verbal cues such as wishing for death, feeling tired, and so forth
4. single or widowed marital status
5. solitary living arrangements
6. recent loss of a loved one
7. previous psychiatric illness or alcohol or drug abuse
8. previous suicide attempts or threats
9. diagnosis of a degenerative mental disorder such as Alzheimer's disease
10. diagnosis of terminal illness in self or spouse
11. chronic mental illness

Alcohol Abuse

Compared to alcohol abuse among adolescents and younger adults, the misuse of alcohol among the elderly has received relatively little attention from researchers and practitioners. This neglect occurs despite the fact that research consistently finds that 4 to 10 percent of all elderly persons abuse the drug (Pruzinsky 1987). Translated into real numbers, as many as 3 million people sixty-five years of age and older have a drinking problem.

Researchers usually divide elderly problem drinkers into a dichotomy based on when the abuse began. The first and numerically largest group is known as early-onset heavy drinkers. This group is composed of aging, long-term alcoholics whose drinking started relatively early in life and has continued into old age. They have a more severe drinking problem and consume more alcohol than the late-onset group (Pruzinsky 1987; Schonfeld & Dupree 1991). The second group, late-onset problem drinkers, started drinking heavily later in life. This group has more education and a higher income than the early-onset group. They have more stable residential patterns and are more satisfied with life as well.

These groups vary greatly in health and psychosocial functioning. Early-onset problem drinkers suffer worse general health and have far more acute health problems than late-onset problem drinkers (Colsher & Wallace 1990). The early-onset group is more likely to show the signs of long-term effects of abusing alcohol. This group has significantly higher rates of strokes, heart attacks, stomach and intestinal ulcers, glaucoma, asthma, bronchitis, emphysema, sleep disturbance, and bowel and urinary problems. Early-onset drinkers spend more time in physicians' offices and hospitals and are able to perform fewer activities of daily living.

People with a history of heavy drinking have more psychosocial deficits as well (Colsher & Wallace 1990; Schonfeld & Dupree 1991). They present more depressive and anxiety symptoms and perform more poorly on mental status examinations. They have learning and memory deficiencies, which have been shown to persist even after seven years of sobriety. Long-term elderly problem drinkers demonstrate a preference for solitary activities and have lower self-esteem.

The two groups are similar in one important way. Prior to taking the first drink on days in which they consume alcohol, both groups report that they feel depressed and excessively lonely (Schonfeld & Dupree 1991). That the antecedents to drinking for the groups are similar may be the result of diminished social support along with brief episodes of depression. According to Schonfeld and Dupree (1991), reduced social support for late-onset drinkers results from recent losses which in turn contribute to the onset of alcohol abuse. For early-onset, a small social support network may be due to others becoming alienated in reaction to persistent heavy drinking over the years. For both groups, these researchers add, social support networks may be composed of formal or task-oriented relationships with people such as apartment managers and agency personnel, rather than with relatives and close friends.

Mental health professionals do not agree on the best course of treatment for elderly alcoholics. Some suggest that treatment modalities should not differ for younger and older persons with drinking problems because there are not many differences between the two groups. Others, including Schonfeld and Dupree (1991), believe that treatment plans for elderly alcoholics should be less confrontive and more supportive. Intervention based on providing a supportive environment helps elderly persons cope with their losses and negative emotional states and assists in rebuilding supportive networks.

Elder Abuse

Elder abuse has not received the attention that child abuse has in recent years, despite the fact that 32 out of 1,000 noninstitutionalized elderly persons admit being maltreated (Pillemer & Finkelhor 1989) and that abuse and neglect complaints comprise about 28 percent of all resident care complaints (Paton, Huber, & Netting 1994).

The stereotyped picture of elder abuse is that of the infirm, dependent parent being maltreated by an overburdened, "stressed-out" caregiving son or daughter. Recent research, however, dispels this assumption and shows that elder abuse correlates with abuser traits rather than the traits of victims (Pillemer & Finkelhor 1989). Maltreated elderly are no more ill or functionally disabled than non-abused older people and they are more likely to be abused by spouses than children. What's more, abusers tend to be dependent on their victims for financial assistance, household repairs, transportation, and housing. Perpetrators often become increasingly dependent on victims prior to the onset of maltreatment because of the loss of other family members, increased social isolation, and increased financial needs (Godkin, Wolf, and Pillemer 1989).

Elder abusers have a number of other qualities in common as well. They have a high incidence of having been arrested, hospitalized for a psychiatric condition, involved in other violent behavior, or limited by some health problem (Pillemer & Finkelhor 1989).

Dementia

Formerly known as organic mental disorders, the dementia disorders are characterized by cognitive deficits, such as memory impairment, that are due to the direct physiological effects of a medical condition or prolonged substance abuse (American Psychiatric Association 1994). Of the several types of dementia, *Alzheimer's Disease* is the most common among the elderly. *The Diagnostic and Statistical Manual of Mental Disorders* (DSM-IV) estimates that 2 to 4 percent of the population over sixty-five years of age have Alzheimer's Disease. The prevalence of Alzheimer's increases with age—as many as 20 percent or more over age eighty-five years may be inflicted. Other forms of dementia are much less prevalent.

Alzheimer's is a degenerative disease and ultimately leads to death, which is caused by a secondary infection. The onset of symptoms is gradual and involves continuing cognitive decline. Until very recently, a certain diagnosis of Alzheimer's Disease could be made only by ruling out other potential disorders.

Reisberg and associates (1989) described several stages in the progressive decline in cognitive abilities. These stages describe observable behaviors listed in the order in which they occur. The stages place a person with Alzheimer's on a continuum in order to educate the family and patient as to what to expect next (Berila 1994). The first stage involves changes in memory that are neither significant in nature nor noticed by others. These lapses in memory do not interfere in functional ability. The second stage involves changes in functional abilities related to complex social or occupational tasks. People with Alzheimer's may withdraw from these situations and hide the declines. Examples include forgetting important appointments, decreased ability to complete complex, familiar tasks, and impaired ability to travel independently.

Stage three marks a decline in abilities to handle complex tasks without assistance. These tasks include balancing a checkbook and remembering to buy certain items while shopping. Stage four involves requiring assistance to choose proper clothing. People with Alzheimer's may need reminders to change their clothes daily and alter their clothes to suit the weather.

In stage five, assistance is required to clothe, bathe, and toilet oneself. Speech is grossly affected; the ability to speak in complete sentences is lost during this stage. During the final stage, stage six, all speech and motor abilities are gradually lost. Vocabulary declines and the ability to move about freely disappears. Eventually the ability to sit without aid, smile, and hold the head up deteriorate.

The symptoms of Alzheimer's Disease are more than memory loss. Hall (1988) has grouped the symptoms into four clusters (see Table 6.2). Organizing the wide range of symptoms grouped this way helps families understand that many of the symptomatic behaviors they see are actually related to the disorder. The first cluster of symptoms, intellectual losses, are often the first to appear. Early-stage Alzheimer's begins with such problems as forgetfulness, trouble making decisions, and difficulties in perception. The second set of symptoms are affective or personality losses. These deficits are recognized by diminished affect and inhibitions, decreased attention span, social withdrawal, and other problems. Third, planning losses involve declines in the general ability to plan activities. Alzheimer's patients experience functional losses in self-maintenance activities such as money management and personal hygiene. Cluster IV symptoms, according to Hall, refer to increased frustrations due to planning deficits, intolerance of multiple stimuli, and increased fatigue from processing information about their environment. Hence, "the tolerance for stress is lowered by negative feedback from caregivers and others who constantly test the client and tell [him or her] that [he or she] is wrong. When the patient's lowered stress threshold is exceeded, the behaviors listed in cluster IV often result" (Hall 1989: 32).

Five groups of stressors can worsen temporarily these behavioral symptoms by heightening stress, which can produce dysfunctional behaviors (Hall 1988). Once these stressors are removed, the dysfunctional behaviors decline. Fatigue, change of routine, excess demands, overwhelming stimuli, and physical stress, such as illness or pain, can aggravate specific symptoms of dementia.

When people with Alzheimer's Disease are no longer capable of safe, independent living, family members have a difficult set of decisions to make. Depending on the family's resources, capabilities, and emotional closeness, the family must choose between institutional care and family, in-home care for the loved one with Alzheimer's. Many choose institutional nursing care. About a third to half of those confined to nursing homes are diagnosed with Alzheimer's Disease and it is the most common reason for admission to long-term care programs (Beaver & Miller 1992). For the others, family members provide care on a daily basis.

Caring for a loved one with Alzheimer's Disease generates significant stress on family members. Understanding the disease is hard and providing around-the-clock attention strains resources, relationships, and nerves. Among the major stressors in families are the change in roles, family conflicts that occur when emotions are tense, and the physical toll of providing care (Mace & Rabins 1981).

TABLE 6.2 Symptom Clusters Associated with Alzheimer's Disease

I. INTELLECTUAL LOSSES

Loss of memory, initially for recent events

Loss of sense of time

Inability to abstract

Inability to make choices and decisions

Inability to reason and problem-solve

Poor judgment

Altered perceptions and ability to identify visual and auditory stimuli

Loss of expressive and receptive language abilities

II. AFFECTIVE OR PERSONALITY LOSSES

Loss of affect

Diminished inhibitions, characterized by emotional liability, spontaneous conversation with loss of tact, loss of control of temper, and inability to delay gratification

Decreased attention span

Social withdrawal and avoidance of complex or overwhelming stimuli

Increasing self-preoccupation

Antisocial behavior

Confabulation, perseveration

Psychotic features, such as paranoia, delusions, and pseudohallucinations

III. CONATIVE OR PLANNING LOSSES

Loss of general ability to plan activities

Inability to carry out voluntary activities or those activities requiring thought to set goals, organize, and complete tasks

Functional loss, starting with high-level maintenance activities such as money and legal management, shopping, and transportation; these progress to losses of activities of daily living, generally in the following order: bathing, grooming, choosing clothing, dressing, mobility, toileting, communicating, and eating

Motor apraxia (inability to carry out motor activities despite intact motor function) (American Psychiatric Association 1994))

Increased fatigue with exertion or cognition, loss of energy reserve

TABLE 6.2 *Continued*

Frustration, refusal to participate, or expressions of helplessness when losses are challenged

Increased thought about function tends to worsen performance

IV. PROGRESSIVELY LOWERED STRESS THRESHOLD

Catastrophic behaviors

Confused or agitated night awakening

Purposeful wandering

Violent, agitated or anxious behavior

Withdrawal or avoidance behavior, such as belligerence

Noisy behavior

Purposeless behavior

Compulsive repetitive behavior

Other cognitively and socially unacceptable behaviors

Hall, G. R. 1988 Care of the patient with Alzheimer's Disease living at home. *Nursing Clinics of North America,* 23(1):31–46, p. 33. Reprinted by permission of the author.

Families respond uniquely to the demands of caregiving, but several factors predict the quality of care (Given, Collins, & Given 1988). First, the quality of family relationships prior to the diagnosis affects the type of care that is offered. Research shows that if family relations were strong, then the duration of care is much longer and the amount of stress caused by caregiving is reduced. Second, if caregiving roles are assumed voluntarily and arise from a sense of dedication and commitment, they are more enduring and have a less negative emotional impact. On the other hand, if caregiving roles are assigned and become an unwanted set of imposed obligations, then the quality of care is likely to be poor. Third, social supports improve quality of care and the well-being of both the sufferer and the caregiver. Emotional support in terms of making caregivers feel valued, and instrumental support in the form of actual assistance are greatly beneficial to the caregiving process. Fourth, utilizing community re-

sources improves the caregiving environment. Utilization of services such as respite, adult day care, and in-home care are affected by the availability, affordability, and the lack of knowledge of the services. Finally, the financial conditions imposed by caregiving have a profound impact. If rendering care creates an economic burden on the family, then caregiving will cause more dissatisfaction and family tension.

CONCLUSION

The "graying of America" will have a major impact on all aspects of social living. This changing demographic profile is a call for the mobilization of resources to meet the needs of an aging population. The increased demands on social and health services, housing, recreation, and transportation to older people will push service delivery systems beyond their current level of productivity.

Aging makes individuals vulnerable to a number of risks. The resources available to aging persons, however, can reduce those risks significantly. As individuals grow older, biological, social, and psychological changes occur that lessen their ability to care for themselves. Using the structural social work model as a guide, social workers can minimize risks and enhance functioning by mobilizing resources to improve compensatory, selection, and optimization skills.

CASE STUDY REVIEW QUESTIONS

Refer to the case of Cynthia and her father Edward at the beginning of Chapter 6. Having read this chapter, how might you answer the following questions?

1. Edward's wife had been compensating for, and thus concealing, Edward's decline in abilities. As it turns out, Edward had Alzheimer's Disease. Given what you know of his condition, what are some other impairments he might suffer? What is the likely course of his disorder?
2. How might you prepare Cynthia for her father's declining health? What supports is she likely to need?

3. What kind of changes are likely to occur in Cynthia's own family? How could social work intervention help?

4. What stressors is Cynthia likely to face herself?

5. What kind of supports and resources would you recommend for Edward?

KEY TERMS

Activity theory: Theory that suggests successful adaptation to aging occurs by staying active.

Ageism: The differential and unfair treatment of older people.

Alzheimer's Disease: A degenerative disease that affects cognitive skills, personality, affect, and the ability to plan activities.

Assisted living facilities: Residential centers that provide services to individuals who are able to get around in their apartment or room by themselves, get to and from meals, and do not require any ongoing nursing care.

Compensation: The second process of successfully adapting to losses due to aging; compensation is the process of counterbalancing, or compensating for, a particular functional or behavioral loss.

Continuity theory: A theory of aging that suggests that older adults adapt to the changes of later adulthood by preserving and maintaining existing internal and external structures; the elderly are motivated and predisposed to use familiar strategies for dealing with changes associated with aging.

Crisis competence: The ability to manage difficult problems.

Disenchantment stage: A stage of retirement in which retirees often experience a letdown as feelings of life satisfaction and physical activity decline.

Disengagement theory: Theory of aging that suggests that the elderly disengage or withdraw from society, and that society withdraws from them; disengagement theory posits that as people age they have less ability and fewer interests in maintaining social connections and performing their roles.

Double standard of aging: Concept that suggests that being old may be a different and in some ways a more negative experience for women than men.

External continuity: Concept within continuity theory that pertains to maintaining familiar physical and social environments.

Free radical theory: Free radicals are highly unstable atoms that are found in human cells and are by-products of normal cellular processes involving oxygen; the accumulation of free radicals may contribute to the aging process.

Hypochondriacal: A condition in which a person is preoccupied with or has an irrational fear of having a serious medical problem when none exists.

Integrity vs. despair: The last stage of the life cycle, according to Erikson; during this stage, people are confronted with their impending deaths and review their lives; when people are satisfied with their lives, they will look back with pride and acceptance and willingly embrace the tasks of old age with less distress and more tolerance.

Intermediate care nursing home: Residential facility based on a medical model; in these facilities, there is an expectation that residents are able to cooperate in their treatment and be involved in the everyday life of the home.

Internal continuity: Concept in continuity theory that refers to the continuation of psychological qualities such as temperament, affect, preferences, dispositions, and skills.

Optimization: Baltes' third process of successful aging, which suggests that old age can be a time of growth, fulfillment, and engagement; optimizing strategies may be applied to existing goals or reflect new goals and expectations.

Pseudodementia: A condition in which a depressed older adult does not complain of melancholia, hopelessness, or physical symptoms, but presents with cognitive and memory deficits; often confused with true dementia.

Retirement: A developmental milestone that marks a person's transition into late adulthood; the term refers to separation or withdrawal from participation from work in which the person was employed.

Retirement home: The least restrictive of the two types of residential settings in which nurses or other trained caregivers are present.

Reorientation stage: The final stage of retirement when retirees have settled into predictable and satisfying stable routines.

Role theory: A theory of aging that focuses on the loss of roles due to aging; adapting to aging is based on readjusting roles and avoiding stereo-typed roles.

Selection: A process of aging in which individuals restrict their "life world" to include fewer areas of functioning; the narrowing of activities may be a consequence of or in anticipation of losses in personal and environmental resources.

Skilled care nursing homes: Residential facility in which residents are unable to care for themselves.

Somatic depression: Type of depression in which depressive symptoms are masked; older adults will complain of changes in sleep, appetite, weight, energy levels, and sexual functioning rather than changes in mood; somatic depression is more common among individuals who have their first depressive episode after age sixty-five.

Subjective health: Refers to how individuals perceive their physical well-being.

CHAPTER 7

DIVERSITY IN COMMUNITIES

OBJECTIVES

After reading this chapter, you will be able to answer the following questions:

1. In what ways are social populations diverse?
2. What are communities?

3. How does group membership impinge on behavior? What are the positive and negative factors of belonging to communities?
4. What are prejudice and discrimination and what are their causes?
5. What is the best way to describe the relationships between communities?
6. What is the nature and history of the social policies that guide dominant/subordinate group relationships?
7. What is the significance of studying communities for social work practice?

CASE STUDY

William, a thirty-eight-year-old African American, saw a social worker in a medical setting after having a car wreck. His doctors expected that he would recover fully from his injuries and would soon be able to return home and to his high-income senior managerial position. During the interview, the social worker learned a great deal about the significance of community membership in the course of helping him adjust to his injuries.

Janice, William's wife of fifteen years, is also thirty-eight and African American. She is a practicing dentist with a high income.

William and Janice have a twelve-year-old daughter, Anna, who is in the seventh grade. Until recently, William and his family lived in an upscale neighborhood in a region of the city that has very few African American residents.

Though Janice and William are successful in the "white world," both felt alienated and disenchanted while living in the Anglo-dominated "Southside." William complained that he and his family felt no sense of community there, unlike their experience in the predominantly African American "Northside" where they grew up.

In their fashionable Southside neighborhood, Janice and William felt out of place and had little in common with the other residents. They discovered that, in the suburbs, people tended to live in their own separate worlds. Consequently, they did not know their neighbors beyond exchanges of cordial greetings. To make things worse, the family felt a lack of trust between their Anglo neighbors and themselves. For example, while taking after-dinner walks in the area, they noticed that Anglos often stared at them as if they were not where they belonged. Suspecting neighbors' distrust towards them, they were never able to make close friends or feel completely comfortable in their own neighborhood. When they did interact with neighbors, they quickly learned that they did not share their tastes in decor, music, diet, and neighborly expectations.

Religion is important to the family, but they had long stopped attending church because the Southside churches they tried over the years lacked the feelings of togetherness they enjoyed in Northside churches. To the family, predominantly European American churches seemed more staid, less emotional, and less supportive than the churches with which they were accustomed.

Before the move, Anna began having difficulties. Although she did well in school, she began having trouble relating to age-mates at school and around home. Her peers were virtually all European Americans. Anna started rebelling against middle-class Anglo values. For example, she only listened to music performed by African American musicians and she vehemently discounted European Americans' art and literature. She often reacted defensively about being African American.

Shortly before William's accident, the family had moved back to the Northside, though William and Janice continued working in the Southside. Several factors led to their decision to return to the African American community. In the Northside, they were closer to their families, which helped Anna maintain a sense of family history and identity. The move back was also designed to avoid additional pressures for Anna. She could see her parents as role models in the Northside rather than seeing them as separating her from her sense of "peoplehood." In her new home, Anna looked like everyone else instead of always sticking out. Now she had peers with whom she could talk about common experiences, styles, and tastes.

William said that he and his family were much happier living in the Northside. They became involved in African American institutions such as their church and organizations such as the Urban League. They had more friends and family there and were able to develop the feelings of community they lacked while living in the Southside.

INTRODUCTION

In Chapter 1, you learned that human development depends on the interaction of the various domains of the environment that shape the course of a person's life. The sociocultural environment is not a homogeneous entity that everyone faces equally. The macro environment has many subsystems that mediate between it and individuals and you will now examine those macro subsystems that have an impact on human development and growth.

No matter how similar some groups may seem, human populations are never homogeneous. Even the narrowest of societies is comprised of people of great diversity. All populations have divisions in experience, expectations, skills, resources, and status. Few contemporary societies maintain traditional cultural and social patterns in which emphasis is placed on similarities rather than functional differences. Modern societies, in fact, function as they do because they are composed of the interaction between and interdependency among human groups. This chapter examines the concept of community and its relevance for human development and social work intervention.

THE DIVERSITY OF HUMAN POPULATIONS

The great French sociologist, Emile Durkheim, observed the progression societies undergo as they evolve from relatively simple organizations to complex ones. In preindustrial societies, people tend toward conformity in all aspects of life. Economic and social roles are about the same, and personalities are very much alike as well. A society such as this is held together by what Durkheim (1893/1964) called *mechanical solidarity,* a form of cohesion based on similarity. Members of the society are expected to conform to the same patterns of living. Most people in the group share common experiences. A mechanical solidarity society usually is small and there is little tolerance for deviating from the norms and values that all members are supposed to follow.

Industrial and postindustrial societies, said Durkheim, are characterized by diversity. Here individuals perform a multitude of tasks in countless specialized status-positions and roles. Individuals and groups hold assorted values and ideologies and pursue dissimilar tasks. Hence people have quite disparate life experiences. If everyone is doing and thinking something different, what binds them together? Durkheim's term *organic solidarity* refers to social cohesion based on interdependence. In modern societies, roles are so highly specialized that any individual is incapable of surviving without others similarly performing their specialized roles. In other words, people have to be unlike each other, in order to perform their different roles, for modern societies to prosper.

Tonnies (1887/1957) distinguished between the types of relationships that people have in groups. His concept *gemeinschaft,* which loosely translates to mean community, represents a communal way of living. A group's gemeinschaft is its members' sense of unity, strong feelings of social solidarity, and commitment to tradition. *Gesellschaft,* on the other hand, implies behavior based on rational self-interest, often at the expense of traditional practices. Gesellschaft is characterized by impersonal, contractual relationships, and individualism. Gesellschaft comes at the expense of allegiance to the group and other individuals.

Without question, organic solidarity and gesellschaft best describe social life today. Yet elements of mechanical solidarity and gemeinschaft remain. Within the diversity of populations are associations of people who are bound together for reasons other than rational contracts and mutual interdependence. These affiliations are called *communities.*

COMMUNITIES

The historical shift from traditional social organizations to complex structures and individualism left people more isolated and alienated than in pre-industrial societies when everything people needed was supplied by the immediate family and other residents of the village. With the advent of capitalism and industrialization came large, impersonal institutions that eroded gemeinschaft relationships and transformed family and community life. The more people became detached from social groups, the more their behavior became self-serving.

In the twentieth century, communities became less essential for living. Replaced by the impersonal, contractual ties inherent in the organic solidarity society, gemeinschaft relationships deteriorated. As capitalism made individuals more and more socially independent in terms of fulfilling needs, many people found that they longed for the social support, personal affirmation, and affiliation with others characteristic of gemeinschaft communities.

No longer secure in the competitive, impersonal nature of social life, many people long to feel a sense of attachment and belongingness to a social group and are turning to volunteerism, religion, and other community activities to restore values of cooperation, helping others, and committing to towns and neighborhoods. Indeed, in recent years there has been a revival of several communities that have created bonds of attachment that provide members with meaningful social affiliations, security, and identity (Yankelovich 1981). There is also evidence that people are identifying more with groups with whom they share some personal or emotional attribute. For example, the recent emergence of gays and lesbians into an organized movement has led to more than political action. Gay and lesbian institutions have developed to serve the needs of the community and have become the emotional locus of gay and lesbian social life. Meeting the spiritual needs of many gays and lesbians is the Metropolitan Community Church, which performs important social functions as well. The church conducts gay and lesbian wedding ceremonies and often serves as a community center offering recreation, cultural events such as concerts, and social services such as counseling and AIDS education. Many large cities sponsor annual gay film festivals, musical and theater groups, business alliances, and charities to help disadvantaged gay men and lesbians. Terms such as "pride" and "community" are frequently used to describe the attachment lesbians and gay men have toward their infrastructure and one another.

The concept *community* is difficult to define, primarily because it is used in several different and often contradictory contexts. In fact, the term has been used in so many opposing ways "as to render it almost useless for describing a specific system" (Hillary 1968: 151). In the broadest sense, communities are the macrolevel intersections of the several domains of the environment.

Communities are broad associations in which people have a common identity and, to varying degrees, feel a sense of unity and common purpose. According to Fellin (1987), communities are social units with one or more of the following three dimensions: (1) a functional spatial unit meeting sustenance needs; (2) a unit of patterned social interaction; and (3) a symbolic unit of collective identity. There are two categories of communities: locality and nonplace communities. *Locality communities* usually have all three dimensions to some degree. Villages, towns, cities, and neighborhoods are examples. *Nonplace communities* are often referred to as communities of interest or identification (Bernard 1973). The "glue" that cements communities such as race or ethnic groups, gays and lesbians, and a professional group like social workers, is a common sense of identification, history, purpose, and interest. These communities are not necessarily connected to localities, although they may have a geographical component. For example, racial and ethnic groups are communities of interest and often live together within specific spatial boundaries. In addition, many communities have biological and natural components, such as shared genetic qualities and climate, that can affect development, health, and lifestyle.

Locational communities are important targets for social work intervention because the environmental features of neighborhoods, towns, and cities vary significantly. Lifestyles, problems, and concerns in rural areas differ in many ways from those in urban areas, though not as much as in the past. People who live in rural areas tend to have a greater sense of gemeinschaft than urban dwellers and demonstrate more traditional values regarding sex roles, heterosexuality, and racial segregation. Rural areas also challenge the mobilization of resources in confronting psychosocial problems. Rural poverty, isolation, and conservatism may interfere with delivering services, such as programs to help persons with AIDS, and resolving social conflicts, especially those of an ethnic and racial nature.

Identificational communities of socially disadvantaged people often offer secure relationships that provide support to their members. When interacting with other members of the community, an individual can have his or her experiences and sense of self validated. Communities can reaffirm the integrity and value of members who may be ill-treated by out-groupers. Identificational communities provide an emotional and social sanctuary of sorts for members of vulnerable groups. Jewish Community Centers and VFW posts, for instance, provide means for community members to feel in solidarity with one another, feel safety by associating with people similar to themselves, and reinforce their own qualities that qualify and define them as members of a particular identification community.

Social work interventions with identificational and interest communities deliver services to social groups that are oppressed and disenfranchised. Lines of inequality in the distribution of wealth in American society are drawn along community boundaries. Racial and ethnic groups and women, for example, are systematically underrepresented in the political and economic realms of society and are subject to special problems such as poverty and violence. Social services often target identificational communities to ameliorate the negative conditions that face the community-at-large.

The types of communities are rarely discrete categories; there is considerable overlap among them. Identificational and locational communities, for instance, often coincide. Members of the same social class or racial and ethnic group, for instance, tend to live in segregated neighborhoods and attend largely segregated schools. When this occurs, residential structures take on the norms and values of the identificational community.

A case in point are the Seventh-Day Adventist enclaves in Keene, Texas, and Loma Linda, California. Institutionalized social practices in these towns reflect the norms and values of the Adventist religious community and contradict those of surrounding communities. For example, there is no mail delivery on Saturday (Adventists' Sabbath) and most businesses are closed. The supermarkets stock vegetarian "meats" and it was practically impossible to get coffee or a caffeinated soft drink in Keene until recently. Keene's public high school, which only opened in the mid-1980s, is under public pressure not to hold sporting events and other extracurricular activities on Friday night and Saturday. The school does not field a football team and must seek permission from other schools to play basketball on Saturday nights after sundown, rather than the usual Friday night. The school never holds open houses and other programs on Friday night and the cafeteria serves vegetarian meals for its students. Conforming to these practices ensures the community's social solidarity and is exemplary of gemeinschaft relationships.

Geographic location is not a necessary condition for identifying with a community. A specific member of an identificational community may change residence and remain psychologically connected to and socially identified with that community. In these types of communities, individuals develop a sense of belongingness to a local community as well as membership in a broader, more global group (Fellin 1987).

A number of identificational communities have organizations that represent the goals and interests of the larger group. For example, members of the National Gay and Lesbian Task Force, NAACP, La Raza Unida, NOW, and the Jewish Defense League may think of themselves as a service community of people dedicated to helping the identificational community reach specific goals. Identificational communities often have social clubs and businesses that cater to the specific needs of the group. Fraternities and sororities, hair salons, nightclubs, and funeral homes are examples of instrumental organizations that work within the context of the norms and values of identificational communities.

Many interest communities, of course, transcend identificational boundaries. For example, social workers consider themselves a professional interest community. It is composed, however, of persons of divergent ethnic origins, gender, philosophies, sexual orientation, and physical capabilities who come together to practice the profession. Within the broad social work spectrum, there are interest affiliations that overlap with identificational communities, such as the National Association of Black Social Workers and the Christian Social Workers Association.

Because each individual belongs to a number of communities, each having its own importance, it is critical to avoid thinking of communities as discrete categories in which the experiences of members are alike. The phrase "communities within communities" best represents the true picture of social groupings. Additionally, the boundaries demarcating communities are not always clear. Therefore, when speaking of a community, it is imperative to define the exact characteristics of the group in question.

People who share an identity, and are thus considered part of a community, may actually not hold common interests. Not all African Americans, for example, have the same experiences; wealthy and middle-class African Americans have

different life needs than poor African Americans, who may have more in common with poor European Americans and Hispanics. If a person of African descent invests little of his or her identity in being an African American, then he or she is not represented by that community and is not a part of it.

How does a person come to belong to a community? Community membership is based on several criteria: shared attributes, self-definition, and community acceptance. First, an individual must share identificational qualities with the community. These characteristics or credentials define the boundaries of community inclusion. Second, individuals must define themselves as members of the community. Individuals may possess the characteristics necessary to gain entry into the community, but choose not to define or identify themselves as affiliated with it. Many people of Hispanic origin, for example, do not consider themselves Latinos. If they are multigenerational American, they perhaps do not speak Spanish and have fully adopted mainstream American culture. Their Hispanic roots may not carry the same degree of identificational importance.

The final criterion for membership is acceptance. Individuals must be defined by others as qualified for community membership. They must be received by members of the community and integrated into its social fabric.

COMMUNITIES AND HUMAN DEVELOPMENT

Behavior is largely understood by taking into account the social reality that gives meaning and definition to "in-group" members and "out-group" people. Communities construct their own rules of inclusion and boundaries and set many of the norms and values that guide individuals' behaviors, influence their attitudes, and shape their personalities. Communities are systems of orientation that help to create and define an individual's place in society (Tajfel 1978) and to organize the behavior of their members. Furthermore, community membership affects how one is treated by people and institutions outside the community. Communities, consequently, have important implications for human development. It is through community dynamics that people interact with many environmental processes.

Innumerable research articles and books have demonstrated differences in behavior and attitudes based on community associations. These differences range from attitudes toward government policies to intimate and sexual behavior. The section that follows identifies several positive and negative effects of community membership on human development.

Positive Effects of Community Membership

Values and Norms. Most communities develop a set of values and norms. Community values and norms serve four purposes: they (1) define the community and set system boundaries; (2) give a community distinction and notoriety; (3) help members interpret the world around them and prescribe appropriate behavior; and (4) function to enhance community cohesion and solidarity. Despite great behavioral differences within most communities, there is also considerable attitudinal and behavioral uniformity among members of large-scale social categories. How does this occur? This uniformity, explains Turner (1982), is created in three stages called *Referent Informational Influences.* First, individuals define themselves as members of a distinct social category. Second, individuals must learn the stereotypical norms of that community. They must ascertain that certain appropriate, expected or desirable behaviors are used to define the community as different from others. And third, individuals assign these norms to themselves and internalize them. Furthermore, adds Turner, people continuously evaluate themselves in terms of their group memberships, and are willing to identify with communities defined as positive. Groups that provide the standards by which individuals evaluate themselves are known as reference groups.

Not only is behavior affected by internalizing a community's expectations, so are perceptions.

The wish to belong is so great that people often change their own thinking and behavior to conform to group pressure. In fact, individuals with group support will maintain a certain conviction despite contrary evidence. For example, members of hate groups such as the Ku Klux Klan and various neo-Nazi groups deny unequivocal evidence of the equality of all human beings in exchange for the sense of belongingness they receive from being accepted into the group. Group solidarity and avoiding rejection are more important to Klan members than questioning their beliefs about the inherent inferiority of people unlike themselves.

Social Identity. Communities define individuals as eligible or ineligible for community membership. By accepting someone as a member, communities award individuals by providing them with a sense of social purpose and meaning, i.e., an identity (Turner 1982). *Social identity* is that part of an individual's self-concept that derives from one's knowledge of membership in a social group or groups together with the value and emotional significance attached to that membership (Tajfel 1978).

Social identity is an important part of self-concept. Identifying with a community involves conforming to varying degrees with the established, validated norms, roles, and values that identify the community and its members as distinct.

Social Cohesion. People tend to be attracted to people with whom they share a common social identity. The term *social cohesion* implies a connectedness among people who have similar experiences. Therefore, identifying positively with a community of people gives rise to a favorable evaluation of in-group behavior, expectations, and attitudes. A negative view of the group to which one belongs would likely lead to a negative self-evaluation. Social psychologists have found that people generally feel secure with people akin to themselves and project positive qualities onto in-group persons, thus promoting group formation and social cohesion (Turner 1982; Hogg & McGarty 1990). Strong community identity and participation help fulfill human needs for acceptance, belongingness, and intimacy.

Supportive community settings are important for members' well-being. Maton (1989) found that community support serves as a buffer to stress. Attachment to a community provides three buffers from stress. First, attachment provides personal caring from other community members. Second, a person with role responsibility within the community feels a greater sense of belongingness and acceptance. Roles provide meaning and structure in everyday living. Finally, attachment to a community provides mutual help groups and extramural activities. Friendships are important stress-buffers because they are outlets for expressing emotions and solving problems (Maton 1989). Communities must have sufficient commitment from members, organization, and resources to provide strong attachments for their members.

Support Systems. Belonging to a community usually entitles members to the *support systems* available to it. These resources can be formal, such as minority fellowships, neighborhood associations, and business alliances, or informal, such as mutual self-help groups and peer support.

Communities differ in their ability to resolve the problems that affect members. Competent communities are those that effectively identify the problems and needs of the community and can achieve a working consensus on goals and priorities. Communities that best engage in problem-solving agree on ways and means to implement agreed-upon goals and utilize or develop the necessary resources and strategies (Fellin 1987). Several conditions, according to Fellin, can enhance the functioning of a community: (1) members must have a commitment to their community; (2) there must be self-awareness among community groups of their own values and self-interests; (3) community subsystems must articulate effectively their own diverse interests and needs; and (4) community members must participate in identifying goals and implementing them.

There are several barriers, however, that hinder a community's ability to resolve its own problems (Warren 1978). First, the source of many problems affecting a community may not lie within the community itself, but may stem from the larger social context of which the community is a part. In such a case, the community's efforts to effect change may be futile because the scope of the problem extends beyond its boundaries and resources. High unemployment rates among African American youths, for example, are directly connected to the ability of the economic system to provide jobs for teenagers, the government's willingness to create incentives for businesses to hire youths, and prejudice and discrimination practices that limit the opportunities for African American teenagers compared to those of European American adolescents. Businesses owned by African Americans lack the capital necessary to hire large numbers of teenagers.

Another problem, marital dissolution, affects some communities disproportionately, largely as a result of forces in the wider sociocultural environment. Marital dissolution is often associated with conflicting role expectations and economic tension, which are common problems among communities with high poverty rates.

The above examples show that communities are not cultural islands isolated from the larger social system or separated from broad forces of cultural development and change that are characteristic of the major institutions of society (Warren 1973). Despite boundaries that set them apart, communities are interconnected with other social systems. These relationships are of most interest to social workers. As Warren states:

> *In sum, many problems which communities face are simply beyond any realistic expectation of resolution through the effective mustering of resources at the community level alone (1973: 16).*

Negative Effects of Community Membership

Unfortunately, community membership is not without costs. Unwittingly people may be exposed to the social and biological issues that are of concern to the communities to which they belong, thereby experiencing problems in common with other community members. Important transactions with systems outside the community may be neither symbiotic nor equitable. Unequal economic and political exchanges in particular may in fact deprive groups and communities of the resources necessary to achieve maximum social and psychological functioning.

The consequences of unequal exchanges with other communities are often pervasive; that is, they may affect community subsystems. For example, women have been denied access to full participation in male economies for centuries. Although women's economic position has dramatically improved, they remain highly vulnerable. One evidence of this vulnerability is what happens to women after divorce. Weitzman (1985) found that the economic quality of living for women and their children fell some 42 percent one year after a divorce, whereas men's standard of living increased 72 percent in the same time period. This economic change has a pervasive effect on these women. Newly divorced women living on lower income may have a drastic reduction in health and retirement benefits and they may have to move to a less desirable neighborhood because their income cannot maintain their former residence, and so forth.

Community-based mental health and service programs are designed to deliver services to groups that are systematically disadvantaged and oppressed and that require action directed toward a class of people experiencing similar needs. Assertiveness training for women and social support services for chronically unemployed and underemployed people in job-training programs are examples of programs that tackle problems structurally produced because of unequal exchanges between communities.

Oppression. Many communities are subject to oppression—wholesale irrational, hostile treatment. These groups are exploited or repressed by a more dominant community in order to maintain the advantages the dominant group enjoys. Individuals are judged as members of the community, not on their personal merits.

Regardless of a person's station and accomplishments, belonging to a community that is perceived to be inferior or undesirable often elicits differential treatment from out-groupers. The effects of prejudice and discrimination, as you will see later in this chapter, penetrate all aspects of people's psychological and social life and can lead to interpersonal conflicts. Oppression is about restricting opportunity and it would be foolhardy to assume that it is an anachronism. Several jurisdictions, such as the state of Colorado, have recently passed laws curbing the civil rights of gays and lesbians. Unlike most laws that seek to define individual deviant behavior, these measures question the legitimacy of an identification community, while denying its members the same constitutional rights people in other social categories enjoy. Laws such as these do not consider individual needs; they are intended to insure the systematic control of the communities that are perceived to threaten the dominant group.

Communities do not share society's benefits equally, nor are they similarly ranked in prestige. As communities intersect with larger social systems, many find relationships unequally reciprocal, that is, some groups benefit disproportionately from the transaction. Social work has traditionally addressed the needs of communities that are systematically disadvantaged and are subordinately ranked by other groups. People from oppressed groups are likely to act out the frustrations and anger of being disadvantaged and so are at higher risk for unconventional and dysfunctional behavior.

Stereotyping. *Stereotypes* are "static and oversimplified ideas about a group or social category that strongly influence our expectations and behaviors" (Thompson & Hickey 1994: 147). Stereotypes are mental images people have of groups that support negative beliefs. Once they learn the stereotypes attached to particular groups, they tend to project that image onto individuals. Stereotypes are overexaggerations of characteristics attributed to various groups. They are irrational, disparaging assumptions used to prejudge a person's behavior and potential.

Through stereotypes, minorities are often depersonalized. Minority people are often not judged on their own merits, but are evaluated on the basis of an impersonal, derogatory characterization of the entire group. Simply to be a member of a minority is considered a basis for contempt (Kameny 1971). Holding negative assumptions of groups functions to support prejudiced beliefs, rationalize scapegoating, and justify inequality.

Role Mediation.   Membership in communities affects the distribution of roles and role expectations. Individuals are often perceived as members of groups rather than as autonomous persons. Images of what the group is like are projected onto individual persons; these projections become the behaviors and potentials expected of the stereotyped person. When an individual takes on a role, out-group members may expect the role to be performed according to their judgment of the group. Further, group members are less likely to assign important roles to out-group members whom they may perceive as untrustworthy or incompetent.

Members of disadvantaged communities are not proportionately found in senior positions of authority in government and business organizations. African Americans and Hispanics are rarely promoted to upper management positions and are grossly underrepresented in professional schools such as medicine and law. Research indicates that many European Americans who are in positions to promote employees in management stereotype them based on race, ethnicity, and gender and treat women and people of color as groups, rather than individuals (Jones 1986).

In his study of corporate managers, Jones found that there is a systematic double standard for European American managers and African American managers. He found that the same qualities that are rewarded in European American managers become the reasons African American managers are often disliked and penalized. "For blacks, aggression is arrogance, but if one is not aggressive then he is labeled not assertive" (Jones 1986:91). African Americans are frequently treated worse during performance evaluations and are given less room for mistakes. When African American managers make a mistake, they may be labeled incompetent, whereas a European American manager's mistake is likely to be dismissed as simply an error. In the business world, African

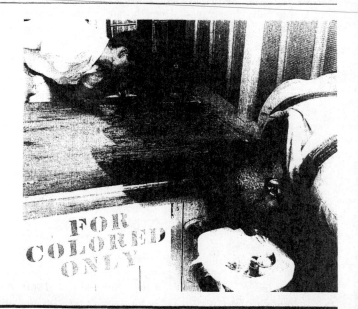

It has not been that long since scenes such as this were common in the United States. Maintaining separate social structures was a strategy of denying minorities access to the benefits of the society-at-large. Many communities today are experiencing the socio-historical residuals of past oppression: poor performance in school, high rates of destructive behavior, higher morbidity and mortality, and poverty.

American managers are often channeled into positions that, though important, do not enable them to function as key decision-makers for the company. These positions, such as community relations, industrial relations, public relations, and personnel relations, are not usually in the CEO track.

Even in sports, where racial and ethnic communities are highly visible, community membership mediates the roles they will play. Despite their high rates of involvement, African Americans are tracked away from the so-called "thinking positions" such as quarterback in football and pitcher and catcher in baseball (Blackwell 1991). African Americans and Hispanics are underrepresented among coaches, college athletic directors, and front-office personnel, such as general managers and vice-presidents, and are rarely involved in the ownership of professional teams.

Marginality. *Marginality* refers to the status of being between two cultures or communities at the same time (Schaefer 1993). Some individuals find themselves unable to feel fully part of the larger society or a particular community. People who are marginal to one community or another may experience emotional distress, isolation, or even ostracism. A child of one Jewish and one Gentile parent may have trouble identifying with either community and feel out of place in both cultural settings. First-generation immigrants are caught in a social and psychological struggle between the cultural demands of their new residence and their cultural and psychological ties to the "old country." Should an individual not clearly fall within the definitional boundaries of community membership, he or she may lack a community-based frame of reference on which one's social identification rests. The absence of social identification can leave a significant void in his or her self-concept.

Stigma. Community membership may carry a stigma. A *stigma* is any attribute that discredits or disqualifies an individual from full social acceptance (Goffman 1963). Stigmas are such powerfully negative labels that they can radically change a person's self-concept and social identity. Goffman identified three types of stigmas, characteristics that are considered outside of society's range of acceptability. The first category of stigma Goffman called abominations of the body, which refer to physical limitations, deformities, or other visible and identifiable characteristics. The second type consists of perceived blemishes of individual character. Goffman noted that society often interacts with mentally ill persons, criminals, and drug addicts, not as individuals with particular problems, but as a common group afflicted with deep-rooted flaws. Goffman's third category is tribal stigma. Society often discredits people because of their race, religion, or ethnicity. Members of stigmatized communities and groups are not only ostracized and often regarded as pariahs, but their humanness is stripped away and they are perceived as "not quite human" (Goffman 1963:5; Thompson & Hickey 1994). The ramifications of social stigma are devastating and, when confronted by stigma, communities attempt to reframe the stigmatizing quality and come together to extol and reinforce the community's positive qualities.

In all three categories, the stigmatized feature becomes the individual's master-status, a status-position or attribute of such importance that it defines a person's social identity and may shape the person's entire life. Many children are taught to stigmatize communities through what Garfinkle (1956) called the degradation ceremony, which is the systematic condemnation of an entire community. The degradation process obscures personal accomplishments and positive attributes and reduces the stigmatized group to an inhuman caricature.

Morbidity and Mortality. Because of the interaction between biological and social environments, membership in communities may affect one's health and even life itself. Community members, in some cases, are unequally vulnerable to certain health risks. For example, African Americans predominantly develop sickle-cell anemia; Tay-Sachs disease, another blood disorder, mostly afflicts people of Semitic origin; hemophilia and color-blindness occur exclusively in men; and infectious diseases are more likely to cause death among the poor than other social classes. The relationship between community and health is not necessarily static; community health can change through community action. At the beginning of the AIDS epidemic, gay men were the primary carriers of the HIV virus in the United States and Canada. Through community organization and education, gay men became more aware of the course of HIV disease and began to practice safer sexual techniques. Now the rate of HIV infection among gay men has dropped considerably.

Belonging to certain voluntary groups may affect health as well. Members of fundamentalist religious sects who reject scientific medicines and treatments for theological reasons prefer healing through spiritual faith. Sadly, these beliefs have resulted in suffering and deaths that could have been avoided. At some point this value that rejects normative health care counters the values of the dominant community and the law. When a child whose parents belong to such a group dies and the death could have been avoided by medical intervention, the parents are usually charged with negligence and failure to protect the child. The religious group's values legitimate the parents' behavior, but opposing mainstream values steer the parents into a cultural harm's way.

PREJUDICE AND DISCRIMINATION

Prejudice and discrimination are further negative consequences of a homeogeneic society. *Prejudice* can be defined as hostile attitudes or antipathy toward members of unequally evaluated groups. *Discrimination* is hostile behavior aimed at maintaining social divisions and community inequality.

Prejudice

There are a number of explanations for prejudice. Some approaches to understanding prejudice focus more on the character of the prejudiced person while others emphasize the social environment that produces and rewards hostile attitudes.

Psychological Theories. Psychological theories of prejudice focus on how prejudicial emotions fulfill certain emotional and cognitive needs in an individual. Perhaps the most well-known of these approaches is Adorno's (1950) *authoritarian personality* theory. Adorno argued that certain personality attributes were common to people who held strong prejudices. The authoritarian personality is paradoxical: on the one hand, this person is gratified by bullying and controlling individuals and groups weaker than her- or himself, while on the other hand strictly conforming to some higher authority. This quality fits the character of the typical member of the Ku Klux Klan, who feels highly validated socially by engaging in hateful, inaccurate rhetoric that presumes his or her own superiority over others. Yet at the same time the Klan member also accepts and succumbs to the absolute authority of Klan leadership and dogma. The authoritarian personality is rigid and intolerant and has a strong concern for social status. These persons are believed to be willing to act aggressively toward people who do not conform to their norms and values.

At first glance, this theory appears to provide considerable insight into understanding the existence of prejudice. Subsequent research, however, has learned that this model does indeed fit members of hate groups and other highly prejudiced people, but that it fails to explain expressions of prejudice in people who do not match the authoritarian profile. In other words, not all prejudiced people are authoritarian. Prejudice is not a characteristic of any one personality type or style; it occurs in people with all kinds of personality traits and social groupings. Furthermore, prejudiced feelings can change without any concurrent shift in personality. In sum, this theory only explains prejudice in limited situations and has little utility beyond those cases.

A second psychological theory of prejudice is *frustration–aggression theory.* In this approach, antipathy arises from frustration. Frustration is believed to be a natural response to failing to reach one's goals. Among prejudiced people, the real source of the frustration is not safe to blame because it is one's own shortcomings, the social system that the person is committed to, or is too powerful to confront. The coping strategy that is relatively safe, however, is *scapegoating,* misplacing blame on a group weaker than one's own. In this view, prejudice is the emotional component of laying blame for one's social troubles. Some research supports the frustration–aggression theory. For example, prejudice against race and ethnic groups in particular has been shown to increase during periods of economic instability.

Despite the apparent utility of psychological theories, they perhaps raise more questions than they answer. First, which conditions create sufficient frustration to lead someone to feel antipathy towards a group? Frustration and aggression are not necessarily inevitable consequences to failed goal-seeking behavior. Second, prejudice exists among wealthy people and those who have reached highly desired economic, social, and political goals.

Social Theories.   Theories that explain prejudice in terms of situations and conditions within the social environment are perhaps the most successful. Three theories will be considered: ethnocentrism, cultural transmission, and power differentials.

All communities believe that their cultural patterns, their ways of doings things, are right and "natural," a frame of mind known as *ethnocentrism.* Because people internalize their cultural foundations, making them part of their identity, they have a strong need to perceive their culture and community as superior to others. People judge others' social and cultural practices from the standpoint of their own ethnocentric beliefs (Kitano 1992). Groups that deviate, therefore, are unnatural and are held in suspicion because they threaten one's group and personal sense of identity and normalcy.

Cultural transmission theory suggests that children (and adults) learn prejudiced attitudes in much the same way they learn everything else. Prejudice is contained within the traditions of a family or community and repeatedly exposed to children. These groups exert pressure on individuals to conform to the rigid attitude (McLemore 1982). Conforming to the prevailing beliefs allows individuals to gain acceptance by an important reference group and perhaps avoid punishments. Furthermore, accepting the group's prejudices provides information, albeit incorrect, that is useful to clarify and give meaning to situations that are perceived as vague or ambiguous.

Power theory stresses that prejudice (as well as discrimination) is associated with economic and political advantages. Holding negative views of an oppressed group legitimizes unequal treatment; a group cannot systematically exploit another if it believes that group to be equal to itself. Hostile attitudes toward that subordinate group, therefore, sanction maltreatment.

Discrimination

Discrimination is any behavior that maintains dominant–subordinate group relationships. It aims to deny members of minority communities equal access to societal benefits. Discrimination is the actual social action of oppressing subordinate communities and it is what makes certain groups vulnerable to high-risk behaviors and continued social disadvantage. Like prejudice, discrimination is applied on a basis of group membership, not individual attributes (Marger 1994).

There are three types of discriminatory social action: derogation, denial, and violence. *Derogation* refers to epithets and rhetoric that put people down. Derogatory words, expressions, images, and humor that cast people in a negative light or that humiliate them are examples of derogatory discrimination. *Denial* discrimination is behavior that limits access of certain groups to opportunities, resources, places, and services. *Violence,* the third type of discriminatory action, is the most severe and involves physically harming or endangering a minority person or destroying minority-owned property.

Discriminatory behavior can be carried out by individuals, groups, or institutions (see Table 7.1). Individual discrimination is a harmful action

TABLE 7.1   Examples of Discriminatory Behaviors and Their Actors

	DEROGATION	DENIAL	VIOLENCE
Individual	Epithets Jokes Expressions	Avoidance	Assault
Group	Rhetoric Ideology	Exclusion	Mobs Bashing
Institutions	Stereotypic media portrayals	Red-Lining Residential segregation Unfair hiring	Unequal execution of death penalty

taken intentionally by a member of a dominant group against members of a subordinate group. Feagin (1989) refers to this behavior as *isolate discrimination* because the act is not socially embedded in the larger organizational or community context. An example might be a social worker who shows less interest in minority clients and does not work as hard on their behalf. Telling racist or sexist jokes or using a derogatory epithet or expression might be viewed as this form of discrimination as well. Feagin cautions that the term "isolate" does not mean that this kind of discrimination is rare, for it is actually commonplace. The term refers to an individual's action taken without immediate support of organizational or community norms.

Group discrimination is harmful action taken by a small number of dominant group members acting in concert against subordinate group members, without the support of the norms of a large organizational or community context (Feagin 1989). Vandalizing Jewish synagogues by hate groups, excluding minority community members from social clubs, and mean-spirited ideology are examples of this type of discrimination.

The most destructive discrimination is wrought by institutions. Feagin defined *institutional discrimination* as organizationally or community prescribed action that has a negative or differential impact on subordinate group members. Institutionalized discriminatory practices systematically ensure that the dominant group benefits economically, politically, and psychologically. This type of discrimination may be intentional or latent, yet it is central to the offending system's structure and represents that system's norms and values. Examples of institutional discrimination are economic development programs that ignore city districts dominated by minorities. The 1992 riots in south-central Los Angeles exposed the dramatic decline in jobs and economic progress in that poverty-stricken area. Other examples include the last-hired, first-fired policy for laying off workers. Since minorities are likely to be the most recently hired employees at most corporations, they have accrued less seniority, and thus are disproportionately affected during periods of corporate downsizing.

Prejudice and discrimination, in sum, are largely the results of situational and economic conditions. They are protective mechanisms used by the dominant group to assure its majority position. When minorities directly compete with the dominant group and its members perceive themselves to be threatened by the minority, hostile feelings surface and retaliatory behaviors emerge (Marger 1994).

RELATIONSHIPS BETWEEN COMMUNITIES

Americans use the term "melting pot" to describe their national persona. The idea goes that peoples from all over the world migrated to North America and melded together to invent a new nationality, a new "tribe," that would represent only the best qualities of the groups contributing to it (Schaefer 1993). The melting pot metaphor, in reality, is more wishful idealism than accurate portrayal of the populace. The American national image is not that of a harmonious homogeneity, but more a mosaic of persisting group diversity and antagonism. Groups and communities maintain separate identities, and, to a large extent, lead separate lives from each other.

The histories of most industrialized societies, however, are filled with struggles between communities and groups that compete for treasured, but scarce, resources. These conflicts over power, wealth, and social justice are evidenced in both the macro social arena, through political movements such as the civil rights movement, labor unions, and political action groups, and at the microlevel of interpersonal interaction.

Minorities

Most of the negative consequences of community membership discussed earlier are derived from a group's unequal position in the larger society. A group that is dominated by another and experiences unfavorable outcomes because of that domination is called a *minority*. Mainly due to its confusing reference to a numerical minority, the term *minority* has been difficult to define because it was first coined in the 1930s. The concept, however, suggests a position of social subordination and having insufficient social power to confront successfully that subordination. Louis Wirth (1945) offered one of the first, and perhaps the best, definitions of the concept of *minority:*

> We may define a minority as a group of people who, because of their physical or cultural characteristics, are singled out from the others in the society in which they live for differential and unequal treatment and who therefore regard themselves as objects of collective discrimination (347).

Explicit in this definition is the fact that minority groups are targeted for differential, unfair, and unequal treatment (Sagarin 1971). Thus members of minority groups hold lower-paying jobs, live in less desirable places, receive an inferior education, exercise less political power, and are subject to interpersonal indignities. These inequalities are the result of the social definitions of those physical and cultural characteristics that distinguish them from the dominant group (Marger 1994). Dominant groups achieve social superiority by controlling society's institutions and wealth and having the power to socially legitimate themselves while simultaneously denigrating competing groups and limiting their access to the social structures and resources on which their domi-

nance is based. In sum, a minority can be defined by three criteria: (1) It has a characteristic that differs from the dominant group; (2) this trait is stereotyped and devalued; and (3) members of the group are treated unfairly and unequally.

From this definition, several groups can be identified that qualify as holding minority status: racial and ethnic groups, women, the elderly, gays and lesbians, the physically disadvantaged, cognitive minorities, and behavioral minorities.

Racial and Ethnic Groups

Racial and ethnic groups probably come first to mind as examples of minority groups. In fact, the term is often used interchangeably with race and ethnicity. History shows that interracial and interethnic conflict are among the defining themes of western cultures. Our history of slavery, oppression, and bigotry openly contradict the core values on which western civilization is based and continue to defy the spirit of equality and democracy.

Subordinate group status based on race and ethnicity is created through four sociohistorical processes: voluntary migration, involuntary migration, annexation, and colonialism (Mack 1968). A number of community groups in North America first arrived here as voluntary immigrants, though leaving their home country may have not been completely voluntary, as in the case of Cubans, Vietnamese, and Russian Jews. These groups and others emigrated to seek out new opportunities, escape war, or flee from social injustice.

Other subordinate status groups were created through involuntary migration. The slave trade forcefully relocated about 400,000 Africans to the United States. Hundreds of thousands more were transported to the Caribbean islands and South America. Coming as slaves guaranteed Africans minority status and set in motion the legacy of African American poverty and frustration that continue to the present day.

Africans were the only peoples that were successfully enslaved. Other groups, such as the Irish, Chinese, and Japanese, came as contracted indentured workers. European Americans usually think of the indentured servant as a voluntary migrant; however, many contract workers were coerced into working in Hawaii or California during the late 1800s. Unlike slaves, indentured workers could return home at the completion of their contracts. Indeed many remained and formed new community groups with minority status (Schaefer 1993).

As a result of wars and treaties, the United States has gained new territories. In the southwest, particularly, regions that were formerly under the control of Mexico were incorporated into the country. Consequently, Spanish-speaking people became a part of the American mosaic. In most cases of annexation, the dominant group attempts to suppress the culture and language of the minority.

Groups become minorities through colonialism. When a dominant power moves into a region with the intention of exploiting its resources and controlling its residents, the result is that the native population becomes a minority subject to unfair treatment on its own land. Usually colonized peoples are not integrated into the cultural fabric of the conquering group.

Women

Women constitute a second category of minority. The Women's Movement has shown us the degree to which women have long been subjected to severe treatment in all parts of the world. Women are traditionally stereotyped as emotional, inferior, less intelligent, and irresponsible when compared to men. Euphemistically known as the "weaker sex," women are unfairly treated in numerous ways. First, women are treated differently than men economically. As a category, women earn far less than men. Furthermore, for most occupations women are paid less than men for doing the same work. Women are less likely to be promoted to upper management positions. Senior managers who are men tend to discount women's abilities and question their dedication to the "team." Second, women are more likely to be victims of sexual assaults and domestic violence.

Rape victims are almost exclusively women and most victims of child sexual abuse and domestic violence are women. Third, men dominate women in social interactions. Men often interrupt women during conversations and discount their ideas and contributions.

The Elderly

Older persons constitute a minority group as well. Being old in a youth-oriented culture places the elderly in a precarious position. People are living longer and U.S. culture has few norms and values to tell people how to be old and how to be around and value older people. Older persons are stereotyped as incompetent, useless, and frail, and are often viewed as a menace. Age is popularly believed to be antithetical to cultural standards of beauty and sexual attractiveness. Many people are shocked when they realize that the elderly are sexual, sensual persons.

The elderly are often discriminated against as they try to secure employment. With more people living into their late sixties and seventies, many want or need additional incomes. Younger persons, however, often believe seniors' skills are of no value and are reluctant to hire an older person. If company benefits are involved, the company may fear rising costs of its employee health insurance program if it hires older persons whose health care needs may be high.

Sexual Orientation

Gays and lesbians qualify as a minority community. The defining characteristic, of course, is a dominant or primary orientation toward sexual or affectionate intimacy with persons of the same gender. Gay men have been stereotyped as effeminate and passive; lesbians as "butch" and "manlike." Homosexuals live in perpetual social rejection by nongays and are subject to ridicule and derogatory rhetoric.

Heterosexuals have felt threatened by homosexuality for centuries. Homophobia, the fear and hatred of homosexuals, remains a strong emotion among many heterosexuals. This animosity continues to produce considerable resistance to social and legal justice for gay men and lesbians.

It may be impossible to list all forms of discrimination that gays and lesbians endure. Several examples can easily make the point that the gay community meets the definition of a minority. First, and perhaps most important, gays and lesbians are not protected by federal civil rights legislation. Not being a protected category makes homosexuals vulnerable to discrimination in hiring and housing. The following case illustrates how far-reaching the effects of this omission can be.

The social services department of a major hospital in a large city had agreed to supervise undergraduate social work internships from a nearby university. It was the first time the hospital had contracted to accept undergraduate students. Hospital policy required the facility's in-house attorney to review all contracts involving the hospital. On receiving the contract from the attorney, the university faculty noticed that he had deleted gays and lesbians from the contract's affirmative action statement, which protected the rights of homosexuals, among other groups. The director of the social work program questioned the attorney about the expunging. He said that since the federal government did not require the hospital to protect gays and lesbians on the basis of sexual orientation, it did not do so. To enter into the field placement contract as it was written would open the hospital to lawsuits by its lesbian and gay employees should they ever be fired or penalized for their sexual orientation. The social work program was left with only one ethical choice and it terminated the relationship with the hospital.

Gays and lesbians are subject to discrimination throughout the social environment. The resistance to the open admission of gays in the military in the early and mid 1990s demonstrates how entrenched the prejudice toward lesbians and gays is. Gays' partners are not always eligible for insurance and pension benefits from employers and gay marriages are not recognized by any state. Gay men and lesbians are subject to random, violent assaults known as "gay-bashing." These attacks stem from the offender's irrational fear of homosexuals. Gays and lesbians are often shunned or rebuked in interpersonal interaction.

Physically Disadvantaged

People whose bodies are different due to developmental disorders, disease, or accidents constitute a minority group. People whose body size falls outside the cultural standards of height and weight are included here as well. Dwarfs and physically and developmentally disabled persons are negatively stereotyped and are subject to unfair treatment.

Disabled people are often the "recipient of unasked-for attention" (Kriegal 1971: 174). They are stared at and others often intrude upon their personal "space." The victim of the voyeurism by non-disabled persons leaves disabled persons feeling self-conscious and angry. Many disabled persons resent having things done for them, because help is often rendered in a depersonalized, patronizing way without recognizing the individuality of the person (Kriegal 1971).

Section 504 of the Rehabilitation Act of 1973 sought to combat discriminatory practices aimed at disabled persons. This measure prevented discrimination against disabled persons in hiring, housing, and accessibility to public buildings. Discrimination persists, however, against persons with functional limitations. One institutional example is that the health care needs of the various disability groups are often overlooked by the health care system. Many health insurance programs limit coverage of or payment to their disabled subscribers (DeJong et al. 1989).

Disability or body size can be a masterstatus and stereotyped. An attorney who is blind is usually referred to as a "blind attorney"; Beethoven is often remembered as a deaf musician. Special skills and abilities are secondary traits when combined with a specific disability (Wertleib 1985). Non-disabled persons often feel repulsed by certain physical incapacities and seek to distance themselves from any contact with disabled people.

Cognitive Minorities

Some groups can be defined as a minority on the basis of the ideas they share. Religious groups are good examples of cognitive minorities. Jews, though well assimilated into mainstream society, are denigrated in political rhetoric by Muslims and right-wing extremists and are often the victims of anti-Semitic harassment, threats, assaults, bombings, arson, and vandalism.

Behavioral Minorities

Some groups qualify as minorities because of behavior that deviates from cultural norms. The fact that a person has been incarcerated for a crime, thus having "paid one's debt to society," invokes an immediate negative response from other people (Kuehn 1971). Ex-convicts have difficulty gaining meaningful employment and their record appears on their credit reports, which makes it difficult to buy a house, secure a loan, or get a job.

Consider the following true event. A highly qualified candidate for a professor's position at an urban community college was unanimously recommended for the job by the department's personnel committee. On his application, the candidate wrote that nine years and six months prior to applying for this position he had been convicted of minor marijuana charges that resulted in probation. Since completing his sentence, he had finished college and went on to earn a doctorate degree. He had no further law violations. The president of the college reacted angrily to the committee's recommendation and called the attorney for the state university system that the college belonged to. The attorney said that the university system, with support of the law, could refuse to hire anyone within ten years of a felony conviction. Armed with this information, the president overruled the professors' recommendation and the candidate was rejected.

Former psychiatric patients meet similar discrimination. Stereotyped as dangerously "sick" and unstable, people who have been hospitalized for psychiatric reasons are often rebuffed in interpersonal relationships and in hiring. The story of former Senator Thomas Eagleton highlights how one's minority status becomes one's master-status. In 1972, the senator from Missouri had been nominated by the Democratic Party for the office of vice-president of the United States. Shortly thereafter, it was revealed that, a number of years earlier, Eagleton had been hospitalized for depression. The press and the public outcry was vociferous. Eagleton became feared, for if George McGovern, the party's presidential candidate, had been elected and died in office, then the country would be in the hands of a "mad man." The pressure was so strong that Eagleton resigned the nomination and was replaced by Sargeant Shriver, a respected member of the Kennedy family.

Consumers of psychiatric and social services are no longer stigmatized as they once were. Nevertheless stereotyping them as failed or broken persons continues.

As I noted in Chapter 1, the broad sociocultural environment most closely resembles the culture of the dominant group. The majority group not only controls society's institutions, but also successfully enforces stereotypes and stigmas. When a particular social group has power over the material culture (e.g., production and distribution of wealth) and the nonmaterial culture (e.g., ideas, values, and laws), and thus reaps the greatest benefits, what relationship does it have with the other communities in the same society? How do groups of unequal power relate to each other and what are the consequences? Power differentials among communities in the social environment are among the most salient factors in understanding human development and are a critical antecedent for charting an individual's course through life.

POLICIES

Once a minority group is created, what is the relationship between it and the dominant group? What policies govern those relations? There are four types of policies that dominant groups in America and Canada have used in regard to minority groups: annihilation, removal, separation, and assimilation.

Annihilation

The policy of *annihilation* directs and justifies the extermination of a social group. The attempts at "ethnic cleansing" in Bosnia–Herzegovenia exemplify the intolerance and hatred communities can have for one another. North American history reveals an extermination policy aimed at Native Americans: Anglos desired Indian lands and embarked on a program that would eventually destroy virtually all vestiges of Indian life. The extermination policy devastated Native Americans socially, economically, and culturally.

Many Holocaust survivors migrated to North America following their liberation at the end of the war with Germany in 1945. The experiences of survivors and their children have provided an opportunity to learn the direct psychosocial effects of extermination policies. Many European Jews who survived massive traumas developed symptoms typical of chronic depression, suffering emotional and cognitive impairment. Problems that manifested among victims included: undifferentiated emotions, difficulty expressing emotions, diminished emotional involvement with others, a lowered capacity for empathy, trust, and love, cognitive em-

---

EXPLORING THE ISSUES 7.1

Who Are the Skinheads?

Skinheads are perhaps the most violent group of white supremacists. They promote bigotry, hatred, and violence toward minorities, especially African Americans, gays, and Jews. Skinheads have been responsible for many of the worst racial assaults committed in the United States in the last twenty years (Clark 1992).

Skinheads, like other gangs, have a style of dress, body adornment, and behavior that is unique and alluring to prospective recruits. Most skinheads shave their heads, wear rolled-up blue jeans, flight jackets, skinny suspenders called braces, and steel-toed boots, preferably Doc Martens. The laces of the boots are usually white representing "white pride" or red indicating "white power." Yellow bootstrings indicate a hatred of police officers or that the wearer has killed one (Zellner 1995). Tattoos are common. Many tattoos feature eagles and skulls, but truly devoted members tattoo the word "skins" or a swastika on the insides of their lips. The appearance of skinheads is meant to shock, intimidate, and inspire fear. It also serves another purpose as well. Conforming to the "look" provides order and stability, acceptance, and meaning to members' lives.

Skinheads preach a philosophy of "us" against "them." This rhetoric is found in their literature and in the music they listen to. The music, often called "oi," from the Cockney word for "hey," or "white power music," is characterized by a hard-driving rock and roll beat that stirs audiences into wild

frenzies. Many Skins enjoy a dancing style in which they literally slam into each other and knock each other about.

Who are the Skinheads? Most Skinheads are teenagers from broken homes who were also abused as children. Most, but not all, come from working-class families and have limited economic resources available to them. They have had trouble finding meaningful employment and usually have few marketable skills. They are very fatalistic and believe that they have little or no control over their futures.

Youths join a Skinhead organization to regain a sense of attachment with others, express a political philosophy of racial purity, and escape some negative situation or condition. As a family substitute group, Skinheads provide a sense of social belongingness and intimacy to alienated adolescents who are isolated by their families, have difficulty developing relationships, and feel "lost."

Not all Skinheads fit the alienated rebel-without-a-cause image. Hamm's (1993) study of Skinheads learned that many are employed, good workers, responsible students, and have good relationships with their parents. A substantial number do not have tattoos or wear swastikas or other Nazi paraphernalia. Hamm believes that in addition to alienation, there are other forces that attract youths to the Skinhead movement: influential leaders, TV shows that make Skinheads look desirable, free-and-easy alcohol use, and white power rock music.

phasis on mundane and banal details of the things in their lives, loss of interest in formerly pleasurable activities, limited capacity for wish-fulfillment and fantasy, shame, uncontrollable anger, denial, guilt, and repression (Danieli 1988).

Many children of survivors seem to have consciously or unconsciously absorbed their parents' Holocaust trauma into their lives. Parents, attempting to give their children the best, stressed survival to their children and latently transmitted to them the life conditions under which they had survived the war. Many of the children of Holocaust survivors have characteristics similar to the victims themselves: a strong need to "escape" or run from relationships or careers, live in isolation, and either become manipulators or dysfunctionally passive (Danieli 1988).

Forced Resettlement

Involuntary resettlement is a second policy a dominant group can enforce against a weaker community. Use of this policy in the nineteenth century has present-day implications. The governments of the United States and Canada relocated thousands of Natives from their national territories to reservations. Indians were resettled on remote lands that held minimal economic value. The infamous "Trail of Tears" journey of southeastern Indians to geographically foreign land in Oklahoma took the lives of untold numbers of men, women, and children and literally dumped people on a terrain for which their survival skills were not suitably adapted. Other Indians were confined to lands that European Americans did not want in the western part of the continent. In later years, when Anglos coveted tribal resources for their own use, the government and courts upheld numerous land thefts and treaty violations. As you saw in Chapter 4, Native Americans, having been abandoned in remote areas, continue to pay the price of losing American wars of aggression that ended over one hundred years ago.

Many Native Americans and Canadians were awarded their ancestral lands only to be denied their traditional economies. Only recently have U.S. and Canadian courts allowed Native groups in Oregon, Washington, and British Columbia to fish on their rivers without interference and unfair competition from Anglos.

Separation

Separation refers to the policy of segregating communities by residence, workplace, and social functions (Schaefer 1993). In most cases, segregation is imposed by dominant groups on minorities to avoid contact with them. Separation policies such as the legally enforced "separate but equal" laws that regulated the behavior of African Americans until the mid-1960s set rigid boundaries between communities and restricted the interaction between community members and their institutions.

Freeing slaves did not constitutionally require Anglo-dominated institutions to serve African Americans or provide opportunities for them. Later legislation required states, especially in the South, to offer comparable services to African Americans and other minorities, but made no statements regarding the efficacy of those services or the amount state and local governments should spend to develop and maintain them. Throughout America, two societies existed: one for dominant Anglos and a second for racial minorities. Unless you are old enough to have lived in this time, it is hard to imagine adjacent water fountains—one marked "White" and the other marked "Colored." African Americans were required to sit in the back of publicly funded buses and sit in separate waiting rooms at physicians' offices. Most hotels and restaurants that served European Americans refused to serve people of color. Interracial dating and marriage were considered taboo. In fact, many states had miscegenation laws that barred such unions.

The so-called Jim Crow laws saw to it that African American institutions like schools and neighborhoods remained inferior to those of European Americans. Health and social services for people of color never matched those received by the dominant group. Hospitals, for instance, routinely denied African Americans treatment. One famous case was that of well-known singer Bessie Smith, who was refused emergency treatment at a nearby hospital following an accident. She died shortly thereafter while in route to a hospital farther away, one that would treat African Americans. African American professionals were denigrated and publicly ridiculed and lacked the wealth and respect European American professionals enjoyed. Jim Crow segregation functioned to keep dominant group members separated from other "undesirable" communities and further maintained and perpetuated the inequality of those groups. Communities were indeed largely separate, but they were by no means equal.

Now that Jim Crow laws are years behind for the United States, much of contemporary social life remains segregated. Separation continues in voluntary associations such as peer groups, friendships, churches, and marriages. And after over two decades of fair housing legislation, there is little breakdown in the residential segregation of African Americans and Hispanics, regardless of education or income level (Zweigenhaft & Domhoff 1991).

Assimilation

Assimilation, from the Latin word *assimulare,* which means "to make similar," occurs when a minority group adopts society's core culture and abandons its own traditions. When a group assimilates, it begins to resemble the mainstream culture more than its own and gradually disappears as a culturally autonomous community. Encouraging assimilation has been the official American and Canadian policy, more or less, toward minorities in recent decades. Assimilationists, those who want minorities to conform to the norms and values of the core culture, see cultural homogenization as advantageous and desirable for society to reach its goals.

Some assimilation to a common cultural core is necessary for macrolevel social systems and institutions to function smoothly and to keep diverse communities interconnected. Groups need to be in agreement on values basic to the maintenance of social living, agree on an economic system of production and distribution, develop a common body of law, and so forth. The key question eventually arises: At what point should identificational and locational communities maintain their own cultural traditions without intrusion from the dominant culture?

Anglo-conformity has been forced on virtually all groups that have entered the United States. Schools have been reluctant to offer instruction in any language but English. European codes of dress are expected. Non-Judaic-Christian religions are uncomfortably tolerated. Anglo standards of beauty, art, and family life are the standards by which other standards are judged. Non-Anglos are expected to adopt these social criteria and are evaluated by the degree to which they conform to the core.

Despite the dominant group's assimilation policy, there is a great deal of core resistance to assimilation. The dominant group is often unwilling to pay for programs to help minorities survive in the mainstream. Furthermore, the dominant group is reluctant to motivate minorities to be like them by sharing the wealth they control. African Americans, Hispanics, some Asian groups, and Native Americans attend inferior schools, live in segregated neighborhoods, and are victims of discrimination, all of which constitute barriers to assimilation.

Many racial and ethnic minorities resist assimilation as well. Some communities fear that Anglo-conformity foreshadows the death of their traditional culture and heritage. Many minority group leaders are apprehensive that their community's traditions and native skills will be lost. In addition, some communities are concerned about changing social identities. Losing one's ethnic identity decreases one's attachment to the social conventions and the saliency of the community in everyday life. As a consequence, many groups are attempting to rejuvenate ethnic traditions among their members. For example, the University of Oklahoma teaches classes in Cherokee language and African Americans are becoming increasingly interested in African practices and knowledge.

Many groups have reached fairly high levels of assimilation. Japanese Americans and Jews, for instance, marry out of the community at high rates and have embraced Anglo culture. With the election of many African Americans to public office, African Americans are slowly beginning to achieve what Gordon (1964) called civic assimilation, the acquisition of power. The struggle for political parity for all minorities, one should remember, is far from its conclusion. Social injustice for minority communities remains the defining outcome of the interaction between communities and the social environment.

CONCLUSION

Differences in communities imply differences in people's lives, experiences, and opportunities. Membership in communities affects human development and the chances an individual has for physical and mental well-being. Mental health workers, however, have been criticized for their insensitivity to the cultural diversity of communities (Latting & Zundel 1986). Most theories of psychosocial development have been developed by middle-class scholars of European descent and may hold little relevance for minorities. Many of the problems communities and their members face are situational due to racism, sexism, and poverty rather than intrapsychic factors. For members of oppressed communities, intrapersonal problems may well be functions of negative circumstances or life conditions in which the person lives day-to-day. Minority clients may need help from social workers with negotiating the environment rather than attempts to ameliorate personality flaws.

Many minority clients believe that they are controlled by external forces, but take individual

Ethnic groups have distinct cultural patterns. In some cases, an ethnic group holds minority status and may differ significantly from the dominant culture. As this picture of a New York storefront illustrates, numerous ethnicities co-exist in this society, often in stark contrast to one another. Learning the behavioral styles of diverse groups is imperative for social workers who practice in communities different from their own.

responsibility for their problems. In those cases, Sue recommends helping clients understand the political forces that shape their problems and pointing out how a client's behavior may be their way of adapting to a hostile environment (Sue 1981; Latting & Zundel 1986). Social problems such as poverty and discrimination are best addressed at the community level by helping to change the type of transactions members of a community have *en masse* with other, especially dominant, groups. As Harrison says, "Social work is concerned fundamentally about the relation of individuals and their community" (1989: 74). The objective of community social work, therefore, is to find, strengthen, or build the resources and structures that enhance the likelihood of a community reaching its goals and improving the psychosocial functioning of its members. One example of such a successful outcome was discovered by Cotterel (1986), who found that community support for parents, especially single mothers in the paid labor force, improved childrearing practices.

Understanding the dynamics of community systems is important for accessing formal and informal social supports that exist within the community (Harrison 1989). If those supports are not extant, then social workers should facilitate their development. Reliance on intracommunity support structures, such as networks, self-help groups, volunteerism, and collective caring, builds stronger communities and improves individuals' sense of acceptance and belongingness. In turn, secure bonds are formed and ego functions are strengthened.

CASE STUDY REVIEW QUESTIONS

Refer to the case of William, Janice, and Anna presented at the beginning of the chapter. Given what you have learned in this chapter, respond to the following questions.

1. When William spoke of a "sense of community," what did he mean? What do you think he was looking for by moving back to the Northside?

2. What advantages did the family gain by living within the African American community? How does the concept of social identity relate to the members of the family?
3. The family is clearly successful economically, yet they continue to be the victims of prejudice and discrimination. Give examples of this and show how prejudice may affect the family's psychosocial functioning.
4. How does community membership shape the family's perceptions, tastes, and expectations? How did these perceptions distinguish the family from their Southside neighbors?
5. In what ways do the concepts of stereotyping and marginality apply to this family?
6. To what degree has the family assimilated into the dominant culture? In what ways has the family not fully assimilated?
7. How were Janice, William, and Anna better integrated into social groups and organizations in the Northside? What benefits does social integration provide them?

KEY TERMS

Annihilation: A policy relating to the treatment of a minority group that directs and justifies the extermination of that group.
Assimilation: The process of adopting society's core culture; when a group assimilates, it begins to resemble the mainstream culture more than its own and gradually disappears as a culturally autonomous community.
Authoritarian personality: A rigid personality style in which a person is gratified by bullying and controlling weaker individuals and groups while strictly conforming to some higher authority.
Communities: Associations of people who are bound together for reasons other than rational contracts and mutual interdependence.
Cultural transmission theory: Social theory of prejudice that suggests that prejudiced attitudes are learned from the traditions of a family or community that exerts pressure on individuals to conform.
Denial: A discriminatory behavior that limits access of certain groups to opportunities, resources, places, and services.

Derogation: A type of discrimination that includes epithets and rhetoric that put people down.

Discrimination: Hostile behavior aimed at maintaining social divisions and community inequality.

Ethnocentrism: The belief that a culture's ways of doings things are right and "natural" and superior to others.

Frustration–aggression theory: A theory of prejudice in which antipathy arises from frustration in failing to reach one's goals.

Gemeinschaft: Represents a communal way of living; a group's sense of unity, strong feelings of social solidarity, and commitment to tradition.

Gesellschaft: Behavior based on rational self-interest, often at the expense of traditional practices; gesellschaft is characterized by impersonal, contractual relationships, and individualism.

Institutional discrimination: Organizationally or community prescribed action that has a negative or differential impact on subordinate group members.

Involuntary resettlement: A social policy that forces minorities to relocate on less valuable lands.

Isolate discrimination: A discriminatory act without the immediate support of organizational or community norms.

Locality communities: A functional spatial unit meeting sustenance needs with a common way of doing things and which shares a collective identity.

Marginality: The status of being between two cultures or communities at the same time.

Mechanical solidarity: Social cohesion based on similarity.

Minority: A group that is dominated by another and experiences unfavorable outcomes because of that domination.

Nonplace communities: Associations due to common interests or identification; also called identificational communities.

Oppression: Wholesale irrational, hostile treatment; oppressed groups are exploited or repressed by a more dominant community in order to maintain the advantages the dominant group enjoys.

Organic solidarity: Social cohesion based on interdependence.

Power theory: A social theory of prejudice that contends that holding negative views of an oppressed group legitimizes unequal treatment.

Prejudice: Hostile attitudes or antipathy toward members of unequally evaluated groups.

Referent Informational Influences: The three-stage process by which attitudinal and behavioral uniformity is achieved among members of large social categories.

Scapegoating: Misplacing blame for one's problems on a weaker individual or group.

Separation: The policy of segregating communities by residence, workplace, and social functions.

Social cohesion: The connectedness and feelings of attachment among people who have similar experiences.

Social identity: That part of an individual's self-concept that derives from one's knowledge of membership in a social group or groups together with the value and emotional significance attached to that membership.

Stereotypes: Exaggerated and oversimplified mental images that support negative beliefs and that strongly influence expectations and behaviors about a group or social category.

Stigma: Any attribute that discredits or disqualifies an individual from full social acceptance; stigmas are powerful negative labels and can radically change a person's self-concept and social identity.

Support system: The formal and informal resources of a group or community to help members reach their goals and meet their needs.

Violence: The most severe form of discrimination; it involves physically harming or endangering a minority person or destroying minority-owned property.

SOCIAL CLASS

OBJECTIVES

After reading this chapter, you should be able to answer the following questions:

1. What are the origins of contemporary social inequality?
2. How is social inequality created and what are the social classes?
3. What are the causes of poverty in America?
4. How does social class affect behavior and influence human development?
5. How is social class relevant for social work practice?

CASE STUDY

Tricia, a thirty-five-year-old housewife, came to a social worker complaining of marital difficulties. She described her marriage as "lackluster," and said that she was very dissatisfied with how her life was going. Tricia and Jonathan, her husband, had been married for six years and had two children, ages two and four.

Tricia's father was an executive in a large corporation. Throughout Tricia's life, he had earned a large salary and gave his family a very comfortable lifestyle. Tricia's mother never worked outside the home, largely because an additional income was not necessary for the family's welfare. Tricia grew up very liberally, in financial terms, and her childhood offered her every opportunity to learn, travel, and enjoy a good life.

Jonathan's family background was quite different from Tricia's. His father worked for a large bakery and delivered bread to supermarkets. His mother worked as a secretary. Both were steady, dependable workers and together their incomes allowed them to own a modest home and provide the necessities for their family.

Jonathan, thirty-three, graduated from high school and had completed one year of study at a community college before going to work full-time. For the last six years, he had worked as an assistant department manager in a large retail store. The job's salary was inadequate to support a family of four. Consequently, Tricia worked part-time to make ends meet. The family had no savings, and lived from check-to-check.

Tricia seemed very frustrated with her husband. She wanted him to move into upper management, but he showed no interest in a promotion. On two occasions, Jonathan's manager asked him to apply for a supervisory position, but he declined. Tricia further complained that her husband was "vulgar." He had poor manners and often spoke inappropriately.

She described Jonathan as rigid with the children. Tricia said that he was less flexible about family rules and authority than she. In addition, Jonathan stereotyped his son and daughter in ways that she disapproved of. He spent a great deal of time with his friends and went hunting and camping at least once a month. Tricia resented these absences and had become increasingly angry.

INTRODUCTION

All societies have mechanisms, called stratification or class systems, for distributing the wealth, resources, and power they produce. Society's resources are not allocated equally because some groups control the places where people work and generate wealth and other groups exist solely on their labor to provide a livelihood. As a result of these different relationships to production, many persons and groups are socially and economically disadvantaged. Inequality affects people's ability to live comfortably and safely and access social supports. Social supports are the resources and processes by which personal and social resources are brought to bear to meet human needs (Lin & Ensel 1989).

Social class differences strongly influence behavior, attitudes, values, and development and constitute one of the most salient divisions in a community. This chapter examines how the class system works, the effects of unequal distribution of wealth, and the relevance of social class to social work practice.

SOCIAL INEQUALITY

The history of social inequality is perhaps as old as human civilization itself. Our prehistoric ancestors who lived in relatively simple hunting and gathering communities shared the food, water, and other resources available to them. However, they likely made distinctions between the young and old and women and men in terms of who received the most of the group's benefits. Though anthropologists speculate on the exact origins of social inequality, the modern stratification system in North America is rooted in medieval Europe and the feudal economic system. Before the

Industrial Revolution, which began in the middle eighteenth century, European society was agricultural and most people fell into two distinct castes, the nobility who owned the land and the peasants who worked it. A small cadre of artisans and craftworkers ranked between them. As is characteristic of a *caste system,* social mobility, moving from one station to another, was not allowed, and people lived their entire lives in the caste in which they were born. Consequently, serfs were bound to the land in a slavery system that lasted several centuries, and did not end until the late 1800s in eastern Europe.

Villages in medieval Europe were organized around the estate and the large house or castle where the "lord of the manor" resided. Serfs could not leave the feudal estate, and their labor, and the fruits of their labor, belonged to the master of the estate. Life for the serfs was dirty, brutal, and void of civil rights. Serfs could sell their children to craftworkers in the villages as apprentices. Serf children were routinely abandoned. Although life for the nobility during the middle ages was harsh by contemporary standards, the aristocracy singularly enjoyed the advantages society offered and lived safer, more comfortable lives, relative to the peasantry.

By the 1600s, following a long period of plague, famine, and war, the feudal system gradually began to disintegrate as European societies emerged from the so-called Dark Ages. During the Middle Ages, the Church was the foundation of European culture. The Church legitimated the rights of the aristocracy to rule without public review, delimited appropriate values and behaviors, and defined "truth." It declared other knowledges as blasphemy or delusion. The relentless horrors of the Plague, which killed about 25 percent of Europe's population, the Church's failed explanation of it, and the complete absence of freedoms for commoners, intellectuals, and skilled workers, led European scholars to question the validity of the Church's dominion over secular matters and its repression of the new knowledge gained from early scientists such as Copernicus, Galileo, and Kepler.

As science opened up a new way of understanding the world, urban technologies and advanced forms of social organization developed, and the climate of European culture evolved into a form recognizable today. Jobs in urban factories attracted rural peasants, who gradually gained some semblance of civil rights, to the cities with the promise of new opportunities and a better life. The newly formed factory-owning class soon commanded great riches that challenged and eventually exceeded that of the landed gentry. The capitalists began to demand a voice in the political apparatus of European states, and the old social order crumbled.

The early years of capitalism failed to change the social and economic conditions of the peasantry. Although they had their "freedom," urban workers did not have the relative comforts that serfdom provided: guaranteed residence, work, and sustenance. Instead, the seventeenth century introduced wage labor, poverty, unemployment, crime, and other urban problems associated with overcrowded conditions and unequal distribution of wealth. Workers had no protections or insurance. When workers were disabled in an industrial accident, which was common, they were simply discharged. Because they had no other sources of income, the disabled lost their housing and the families often fell apart. Wages were low, as capitalists learned early that the shortest path to high profits was to reduce production costs, particularly the cost of labor. The urban poor during these years lived in squalor; low wages, chronic health problems, and violence were commonplace.

As this new urban poverty grew, society's elites, those who controlled the land, the factories, and the other social institutions, began to fear and detest people whom the system was not sufficiently supporting. Poverty was defined as an immoral, sinful lifestyle deliberately chosen by the poor, and many of the poor were sentenced to slave labor in almshouses. New ideologies legitimated oppressive treatment of the poor; some of these philosophies remain influential today in lay thought and public policy. One such philosophy was that of the early Protestant reformer, John

Calvin, whose writings and sermons declared that high social class and wealth were signs of God's grace. God, it was believed, preordained those who were wealthy to enter heaven; those who were poor were not and were destined to live their lives on earth in misery. Calvin contended that owning wealth was God's will and that the accumulation of wealth was rational and honorable. The accompanying comfortable life was the earthly precursor to the heavenly life that would follow.

Herbert Spencer, writing in the 1800s, similarly validated the differences in classes. He believed that differences in wealth were the results of natural selection processes. The rich were the "fittest" and best able to survive the challenges of the world, as proven by their observable success. The poor, on the other hand, were biologically inferior. Reform programs and well-paying employment to benefit the poor were unjustified because

their inherent frailty rendered them unable to utilize any such opportunity. His philosophy, called Social Darwinism, recommended no governmental actions on behalf of society's disenfranchised; any such aid, he believed, would be a wasted effort. (Darwin himself disapproved of Social Darwinism and sought to distance himself from Spencer.)

It was not until Karl Marx began writing in the 1800s that the poverty classes had an advocate among important intellectuals. Marx was among the first scholars to theorize that poverty was not the result of biology or spiritual intrusion, but the consequence of normative human social constructs that allowed certain groups to oppress and exploit others. In capitalism, some people own the means of production—the places where people work and the tools that generate wealth. Because everyone else does not have an ownership relationship to work, they must sell

Western societies demonstrate great gaps in wealth and opportunity. The contrast between comfort and desperation is often ignored.

their labor to the owning, or capitalist, class for whatever wage the owners are willing to pay. In Marx's view, when people lose control of their labor and have little wealth, they feel alienated and detached from social life and other people. The material conditions of life, said Marx, shape the nonmaterial culture, such as ideas, personality, emotions, and so forth.

INEQUALITY TODAY

Inequality is a pervasive condition in American society. In the last decade, changes in public policy have not only assured the persistence of inequality, but have solidified it. Relocating manufacturing facilities outside of the United States, tax advantages for upper income families and corporations, and reductions in government programs for the poor have resulted in two significant trends: (1) while the value of the income of the top fifth of all households increased, (2) the incomes of the lower 20 percent have dropped in value (Jaeger & Greenstein 1989). The poorest 40 percent of the population earn only 13.5 percent of the country's income and hold less than two percent of all wealth. The poorest fifth earn only 3.9 percent of the income. The richest 20 percent of American families receive almost 47 percent of the income and own about 80 percent of the nation's total wealth. The most affluent families, the top .5 percent, control one-third of all assets in America (U.S. Census 1991; Macionis 1993).

These trends have important implications beyond the economic ramifications. Many psychological and social problems are directly related to the dynamic interplay between income and psychosocial development. Wealth in a society is a zero-sum equation; there is a finite amount to go around. As one group takes a larger slice of the pie, one or all of the remaining groups get less. The expansion of the more affluent families' accumulation of wealth has largely come at the expense of the poorest strata. As the poor become more entrenched in poverty, their quality of life diminishes and psychological and social problems harden.

Social class cannot be understood from an individual, psychological perspective. There are no

recognized character or physiological traits that cause poverty. Rather, poverty, as with wealth, is the consequence of dynamic processes of social systems, despite the persistent belief that the poor and working class choose economic and social deprivation.

SOCIAL CLASSES

One question that puzzles sociologists is: What are the social classes in America? *Social classes,* which are categories of people holding similar economic and authority positions, can be conceptualized by two distinctly different theoretical constructs. The first framework, *continuum class theory,* defines social class positions as falling on a continuum based on several variables such as income, occupational prestige, and education. Davis and Moore (1945) theorized that social classes are determined through a meritocratic mechanism in which wealth, prestige, and power are dispersed according to individual talents. According to this conservative view, jobs are rank-ordered by the perceived importance of their contributions to the efforts of groups and society to survive and function smoothly. The important jobs are thought to be the most difficult to perform, and thus require the most gifted persons to fill them. Consequently, these highly prized occupations are well compensated. This theory assumes that people start off equally competing for the "good" jobs. Schooling provides the sifter: those who do well and go the furthest in school are awarded with better paying positions. This perspective is outlined in Figure 8.1.

The conventional terms designating the classes stem from this view: upper-upper, lower upper, upper-middle, middle-middle, lower-middle, and lower.

In the second framework, *categorical class theory,* society is composed of opposing, antagonistic groups competing over resources and opportunities. Rooted in Marxist sociology, this view sees classes as discrete categories that vary in their formal positions of authority over economic and political institutions and resources.

The Bell Curve—Here We Go Again!

In 1994, Richard Herrnstein and Charles Murray published their controversial book, *The Bell Curve*, in which they argued that social class position, crime, and welfare dependency are connected to low IQ, which is genetically based. To Herrnstein and Murray, society is organized as an intellectual hierarchy headed by a "cognitive elite." A "cognitive underclass" falls to the bottom of social strata. People are poor because they inherited inferior genes; therefore, education, affirmative action, and other programs and policies that strive to eliminate poverty are wasted efforts. The inferior genetic makeup of the poor prevents them from taking advantage of opportunities to improve their lot in life.

Their argument is particularly pernicious toward African Americans, who are overrepresented in poverty. *The Bell Curve* argues that, if intelligence is genetic and genes predict social class position, then African Americans must be inferior to Europeans.

Efforts to use science to "prove" the inferiority of Africans hardly began with the publication of *The Bell Curve*. As early as the sixteenth century, English and Dutch travelers and intellectuals hypothesized that Africans were some sort of biological link between humans, meaning Europeans, and apes. This conclusion was deduced simply because Africans lived near apes, had a dark skin hue, and were not Christian. Many serious writers of the day believed that Africans were the product of bizarre bestiality between apes and black women.

William Petty, one of the founders of the Royal Society, wrote in the 1600s that "the Europeans do not onely differ from...Africans in Collour...but also in their Haire...[and] in the shape of their Noses, Lipps, and cheek bones.... They differe also in their Naturall Manners, and in the internall Qualities of their Minds" (Lyons 1975).

By the middle 1700s, the notion of a racial hierarchy was firmly entrenched in European scholarly circles. Classification schemes universally placed Africans at the bottom, and Europeans at the top. In 1758, the Swedish botanist Charles Linnaeus described the Europeans as gentile, inventive, brawny, and governed by customs. Africans were described as phlegmatic, crafty, indolent, negligent, and governed by caprice. These qualities were assumed to be inherent in physiology.

From the late eighteenth century to mid-nineteenth century, many noted scholars of the day tried to show the superiority of Europeans by studying skulls and other anatomical features. Most "studies" concluded that Africans were the lowest form of humans and were akin to high-order apes such as orangutans. Many argued that Africans actually were not fully human and were a separate species. The offspring of mixed parents were thought to be sterile, hence the term *mulatto*, which is derived from the Spanish term for mule.

The research was occasionally underhanded as well as misguided. Samuel George Morton, in the middle 1800s, collected over 1,000 skulls and filled them with lead bb shot to determine cranial capacity. Morton "discovered" that Europeans' crania were larger, which gave them larger brains. He reached this conclusion only after culling out skulls that did not suit his hypotheses (Gould 1978)!

Since then, similar research using so-called objective intelligence tests, among other techniques, has tried to show Africans' inherent inferiority.

Why has this particular line of research persisted for so long? Serious concerns regarding the inferiority of Africans began when Europeans started exploiting African labor and resources. Slavery and oppression were in direct opposition to blossoming ideals of equality and democracy. If scientists could prove that Africans were inferior, and not fully human, then their exploitation was legitimate and no different than the domestication of any other animal. Racist research strives to legitimate an unequal distribution of wealth, power, and opportunity. People and systems that discriminate can do so without guilt or contradiction if they believe that inequality reflects the natural order of genetic differences.

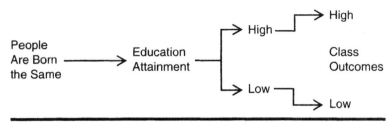

FIGURE 8.1   Continuum Model of Social Class

People with the most control over society's resources reap its rewards and have a higher quality of life. This way of understanding class is based on relationships to authority in the workplace, specifically the degree of control one has over his or her own labor. In this approach, social class is determined by three dimensions: (1) ownership of productive property, (2) authority over the assets of productive organizations and labor, and (3) skill and expertise (Wright & Cho 1992).

According to this theoretical framework, social class is determined in large part by the social class into which one is born, rather than by purely personal qualities. Unlike the Davis and Moore hypothesis, this theory predicts that class of origin is associated with access to quality schools, social supports for educational attainment, and economic opportunities. That most children eventually reproduce the class status of their parents supports this approach, which is diagrammed in Figure 8.2.

Both frameworks are useful in assessing client systems. The continuum model of Davis and Moore points assessments in the direction of resources available to clients. This approach considers the relative weights of several variables, which combined, add to a person's class position. Understanding clients' income and wealth, the objective and subjective aspects of their employment, and their educational attainment contribute to two significant parts of the assessment process: (1) diagnosing human problems in terms of person/environment dynamics and (2) determining the stock of resources that clients bring to a social work intervention.

The categorical approach identifies a person's relationship to authority and working conditions, which have been shown to affect self-esteem, material and psychological well-being, and adaptation to the social environment. Kohn and Schooler's (1983) work discovered that the social dynamics inherent in the work people do are related to virtually all aspects of values and orientation to life. Occupation is central to people's lives and the social experiences of work can facilitate or deter self-determination.

People who are closely supervised tend to be more *other-directed;* that is, they place a greater emphasis on conformity and staying "in line." Following orders becomes a mandate for surviv-

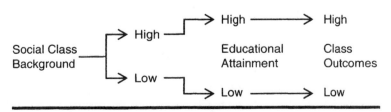

FIGURE 8.2   Categorical Model of Social Class

ing work and keeping jobs. Those without authority realize there is no room for deviating from the demands of the job and the supervisor. As parents, they value conformity for their children, too, knowing strictly that following workplace rules is a necessary adaptation to the work environment.

Persons who work more independently, without close supervision, tend to be more *self-directed* (Kohn & Schooler 1983). Self-directedness affects values very differently. Work that fosters thought and initiative broadens a person's self-confidence. People in these positions feel more in control of the forces that affect their lives and demonstrate less anxiety than people in positions without authority. People who hold formal authority are more trustful of other people and social institutions and are open to innovations. Those without authority are more resistant to change (Kohn & Schooler 1983). As parents, self-directed people pass along the personality orientations best suited for this kind of labor.

What Are the Classes?

For simplicity, the conventional terms designating the classes are the most appropriate for assessing clients. Concepts from both models, however, should be included in an actual assessment.

Upper Class.   This group represents the most wealthy families in American culture. Their wealth stems not from work and salaries, but from unearned income derived from owning controlling interests in the major corporations in the country. Because this group benefits most from the social structure, it tends to be very conservative politically. This class has a strong sense of family history, because their wealth and influential position in society are rooted in previous generations. Compared to the rest of society, the wealthy enjoy high life expectancies, good health, sound mental health, and higher life satisfaction. The upper class is the only class with true boundaries, listing many members in social registries and expecting endogamy, marrying within the group. Members of the upper class take great pride in attending and

successfully completing elite prep schools and see themselves as accomplished persons (Zweigenhaft & Domhoff 1991). Wealth and authority bring them stature in the community and all the trappings of success in a culture that often equates personal success with economic prosperity.

Middle Class.   This class is the largest and most diverse. The upper middle class is made up of professionals and senior managers. The remainder of the middle-class is composed of middle managers, lower ranking professionals, and other traditional white-collar workers. Middle-class jobs are those that typically work with abstractions and symbols. These positions hold various levels of authority and the people in them are order-givers; they plan the work of others. One's social identity, which is understood in terms of the salience of the reference groups people use to define themselves, differs by social class. Middle and upper class persons usually define themselves on the basis of advanced educational and professional credentials—as doctors and lawyers, for example (Zweigenhaft & Domhoff 1991).

The middle class once carried the promise that one's standard of living would steadily improve over time. Now the middle class, once the anchor of American life, is shrinking due to layoffs, the shift to a service economy, and the decline in the value of middle-class incomes, which have not kept pace with the costs of living (Mantsios 1992). As the social and economic conditions of middle America become increasingly more precarious, more middle-class individuals and families, who thought they were inoculated from economically related apprehensions, are experiencing tensions and frustrations that they used to believe were limited to the working class and the poor. Consequently, more middle-class people are presenting with stress-related disorders due to loss of status.

Another source of stress for middle-class families is repeated job relocation, which has emerged as a significant issue for corporate employees, particularly those in high-tech industries. Studies estimate that corporations resettle about 100,000 employees and their families each year; many employees, especially managers and high-tech engineers, can expect transfers every two to three years (Anderson & Stark 1988). People in occupations with high rates of relocation develop a set of stress symptoms called mobility syndrome (Anderson & Stark 1988; Marshall & Cooper 1979). These symptoms include depression, poor health, social isolation, strong dependency on the marital relationship for emotional satisfaction, high risks for alcoholism, pervasive feelings of social anonymity, destructive aggression, marital conflict, and a high divorce rate. When families relocate, they lose important support networks, valued persons, and things such as their house and familiar surroundings. Family roles are disrupted and developmental tasks may be interrupted. For example, a teenager who was working a part-time job may forfeit some autonomy when forced to move to a new city (Anderson & Clark 1988).

Working Class.   The working class includes skilled and unskilled workers whose relationship to authority is that of order-takers. Working-class positions are at the bottom of the employment hierarchy and execute labor rather than plan it. Members of the working class make few decisions affecting their day-to-day work, which is often seasonal and unstable. The working class lives continuously in financial uncertainty, on low incomes, and without job security. Working-class positions are less likely to receive benefits such as health insurance and retirement accounts. Blue-collar jobs often involve routine, monotonous work that requires minimal thinking and creativity. Persons in the working class hold jobs that are low in social prestige, which often leave them feeling as though they have failed for not achieving middle-class success. They are often denigrated as untalented and may assume feelings of personal powerlessness, believing they are "nobody special" (Sennett & Cobb 1973). Ethnic and religious identities may be more important than class to people at the lower levels of the social structure, although they are very conscious of class divisions. Working-class people tend to define themselves first as Italian, Irish, Catholic,

Jewish, or Protestant, "a fact that reflects itself in political attitudes, voting patterns, and marriage patterns" (Zweigenhaft & Domhoff 1991: 168).

Poverty Class.   The poor are those people who are chronically unemployed or acutely underemployed and are unable to enjoy the minimum benefits of society. As shall be seen in the next section, those in poverty suffer the most severe living conditions in society. People in poverty are poorly educated and trained and experience social problems and psychological pathologies at greater rates than the other classes. Poverty is clustered in inner cities and rural areas, especially in the South. In these areas, educational and economic opportunities are insufficient to alleviate poverty.

POVERTY IN AMERICA

Probably no condition in society is more foreign to the American dream than poverty. *Poverty,* according to Townsend (1979, cited in Oyen 1992), is the "lack of material resources of a certain duration and to such an extent that participation in normal activities and possession of amenities and living conditions which are customary or at least widely encouraged or approved in society become impossible or very limited." In its simplest terms, poverty refers to complete economic and social deprivation.

Poverty is characterized by low and usually unstable income, meaningless employment when it's available, poor nutrition, and an often unsafe living environment. Those in poverty are persistently exposed to the worst of society: poor sanitation, less reliable social and medical services, prejudice and discrimination, crime, and violence. Given this plight, people in poverty may experience chronic life stress (Mirowsky & Ross 1989); every day is an exercise in futility, despair, and, in many cases, danger.

Counting the Poor

Defining poverty is not an easy task. Thus it is difficult to determine the number of people who are actually poor in America. Official statistics on poverty are based on *absolute poverty,* a term that defines poverty as those people who fall beneath a fixed income level set by the federal government.

The Social Security Administration sets poverty levels based on its consideration of the minimal amount of income required for subsistence living. This calculation of poverty has several liabilities. It can be argued that access to government programs must be means-tested—there must be some point at which people are qualified for those services and when they are not. Absolute poverty, however, forces services not to consider an individual's or a family's needs, only whether or not the client's income qualifies under government rules. A second problem with the absolute definition is that it does not observe regional differences in cost-of-living. Finally, regardless of the mathematical formulations used to calculate the guidelines, the resulting poverty levels remain subjective and arbitrary. Relative to the quality of life of upper-class families and the wealth that exists in American society, poverty could just as easily be set at $35,000 a year for a family of four.

Perhaps a better way to think about poverty is illustrated by the concept *relative poverty.* This term defines poverty in relation to the average lifestyle in society. If this definition were used, the number of poor people would expand to include those at 101 percent and more of the official poverty levels. Those who support broadening social services to poor people prefer the relative poverty idea. They argue, for example, that there are no significant differences between people in official poverty and those near poverty, yet the income of persons over the official line disqualifies them from services.

Explanations of Poverty

What causes poverty? There are two quite different responses to this question. The first suggests that the poor themselves are responsible for their plight. Though many people experience class mobility, those who change class positions do not make extreme leaps on the economic ladder. Those who are poor are likely to come from poor or nearly poor family backgrounds. Because of the "momentum" of social class throughout a family's generations, many have come to believe that poverty is the consequence of innate biological or cultural inferiority.

A second response blames the organization of social institutions for poverty. Institutions fail to provide certain people and groups adequate opportunities to advance economically and socially by systematically discriminating against their attempts to succeed. People are trapped in poverty because the economic institution, for example, does not provide enough good paying jobs to allow families to live well.

Three approaches to understanding poverty stem from these paradigms: (1) blaming the poor, (2) the culture of poverty, and (3) the structural perspective.

Blaming the Poor. "Blaming the victim" perhaps remains the most accepted explanation of poverty among the general public, though it is unpopular among social workers. In this framework, the line of thinking is relatively simple: the poor are responsible for their poverty. Derived directly from Herbert Spencer, who argued that poverty was inherent in the physiological character of the poor, blaming the poor contends that people are poor because of either bad genes or by bad choices (e.g., laziness, drug addiction, and bad values). Figure 8.3 illustrates the causal pattern in the blaming the poor view.

The theory has limited support within the academic community, however. Psychologists Arthur Jensen (1969) and Richard Herrnstein (1973) have argued that intelligence is inherited. Groups at lower social and economic strata, especially people of African descent, they contend, are intellectually and genetically inferior to those at higher

Personal Characteristics ——————————→ Poverty

FIGURE 8.3 Blaming the Poor

levels. Economic success, therefore, is a function of innate mental ability. Despite flaws in their research techniques and theories and renunciation by most scholars, these writers have contributed to the legitimization of poverty and validated racists who opposed any interference in the "natural" order of the social classes.

Many studies have demonstrated that the poor share essentially the same orientation to life as the middle class. Like the middle class, the poor value cleanliness, family togetherness, hard work, personal integrity, consumerism, and individualism, despite the middle class's criticisms that the poor deliberately reject these core cultural values. As Liebow (1967) points out, poor people place no lower value on a job than does the larger society. In other words, laziness in the ghetto is the same as laziness in suburbia.

Culture of Poverty. Just as wealth is inherited, so is poverty. The phrase *culture of poverty* was coined by anthropologist Oscar Lewis in 1959 and describes how some groups never escape poverty. The assumption of the culture of poverty is that the economic progress of these groups is impeded by a set of dysfunctional and crippling cultural values (Steinberg 1981). The poor, according to this perspective, are excluded from mainstream society and subsequently develop a way of life that is different from the middle class. This culture is designed to adapt to the material and emotional circumstances of long-term material deprivation. The pressure of coping with everyday survival leads to: a present-time orientation; the lack of opportunity; low aspirations; exclusion from the political process; feelings of powerlessness and inferiority; and the inability of men and women to provide adequately for their families (Steinberg 1981).

Poverty is reproduced as children are socialized into this culture, which constitutes the social foundation of the poor's environment. According to this view, poor children and adults would be unprepared to take advantage of economic and educational opportunities should they be presented to them because the poor lack the cultural tools to meet the personal demands of working and managing money. The causal model of the culture of poverty is diagrammed in Figure 8.4.

The culture of poverty perspective is a conservative approach to understanding poverty. It argues that changing the external conditions of life and opening opportunities would have little effect on reducing the self-perpetuating nature of poverty because it is rooted in "deeply ingrained habits" and is "inwardly caused" (Banfield 1974: 143). Reversing cultural patterns, rather than "throwing money" at the poor, is the key to eliminating poverty. Most government and private programs aimed at the poor follow this prescription.

Despite the popularity of this theory, there are several serious criticisms that jeopardize its validity. First, it blames the victim and conceals the social causes of poverty. Programs such as inner city religious programs and the War on Poverty, for example, have failed to eliminate poverty because they focus on value clarification, ideological training, and job skills as the goals for helping people escape poverty. These programs assume that the macro social environment is equally interested in alleviating poverty and that the economic, social, and political systems are prepared to accommodate the needs of the poor. These programs seek to change individuals, not elements of the social structure that create jobs and minimize wage disparity.

A second criticism of the culture of poverty is that those traits thought to be core values of the poverty culture do not constitute a culture (Liebow 1967). This perspective fails to see that the lifestyles of the poor are consequences of the fu-

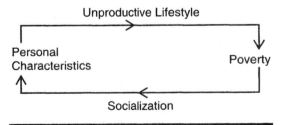

FIGURE 8.4 The Culture of Poverty

tility of deprivation. For example, the poor often exhibit a present-time centeredness: immediate pleasures are often pursued without regard to long-range implications (Steinberg 1981). Most poor people have never experienced anyone in their family escaping poverty. The jobs that are presented to the poor are hard, often dirty, and always unrewarding. The poor may have low aspirations and live for the present because the future promises nothing different from the present. Poor men and women are unable to find jobs that allow them to live according to conventional values.

Structural–Environmental Approach. A third perspective for explaining poverty is the *structural–environmental approach*. Diagrammed in Figure 8.5, this view reverses the causal arrows in the previous two theories.

The structural–environmental theory emphasizes the macro social organizations that impinge economically and politically on individuals, families, and groups. This theory acknowledges that poverty is a preexisting condition into which people are born. Poverty is not created by individual actors, but by social mechanisms that systematically disqualify some status-positions from attaining wealth. Salaries are based on the positions one holds, and positions are differentially ranked. Therefore the same system that creates the wealthy and the middle class also creates the poor.

In this perspective, the economic institution is the primary "cause" of poverty. The economic structure controls the employment and unemployment patterns related to poverty. The stereotype that poor people are unwilling to work is undermined by the fact that most of those in poverty are employed. The contributions of some positions

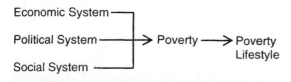

FIGURE 8.5 The Structural–Environmental Approach to Poverty

are deliberately devalued by those who decide how to distribute corporate resources. Many are so poorly paid that they do not allow the worker to live above the poverty line. Government records indicate that 5.6 percent of all workers are within poverty limits. Among workers, low pay is the primary cause of poverty. Research has found that even increasing the amount of hours for which poor workers were paid would remove few of their families from poverty status (Klein & Rones 1989).

The economy further creates poverty by maintaining steady unemployment, what Marx called the industrial reserve army. Capital needs a certain percentage of the labor force unemployed. Corporations can draw upon those not working for temporary or permanent expansion and use unemployment as leverage to keep wages low. Most capitalist societies do not consider work as a right and refuse to pass legislation guaranteeing employment, a policy not considered in the United States since George McGovern's bid for the presidency in 1972. Should holding a job become a civil right, the balance of power would shift dramatically, the wealth and power of the upper classes would decline, and poverty would diminish.

The political institutions reinforce poverty as well. As stated earlier, there has been no federal or state policy to reduce the incidence of poverty since the mid-1960s. Since 1980, the government has supported policies that virtually ensure the continuation of poverty in America. Minimum wage standards and welfare transfers do not have built-in cost-of-living adjustments as do social security benefits. Consequently, over the last two decades the actual value of low-income workers' and welfare recipients' money has declined. The poor have no political advocate inside the decision-making process. Jesse Jackson's two campaigns for the Democratic Party's presidential nomination in 1984 and 1988 have been the only venues for expressing the needs of America's poor since 1964.

The poor nominally participate in the electoral process. Because candidates typically do not address their concerns, the poor have a limited investment in government. When the poor have a political grievance, they usually resort to nonconventional behavior such as demonstrations and riots to express their needs. Other classes exert political influence through more legitimate means. The wealthy lobby, contribute to campaigns, run for office, and are appointed to political positions. Due to their sizes, the middle and working classes control a large number of votes and will use them to influence policies such as taxes and economic development.

Social processes also perpetuate poverty, especially the makeup of the poverty population. Prejudice and discrimination function to deny women and racial and ethnic minorities access to economically secure positions in society. Although women, African Americans, and Hispanics have begun to enter mid-management positions, few climb to senior management ranks. Many lower paying jobs are seemingly designated for minority group members. Women are secretaries and day care workers for example, racial and ethnic minorities are overrepresented in occupations such as food service and janitorial work.

Social services are not equally dispensed either. Welfare programs, for instance, do not allow families to escape poverty. Government benefits lower the poverty rate only 2.5 percent, from 13.5 to 11 (Lamison–White 1992) and provide little incentive to work, given the low wages offered by the economy. Other research and popular media indicate that other services function differently in low income neighborhoods than they do in non-poor areas. Police and fire calls are answered more slowly, banking services are less available, and grocery and retail products cost more in poor areas. Schools in the inner city, where poverty is highly concentrated, are unequally staffed, funded, and equipped. In these schools, curricula have little cultural or social relevance to students. With inadequate facilities and no expectations for doing well, students in low-income schools have high rates of failure and dropping out (Kozol 1991).

The poor's interaction with the criminal justice system is not comparable to that of other social classes. Poor people stay in jail for longer periods of time because they cannot make bail, cannot afford adequate legal defense, are not likely to be judged by a jury of their peers (because the poor rarely serve on juries), receive longer sentences, and are more likely to receive the death penalty (Eitzen 1986).

Poor families and neighborhoods are unable to help themselves pull out of poverty's despair because of the absence of capital and the reluctance of investors to develop poor areas. The loss of well-paying jobs to automation, corporate mergers, and factory relocations has been documented in the scholarly and popular presses. What has often been lost in the sea of economic numbers is the deprivation this has caused. With the loss of industry, the tax base in central cities has been eroded and fewer people are working for higher wages. They now spend less money on consumer goods and pay fewer sales and personal income taxes. Because governmental revenues have declined, the poor and near poor have been hit particularly hard by economic changes. Working for lower wages, or not working at all, prevents families from saving money and investing it.

Because the structural features of society are relatively fixed, poverty is reproduced not through the socialization of young people into a set of dysfunctional values, but through the repeated interactions of social organizations and processes that produce social inequality. Figure 8.6 details the reproduction of poverty. Notice that individual characteristics are presented as outcomes, not causal factors.

Who Is Poor?

There has been no concerted national anti-poverty policy since Lyndon Johnson's Great Society Movement and the War on Poverty programs of the 1960s. The War on Poverty initiated a number of sweeping social changes that resulted in a dramatic decline in poverty rates. In 1959, 22.4 percent of all Americans were under the poverty line. By 1970, that figure had quickly dropped to 12.6 percent as training and employment programs and

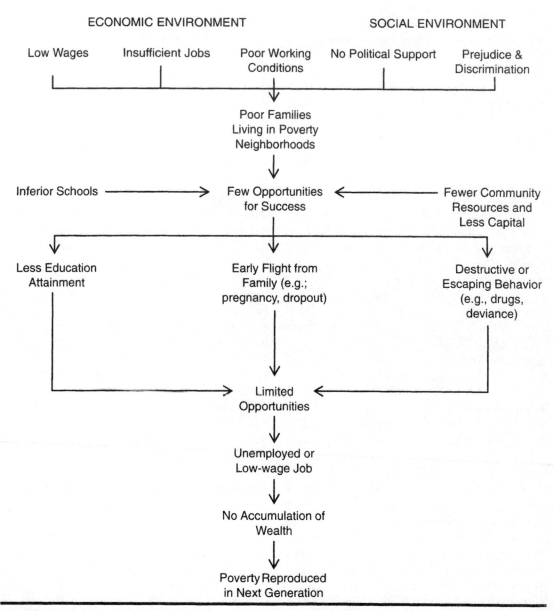

FIGURE 8.6   The Reproduction of Poverty

social services improved the social and psychological conditions for the poor. Since the War on Poverty ended, however, poverty levels have remained somewhat steady and currently stand at 13.5 percent (1990), but were as high as 15.2 percent in 1983 (U.S. Census 1991). Without a speci-fied national policy and the collective will to alter the causes of poverty in America, no significant change has occurred. In fact, in the absence of an anti-poverty agenda, the number of people under the poverty line has increased since 1970 to almost 34 million.

Though all social groups are represented in poverty, some groups are overrepresented; their poverty rates are higher than their percentage of the population as a whole. Poverty, therefore, is concentrated among certain groups in society. Persons who are or who become poor are usually members of groups that are relatively powerless in society such as women, children, ethnic minorities, and the elderly.

Women and Children. Families headed by women, especially women of color, with no husband present, constitute the fastest-growing category below the official poverty line. In 1988, about 17 percent of all households were headed by unmarried women, yet 53 percent of all poor families were headed by women (Lamison–White 1992; Segal 1991). Only 12.7 percent of non-poor families are maintained by a female householder yet a third of female headed households are poor (Lamison–White 1992). This increase in poor, female-headed households is known as the *feminization of poverty.*

The rate of poverty among children is the highest in several decades. Childhood poverty averaged about 25 percent in years immediately preceding the War on Poverty. Following the War on Poverty, the poverty rate for children fell to an average of 15.7 percent during the 1970s. During the 1980s, when federal programs no longer aimed to reduce the incidence of poverty, the poverty rate for children soared to 22 percent in 1983 and averaged 20.6 for that decade (Segal 1991), a trend called the *juvenilization of poverty.* The poverty rate for children remains about one in five and over 40 percent of all persons in poverty are children.

Similar to the total population, children are not equally at risk for poverty. Of children in female-headed households, one in two is in poverty. Furthermore, of children whose parents are themselves children, 70 percent are poor (Children's Defense Fund 1990). Although most poor children are European American, children of color have increasingly high poverty rates in relation to their numbers in the general population. Table 8.1

TABLE 8.1 The Ethnicity of Poor Children

	PERCENT	PROBABILITY
European Americans	5.1	1 in 7
African Americans	44.2	4 in 9
Hispanics	39.7	3 in 8

Sources: Statistical Abstract of the United States (1992) and the Children's Defense Fund (1990).

shows the percentages and probabilities of children being in poverty.

Although the poverty rate for children has been as low as 14.4 percent (in 1973), there has been steady growth in the percentage of children who are poor. The proportion of American children living in poverty grew over 25 percent between 1979 and 1990 and if this trend is sustained, one in four will live in poverty by 2000 (Children's Defense Fund 1990).

The feminization and the juvenilization of poverty are the result of marital disruption and limited economic opportunities for women. Although increases in marital dissolution have paralleled historically the feminization of poverty, only a small percentage of female head-of-household poverty is due in fact to simultaneous changes in household composition (Bane 1986). Weitzman's (1985) study of divorced men and women revealed important economic consequences within a year after the marriage dissolved. The standard of living of divorced women and their children decreased some 73 percent while that of divorced men increased over 40 percent. Because women often have fewer and perhaps outdated marketable job skills and less seniority, they have less earning power than men. Furthermore, numerous studies and government reports indicate the inability and/or unwillingness of noncustodial parents to pay child support following divorce. These studies estimate that about a third pay no support at all and another third do not pay the full amount awarded or are required to pay amounts that are not sufficient to support their children. Child support payments usually are discontinued when the child reaches age eighteen, though the child may continue to be economically dependent as a college student (Grisset & Furr, 1994). Should child support compliance improve, a number of families would rise above the poverty line. Many children, however, who are entitled to support have fathers who are unable to comply with the court order, despite their willingness to do so, because they earn low incomes themselves.

Most female and child poverty is the result of (1) income or job changes due to recessionary layoffs, factory closings, and underemployment that leave single women with insufficient financial resources, and (2) the premarital poverty of many single parents, especially African Americans. The feminization of poverty then is not the province of family breakups, but rather the inability of the economic sector to supply enough well-paying jobs for women to support themselves and their families. Furthermore, women continue to face discrimination in the workplace. Women make about 72 percent of what men are paid and rarely are found in senior positions in corporations. Consequently, basic necessities are often out of reach to single women and their children.

For many single parents, the cost of working is too high, vis-à-vis their earnings from employment. Transportation, day care, clothing, and training price many women out of the job market. The psychological benefits of working are sacrificed in exchange for welfare benefits that offer expensive services and commodities such as housing, health insurance, and day care.

Ethnicity.   Most poor people in America are European Americans, although the public image of the poor is that they are African American or Hispanic. In 1990, 22.3 million European Americans (10.7 percent) were poor. African Americans, who make up approximately 12 percent of the population, had three times the dominant group's rate: 31.9 percent or 9.8 million. Among Hispanics, 28.1 percent were in poverty. The War on Poverty had a significant impact on ethnic groups' poverty status. In 1959, the year preced-

ing the election of John Kennedy and Lyndon Johnson, over 55 percent of African Americans were poor. By 1965 and the initiation of antipoverty programs, that figure dropped to 41.8 percent. The rate of African American poverty has never fallen beneath 30 percent. Hispanic poverty, which was first measured by the United States Census in 1973, has increased from 21.9 percent in that year to 28.1 percent in 1990 (Lamison-White 1992).

Elderly.   Half the nation's poor are either children or over 65. After many years of decline, poverty among the elderly (12.2 percent) is slightly below poverty figures for the population at large. The proliferation of retirement funds, increased services for the aging, and conscious planning by the government have lowered the number of poor elderly people.

Despite this optimistic trend, there is cause for concern. Older African Americans and Latinos remain poor at much higher proportions than European Americans. As Table 8.2 shows, European Americans' rate of absolute poverty is half of elderly Hispanics' and less than a third of African Americans'. Table 8.2 further illustrates how economically fragile the aged are. Many elderly are among the "near poor," those persons just above the poverty threshold (Lamison-White 1990). When government transfer payments are subtracted from the elderly's income, the poverty rate increases almost four-fold (U.S. Census 1991). These statistics indicate that European Americans

TABLE 8.2   The Poor Elderly

	PERCENT	EXCLUDING TRANSFERS
All Groups	11.2	46.4
European Americans	10.1	44.8
African Americans	33.8	65.6
Hispanics	22.5	54.6

Source: U.S. Census, 1991

have more access than African Americans or Hispanics to retirement and pension benefits during their working years. Minorities are more dependent upon the government for maintenance.

LIFE CHANCES

Social class is perhaps the most significant feature of the macro social environment and accounts for wide variations in behavior, attitudes, values, and development. Socioeconomic environments set the boundaries for the ways people live and affect *life chances,* which are the opportunities to experience the good things in life. Those in higher class positions, for example, can acquire the resources necessary to maintain psychological and social well-being. Styles of life, for both rich and poor, are functions of the material realities of the immediate social environment. The section that follows describes several differences in life experiences that are consequences of class. It is important for social work practitioners to understand these differences to improve the quality of assessments and enhance treatment and intervention plans.

Class and Values

The middle and upper classes create very different kinds of people than do the working and poverty classes. Changes in class indicators such as wealth and income, education, occupational prestige, and authority correlate with differences in personal values and behavioral styles. Most of these variations result from strategies people use to adapt and adjust to the amount of material comforts and security they have in their lives.

There is a difference, for example, in the subjective nature of employment. In the higher classes, jobs are regarded more for their intrinsic qualities such as how interesting and challenging they are. The lower the class status, the more jobs are judged on extrinsic criteria such as pay, benefits, and the supervisor (Kohn & Schooler 1983).

People in higher class positions have been shown to demonstrate a greater interest in how and why things happen. They exhibit more self-control, responsibility, and empathy. As class status declines, on the other hand, there is more emphasis on conformity and how one's performance is judged by others. The higher the class position one holds, the greater the self-confidence; as class position decreases, people tend toward *fatalism,* a sense of feeling out of control of one's future (Kohn & Schooler 1983). People who are more economically insecure and have fewer opportunities are more likely to be present-time centered and unable to think of the future as possibly different from the present. As class levels rise, people have more tolerance of controversial behavior such as homosexuality and premarital sex (Macionis 1993).

Jencks and his associates (1979) found that middle-class children rank higher than working-class children on six social-psychological factors. Middle-class children demonstrate more executive ability, emotional control, industriousness, initiative, integrity, and perseverance. These traits, though not a major part of explaining and predicting the social class of a person, contribute to maintaining middle-class status as children reach adulthood.

Class and Health

The relationship between social class and health has a strong positive correlation, the higher the class position the better one's health. Research and health statistics clearly show that wealth and occupations that are less physically demanding are clearly associated with greater physical and mental well-being and extended life expectancy. Not only do health problems become more common and serious as income declines, the poor have not obtained equity in access to health care (Berk, Cunningham, & Beauregard 1991).

Physical Health.   The lack of social resources exerts a strong impact on health (Lin & Ensel 1989). Meager diets and stress due to economic deprivation set up poor and working-class people for greater health problems than people in the middle and upper classes (Foley 1992). One in three low-income people without a high school education, for example, assess their own health as fair or poor, whereas only 3.7 percent of higher income and college-educated people similarly rate their health (Vital & Health Statistics 1990). Low income, less education, and physical labor bring higher risks for both morbidity and mortality. People in lower income groups are more likely to suffer infectious diseases such as pneumonia, influenza, tuberculosis, and AIDS (Vital & Health Statistics 1990).

Poor people are more likely to be admitted to hospitals as well. Low-income persons are about two times more likely to be hospitalized than moderate and high-income people. Similarly, people without a high school diploma are significantly more at risk of a health condition that warrants hospitalization than someone with a high school or college education. It is interesting to note, however, that high income and highly educated people are more likely to see a physician for their maladies than poorly educated persons. Chronic health problems, which the poor are more likely to suffer, make people less ambulatory, which translates into greater limitations of activity (Vital & Health Statistics 1990). Lower income people are more likely than middle and upper income people to miss school and work days due to health problems.

Mortality Rates.   Social class influences one's chance of staying alive (Antonosky 1967; Keil et al. 1992). Socioeconomic status is a key predictor of mortality and varies inversely with family income. People with incomes under $5,000 (1990 dollars) had twice the mortality rate of people with family incomes over $50,000. In addition, cause of death and income are related. Persons in lower income groups are more likely to die from violence, accidents, cancer, diabetes, diseases of the heart, pneumonia and influenza, and chronic obstructive pulmonary disease. For poor European American men, liver disease and cirrhosis, automobile accidents, and suicide were common causes of death. People in professional or technical jobs have the lowest mortality rates of all occupation groups (Rogot et al. 1992). The effects

of income distribution on health are significant, and as Wilkinson (1992) contends, if America dispersed wealth more equitably, as is done in other industrialized countries such as Japan, Sweden, or Norway, then it is possible that life expectancy would increase two years.

Children's Health and Mortality.   Children's health and mortality are also affected negatively by the social class of their families. Nelson's (1992) study of children's death rates compared AFDC eligible children with non-poor children and found that poor children are more likely to die from endogenous causes such as cancer, heart disease, pneumonia, and influenza. Nelson's data showed further that exogenous causes, especially fire and violence, struck poor children more than the non-poor.

Low-income women are at greater risk for poor birth outcomes such as infant mortality, low birth weight babies, and complicated pregnancies and deliveries (Lia-Hoagberg et al. 1990). Low-income and impoverished women have more reproductive difficulties and ill children for several reasons. The main reason may be that as social class position declines, the probability of receiving prenatal health care diminishes. The primary predictor of infant health is adequate prenatal care. Although prenatal care is available to poor women for free or low cost, many do not utilize the service.

Lia-Hoagberg (1990) identified three types of barriers that reduce the likelihood of getting adequate care. Sociodemographic factors comprise the first category of barriers to prenatal health care. Women who are in poverty, have less than a high school education, are unmarried, and are under twenty years of age are less likely to receive adequate care. A second barrier, psychosocial factors such as unplanned pregnancy, general feelings of unhappiness, ambivalent feelings toward the pregnancy, and failure to recognize and confirm the pregnancy, interfere with receiving prenatal care. The third set of barriers are structural factors: the lack of money, insurance, child care, and transportation.

The physical and spatial environment has a strong impact on the future of young people and their ability to improve their life chances. Compare and contrast the environmental qualities of these two schools. In the picture of the rural school, notice how the grass is overgrown, the playground is not fenced despite being close to the road, and the pile of dirt. Several buildings are temporary structures and several classes are taught in the gymnasium. This school, which is a consolidation of three differenct school districts, has not been substantially renovated since the 1930s. In the picture of the more affluent public school, however, the grounds are manicured and the building is newer and better maintained. In front of the school is a relaxing pond and park area. The grounds are spacious, well-protected from traffic, and utilized for education. For example, on one side of the campus the school has established a living tree "museum." In rural areas, people have fewer chances to select the kinds of environments they desire and that can improve opportunities for themselves and their families.

What explains these differences in health? Limited personal and family resources stress health in three ways. First, fewer household resources means discretionary income is not readily available to purchase preventive health care services and supplies, health services when ill, and insurance. Second, low-income families typically can only afford to live in housing that is poorly constructed and maintained. Low-income housing is often inadequately heated or cooled or protected from disease-carrying insects and rodents. Third, inadequate education and a lack of simple, routine medical care ill-equip low-income people to recognize ailments and purchase appropriate care.

Another factor involved in the reduced quality of health and higher death rates among the poor is that the parents and guardians of poor children either postpone seeking medical care until it is too late to benefit from it or have less access to health services (Nelson 1992). Numerous studies point out that the underprivileged, especially those without insurance, are subject to ridicule and demeaning treatment in public health clinics and hospitals. One frightening example of this occurred in a Louisville, Kentucky, charity hospital when a resident physician for "fun" attached a "DNR" ("Do Not Resuscitate") tag to the back of a homeless man whom the physician had treated.

Day-to-day life for low-income families is full of stress, which can have a negative impact on health. Fear of losing a job, living on the edge of financial ruin, unemployment, and feelings of failure when one is unable to buy products and services that are the basic lifestyle accouterments of middle-class life, undermine physical and mental health in families whose financial resources are limited.

Economically deprived families have fewer social supports available to meet health and financial problems. They live in unsanitary, overcrowded conditions, exposing themselves to serious health risks. Doctors are in short supply in poor neighborhoods, so traveling to a clinic adds to the cost of health care. When income and physical conditions of life are improved, health improves.

Alienation

Satisfaction with work and alienation are associated with job status and the degree to which one is supervised. Managers, for example, have higher job satisfaction than laborers and clerks. Satisfaction declines as one moves down the occupational ladder. Managers and professionals are in a better position to avoid the undemocratic nature of work that makes the worklives of many Americans frustrating, stressful, and unrewarding (Schor 1991).

Karl Marx believed that our capacity to be productive is our primary means of creativity. He wrote that people reach their fullest human potential through work, in which they construct something of value from raw materials. Labor, to Marx, is unique to humans and is our way of creating the world in which we live. Because of the social organization of work in industrial, and now postindustrial societies, people become estranged from

their work and consequently from each other and themselves. Marx referred to this sense of detachment as *alienation.*

When people lose control over the forces of their lives, especially productive forces, they begin to feel "alien" in a hostile world. Because workers are subject to manipulation by managers, work in large and impersonal settings, and work at specialized tasks that are typically mundane and boring, they use only a fraction of their talents and have no pride in their own creativity and their final product. Without satisfaction, work becomes meaningless (Eitzen 1986). Marx saw work becoming an enforced rather than a satisfying and creative activity.

Higher up the class hierarchy people are generally more contented and satisfied with their relationships and their lives in general. As income declines, conversely, people feel more discontent and experience more discord in relationships. Low-income people are rejected and even despised by others in society. Being pushed away by society breeds self-defeating self-concepts, anger, and apathy (Eitzen 1986).

Social Class and Self-Esteem

Social classes are further contrasted by differences in self-esteem and feelings of self-worth. Poor and working-class people are more likely to feel inferior and inadequate than middle-class individuals. Middle- and upper-class people are the most successful according to society's standards and therefore have reason to believe in their own superiority. They do well in school and business and communities look up to them for leadership and guidance. The working-class and poor, on the other hand, blame themselves for not succeeding in school and "being at the bottom of society" (Sennett & Cobb 1973: 96). They tend toward fatalism, feeling out of control over what happens to them, whereas the middle- and upper-classes feel in control of their destiny.

These differences are functions of a cultural environment of individualism and social inequality. In a society that places a high social premium on material accumulation and occupational prestige, personal value is often equated with economic success. As a core value of American culture, rugged individualism, the philosophy that everyone is on their own economically, rewards those who are prosperous with the aura of personal superiority. On the other hand, those who are less successful are perceived by society as having more undesirable qualities and characteristics.

Social Class and Gender Roles

Gender roles are expected behaviors identified with sex. Traditional gender role orientations are those in which men and women have clearly different behavioral and emotional scripts: tasks are sexually divided—some are "women's work" and some are men's.

Orientation to gender roles varies by social class. As social class status declines, people hold more traditional expectations of men's and women's roles in friendships, families, public life, and work and professional activities. The poor and working-class see women and men as having distinct differences in character and abilities; men are the legitimate heads of households and women have no business competing with them. Men's work is the primary economic activity and women tend to the children and home. Society is stratified not only by wealth, but by gender, and men enjoy the advantages.

The middle- and upper-classes, however, demonstrate more flexibility. Middle class men are more likely to help with household tasks and childraising, and will attend to the emotional needs of their spouses and children more than working-class men. Men with higher incomes, education, and occupational prestige think of their wives' work as equally important to their own and consider them when making personal and professional decisions. Power is more likely shared in middle-class families.

Traditional gender roles are important for lower-income people whose lives are economically unstable and powerless. As income declines, so do stability and a predictable future. In light of the discord and stress that accompany low incomes (Kessler & Cleary 1980; Mirowsky & Ross 1989), the poor and working class are in need of a social structure that is meaningful to them and provides them a sense of purpose and predictability. Understanding their situation explains why the women's movement never caught on among poor and working-class women. They have always worked, albeit in unrewarding jobs and for low pay. The interest of these women, therefore, is to be liberated *from* work, not liberated *to* work. For the working class, traditional gender roles function to create order in the face of meaningless and powerless work environments, the economic powerlessness of men, and the desires of poor women to enjoy the comforts of middle-class women, who, until recently, married men who could support them (Lengermann & Wallace 1985).

Feminism has been largely a middle-class phenomenon. In the past, women from higher income families often received first-rate educations, only to be stifled afterwards by the expectation that they would and should become housewives. These women were denied access to the professional world of men, and organized a series of social movements, dating back to the 1840s, to break gender barriers. Low-income women were already working in factories, retail outlets, and other places because their husbands' wages were insufficient to make ends meet. The women's movement holds little significance for them.

Traditional gender roles provide social relevance to poor and working-class men and women and help define their places in a world that denies them power, wealth, and status in the community. An orderly gender-based division of labor compensates for the anomie, or normlessness, that low-income life causes, by providing *nomos*, a sense of order and meaningful existence.

CONCLUSION

Social class differences have a number of implications for social work practice. Low and high status clients present with different types of problems and react differently to efforts to change.

Davis and Proctor (1989) have found that the number of problems presented by clients appears not to vary by social class. Types of problems, however, do differ. People in higher economic brackets are more likely to report problems with personality adjustment and personal relationships, while poorer clients present problems related to economic resources and caretaking of family members. Low-income clients and unemployed clients are more likely to present physical, medical, or somatic complaints, whereas higher income people are more likely to present emotional, interpersonal, and personal problems such as tension, anxiety, insecurity, and negative self-image (Davis & Proctor 1989).

Using the structural social work model, these differences are easily explained. The relationship between needs and resources is an important one. As needs become evident, resources necessary to satisfy them must be available. When needs exceed the resources on hand, problems arise. If an individual's or a family's unmet needs are basic to survival, e.g., housing, money, health care, and stability, then the problems that emanate will reflect that condition. If survival needs are assured, as in the case of middle- and upper-class families, then the focus of their lives shifts to emotional gratification in their interpersonal relationships.

While interacting with low-income clients, it is imperative to be attentive to differences in tastes, values, and language. Much of the variation in everyday life is attributable to differences in styles that are reactions and adaptations to unequal resources and living conditions. Therefore reducing all problems to psychological phenomena is unsound practice. Economic stress, alienation, and powerlessness may bring about emotional and behavioral problems.

Working-class individuals may show more resistance to change than middle- and upper-class people. Because of the nature of working-class life, direct concrete interpretations and interventions are of more value than abstract theoretical insight.

CASE STUDY REVIEW QUESTIONS

Now that you have finished reading this chapter, refer back to the case study at the beginning. Using what you have learned, how would you answer the following questions about the case?

1. How might sex roles and social class be connected in this family?
2. From what you know of Jonathan, how would his social class background influence his lack of occupational initiative? In what ways do conformity issues affect Jonathan?
3. Social class most likely influenced Jonathan and Tricia in diverse ways as children. How can you see these differences in them as adults? Do you see self-esteem differences between them. If so, how are they related to social class?

KEY TERMS

Absolute poverty: A way of defining poverty as those people who fall beneath a fixed income level set by the federal government.

Alienation: A sense of detachment.

Caste system: A system of social stratification in which social mobility is not allowed.

Categorical class theory: An approach to social classes that sees society as composed of opposing, antagonistic groups competing over resources and opportunities; classes are discrete categories that vary in their formal positions of control over economic and political institutions and resources.

Continuum class theory: A model of social class that sees classes as positions falling on a continuum based on several variables, such as income, occupational prestige, and education.

Culture of poverty: A theory of poverty that claims that the poor develop their own culture that includes values and norms that hinder their abilities to escape poverty; poverty persists because children are socialized by these values.

Fatalism: A sense of feeling out of control about one's future.

Feminization of poverty: The processes that have resulted in a dramatic increase in poor households headed by women.

Juvenilization of poverty: The processes that have resulted in a rising percentage of children in poverty.

Life chances: The opportunities to experience the good things in life.

Other-directed: Placing a high emphasis on conformity.

Poverty: The lack of material resources, which negatively affects participation in the normal activities and living conditions that are customary or at least widely encouraged in society; social and economic deprivation.

Relative poverty: A means of defining poverty by comparing individuals' and groups' lifestyles to the average lifestyle in society.

Self-directed: The ability to work independently.

Social classes: Categories of people holding similar economic and authority positions.

Structural–environmental theory of poverty: A theory of poverty that claims that poverty is caused by social, economic, and political forces rather than individual or cultural factors.

CHAPTER 9

RACE AND ETHNICITY

OBJECTIVES

After reading this chapter, you will be able to answer the following questions:

1. What do the terms *race* and *ethnicity* mean? How are they relevant to human behavior?
2. What are the several theoretical approaches to analyzing ethnic groups?
3. How have the histories of large ethnic groups influenced present conditions?
4. What are some of the cultural features of the major ethnic groups in America?
5. How are self-esteem, mental health, and physical health affected by ethnicity?
6. What is racial identity? How is it formed?

CASE STUDY

After eighteen months of marriage, Shige (pronounced SHEE-GAY) and Maria began to argue practically daily. Disagreements over minor and trivial differences in opinion or tastes quickly escalated to major arguments. Everything about the other person seemed to spark anger and resentment. When they decided to seek assistance from a social worker, both quietly felt hopeless that their marriage would survive.

Shige is a first generation Japanese American. He came to the United States at age eighteen to study at a university. After graduating, he gained employment and decided to reside in the United States. A short while later, his widowed mother moved to this country to live near her only child. Shige is bilingual and speaks English flawlessly.

Maria is a third generation Mexican American. Her grandparents immigrated to the United States from Mexico shortly before her parents were born. Maria comes from a large family. The members of her family are emotionally close and maintain strong friendship ties with each other. Maria is fluent in both English and Spanish, but usually speaks Spanish with her family.

Shige is a very traditional person. He is shy, quiet, stoic, and dislikes gregarious behavior and loud displays of emotion. He is uncomfortable with public expressions of affection, or any other emotion for that matter. Shige feels a strong sense of duty to his family; he spends one day a week attending to the needs of his mother—mowing her lawn, cleaning, maintaining her household bookkeeping, and so forth. Shige has a firm belief in divisions of labor between men and women. He believes that there are some behaviors and tasks suited for men and others appropriate for women. He is highly protective of Maria.

Maria is a very demonstrative person. She is sociable and unreserved and readily speaks what is on her mind. Expressing emotions comes easily to her and her family. Family affairs are usually open and everyone attends to the needs of others. When her family gets together, there is laughter and conviviality.

After several meetings with the social worker, several themes to their arguments appeared. Shige felt embarrassed when he was with his in-laws. He felt disgust at their communication and affection styles. Maria's family spoke Spanish during get-togethers, further alienating him from the family. A second theme that surfaced was that Maria resented Shige's traditional orientation to sex roles. Though her family was very traditional, Maria saw herself differently in that regard.

Third, Maria resented Shige's attention to his mother. Shige rarely included Maria in his weekly visits, which left Maria feeling that he was ashamed of her and that his mother disapproved of her. He fulfilled his commitment to his mother each week regardless of plans Maria may have made for them.

INTRODUCTION

The environment mediates behavior and development according to individuals' racial and ethnic identity. Ethnic identity usually commands strong feelings of loyalty and allegiance and is a core feature of how people feel about themselves and relate to others.

Racial and ethnic groups influence behavior in two general ways. First, as salient social systems of norms and values, these communities define many of the rules members are expected to follow. They are socialized in an ethnic environment that presents its norms and values as inherently natural; therefore, members see them uncritically as the way life is.

Second, the majority or minority status of the racial or ethnic group a person belongs to affects behavior. Members of dominant ethnic groups have a much different social and psychological experience than members of subordinate ethnic groups, which frequently receive mixed messages from the core culture. On one hand, the predominantly Anglo society expects young minority group members to conform to the majority culture while also saying that they cannot do so because they are, by European American standards, "inferior" (Rappaport 1977). Discrimination, whether covert or overt, intentional or unintentional, sends strong signals to racial and ethnic minorities that their boundaries are limited and constrained. Social work has long intervened on behalf of disenfranchised racial and ethnic groups. Doing so requires an understanding of the unique cultural and social conditions of the groups whom social workers encounter in their professional practice. This chapter explores the relevance of race and ethnicity on human development and behavior.

THE MEANINGS OF RACE AND ETHNICITY

What do the terms *race* and *ethnicity* mean? The answers are not as clear as one might imagine and vary from culture to culture. *Race* is a biological term that refers to immutable genetic marks that are transmitted from one generation to the next. Despite centuries of race research that has strived to create human taxonomies comparable to breeds or subspecies, biologists have been unable to classify variables uniquely characteristic of a so-called racial group. Research that attempts to create pure biological divisions among humans has a hidden agenda: if there are true (and significant) genetic differences in peoples, then variances in behavior must be attributable to those physiological factors. If this were true, these biological, hence natural, strata could be evaluated and ranked from superior to inferior. Racist thinking such as this assumes that Europeans have more wealth and power because they are biologically superior, thus having the wits to dominate other groups much as humans dominate other animals. There is no biological or anthropological data to warrant this conclusion. Brain size, cranial capacity, chromosomal makeup, genetic coding, and cellular construction all indicate that humans are of one species with no subspecies classes. Biological differences that do exist are superficial.

In fact, the traits that are commonly used to distinguish racial groups are not neatly clustered into racial categories. Skin color, the trait used most often, is not an absolute indicator of biological race. There are light-skinned people of African descent and the people of India, Pakistan, and Iran are very dark-skinned, though they are considered Caucasian.

If race has no biological importance in terms of creating taxonomies of the Homo sapiens species, then why is race so important in modern social life? If racial groups do not exist biologically, they certainly exist socially. Van den Berghe's (1967) classic understanding of race is among the best. He suggested that race is a group socially defined on the basis of physical characteristics.

Race, by the way, is not biologically irrelevant. For example, racial groups are unequally susceptible to certain diseases and other health conditions. Many of these conditions, however, may not be attributable to a racial group's physiological makeup, but to its economic and social position vis-à-vis other groups.

The relationship between racial groups is largely antagonistic. European Americans have conquered and exploited groups unlike themselves since the colonists first arrived in the western hemisphere. Because of the history of conflict between racial groups, racial assignments in North America are discrete. Each category is based on national heritage, that is, where your ancestors originated. In Latin America, conversely, the boundaries between racial assignments are less discrete, being based on a continuum of skin color. For example, Puerto Ricans do not relate to the conventional black–white racial dichotomies used on the mainland. Instead racial identity is contextually influenced. Rodriguez and Cordero–Guzman (1992) made the interesting observation that a person traveling from Puerto Rico to Mexico to the United States could easily change "race" with each border crossing, going from white to mulatto (mixed racial heritage) to black. In the United States, white is defined as the absence of nonwhite blood and a person is black if any black blood is present. Categorical racial assignments reflect the need of society to maintain separate and readily identifiable groups so that people will know how to act towards others and what futures they can expect.

Historically, absolute racial separations have played important social functions and laws were in place as recently as the mid-1980s that specified how to determine a person's racial category. The social category you were in spelled out where you went to school, whom you could marry, who deferred when passing on a sidewalk, what kinds of jobs you could hold, and how much money you could make.

One of the most interesting race definition laws was the "One-Sixty-Fourth Law" that stipulated that anyone found to be one-sixty-fourth black, was all black. In this case $1/64 = 1/1$! For a person to be one-sixty-fourth black, he or she must have had one great-great-great-great-grandparent who was of African descent. The law was easily enforced by hospitals because under the law a parent was always either 100 percent white or 100 percent black. By modern standards, laws such as this sound ridiculous. In their time, these laws served as the foundation of social life. Essentially they specified who had access to social benefits, in other words, who had access to European Americans' society.

Legislation and court rulings have stricken down laws that create absolute racial categories. Yet such laws have left a legacy of categorical thinking and social divisions. Racial boundaries, consequently, remain fairly impermeable. This is the social meaning of race.

Ethnicity refers to distinct sociocultural systems. Ethnic groups are set apart from others because of their national heritage or distinctive cultural patterns. Ethnic groups vary in the degree of their distinctiveness. Hispanic groups and Chinese Americans retain much of their traditional culture through language, diet, friendship networks, religion, values, and endogamy. Other groups, such as Italians, Jews, Irish, and Poles, have abandoned much of their homeland culture, but maintain distinguishing cultural practices through associations and organizations. *Ethnic enclaves* in urban areas also perpetuate cultural boundaries (Schaefer 1993).

Ethnicity, like social class, affects a person's living conditions and life experiences. It is a strong predictor of attitudes, beliefs, and behavior. Yet ethnicity, also like class, does not explain these phenomena independently. Gordon (1978) sought to understand the relationship between class and ethnicity by merging the concepts to form a new status he called *ethclass*. This concept considers the influence of both class and ethnicity on behavior. For example, middle-class African Americans have more in common with middle-class Anglos than they do with poor or working-class African Americans. They are politically and economically more conservative than lower-income African Americans, though not quite as conservative as their Anglo counterparts, and engage in family behaviors and achieve educationally similarly to middle-class European Americans. Middle-class African Americans differ from middle-class Anglos because they retain many of their African cultural characteristics and are subject to racial discrimination.

The prejudice and discrimination that non-European racial and ethnic groups face separates them from social classes. Jews, African Americans, Latinos, Asians, and Native Americans, among other groups, encounter stereotyping at best and hostility at worst at all social levels. The debate over which variable, class or ethnicity, has the most impact on a person's behavior and life outcomes is a rich one. The likely conclusion to this argument is that both factors influence behavior, but in different arenas of life.

Ethnic Groups as Cultural Systems

The social work practice research rigorously emphasizes that social workers must learn the culture of their clients. Indeed, working within the cultural system of a client facilitates mutual understanding, keeps the social worker consistent with the client's values, and allows clients to engage the professional without compromising their indigenous culture or feeling uncomfortable. Staying within the parameters of clients' cultural environment builds rapport and trust and enhances the effectiveness of the intervention. Some ethnic groups' norms and values contrast significantly with the dominant culture, while other groups have acculturated to varying degrees. Ethnic communities are cultural systems and a significant segment of the system's constituents shares norms, values, sentiments, and expectations. Social structures, which are developed to meet community-defined needs, are hierarchically arranged to respond to certain needs. Thus roles and statuses emerge within the community in relation to social expectations. Differential rewards are assigned to those statuses (Blackwell 1991). Consequently, there is diversity within the community system, but members are held together by adherence to commonly shared values, experiences, history, and goals.

Not all people from the same ethnic group experience life the same way. Cultural traits typical to groups represent qualities of the group in general; any given individual member of the group may or may not behave according to the cultural expectation. Some members of a racial or ethnic group may not strongly identify with that group or feel personal loyalty or attachment to it. Their personal self-esteem is unrelated or only marginally related to their ethnic ancestry and they feel little or no sense of loss for not having a strong ethnic identification. Their behavior, values, and aspirations are consistent with the dominant culture or some other value system. Predicting individual behavior by a group's profile and judging what a person should be like without first observing the person's behavior, risks stereotyping and obscuring the person's individuality rather than understanding the person as an individual (Berg & Miller 1992). Being aware of clients' ethnicity means (1) to be prepared for a client to show his or her system of meaning and expectations and (2) knowing in advance how to work within that system once it is learned that those values play a central role in the way the client relates to the world.

PERSPECTIVES ON RACIAL AND ETHNIC GROUPS

To understand the sociocultural dynamics of race and ethnicity, one must review several perspectives from the literature. Using Padilla's (1990) typology as shown in Figure 9.1, each theory of ethnicity can be classified according to its level of analysis (culture vs. social structure) and by the target it proposes to change (the individual vs. community).

Padilla's review of theories begins with cultural theories that target the individual for social change (cell A). This theory suggests that the inherent "cultural" characteristics of ethnic groups are the source of their inability to succeed in the host society. A disadvantaged group's cultural orientation is seen as backward and poorly developed when compared to the affluent, dominant core. To change their current condition, a transition to more modern cultural norms and values through acculturation is necessary. Assimilating to the dominant, and supposedly more advanced, core culture is achieved by changing individuals so that they think and act like dominant group members.

Level of Analysis

		Cultural	Community
Target of Change	Individual	A Cultural Theory Individual Level	C Structural Theory Individual Level
	Community	B Cultural Theory Community Level	D Structural Theory Community Level

FIGURE 9.1 Padilla's Typology of Theories of Ethnicity

There are numerous criticisms of this idea. First, Padilla cites research that shows that much of what has been considered the cultural distinctiveness of groups such as Mexican Americans is basically a myth. There are perhaps as many similarities among ethnic groups as differences; this approach does not account for this fact. A second criticism of cultural theories at the individual level is that it fails to incorporate inequality caused by social, political, and economic discrimination and oppression. Social inequality and discrimination are not reversible by simply changing individual members of the ethnic group to conform to the dominant culture.

The view of culture at the community and society level (cell B) emphasizes the relations between, and the integration of, different cultural groups. The assimilation or acculturation of ethnic groups that differ from the dominant culture is not limited to individuals' ability to adjust to the core, as in the first type. Full assimilation assumes complete integration, which Padilla defines as "the degree to which members of a group are distributed across a full range of associations, institutions, and regions of a society" (1990:264). In other words, assimilation does not occur by individuals independently acculturating themselves to the main culture, but by ethnic groups *in toto* effecting change. The main criticism of this approach is that it presupposes that ethnic groups face similar social and economic opportunities in the dominant society. A sociohistorical perspective demonstrates that social relations circumvent assimilation, thus perpetuating ethnic divisions and the continuity of a group's cultural heritage.

The third approach to ethnicity is structural theories, individual level (cell C). This theory type suggests that the problems of ethnic groups originate from the organization of economic, social, and political structures that fail to meet the unique needs of ethnic groups. The oppressive nature of these systems does not prepare members of ethnic groups with the skills necessary to function successfully in society. The target of change is the individual and the goal is to help individuals improve education achievement and work skills.

Research shows that education and English proficiency are significant factors in the occupational attainment of Latino men. If education levels were raised three grades for Latinos, their average wage would increase 16 percent (Padilla 1990).

The primary criticism of this approach is that it argues that the social structures and individual members of disenfranchised groups are ultimately responsible for their own inequality. Therefore the structures of the larger social context are still avoided as targets of change.

The fourth theory type Padilla discusses is the structural theory, community level (cell D), which is predominant among social scientists. These theories hold that race and ethnic relations reflect historical patterns of domination and subordination, and oppression and resistance. Ethnic inequality is the consequence of structural, institutional discrimination that channels ethnic workers into low-paying jobs and denies them equal social justice. These conditions place members of ethnic groups in desperate social situations and push them into high-risk, destructive behavior. By focusing on the unevenness of labor markets and the interplay of social and economic factors, these theories have successfully linked labor-repressive techniques used by those who control economic systems with long-term racial inequality. The goal for change in this approach is to alter structured community and societal mechanisms that result in inequality in accessing social resources and benefits.

PROMINENT RACIAL AND ETHNIC GROUPS

The following discussion looks at several racial and ethnic groups prominent in American and Canadian social life that are frequent consumers of social work services. A brief history of each group and the qualities that generally represent the cultural core of the group are discussed. Later chapters will discuss specific differences in family systems.

Native Americans

Some 30,000 years ago, the ancestors of Native Americans and Canadians crossed the Bering Sea on a now submerged land bridge that connected eastern Asia to Alaska. These peoples evolved into hundreds of distinct ethnic groups spread throughout North and South America. Pre-Columbian native cultures built great cities in Mexico and Central America, complex economic systems in New Mexico and Arizona, devised complex mathematical formulations, advanced agriculture, engineered buildings that rivaled those in Europe in architectural accomplishment, made war and peace, engaged in trade, and developed artistic and literary traditions.

Columbus's "discovery" disrupted the course of social evolution of native peoples. Contact with European nationalities and later the Euro-Americans brought immediate suffering, destruction, and chaos to native peoples and their ways of life. No native nation escaped the European onslaught that would cause the total native population to dwindle to a mere quarter of a million people by the early 1900s.

The only historically accurate way to understand the treatment of Native Americans today is to see them as defeated nations whom the society continues to punish for being here first. The Indian Wars, glorified by Hollywood and folklore, were actually American wars of aggression. European Americans believed in a "manifest destiny," which held that God ordained them to occupy and control the lands that would become the United States. Unfortunately, sovereign nations, i.e., the Indian tribes, held those territories.

After conceding defeat, many native ethnic groups were resettled onto lands set aside for Indian habitat. These lands were not selected with the goal of enabling tribes to thrive economically. Instead they were often isolated, desolate, nonarable lands European Americans then judged to have little or no economic value. The geographic isolation of Native Americans on reservations partly explains their present extremely high rates of poverty. Because many Indian enclaves are distant from transportation lines, markets, and raw materials, the costs of economic activity on reservations are high. Thus corporations are hesitant to develop industries on or near reservations. Most

Native American poverty, however, is directly attributed to historic discrimination and the lack of a national will to incorporate Native Americans into the economic mainstream.

Many Indian ethnicities, such as the Pueblo communities in New Mexico and the tribes in the Pacific northwest, have remained on traditional lands. The government and European American competitors, however, have not allowed them to carry on their traditional economic activities.

Until very recently, the United States government had broken virtually every treaty it had signed with an Indian nation. Even as late as the 1990s, many corporate leaders were urging Congress and the courts to declare Indian reservations unconstitutional for the purpose of exploiting grazing lands and newly discovered mineral deposits. Nonetheless, the legal tide is now turning in favor of Native Americans. Courts have awarded tribal governments large settlements as compensation for lands stolen with federal support. Congress now allows tribal governments considerable political and judicial autonomy.

One example of this autonomy is the Indian Child Welfare Act of 1978. Prior to this bill, child protective services removed Native American children in need of foster care from the reservation and placed them with European American families or institutions. Native communities complained that this practice further injured the Native American children by subjecting them to a foreign culture at a time of tremendous individual trauma. The passage of this act gives Native American foster homes and shelters priority in receiving an Indian child.

Anglos' perceptions of Native Americans, according to Mary Anne Broken Nose (1992), is often characterized by three factors: (1) the tendency to generalize the behaviors and values of one tribe to all Indians; (2) perceiving Indians in terms of deficiencies according to European American ideals rather than in terms of their own traditional culture; and (3) using moral evaluations as descriptions of Native Americans. She points out that the media coverage of Native Americans is usually negative. The media focus on alcoholism, poverty, and family violence to the degree that the public believes that Native American problems are insurmountable and beyond hope. Many non-Indians conclude that Native Americans' situation is desperate. Broken Nose argues that other people rarely hear of the strengths of Indian families, deeply felt spiritual beliefs, and positive values of generosity and courage.

Native American lifestyles perhaps have the least European influence outside recent Asian immigrants. The cultural systems of American Indians, therefore, often include values and behaviors that contradict core cultural expectations and seem foreign to other Americans. Indian nations are distinctive cultures, differing not only from European America, but from each other as well. There is not a single Indian culture. Nevertheless, Lazarus (1982) found similarities in value orientations among Native American peoples. The following list describes many of these values.

1. The community affords children the same degree of respect as adults and considers them important members of the family. Children are not accustomed to an adult-imposed structure such as that found in a school setting. Talking loudly to and reprimanding children are considered ill-mannered.

2. Native Americans place great importance on the values of cooperation and harmony with the natural environment. One accepts the natural world and does not try to change it.

3. The community judges individuals by their relative contribution to the group. Generosity and sharing are prominent attributes.

4. Competition is encouraged, but is only acceptable as long as one does not try to hurt anyone. Cooperation is highly prized.

5. Native Americans desire to live an unhurried lifestyle and work to meet present needs.

6. Native Americans venerate and respect the elderly as wise and knowledgeable.

7. There is a premium placed on the traditional lifestyle. Elders and schools teach children ancient legends, knowledge, and rituals specific to their nation. Fostering an ethnic identity in chil-

dren is important to parents and community leaders (Lazarus 1982: 84).

Native Americans highly value cooperation and harmony. Being first, the best, and the smartest are important individual qualities, but they are evaluated in terms of how they benefit the group to which one belongs. To stand out and speak of one's accomplishments separate from the group is considered poor manners. Children may feel uncomfortable if singled out and labeled as better than others.

Native Americans often interpret eye contact as disrespectful. A younger person demonstrates respect to elders by avoiding eye contact. Thus, Native American children might experience discomfort if told to look an older person, especially one in authority, directly in the eye (Mitchum 1989). Many Native American religions teach the interconnectedness of the material and spiritual worlds. Beliefs in spirits and having hallucinations and visions are considered normative experiences. Western-oriented professionals may be quick to label such behavior as delusional or psychotic, yet many Native American cultures revere having such experiences and cherish them as a blessing or message from a supernatural being. Rather than labeling spiritual behavior as deranged or heretical, social work professionals should first be mindful of the cultural context in which the phenomenon occurs. Second, workers should be self-reflective about their own personal religious beliefs. An ethnocentric response typifies the westerner who compares the moral validity of Native American spirituality to Christianity or other spiritual or moral philosophy and practice.

Mary Anne Broken Nose (1992) found that the Lakota people have specific cultural practices designed to "treat" the psychosocial problems that people may develop. These practices may seem foreign to outsiders, but are viewed as culturally normative to the Lakota and are thus successful interventions. For example, the Lakota have cultural rules to handle grieving that differ from European-influenced standards. Ventilating emotions by a bereaved person is often unacceptable. To

EXPLORING THE ISSUES 9.1 _____

Opposing Value Systems

Values are systematically transmitted through social groups and institutions. Even when social groups mingle, values may differ dramatically because they are promoted by different social systems. Here is how two neighboring value systems compare on ten different concepts.

On Nature
Navajos believe in living harmoniously with nature. Anglos believe in mastering nature.

On Time
Navajos are oriented to the present. Anglos are oriented toward the future.

On Goals
Navajos believe in traditions and being a good person. Anglos believe that one must climb the ladder of success.

On Social Living
Navajos believe in cooperation. Anglos believe in competition.

On the Self
Navajos strive for anonymity. Anglos strive for individuality.

On Relating to Others
Navajos reward submissiveness and politeness. Anglos reward aggression.

On Work
Navajos believe that one works to meet present needs. Anglos believe that one works to get ahead and acquire things.

On Wealth
Navajos share wealth. Saving is stingy and selfish. Anglos save for the future.

On the Pace of Life
Navajos believe that time is always with us and clocks are unnecessary. Anglos are clock watchers and adhere to strict schedules.

On Winning
Navajos prefer to win once with humility and then let others win. Anglos prefer to win all the time and at all costs.

Adapted from: Lazarus (1982: 88); Zintz (1969: 183).

---

grieve before ill people die is believed to hurry death and to talk about persons who have died is viewed as preventing their spirits from entering the spirit world. Wakes usually last four days, but grievers do not talk about the dead person, they speak to him or her. Other grieving behavior varies by context. A woman may cut her hair if the dead relative is a mother or grandmother, but not for a father or grandfather. A man may wear an eagle feather for his father-in-law.

Another example of traditional Lakota intervention is the sweat lodge ceremony. The sweat lodge is a domelike structure that is a sacred place of prayer. Lighted fires fill the lodge with steam. Troubled persons, such as a group of adolescents, enter the lodge to speak of their problems. There they find support and guidance. Sometimes participants will receive a spiritual sign. Broken Nose reports many successes for the sweat lodge ceremony in relieving emotional stress and helping individuals find solutions to their problems.

Latinos

As with Native Americans, the Latino community is heterogeneous, composed of groups of diverse historical and national origins. The three largest Hispanic groups, Mexican Americans, Puerto Ricans, and Cuban Americans, have a number of dissimilarities, owing to their own cultural heritage and historical relationship to the United States. Another Hispanic group are those Latinos, most notably the Hispanos of New Mexico, who settled in what would become the United States before Mexico's independence from Spain. These peoples often refer to themselves as Spanish Americans or Latin Americans because their cultural focus has long been towards the United States rather than Mexico or another country. When you add people from Central and South American countries, you can easily see the mistake of assuming a homogeneous Latino culture.

Latinos of all national origins are especially retentive of their culture. Even after three or four generations in the United States, Latinos usually continue to speak Spanish, interact with other Hispanics, retain ethnic loyalties and identities, consume Hispanic music, art, and food, and celebrate the national holidays of their homelands. It is no coincidence that prejudice against Latinos often targets Hispanic culture, rather than assumed inherent biological–racial qualities, which are often stereotyped in other groups.

If Latinos are expected to maintain their traditional culture, does acculturation produce stress? Vigil (1979) researched this question and found that the answer depends on the setting. In barrios, unacculturated Mexican-oriented adolescents enjoy greater psychological well-being than Anglo-oriented Mexican Americans and Chicanos, those who are partly acculturated and thus marginal to both groups. Vigil suggested that the strong family ties of traditional Mexican culture protect youths from stress and provide social integration. In suburban areas, however, unacculturated teens have a more difficult time, whereas acculturated adolescents show less stress and anxiety. Vigil's findings indicate the importance of individuals being in sync with their social environment. When there is greater consonance between individuals and their environments, the greater the likelihood that their well-being will improve.

Mexican Americans. Mexican Americans are the largest Latino group in the United States. With high fertility and immigration rates, it is also among the fastest growing communities.

Mexicans first encountered Anglos in Texas and the Southwest as American expansion pushed forward into Mexican territories. From mid-nineteenth century conflicts, such as the Texas War of Independence and the Mexican–American War, came Anglo stereotypes of Mexicans as lazy, dangerous, unproductive, and inferior. These stereotypes rationalized horrendous discrimination against Mexicans and Mexican Americans in Texas and throughout the American west well into the twentieth century. The stereotypes, of course, held no basis in truth, but were necessary to justify taking Mexicans' lands, disrupting villages and commercial activity, and denying Mexicans access to democratic processes. Anglos denigrated Mexican culture as inferior and quickly assigned Mexican Americans to the roles of second-class citizens.

Mexican Americans continue to suffer from Anglo prejudice and discrimination. Mexican Americans are overrepresented in poverty and mostly live in segregated urban enclaves where they are isolated from Anglo society (Parillo 1994). Many live in substandard, overcrowded housing and survive on minimal incomes. They frequently underachieve in states' education systems, partly because of their high rates of poverty, but also because of education policies embedded in the principles of *cultural imperialism*. Cultural imperialism refers to the practice of forcing Anglo-dominated culture on all citizens, regardless of the community's cultural heritage and practice. Denying Spanish-speaking children access to classes taught in Spanish dooms Latino children to school failures. Poor educational accomplishments increase the likelihood of attaining a low-income job and engaging in high-risk behavior.

Delgado–Gaitan and Truebor (1991) discuss three value and behavioral differences between Mexican Americans and Anglos. First, Mexican Americans consider inappropriate shows of aggression or free public expressions of one's own feelings of pain, anger, jealousy, or love. As Chicanos become more acculturated to Anglo norms, they experience greater pressure to express personal feelings openly and unhindered. These different cultural expectations regarding self-expression place many Mexican Americans in a cultural gap. In one context, the free expression of emotions and ideas is appropriate in the presence of Anglo friends and other Chicanos who are equally acculturated. In another context, older and more traditional Mexicans may interpret such expressions as lack of control or *mala educación*, bad manners.

Another important value that differs from Anglo culture is how displays of wealth are perceived. It is important not to exhibit one's wealth or good fortune in a conspicuous way, especially when extended family members and close friends are poor. Ostentatious behavior demonstrates disloyalty to the family and the community. There is honor in being discrete and humble. To display wealth is to be insensitive to other Mexican Americans and show a lack of hospitality, embarrass the elderly and one's parents, and side with Gringos.

Mexican Americans often identify themselves as members of a family instead of as individuals, which is common among Anglos. Parents occupy places of the highest respect and authority. Social networks are based primarily on kinship or familial ties and provide emotional, social, and economic support. This cultural orientation and structure lead many Mexican Americans to distrust the impersonal character of public institutions. Chicanos often seek out and feel more comfortable in institutions in which they can develop and rely upon personal relationships (Delgado–Gaitan & Truebor 1991).

Moore and Pachon (1985) present other value differences between the two cultures. These authors suggest that Chicanos stress enjoying life and cooperation over competitiveness and that they seek intangible gratification and downplay the intrinsic value of material rewards.

A number of studies suggest that many Mexican Americans are oriented toward the present rather than the future. It is possible that this conclusion is due not so much to cultural differences, but to poverty. For the poor, regardless of ethnicity,

there is little value in planning for the future because they have few resources with which to fulfill those plans. Furthermore, to suggest that Mexican Americans do not plan for the future smacks of prejudicial thinking in which stereotypes, such as irresponsibility, figure. Few Mexican Americans at all income levels are "wholeheartedly in favor of thinking only about the present without worrying about the future" (Moore & Pachon 1985: 128).

Cuban Americans. Cuba's relationship with the United States has similarly been marked by wars, military control, and cultural tensions. Cuba and Puerto Rico became U.S. territories after an American victory in the Spanish–American War in 1898. Four years later, Cuba gained independence, but maintained close, dependent relations with the United States.

Emigration out of Cuba was negligible until the revolution of the late 1950s, which changed the demographic profile of Hispanics in America and the social landscape of south Florida. Since 1959, four waves of immigrants have expanded the Cuban population in the U.S. to over one million by 1990. Cuban Americans now constitute about 5.5 percent of the Latino population in this country.

When the Castro-led revolution seized control of Cuba's institutions, the government began to resocialize the nation to different social priorities and policies, most of which were not to the advantage of wealthier Cubans. The new national agenda threatened the means affluent Cubans used to gain their prosperity and power. Consequently, the first major immigration of Cubans to the United States included many members of the middle and upper classes, people whose wealth and knowledge of social, commercial, and technical systems in effect fueled the society. This immigrant group, which is often referred to as the "displaced bourgeoisie," totaled about 200,000 persons. These early Cuban immigrants settled primarily in the Miami area. Others ventured north to New York City.

After two or three years of virtually no immigration, a second wave of Cubans entered the United States. From 1962 to 1965, about 30,000 people clandestinely left Cuba in unsanctioned flights and boat crossings to Florida. A large portion of this group was educated and skilled persons who chose not to emigrate or were unable to leave in 1959 and 1960.

The third and fourth waves of Cuban immigration brought people to the United States who were quite different from the first two groups. From 1965 to 1973, the Castro government allowed two flights each day to take those who wanted to leave the island for Florida. Only one-sixth of the 250,000 who came in those years were middle class. The remainder were working class or poor. The final wave, the Mariel boatlift, brought over 125,000 Cubans to America within a few months. The Marielitos, as they were known, were mostly working-class persons and poor, unskilled laborers. This was the least educated of the four waves of immigrants and included several thousand convicted criminals, many of whom had committed violent offenses. A high percentage of the Marielitos was black and found themselves marginal people in the United States. They were peripheral to the established Cuban community and were unable to assimilate into Miami's African American community. This group had the most difficulty making the transition to social and economic life in America.

Cuban culture is a rich blend of European and Caribbean lifestyles. Cubans take great pride in their heritage and tend to maintain a strong Cuban identity, having held onto the old culture more than most ethnic groups in the United States. Family cohesion, traditional sex roles, and loyalty to the community are common traits among Cubans. Cuban culture expresses individualism as national and personal pride, which Anglos often misperceive as haughtiness (Parillo 1994). Gomez (1990), however, found that being bicultural has significant benefits for Cuban Americans. Adapting to the majority culture while retaining ethnic culture improves psychological well-being, self-esteem, and job satisfaction. Studies of other ethnic groups show similar results as well.

Cubans are the most successful Latino group in terms of income, accumulation of wealth, and educational accomplishment. Primarily three factors led to economic success for Cubans: (1) The early arrival of educated technocrats, business leaders, and intellectuals allowed the Cuban community to start businesses, newspapers, political organizations, and commercial networks. Cuban professionals provided legal and health services to the community. (2) The Cuban community had substantial capital to invest in business and other

All ethnic groups have a unique history. This monument in Miami, Florida, represents not only an important event in Cuban history, but the ethnic diversity in American society. For social workers, knowing a group's past helps understand its character, meanings, and relationship to the social world.

endeavors. (3) Assistance from the United States government facilitated the development and expansion of Cuban enterprises and culture.

The Cuban community in Miami is a good example of an ethnic enclave economy. Cubans engage in high rates of entrepreneurial activity and have built a solid economic infrastructure within the community. Cuban-owned businesses dominate the Cuban American market and provide jobs for Cuban workers.

Cubans share certain values that differ from the dominant American culture. Like the dominant culture, Cuban culture stresses hard work. In the mainstream, working hard is a means to material comfort. In this culture, Cubans should pursue work for personal freedom; work is not considered an end in itself. One should enjoy life and work is the way to gain the freedom necessary to do so. The Puritan values of thrift and frugality are not typically shared among Cubans. Cubans are fervent believers in generosity. Sharing good fortune and reaching out to others are important traits. As Parillo notes, being a *tacano,* a cheapskate who does not readily show affection and friendship through kindness and hospitality, is among the worst sins one can commit (Parillo 1994).

Despite the achievements of Cubans, the community faces a number of serious issues. The most notable include poverty, ethnic tension with Anglos and African Americans, and generational cultural continuity. Cuban Americans are overrepresented in poverty, though their poverty rate is considerably lower than other Latino groups. Just over 15 percent of Cubans are poor, which compares favorably to the 26.2 percent of all Latinos. The Cuban rate is four percentage points higher than Anglos'. As a group, Cubans fall behind European Americans in income, number of professionals, and employment rate.

There is considerable ethnic tension in Miami between Anglos, Cubans, and African Americans. Because of the political tensions between the American and Cuban governments, the United States warmly welcomed the arrival of the first Cubans as both a propaganda and humanitarian triumph. The political implications and the fact that Florida had to handle the needs of a quarter million refugees in a short period of time prompted the American government to provide financial and various kinds of support to Cubans to improve their chances of success. The government assistance to Cubans angered African Americans, long overrepresented in poverty in South Florida, who felt ignored by the government. European Americans were similarly angry at the "hand outs" offered to "foreigners." Skilled and unskilled Cubans competed with European Americans and African Americans for jobs and housing. Schools and medical and social services were heavily taxed as they struggled to meet the needs of the growing Cuban community. European Americans blamed Cubans for local problems. The succeeding tension has resulted in a stormy political climate in Miami and Dade County, Florida, and major ethnic rioting.

Within the community there are problems between the generations. Elders want their children and grandchildren to maintain a strong Cuban identity and retain the values and customs of the home culture. Most younger Cuban Americans have never seen Cuba and only know of it vicariously through their family and community. Many young people have assimilated to core Anglo values and norms, which disturbs elder Cubans who dream of returning to a "free" Cuba and restoring a capitalist economy and a government there that is friendly to the United States.

Puerto Ricans. Since the late fifteenth century when Spanish imperialists first reached the island, the history of Puerto Rico has been a lesson in oppression. The Spaniards enslaved the native population to work in mines and the fields. Forced labor, disease, and violent suppression decimated the original inhabitants of Borinquer, the original name of Puerto Rico. Spanish traders then imported African slaves as cheap labor. By 1530, African slaves represented over 50 percent of the Puerto Rican population.

Puerto Rico remained a Spanish colony for some 400 years until Spain ceded the island to the United States when the Spanish–American War ended in 1898. Puerto Ricans today are descendants of this varied ethnic background of Africans, Indians, and Spaniards. Spanish influence integrated all three groups into a unique, vibrant Caribbean culture.

The major difference between the two conquering nations was that the colonial power changed from the culturally harmonious Spaniards to the culturally dissonant Americans. Under American control, Spanish culture suddenly became a liability and an obstacle to modernization (Schaefer 1993). One thing did not change: Puerto Rico continued to be exploited economically.

Although Puerto Rico was subordinate to Spanish rule, the island was economically self-sufficient. The Americans, however, destroyed the traditional economy and converted Puerto Rico to an import-dependent country. Attempts to Americanize Puerto Rico displaced traditional agriculture by establishing large plantations controlled by absentee owners. Cash crops were grown rather than food crops. Eventually Puerto Rican agriculture relied on a single cash crop, sugar, because farming priorities favored profits for American investors. During the 1930s, Congress passed laws limiting the amount of land Puerto Ricans could own (Feagin 1989). These economic changes in the first half of the twentieth century created a large rural poverty class. Unable to survive in the country, many moved to the cities only to find that slums and unemployment awaited them.

In the 1960s, following decades of political reform, a new program, "Operation Bootstrap," sought to improve the economic well-being of Puerto Rico. Operation Bootstrap enticed multinational corporations to the island to supply jobs in exchange for wages lower than they would pay on the mainland. In many ways, urban industry benefited the corporations more than Puerto Ricans. The transition to manufacturing actually increased unemployment and the low wages paid to Puerto Ricans were not sufficient to improve the quality of life significantly.

To relieve the social pressures of high unemployment, hundreds of thousands of Puerto Ricans have migrated to the eastern United States, especially the New York and New Jersey region. Today, Puerto Ricans account for about 12 percent of all Hispanic Americans.

An organized Puerto Rican community developed rather slowly on the mainland because of two-way migration between the island and the mainland. In recent years, a number of community institutions have sprung up to meet the people's needs. Hometown clubs, voluntary associations based on one's place of birth, offered social opportunities by providing a place for weddings, birthdays, communions, and confirmations (Parillo 1994). The neighborhood grocery store, the *bodega,* serves as more than a source of Hispanic food; it is also a gathering place where adults and children meet to visit, exchange news, or gain information on jobs, cars, and other items important for living on the mainland. The community has founded other civic and social organizations that work to enhance the self-esteem of Puerto Rican children, instill community pride, and build community resources (Parillo 1994).

The Puerto Rican family is the cornerstone of national as well as individual identity. Like other Latino groups, Puerto Ricans feel a deep commitment to family responsibility and family members. A century of American influence and industrial poverty, however, has undermined the family structure to a certain degree. Puerto Ricans have the highest proportion of female-headed households among all Latinos. The best explanation of this fact is that a major concentration of Puerto Ricans live in New York City where jobs are scarce and the cost of living is high. Outside the New York metropolitan area, single-parent Puerto Rican families are rare (Moore & Pachon 1985).

Anglo-Americans often regard Puerto Ricans as foreigners, though they are citizens of the United States. As "outsiders," Puerto Ricans are subject to unnecessary stereotyping, discrimination, and poverty. Evidence of stereotyping Puerto Ricans dates back to the 1890s when Anglos first gained military control of the island. Images of Puerto Ricans as lazy, docile, immoral, and criminal persist today, even among teachers, journalists, and other professionals (Feagin 1989). Puerto

Ricans are discriminated against in ways that affect their quality of life. One example is housing. Puerto Ricans, especially in the northeast, are steered away from most housing markets. In this scenario lies a double jeopardy. Since Puerto Ricans are systematically led to housing other groups do not want and are disproportionately poor, they frequently live in substandard, inadequate housing. Because of their poverty, Puerto Ricans devote a higher percentage of their income to paying for that housing.

Education is another area of discrimination. Like other Latino groups, access to Spanish language instruction and bilingual and bicultural teachers and administrators is inadequate. Many screening exams for government jobs and higher education are needlessly available only in English.

Poverty is also associated with high rates of crime for Puerto Ricans, as well as Mexican Americans. Criminal activity is a means to several ends for poor Latinos. Theft, burglary, and other property crimes may be sources of income for economically disenfranchised persons. Crime may provide status and individual enhancement. This route to status is made possible by the absence of legitimate opportunities to gain status. Many Puerto Rican youths are members of violent gangs as well. The minority context of poverty and hopelessness about a better future encourages adolescents to form groups in which they control some portion of their own fate and express their own sense of courage and dignity (Moore & Pachon 1985).

African Americans

African Americans are the only people that immigrated to North America involuntarily. Captured and sold as slaves, Africans and their descendants were brutalized by savage slave traders and masters and held in disgust by the communities where they worked and lived. No slavery system in world history matched the uncompromising and relentless control of its "chattel" as did American bondage. Despite the rhetoric of the United States constitution, which guaranteed rights to all persons, slavery persisted almost 100 years after American independence. African Americans as slaves were seen as "the missing link," the human subspecies that connected humans, meaning Europeans, to lower primates. Therefore enslaving and denying Africans even the most basic human privileges were justified. The rationalization that Africans were not fully human meant that they could not be educated, free to make decisions, did not have "human" emotions, and needed to be controlled. In fact, many slave owners believed they were providing a great cultural justice to African Americans by exposing them to European culture, especially Christianity!

Slavery was about cheap labor. For almost four centuries, slave labor was the most economical mechanism for exploiting the raw materials and developing the agricultural resources of much of the western hemisphere. Slaves were bought and sold, bred, and used as collateral like any other property. Plantation owners broke up slaves' families by selling off relatives. Slave women were sexually exploited by many European Americans and were encouraged to produce many babies, which were capital to the slavers.

The American Civil War, which was fought over the rights of states to make their own decisions about slavery, dissolved the institution of slavery. It did not, however, completely free African Americans from oppression. The second major period of African American history in America, the era of segregation, was characterized by continued efforts on the part of the dominant social structures to exploit African Americans economically and to repress their social and political activities. Numerous state and federal laws and court rulings legitimated the establishment of two "separate but equal" societies. Of course, African American and European American "societies" were not separate and they certainly were not equal. Subjugating African Americans served the interests of European Americans. Keeping an entire class of people, easily defined by ancestry and skin color, poorly educated and economically repressed translated into: (1) economic benefits for business and farm owners, and (2) less competition for working and middle-class European Americans.

In many ways the church is the center of African American life. Long a voice of secular and sacred messages, the church is the focal point of social action and is one of the primary organizers of community resources. Historically the church has been at the forefront of the community's efforts to improve its economic and social welfare and continues to provide many of the community's leaders.

The civil rights movement of the 1950s and 1960s resulted in the termination of Jim Crow segregation and undermined the moral, legal, and social underpinnings of segregation policy. Just as the end of slavery did not result in legal and social equality for African Americans, the outcome of the legal equality gained during the civil rights movement has not been social equality. Compared to European Americans, African Americans continue to fare poorly economically, have higher rates of unemployment, underachieve in school, experience discrimination in the judicial system, have more family disruptions, engage in more high-risk behaviors, and have higher rates of physical and psychiatric illness. Furthermore, the economic future of African Americans is not particularly encouraging.

Segregation and discrimination forced African Americans into ethnic enclaves with rather inflexible boundaries. Even today neighborhoods, churches, and interpersonal relationships remain largely segregated. Informal rules about where European Americans and African Americans "belong" are extant throughout America. Persistent efforts on the part of European Americans to keep the groups apart and to deny African Americans access to the benefits of society has resulted in a unique African American culture. Though similar to European ways of life—speaking English, sharing Christianity, and so forth—African American culture is a mixture of remnants of African ethnic heritage, European influence, and centuries of adapting to poverty and oppression.

Like other groups, there is considerable diversity within the African American community. In spite of this variation, African Americans share or at least are influenced by the following characteristics: fictive kinships, the value of the extended family, expressive language patterns, and the shared experience of societal discrimination (Wilson 1986; Fordham 1988).

Fictive Kinship. *Fictive kinship* refers to a "kinship-like connection between and among persons in a society, not related by blood or marriage, who have maintained essential reciprocal social or economic relationships" (Fordham 1988:56). Among African Americans, the term conveys more than social and economic connections; it also connotes a sense of "brotherhood" and "sisterhood" of all African Americans. As Fordham explains, African Americans have a sense of peoplehood or collective social identity that implies a particular mind-set or worldview of what it means to be African American. The fictive kinship system has two important psychosocial functions for African Americans. First, it facilitates community allegiance and involvement and second it symbolizes African Americans' opposition to a European American social identity. In fact, the system was developed in part as a response to the exclusion and maltreatment of African Americans by Anglo-controlled social structures and the persistent tendency of European Americans to treat African Americans "as an undifferentiated mass of people, indiscriminately ascribing to them certain inherent strengths and weaknesses" (Fordham 1988:57).

As African American children learn the meaning and importance of the fictive kinship system from their elders and peers, they also learn that it places them at odds with dominant cultural institutions and relationships. The collective character of the fictive kinship system conflicts with the individualist orientation of the mainstream culture. What's more, when African American youths become successful in social institutions controlled by European Americans, including schools, they often believe or are pressured to believe that they are betraying the African American community. Many inadvertently ensure their own failure by maximizing their connection to the indigenous culture and resisting assimilation into the school culture. Success in school and employment improves young African Americans' chances of economic self-sufficiency, yet it may lead others who maximize fictive kinship relationships to accuse them of "being white" and aligning with the dominant group. A task for African American youths, therefore, is to reconcile and mediate the cultural forces that tug at them.

Research supports the notion of fictive kinship. Whittler, et al. (1991) found that African Americans with a strong racial identity participate in causes and activities involving their community and have more African American than Anglo associates than African Americans with less identity attachment to the community.

Extended Family. The extended family is very important to African Americans. Numerous studies show that African Americans, more than European Americans, give and receive more assistance from family members. Family support may include cooperative living arrangements, sharing wealth, exchanging services such as day care, and sharing informational and emotional support.

The significance of extended family networks is believed to have its roots in Africa, where in some regions the entire tribe is viewed as family and kinship bonds are valued. A vestige of these roots may be seen today. Many African Americans refer to each other as "brother" and "sister" and may call close family friends "aunt" or "uncle" (Wilson 1986).

Some research contradicts the cultural explanation of family sharing and assistance. Relying on a pragmatic model, Mutran (1985) learned that to a large extent the greater amount of help younger African Americans give older family members, when compared to European Americans, is due to economic necessity. Similarly, assistance from older to younger generations exists largely because of the greater need of younger generations for continued help. Some cultural differences in extended family support between African Americans and European Americans do occur, however. The main difference is the influence of attitudes on helping behavior. Among African Americans, the feeling that the younger generation deserves more respect influences the elderly person's extension of aid. Mutran found no comparable feeling among European Americans. Furthermore, African Americans are more likely to regard the elderly with greater respect.

Expressive Language Patterns. The expressive manner in which many African Americans communicate is believed to be a cultural trait retained from Africa. Contemporary African Americans' communication style is an extension of the eloquent use of speech, descriptions, and the oral traditions common to African cultures. Demonstrative expressions and pronunciations of vowels have been traced to linguistic patterns from Africa as well.

African Americans' language patterns reflect several themes, according to Joseph White in his book *The Psychology of Blacks* (1984). These recurring psychological themes include:

1. Emotional vitality: A sense of aliveness, symbolism, figures of speech, and personification.
2. Realness: Talking openly about pain and distress and seeing reality in concrete terms.
3. Resilience: Laughing in the face of adversity without denying the gravity of an adverse situation.
4. The value of direct experience: Common sense and direct experience often carry more weight than information gained by reading or taking a course.
5. Distrust and deception: Reflected in the language and expressive patterns of blacks as a cultural response to oppression.

Shared Experience of Societal Discrimination. All African Americans, regardless of economic success and occupational status, encounter direct or indirect expressions of prejudice or discrimination. At all levels of the economic spectrum, African Americans must concern themselves with the reality that race is a master-status and one that often elicits emotional responses from others. Many successful African Americans have found that European Americans often do not see them as black, but as "raceless." Indeed, many African Americans who have prospered find themselves developing a raceless identity in order to do well outside the fictive kinship system (Fordham 1988).

Racism remains a deeply entrenched belief in the American psyche. The consequences of both historical and contemporary discrimination persist in virtually all aspects of African American life. Nonetheless, African Americans have developed many positive cultural qualities in order to adapt to oppression: extended family relationships, deeply held spiritual beliefs, fictive kinship ties, and artistic expressions, among many others.

African Americans are as socially and psychologically diverse as any ethnic group. Status within the African American community is based not only on income and occupational prestige, but on one's ability to hold a steady job, provide for one's family, keep alive African American traditions, and remain committed to the community by supporting the church and other African American institutional groups (Kimbrough & Salomone 1993). In important ways, African Americans are no different than any other group in America. Contrary to stereotypic myths, African Americans hold strong intrinsic and extrinsic work values. Work is not only important as a livelihood, but as a way of achieving independence, self-esteem, and autonomy (Thomas & Shields 1987). Like European Americans, most African Americans look toward the future in hopes of attaining a rewarding career and bettering the lives of their children.

Asian Americans

The term *Asian American* is more a misnomer than an accurate descriptor of a social group. At best, *Asian American* is an umbrella term for several groups of Asian descent that represent many different cultures and histories.

Asian Americans are often hailed as a model minority. Media and government reports and social scientists often present an idealistic image of Asian communities as hardworking, law-abiding groups that essentially pose no problem to the society-at-large. Like most stereotypes, this idealization has some basis in truth. Indeed, median family income for Chinese and Japanese is higher than the national level. Filipino family income matches the national median. The incidence of poverty in these groups is the same or lower than the general population as well. Asian Americans attain more education than is average for other

Americans and are underrepresented in admissions to psychiatric hospitals (Crystal 1989).

These statistics and the exemplary public mythological image conceal very real problems within Asian American communities. Reports of the incomes of Asian families, for example, can be misleading. Unlike other American groups, Asian households have more workers per household. Further, Asians are concentrated in states such as California and New York where wages, and the costs of living, are high. Asians appear to be underpaid, given their high levels of education. They earn about 88 percent of what European Americans earn, even at comparable educational levels (Feagin 1989).

A second problem for Asian Americans is that immigrants who were professionally trained and credentialed in their home countries find it difficult to practice or find work within their areas of expertise. Third, low overall poverty rates conceal high rates of impoverishment among the Asian elderly. The incidence of Asian elderly poverty exceeds that of elderly African Americans and Hispanics. Fourth, although studies consistently reveal low admission rates to psychiatric hospitals, these findings need not suggest low rates of mental illness or emotional distress. Sue and McKinney (1980) found a significantly higher proportion of psychotic diagnoses among Asian patients. Moderately disturbed Asians are less likely to seek out formal mental health services because of cultural differences in approaching and treating emotional stress and values that regard exposing family problems to outsiders as shameful and evidence of weakness (Crystal 1989).

A large percentage of Asian Americans are new arrivals. Most have come to escape political persecution or to improve their economic and social standing. Virtually all are optimistic that their lives will be better for having come to America. These idealistic expectations often fail to materialize once the reality of living in a discriminatory and prejudiced society is apparent. Shon and Ja (1982) found that Asian families go through several phases of reaction after moving to the new culture. These reactions may include:

1. Culture shock and surprise at the disparity between what was expected and what actually exists;
2. Disappointment over the prevalent social conditions of America in general and their lives in particular;
3. Grief at separation from and loss of what was left behind;
4. Anger and resentment;
5. Depression over the family situation;
6. Some form of acceptance of their situation; and
7. Mobilization of family resources and energy (118).

Many new immigrants struggle to meet basic survival needs. Adequate housing, health care, and vocational training are among the most pressing needs for the newly arrived. English proficiency deficits hinder employment, which is already impeded by racial prejudice and discrimination.

The differences between Eastern and Western cultures add to problems of immigrants and existing Asian communities. Eastern philosophies acknowledge that individuals are products of their relationships to nature and other people, particularly the family. American mainstream values such as self-sufficiency, self-reliance, and individuality are therefore not highly prized among most traditional cultures (Shon & Ja 1982).

Social workers must adjust their interventions from an individualistic orientation to one where the family is the basic unit of culture and organization. For example, in times of crisis, it is acceptable for Asian Americans to assume a very dependent role in their families. Dependence in Asian communities is closely interwoven with family loyalty and a sense of obligation (Crystal 1989). Westerners, whose cultural focus begets individual autonomy and self-differentiation, may see dependency as continued pathology and attempt to impose values of self-assertion to "correct" the condition.

Communication styles also differ among many Asians. The manner of communication among Asian Americans is often determined by individual characteristics such as age, gender, and marital status. For example, it is unreasonable to expect a younger person to express a negative feeling in front of or toward older persons (Lum 1986; Crystal 1989). Silence and nonverbal communications have great meaning to Asian Americans, but can easily be misunderstood by westerners as incommunicative or resistant. Indirect dialogue is often preferred over direct, confrontational styles of communication.

Chinese Americans.   The first immigrants to arrive in the United States from Asia mostly came from China and Japan. People were recruited for unskilled agricultural and construction work in the American West and Hawaii. Most who emigrated were single males who planned to return after bettering themselves economically (Marger 1994).

European American resentment of Chinese workers resulted in one of the most nefarious movements against an ethnic group in American history. Because the Chinese were perceived to be a labor threat, European Americans drove Chinese workers from their jobs and homes and subjected them to harsh restrictions. To accommodate the fears of European Americans, Congress enacted the only immigration law that singled out a specific group by name. The Chinese Exclusion Act, passed in 1882, banned the entry of Chinese for ten years. In 1907, the prohibition on Chinese immigration became permanent and continued for several decades before it was repealed.

Because of the limitations placed on Chinese Americans' freedoms, they clustered into urban residential ghettos, known as "Chinatowns." In these enclaves, Chinese Americans sought refuge from discrimination, though Chinatowns owe their very existence to social barriers that prevented Chinese from moving about freely. Because the vast majority of early Chinese immigrants were men, the Chinese were slow to coalesce into a viable community. In fact, the population of Chinese Americans did not change appreciably until after World War II, when many Chinese men and women fleeing the Communist revolution entered the United States.

Chinese culture is rooted in the kinship system rather than the individual. Instead of stressing personality development, as individualistic Westerners do, Chinese focus on interpersonal involvement with other people, gods, and objects. Chinese families are stable and accessibility to individual members is predictable and automatic. In contrast in the West, individuals are expected to leave their family of origin to find their own identity in a self-created world where relationships are voluntary and conditional (Tung 1991). To maintain the stability of families and the social order, according to Tung, the Chinese community values attachment to rational control, compromise, patience, and denying one's own feelings to do what is right in a particular situation.

An indication of Chinese Americans' integration into cohesive family life is their relatively low rate of problem drinking (Chi, Lubben, & Kitano 1988). Heavy drinking among Chinese women is rare and among men is the lowest of all Asian groups. Chi and associates found that having a friend who drinks heavily is the main determinant of heavy alcohol consumption. Chinese Americans apparently have fewer such associations, thus they may be less willing to make friends that would provide opportunities to engage in risky behavior. Pressure to conform to community and kinship values supersedes a need to commit highly individualistic and self-indulgent behavior such as heavy drinking.

Despite the glitter of Chinatowns, many Chinese Americans live in poverty (Kitano 1991). The tourist-based ethnic economy of most Chinatowns creates jobs, most of which, however, are low-paying with few benefits. Chinese Americans' economic distribution is bimodal: Many Chinese have highly skilled, well-paying positions, while many others hold poorly paid jobs. Relatively few are in the middle.

Japanese Americans.   Japanese first entered the United States under circumstances similar to the Chinese. Most were unskilled men who came under an agreement for labor. As with the Chinese, European Americans grew intolerant of Japanese workers and pressured governmental leaders to undermine the Japanese population. The Gentleman's Agreement with Japan and the Oriental Exclusion Act of 1924 restricted Japanese immigration to the United States. Other state and federal legislation limited the amount of land Japanese farmers could own and denied them citizenship.

The early Japanese and Chinese experiences in the United States differed in several significant ways. First the Japanese established a more successful community before the Chinese. Because more Japanese women immigrated, Japanese formed families and other social institutions that allowed them a more "normal" lifestyle. Second, the Japanese resisted European Americans more than the Chinese. Groups such as the Japanese American Citizens League were successful in defending the rights of the group. Third, before moving to the cities, Japanese Americans carved an economic niche for themselves in agriculture, unlike the Chinese who were unable to form significant economic enterprises. A final difference between early Japanese and Chinese American history occurred during World War II when thousands of American citizens of Japanese ancestry living on the west coast were incarcerated in concentration camps for fear of sabotage. Their property was seized and their rights were suspended without due process of law. Unlike other Americans, the Japanese had to sign loyalty oaths and had to serve in the military to prove their loyalty. The federal government has repaid Japanese Americans only partial value of the property that was seized, and did not formally apologize to Japanese Americans until the 1980s.

Today Japanese Americans are highly assimilated into the core culture. Their out-group marriage rate is high and they are integrated into the social and political fabric of the mainstream community. Furthermore, Japanese Americans have enjoyed economic success. Prosperity has other payoffs as well. Rates of divorce, crime, delinquency, and mental illness among Japanese Americans are low. The probable explanation of this group's overall well-being lies in several factors: Strong in-group values of unity, respect for authority, politeness, a community orientation, and a focus on high achievement.

Few Japanese Americans have completely rejected their ethnic heritage. Many hold traditional values, such as maintaining a sense of duty to one's family obligation and to the community. Despite high levels of assimilation, outbreaks of Japanese "bashing," such as that which occurred in the early 1990s, indicate anti-Japan sentiments persist among many other Americans and that this group is not fully accepted into the core culture.

Koreans, Indochinese, and Filipinos. A second wave of Asian immigration began in the 1960s. Not only did Chinese make the long trek to America during this time, so did large numbers of Koreans, Indochinese peoples (Cambodians, Laotians, and Vietnamese), and Filipinos. The lure of economic opportunity drew Koreans and Filipinos to the United States, while many Cambodians, Laotians, and Vietnamese fled political persecution and war.

The Korean American population increased from 70,000 in 1970 to about 800,000 by 1990. Most live in California. Korean immigrants differ from other recent Asian immigrants. They tend to be from Korea's middle class and include many college-trained professionals. Moreover, they frequently have come as families and many are Christians (Marger 1994).

Indochinese peoples are often discussed together because they share the experience of the Vietnam War and Communist takeovers in their countries. Though their nations share certain facets in their political histories, these groups are culturally quite different. Southeast Asians arrived in two waves of immigration. The first period, 1965–1969, included mostly college graduates and professionals; the second, 1975–1980, included primarily unskilled, poorly educated, and English-deficient persons. The adjustment to American society has been difficult for the latter group and they remain the most economically depressed Asian American group (Marger 1994).

McQuaide's (1989) study of Southeast Asians provides insights into providing social work services to this population. McQuaide found that Southeast Asians typically rely on their families to solve problems; hence, bringing in a nonfamily member may be seen as family and ancestor betrayal. Emotional problems are often understood as a hereditary trait, punishment for past behaviors of the family, or poor guidance from family leaders. Southeast Asians consider the open expression of emotions in bad taste and believe that self-control and denial are preferential behaviors. Many Southeast Asians believe that discussing traumas and losses, such as the stresses of acculturation, does not improve their situation or relieve emotional distress.

ETHNICITY AND ECONOMIC STATUS

To some extent, the defining criterion of the powerlessness implicit in the definition of "minority" is a group's economic impotence. The history of race and ethnic relations in North America is essentially about western Europeans and their descendants economically exploiting weaker peoples. Native Americans' lands were coveted, then taken by European Americans for economic gain. The labor of Africans and later African Americans was exploited first in slavery and then by laws and customs disqualifying African Americans from social and economic mobility. Japanese and Chinese immigrants first came to American territories and the mainland as cheap labor. For those who stayed in the United States, laws were passed in the early and mid-1900s prohibiting them from citizenship and land ownership, thus limiting many Chinese and Japanese Americans' economic activity to low-wage jobs. Business owners have sought to discourage lawmakers from controlling the entry of Mexicans into the United States because the lower the wages they are paid, the bigger the owners' profits.

With a long legacy of the Anglo-dominated economic system's repression of minority groups' economic development, most racial and ethnic minorities continue to endure financial and occupational hardships, which in turn perpetuate their relative powerlessness, that create barriers for resolving community problems. An economic system usually favors those who exert the most control over that system. The economic environment is hostile to most people of color, who, coincidentally, do not have much voice in economic decision-making, and fails to consider and attend to minorities' material needs.

As I have stated, human communities are never homogeneous populations. Diversity within a community is due in part to the internal economic divisions within it. Class strata account for most of the variations in attitudes, values, and behaviors of an ethnic group's members. The economic resources of client systems are among the most critical for dealing with many kinds of psychosocial problems. European Americans, as a general rule, have more economic assets than people of color, even when compared against minorities of the same occupational and social class category. African Americans enter the middle class with only a fraction of the assets of middle-class European Americans, whose parents and grandparents were middle class (Wilkerson 1992). European Americans have a longer history of accumulating wealth and other kinds of assets, such as home ownership, than minorities, who only recently have been given the opportunity to enter the mainstream labor market. Racial differences in inheritance and other intergenerational transfers account for differences in assets when income is controlled (Blau & Graham 1990). African Americans and other minorities thus have less capital with which to buy a house, finance college for their children, or weather a catastrophe (Wilkerson 1992). In fact, the property and business assets African Americans and other ethnic minorities own have lower market values than property owned by European Americans (Long & Caudill 1992).

SELF-ESTEEM AND RACIAL IDENTITY

The self-esteem of ethnic groups has long been researched by social and behavioral scientists. Early research suggested that individual self-esteem among minority groups would be low because, in making social comparisons with European Americans, racial and ethnic group members would evaluate themselves negatively and internalize the messages of inferiority delivered by a racist society. Methodologically superior studies, however, have since revealed that the self-esteem of African Americans is equal to or even greater than that of European Americans. How is this so?

Research by Krause (1983), Hoelter (1982), and Bowler et al. (1986), among many others, shows that self-esteem for African Americans is not based upon social comparisons and interracial contact with European Americans in schools or other contexts. The major determinants of self-esteem lie in the feedback received from significant others, people defined as being important, and not from the majority of persons with whom a person merely comes in contact (Krause 1983). The *principle of reflected appraisals* suggests that a person's self-esteem is a product of how that person believes others see him or her. For African Americans, the feedback from dominant group members, which may include prejudice and discrimination, has no effect on self-esteem. The reflected appraisals of family and friendship networks and African American institutions such as the church have a much stronger influence on self-esteem (Hughes & Demo 1989). By not comparing themselves with the dominant group, minorities avoid the potentially damaging consequences of failing to compare favorably to relatively objective standards of social success as defined by the dominant group (Hoelter 1982). Since most racial and ethnic minorities are overrepresented in poverty and are underrepresented in positions of authority, to internalize personal meanings from these social realities would be devastating. European Americans, in forming self-esteem, focus more on objective standards of comparison such as income, occupational prestige, and material gain, than racial and ethnic minorities. African Americans, unlike European Americans, maximize the rewards of their interpersonal relations, and the community enhances rather than inhibits its members' self-images.

Racial groups may not contrast significantly in self-esteem, but studies show differences in *personal efficacy* between African Americans and European Americans. Personal efficacy suggests self-evaluations of one's usefulness and utility. Whereas social class does not predict self-esteem for African Americans, class does influence personal efficacy. Hughes and Demo (1989) found that personal efficacy is a product of one's location in the social order. Institutional inequality deprives African Americans of opportunities that would enable them to feel efficacious. "Discrimination in institutional life has largely relegated blacks to subordinate positions and excluded them from positions of power, resources, and contexts of action that afford individuals the best opportunities to experience themselves as powerful and autonomous" (1,530).

Research on minority status and self-esteem has focused primarily on African Americans because of the severity of the discrimination they have endured. But what of other groups? Porter and Washington's extensive literature review (1993) shows that most studies of children found that Asian American and Mexican American children have lower personal self-esteem than do Anglo Americans and African Americans. Bowler and her associates (1986) found that both African Americans and European Americans have higher self-esteem than Filipino, Hispanic, and several Asian groups. This research concluded that the relatively low self-esteem of these groups is a product of their more recent arrival in the United States and having to cope with greater acculturation challenges and threats. Furthermore, these groups may feel more racially self-conscious when in the presence of other ethnic groups because of cultural dissimilarities in language, religion, and national heritage. One example is that several studies have found that Koreans and Japanese Americans have a poor body image compared to African Americans and Anglos. Becoming bicultural, and thus socially competent in the dominant culture, improves psychological adjustment among Asians and Latinos (Porter & Washington 1989).

Forming a stable minority *racial identity* improves self-esteem and overall mental health among racial and ethnic minorities. In a multicultural and discriminatory society, however, developing positive attitudes toward one's own racial or cultural group and his or her place in it requires attaching psychologically to a status that is denigrated by the environment-at-large and then defending oneself against prejudice and hostile treatment.

Cross (1971) developed a cognitive model of how racial identities are formed. According to the model, an individual progresses through a sequence of five stages in developing a positive identity as an African American. In the first stage, *preencounter,* the person has a Euro-American worldview and devalues his or her ascribed race in favor of Anglo culture. Second is the *encounter stage.* It begins when the person experiences some critical incident that challenges the person's existing, pro-Euro-American worldview and related personal identity. The person starts searching for a new identity. The third stage, *immersion–emersion,* is characterized by a deep involvement in African American experiences and culture. European Americans' culture is denigrated and African American culture is idealized. Positive attitudes about being African American have not yet been internalized, but the individual is actively engaged in learning the meaning and value of his or her race and distinct culture. Stage four is the *internalization stage.* The person emerges from stage three to internalize African American identity. The individual feels pride and security in the new identity. At this stage the person has a secure sense of self and a more flexible vision of the world that neither puts down Anglos nor idealizes African Americans. *Internalization–commitment* is the final stage and is similar to the fourth stage except that the person is involved in political action and social movements to ameliorate the problems of racial inequality (Cross 1971; Pyant & Yanico 1991).

Racial identity is not an "all or none" unitary concept. A person might have varying group identity orientations. Racial identity can be broken down into separate parameters, or aspects, of group identity (Hilliard 1985; Thompson 1992). Thompson's research found racial identification to hold different aspects: psychological and cultural. The psychological factor refers to an individual's level of concern for and committedness to African American issues and other African Americans. The second aspect of racial identity is cultural and pertains to a person's awareness of and respect for African American culture. A person's racial identification is important because it affects how an individual perceives the world and experiences reality (Thompson 1992). A weak racial sense of self may negatively affect the ability to feel comfortable with oneself and could lead to social malintegration. Self-doubts about who one is and where one belongs can debilitate social functioning in that the individual's confusion and isolation reduces effective coping and undermines relationships.

In fact, racial and ethnic identity has been shown to affect psychological health. Pyant and Yanico (1991) found that among African American women who were pre-encounter, using Cross's term, and endorsed a pro white/anti-African American attitude, reported more psychological and physical symptoms and lower self-esteem. This finding fits Cross's model of racial identity formation well. Individuals who have not yet come to terms with their racial and ethnic selves may internalize stereotypes of their own racial group. The result is self-alienating. The overwhelming majority of people of color have stable racial identities and do not lament their ethnicity. For those who do question the meaning and saliency of their ethnicity, there are psychological costs to pay.

ETHNICITY AND MENTAL HEALTH

As Cockerham's (1989) literature review shows, research has uncovered no differences in psychological functioning and overall mental health that can be attributed directly to race and ethnicity. When differences between groups do appear, they are caused by factors that are socioeconomic rather than racial. Socioeconomic status interacts with race to increase psychological distress and research points out substantial racial differences in psychiatric disturbances at lower levels of both income and occupational status (Ulbrich et al. 1989).

In general, having a low income subjects people to two kinds of stress: (1) economic problems and (2) greater vulnerability to undesirable life events. These stresses create problems independent of the other as well as being interactive. However, there are key differences in the way these stressors affect racial groups. Working-class and poor African Americans differ from European Americans in the ways they respond to stress. Lower income African Americans are more vulnerable to the impact of undesirable life events, but less vulnerable than European Americans to the effects of economic problems. That low-income African Americans are less vulnerable to economic problems perhaps suggests that they have developed adaptive strategies that enable them to avoid the debilitating impact of the daily strains inherent in poverty. Three mechanisms may help African Americans cope with economic problems. One, African Americans can attribute their life situation to social inequality and discrimination (system blame), rather than personal failure. Two, resources of extended African American family systems are often pooled for mutual assistance. Commodities and services such as money, child care, and emotional support are commonly exchanged and shared (Ulbrich et al. 1989). Finally, African American institutions, most notably the church, play an important role in buffering economic stress. Interestingly, religion itself may not be the factor that reduces the impact of stress. Jones–Webb and associates (1993) found that African Americans who belong to non-Western religious groups are at higher risks of depression than those who belong to traditional African American churches. Therefore the *social* significance of the church must provide the protective function for African Americans.

The hypothesis that states that mental health and socioeconomic status are positively related may not hold true for Hispanics. Contrary to expectations, the personal and community stress associated with high rates of poverty does not translate into more psychological problems for

Chicanos (Cockerham 1989). Immigrants from Mexico to the United States show relatively positive levels of mental health (Burman et al. 1987; Cockerham 1989).

What features of Hispanic communities offset the impact of low income, limited educational opportunities, prejudice, discrimination, and language differences that impede efforts to take advantage of social opportunities? Several facets of Hispanic cultures may reduce poverty-derived anxiety among Latinos. Mirowsky and Ross (1984) found that a community emphasis on strong personal relationships with family and friends helps resolve psychological problems. In comparison to Anglos, who are more alone in confronting emotional and situational distress, Latinos often have extensive informal supportive relationships and an enhanced sense of community solidarity reinforced by nationalism and institutions such as the Catholic Church.

These community inoculations against psychiatric distress may not hold true for Puerto Ricans. Less recent studies suggest that the rates of emotional disorders for Puerto Ricans may in fact be higher than the national average. Some suggest that migration experiences take a higher toll on Puerto Ricans than Chicanos and that the ethnic identity of Puerto Ricans is more fragmented because of the island's commonwealth status. Many who emigrate from the island to the mainland are surprised to be discriminated against and to find that they are not considered "real" Americans by Anglos and other groups.

Few studies have researched the incidence and prevalence of psychiatric disorders among Native Americans. Nevertheless, there is an acute need for mental health services among American Indians. Perhaps the best way at the present to make inferences about Indian mental health is to look at two measurable indicators of psychiatric distress: chemical dependency and suicide. Extremely high rates of alcoholism and fetal alcohol syndrome among Native Americans is well documented. Medical research has dispelled popular myths that the genetic makeup of Indians predisposes them to alcoholism. Native Americans metabolize alcohol no differently than any other group. What they face, however, is a lack of meaningful economic and social opportunities that can provide them purpose and material prosperity. Reservation life may relegate Indians to such an isolated and frustrating existence that other, more functional coping strategies are rendered ineffective. Alcoholism is reported to be two to three times the national average and associated with high rates of accidents and interpersonal violence.

Suicide among Native Americans is also extremely high. For Indians, the suicide rate is 20 percent greater than that of the general population. Among some tribes, the rate is even higher (Cockerham 1989). Most Indian suicide victims are adolescent and young adult males who are perhaps most frustrated at the lack of opportunities and the repression of their ethnic, tribal identity.

For Asian groups, the overall prevalence of psychiatric disorders is low in relation to other racial and ethnic groups. Studies reported by Cockerham indicate that low rates of psychological distress are the result of social environmental factors such as family solidarity, social integration and networks, and a strong community identity. Japanese Americans appear to have especially low rates of psychological problems. This is most likely a consequence of high occupational and educational achievements. Research on the mental health of newly arrived Asians is needed because of their high rates of poverty, their stressful migration history, and the impact of wars in southeast Asian and Korea on psychosocial development.

ETHNICITY AND HEALTH

For the most part, the physical health of racial and ethnic minorities falls well below that of European Americans. Despite their greater needs, the health care system fails to meet the needs of these communities through limited access to services, few minority physicians, and the relative lack of knowledge of the health needs of these communities. This section looks at the relationships between the social status of racial and ethnic communities and health patterns.

Hispanics

The health of Hispanics, Mexican Americans, and Puerto Ricans, particularly, is substantially worse than that of Anglo Americans. Hispanics are clearly disadvantaged in a number of morbidity categories. Mexican Americans acquire diabetes at rates of three to five times the general population. Chicanos have higher probabilities for developing stomach, gall bladder, and cervical cancers. Puerto Ricans have disproportionately high rates of breast and cervical cancers. Mexican American cancer rates for lung, colon, breast, and prostate cancers, however, is only one-half to two-thirds the general population's. Hispanics in general experience high rates of AIDS, hypertension, injuries, violent death, lead poisoning and measles among children, infectious and parasitic disorders, and tuberculosis (Novello et al. 1991; Markides & Coreil 1986).

What explains high health risks for the fastest growing minority in the United States? Except for evidence that suggests that a percentage of Hispanic diabetes cases may be attributed to genetic predisposition to the disease, the high incidence of diabetes is primarily due to dietary factors (Markides & Coreil 1986). Poor nutrition could account for high rates of stomach cancer as well. Cervical cancer, which afflicts Hispanic women at two times the rate incurred by European American women, is perhaps due to early and high fertility (Novello et al. 1991).

The main explanation of the poor health of Hispanics is their relationship to the health care system. Schaefer notes that Hispanics are locked out of the health care system more often than any other racial or ethnic group. Compared to 13 percent of European Americans without health insurance, the rate of Hispanic uninsureds ranges from 33 percent to almost 42 percent at any one time (Schaefer 1993; Novello et al. 1991). Chicanos often hold jobs that provide no health benefits and do not earn enough to purchase insurance privately. Their incomes, though meager, are sufficient to exclude them from many government entitlements.

Another barrier to getting health care is language (Furino & Muñoz 1991). Health care providers rarely speak Spanish, making it hard for physicians and patients to understand each other. Plus language differences may keep Spanish speakers from seeking services. One study showed that 86 percent of Spanish-speaking women had never had a mammography, whereas 53 percent of bilingual Hispanic women did use the diagnostic and preventive examination (Stein et al. 1991).

Because of these barriers, Hispanics often access the health care system after their condition reaches crisis proportion. Many access health care through hospital emergency rooms (Furino & Muñoz 1991). Consequently, Hispanics have less favorable outcomes to their health problems.

Hispanics have a number of other predisposing characteristics that differentiate them from the rest of the population and may influence the health services they receive (Anderson 1986):

1. Hispanic families are often headed by adults with lower education.
2. Hispanic families are, on average, larger in composition. Large families decrease health quality.
3. Many Hispanic families are recent arrivals to their communities. Therefore they may not have an informal network for assistance and for getting referrals to health providers.

The health report of Hispanics is not all bleak. Despite generally low incomes, the likelihood of being born away from a hospital, and lower usage of formal prenatal care, infant mortality rates among Hispanics are low (Novello et al. 1991; Becerra et al. 1991). For the general population, infant mortality rates are inversely related to socioeconomic resources and prenatal checkups and intervention. Hispanic women, especially Mexican Americans, are likely to seek informal family and community support and paraprofessional assistance. Hispanic mothers may not pursue professional help as often as Anglo women, but they receive help elsewhere.

African Americans

African Americans similarly have disproportionately high rates of morbidity and mortality in almost all medical categories (Potter 1991). African Americans are more likely to get and die from diseases that can be prevented or treated. Seventy percent more African Americans die from infectious diseases such as TB, cholera, measles, and syphilis than European Americans. These diseases can be preempted by immunization, vaccination, or antibiotics (Rogers 1992).

The spread of AIDS among African Americans is disastrous. African American men are three times more likely to die from AIDS than European American men and African American women are nine times more likely to die from AIDS than European American women (Vital Statistics 1992). In comparison to death rates of the general population, African Americans are two to three times more likely to die from obesity, alcohol dependency syndrome, meningitis, conditions originating in the perinatal period, excessively cold temperatures, and accidental poisoning. African American men are over eight times more likely to die from assaults with firearms than European American men (Vital Statistics 1992).

In the last several decades, the life expectancy gap between African Americans and European Americans has narrowed to just over six years. Most recently, however, the gap has begun to increase (Rogers 1992). Four health problems account for the difference in life expectancy: cardiovascular disease, strokes, and cancers in both African American men and women, and homicide rates for men (Keith & Smith 1988; Otten et al. 1990).

Virtually all research on the state of African American health links morbidity and mortality rates with poverty. The social and economic conditions of poverty have a negative affect on health. Furthermore poverty creates barriers to accessing the institutional health system. Of African Americans, 42 percent have no regular health insurance (Rogers 1992). If low income and no insurance are combined, then it's no surprise to learn that African Americans see physicians less often than European Americans, even though their health is worse. A greater percentage of African Americans than European Americans have not seen a physician within the previous year. Access to government assistance is not necessarily a panacea for their problems. Many African Americans live in states, such as in the deep South, that operate less generous Medicaid programs (Blendon et al. 1987). Government health programs get bogged down in a mire of paperwork that often results in aggravating delays in paying service providers. A substantial number of health providers refuse to accept Medicaid insurance because they cannot support their practice on the amounts the government reimburses for their services and the costs of submitting claims.

The social characteristics hypothesis suggests that once pertinent social, demographic, familial, and economic qualities are controlled, race differences in mortality disappear. Rogers's data show that the mortality gap between European Americans and African Americans is explained by the latters' likelihood of falling into high risk social categories. Not only are African Americans overrepresented in poverty, they are less often married and live in larger families—factors related to poor health. When socioeconomic, demographic, and familial factors are controlled in researching black–white health differences, differences in mortality are *eliminated*. The health of African Americans, therefore, can be improved through reducing poverty and its outcomes: substandard housing, nutrition, and sanitation.

The infant mortality rate in the African American community is one of the most critical health concerns in American society. It is about double that of European Americans and compares to infant mortality rates in poor, developing nations. The main medical predictor of neonatal death is low birth weight, usually measured as 2,500 grams or less, which is caused by a subnor-

mal rate of fetal growth and shortened gestation. African Americans are more likely than European Americans to experience both conditions (Kallen 1993). Laveist (1993) and Kallen (1993) have found that African American infant mortality is related to social factors such as the mother being unmarried, the mother not wanting the pregnancy, smoking, hypertension, and other diseases common to poverty. African American infant mortality is higher in cities in which residential patterns are heavily segregated by race (Laveist 1993). Segregation means that African Americans' proximity to physicians, other health providers, and employment opportunities is not advantageous to proper prenatal and postnatal fitness. In cities where African Americans have gained political control, infant mortality is lower (Laveist 1993). Political empowerment reduces, but does not eliminate, the negative consequences of segregation, by having an effect on services and opportunities that influence infant mortality.

CONCLUSION

The structural model of social work practice points to the ecological inequalities among ethnic groups. The systematic discrimination that disadvantages minorities takes the form of limited resources and opportunities that prevent groups from realizing their goals. Ethnicity is important for social workers on two fronts. First, social workers should be sensitive to cultural differences and work within the boundaries of the client's cultural system. From a structural point of view, understanding a client's culture allows social workers to see how the culture affects social roles, beliefs, and expectations. Second, social workers must analyze the group's relationship to the dominant culture.

A core value in the social work profession is that maintaining ethnic diversity is enriching, not divisive. Helping clients utilize the resources and energy of their community, feel connected to their ethnic heritage, and overcome unfair barriers, are goals and values that everyone in the profession should proclaim.

CASE STUDY REVIEW QUESTIONS

1. What are the generational issues, vis-à-vis Maria's orientation to Mexican and American cultures, that she might be experiencing? How might these issues affect her perception of how she sees herself as a woman and her expectations of Shige?
2. Although everyone in both families spoke English, why was language a barrier in this situation?
3. How might each group, Mexican Americans and Japanese Americans, view the marriage of Maria and Shige? What cultural pressures concerning marital assimilation may be at work here?
4. How might cultural differences interfere with Shige and Maria meeting their personal needs and the needs of their marriage?
5. How do Shige's sense of family duty and Maria's ties to her extended family create cultural conflicts for the couple?

KEY TERMS

Cultural imperialism: Forcing dominant-group culture on all citizens, regardless of their cultural heritage and practice.

Encounter stage: A stage in the process of forming a racial identity in which people experience some critical incident that challenges their existing, pro-Euro-American worldview and related personal identity; during this stage the person starts searching for a new identity.

Ethclass: A way of defining social status that considers the influence of both class and ethnicity on behavior.

Ethnic enclave: Geographic and/or economic patterns of ethnic homogeneity.

Ethnicity: Distinct sociocultural systems.

Fictive kinship: Kinshiplike connections between unrelated persons who have maintained essential reciprocal social or economic relationships; a sense of peoplehood or collective social identity.

Immersion–emersion stage: A stage in the process of forming a racial identity; this stage is characterized by a deep involvement in African American experiences and culture; dominant culture is denigrated and African American culture is idealized.

Internalization stage: A stage in forming a racial identity; the person internalizes an African American identity and feels pride and security in the new identity; there is a secure sense of self and a more flexible vision of the world.

Internalization–commitment stage: The final stage in forming a racial identity; the person is involved in political action and social movements to ameliorate the problems of racial inequality.

Personal efficacy: Self-evaluations of one's usefulness and utility.

Preencounter stage: The first stage in forming a racial identity; the person has a Euro-American world view and devalues his or her culture in favor of Anglo culture.

Principle of reflected appraisals: The idea that people's self esteem is a product of how they believe others see them.

Race: A biological term that refers to immutable genetic marks that are transmitted from one generation to the next.

Racial identity: Individuals' level of concern for and committedness to the issues that affect their racial or ethnic group; being aware of and respecting one's ethnicity.

CHAPTER 10

GENDER

OBJECTIVES

After reading this chapter, you should be able to answer the following questions:

1. What is the breadth of gender roles and how do expectations differ for males and females?
2. How do social systems influence gender development?
3. What is gender identity and what are the different theories pertaining to forming a gender identity?
4. Is there such a thing as a "gender profile?" How do men and women differ and how are they the same?
5. Are there gender differences in mental health? How do roles affect women's psychological adjustment?
6. Do men's and women's physical well-being differ?
7. How does gender affect behavior in groups?

CASE STUDY

Susan is a forty-six-year-old woman with two grown sons, neither of whom lives with her. Her boyfriend, Bob, accompanied her during her first interview with a social worker. Susan complained of experiencing "fits" of raging anger at Bob and of feeling "lost" and "out of control" of her life. Bob corroborated Susan's assessment of her anger, and added that it threatened their relationship. He said he would attend sessions to "help Susan."

Susan was well dressed and she looked as if she devoted time and care to her hair and makeup. She maintained good posture and carried herself with an air of confidence.

About eighteen months prior to meeting the social worker, Susan divorced her husband, Tom, of nineteen years. She described the relationship as severely abusive. Her husband's physical abuse escalated over the years, finally reaching the point that he began using weapons against her. After her husband threatened her with a pistol, she fled the marriage. Within a short time, she secured a good job in an office, and established a life for herself.

During her marriage, Susan assumed responsibility for all household chores. She did the lion's share of the child-raising, cleaning, and cooking. She paid the bills each month and basically "did everything around the house except mow the lawn." Because of his inattention, she often felt frustrated and angry at her husband.

Her childhood was tense and highly conflicted. Susan portrayed her mother, Florence, as a loud, arrogant woman who was not very nurturing. Her mother, according to Susan, was a person who needed to be in control of everyone around her, especially her household. She used to humiliate Susan in public and tease her mercilessly. In fact, Susan complains that her mother still criticizes her appearance and life-choices in front of other people. Florence would beat Susan relentlessly during her daughter's teenage years, often leaving bruises on her body. Florence also lived her life somewhat vicariously through Susan. Susan was popular in high school and was a cheerleader. Florence encouraged Susan's extracurricular activi-ties and often took credit for her successes. Susan's mother, however, was not supportive of her academic responsibilities and she maintained less than average grades. She never seriously planned for an adult career.

Susan had one sibling, an older brother, who was spared the physical abuse. His and Susan's parents encouraged him to go to college, which he did. He later became an engineer. After graduating, he left the state.

Susan's father was a gentle, loving, but underfunctioning man who provided an emotional safety zone for the family. He stayed detached from the family's troubles and rarely involved himself in family activities. He died when Susan was in her early twenties.

Bob and Susan's relationship was a "roller coaster" affair. There were peaks of elation and valleys of despair. She fell in love quickly and was eager to marry or cohabitate with Bob. She repeatedly offered to fulfill any wish he might have; Bob could do no wrong. As in her marriage, Susan overfunctioned in her relationship with Bob. Bob, however, felt smothered. Himself recently divorced, Bob tried to tell Susan that he did not feel as strongly as she did and that he wanted to date other women. It was during those talks that Susan would explode with rage.

After several weeks of working with the social worker alone, without Bob's presence, Susan revealed two important pieces of information. First, she had been married before meeting Tom. She married her high school boyfriend immediately following graduation. The marriage lasted only a few months. Second, she revealed that Bob had struck her a month or so before she first saw the social worker.

INTRODUCTION

Like class and ethnicity, gender is an important factor that mediates people's relationship with the social environment. On our *sex*, which refers to identification of male or female based on genetic and anatomical characteristics, hinges our first recognition that the environment differentiates between categories of people. Our sex also introduces us to our first social label, and to the realization that these labels are indeed meaningful. Our gender identity is our first and perhaps most salient social identifier. *Gender* refers to the social and cultural characteristics associated with being male or female.

There are, of course, biological differences between the sexes that may account for some gender-based variation in psychological temperament and style. Beyond these biosexual differences, however, most of the ways that men and women are unlike stem from disparity in the opportunities the environment presents to play roles and demonstrate certain emotions with equanimity. Innate biological differences do not account for troubling social problems, such as unequal pay, the feminization of poverty, rape, political underrepresentation, more household responsibility, and more psychological distress, that systematically disadvantage women. The underlying basis of gender identity may be sexual physiology, but the symbolic meanings of social and psychological gender are defined by the psychosocial environment.

GENDER ROLES AND GENDER IDENTITY

Gender roles are socially prescribed behaviors and emotions that are considered sex-specific. All cultures have a unique system of behavioral expectations for women and men, consequently differences in gender appropriate behavior are very broad. In this culture, men are socialized to be more assertive, autonomous, competitive, and logical. Conventional rules instruct women to be passive, dependent, emotional, and concerned with others. Other cultures have different expectations. In some Middle Eastern cultures, for example, men are expected to be emotionally demonstrative and women more stoic. Cultural variations in gender expectations are countless and provide considerable evidence that gender-specific behavior is socially arbitrary and not fixed in biological makeup.

Gender roles are changing in this society. More women, especially those with children, are entering the paid labor force and moving into higher levels of authority than ever before. In increasing numbers, women are becoming physicians, scientists, politicians, veterinarians, engineers, police officers, soldiers, and truck drivers, positions historically the province of men. Similarly, social rules are becoming increasingly tolerant of men's involvement in activities that once were reserved for women: cooking, housecleaning, and child care. More men are not only realizing that they are capable of nurturing their child, but they are finding the experience enriching. Differences in sex-typed personality qualities are also blurring as women are learning to be assertive and men are learning to express their emotions. In sum, men and women today have more freedom of choice in virtually all areas of life than was traditionally available to them (Denny & Quadagno 1992).

Specific gender roles are usually thought of as falling on a masculine–feminine continuum. The more feminine a person is, the less masculine that person is, and vice versa. Bem (1981), however, dismisses the continuum models and argues that femininity and masculinity are two independent dimensions. Therefore, a person could exhibit any combination of both masculine and feminine qualities.

Life is thought to have two basic dimensions: the "people side of life" or *expressiveness,* and the work and activities side, referred to as *instrumentality.* Expressive behaviors are those that are concerned with interpersonal interactions. Examples of expressiveness are friendliness, caretaking, empathy, nurturance, and showing affection. Instrumentality is about "getting the job done." It includes attributes that facilitate accomplishing tasks. Ambition, courage, assertiveness, authoritativeness, autonomy, and creativity are instrumental behaviors.

Assigning expressiveness and instrumental behaviors a gender label is fairly easy using stereotypes as a guide. Expressiveness skills are thought to be the domain of women, while men are expected to be instrumentally oriented. As Bem suggests, a person is not completely without one or the other quality. No woman lacks instrumental skills and no man is completely unable to show any kind of expressive quality.

Nonetheless, men, as a rule, are expected to be independent, unemotional, competitive, and ambitious. The tough male is still the ideal norm in this culture. These traditional expectations collide with contemporary expectations that not only must men have stereotyped qualities, but that they must also be open, gentle, warm, and compassionate. These latter expectations conflict with how men are usually socialized and force them to act in ways they know little about.

Conforming to masculine stereotypes feels good to many men. One reason, of course, is that instrumental traits have excellent payoffs. These qualities are most useful for ascending to power, gaining wealth and status, being self-reliant, and being in charge. There is most certainly a self-esteem enhancer in assuming control of one's environment and instrumental attributes are best-suited for acquiring that control.

Men who invest heavily in traditional masculinity pay a price for those benefits. There are numerous built-in, contradictory social expectations placed on men by the male gender role. For example, it is inconsistent with human experiences to expect males not to feel and discuss their emotions. Another example: Males who strive for complete autonomy have difficulty fitting into groups and developing intimate social relationships. Men may think of themselves as inadequate and insecure, and experience role strain if they believe they have failed to live up to society's expectations. If a man feels he is not aggressive, successful, or as tough as he thinks other males are, he may blame himself rather than looking at the unrealistic nature of the role he is trying to fulfill (Doyle 1983). He may try to compensate for his perceived shortcomings and act "macho," behavior that could stress relationships, push others away, and isolate him.

Gladding (1991) lists six negative outcomes of conforming to traditional male gender roles:

1. restrictive emotionality
2. a high preference for and prevalence of control
3. homophobia
4. restrictive sexual behavior
5. obsession with success
6. health problems

The range of emotional expressions in men is limited, compared to women. Many men have trouble identifying and labeling their feelings, much less talking about them. Therefore they often feel uncomfortable talking about emotions and intimate relationships because they do not know how to do it and because they are afraid that demonstrating an expressive quality makes them feminine. Stereotypical men do, however, approve of emotions, such as anger, that indicate strength and power (Doyle 1983).

Men have stronger needs for power and control than women. The traditional male sex role is validated primarily by physical strength and aggression (Doyle 1983). These needs are often manifested through actions such as domestic violence and other violent crimes. Men are more likely to develop psychological disturbances, such as narcissism, that are related to controlling others.

Men, in general, question their sexuality more than women, and often engage in sexual and physical activities to assert their "manliness." Homophobia, which is an irrational fear of homosexuals, is an expression of men's (and women's) insecurity and uncertainty in understanding themselves. Condemning homosexuals becomes a way of asserting traditional masculinity publicly, proving to everyone that there are no doubts that they conform to the public image of being a man.

Restricted sexual behavior is also a liability of stereotypical masculinity. Sexuality is viewed as primarily a male activity. Women, if they are to maintain their "value," are expected to refrain from premarital sex. The sexual double standard, however, allows males complete sexual freedom, which paradoxically has its liabilities. Men are expected to be sexually "on call," ready to go at all times. This expectation does not allow men the choice not to have sex if they do not feel like it.

Furthermore, it leads men to see women as sexual objects and sex itself as a means to an end.

Traditional masculinity leads men to have an obsession with success. Material acquisitions and occupation become the criteria on which their self-esteem is based. Economic success equals personal success for these men, and not to "succeed," by whatever standards they have set for themselves, is to fail to measure up in the competition among males.

Finally, men pay a price for masculinity with their health. As you will see later in this chapter, men do not live as long as women and are far more vulnerable to chronic illness. Sex differences in health are largely a consequence of gender role expectations.

The modern women's movement has led to important cultural trends in how women see themselves and live their lives. One of the most significant cultural changes in the twentieth century has been the social and political emergence of women. Unlike previous generations, women now enter the paid labor force without being questioned and challenged. They are delaying marriage and parenthood to pursue individual wishes and goals. The feminist movement is highly organized and supported by female as well as male intellectuals, officials, and laypersons.

Feminism has not only caused a rift between men and women, but also among women. Many females maintain traditional roles and identity and reject the notions that women should behave in stereotypically masculine ways and compete with men economically and socially. Conservative women of today, however, are not as conventional as their grandmothers may have been. Virtually all women now agree that civil rights should be extended to women without compromise and that women who choose to enter the paid labor force should receive pay equal to what men receive. The old stigma against divorced women is for all practical purposes extinct, and though troubles remain, working women are no longer punished for getting married as they were in days past. Laws and judicial precedents protect women to an extent previously unknown in American history.

This is not to say there are no gender problems in social institutions. Women are grossly economically disadvantaged. Their earnings are considerably lower than men's, and women have difficulty getting promoted beyond middle management levels in the hierarchy. Male executives are reluctant to trust women with important decisions and routinely discount their opinions. Family leave policies in the United States provide advantages to businesses over parents. In families, women are still expected to carry out traditional roles. Women who work as many as thirty-six hours per week still perform two-thirds of the household chores. Women are victims of domestic violence more than men and are economic losers following a divorce. Women are exploited and disadvantaged in countless ways, such as being victims of rape, incest, and other crimes, underrepresented in government, and understudied in medical research.

The consequence of pervasive *sexism,* which is prejudice and discrimination based on sex, is that women have to adjust their lives in response to oppressive challenges from the environment. Women often live in fear for their safety and have their freedom of movement curtailed. They are victims of sexual harassment in groups and organizations, and are needlessly vulnerable to poverty. Feedback from the social environment often minimizes the contributions of women at both macro and micro levels. The incongruence between the male-dominated social world and a woman's aspirations are significant obstacles for women to overcome.

Nonetheless, things are changing. At the micro level, differences between women's and men's values have narrowed (Fiorentine 1988). Since the 1960s, society has witnessed a dramatic increase in women valuing and reaching status-attainment goals such as professional education, executive careers, and independent living. At first glance, this would seem to suggest that women's values are becoming masculinized, which means to value status-attainment goals while relinquishing domestic–nurturance values and activities. These changes in women, however, are accompanied by traditional domestic and nurturance values and goals. This process reflects an amalgamation of feminine and masculine values in which women are acquiring status goals without necessarily giving up expressive attributes. Boys and girls continue to be socialized differently, according to Fiorentine, but social differences are no longer so effective that boys and girls pursue extremely different life goals.

Many gender role experts agree that men and women are slowly becoming more similar and are merging instrumental and expressive attributes, a personality quality known as *androgyny*. Androgynous personalities have certain advantages over those who are stereotypically masculine or feminine. Androgynous people are more flexible in their gender roles and social skills, which means that they are generally more competent and have a high sense of self-esteem. They have positive attitudes regarding sex and are more achievement oriented.

As you learned in Chapter 1, roles are created and reinforced by the social environment. How then, does the environment structure roles based on a person's sex? How does the environment affect one's sexual sense of self? In other words, how do the social meanings of sex intersect with psychological meanings?

THE SEX-CHARGED ENVIRONMENT

For decades, sociologists and psychologists have contended that gender role development was the result of socialization, the general process by which people learn the ways of society or a social group in order to function in it. Among scholars and students, socialization is the most given "explanation" of why men and women are different.

Socialization, however, is far too broad and ambiguous a concept to account for how gender roles are presented by the environment and internalized by an individual. It suggests that appropriate gender learning is a one-way transaction in which parents and other agents of the environment "shape" children to act in accordance with a socially defined gender script.

A structural social work perspective redefines the gender exchanges between the sexually-charged environment and the individual as a system of sex-specific opportunities. Once children are assigned a sexual identity as male or female based on biological appearance, the environment mobilizes to treat them differently, giving boys opportunities to do some things and girls others. Feedback from the environment lets children know if they are doing the right thing according to the environment's expectations. Not only are boys expected to be tough and assertive and are rewarded for it, as traditional socialization practice runs, they are given concrete opportunities to act that way. Girls, likewise, are given more opportunities to develop their emotional maturity, verbal skills, and relationship skills.

In general, women are raised in a network of intimate, interpersonal ties, especially with their mothers. These early affiliations award women more opportunities to become compassionate and responsive to the needs of others, resolve conflicts while making sure no one gets hurt, and to make personal sacrifices for significant others. Hence women learn to emphasize what Gilligan (1982) calls a "web of connectedness" and an "ethic of care." Men's early ties, however, are weaker. Rather than having chances to learn intimacy skills and to have a deeper sense of personal attachment to others, men search for personal power and place a high priority on individual rights. Having been left alone more and shown less affection gives men the chance to seek personal fulfillment while to a certain extent sacrificing relationships (Gilligan 1982).

Because this process of opportunity is structured along gender lines, it often presents unequally to males and females. Men are more likely to be given the opportunity to development personality traits that allow them to gain entry to and be successful in the status-positions that society prizes and rewards the most.

How does the environment create different opportunities to develop gender identities? The following section illustrates the impact of differentiating messages sent by the environment to

The Couvade Syndrome
BARBARA GRISSETT

Women experience a number of symptoms related to pregnancy. For example, the hormonal changes that occur in early pregnancy are related to such discomforts as nausea and vomiting (commonly called "morning sickness"). In late pregnancy, the uterus, greatly increased in size, crowds other internal organs, producing such conditions as heartburn and frequent urination.

Cultures vary in their response to these and other related symptoms of pregnancy. Each culture prohibits certain foods during pregnancy to assure a healthy baby and easy childbirth. Some cultures proscribe postpartum sex and isolate new mothers in the days following childbirth. Cultural expectations of fathers' roles in pregnancy and childbirth vary widely as well.

One of the most interesting cultural practices associated with pregnancy is called the couvade syndrome. During the couvade, a new father behaves in ways that resemble the mother's physiological symptoms. He might stay in bed for a few days to recuperate from the ordeal of childbirth, while his child's mother returns to her ordinary activities as if nothing had happened to her. During his postnatal confinement, the father observes culturally-imposed social isolation. This custom is rare, but has been observed among the Garifuna of Central America, the Ainu of Japan, and some tribes in south India.

Traditionally, among the Ainu, new fathers rested for twelve days (twice as long as new mothers), lying near the hearth, wrapped up as though sick (Murdock 1934). The Shoshone also practiced the couvade in the past. At the beginning of the childbirth process, the mother-to-be entered a birth hut, and the father-to-be went to a separate hut that his mother had made for his use. He stayed there, isolated from the community, until the newborn's umbilical cord detached. While in isolation, the father was expected to observe the customs culturally appropriate for women during menstruation (Hoebel 1972). The couvade remains a part of the culture of the Garifuna of Central America. New fathers avoid any activity, such as cutting wood, that involves jerking movements. They are also forbidden from having intercourse with any woman except the mother of their children. These restrictions are observed in order to protect the children's health (Kerns 1989).

Prenatal experiences of fathers often include pregnancy-related symptoms. These are much more common than the postnatal manifestations of the couvade. Expectant fathers in all cultures have reported suffering from nausea, vomiting, lethargy, dizziness, and excessive thirst during their wives' pregnancies (Lamb 1987). These symptoms, however, may be more prevalent in cultures that practice the couvade. Munroe and Munroe (1971), for example, found that 92 percent of the Garifuna males experience prenatal symptoms such as lassitude, food cravings, vomiting, and headaches. By contrast, only half of the Americans they studied experienced those symptoms.

Interpretations of the meaning of the couvade usually contain themes of psychological and biological connections between father behavior and infant well-being. Fathers are expected to observe culturally prescribed pre- and postnatal behaviors in order to ensure the baby's safe arrival and subsequent health. In these cultures, the couvade is an expected ritual in which virtually all men experience the rigors of pregnancy and childbirth. In others, the couvade occurs more spontaneously, usually as a result of the father's empathy with his wife's condition.

young and adolescent children. It is theorized here that many of the environmental *sexual cues* that a child uses to form a male or female identity are frequently subtle and indirect, rather than overt and directly rewarded or punished.

Parents

Children first learn gender-coded messages from their parents. From birth, parents appear to map out their baby's life in terms of its sex (Lewis 1987) and boys and girls are treated differently from the very start. An interesting study of new parents' attitudes soon after delivery found that they described their daughters as "softer" and "finer featured," and their sons as "firmer," "alert," and "stronger" (Rubin et al. 1974). Giving newborns sex-appropriate names, dressing them in gender-specific clothing, and color-coding their toys, furniture, and other belongings, make the baby's sex obvious to the social world. These early gestures of gender tracking are not meaningful to the infant, of course, but they set in motion the process of differentiating experiences by sex and showing children that there are some things just for girls and some just for boys.

Parents have been shown to handle their boys and girls in subtly different ways (Lewis 1987). Shortly after childbirth, fathers stay in the delivery room longer, make six times more comments about the baby, and hold their baby two times longer if it is a boy. As children get older, parents continue to separate their experiences. Girls are given dolls and encouraged by parents, especially mothers, to play toy-based, conventional games like "pat-a-cake." Many fathers like to engage in rough and tumble spontaneous play, especially with their sons, and prohibit them from doll-playing and other sex-inappropriate play. Affection is also displayed differently to boys than girls. Parents begin to show fewer gestures of intimacy to sons during the toddler years. Mothers, according to Malatesta and associates (1989), react more emotionally toward young daughters than to their sons.

Children learn what is important from the different reactions girls and boys receive when performing the same behaviors (Fagot 1984a). Fagot (1978) studied both parents at their home interacting with their twenty- to twenty-four-month-old children. She found that boys and girls were treated differently in the following ways:

1. Boys are more likely to be left alone in play or to be joined by their parents;
2. Parents reacted negatively to boys when they were engaged in doll play;
3. Parents reacted negatively to boys when they asked for help;
4. Girls received positive parental reactions when they played with dolls or asked for help;
5. Girls received positive parental reactions when they followed a parent around;
6. Girls received negative reactions for manipulating objects, running, jumping, and climbing.

From these observations, Fagot concluded that "parents are not fully aware of the methods they use to socialize their young children" (1978: 464).

Adults will treat infants generally the same until they learn the baby's sex. In experiments where parents were watched playing with a baby whose sex was hidden, the parents changed their interaction style with the baby when its sex was revealed. When told the infant was a boy, the adults began to encourage the infant to exhibit vigorous motor activity. When the infants were identified as girls, the adults talked more to them or provided them with dolls (Frisch 1977; Smith & Lloyd 1978).

These early differences in the ways parents relate to children are more significant than just patterns of learning and imitating. Parental pressures set limits for what is available to children because of their sex. Differential socialization models are real opportunities for boys and girls to develop certain skills and traits. Based on what toddlers and preschoolers are told, they have in mind a perception of sexual difference, and with this difference, limits and boundaries are implied.

Teachers

It has been well documented that schools teach and influence behaviors as well as the development of thinking skills in students. One such area in which teachers affect children is gender-specific behavior. Teachers, either deliberately or inadvertently, reinforce sex-typed behaviors in young girls and boys. In most schools there are two codes of etiquette—one for boys and another for girls. Boys, for example, are given greater license to run, jump, play, and sprawl on the floor in virtually any position. Girls, however, are reminded to sit and act in a "ladylike" fashion (Thompson & Hickey 1994). Some teachers have been observed asking boys and girls to perform sex-typed chores in the classroom. For example, boys are more likely to be told to empty the wastebaskets, while girls were instructed to water the plants. Teachers reward girls who are passive, well-behaved, and well-mannered, but reinforce boys for being assertive and asking questions (Morrison 1988; Eccles & Midgley 1990; Turner & Rubinson 1993).

Teachers influence gender-typed behavior by persistently acknowledging certain actions in boys

Are boys naturally more aggressive? Whether or not body chemistry makes boys more impulsive and aggressive may not be as important a question as how the psychosocial environment reinforces these behaviors in males. Boys and men are given more opportunities and rewards for aggressive behavior, whereas aggressive girls and women are often threatening and devalued. Judging from this photograph, these lessons begin early in life.

and others in girls. Fagot (1984b) found that teachers pay more attention to boys' aggressive behavior than to aggression in girls, and react more to dependency behavior in girls than in boys. The effect of these patterns is that the behavior not acknowledged, dependency in boys and aggression in girls, is likely to be extinguished because of the absence of any reinforcement.

In terms of instruction and advisement, teachers handle boys and girls differently. In the classroom, boys are called on more and receive more encouragement from teachers than are girls (Kantrowitz et al. 1992). Teachers often expect boys to perform well in the sciences and math, and girls to do well in language and arts. Many academic counselors persist in tracking boys into traditionally masculine courses and careers, while steering girls into traditionally feminine areas. Advisement is an important step in choosing a career and if girls are presented limited options, many may accept those choices as all that are available to them. Consequently, they may then be charted on a course toward adult jobs with limited authority, low income, and little future.

Peer Influences

As children grow older, they spend more time with nonrelated children. Peer relationships, developed in day care and school and in voluntary organizations such as church or scouts, become highly influential in reinforcing appropriate gender role expectations. Children learn from each other and what they learn from other socializing agents, e.g., parents and teachers, they practice with other children. Peer groups and play activities are sex-segregated throughout childhood, and in these groups youths rehearse behaviors and roles independent of parents' scrutiny (Doyle 1983). Acceptance by peers often depends on how well a child conforms to certain gender standards.

Teaching and maintaining sex-typed behaviors by peers has been shown to be powerful among children, especially boys. Preschool and kindergarten children tend to castigate peers for violating sex-typed norms by criticizing them, asking them to stop engaging in disapproved behavior, refusing to play with them, diverting their attention, or physically intervening to stop the behavior. These interventions are effective; children who are violating gender norms usually will stop their behavior (Lamb, Easterbrooks, & Holden 1980). During adolescence, especially, boys' influence on each other is perhaps without parallel. Proving their masculinity through "dares" and tests of aggression and toughness is a necessary part of peer acceptance among many adolescent male groups. The male that acts as a "sissy" or a "chicken" quickly finds himself shunned by his male peers. The adolescent male is often confronted by peer demands to prove his manliness. These confrontations are usually anxiety-inducing and perceived defeats may leave the child with self-doubts (Doyle 1983).

Teenage girls are similarly met with pressures to conform to traditional expectations. Today young women face more mixed messages than boys. On the one hand, girls hear that they can achieve anything they want, that there are no longer any sex boundaries that can hold them back. At the same time, years of traditional influence by parents and others conflict with those nontraditional messages. Many girls begin to underachieve in school and have emotional troubles during adolescence because of the mixed signals they have received. Playing "helpless" and worrying about appearing too smart, i.e., out-competing their male peers, are still familiar themes among adolescent girls.

**THEORIES OF GENDER
IDENTITY FORMATION**

Gender identity is the feeling or belief that one is a male or female. It is the cognitive process by which people come to include sex as a meaningful part of their personality.

Among contemporary scholars, two broad theories of gender identity formation predominate: social learning theory and cognitive theory.

These theories describe how individuals internalize sexual messages from the environment, incorporating them into their sense of self.

Social Learning Theory

Social learning theory postulates that an individual learns a gender script through a persistent conditioning process and imitation. This theory emphasizes the observation that gender-appropriate behaviors are rewarded through praise and encouragement, thus improving the likelihood that they will be repeated, and that unsuitable behaviors are punished by anger and disapproval. In this way, people learn to act sex-appropriately. Boys, for example, are usually discouraged by parents, other adults, and peers from playing with "girl toys" or acting out stereotypical female roles. They are rewarded, however, for playing "army" and other active, competitive games. As a result of this conditioning, children will identify with and imitate the same-sex parent. From this process, an appropriate gender identity is formed.

Many sex-specific behaviors are learned observationally, without direct reinforcement. The concept of *modeling* suggests that a child observes another's behavior and imitates it. A child is most likely to imitate a person perceived as nurturing, powerful, and similar to themselves, usually a parent or significant other with whom a strong attachment or identification has occurred (Bandura 1977; Mischel 1979). If that person is the same sex, and the theory would argue that this is usually the case, then the child will mimic that person's behavior and internalize it.

A great deal of gender identity is indeed learned through reinforcement and simple imitation. The process of rewards and punishments, however, falls short of explaining *in toto* all the gender roles and the persona people come to possess. There are simply too many gender-related rules of acting and emoting to be explained by the conditioning process. Furthermore, there is no evidence to suggest that children always identify with their same-sex parent. It happens of course,

but critics of this approach contend that it does not occur sufficiently often to lend high validity to the theory.

Cognitive Development Theory

The second major theory of gender role learning is *cognitive development theory,* which takes the view that the mental maturity of a child is a prerequisite to the acquisition of a gender identity. This approach focuses on how children perceive the people and the world around them. Whereas social learning theory suggests that the internalization of gender-appropriate behavior stems from the rewards and punishments associated with different sex-typed behaviors, cognitive development theory takes the opposite view, that imitation and reinforcement of sex-typed behavior is actually caused by a preexisting gender identity (Hargreaves 1987).

Cognitive theory hinges on a child first developing the mental maturity to recognize that sex is a relevant and important self-identifier. Children first realize their sex as early as eighteen months of age (Lewis 1987). Until ages four or five, however, children are not mentally able to understand that their sex will not change. Little girls may believe that they can become a boy by cutting their hair; a little boy may think that wearing a dress changes him into a girl. Acknowledging *gender constancy,* a term that describes the recognition that sex is immutable and permanent, sets the child on a new course of action. At that time, the child will begin to seek rewards for acting out gender-correct behaviors and strive to become a competent actor of the expected gender script. Children begin to evaluate themselves and others in terms of the gender expectations they have learned. Gaining approval for taking the correct gender role becomes a rewarding endeavor. Identifying with the same-sex parent or significant other is caused by the cognitive development of a gender identity.

Although much of this theory has the support of empirical evidence, the relationship between gender constancy and motivation to act gender-specifically has not been confirmed. Before they have acquired an awareness of gender constancy, children have an elaborate understanding of gender roles and already act in many sex-typed ways (Berger 1994; Fagot 1985; Huston 1985).

Other cognitive theorists, such as Sandra Bem (1981), contend that young children's motivation to behave in gender-appropriate ways derives from their *gender schemas,* the ways they organize their knowledge about people in terms of gender-based categories. For example, a gender schema might have women caring for children and men performing heavy outdoor work. Children acquire gender schemas early in life because the sociocultural environment makes so many sex-specific distinctions in behavior, emotions, and images. These messages are easily understood by children. Once children learn these schemas and identify their own sex, they try to conform to the correct schema and use them to evaluate themselves and others' behavior (Berger 1994).

Social learning theory and cognitive development theory differ on several key assumptions of developing gender identity. However they share several important conclusions. First, gender identity is learned, not innate to any biological predisposition. Second, modeling is significant in incorporating gender meanings in personality. Children will use the gender models presented them to form mental images of what gender means. Acting on those images will most likely be rewarding internally and rewarded externally by the environment.

THE GENDER "PROFILE"?

Is there such thing as a gender profile? Watching reruns of television shows from the 1950s would lead you to believe that men and women were different species! In those programs, men and women followed very traditional gender scripts that depicted them as having completely separate orientations to life, mental capabilities, and emotions. These popular images were reflections of similar scientific views. From the early to mid-twentieth century, it was not uncommon for scientists to believe that males and females were innately different in all aspects of biological and behavioral life.

Contemporary research has demonstrated that there are some basic differences between men and women. The prevailing thought, however, is that there are more similarities and fewer differences than what one might imagine. Most sexual differences other than reproductive capabilities do not represent qualities that are exclusive to one gender or another. For example, men are larger, faster, quicker, and stronger than women on the whole. This is not to say that all men are more athletic and powerful than all women. Indeed, female athletes outperform many men and there are a number of women who are taller and stronger than a lot of men. The idea here is that *in general* men are larger than women. The same concept applies to psychosocial phenomena, as you will see.

Aggression

Historically, research has demonstrated what people have always assumed—that men are more aggressive than women. Although many studies continue to show that men are more aggressive, some researchers have challenged that idea and have found women to be equally aggressive as men, albeit in different styles.

Men are more likely to be aggressive when a situation requires the person to make the first move, to initiate the action rather than respond to the action of another (Deaux 1976). In an interesting study that demonstrates this point, Doob and Gross (1968) studied how male and female drivers responded to a stalled car at an intersection. The driver of the stalled vehicle, a confederate of the researchers, acted benignly and without provocation. The researchers observed that men were more likely than women to act aggressively toward the stalled driver with aggravated honking and shouting.

Women, on the other hand, become aggressive when responding to an action of another person. A second interesting experiment illustrates this phenomenon. Harris (1974) had her assistant cut into supermarket waiting lines while she recorded the reactions of the "victims." Harris noticed that the female "subjects" showed more aggressive responses to the intrusion than did the men. This indicates that when an aggressive reaction is called for, women are equally, if not more likely, to act aggressively.

Men's aggressive behavior is often more overt and directly observable than women's. For example, men commit a majority of violent crimes and engage in more aggressive play activities than women. Men's aggression tends to be more physical and to produce more serious consequences. The visibility of male aggression may account for the perception that males are overwhelmingly more aggressive than women.

The conditions for learning an association between gender and expectations for aggressive behavior are present early in a child's life (Lott & Maluso 1993). One important difference in parental socialization of girls and boys is that parents prohibit aggression in girls. Other studies of aggression in children support a social learning interpretation of sex-typed behavior. In an extensive literature review, Lott and Maluso (1993) discovered the following about environmental influences on enabling boys' aggression:

1. Teachers recommend more severe punishment for boys than girls;
2. Fourth- to seventh-grade boys are more likely to believe that aggression increases their self-esteem and feel less guilty about aggression than a comparable sample of girls;
3. Unlike unaggressive children, aggressive boys and girls expect tangible rewards from aggressive acts;
4. A study of eight-year-old children associated aggressive behavior with a lack of parental nurturance and with parental punishment;
5. Boys are more consistently aggressive, whereas girls are intermittently so;
6. Excessive exposure to violent television programs is associated with a long-term increase

in the aggressive behavior of boys but not of girls. Boys' aggressive behavior is more often reinforced than girls' who learn early in life that physical aggression is an undesirable behavior (Eron 1980; Lott & Maluso 1993).

There appears to be little substantial evidence that sex-typed aggression is caused by innate predispositions. Observing male aggression, rewarding it, and attributing boys' aggression to some normal expectation that "boys will be boys" give males of all ages not only the opportunity to be aggressive, but social permission as well.

Intelligence

Scientific research in the nineteenth and early twentieth centuries "found" that men's brains were far superior to women's, thus explaining why men were so much more intelligent than women! Scholarly reports went to great pains to document the "facts" that proved without doubt that men were anatomically further along the evolutionary path. These scientists believed that educating women would even endanger women physiologically. If women engaged in the same intellectual activities as men, it would adversely affect their reproductive organs and cause sterility (Bealle 1993)!

Of course, the primitive scientific technologies and theories of these scientists did not allow them to minimize the intrusion of their own Victorian values, which denigrated women and suppressed them in all ways. Women's intellectual achievements have been overlooked throughout history. Even today, many women have difficulty having their ideas accepted and being taken seriously by men, who continue to believe that women's intellectual acumen is inferior to their own.

Although there is no difference in the intelligence of adult men and women, their cognitive maturation patterns differ slightly. Girls develop more quickly than boys for the most part. This is due to two factors: (1) girls physically mature faster than boys, and (2) girls are more highly motivated to learn school-related materials than boys. Maturation factors soon even out between the sexes, but the second factor is caused by social processes. Girls are usually more compliant with adult demands and display greater concern about doing well in school (Singleton 1987).

Early on, girls usually have better reading and verbal skills than boys. Sex differences in reading are largely a function of the child's perception of reading as sex-appropriate or inappropriate (Singleton 1987). Boys often see reading as a feminine activity and are less interested.

It has been generally accepted that males are superior to females in mathematical skills. This belief was reinforced by the fact that girls often avoid mathematics and science subjects in high school and college and are more likely to claim a "math phobia." Differences in the ability to perform mathematical computations can be explained in cultural terms. Males are likely to see math as a useful prerequisite for the adult roles they are likely to achieve. Math and science are consistent with their expected futures. The career signals to girls, however, are less clear, therefore mathematics is not as clearly relevant to them. And although males score higher on the math sections of standardized exams, females receive the same marks as males in math courses in school.

Visual–spatial abilities are those that allow people to pick out and make sense of objects in their field of vision. Spatial abilities include finding one's way around a town or building, recognizing upside-down objects, playing movement games, reading maps, and solving puzzles (Singleton 1987). Males are superior to females in these tasks from adolescence onwards, though there is some evidence to suggest this advantage begins as early as four years of age. Boys consistently demonstrate higher levels of ability in comprehending movements of objects in space, three-dimensional configurations, and perception. The exact cause of these differences in ability are not known at this time, though evidence points to physiological structure, rather than sociocultural factors. The ability to do math is not related to visual–spatial ability. Studies that compare males and females of comparable visual–spatial ability show no differences in math skills.

Creative thinking skills do not vary between males and females, though creative tasks that depend on verbal skills tend to favor females (Maccoby & Jacklin 1975). More men are found in creative occupations such as painting, sculpture, literature, and music, and are especially among those who are considered the most successful. This is due to the social environment that provides more opportunities for men to engage in creative activities and is more tolerant of their creative efforts.

Creative content tends to differ by sex. Boys produce more drawings that are technical in nature, while girls produce pictures that are more expressive. Girls, for example, draw pictures of landscapes, express fantasies in their art, and include people involved in a story. Boys, on the other hand, are more likely to create images of vehicles and machines.

Self-Esteem

Gender has a near unequaled power to shape people's thoughts, feelings, and actions. It is used to find coherence and meaning in the actions of others and is an important means of self-categorization. For most people it is a core aspect of the self-concept (Cross & Markus 1993).

Despite past beliefs, there are no significant differences between the self-esteem of men and women. It was once believed that women's perceptions of themselves were low because their roles and status were socially inferior, were less rewarding, and more frustrating compared to men.

There is some evidence, however, that sex-role orientation is related to differences in self-esteem. For both males and females, a masculine sex-role orientation (Lamke 1982) and androgynous personalities (Spence & Helmreich 1978) are associated with high self-esteem. A highly feminine orientation to sex-roles correlates with high self-esteem in women as well (Stafford 1984). This latter finding contradicts the traditional notion that housewives experienced deprivations in self-esteem. In fact women who hold traditional attitudes toward women's roles had self-esteem equal to those women who subscribed to egalitarian, liberal role definitions. According to Stafford, this is indication of a shift toward egalitarian values among women.

A main predictor of self-esteem for women is their internal disposition toward their roles. Self-esteem is higher if a woman's perception of her roles is congruent, that is, she is doing what she wants to do. Incongruent homemakers, those whose actual work deviates from their desired work, have lower self-esteem than homemakers who are content with the role. These homemakers are frustrated and dissatisfied with their work roles and selves. The self-esteem of women with careers who desire a more extensive homemaking role, experience no loss in self-esteem because they are likely to have some opportunity to actualize their homemaking desires (Stafford 1984).

A traditional orientation to sex-roles has been shown to have long-term costs for women. Helson and Picano's (1990) longitudinal study of women at ages twenty-one and forty-three revealed that over the course of those twenty-two years the traditional women in their sample experienced a slight decline in overall well-being, more chronic problems, and less energy than nontraditional women.

These studies suggest two themes in the relationship between gender roles and self-esteem. First, socially defined masculine qualities such as assertiveness and independence enhance self-esteem in both men and women. This is not surprising. These traits are confidence boosters and are empowerment qualities that a person can use to gain control over his or her life. The second theme is that an organized sense of self, regardless of the orientation, is critical for healthy self-esteem formation. A person who has an integrated sense of self, whether it's masculine, feminine, or androgynous, may have developed stronger ego boundaries and as a result experience fewer fears of identity loss (Snow & Parsons 1983).

In sum, gender impacts an individual's self-concept in at least two different ways, according to Cross and Markus. First, gender can have an impact on the content of the self-concept, so that gender and gender-related attributes, activities, and dispositions become part of the self-concept. Second, an individual's gender conditions the types of social interactions that characterize his or her experience. Thus gender may be instrumental in the organization and functioning of the self-system (1993:74).

Communication Styles

Folklore fashions the communication patterns of women as gossipy over-talkers who talk more than necessary. Many men, so the stereotype goes, reflecting their stoic approach to the world, minimize verbal communication, using an economy of words, and only speaking when necessary.

Men and women do in fact communicate in different linguistic styles, but not as traditional myths would have us believe. First, numerous laboratory and natural setting experiments and observations conclude that men talk more and initiate topics more than women (Deaux 1976). Women, on the other hand, are more likely to react to the comments of others than to initiate conversation. Men interrupt the speech of other speakers more than women. Unlike men, when women are interrupted, they generally do not attempt to recover the conversational lead.

The content of communication differs by gender as well. Women are much more willing to disclose information about themselves than men. In fact, some men hold other men suspect when they disclose too much too soon. Men usually like other men who disclose relatively little information about themselves, especially early in the friendship (Cozby 1973). Men are particularly less willing to disclose their fears to other men. These findings suggest that male self-disclosure is a disadvantage in a relationship that is essentially competitive (Fasteau 1974).

Many linguists and anthropologists believe that men and women communicate for different goals. Women's approach to communication reflects a sensitivity and connection to others. The goal of women's social interaction is often cooperation and support. Social dialog often has very different meanings for men, whose communication goal is often competitive one-ups-manship (Tannen 1991; Cross & Markus 1993).

Two theories have been suggested to explain these differences in communication patterns. One approach suggests that "women's speech" is characteristic of those low in social power. A second perspective contends that women's desire for equality and harmony in relationships may contribute to speech patterns that minimize hierarchical relationships or status. Instead, women express support for, or attentiveness to, the speaker (Cross & Markus 1993).

GENDER AND MENTAL HEALTH

Overall rates of mental disorders appear not to vary by gender, but women are believed to experience more psychological distress than men. Men and women also cluster in different types of diagnostic categories. Personality disorders and drug and alcohol disorders are more common among men, whereas mood disorders, specifically depression and anxiety, are more prevalent among women. Schizophrenia is found among men and women about equally (Dohrenwend & Dohrenwend 1976).

Several theories have been posed to explain higher rates of depression among women. One theory suggests that women more freely report depressive symptoms than do men. The idea is that a man might believe that admitting psychiatric symptoms is an indication of weakness, a blight on his perceived masculinity. Differences in symptoms, therefore, are a function of women's greater willingness to discuss their troubles. Several studies have shown, however, that men are no more reticent to admit difficulties than women (Fujita et al. 1991).

Differences in mental disorders between men and women may be due to biological factors. Evidence, however, that hormonal changes in women's bodies, particularly those occurring during menstruation and menopause, lead to an onset of depressive symptoms is insufficient to confirm this hypothesis. Women are no more likely to be-

come depressed during the menstrual cycle or menopause than at any other time. Similarly, research on the effects of hormones or chromosomes on male aggression are inconclusive as well (Cockerham 1989).

Other theories suggest that sex-based differences in mental health are the result of gender-specific social roles that lead women to suffer more psychological discomfort than men (McRae & Brody 1989). Contrary to past beliefs, full-time homemakers do not necessarily exhibit more depressive symptoms than working women (Rendely et al. 1984). Homemaking was thought to promote emotional troubles in women because the role is relatively unstructured and carries little prestige or gratification (Gove & Tudor 1973). What has been discovered, however, is that a traditional sex-role identity is associated with psychological symptoms, rather than the specific role one holds. Women who have incorporated more masculine and androgynous traits exhibit fewer depressive, anxious, and relationship troubles than traditionally feminine women. Rendely et al. (1984) found that if women do not develop stereotyped masculine attributes such as self-reliance, assertiveness, and self-sufficiency, they may be subject to psychological distress.

Several of the diagnoses commonly assigned to women are associated with social factors "that foster the development of some traits at the expense of others" (Sands 1991: 137). Diagnoses such as dependent personality disorder, histrionic personality disorder, eating disorders, depression, and agoraphobia may be expressions of role conflict, powerlessness, or unsuccessful attempts to live up to social expectations of women (Sands 1991).

Work Roles and Women's Mental Health

As more women enter the work force, questions about the effect labor has on women's mental health have been raised. Work itself has little impact on women's well-being, but the quality of the work environment does. Women's work roles are often frustrating in terms of both the kind of work that is performed and the social conditions of their positions. Women often find themselves in jobs that require repetitive, mundane, and monotonous tasks. Highly repetitious and dull work is stressful, unstimulating, and threatens emotional and physical health. Women are more likely to hold jobs that are relatively low in power, pay, and autonomy. These work conditions have been linked to depressive symptoms in women (Piechowski 1992).

Marital Roles and Women's Mental Health

Marital roles, which differ greatly between men and women, hold more negative outcomes for women (McRae & Brody 1989). Women often experience the same social situation at home that they encounter at work: considerable responsibility without control and rewards. Women, even those in the paid labor force, work more than twice as many hours at home as their husbands doing household chores and tending to children. As women work more hours, there is less time for relaxation and recreation. Fatigue, anger, and resentment may build up at home, straining a woman's emotions, relationships, and support system.

The degree of husbands' participation in child care and household responsibility has been found to be significantly related to the experience of negative mental health outcomes for women. As husbands contribute more to the completion of household tasks, wives' emotional well-being improves. These problems are relaxed in families with the financial resources to pay for some household services. That increased husband support improves wives' psychological health cuts across ethnic lines as well (Krause & Markides 1985).

In general, marriage is more a central component in women's lives than in men's, who have work and peer relationships that compete with the family. Marriage thus affects women more than their husbands, rendering their mental health more dependent on the perceived quality of the marriage. Therefore marital distress has a greater impact on women's psychological well-being (McRae & Brody 1989).

Multiple Roles

As a majority of women with school-age and younger children are now in the paid labor force, more and more women are combining worker, spouse, and parent roles. What is the impact of multiple roles on the mental health of women? Multiple roles per se do not negatively influence psychological well-being among women, but the attributes of a woman's experience in those roles can have a dramatic affect.

Two seemingly divergent theories have been developed to describe the relationship between women's mental well-being and holding several roles. The *conflict hypothesis* views energies of individuals as finite, but role demands as infinite. Role conflict, therefore, becomes an inevitable, normal, and expected consequence of multiple roles. The *enhancement hypothesis,* on the other hand, emphasizes the potential benefits of multiple roles. In this perspective, multiple roles provide multiple sources of social support, skills that transfer from one role to another, and a sense of meaning, personal worth, and purpose (Tiedje et al. 1990). Conflict and enhancement consequences of multiple roles are not necessarily mutually exclusive as shown in Figure 10.1. Some women experience both conflicting or self-enhancing outcomes of multiple roles. While some women view their roles as either stressful or supportive, others see them as neither. These differences have important implications for women's mental well-being. The presence of pernicious and pervasive role conflict is associated with depressive symptoms and less family satisfaction among women, regardless of their roles' self-enhancing attributes. The enhancement aspect of multiple roles is not sufficiently protective to counter the effects of intense role conflict.

Research suggests that a woman's psychological adjustment is associated with the degree of control she exerts over the demands of her envi-

Enhancement

		Low	High
Conflict	High	Low Enhancement High Conflict *Associated with Distress	High Enhancement High Conflict *Associated with Distress
	Low	Low Enhancement Low Conflict	High Enhancement Low Conflict

FIGURE 10.1   Multiple Roles and Women's Mental Health
Adapted from Tiedje et al. (1990)

ronment. Her sense of control is enhanced when she believes her configuration of roles is of her own choosing (Piechowski 1992).

Work and family roles interact and impinge on each other. For example, married women with significant control over their labor demonstrate fewer symptoms than housewives and employed women with little control over their labor. Family demands, such as the presence of children, affect women with little job autonomy more than wom-

en with greater job independence. Depression is not associated with children per se, but with the degree of role conflict a woman experiences, how she weaves her varied roles together, and with the relative ease or difficulty in arranging adequate child care. As Lennon and Rosenfield (1992) make clear, positive conditions in one sphere of life may offset negative conditions in another. Figure 10.2 indicates factors associated with depression in women.

Political empowerment has been a major force of change in rewriting the cultural stereotypes of women. The traditional feminine script that leads women to be dependent, passive, physically attractive, and adaptable now has a competitor. An emerging model of femininity validates assertiveness, ambition, self-confidence, and competitiveness, though not necessarily in the traditional masculine style.

FIGURE 10.2 Factors Associated with Depression in Women

FAMILY	WORK
Demanding expectations	Demanding expectations
Marital strife	Lack of autonomy
Conflicts over children	Low wages
Spouse's poor health	Conflict with colleagues and supervisor
Caring for frail parents	Impersonalized work environment
Health/behavior problems in children	Employed by necessity
Parenting in blended families	Lack of a commitment to work
Less voice in decision-making	Husband doesn't want her to work
Traditional division of labor	Work and family interfere with each other
Spouse's abusive behavior	Little career growth opportunity
	Job does not fit interests

Source: Piechowski (1992)

Latinas experience higher rates of depression than Latinos, regardless of the levels of acculturation (Amaro & Russo 1987). Latinas, who are overrepresented in poverty, have high fertility rates and are thus raising more children at home on lower incomes. Hispanic women begin childbearing at younger ages than other groups and have high rates of teenage and unwed pregnancy and childbirth. These factors are stress-inducing and have negative mental health implications. The immigration process is depressing by definition. Latinas experience substantial yet normal grief and loss responses to leaving their homes, extended families, and friends. Once in the United States, Latinas are further confronted with job and interpersonal discrimination and cultural barriers to resources, all of which are emotionally distressing.

Differences in emotional distress between men and women appear to be narrowing. According to McLanahan and Glass (1985), this is due to two factors. First, changes in men's employment account for a decline in men's well-being. For men, an employment role is a major source of identity and self-esteem. Historically, men's achievement and status have been measured in terms of occupational status and career mobility. Since the 1980s, men have been working less due to layoffs and long periods of unemployment. Second, there has been an increase in women's employment. Women are gaining the psychosocial benefits of economic empowerment that previously were a male monopoly.

Emotional Differences

While research consistently finds that women express more emotional difficulties than men, studies further show that women report as much overall happiness as do men. What explains this paradox? Fujita and associates (1991) suggest that gender differences in *affect intensity* can explain the difference. Affect intensity simply refers to the intensity of a person's response to an emotion-provoking stimulation. Research on affect intensity has found that people who experience high levels of negative emotional intensity also experience high levels of positive emotional vigor. Women are generally more affectively intense than men, which allows women to experience both joy and sorrow in greater emotional peaks than men might.

This difference may explain why women concurrently report higher levels of depressive symptoms and feeling happy overall. Women experience emotions more strongly and more vividly than men. Because the environment presents more opportunities for women to be emotional and to talk about the emotional aspect of issues and problems, they have more experience with emotions, both positive and negative, and feel more comfortable with emotions and are freer to express themselves emotionally.

Because socialization often limits the opportunities for men to develop their emotional breadth, men may be more inhibited or even incapable of reacting positively to a pleasant event, or negatively to an unpleasant one, and therefore may suffer a more drab emotional life (Fujita et al. 1991).

Gender differences in negative affect may be heightened by different patterns of responding to predepressive episodes. Nolen–Hoeksema (1987) found that women ruminate about the causes of their problems more than men, but that men will distract themselves with other activities when they are confronted with a similarly unhappy event. As women focus their attention on their depressed mood, the probability of actual depression setting in is higher.

Dependency

Many popular and scholarly writings have been devoted to the notion that many women are excessively dependent. In fact, an entire industry has been formed around the idea of co-dependency, which targets "dysfunctional" women who supposedly sacrifice their own needs to attend to the needs of another person. Popular books such as Dowling's *The Cinderella Complex* (1981) contend that many women long to have men take care of them and that individual success is frightening to women who would ultimately prefer to remain dependent economically and emotionally. Indeed, women have been shown to exhibit more pathological dependency than men. Women are less likely to take action to solve their own problems and state clearly their opinions, and are more likely to act out of fear of disapproval and avoid conflict and challenges (Lerner 1983).

Lerner reframes the concept of *dependency* in women. She contends that much of the dependency seen in women is the result of contextual, environmental factors that evoke dependent behavior. Unlike men, who go from mother to mother in the form of a wife, women often relinquish their mothers in order to do the mothering in their own families of creation. As the "good wife," she cooks, cleans, soothes, nurtures, comforts, and supports, although she is less frequently on the receiving end of such caretaking. A woman may consciously or unconsciously anticipate that her own dependency needs will be met by providing for the dependency needs of others. When they are unmet, she may demonstrate behavior that seems excessively dependent or demanding. Women are often unable to pursue actively their self-directed activities that would allow them to provide for their own needs. From this perspective, says Lerner, women are not the excessively dependent sex: "Most women are far more experienced in worrying about needs of others, than in identifying and assertively claiming their own needs" (1987:68). Displays of dependency often have protective and systems-maintaining functions. Taking care of others and avoiding conflict protects the egos of significant others and protects the family system.

GENDER AND HEALTH

Some of the most conspicuous and persistent differences between women and men concern health and mortality. As long as vital statistics have been kept in the United States, evidence has shown higher rates of mortality for men, but higher rates of morbidity and health services use for women (Verbrugge 1985). What is behind these differences?

First let's look at sex differences in health and death rates. A fact that is quite familiar is that throughout all developed countries women outlive men. American females born in 1992 can expect to live 79 years, compared to 72 years for men (Dept. of Health & Human Services 1992). Risks of death are higher for men than women in all ages and cause of death categories.

Women have more chronic diseases than men, despite their greater longevity. The problems that women experience, however, are not as serious as the conditions suffered by men. Men have higher prevalence rates for critical diseases that can cause permanent disability and loss of life. This is not to say that men are not afflicted with ailments such as thyroid disease, which is far more common among women, and that women do not suffer from heart disease, which is more prevalent among men. The causes of death and the types of disorders that men and women endure are the same; it is the frequency with which the two sexes acquire the disorders that distinguishes them (Verbrugge 1985).

What accounts for differences in morbidity? Gender role construction and psychological characteristics have been shown to shape sex-based differences in health perceptions and reporting symptoms. Women and men run different health risks stemming from gender role expectations concerning lifestyle, employment, and psychological and emotional states. Verbrugge (1989) and Anson et al. (1993) have demonstrated that females' higher rates of illness originate largely from less involvement in the paid labor force, greater stress and unhappiness, and a sense of coherence, i.e., a belief that life stressors are comprehensible, manageable, and meaningful. When these factors are controlled, that is, comparing similar men and women, the excess female morbidity disappears. In fact, some health problems become more common among men.

For men, several factors create serious health risks. Many of the jobs in which men are commonly found are more dangerous than jobs dominated by women. Men have more exposure to hazards such as chemicals, lifting, noise, and so forth. They perform more risky household tasks, such as lawnmowing, than women as well. Men smoke, drink, and drive more than women, and these behaviors markedly raise their risk of chronic disease and death. Men may tax their bodies more than women (Verbrugge 1985). Intense motivation to achieve and compete may generate considerable tension that can wear down the body's immune system and impede organ functioning.

Women, on the other hand, engage in more health prevention activities. They take vitamin supplements, consume less alcohol and tobacco, get more preventive health exams, and maintain stronger emotional ties that buffer stress. Women are more attentive to body discomforts and are more willing to seek medical attention for major problems (Verbrugge 1985). The only preventive health activity in which men surpass women is exercise. It is clear that one's relationship to the social environment accounts for a great deal of the difference in health between men and women.

Women's health has been the subject of extensive research the last few years because of overall greater interest in women's experiences and their generally higher morbidity rates. The quality of women's health is related to several psychosocial factors: employment, marriage and family life, and stress.

Employment has a positive effect on a woman's physical health, especially for the unmarried. For married women, health improves when secure employment is gained. Research on African American women with children found that a job was associated with improved health (Repetti et al. 1989). The beneficial health effects of employment are due to several social supports associated with employment such as: income for nutritional diets, better housing, and preventive health care; more control over the psychosocial environment; reduced stress; and health insurance.

The health of unmarried women is superior to that of married women. As noted earlier, women in general suffer more psychological distress than men. One likely source of this tension is marriage and family life, which is more stressful for women. Homemakers are in poorer health than employed women (Verbrugge & Madans 1985).

Inside families, the roles women assume greatly affect their well-being and influence their attitudes and beliefs about personal nutrition care. As part of the caretaking role, which women have traditionally held, women have been responsible for family nutrition, an important factor in predicting the quality of health. Devine and Olsen (1992) found that the more a woman cares for the needs of others, the more likely her attention will shift away from her own needs. Other family roles have a similar effect. If a woman plays a peacekeeping role in a family with conflict, for example, then more attention is focused on keeping the family calm, especially at mealtime, rather than maximizing the nutritional quality of meals. How husbands perform their roles greatly influences the health of wives. If husbands are supportive emotionally and with household tasks, especially preparing meals, then women eat better and have improved physical health.

Lawler and Schmeid (1992) found two psychological factors associated with improved health for women: hardiness and internal locus of control. There are three components of hardiness: a high commitment to life and work, control over life experiences, and a challenging response to life demands. These three factors have been associated with fewer negative stress effects and health problems in women. An internal locus of control is the best predictor of good health in women and in men as well (Cohen & Edwards 1986). Individuals whose self-esteem is self-defined and who are self-validating have fewer illnesses. And when they are ill, their problems are less severe.

Biological Factors

Some differences in health are attributed to genetic predispositions or reproductive physiology, which place men and women at variable risk for illness. In general, males are believed to be less durable biologically than females. Some of women's advantages, however, are offset by the health risks associated with the female reproduction system and breast–genital tract morbidity. Women have greater genetic resistance to infectious diseases and are protected from cardiovascular morbidity by sex hormones up to the time of menopause (Verbrugge 1985).

There are significant distinctions in infant mortality as well. Although more male babies are born, more of them will die in infancy and early childhood. The sex ratio, stated as the number of males per 100 females, is about 105 at birth. That is, about 105 male babies are born to every 100 females. This figure is a constant in all cultures. By age twenty-five, the sex ratio reaches 100, and there are about the same number of males as females. What happens to the male babies? As babies and small children, females are stronger and more hardy than males. A good illustration of this point is that among the poor in the United States and other countries, the sex ratio at birth is lower. Because the poor have considerable more health problems that lead to higher rates of problematic gestations, complicated deliveries, and lower infant weights, infant mortality is high, resulting in more males failing to survive. For babies whose birth weight is under 3,000 grams, the sex ratio is only 81. For babies weighing 3,001 to 3,500 grams at birth, the sex ratio increases to 95. For those with a birth weight greater than 3,500 grams, the sex ratio is 115 (Weller & Bouvier 1981).

AIDS and Women

The spread of AIDS is increasing among African American and Hispanic women. African American women are about fourteen times more likely to develop AIDS than European American women. AIDS is now the eighth leading cause of death among African American women ages fourteen to forty-four. In New York and New Jersey, AIDS is this group's leading killer. According to the Centers for Disease Control (Smith 1996), African American women constituted 57 percent of all new AIDS cases and Hispanic women 20 percent, in 1994. In that same year, African American and Hispanic men totaled over half of new AIDS cases among males for the first time.

Most women (just over 50 percent) acquire HIV, the virus that causes AIDS, through intravenous drug use. About one-third receive the virus through heterosexual contact.

Women of color are at greater risk for AIDS because of their higher rates of high-risk behavior, greater likelihood of male sexual partners denying any homosexual contact, and limited access to health care.

GENDER AND GROUPS

The sex composition of a group can have poignant implications for a group's functioning and outcomes and how members feel about belonging to the group. Men and women reveal different aspects of themselves in a group, depending on the sex of the other members (Aries 1973) and on their own orientation to gender roles.

When in same-sex groups the behaviors of men and women differ from their responses when in mixed groups. Women in all-female groups express great interpersonal concern for each other, discussing themselves, their families, and relationships. In female groups, members feel free to express interest in social relationships and are more at ease in sharing. This has been found to be the case for adolescent girls (LeCroy 1986, cited in Gladding) as well as adults.

Males in same-sex groups tend to focus on competition and status topics (Reid 1991). Their behavior is essentially instrumental in that their communication and behavior are related to pragmatic topics and have some specific aim or competitive agenda.

Same-sex groups for both sexes reinforce traditional gender role expectations for men and women. When groups are mixed, people's behaviors change in interesting directions. Both males and females in mixed-sex groups behave in more traditionally masculine ways, that is, both exhibit more instrumental actions. Females increase their instrumentality in the presence of males (Hans & Eisenberg 1985), but when in groups with females, males show more expressive behavior (Deaux 1976). This process is called the opposite-sex conversion. In mixed-sex groups, men are less tense (and competitive), appear more friendly, disagree less, and are more talkative than when they interact in same-sex groups. Although women are more masculine-acting in groups with men, they are more passive vis-à-vis the men. They allow

men to initiate topics and let men take part in interactions with greater frequency than they do themselves (Reid 1991). Men, however, still exhibit masculine stereotyped behavior in mixed groups. Compared to women, they are less willing to change to accommodate others and they assert themselves as leaders, while eschewing roles such as secretary (Hans & Eisenberg 1985). Men do not always dominate interaction in mixed-sex groups. The focus of a situation, whether it is instrumental or expressive, may determine which gender is dominant in conversation (Kimble et al. 1981). All in all, interaction in mixed groups is more intense and excitement-filled than in same-sex groups (Reid 1991).

A person's own orientation to gender roles affects behavior in groups. Gender mythology portrays women as helpless and incompetent persons, particularly in the presence of men. The powerless, ineffective woman then is rescued by the strong and capable man. Like most such tales, this one serves to denigrate the abilities of women and concurrently instructs women to discount their own skills and settle for, if not hope for, dependency on a "good" man.

Probably individuals have met at least one woman who plays the helpless–dependency game, a woman who has bought into the "Prince Charming" myth. Coutts (1987) was interested in such behavior and learned that some women do actually sublimate their own skills when in mixed-sex groups. Traditionally oriented women who perceive a situation or task as inappropriate for women, she learned, are likely to suppress their abilities even when paired with lower-ability men and masculine, i.e., instrumental, women. Traditional women report more ambivalence over successful performance in group tasks, probably because they are more compliant, and feel discomfort with competition. They are more likely to attribute what success they do have to external forces such as luck than to internal forces such as skill.

If a person is a sex minority in a mixed-sex group, then that person will likely heighten the stereotypical responding of traditional women. Traditional men who are in the minority in a group express little interest in being a leader, perhaps because they feel uncomfortable leading a group of women (Hans & Eisenberg 1985).

Androgynous people demonstrate greater flexibility in groups. They are willing to accommodate other group members' desires. Not only do they prefer leadership roles, group colleagues view them as leaders as well (Hans & Eisenberg 1985).

Men and women respond to group settings differently. Men find crowded situations more unpleasant than do women and prefer a larger personal space separating them from other people. When crowded, men react with more hostility and are aggressive, whereas women feel more anxiety. There are some situations in which men function well in crowded group conditions. In all-male groups that are highly task-oriented, men actually get more accomplished and have more positive cohesive experiences. Women, however, have more negative reactions in problem-solving high-density same-sex groups (Deaux 1976).

CONCLUSION

Although some distinctions between men and women may be due to constitutional differences, most stem from environmental influences that channel males in one behavioral and emotional direction and women in another. The structural model of social work practice helps to understand the differences between those influences. Men reap more advantages in society because it offers men more opportunities to gain those advantages. The environment levies expectations on men to have the personality qualities necessary to take advantage of those opportunities. The environment, on the other hand, presents females with opportunities that are less rewarding financially. Similarly, women are expected to develop personality qualities that are consistent with so-called "pink collar jobs" and domestic activities.

The structural approach identifies those aspects of the environment that favor males and reveals how systems give males instrumental and psychic advantages while restricting females. As a corrective strategy, the model would advocate changing the environment to narrow the gap between the sexes and giving women more opportunities to be self-sufficient in their personal lives and more powerful in their social lives.

CASE STUDY REVIEW QUESTIONS

Refer back to the case of Susan, discussed at the beginning of the chapter. Susan's situation is complex and multifaceted. As in any client system, it is impossible to pinpoint a specific factor as a solitary cause. People are too complicated to reduce their behavior to single causal factors. A number of factors contribute to a person's or group's troubles. Given what you have read in this chapter, how might gender issues contribute to Susan's problems?

1. In many ways, Susan is a traditional woman. She considers herself very feminine. From what you know about her, how does she demonstrate her orientation to sex-roles? How does her femininity influence her relationships?
2. You know a little about her family of origin. How might Bem's theory of gender schema help you understand Susan's expectations of herself and the men with whom she becomes involved?
3. Susan appears to have low self-esteem and dependent qualities. How might Lerner assess those features in Susan? How have Susan's roles contributed to feelings of low self-worth?
4. Susan has difficulty being alone. How do you think Susan became so relationship-centered? How do gender issues play a role in this?
5. Later on, Susan joined a support group of battered women. What kinds of issues could she bring to the group that are likely to be experiences shared by other women?

KEY TERMS

Affect intensity: The intensity of a person's response to an emotion-provoking stimulation.

Androgyny: A personality quality in which instrumental and expressive attributes are merged.

Cognitive development theory: The view that the mental maturity of a child is a prerequisite to the acquisition of a gender identity.

Conflict hypothesis: A theory that describes the relationship between women's mental well-being and performing several roles; this view suggests that energies of individuals are finite, but role demands are infinite; role conflict is an inevitable, normal, and expected consequence of multiple roles.

Dependency: Sacrificing one's own needs to attend to the needs of others; unwillingness to become self-supportive and autonomous emotionally and economically; dependent persons have difficulty solving their own problems and stating clearly their opinions; acting out of fear of disapproval is a common trait.

Enhancement hypothesis: A theory of the relationship between women's roles and mental well-being; this view emphasizes the potential benefits of multiple roles such as social support, skills that transfer from one role to another, and a sense of meaning, personal worth, and purpose.

Expressiveness: Behaviors and traits that are involved with interpersonal interactions.

Gender: The social and cultural characteristics associated with being male or female.

Gender constancy: The recognition that sex is immutable and permanent.

Gender identity: The feeling or belief that one is a male or female; the cognitive process by which a person comes to include sex as a meaningful part of his or her personality.

Gender role: Socially prescribed behaviors and emotions that are considered sex-specific.

Gender schema: The ways people organize their knowledge about others in terms of gender-based categories.

Instrumentality: Behaviors and traits that facilitate accomplishing tasks.

Modeling: Learning a behavior through imitation.

Sex: Identification of male or female based on genetic and anatomical characteristics.

Sexism: Prejudice and discrimination based on sex.

Sexual cues: Direct and indirect environmental messages about how people should act because of their sex.

Social learning theory: A theory that argues that individuals learn appropriate behavior through conditioning and imitation.

CHAPTER 11

SEXUAL ORIENTATION

OBJECTIVES

From reading this chapter, you will be able to answer the following questions:

1. What has been the historical relationship between sexual orientation and Western culture?
2. What is sexual orientation and what different forms can it take?
3. How does sexual identity develop?
4. What is the prevalence of heterosexuality and homosexuality?
5. What causes homosexuality and heterosexuality?

6. What are gay and lesbian relationships like? How do they differ from heterosexual couples?
7. What happens when gays and lesbians live in heterosexual relationships?
8. What are the main issues for gays and lesbians who are parents?
9. In general, what are the mental and physical health considerations of the gay and lesbian community?
10. What are the causes of homophobic attitudes and behavior?
11. What is the experience of gays and lesbians who are also members of racial and ethnic minorities?

CASE STUDY

Charles is a thirty-eight-year-old European American male who identifies himself as gay. He lives with Robert, his lover of eleven years. For the last nine years, however, they have not engaged in any sexual behavior with each other. Charles has had no sexual liaisons outside his relationship and he believes Robert has had no extra-relationship sex either. Charles is a high school science teacher, a profession he loves and has held successfully for 15 years.

Charles sought out a social worker to help him work through problems with overeating. Years of eating out of control has left him quite obese. The social worker recommended a medical examination to determine (1) if a physiological condition could be responsible for his obesity, and (2) if there were any health problems connected to his weight. The exam revealed neither a medical reason for his obesity nor any significant health problems. Therefore, psychosocial intervention was indicated.

Charles was the only child born to very traditional parents. He described his father as domineering and inflexible and his mother as very submissive and passive. She, too, was a teacher. Charles's parents argued frequently. On many occasions, these fights ended with Charles's father physically abusing his mother. During his parents' conflicts, Charles's role in the family system was protector. He often entered the fights to defend his mother from her husband. Charles remains distant from his father and has little significant interaction with him.

His parents never talk about Charles's sexual orientation or his relationship with Robert. His partner has visited Charles's family only a few times over the years. They never consider Robert and Charles a couple. It is clear to Charles that his parents do not fully accept his gayness, but at least, he says, they do not reject him completely.

After a few interviews, the social worker began to sense Charles's own discomfort with his homosexuality. On acknowledging this, Charles eventually admitted that he felt both internal and external homophobia. His internalized homophobia took the form of low self-esteem and self-hatred for being gay. Although he accepted his sexual orientation without question and never tried to think of himself as heterosexual, he struggled with accepting himself as gay. Pressure from external homophobia primarily concerned his employment. As a teacher in a conservative school and city, he knew what might happen if he disclosed his sexual orientation. Fearing for his job, he worked diligently to keep his personal life private. For example, he lived in the suburbs, far from his place of employment and the center of the city's gay community. In addition, many years ago he stopped participating in the gay community. He quit his volunteer and political activities for fear of detection.

Charles is a very lonely, angry person. He comes across as condescending and superior, thus driving away people who might otherwise become his friends. He believes he is always right and is quick to denounce others' opinions and lifestyles.

There is no question that he has the upper hand with Robert. Charles wields more power in the relationship and makes more of the couple's decisions.

After several more meetings, the social worker began to link Charles's weight problems and his struggle to confirm his sexual identity with the tension and oppressiveness of his social environment. Understanding well the stigma many heterosexuals attach to lesbians and gays, Charles feared how other people would respond to his homosexuality. His fear of abandonment and rejection led him to near constant anxiety. Consequently, he would overeat for gratification and be unpleasant around other people to keep from getting close.

INTRODUCTION

Sexual orientation is another mediating factor through which the social environment influences people's psychosocial development. Research is beginning to show that homosexuality and heterosexuality are not preferences, i.e., people do not rationally choose one orientation over the other. Neither heterosexuality nor homosexuality can be explained at this point, but theories that allege homosexuality to be solely a psychiatric condition have been decidedly debunked. Most people feel that their sexual desires are "just there." The feelings of same-sex desire and opposite-sex desire do not differ physiologically or emotionally.

Homosexuality is not a choice of a deviant lifestyle, it is most likely a function of biological propensity. If this is the case, then sexual orientation differences are socially and politically equivalent to differences in race and gender.

Society responds to a person's sexual orientation by attaching values to different types of sexual expression. The subjectivity of social responses to sexual orientation leads to the creation of very different life circumstances for people who are judged unfairly by those values. This chapter looks at the development of sexual orientation and the meanings it has for personal and social life.

SEXUAL ORIENTATION AND CULTURE

The official cultural standard of sexual expression in this society is limited to heterosexuality. In the past, homosexuality, sex between persons of the same gender, has been derided as loathsome, disgusting, immoral, and pathological. In other cultures, however, cultural norms and values accommodate the practice of homosexuality. In fact there are numerous examples of same-sex sex being expected among society's members.

Homosexuality was considered legitimate behavior among many of the ancient precursors of Western culture. Ancient Egyptians regarded homosexuality as an act of submission if an individual took the "passive," or insertee's, position in anal intercourse. It was acceptable behavior for the "active" partner, however. After defeat in battle, the soldiers of a conquered army could expect to be sodomized by Egyptian victors, with stigma attached only to the passive role (Ross et al. 1988).

Greeks during antiquity condoned male homosexuality as natural behavior that carried no shame or sin. Many of the Greek philosophers exalted the expression of love between two men, believing that the affection shared by males was the highest bond of attachment humans could achieve. Homosexual lovers were believed to make the best soldiers and acts of homosexual love were expected between an adult teacher and an adolescent student. In this culture, male homosexuality coexisted with heterosexuality.

In ancient Rome, homosexual behavior was a valid recreational and familial activity and tolerated throughout the society. Among the upper class, whom we know most about, marriages between two men or two women were legal and apparently common occurrences. Several emperors, including Nero, were married to men (Boswell 1980). There were no formal restrictions on how one expressed homosexual desires in Rome, but there were informal norms that governed the behavior. As in Egypt and several other Middle Eastern cultures of the time, it was considered beneath a man's status to take the passive role in anal intercourse. Therefore a man of high social rank would only have homosexual contact with a man of lesser status.

Among ancient Jews, whose culture greatly influenced Christian values, sexual intercourse between two people was intended for the sole purpose of procreation—making a baby. In that sense, sex was an act shared with God, for only through God's divine power could babies be created, so it was thought. Homosexuality, therefore, was an affront to God for the early Hebrews. Actually, the Hebrews had learned early on that survival meant replenishing their numbers. Life in the desert was perilous and there was a stream of never-ending enemies threatening the Hebrews' very existence. Since infant mortality was extremely high in ancient times, the tribal unit could ill afford sexual practices that did not lead to adding members to the society. Making homosexual behavior taboo and sinful functioned to stabilize the population and protect the social system in a hostile environment.

Early Christians, with their antipathy towards any sexual expression, eventually adopted Hebrew codes pertaining to homosexuality. Christian philosophy, largely inspired by the writings of St. Augustine and Thomas Aquinas, branded homosexuality as an evil choice in which people's lust is uncontrolled and unbridled. Sexual intercourse that could not lead to conception was ruled a sin. By the early Middle Ages, known homosexuals in the Christian world were persecuted as witches, heretics, Satan's minions, and threats to the established order. It is these values that persist today and make up the roots of the extensive prejudice and discrimination demonstrated against gays and lesbians in contemporary society.

During the colonial and early years of American history, laws prohibiting homosexual behavior were rigid and were enforced by severe corporal punishment, prison, forced labor, castration, or death. Homosexuality was considered immoral and a "crime against nature." Homosexuals were held in contempt and oppressed throughout Amer-

---

EXPLORING THE ISSUES 11.1

The Sambia of New Guinea

Although all cultures prescribe heterosexual norms and values as normative standards, not all contemporary cultures foster biases against homosexual behavior. One example is that of the Sambia of New Guinea, who hold values opposite those of the Western world. The Sambia characterize homosexuality as a phase of universalized bisexuality. Homosexual fellation is practiced as a means of developing masculinity, as well as having educational and emotional functions (Ross et al. 1988). Avoiding homosexual contact is sporadic among Sambia men and is considered pathological by the sociocultural environment (Money 1987).

To the Sambia, semen is a precious commodity. Not only does semen cause a fetus to develop in the womb, but it is responsible for most of male growth after weaning. Through an institutionalized ritual called *monjapi'u*, which men liken to breastfeeding, oral sexual contacts feed semen into a male's body. The contents of semen are then distributed throughout the body and cause skin, bones, and the skull to grow. The Sambia believe that semen masculinizes the body and produces pubescent secondary sex traits such as muscle tone, body hair, and a mature penis. Because a man's strength is believed to be derived from semen, inseminating another male is to bestow a generous gift to him (Herdt 1984).

ican society. Eventually the scientific community, keeping in line with mainstream thinking, labeled homosexuality a psychiatric pathology, subject to treatment and "cure."

Several events during the 1960s marked a change in the history of gays and lesbians. First, in 1961, the Illinois state legislature passed the first state law that decriminalized homosexual acts between consenting adults acting in private. A number of states have since followed suit. However, many states continue to have antisodomy laws on their books.

The second major event that changed gay and lesbian history occurred in a gay bar called the Stonewall Inn in New York City's Greenwich Village. In June, 1969, police raided the Stonewall in what seemed to be yet another incident of harassment. What was different was that the gay men at the bar fought back and their resistance inspired the Gay Liberation Movement. Gay liberation is an organized social movement designed to support gays and lesbians, educate heterosexuals on homosexuality, and press for civil rights. Though homosexuals are far from enjoying complete equality in American society, they have achieved countless social, political, and economic advantages.

Affectional homosexuality, which can be either homosocial or homosexual or both, refers to the close emotional bonds shared by people of the same sex. The close emotional bonds that same-sex friends and members of athletic teams share for each other is tolerated by Western society if there is no overt sexual component. These homosocial attachments may have a sexual undercurrent about them, but they are rarely expressed. If they are, the "rules" of the relationship are broken and tension, conflict, and perhaps rejection ensue.

These different categories of homosexuality cannot be regarded as a single, coherent behavior. The wide variety of human homosexual behavior is best described in Bell and Weinberg's (1978) term—*"homosexualities."* What is considered homosexuality reflects a multiplicity of motivations and etiologies. Therefore, behavior socially labeled homosexual is inconsistent among cultures.

DEFINING TERMS

Distinguishing between homosexuality and heterosexuality is no simple theoretical or empirical task. Most people, contrary to popular belief, do not neatly fit the traditional perceptions of sexual exclusivity. Consequently, dichotomizing sexual orientation into discrete, mutually exclusive categories is an inaccurate description of how people express themselves sexually.

Alfred Kinsey, the researcher who pioneered the study of Americans' sexual behavior, concluded that sexual orientation is not a set of categories, but a fluid, mutable continuum of expression (1948). His studies revealed that most individuals have sexual fantasies about sex with someone of the same gender at least once in their lives, though they may never act on those urges. A large number, furthermore, experiment with same-sex contact as an adolescent or adult, though they may not consider themselves homosexual or even *bisexual,* sexual orientation in which a person is sexually attracted to persons of both sexes. Portraying sexual orientation as a continuum has been supported by more recent research as well (Ellis et al. 1987).

Most definitions of homosexuality dismiss same-sex sexual behavior as secondary in importance. Because sexual behavior is relevant to time, place, and context, it is not an accurate measure of a person's intrinsic sexual self. Homosexual acts in prison, as experimentation, or as occasional recreation, do not in and of themselves constitute a homosexual identity. Behavior is too shallow a measure by which sexual orientation can be understood.

Sexual orientation may be thought of as basic organized desire that remains fixed throughout the life cycle. It refers to the predominance of erotic responses that hold significance for a person (Reiter 1989). In other words, sexual orientation is a person's essential sexual self, one's core attachments and fantasies that endure over time. Sexual orientation is a sexual point of reference. *Homosexuality,* therefore, is a sexual orientation in which fantasies, attachments, and longings are predominantly for persons of the same sex. These longings may or may not be expressed in overt behavior or accompanied by a homosexual identity (Reiter 1989). *Heterosexuality,* therefore, has the same definition but refers to attractions to people of the opposite sex.

Sexual identity, however, is more subjective. It is the degree to which a person adopts a heterosexual or homosexual self-label. Sexual identity is the experience of clarifying "Who I Am," "This is Me," and "I Am a Homosexual or Heterosexual." Identity formation has two basic components. First is the ability to look objectively at one's self and recognize his or her own characteristics, i.e., orientation. A person may label these characteristics homosexual based on societal and personal definitions of homosexuality. Second, sexual identity involves the feeling or sensation of *being* homosexual or heterosexual. It is a knowing and experiencing of the self. Because sexual identity involves a personal response to one's own qualities based on environmental input, people may differ in the strength with which they feel themselves to be homosexual (Cass 1990). Sexual identity is not fixed, but for most people it is intense with little variation.

Sexual identity may not match one's sexual orientation. Incongruence between homosexual orientation and heterosexual behavior and identity is a common occurrence because of the heterosexual pressures the psychosocial environment levies on adolescents and adults who have homoerotic feelings and the prejudice and discrimination open gays and lesbians receive. Consequently, many people repress their homosexual orientation in favor of a safer, more normative heterosexual identity.

DEVELOPING A HOMOSEXUAL IDENTITY

When a person first becomes aware of homosexual longings, there are several possible routes he or she may go through before self-labeling as homosexual (see Figure 11.1) (Reiter 1989). First, a person may act upon those desires for same-sex contact in overt homosexual behavior and may then self-label as gay or lesbian. Second, conscious homoerotic desires may lead to self-labeling and identity as a homosexual without acting on those longings. In these two paths, sexual orientation and identity are congruent. Three, an individual may repress and deny homosexual longings and avoid any sexual behavior with someone of the same gender. This person constructs a heterosexual identity and may marry and have children. This person's identity is incongruent with her or his orientation and may lead to identity confusion and chronic anxiety. At some point, this person may decide to remove those defenses that caused the orientation–identity discrepancy and engage the homoerotic feelings, eventually changing identity to match orientation. A final route to the construction of a homosexual identity is that of a person who is psychologically heterosexual with a heterosexual identity, but later relabels as lesbian or gay. This path is more common among women than men. This person may have a lesbian or gay relationship, sometimes for political reasons, especially in the case of women who strongly identify with the women's movement and desire to separate themselves from men. Orientation and identity are discrepant in this case as well.

Incongruence between sexual orientation and identity is not without its costs. Blumenfeld and Raymond (1988) cite cases in which those who disclaim their homosexuality often are unhappy and have difficulty feeling fulfilled. One choice for homosexuals in denial is to live double lives by having same-sex liaisons in secret while living a public heterosexual life (Blumenfeld and Raymond 1988). This option, too, usually leads to psychic conflict, game-playing, and deceit.

Coming Out

In the last few years, more and more lesbians and gays are announcing their homosexuality. Known as *"coming out,"* proclaiming a homosexual orientation occurs in stages and is best thought of as a process (Cass 1979).

Stage 1. *Identity Confusion.* After beginning to have sexual attractions to same-sex persons, the

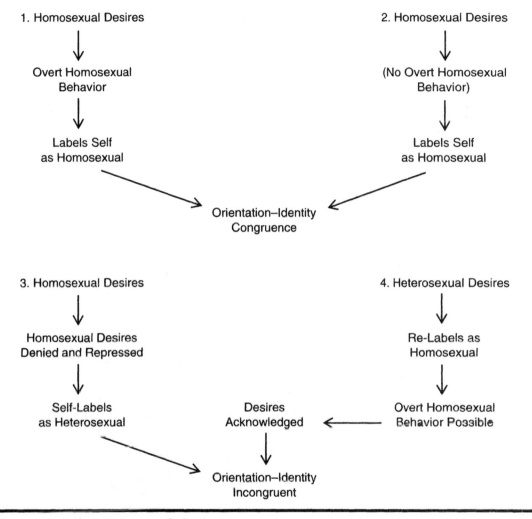

FIGURE 11.1   Paths to Homosexual Identity

"Who am I?" stage is associated with feelings of being different from peers and a growing sense of personal detachment. The person becomes conscious of same-sex feelings or behaviors, but rarely discloses these feelings at this time.

Stage 2. *Identity Comparison.* In this stage, the person rationalizes and bargains homosexual feelings: "I may be a homosexual, but maybe I'm bisexual," "Maybe this is just temporary" (Blumenfeld and Raymond 1988). The person may feel alone and like he or she is the only person with these feelings.

Stage 3. *Identity Tolerance.* Accepting a homosexual identity begins in this stage. Contacting other homosexuals counteracts feelings of isolation and alienation. At this point, the person only tolerates, not fully accepts, a homosexual identity. As Cass points out, the feeling of not belonging with heterosexuals becomes stronger. Interaction with other lesbians and gays is critical to learning the cognitive, affective, and behavioral skills needed to manage the new identity. This interaction provides a guideline for behavior, validation of feelings, and a buffer against self-generated homophobic responses. Associating with supportive gays and lesbians facilitates the cognitive restructuring necessary to shift homophobic attitudes that precluded self-acceptance (Kahn 1991).

Stage 4. *Identity Acceptance.* Following increased contact with other gay and lesbian persons, friendships start to form. Other homosexuals are evaluated more positively and the person's reference group begins to include gays and lesbians. Now being homosexual is incorporated into the self-definition.

Stage 5. *Identity Pride.* At this point, the person becomes aware of social injustice and public issues involving the gay community. The person may feel anger at heterosexuals for these inequities and create distance from heterosexual institutions such as marriage and gender-role orientation. The person discloses to more people and longs to be absorbed into the gay subculture.

Stage 6. *Identity Synthesis.* By now, the homosexual person has fully integrated gay or lesbian relationships into the structure of his or her personality and social life. The anger at heterosexuals subsides and the gay or lesbian person learns to trust them with their own differences. Straights who are not supportive are further devalued, however. Over time, involvement in the public forum is less intense and the person is less likely to perceive a dichotomy between gays and lesbians and heterosexuals.

Research has largely supported Cass's model of "outing." As with most "stage theories," not all people experience the stages in the same order or with the same speed. Kahn (1991) found that, if an individual acknowledges her or his homosexuality early, he or she will pass through the stages more quickly and evenly than those who "come

Gay institutions and organized activities such as the 1994 Gay Games help validate homosexual identity for participants and non-participants alike. The Games were instrumental in fostering solidarity among gays and lesbians. These demonstrations of social cohesiveness make transitions into a homosexual identity easier for individual lesbians and gays. As gays and lesbians create more meso- and macrosystems, they can participate in normative activities without being stigmatized and discriminated against by homophobes.

out" later. Those who identify as homosexual in older ages, on the other hand, often skip the earlier stages. Kahn noticed that some lesbians skip the tolerance stage altogether, while many go through the stages as Cass described them.

Coming out is an anxiety-inducing process in which an individual fears rejection by family members and friends. Coming out is made more difficult by families that hold strong anti-gay sentiments and have poor communication patterns. Family intimidation and intolerance may force lesbian or gay persons to suppress their sexuality, which can lead to depressive symptoms and self-destructive behaviors. Families that are supportive, understanding, and tolerant of differences ease the coming out process (Kahn 1991).

Forming a homosexual identity is a lifelong process. Few gays and lesbians fully succeed in working through their identity issues. New issues or problems challenge their sense of self and threaten their place in the community-at-large.

PREVALENCE STUDIES

Determining how many people are gay, lesbian, bisexual, and straight is an arduous task because of the complexity of the definitions of those concepts. For Kinsey (1948; 1953), precise distinctions between the sexual orientations blur into a continuum of experience and an impossible matrix of possibilities. By clustering together people with similar sexual experiences, however, Kinsey estimated prevalence figures that corresponded with the discrete categories of sexual orientation.

Kinsey estimated that about 10 percent of the adult population was homosexual. Many scientists and activists believed Kinsey's figure represented a constant in all human cultures and it became politically charged through its use by the gay rights movement. The 10 percent figure came to represent the biological naturalness of homosexuality and the powerful political and economic force that lesbians and gays composed. It further meant that there was a safety in numbers, that an individual gay or lesbian was not alone in the world.

A number of recent and more sophisticated studies have seriously challenged Kinsey's 10 percent homosexual rate. Research consistently finds that Kinsey's figure may be about twice the actual occurrence of homosexuality in the general population. Studies on the numbers of homosexuals, using definitions comparable to Kinsey's, find that 3.3 to 7 percent of the population is exclusively gay or lesbian. Table 11.1 reviews the findings of several of these studies.

Variations in the estimates of homosexuality occur for several reasons: locality, age of the sample, and the willingness of respondents to disclose their orientation. Also of importance is the number of people who have participated in a homosexual act, but do not consider themselves to be gay or lesbian. Fay et al.'s (1989) research found that about 3.5 percent of the population engage in "occasional" homosexuality. About one in five adult men have had sexual contact to orgasm with another man at least once at some time in their life; 6.7 percent had this contact after age nineteen and 2 percent had this contact within the last year. Hunt's (1974) study found that approximately 14 percent of women have had at least some lesbian experience.

WHAT CAUSES HOMOSEXUAL BEHAVIOR?

At this time, no one knows why some people are homosexual, bisexual, or heterosexual. The scope of the research on what causes homosexuality has

TABLE 11.1 Prevalence Reports of Homosexuality

STUDY	PERCENT EXCLUSIVELY HOMOSEXUAL
Fay et al., 1989	3.3 to 4
Gebhard, 1992	5 to 6.2
Harry, 1990	4
Rogers & Turner, 1991	5 to 7
Cameron et al., 1989	4

been broad, yet no solution to the problem has yet been found. Tests of interesting theories have not yielded conclusive results. Let's review the biologic and psychosocial literature that addresses homosexual etiology. In general, this literature eliminates potential causes of homosexuality rather than pinpointing specific predictors.

Theories of Biology

Most gays and lesbians believe that their homosexual orientation is a result of innate qualities over which they have no control. Their attraction to same-sex people, they contend, is a primary feeling, one which comes naturally and is not freely chosen. Satisfying those longings feels normal, fighting them creates anxiety. Heterosexuals express their sexual orientation in similar terms. The naturalness of homosexual (and heterosexual) attractions leads researchers to look at predisposing biological factors.

Genetic Theories.   Genetic theories of homoscxuality contend that homosexuality is an inherited trait. Scholars supporting this perspective point to several twins studies that appear to indicate a high prevalence of homosexuality among identical or monozygotic (MZ) twins. One of the best known recent studies was conducted by Bailey and Pillard (1991) who studied 56 homosexual men with identical twins and 54 homosexual men with a nonidentical or dizygotic (DZ) twin. Each pair of twins was raised together in the same family environment. The study found that 52 percent of the MZ cotwins and 22 percent of the DZ cotwins were gay. The concordance rate for nontwin biologic brothers was only 9.2 percent.

These findings at first seemed to suggest that genetic material must indeed be causing a homosexual orientation to develop. There are several problems, though, with the conclusions reached from these results. First, 48 percent of the MZ cotwins were *not* homosexual. MZ twins share completely genetic coding, so if a homosexual gene existed in one brother, it must be present in the other. Second, the twins were raised together, so it

is impossible to separate genetic influence from some environmental effect. Finally, DZ twins are genetically comparable to biologic, nontwin siblings. Therefore, one would expect to find similar rates of homosexuality between them, since they would be equally likely to share the gay brother's "homosexual gene."

Genetic theories of homosexuality have not received adequate support to be considered a valid theory of homosexuality. No one has identified a gene pathway that "causes" homosexuality and twin studies are inconclusive. Consequently, research on prenatal hormones and brain physiology have gained more attention.

Hormonal Theories.   Theories that link hormones and sexual orientation have received the most research attention during the past two decades. Speculation that hormones determine sexual orientation has fallen into disfavor recently, however. Hormonal assays have failed to demonstrate a correlation between sexual orientation and adult hormonal constitution (Byne & Parsons 1993). Hormonal therapies for medical conditions unrelated to sexuality have shown no effects on altering sexual orientation or behavior. Fluctuations in androgen or estrogen levels induced by gonadal neoplasm, trauma, or surgical removal of sex organs result in no changes in sexual orientation (Gooren 1990). Levels of sex hormones such as testosterone do not differ between gay and heterosexual men.

The hormone theory that has gained considerable attention recently is the prenatal hormone hypothesis. This theory postulates that sexual orientation develops during critical periods of fetal brain development. Like genitals, the intrinsic pattern of the fetal brain is female. Once masculinizing hormones, such as androgen, are produced by the male fetus, the male brain begins to differentiate. Unlike genital development, in which a feature loses its female quality in the process of acquiring male characteristics, such as when the labiascrotal fold obliterates the labia as it forms the scrotum, the loss of female attributes of the brain and the acquisition of male characteristics are largely independent (Byne & Parsons 1993).

Brain defeminization and masculinization can occur during different but overlapping periods of fetal development and involve different neural structures and hormones (Goy & McEwen 1980). Female fetuses are possibly protected from defeminization by a chemical that attaches to estrogen and prevents it from entering the brain.

The prenatal hormone hypothesis suggests that male heterosexuals and lesbian women are exposed to high levels of prenatal male hormones and develop masculinized brains, while gay men and heterosexual women are exposed to lower levels and retain a female pattern of brain organization (Byne & Parsons 1993).

As provocative as this theory may be, there is a lack of evidence to support it (Bailey et al. 1991; Money 1987; Doell & Longino 1988). Prenatal hormone differences are not believed by some to be sufficient to explain the complexity of human sexual response. Human sexual behavior is too plastic, that is, preferred modes of sexual expression and stimulation change over time. Disruptions in prenatal hormone levels likely cannot account for this.

A second criticism of the prenatal hormone hypothesis is that disruptions in normal hormone production should produce additional hormonal disorders. Hormone deficiency and insensitivity are not more prevalent among gays and lesbians. For example, men with androgen insensitivity have no higher rates of homosexuality. Other hormone-disturbance disorders show no association with higher rates of homosexuality as well. Prenatal exposure to the very potent estrogenic progestogen diethylstilbestrol has no influence on sexual orientation (Byne & Parsons 1993). This compound inhibits androgen synthesis in women. Only one study of three found a higher rate of bisexuality and lesbianism among exposed females (Ehrhardt et al. 1984).

Another prenatal hormone theory of homosexuality is the maternal stress theory. A stress response to environmental stimuli is believed to affect hormonal production in the fetus. Prenatal maternal stress has been shown to have a demasculinizing effect on rat pups' pregnancy (Money

1987; Bailey et al. 1991). Ellis and associates (1988) found that mothers of lesbians and gay men reported higher than average stressful incidences and stress severity one year prior to pregnancy than other mothers and that mothers of lesbians and bisexual men reported high stress during pregnancy, though the differences were not significantly different from other mothers except during the second trimester of pregnancy. In fact, these mothers claimed to experience stress two times more severe than mothers of heterosexual men.

Maternal stress theories have not received a great deal of support. For one reason, data are based on reports which rely on the mothers' memories. Remembering particular stressful events fifteen or more years in the past is not considered reliable evidence on which to base a theory. A second criticism of this theory is that there is no evidence to suggest that stress responses will have the same effects in humans as they do in rats, which, though physiologically similar to humans in many ways, do not possess comparable brain and neural structures.

Neuroanatomic Studies.   Some research has found that the size of three different brain structures may vary by sexual orientation in men. One, it has been suggested that the anterior commissure of the brain is larger in women and homosexual men than in heterosexual men (Allen & Gorski 1991). The differences, however, are not broad. Furthermore, other studies have reached contradictory results. Two, the corpus callosum may be female-typical in homosexual men. Such speculation is premature as the twenty-three studies researching this hypothesis have also yielded conflicting results (Byne & Parsons 1993). Three, the size of certain regions of the hypothalamus, which plays a role in sexual functioning, may vary with sexual orientation, being as small in homosexual men as in heterosexual women (LeVay 1991).

There is more reason to reject the above hypotheses than to accept them. First, none of these three theories has thus far withstood successful replication. Studies attempting to corroborate initial reports of neuroanatomic differences in sexual orientation have found either no differences or evidence opposite to the original theory. A number of the studies used brain tissues of subjects who died from AIDS and it is plausible that human immunodeficiency virus infection could alter brain structures and affect research outcomes. Finally, these studies are based on observations of small and unrepresentative samples. Furthermore, the medical histories of many subjects in the LeVay study are unknown. Until further research corroborates neuroanatomic theories, support for them at this time is uncertain (Byne & Parsons 1993).

Why Biology? Why search for a biologic etiology of homosexuality? That no stable biological theory of sexual orientation has been derived as of yet does not preclude the importance of searching for one. There are several reasons to continue to look for a physiological cause of orientation. First, there is ample animal evidence that behavior changes with structural and hormonal treatments. It is true that behaviors in animals are poor models of like behavior in humans (Byne & Parsons 1993), yet it is assumed that animal sexual behavior functions on biological imperatives rather than choice. This property appears to parallel human sexual orientation, which emerges as an *a priori* characteristic, rather than a chosen attribute. Second, the most reliable predictor of adult sexual orientation is childhood gender nonconformity (Zuger 1989). Many argue that this happens so early in development that it must be inborn. Third, orientation appears to resist change. A person can change her or his identity, but orientation remains an objective constant.

Psychosocial Theories

Perhaps another reason why biological factors may hold the key to understanding sexual orientation is the absence of an adequate psychosocial theory. Tests of hypotheses that connect family dynamics and personality traits with homosexuality have thus far fallen short of identifying a set of significant psychodynamic predictors of homosexual behavior. This is not to say that family and psychological dynamics are not useful in understanding same-gender sexual behavior. Relying on them to predict the onset of such behavior, however, is not defensible at this time.

Early Gender Nonconformity. The sole consistent psychosocial predictor of adolescent or adult homosexuality is nonconforming sex role behavior in childhood (Bell et al. 1981; Zuger 1989; Hockenberry & Billingham 1987). Compared to heterosexual men as children, gay men were more likely to (a) have a serious fear of injury in childhood (75 percent to 46 percent), (b) avoid baseball (84 percent to 38 percent), and (c) prefer girls as playmates (33 percent to 10 percent) (Bell et al. 1981). Zuger found early nonconformity among males consistent predictors of homosexuality regardless of ethnic and national differences. Nonconformity to male sex roles does not suggest the presence of feminine traits in boys; it is the absence of masculine traits that predicts future homosexual behavior (Hockenberry & Billingham 1987). Note, however, that nonconformity is not an exclusive indicator of future homosexuality. A significant proportion of heterosexual men also demonstrated such behavior.

The relevance of early gender nonconformity remains unclear at this time. Is nonconformity a consequence of biological predisposition, or is it a response to some aspect of the individual's psychosocial environment? The influence of the environment on gender identity, as you saw in Chapter 10, is particularly strong. However, researchers have not identified any psychosocial factors that could account for a child's nonconformity. The present state of research technologies is incapable of answering this question.

Dysfunctional Family Theory. The most well-known of these approaches comes from Bieber's (1962) study which was the first to suggest that the family constellation of a domineering mother and a weak, passive father was causally associated with homosexuality in sons. Other studies have found similar patterns in the families of origin such as hostile, detached fathers paired with domineering mothers to predict homosexuality.

Wolff (1971) compared homosexual and heterosexual women and found that lesbians were more likely to have a rejecting or indifferent mother and a distant or absent father. She concluded that lesbianism is derived from inadequate maternal love, leaving the daughter to search for such love from other women. The daughter's distant relationship with her father impedes her learning to relate to men.

Critics view these studies as seriously flawed. Recent research shows that the differences in parenting styles portrayed in these studies are associated with emotional disturbances, not sexual orientation in children (Ross & Arrindell 1988). If emotional well-being is controlled, parental style is remarkably similar among parents of homosexual and heterosexual children. What parenting differences do correlate with orientations may be an effect, not a cause, of a homosexual child. Parents, in these cases, may become hostile, controlling, and detached as a result of their child's gender nonconformity and homosexuality. In short, improper parenting has no significant bearing on sexual orientation.

Many parents may assume the blame for their child becoming gay or lesbian and doubt themselves as parents. Nonetheless, they should realize that many lesbians and gays come from well-adjusted families. Marmor (1980) believes that, although there may be sufficient evidence to suggest that boys and girls exposed to "dysfunctional" family backgrounds have a greater than average possibility of becoming gay or lesbian, not all people who have this background become homosexual. Homosexuals and heterosexuals come from all combinations of parental styles and traits, none of which is sufficiently predictive of sexual orientation.

Individual Traits Theory.   A number of other causal theories focus on individual qualities that may lead to homosexuality. These approaches usually point toward certain personality traits stemming from childhood sexual abuse or trauma. These theories have lost support in recent years. Dancy (1990) found no significant differences between lesbians and heterosexual women on personality and family factors. She concluded that no single personality factor or combination of factors contributes to sexual orientation. In other words, there is no homosexual personality.

Heterosexual and lesbian women report similar incidences of traumatic childhood sexual experiences. The number of rapes, molestation, incest, and other negative experiences is about the same for the two groups (Brannock & Chapman 1990). The only difference between them is that the median age of lesbians' first negative sexual encounter is seven compared to ten years for heterosexuals, and that heterosexuals are more likely subjected to multiple negative experiences.

Peters and Cantrell (1991) found no relationship between sexual orientation and early sexual trauma, incest, or distressing heterosexual contact. They did find that lesbians have more sexual experience and more forced sex with other children by age twelve than heterosexuals, but there were no differences in the sex of the other person or in their responses to that sexual experience. There is no merit to the argument that gayness and lesbianism result from "seduction" by an older person of the same gender (Bell et al. 1981).

Interaction Model

Since biological and psychosocial models have largely failed independently to identify causal antecedents to sexual orientation, perhaps it is time to abandon discrete models and concentrate on interactive models that combine features of both schools. At this time, it is known that genes and hormones do not specify sexual orientation per se, but do affect particular personality traits and thereby influence the manner in which individuals interact with their environment (Byne & Parsons 1993).

The combined effects of inherited personality traits, hormone disturbances, and social environment may be the best hope for explaining variations in sexual orientation. Such an interactive approach has several theoretical benefits. It would (1) allow multiple avenues to homosexuality,

(2) account for the high concordance rate for homosexuality among identical twins reared together, and (3) account for the failures of the psychosocial theories.

Storms's (1981) theory is one attempt to integrate psychosocial and biological models. His approach links early sexual maturation to sexual orientation. In Storms's theory, early pubertal development, activated by hormones, initiates the sex drive when a young person's social contacts are largely with children of the same sex. While that early maturing adolescent is socially confined to same-sex groupings, erotic feelings become centered on members of the same sex. The stronger sex drive would magnify the impact of any gratifying sexual experience, but the possibility of homosexual experimentation at this age is much easier than heterosexual activity (Masters, Johnson, & Kolodny 1992). If that same child is placed in a heterosexual setting, he or she would likely develop a heterosexual orientation (Storms 1981).

Support for this theory is mixed. Masters & Johnson contend that long-term data on adolescents who undergo early puberty do not have a higher incidence of homosexuality. There is, however, evidence that homosexual men and women report sexual interests and arousal sooner than heterosexuals, though these studies are based on recollection, which is prone to distortion and inaccuracies.

Conclusions on the Nature of Theories of Homosexuality

Because of the varying social and cultural contexts in which same-gender sexual contact is found, the theories that attempt to explain the "causes" of homosexual behavior, as behavior that deviates from heterosexual norms, are vague and incomplete. The noted sexologist, John Money (1987), contends that a theory of homosexual behavior must encompass homosexual behavior that is culturally normative, such as that among the Sambia (see Exploring the Issues 11.1), *and* that

behavior that is the result of a predisposed sexual orientation.

It is unlikely, however, that a single theory can explain this wide range of behavior, because the phenomenon being explained, homosexuality, is a mutable, elastic concept that varies by culture and perhaps by groups of individuals within the same society. A solitary theory of homosexuality cannot explain homosexual behavior that occurs within the context of normative social practices as it would account for sexual orientation, because they are separate phenomena. Among the Sambia and other such cultures past and present, homosexual practices are not engaged in because people are driven by some unexplained sexual desire or need to seek long-lasting attachments with same-sex individuals. The behavior occurs because it is considered socially meaningful by the society for purposes other than permanent love attachments. Sambians who are predispositionally oriented toward homosexuality and heterosexuality alike will follow the cultural scripts that include homosexual contact.

Asking what causes homosexuality is a loaded political question. If it is discovered that a homosexual orientation, in the Western world at least, is due to biological conditions out of the control of the individual, then gays and lesbians could be considered a minority group and then be entitled to government protection as such. Finding a biologic cause of sexual orientation differences may lead some, however, to seek a medical "cure" for homosexuality. Or it could lead, theoretically, to biological engineering to eliminate homosexuality altogether.

Perhaps a more important question than what causes a person's homosexuality is how that person feels about and is adjusting to their same-sex desires. I recall a counselor (who was not a social worker) in a mental health clinic who was discussing a new client who happened to be the first gay person with whom she had worked. After describing the client's stressors in a supervision meeting, she was asked for her first course of therapeutic intervention. The counselor responded, "The first thing I'm going to do is find out why he is gay and connect that to his present problems." This approach is a dead-end, futile exercise that not only is unresolvable, but would distract the client from his real issues, which did not include questioning his homosexuality. The counselor was convinced by her peers to pursue the following course of action: first, accept the client's gayness as status quo reality and work within the parameters of his homosexuality; second, rather than looking at what "caused" his homosexuality, look at how his environment may exert heterosexual pressure on him and how he responds to it; and third, look at her own values on homosexuality to see if she considered it a pathological condition or an immoral choice that should itself be treated.

In summary, there is sufficient biological evidence to support the notion that physiological factors play a role in sexual orientation, both heterosexual and homosexual. The weight of that role, however, is unclear. Furthermore, social and psychological research have not established connections between parenting styles, personality traits, and gender role nonconformity and homosexuality. Practitioners, nonetheless, should approach sexual orientation not as a chosen lifestyle, but as an ascribed status in which the individual has little, if any, control.

GAY AND LESBIAN RELATIONSHIPS

Of all close same-sex relationships, which should be considered homosexual? If mere same-sex sexual contact does not constitute homosexuality, does it imply a relationship? A relationship should be considered homosexual only if the participants define themselves as gay or lesbian (Peplau & Cochran 1990). In other words, relationship definition springs from subjective personal identity. If the partners consider themselves homosexual and label themselves accordingly, then the intimate couples they form may be considered homosexual.

Homosexual relationships are remarkably similar to adult heterosexual couples. There are, however, a number of important differences in style and the kinds of problems they face. For example:

1. Heterosexuals do not struggle with roles, finances, and social obligations the same as gay men and lesbians;
2. Acceptance is almost always a problem for gays, but not for heterosexuals;
3. Gays and lesbians establish their relationships without models to guide them whereas heterosexuals have a wide variety of models to emulate;
4. Nongays rarely must defend their sexuality or worry about issues of self-disclosure (McWhirter & Mattison 1984).

Diversity among Lifestyles

Bell and Weinberg (1978) found that homosexual lifestyles are highly diverse. From data collected from about 1,000 lesbians and gay men, Bell and Weinberg developed a typology of five gay lifestyles that illustrate two points: (1) that certain lifestyles enhance stability and emotional well-being, while others are related to psychological discomfort, and (2) that not all homosexuals are alike. According to their study, about three of four homosexuals fall into one of these relational types. The remaining 25 percent are too divergent to classify.

Closed-coupled homosexuals live together in relationships that resemble heterosexual marriages. Partners are closely attached and feel sexually content. Closed-coupled homosexuals report few sex problems, are mostly monogamous, and are the happiest and most fulfilled of the five categories. Bell and Weinberg estimate that 28 percent of lesbians and 10 percent of gay men fall into this group.

Open-coupled homosexuals live in one-to-one relationships but have outside sexual partners. They spend more time looking for other sexual partners and have more sexual and identity problems than closed-coupled gays. About 17 percent of lesbians and 18 percent of gay men are classified as this type.

Functional homosexuals are uninvolved in a relationship. They have a high number of sexual partners, and few sexual problems. Functional gays and lesbians have a high interest in sex and are comfortable in their sexual identity. Fifteen percent of gay men and 10 percent of lesbians fall into this category.

Dysfunctional homosexuals are not coupled, and have a high rate of sexual problems. Most regret their sexual orientation and their level of psychological adjustment is poor. Dysfunctionals are typically lonely, anxious, unhappy, and depressed and are likely to seek professional help for emotional problems.

Asexuals are low in sexual interest and are single. This group is most secretive about their sexual orientation and have extreme difficulty relating to others. They are generally loners, yet they have little interest in becoming involved with friends or the gay community. Suicidal ideations are common among this group. Sixteen percent of gay men and 11 percent of lesbians are considered asexual.

Stages of Gay Relationships

McWhirter and Mattison (1984) found that gay couples develop through a series of six stages. Each stage holds qualities that serve as balancing characteristics to keep the relationship together. Though not all couples proceed through the stages similarly and may have qualities of different stages at the same time, McWhirter and Mattison found that all couples they studied experienced the stages in somewhat similar fashion.

The first stage is *blending,* which involves the first year or so of being together. In this stage, the couple merges, which these authors suggest is the joining together of two forces to a create a new one. In this stage, the couple falls in love and begins to integrate the various aspects of their lives—work, friends, and family. During the blending stage, most gay men strive to create equality. They negotiate how to share money and other resources and how to divide costs and tasks fairly. Sometimes problems arise when gay men,

without role models to specify behavioral norms, begin to follow traditional male scripts and become competitive, which undermines relationship equity. Like heterosexuals, the early years of gay relationships are sexually intense. There is intense passion and virtually every quality of the other person is sexually exciting. This excitement may wane over time, just as it does among straights.

Stage two is *nesting,* which takes place during the second and third years of the relationship. The transition to stage two is marked by sharing a household. Now the couple is looking to "set up house" and furnish it to meet their needs. They work towards compatibility in living together, negotiating differences in opinion and developing dyad-maintenance behaviors such as problem-solving skills.

Stage three, which usually occurs during the fourth and fifth years, is *maintaining.* McWhirter and Mattison found that stages one and two are satisfying and fulfilling as gay men merge their identities with each other. By stage three, each partner begins to reassert his individuality. Rather than functioning as if they were one person, as in the first two stages, the reappearance of individual identity marks the transition into the next phase. By this time, the couple has considerable trust in each other and each knows the other's habits and traits well. By stage three, however, they begin to feel stagnated as individuals and rediscover old interests and develop new ones that may not involve their partner. The move to greater individual autonomy need not threaten the relationship. By now the couple should have worked out conflict management skills and formed family traditions and rituals.

Building is stage four, years six through ten. During these years the individuals' independence is clearly established, without necessarily damaging the intrinsic value of the relationship. They are more productive as people and have reached a secure level of comfort with their partner.

Stage five is *releasing,* years eleven through twenty. McWhirter and Mattison call this stage "releasing" because "it is during this decade that the couple learns to give the self wholly to the relationship. It is the final giving up of an aloneness that was never wanted. The 'me' is now safe in the arms of the 'we'" (1984: 111). There is a complete acceptance of the other person as he is and the partner is valued for his companionship. There may be some anxiety about the future during the releasing stage. Though they have lost the fear that something may go wrong, they may worry about feeling empty or ambivalent about the future of the relationship.

Stage six is *renewing,* beyond twenty years. As each person in the couple ages, they look to each other to restore the excitement of earlier years and to validate each other as having lived a satisfying life. They must grapple with issues of health and dying, the loss of productivity, and the loss of family members and friends. The renewing stage concerns restoring a sense of partnership in their relationship.

Features of Gay Relationships

Most lesbians and gays, like heterosexuals, are looking for enduring, close relationships. Over one-half of gays and 75 percent of lesbians are involved in an intimate relationship and most perceive their relationships as satisfying. In fact, the levels of satisfaction resemble heterosexuals when matched by age and length of relationship. Gay, lesbian, and heterosexual couples do not differ in terms of feelings of attachment, love, respect, and caring, and they report liking and disliking the same things about their partners (Peplau & Cochran 1990).

The following discussion examines the nature of homosexual relationships on several factors: homogamy, power, roles, and sex.

Homogamy. *Homogamy* is the practice of marrying someone similar in age, socioeconomic status, race, religion, cognitive and personality characteristics, and other traits. Lesbians and gays are slightly less homogamous than heterosexuals because they have a narrower pool from which to select partners (Harry 1984). Compared to hetero-

sexuals, gays are significantly less homogamous only on four factors: age, income, job prestige, and education (Kurdek & Schmitt 1987). Because age is related to income and job prestige, the differences in these two variables are probably due to the disparity in age. The age difference has been found to play an important complementary role for gay couples. The larger the difference between the ages of the partners, the longer the relationship perseveres. Older partners provide direction and stability for younger gay men who may be wrestling with their new identity and facing discriminatory challenges from the social and economic environment.

Whereas gays may operate on the principle of complementarity, lesbians, who are more homogamous than gays, function on equality (Kurdek & Schmitt 1987). Lesbian partners are more homogamous in attraction, levels of attachment, self-concept, and family support than gay men. These similarities underscore the emotional closeness and dyadic bonding of lesbian relationships and the interpersonal locus of female socialization.

Power. Gay and lesbian relationships are more egalitarian than heterosexual couples. Most homosexuals value power equality as a goal, yet holding power is more important to men than women (Peplau & Cochran 1990). Harry (1984) suggests that homosexual couples are more likely to share power equally because (a) there is no specialization of decision-making areas based on gender, (b) both are likely to work for pay, and (c) both partners are subject to the same degree of discrimination, which reduces or eliminates the economic and social differences found between heterosexual husbands and wives.

Despite greater equality among gays and lesbians, power is often unequal in homosexual relationships. One study of lesbian couples found that as many as 40 percent felt power in their relationship was unequal (Caldwell & Peplau 1984). Exchange theory is particularly useful in understanding differences in family power. This theory posits that power is held in a relationship by the person who benefits most from that relationship, has the most resources, and who has more higher ranked status markers such as age and occupational prestige. Just as in straight couples, the person in a gay or lesbian dyad with the highest income or who is eldest in age usually wields the most power (Peplau & Cochran 1990). A lesbian in a relationship is at a power disadvantage if she is more involved than her partner, has less education, is younger, and has a lower income (Caldwell & Peplau 1984). Differences between incomes are not as broad in lesbian households as the disparity between the incomes of gay men in close relationship or in heterosexual dyads where women enter relationships with fewer economic resources than men.

Power affects the interpersonal interaction in homosexual relationships as it does heterosexuals'. Kollock, Blumstein, and Schwartz (1985) compared the conversational patterns of lesbian, gay, and heterosexual couples. More powerful persons in each group disproportionately dominated conversations by talking more and using interruptions to gain entry to the interaction. In addition, gay men who are more powerful are likely to ask more questions as a way of structuring or controlling the conversation.

The balance of power affects relationship happiness. If power in a relationship is greatly disparate, contentedness is jeopardized. When power is equally shared, however, each partner feels a greater sense of satisfaction with the relationship, feels closer to the other, and perceives fewer problems in the relationship (Caldwell & Peplau 1984). These are consequences of power sharing in heterosexual relationships, too.

Roles.   Unlike heterosexual relationships, roles in homosexual relationships lack institutionalized norms, supports, and standards that prescribe roles. Consequently, gays and lesbians rely more on innovative processes of role-making than on enacting culturally defined scripts for homosexual relationships (Peplau & Cochran 1990). One stereotype of gay and lesbian relationships is that they recreate traditional heterosexual sex roles despite the absence of dyad gender differences. The popular image of homosexual relationships portrays the "butch-femme" sex role dichotomy in which one partner is overtly masculine and the other is traditionally feminine. Using heterosexual roles as a model is largely rejected by homosexuals in enduring relationships. For most, clear-cut "husband–wife" roles are not found. Many lesbian and gay couples specialize roles, but these divisions are usually not drawn along gender stereotypes. Traditional masculine/feminine role divisions are the choices of a minority of couples, and are usually connected to temporary situations such as a partner's illness or unemployment (Peplau & Cochran 1990).

Most lesbians and gays in enduring relationships structure roles according to two other models (Harry 1984). One pattern is based on age differences. Similar to other age-structured roles such as mentor–apprentice, teacher–student, labor is divided and decision-making is based on the status of age. A second role pattern in gay relationships, and the most common, is based on peer relations. This model closely resembles friendship patterns. In this case, the partners are similar in age and divide household tasks equally. Decision-making is equally shared and there are no emotional or behavioral differences based on status differences.

Lesbians are more egalitarian in terms of structuring roles in their relationships. They demonstrate greater flexibility and tolerance than those in gay and heterosexual relationships. Satisfaction in lesbian relationships is highly connected to the couple's consensus on important matters and its equitable problem-solving skills (Rosenzweig & Lebow 1992).

Gender identification and personality affect relationships. Androgynous gay and lesbian individuals are more egalitarian and satisfied with their relationships than those who are traditionally masculine or feminine. An excessive commitment to either masculinity or femininity alone can reduce the overall quality of a relationship (Harry 1984).

Androgynous and feminine individuals have qualities that are conducive to positive interpersonal relationships (Kurdek & Schmitt 1986). Androgynous people tend to be socially poised, mature, concerned with others, likable, assertive, and appropriately self-disclosing. Highly feminine people are more submissive, dependent, and sensitive to expressive cues. Masculine and undifferentiated people, conversely, have qualities that are less conducive to maintaining enjoyable, rewarding relationships. Highly masculine people are more task-minded, hostile, dominant, narcissistic, demanding, temperamental, and less nurturing. Undifferentiated gays and lesbians tend to be self-centered, alienated, withdrawn, poorly socialized, depressed, unattractive, lacking in intimacy, and less well-adjusted (Kurdek & Schmitt 1986).

Sex.   Another myth about lesbian and gay couples is that they are sex-centered, not only having frequent sexual contact, but basing their union solely on sex. Like other myths, this one is rooted in heterosexual biases against homosexuals and a false presumption about their lifestyle. In truth, frequency of sex is not significantly different between heterosexual and gay and lesbian couples when length of relationship is controlled.

Gays and lesbians are very different sexually. Single lesbians have sex less frequently and with fewer partners than gay men and more lesbians have had heterosexual sex in the past than gay men. Lesbians are also more likely to have been heterosexually married. Lesbians are less concerned about their partner's age and attractiveness than they are about relationship values concerning equality and how the relationship improves their personal lives. Lesbian sex practices are sensuous, but less genital and orgasm-focused and less oriented to vaginal penetration than heterosexual women's sex. Lesbians in committed relationships have sexual encounters outside the relationship at about the same rate as heterosexual women, but far less frequently than gay men (Nichols 1990).

Lesbians tend to have less sex than those in the other two types of relationships. Nichols (1990) suggests this is due to three factors. First, their low sex frequency reflects women's general socialization that leads them to fear and devalue sex and repress their own sexual desires. Nichols reports that lesbians have high rates of sexual desire disorders.

Second, lesbian relationships often become fused, that is they become excessively close to one another. Lesbians often fail to establish emotional, territorial, and cognitive boundaries for themselves. They typically share all activities together and form few individual friendships outside the relationship (Kaufman et al. 1984).

Sex between two fused people is often strained. A satisfying sexual experience and relationship require focusing on oneself, as well as giving one's partner pleasure. If both partners are concentrating on pleasing the other, they may find that they neglect their own needs and do not enjoy sex.

Third, lesbians, like heterosexual women, tend to fuse sex and love. More than men, they are likely to engage in sex in the context of a relationship. For many women, love becomes a sufficient expression of attachment, thus sex may hold less attraction.

Gay men are more sexually active, as singles and in relationships, than lesbians and heterosexuals. They also are more likely to have sexual affairs outside their relationships as well. The reason gay men are so active sexually may be due to expectations of male sexuality. Blumstein and Schwartz (1983) speculate that traditional socialization, which encourages men to be sexually active, makes men more interested in sex and reduces sexual inhibitions. As among heterosexual men, sex for gays is often a goal and is enjoyed as recreation. It is often seen as an end in itself.

There are, nonetheless, a number of striking differences between gay and heterosexual men in terms of sexual expression. Many gay men are exceptions to traditional male sexual values and styles. These men take their time during sexual interaction, rather than hurrying along in a goal-oriented effort (Masters & Johnson 1979). Like lesbians, they use more freeflowing and inventive styles of sexual play than married heterosexual men. Delaying orgasm by extending arousing sex play heightens physical pleasure and can have the emotional effect of enhancing closeness and attachment.

During the first several years of a relationship, gay men have sex with their primary partner more often than heterosexuals do. As relationships go on, however, gay male couples reverse themselves and engage in fewer sexual acts than heterosexuals. This pattern may be a function of the AIDS crisis. As one partner becomes ill, the other looks outside the relationship to meet sexual needs (Blumstein & Schwartz 1983; Peplau & Cochran 1990).

All-in-all, lesbians and gays report high levels of sexual satisfaction with their partner. Blumstein and Schwartz found that about 70 percent of lesbians, gay men, and heterosexuals were satisfied with the quality of their sex life. In all groups, relationship and sexual gratification were higher among those couples who engaged in fulfilling sexual activities and who engaged in sex often enough to satisfy their needs.

GAYS AND LESBIANS IN HETEROSEXUAL RELATIONSHIPS

Many gays and lesbians have been married heterosexually before socially presenting themselves as homosexuals. About 17 to 20 percent of gays (Ross 1989) and about one-third of lesbians (Masters & Johnson 1979) were married prior to coming out. Many more are presently in heterosexual marriages. According to Masters and Johnson, two-thirds married to try to reverse their homosexual orientation. Bell and Weinberg (1978) found other reasons lesbians and gays chose to enter conventional heterosexual marriages: to hide or deny their sexual orientation, to test their heterosexual responsiveness, to deny their homosexuality, to accommodate heterosexual pressures to marry and have children, and because of previous disappointing homosexual encounters. Homosexuals who marry may feel that their orientation is situational or will disappear on its own. Others may not discover their homosexuality until after their marriage.

The marriages of gays and lesbians are no more unstable than heterosexual marriages, but they often follow different patterns. Ross (1989) calls one such difference "conjugal role separation," which he sees as the predominant pattern of

married life for these couples. The partners in gay–straight marriages are often involved in separate and different activities. These activities are often complementary, however. They are separate but interlocking, with a minimum of interaction. Each person may have his or her own friends and social networks, for example, but does not allow those networks to interfere with tasks needed to maintain certain family activities such as child-raising, going on family vacations, attending office parties, and so forth.

Couples usually adjust to sexual orientation differences in one of four ways, though none is particularly successful (Ross 1989).

(1) *Separation.* Couples often separate once the homosexuality is disclosed, especially if there are no children and marital life is otherwise unsatisfactory. The "straight" spouse may question the fidelity of the partner and the two of them may realize their relationship goals are incongruent.

(2) *"Platonic" Marriage.* In this pattern, the couple abandons the sexual side of marriage and concentrates on other sources of marital satisfaction and outside interests such as work, children, and hobbies. Sexual needs are fulfilled outside the marriage. The homosexual inclination of the gay spouse is usually kept quiet. This pattern can be functional for maintaining the family system, but can cause intense stress as well. Repressing sexual needs or meeting them outside the marriage interferes with the partners being truthful with each other (Van der Geest 1993). Frustration, guilt, devaluation of the spouse, and bitterness are prevalent emotional consequences.

(3) *Double Standard Marriage.* In this marital pattern, the gay or lesbian partner maintains homosexual as well as marital liaisons. Both people may eventually realize that they are unable to sustain a dual commitment. Resentment by both spouses commonly follows.

(4) *The Innovative Marriage.* This style is comparable to an open marriage and does not fit the conventional marital picture. In this case, frequent heterosexual as well as homosexual relations are all open. When these marriages are happy and

successful, the heterosexual spouse is usually one who does not depend solely on the marriage for identity and primary support. The level of dependency on each other is minimal (Van der Geest 1993). It is perhaps the most successful of the four styles, but success depends on the versatility of the homosexual partner and the broad-mindedness of the straight spouse. Usually these marriages have boundary problems and there is much contentiousness, jealousy, and competition.

Women who divorce their homosexual husbands do not differ from women divorced from heterosexual men in psychological symptoms or in overall divorce adjustment, with one exception. Women divorced from gay men carry more anger than other divorced women. They focus their anger on their ex-husband as well as themselves. They feel used, betrayed, and cheated from an honest chance of having their marriage work and living up to the heterosexual ideal (Smith & Allred 1990). Their self-anger is primarily a function of feeling naive and perhaps exposing themselves to HIV.

On the other hand, most of the women divorced from gay men felt they had grown from the experience. They felt pride and confident in having handled a difficult situation well and believed they had become more compassionate for and accepting of others.

LESBIANS AND GAYS AS PARENTS

As parents, lesbians and gays challenge society's assumptions about the traditional structure of the family and threaten the definitions of motherhood and fatherhood sanctioned only within institutionalized heterosexuality (Levy 1992). Homosexuals' parenting is falsely believed to damage the welfare of the child and to promote or "cause" homosexual lifestyles. Nonetheless homosexual couples adopting children is becoming increasingly accepted and many lesbians opt for artificial insemination to become parents naturally (Salholz et al. 1990).

Openly gay and lesbian people who are raising children face problems that heterosexual parents do not because of the hostile response they receive from heterosexual-based social institutions. Hostility from the social environment takes the form of discrimination in child custody decisions and being less likely to be awarded custody of their child; other legal discrimination; unfair housing and employment practices; and persistent confrontation with prejudicial attitudes.

Gays and lesbians further face micro system problems not present among heterosexuals. Homosexuals must confront and defend their own sexuality to their children, who are no more likely to be gay than children of heterosexual parents. Gay fathers have more difficulty acknowledging their homosexuality than lesbian mothers do (Masters et al. 1992). This may be a consequence of the subjective belief that the father role must follow certain masculine expectations. The father may believe his children will interpret his homosexual orientation as weak and unmasculine. Thus the father fears rejection by his children. Gay fathers, however, report tolerance and acceptance by their children, and though there may be short-lived problems when they disclose their orientation, few complications endure.

Gay parents facing discrimination and interpersonal problems must develop functional coping strategies. Levy's (1992) study of lesbian mothers revealed that they look for support in relationships and activities that validates both their lesbianism and their identity as mothers. Those that handle difficult situations best draw personal strength from their independence, yet strive to maintain appropriate family cohesion and organization. Asserting a high level of self-acceptance is one key for successfully facing their problems.

MENTAL AND PHYSICAL HEALTH

Mental Health

Researchers have long compared the personalities of heterosexuals and homosexuals. One might expect the mental health of gays and lesbians to be low due to homophobia, social stigma, and the social view of homosexuality as abnormal (Christie & Young 1986). Research shows, however, that homosexuals fall within the normal range of mental health and psychological adjustment. There are few if any psychological differences between gays and lesbians and heterosexuals (Ross et al. 1988). As such, there is no homosexual personality profile. Lesbians and gays can have many types of personalities within socially defined normal limits (Wilson 1984).

There is some evidence that lesbians and gays may develop different personality patterns, though they constitute neither a clinical entity nor pathology. Personality inventories have found traits such as endurance and dominance to be slightly higher among homosexuals, but far short of any pathology (Wilson 1984). There are possibly two reasons why homosexuals develop certain personality traits differently from heterosexuals. First, gays and lesbians may develop patterns consistent with the expectations of the gay community, and second, they develop traits based on individual, subjective interpretations of being gay.

Like straight people, lesbians and gays are subject to the same factors that "cause" good and bad mental health. When controlling for those variables, researchers have found several other correlates of mental health status among homosexuals. Pathology among some homosexuals is connected to the stresses of being a gay man or lesbian in a society that stigmatizes homosexuality. As Ross and his associates (1988) point out, homosexuality per se has no implications for mental health, although the society in which a person lives and its reaction to homosexuality may affect psychological well-being. In other words, anxiety and neurosis among homosexuals are frequently products of the social stigma attached to being gay.

In another study of homosexual mental health, Ross (1989) outlined specific factors associated with emotional well-being and poor psychological adjustment. He found that the following variables correlate with poor mental health: infrequent homosexual sex, loneliness, never having had an exclusive homosexual relationship, and worries over exposing their homosexuality. Lesbians and gays who are involved in the gay community, receive greater support, and feel less threatened by the heterosexual world have stronger mental health.

Physical Health

There are no health problems associated with homosexuality per se. In general, the physical health of lesbians and gays matches the health of heterosexual men and women. The overall health status of lesbians, in fact, exceeds that of other groups. Gynecologic disorders, for example, are far more common among heterosexual women. Gonorrhea, syphilis, and chlamydia are rare among lesbians and pelvic inflammatory disease is unlikely. Herpes can occur, but is not identified by public health officials as a specific problem for lesbians. Rates of cervical intraepithelial neoplasia are low as well. Lesbian and heterosexual females experience the same rates of menstrual problems, though some data indicate lesbians have fewer menstrual complications. There are no differences in the sexual response cycle as well (Johnson & Palermo 1984).

Two health problems related to lifestyle factors affect gays and lesbians more than heterosexuals. The rate of alcoholism among homosexuals exceeds that of heterosexuals. Some studies report alcoholism among lesbians to be five to seven times higher than among nongay women. Alcohol abuse is a consequence of three social features of the gay community (Johnson & Palermo 1984): (1) the importance of gay bars as a social community; (2) the alienation and isolation that result from social rejection and oppression; and (3) the failure of the health care system to provide adequate treatment services for gays and a reluctance on the part of gays to seek treatment for alcohol abuse.

The second health problem in the gay community, particularly among men, is the high prevalence of sexually transmitted diseases (STD). Most studies have found that the rate of STD among gay men is three times the rate of heterosexual men. The incidence of STD is much higher among gay men primarily because of their frequent sexual contact with a variety of partners, the type of sexual practices they engage in, and the anonymity of many partners that makes contact-tracing difficult (Ross 1992).

As is well known, the most devastating of these diseases is AIDS, which affects gay men at a far higher rate than lesbians. HIV disease (Human Immunodeficiency Virus) has ravaged the gay community and has induced changes in behavior at the micro and community levels. The fear of acquiring AIDS has affected the psychological well-being of many gay men. AIDS anxiety often affects men's willingness to establish relationships. The anxiety is so strong that many gay men opt for celibacy to avoid contracting the disease. There are oft-reported cases that worrying about AIDS can worsen into more serious psychological problems. Valdiserri (1986) found that in fearing AIDS, gay men often develop hypochondriacal preoccupations, obsessional ideations, and other anxiety-related disorders.

At the community level, AIDS has sparked widespread action. Gay networks in most cities have in-community nursing and care programs to attend to those in the late stages of the disease. Fund-raising to help indigent persons with AIDS is another support service found in most urban areas. AIDS education has been a particularly significant service of the gay community and its success is largely responsible for lowering the rate of new AIDS cases among gays. AIDS support groups have been formed all over the country to attend to sufferers' emotional needs and to exchange information. Militant groups such as ACT UP (the AIDS Coalition to Unleash Power) have succeeded in creating change through acts of civil disobedience. ACT UP demonstrated on the floor of the New York Stock Exchange to protest the price of drugs used to treat AIDS, forced the U.S. Food and Drug Administration to approve more rapid testing of new drugs, and disrupted mass at St. Patrick's Cathedral in New York to protest the Catholic Church's policy against the use of condoms as a means of preventing the transmission of HIV (Masters, Johnson, & Kolodny 1992). Other groups have been equally successful in bringing AIDS to the public theater and increasing the pub-

lic's knowledge and awareness of the disease. The AIDS epidemic has taken its toll on gay institutions as well. Gay bathhouses have virtually become a thing of the past and the number of gay bars has declined.

Unfortunately AIDS has fomented new forms of anti-gay discrimination. Insurance companies have changed their rules to avoid paying benefits to HIV-positive people, or those the companies believe to be at risk for contracting the disease. Insurance companies have withdrawn coverage from AIDS sufferers, denied them benefits under "previous conditions" exemptions, and refused to cover single men in high risk areas unless they are tested for HIV. Thousands of HIV-positive employees have lost their jobs. HIV-positive servicemen and women are routinely discharged from the military when their infection is disclosed. The rate of violence against gays has increased since the beginning of the epidemic.

HOMOPHOBIA

Hostility directed at homosexuals, known as *homophobia,* is unlike the prejudice and discrimination aimed at racial and ethnic groups, women, and other communities. First, because sexual orientation has no outward signs like gender and race, discriminating against specific homosexuals is only possible once their orientation is identified. Consequently, discriminatory action against lesbians and gays has less of a history of economic exploitation. Anti-gay discrimination is a social control mechanism that functions to force people to live a life-style that is consonant with the religious and moral ideologies of the dominant groups.

A second difference is that hostility directed towards homosexuals often has the sanction of government. Homosexuals are not a protected federal category. In fact, governments in several jurisdictions have moved to curtail the rights of gays. Consider the following examples: Cobb County, Georgia, declared gays officially unwelcome; all but eight states allow employers to fire people simply for being gay; no state recognizes gay marriages; Montana's "deviate sexual conduct" law makes homosexual behavior a felony and carries a penalty of ten years in prison, though it is rarely enforced; voters in Colorado and Oregon approved measures in the 1990s that limit the rights of homosexuals; and state courts are reluctant to award custody to "outed" gay and lesbian parents and resist approving their attempts to adopt children.

As the public presence of homosexuals becomes more conspicuous, homophobia rises (Henry 1994). Gay persons are unwelcome in many churches and landlords routinely deny them housing. Employers frequently deny gays and lesbians promotions on the basis of their sexual orientation. The most insidious form of discrimination against homosexuals is violence. "Gay bashing" continues, though there is evidence of its decline in some major cities. As gays assert themselves politically and socially, violence against them increases. For example, in Denver anti-gay violence increased 12 percent in 1992, the year Colorado voted to restrict gay rights (Henry 1994).

Finally, anti-gay sentiment extends into family and private life. Many heterosexuals do not endorse basic civil rights for gay and lesbian persons. In a study of heterosexuals' attitudes toward lesbians and gays, Beran and associates (1992) found that:

- 54 percent are against gay parents gaining custody of their children;
- 22 percent believe that homosexuals' free speech should be limited;
- 43 percent would not vote for a known homosexual for public office;
- 37 percent object to working with a gay or lesbian person;
- 41 percent are averse to working for a homosexual;
- 34 and 48 percent object to gays and lesbians as teachers and clergy, respectively;
- 20 percent would not want homosexuals as neighbors.

If homophobia is not economically-based like discrimination against other groups, what is it about? The classic explanation of homophobes suggests that they are people who are insecure in their own gender identity or sexual orientation. These insecurities, so the theory goes, translate into hostility that they defensively project onto those people who symbolize the homophobe's own unacceptable urges or identity confusion (Herek 1988). In this case, homophobia is a defensive strategy for avoiding anxiety generated by intrapsychic conflicts. No doubt this theory explains some individual cases of homophobia. It is not broad enough, however, to account for other kinds of antigay behavior and rhetoric.

Herek (1988) identified four sources of hostility against homosexuals.

(1) *Traditional attitudes about gender and family roles.* Prejudiced people see homosexuality as violating traditional gender role standards. Those who hold less fixed ideas of the roles of men and women are more tolerant of homosexuality (MacDonald et al. 1973). Adherence to traditional sex roles is the primary predictor of anti-gay prejudice among heterosexual males. Homosexuality contradicts their ideology of appropriate gender role behavior. Females' attitudes are a product of a wider array of variables and reflect variables similar to other kinds of prejudice (Newman 1989). Sex roles, parental attitudes, authoritarianism, and educational and media influences make a contribution to female attitudes toward lesbians.

Families provide the earliest teaching of what behaviors are acceptable and unacceptable in given contexts. Families that are secure, tolerant, and respectful of differences allow children to resolve conflicts and integrate a wide spectrum of information about people. Conversely, if a family's values are rigid, it will exclude new incongruous information, such as homosexuality, as a survival strategy. Closed, rigid families are less tolerant of individual differences because differences are threatening to these values (Kahn 1991; Kurdek 1988).

(2) *Perceptions that one's friends hold similarly negative attitudes.* Sharing in a reference group's values of anti-gay sentiment may gain a

person acceptance into that group. It may signal to the group that a particular person is "one of us" and gain him or her status that would not otherwise be won. On the other hand, failure to hold such values may result in being avoided by key persons or barred from the group. Group pressures to hate gays may be all the motivation some people need to be homophobic. Homophobia therefore affirms a sense of self through expressing values integral to personal identity as defined by the group in which the person wants to belong. When confronted by evidence that suggests physiology may play a role in sexual orientation and that sexual orientation is not a choice, prejudiced individuals will shun those facts in preference for group acceptance.

(3) *Strong adherence to an orthodox religious ideology.* Homophobia is particularly intense among individuals and groups who hold conservative religious beliefs (Herek 1987). This relationship points to the philosophical and moral issues central to anti-gay values and behaviors. Homosexual behavior is feared because it threatens religious principles, most of which go back thousands of years to a time when it was believed that sex existed to produce children, who were needed for economic survival. Homosexuality was labeled sinful to dissuade individuals from engaging in behavior that might damage the group. These values persist today as religious rhetoric. The derogatory statements made by the religious right at the beginning of the AIDS epidemic illustrate such rhetoric, which claimed that AIDS, which initially was predominantly striking gay men, was "God punishing homosexuals." Conservatives continue to define sexual orientation as a "choice" and, in this mindset, the choice is immoral. Attitudes are more negative among people who believe that homosexuality is a choice (Whitley 1990).

(4) *Past negative experience with gay people.* A great deal of prejudice against a group comes about when a person has a negative experience with a member of a minority group. The prejudiced person then generalizes the hostile feelings derived from the negative interaction with one person to an entire group. Many straights falsely believe that homosexuality is somehow conta-

gious or that one can be seduced through some enchantment to become gay or lesbian. Anxiety over becoming gay can cause a straight person to fear homosexuals and acts as a setup to have an anxious and unpleasant encounter with a gay or lesbian person. What is interesting is that one predictor of nonprejudice among heterosexuals is a positive experience with a homosexual, especially when paired with the belief that the controllability of sexual orientation is slight (Whitley 1990). Having been subject to a sexual advance is not related to discomfort around homosexuals (Gentry 1987).

In some ways, homophobia has lessened since the Stonewall Riot. Some states have decriminalized homosexual acts of love and a growing number of corporations give gay and lesbian partners of employees "spouse-equivalent" benefits. Many companies have incorporated special policies banning in-house discrimination and television programs occasionally have shows dealing with gays and lesbians in a supportive way. More and more gays and lesbians are living open, secure lives, freed from the closet to express their love as any other citizen. Yet some things have not changed. A 1994 Time/CNN poll of heterosexuals learned that 53 percent of adults believe that homosexuality is morally wrong. This represents no change since 1978 (Henry 1994).

ETHNICITY AND HOMOSEXUALITY

Homosexual life is even more difficult for gays and lesbians who are also members of racial and ethnic groups. Homophobia is greater within many minority subcultures than in mainstream American culture. Tension between racial and ethnic communities and the gay community contradicts the similarities they share as disadvantaged groups. Nevertheless, there is considerable antigay sentiment among African Americans and Hispanics. Furthermore, racism within the gay community creates resentments and conflict among gays themselves.

Lesbians and gays of color experience "double minority" status. They are members of two (or three in the case of lesbians) social groupings that are each subject to categorical discrimination. Double minority status has real consequences in terms of economic success, social life, and personality development issues.

Values about homosexuality are particularly negative among African Americans. According to Icard (1986), the African American community's emphases on the group for economic and social survival and traditional sex role expectations provide the cultural context for its anti-gay sentiment. For many blacks, homosexuality is a cultural phenomenon of European Americans. To be black and gay is to betray African Americans. The African American church influences the community's animosity toward gays and lesbians. African American churches routinely portray homosexuality as a corruption and perversity. Another heterosexual pressure exerted on African Americans within their community is the pressure to have children and orient themselves toward the family. These pressures are so strong that many African Ameri-

cans who have sex with persons of the same gender do not identify themselves as gay or lesbian.

At the same time the African American community is rejecting them, African American lesbians and gay men find they are not necessarily welcome in the gay community either. The gay community is predominantly Euro-American in terms of its culture and value system.

Faced with this conflict, Icard notes that African American gays typically follow one of two types of race and sexual identity formations: those who identify more with the gay community and those who place emphasis on the African American community. Attempts at reconciling the incongruence of rejecting one aspect of identity in favor of another often result in exaggerated identities. One common outcome is the "Miss Thing" syndrome among gay men, which includes exaggerated effeminate behavior and affect and excessive dependence. Another behavioral style common to gay African American men is the "Super Stud." These men assume an aggressive,

Many people feel threatened by homosexuality. This picture of a person with AIDS being harassed is a good example of how people hold onto beliefs with strong group support despite evidence that demonstrates the beliefs to be false. Homophobia is associated with ideologies that assume (1) homosexuality is completely and freely chosen and (2) homosexuality is morally wrong. Homophobia represents political aggressiveness attempting to force people to conform to one group's expectations of how one should live.

defensive posture and take on the dominant role in all relationships.

In sum, many African American lesbians and gays have difficulty solidifying and stabilizing their gay sexual identity because they feel detached and alienated from the European American-dominated gay community.

Hispanic cultures similarly expect exclusive heterosexual behavior. Latino cultures, for the most part, are patriarchal, emphasizing compulsory heterosexuality, especially among men. These norms are of such magnitude that discrete lesbian or gay male identities, based on self-definition and involving emotional as well as physical aspects of same-sex relations, are unusual among Hispanics (Arguelles and Rich 1984). Like African Americans, many Hispanics who engage in same-sex contact do not consider themselves homosexual.

Enforcement of heterosexual norms has eased somewhat in Latino communities, but coming out of the closet still carries certain risks, such as rejection by friends and family, isolation from the community, and being ostracized by the church.

The conservative political values of Cubans, for example, have increased restrictions of gay social life and narrowed sexual tolerance in Miami. For Cuban lesbians and gays, coming out is particularly painful and possibly a violent experience. There is less tolerance for working-class gays than for those in other classes. Homosexuals who manage to escape the anti-gay wrath of the community despite their open lifestyles are generally those of considerable income and resources. In other words, coming out is a class privilege (Arguelles & Rich 1984; Rich & Arguelles 1985). In general, there appears to be a quiet acceptance of Latino homosexuals. For most Latin Americans, the rule is *se dice nada, se hace todo,* say nothing, do everything (Arguelles & Rich 1984).

CONCLUSION

This chapter examined the development of sexual orientation and the meanings it has for personal and social life. If, in fact, sexual orientation is biologically predisposed, as research suggests, then gays and lesbians should be offered the same civil rights protections as other groups defined by ascribed characteristics, e.g., sex and racial groups.

Homosexuals have more difficulty establishing a stable sexual identity because of the stigma attached to them and the prejudice and discrimination they continue to face. The structural model of social work practice contends that environmental disadvantages account for most of the troubles gays and lesbians face. If those who control macro systems in the environment were not so hostile toward homosexuals, then housing and employment discrimination would not exist. If people were not so hostile in their interpersonal interactions with gays and lesbians, then coming out would not be a traumatic experience and there would be less ambiguity in the norms and values that guide the behaviors of gays and lesbians.

The structural model analyzes the transactions between lesbians and gays and their environment. When such an analysis reveals that the environment presents few barriers to normal living, gays and lesbians have fewer psychosocial problems. However, when the environment denies tangible and/or psychic resources for homosexuals, they are more likely to suffer inter- and intrapersonal distress.

CASE STUDY REVIEW QUESTIONS

Refer to Charles's case at the beginning of this chapter. Given what you have learned, how might you address the following questions?

1. How does Charles's family of origin impact his self-understanding and self-awareness as a homosexual?
2. At what stage of sexual identity formation would you assess Charles? In what ways has his denial of his homosexuality affected him?
3. Using Bell and Weinberg's typology, how would you describe Charles's homosexual lifestyle?
4. How do homophobic reactions in the environment affect Charles?
5. What can men and women with heterosexual orientations learn from those with gay or lesbian orientations?

KEY TERMS

Affectional homosexuality: Close emotional bonds shared by people of the same sex.

Asexual homosexuals: Gay people who have low sexual interest and are single; they are usually secretive about their sexual orientation.

Bisexuality: A person who is sexually attracted to people of both sexes.

Blending stage: The first stage in gay relationships when the couple falls in love and begins to integrate the various aspects of their lives; during the blending stage, most gay men strive to create equality.

Building stage: A stage in the development of gay relationships in which individuals' independence is clearly established and they have reached a secure level of comfort with their partner.

Closed-coupled homosexuals: Gay people who live together in relationships that resemble heterosexual marriages; partners are closely attached and feel sexually content; they tend to be happy and satisfied with their lives.

Coming out: The process of acknowledging a homosexual orientation.

Dysfunctional homosexuals: Gay people who are coupled and who have a high rate of sexual problems; most in this category regret their sexual orientation and their level of psychological adjustment is poor.

Functional homosexuals: Gay people who are not involved in a relationship, but have a high number of sexual partners with few sexual problems; they have a high interest in sex and are comfortable in their sexual identity.

Heterosexuality: A sexual orientation in which fantasies, attachments, and longings are predominantly focused on or directed toward people of the opposite sex.

Homogamy: The practice of marrying someone similar in age, socioeconomic status, race, religion, cognitive and personality characteristics, and other traits.

Homophobia: Prejudice and discrimination aimed at gays and lesbians.

Homosexuality: A sexual orientation in which fantasies, attachments, and longings are predominantly focused on or directed toward people of the same sex.

Identity acceptance: A stage in the coming out process in which other gays and lesbians are evaluated more positively and the person's reference group starts to include the gay community.

Identity comparison: A stage in the coming out process in which the person rationalizes and bargains homosexual feelings.

Identity confusion: The first stage in the coming out process in which people begin to recognize sexual attractions to their own sex; this stage is associated with feelings of being different from peers and a growing sense of personal detachment.

Identity pride: A stage of the coming out process in which people become aware of social injustice and public issues involving the gay community; people may feel anger at heterosexuals for these inequities and distance themselves from heterosexual individuals and institutions.

Identity synthesis: A stage in the coming out process in which the homosexual person has fully integrated gay or lesbian relationships into the structure of his or her personality and social life.

Identity tolerance: A stage in the coming out process in which people begin to accept a homosexual identity; at this time, people only tolerate, but do not fully accept, a homosexual identity.

Maintaining stage: A developmental stage in gay relationships marked by the partners beginning to reassert their individuality.

Nesting stage: A developmental stage in gay relationships in which the couple works toward compatibility in living together.

Open-coupled homosexuals: Gay people who live in one-to-one relationships but also have outside sexual partners.

Releasing stage: A stage in the development of gay relationships in which partners are valued for their companionship and acceptance of the other is complete.

Renewing stage: The last stage of long-term gay relationships in which each partner looks to the other to restore the excitement of earlier years and validates the other as having lived a satisfying life.

Sexual identity: The degree to which a person adopts a heterosexual or homosexual self-label.

Sexual orientation: A person's sexual point of reference; it includes one's core attachments and fantasies and represents a person's basic organized sexual desire that endures over time.

CHAPTER 12

FAMILY ORGANIZATION

OBJECTIVES

After reading this chapter, you should be able to answer the following questions:

1. What are the origins and functions of the family?
2. What are the images of the modern family? How do romantic ideals and myths affect family life?
3. What is the difference between healthy and dysfunctional families?
4. How do family tasks differ during the family life cycle?

CASE STUDY

Carla and Matt called a social service agency and asked for help in dealing with a family problem. Until now, they had been able to solve their own problems and had never needed outside help before.

Carla and Matt have three children. Alice is nineteen and recently left home to attend college. Paying for her college has been a financial burden for the family and has added unusual stress. Beth, who is fourteen, is active in school and extracurricular activities. She makes good grades, is popular, and gets along well with almost everybody. Lee, twelve, is in the sixth grade. He has been diagnosed with a learning disability and is in special education classes. He does well in school, but has a hard time with homework. Lee tends to be very sensitive and has little self-confidence.

Matt works full-time and lately has been working extra hours to make money for Alice's college. Carla works part-time outside the home and is highly involved in the children's activities. Matt has always helped Lee with his homework. This arrangement has worked well for the family until recently.

Lately, Matt has begun to lose his temper with Lee. He is becoming increasingly irritable and impatient and often storms out of Lee's room yelling, "Why can't you do it yourself?" The tension is reverberating throughout the family and everyone is uncomfortable.

The social worker helped this family see what stressors were affecting the family and together they worked out a plan to solve the problem. First, Matt agreed to work fewer hours. Second, Carla and Matt would share the load of helping Lee with his homework. Third, the couple joined a bridge club. They used to play bridge regularly, but had stopped this enjoyable activity long ago. Fourth, they talked with Alice honestly about the financial realities of the family. Though her parents felt responsible for her college education, Alice offered to get a job to help with expenses.

INTRODUCTION

The family is the bridge that connects individual experience and development with communities and social institutions. As a particularly influential aspect of the environment, families reproduce the culture and community standards by teaching members how to get along in the social world. Family membership affects society's reaction to individuals. From families people get their ethnicity and economic standing.

As systems, families have dynamics that exert pressure on the individuals within them. Families form patterns of interacting that foster or inhibit individual development. By focusing on family interaction styles rather than the psychological status of individual family members, it becomes possible to understand the family as a systematic environmental force and how it influences human behavior.

It is often the case that social workers' clients are family systems rather than individuals. This means that the social worker is working with a recurring, interrelated, interactive system of people who live together within the context of a broader sociocultural environment. Visualizing the family as a constellation of roles organized within a behavioral framework yields a superior understanding of family phenomena than simply observing the intrapersonal, psychological qualities of individual family members.

This chapter introduces basic concepts of family dynamics and is the first of three chapters that discuss the family as a core feature of individuals' social environment. Although kin create their families, what they form has a reality and force all its own. Like all other groups, families are structured by roles, norms, and values. Paired with the emotional intensity of family life and the social identity and status derived from the family's position in the community, the family structure has more direct influence on human behavior than any other social system.

ORIGINS AND FUNCTIONS OF THE FAMILY

Family Origins

Anthropologists are not certain about the prehistoric origins of human families. Several theories have been offered since the 1800s, though there is little evidence that supports any of them. The sociobiological approach probably contributes the most toward understanding the beginnings of the family. This approach suggests that families began once human females no longer came into estrus, which means going into "heat." Losing the biological mandate that determined when mating occurred allowed humans to focus on permanence in relationships. Sexual urges could be satisfied at any time, not just when biological processes switched them on. From this viewpoint, it is possible that relationships were formed for reasons of sexual protection. Consequently, attractiveness and choice became a part of mate selection and bonds between males and offspring were formed.

By the beginning of written history, marriage and the family were well-established social systems in all cultures. Family systems have evolved throughout history and vary in composition, style, and how they interact with the society-at-large.

Differences in family systems are based on environmental conditions. For example, marriage systems in which women could take multiple husbands (*polyandry*) were found in cultures that lived in extremely impoverished conditions. These systems were not female-dominated, as one might think. Actually, in polyandrous cultures, which historically were rare and no longer exist, the status of women was extremely low and sharing wives was an adaptive strategy to a short supply of food. In other words, it took two or more men to produce enough food to support one woman, who was considered a burden on the community.

Family systems are products of the cultural and economic environments in which they are situated. Not all family systems follow the cultural expectations found in the West. In many cultures, polygyny is the norm. Despite the temptations to label these families as bizarre and immoral, it is important to understand these systems within their own cultural and historical context.

Polygyny, a marital system in which men can legitimately take more than one wife, is a very common marriage system. It is found in non-Christian, preindustrial or industrializing cultures that do not value women politically, economically, and socially. Having multiple wives is a status marker of the husband's wealth. The more money he has, the more wives he can support. Most polygynous cultures are poor; therefore most marriages in these societies are actually *monogamous,* having one spouse at a time. Furthermore, if every man expected more than one wife, there would not be enough women to go around.

Contemporary family systems within Western culture also take their forms via interaction with the environment. Changes in fertility patterns, parents' relationships with their children, and divorce are associated with changes in the non-family environment. Many of these relationships will be explored in the following chapters.

Family Functions

Every system must have goals or imperatives that define its purpose and give it meaning. Like other institutions, the family functions at different levels of the social structure. For this reason, any analysis must consider the role of the family in the perpetuation and integration of society in general as well as how the family operates in terms of meeting the needs of each of its members.

The functions of the family have changed dramatically in the last half century. Several examples illustrate this point. First, the family used to be a unit of production; that is, the family was both a producer as well as a consumer of wealth. Family members participated in the productive activities that were necessary to generate the food and products they required for survival. In an urban, industrial–service economy, however, most economic production occurs outside the home and children do not contribute to the economic welfare of the family. Family members do not produce their own wealth per se, but depend on organizations in the broader economic system to provide jobs that exchange money for labor. Today, the family is a unit of consumption, which means that families share the wealth that the adults bring to the family from outside its boundaries.

Over time, other family functions have been taken over by outside organizations and institutions. For example, most of the education children needed to perform their expected adult roles was provided by other family members. Formal schooling was limited and often did not correspond to what people needed to know to survive in their particular social environment. Additional examples of previous family functions that are now the province of outside agencies include health care, day care for children, elderly care, and welfare for economic support.

Contemporary family systems are unlike any others in history. Whereas in the past family cooperation and resources determined survival and were the primary foci of family relationships, now the emotional aspects of family relationships are paramount to the family's relationship to society-at-large. To accommodate the dynamics of the companionship aspects of family life today, theorists have defined three types of family functions: institutional functions, system functions, and individual support functions.

Functions of the Family as an Institution. Universally, societies have relegated several important integrative tasks to the family institution. These tasks are concerned with regulating sexual behavior and reproduction. Though it would certainly be naive to believe that all sex, now or in the past, takes place after the legitimating social ceremony of marriage, there is the expectation that the products of sex, namely children, are the responsibility of families. Governments and other social agents reluctantly involve themselves in the rearing of children and do so only when the child is at risk of maltreatment. Otherwise, for better or worse, children are the wards of the families into which they are born.

Families function not only to have, but to socialize children. This means that families are obligated to prepare children for social living. They teach children the basic tools of the culture, e.g., the language, and the culture's precepts of right and wrong. Families teach children to conform to social rules and etiquette and to become good citizens. In general, families perform a major role in adaptation, which means teaching children to learn the vital aspects of modern life (Vincent 1966). This function requires the family to have some degree of connectedness to an external community that defines the norms, values, and roles prerequisite to social integration.

Functions of the Family as a System Itself. Families are systems; therefore, there are certain tasks that families must accomplish to maintain themselves and maintain the welfare of individual members. Family systems are divided into three subsystems that are responsible for accomplishing these tasks: the marital subsystem, the parental subsystem, and the sibling subsystem. The responsibilities of the subsystems are outlined in Table 12.1.

Economic cooperation is necessary for meeting the biological needs of family members. Family members produce wealth and then share it with kin in the form of food, shelter, protection, and recreation. As I stated above, families are not economically self-sufficient or self-determining; they are dependent on the political economy for jobs or assistance. No matter how hard adults in a family work, what they make is arbitrarily set by employers. Therefore, how a family performs this self-maintenance task is highly influenced by external, non-family processes.

A second task for self-preservation is a family division of labor. Families must have an organization in order to avoid chaos. This structure should include leadership and an allocation of tasks, such as the various instrumental household chores, that keep the family system functioning smoothly. Families must also tend to the emotional needs of regulating the system. This includes problem-solving and handling crises and emotional distress when they occur.

Family Functions that Support Individual Members. In this existentialist age, marriage and family life is less about economic survival

TABLE 12.1 Differentiation of Family Tasks by Family Subsystems

MARITAL SUBSYSTEM

- Provide emotional satisfaction of adults without compromising the psychosocial development of each individual;
- Be supportive of spouse's needs, activities, and aspirations;
- Develop problem-solving techniques that allow individual needs to be fulfilled, but also facilitate feelings of closeness, shared identity, and mutual accommodation;
- Foster creativity, learning, and personal growth;
- Maintain boundaries to separate marital functions, such as sex, from the other subsystems.

PARENTAL SUBSYSTEM

- Protect and show affection to children;
- Socialize children through guidance, rules, and appropriate discipline;
- Adapt flexible parenting styles to the age and specific needs of the child, rather than the needs of the individual parent;
- Develop communication and effective problem-solving techniques that foster developmental growth in children.

SIBLING SUBSYSTEM

- Learn to relate to peers through negotiation, cooperation, and competition;
- Learn how to make and keep friends;
- Learn how to achieve recognition through use of skills;
- Adapt to the adult world by following rules, mastering school assignments, and learning to respect others as human beings;
- Strive toward independence and develop a personal identity and code of ethics.

and more about emotional contentment. Families must succeed in enhancing the development of both adults and children.

Just as families should help spouses realize their own human potential and maximize emotional fulfillment, families should foster the development of emotionally secure children as well. Families have the most important influence on the personality development of offspring. To accomplish this goal, family systems must create a secure, stable, and safe environment.

Families affect personality development by the ways they manage affect in children (Farley 1990). Children signal internal tensions through expressions of emotion. If families acknowledge and differentiate one emotional state from another, then the child's distress is resolved with help from caregivers. If, on the other hand, the family fails to identify and respond to children's emotional signals, children are left to deal with problems individually and in isolation, a situation that usually leads to anxiety and depression. Successful families have the ability to express and respond to affect messages in children, who in turn learn to trust their environment and articulate their feelings and ideas. One critical task for families, for example, is to teach children how to regulate sexual and aggressive impulses and express them in socially acceptable ways. If a family is well organized with an appropriate system of rules, children will learn alternative strategies for dealing with aggressive impulses.

Despite their appearance, supporting individual development is not confined to the internal interactional patterns of families. The external environment has a profound impact on how families perform these tasks. Stress from unemployment and poverty, a poor social structure in neighborhoods, and a lack of meaningful educational opportunities make it hard for families to provide the kind of stability they need to rear emotionally secure children.

In summary, families have requirements that must be satisfied in order for society, the family system itself, and individual members to thrive. These tasks are best performed when the family is well organized, attuned to the emotional needs of adults and children, receives adequate resources from social institutions, and is aligned culturally with the community in which it is embedded.

FAMILY IMAGES AND MYTHS

Because of the importance of families in human development, family life invokes strong emotional responses and often carries unreasonable expectations. Furthermore, the family has become politicized in recent years, a process that has promoted a nostalgic movement to return "traditional values" to families. This agenda suggests that family life in the past was simpler and more important.

However, family life historically has been anything but the utopian picture many ideologues paint. In the "old days," men were the legal and factual heads of the household; therefore women and children had few rights and could not make major family decisions. Abusive behavior was tolerated and escape through divorce was difficult, and in many instances impossible. The sexual double standard was more powerful than today and minority families were largely excluded from important social institutions. Families that differed from the middle-class, nuclear model were viewed as illegitimate or pathological.

There are several false beliefs about what today's families are like as well. People's expectations of what families should be like color the family system of which they are a part. When these myths are held, disappointment, frustration, and anger are likely consequences when the beliefs are revealed to be false.

Families as "Havens in a Heartless World"

Many people think of the family as a "haven in a heartless world," where the family is a private island of love, warmth, and togetherness, separated from the rest of the world. As a "haven," the family insulates and protects adults and children from the demands and conflicts of society. In other words, the family is an escape from the antagonisms of work, community problems, and other conflicts and is a place where people renew their spiritual resources (Keniston 1965).

The Tale of the Gypsies

Gypsies are among the least understood and most stereotyped ethnic groups. A recent poll showed that Americans rate Gypsies as having the lowest social desirability of all groups in the country (Marger 1994). Gypsies are notorious for being nomadic, cunning, sly, and sexually immoral. Is this reputation fair? How did they receive this characterization and why are Gypsies so mysterious?

Gypsies, who call themselves the Rom, have a distinctive culture and language, though they have no national homeland. The Rom keep few records; therefore little of their early history is known. Most likely, the Rom originated in Northern India because their language, Romany, is a form of Sanskrit (Cohn 1969). It is beyond doubt, however, that the Rom have been the target of prejudice and discrimination throughout their history. For example, over 250,000 Gypsies were killed by the Nazis in World War II.

The core of Rom culture is the concept of *marime'*, which means pollution or defilement. *Marime'* refers to social rules that divide the world into clean and unclean, good and bad, pure and impure (Clebert 1963). It draws the line between what is Rom and what is *gadje*, or non-Gypsy. *Marime'* is particularly relevant in reference to the upper and lower halves of the body. The upper parts, notably the head and mouth, are believed to be good and clean. The lower half, especially the genitals and anal region, is unclean, or *marime'*. The Rom never "mix" the two regions of the body. Underwear and shirts are never washed together. Different towels and soaps are used for the face and for the lower body.

Marime' affects relationships as well. Women who are menstruating, pregnant, or new mothers are *marime'*. During these times, they may not cook or serve food to men. A *marime'* woman "may not step over anything belonging to a man or allow her skirts to touch his things...[and her] clothing must be washed separately from men's" (Gropper 1975: 92–93). Women's breasts, however, are not *marime'*, and bras are often used to carry personal items and money. Children and men freely reach into their mothers' and wives' brassieres to retrieve items. Rom women often greet each other with gentle twitches of one another's breasts. In this sense, breasts are no different than hands!

The concept of *marime'* also separates the Rom from the *gadje*. To Gypsies, the *gadje* are a different and offensive race of people who are predisposed to *marime'*. *Gadje* wash underwear and tablecloths together, forget to wash their hands after using the bathroom, put their feet on the table, and engage in oral sex (Sutherland 1975).

Because the *gadje* are *marime'*, the Rom limit contact with them and consider them fair game for con games, fortune-telling scams, and other illegal activities. If *gadje* are *marime'*, then so are their social organizations. Gypsies believe that bureaucracies are *gadje* institutions that strive to control them. Consequently the Rom have no respect, or any need, for bureaucratic organizations. They often carry several drivers' licenses and credit cards, each with a different name, have no formal recording of their business transactions, and resist formal education. They work hard to elude *gadje*.

Their reputation for being nomadic is based on fact. Most Gypsies are vigorous travelers. Though some prefer a sedentary lifestyle, most maintain a fondness for travel. Gypsy culture associates mobility with freedom, health, and good fortune. Gypsies move to follow job opportunities, maintain social and family obligations, avoid discrimination, and, to some extent, to avoid the law.

The culture of the Gypsies is organized into three structural units or layers: *familia, vitsa,* and *natsiyi*. The *familia*, the basic unit of social life, is a functional, extended family. Aunts, uncles, cousins, parents and their children, and other relatives work and live together. The *familia* are highly supportive and protective of their members and command strong loyalty. The *familia* often own property collectively and provide most of the family's health care, social life, and economic well-being.

A *vitsa* is a clan or band composed of up to 100 *familias*. Several *vitsa* belong to a *natsiyi*. The *vitsa* and the *natsiyi* are important social identifiers. Members of a *vitsa* feel a kindred relationship, even though they might come together only during special occasions (Kephart 1987). The *natsiyi* and *vitsa* perform important social functions for the Rom. They resolve conflicts, provide economic assistance, protect members from police harassment, and provide an immediate supply of marriage partners.

continued

Gypsy families are among the most diverse in North America. The traditional practice of arranged marriages, long abandoned in Western societies, persists among the Rom. Though young people are not obliged to accept their parents' selection of a mate, parental influence is quite strong. Marriages among the Rom are more than unions between two people; they are the union of two *familias*. Therefore, marriages have political significance and the parents must protect the *familia's* interests. *Gadje–*Rom intermarriages are rarely tolerated.

If parents' authority in mate selection has its limits, they maintain complete control of the *daro*, or bride price, which is paid by the groom's family to the bride's. The *daro* differs from dowries paid in India and other places in that it is a deposit against maltreatment of the woman. If a husband mistreats his wife, she can return home and the husband forfeits the money paid to her family. Attractive women and women from prestigious families and *vitsas* command high *daro*.

Gypsy families have other distinctive features. For example, husbands and brides are unusually young. This may be one reason why Gypsy marriages have a high rate of failure. The customary age for first marriages ranges from twelve to sixteen. Marrying past age eighteen is uncommon (Sutherland 1975). Rom families are generally quite large, primarily because birth control and abortions are rarely practiced. Reliable data on Gypsy marriage, divorce, and fertility are virtually impossible to obtain because the Rom have no interest in recording their marriages or other family activities with government authorities. Rarely do Gypsies have marriage certificates, legal divorce decrees, or birth records.

Many traditional images of the Gypsies have some degree of truth to them. Placing Rom behaviors within the cultural context of *marime'* and *gadje*, however, makes their actions seem more rational and less immoral to outsiders.

This is perhaps the greatest myth of family life: that terms such as *isolation* and *privatism* are accurate descriptors of families. In reality, families embody the antagonisms that exist in the general society (Lasch 1978). Sexism in politics and the workplace appear as domestic violence and higher domestic workloads for women, even when they are employed full-time. An unequal division of wealth in society translates into more tension, divorce, and discord in families whose incomes are low. Losing a job, which often leads to low self-esteem, frustration, and anger, becomes the basis for abusive behavior and scapegoating. A complete list of examples that shows the fluidity of the boundary that separates family from non-family indeed would be quite long.

Without question much of a particular family's behavior is the result of personality issues and the continuation of the family's behavioral history. Nonetheless, it is important to realize the pressures of non-family forces on family functioning as well. Over time, family styles and composition probably would change very little if it were not for the extensive social changes that have occurred during the last several decades (Glick 1989). Two examples illustrate this point. First, advancements in education and technology have led to the rapid diffusion of ideas that affect the motivation of individuals about forming families and rearing children. Education and technology are used to seek out higher wages and to expand interests in status, consumerism, and materialism, while forgoing interests in family life. Second, women have experienced faster increases in education than have men. As a result, women are pursuing educational, career, and personal interests at the expense of the traditional expectation of forming families.

In sum, families are never isolated from the social world. Exchanges between family and non-family systems are continuous. The forms families take are actually reflections of non-family social processes. Therefore, thinking of the family as a "haven in a heartless world" assumes that families are essentially separate systems completely detached from the rest of the world.

Family Self-Reliance

Another myth of family life is the belief in family self-reliance (Coontz 1992). The popular image of the family standing on its own feet, not taking "handouts" from anyone, is firmly ingrained in the minds of Americans. Television and other media reinforce this image with shows and stories that portray the family as autonomous, rugged, and self-sufficient. Families that receive outside help are portrayed as weak and unfit. As much as this idea is believed, it is also incorrect.

Families have a long history of receiving assistance from non-family institutions, communities, and acquaintances. As Stephanie Coontz (1992: 69) argues, "depending on support beyond the family has been the rule rather than the exception in American history, despite recurring myths about individual achievement and family enterprise." This rule of assistance is not limited to poor, "welfare" families. All families receive some kind of help. For example, federal tax subsidies for homeowners are about four times higher than direct public spending for low-income housing programs. The richest 20 percent of the American population receives over 52 percent of all federal housing subsidies, which is three times as much as the poorest 20 percent of American families (Leonard, Dolbeare, & Lazere 1989). Other examples of welfare that families receive, but often do not consider when casting themselves as self-reliant, include: Social Security, tax relief for dependent children, publicly funded education, protection services, subsidized transportation, food price stabilization programs, government supported health programs, and countless others.

Because families believe they are self-reliant, they may resist intervention when they are no longer able to cope with a particular problem. It is ironic that many families will resist intervention from professionals, yet will turn to judges to make child custody decisions when their marriage dis-

solves. In short, the philosophy of the rugged individual is mythological and short-sighted.

Romancing the Family

Marriage has a profound meaning for most people. Although half of all marriages will eventually end in divorce, most people believe that their marriages will last "till death do they part." By law, marriage is a formal, legal union in which debts and assets are shared and tax benefits are awarded. Interpersonally, marriage is a public declaration of commitment, companionship, and love. For many people, marriage also carries expectations of being a "cure-all" for their problems. These families have love, but they idealize what love means. Herein lies a third important myth: Marriage and family are panaceas to problems.

Most certainly dating and getting married are, and should be, romantic times in which couples court each other, fall in love, and plan their lives together. There are occasions when troubled individuals will add an additional agenda to the courtship process and expect that getting married will magically end their chronic loneliness, despair, and anxiety. These marriages are doomed from the start because one of the spouses has entered the relationship for self-serving reasons and the exchange of support and affection is likely to be one-way. Dependent spouses are usually either very demanding and expect their partners to fulfill their personal needs, or they will be passive and abandon their own needs to fulfill the partner's needs to prevent the partner from leaving.

This can apply to having children as well. Many children enter the world unwittingly in the role of marriage-saver and depression-reliever. Spouses who are depressed or whose relationship is not going well may hold the false belief that having a baby will bring them closer together and make them the stereotypical happy family. This strategy not only does not work to resolve marital problems, it also places the child in an unfair position in the family system. Parents may become angry at the child who fails to save the troubled marriage or emotionally abandon the child who is no longer needed, or is symbolic of the marriage after it has dissolved. These parents may opt to overwhelm their children, essentially fusing their identities and not allowing the child to achieve autonomy.

Producing a baby because of marital strife is an attractive proposition for people who may feel helpless and desperate in their marriage. The baby diverts attention from specific problems, at least for a while, and the couple may feel temporarily recommitted to the relationship. This may renew hope that they will indeed become a happy family and fulfill their earlier expectations. It is also easier to relate to a baby than it is to confront difficult marital problems. Many people who consciously or unconsciously have a baby to avoid problems will stay married for a long time. As long as they can focus on the child, they can push their problems aside and essentially pretend they do not exist. These marriages may appear happy in public, but the couples are often tense or discontented when alone.

Eventually the couple will have to confront their problems. When children reach adolescence or adulthood and begin to spend more time away from home, parents no longer have them as a buffer and diversion. Divorce is common during this transition because parents have to deal with long-standing, but ignored problems without any experience at resolving major conflicts. Furthermore, because of the underlying tension caused by the unresolved problems, the couple has not been mutually supportive or loving over the years, and so they enter the postparenting stage of their marriage without the momentum of working together and strengthening the attachments between them.

Family Myths and Rules

The myths described above are some of the beliefs that are commonly found throughout the culture. Individual families also develop their own false beliefs out of their own situations.

Families develop rules to govern their interactive patterns. *Family rules,* using Hepworth and Larsen's definition, are shared cognitive perceptions about each other, the family unit itself, and the world at large. These perceptions may be consistent with community and cultural standards or they may be distortions of reality, "that is, ill-founded, self-deceptive, well-systematized beliefs uncritically held by members" (Hepworth & Larsen 1993: 310). These myths function to help shape, maintain, and justify family interactional patterns.

DEFINING THE HEALTHY FAMILY

Perhaps the most overused term regarding family life today is *dysfunction.* The concept of the dysfunctional family is readily applied to families by mental health professionals and lay persons without actually qualifying what the term is meant to describe. Used freely and without being defined operationally, the term *dysfunction* proffers little useful information about the functional strengths and weaknesses of a given family system (Beavers & Hampson 1993). The best approach to take while defining a dysfunctional family is to avoid vague, ambiguous labels such as "schizophrenic," "addictive," and "codependent," in favor of specifying multidimensional measures of family functioning (Epstein et al. 1993).

Not all "dysfunctional" families are alike, nor are they unhealthy in all facets of family living. Similarly, not all healthy families work smoothly in all areas. Some are efficient in some areas, but stumble in others. Family competence, therefore, is measured by a progressive continuum, rather than discrete categories. Conceptualizing family health in this way promotes the view that observable growth and adaptation in families is possible (Beavers & Hampson 1993).

The McMaster Model, a well-known measure of family health, identifies six dimensions of family functioning: problem-solving, communication, roles, affective responsiveness, affective involvement, and behavior control (Epstein et al. 1993). According to this model, outlined in Table 12.2, these factors have the most impact on the emotional and physical health or problems of family mem-

TABLE 12.2 The McMaster Model of Family Functioning

PROBLEM-SOLVING

Two types of problems:
Instrumental and affective
Seven stages to the process:
1. Identification of the problem
2. Communication of the problem to the appropriate person(s)
3. Development of action alternatives
4. Decision on one alternative
5. Action
6. Monitoring the action
7. Evaluation of success

Postulated:
- Most effective when all seven stages are carried out.
- Least effective when families cannot identify problem (stop before step 1).

COMMUNICATION

Instrumental and affective areas
Two independent dimensions:
1. Clear and direct
2. Clear and indirect
3. Masked and direct
4. Masked and indirect

Postulated:
- Most Effective: Clear and direct
- Least effective: Masked and indirect

ROLES

Two family function types:
Necessary and other
Two areas of family function:
Instrumental and affective
Necessary family function groupings:
1. Instrumental
   a. Provision of resources
2. Affective
   a. Nurturance and support

b. Adult sexual gratification
3. Mixed
   a. Life skills development
   b. Systems maintenance and management
Other family functions:
Adaptive and maladaptive
Role functioning is assessed by considering how the family allocates responsibilities and handles accountability for them.
Postulated:
- Most effective when all necessary family functions have clear allocation to reasonable individual(s) and accountability is built in.
- Least effective when necessary family functions are not addressed and/or allocation and accountability are not maintained.

AFFECTIVE RESPONSIVENESS

Two groupings
Welfare emotions and emergency emotions
Postulated:
- Most effective when a full range of responses is appropriate in amount and quality to stimulus.
- Least effective when range is very narrow (one or two affects only) and/or amount and quality is distorted, given the context.

AFFECTIVE INVOLVEMENT

A range of involvement with six styles identified:
1. Absence of involvement
2. Involvement devoid of feelings
3. Narcissistic involvement
4. Empathic involvement
5. Overinvolvement
6. Symbiotic involvement

Postulated:
- Most effective: Empathic involvement
- Least effective: Symbiotic involvement and absence of involvement

continued

TABLE 12.2 *(Continued)*

BEHAVIOR CONTROL

Applies to three situations:

1. Dangerous situations
2. Meeting and expressing psychobiological needs and drives (eating, drinking, sleeping, eliminating, sex, and aggression)
3. Interpersonal socializing of behavior inside and outside the family

Standard and latitude of acceptable behavior determined by four styles:

1. Rigid
2. Flexible
3. Laissez-faire
4. Chaotic

To maintain the style, various techniques are used and implemented under "role" functions (systems maintenance and management)

Postulated:

- Most effective: Flexible behavior control
- Least effective: Chaotic behavior control

Source: Epstein, N. B., Bishop, D., Ruan, C., Miller, I., & Keitner, G. 1993 The McMaster model: View of healthy family functioning. In F. Walsh (Ed.), *Normal Family Processes*, 2nd ed. New York: Guilford Press, pp. 138–160.

bers. Families' performances in these areas can range from "most effective" to "most ineffective." Let's review these six areas of family behavior and try to determine what makes a family "healthy."

Problem-Solving

In the McMaster Model, problem-solving is defined as a family's ability to resolve problems to a degree that maintains effective family functioning. Although effective and ineffective functioning families encounter about the same number of problems, they handle them quite differently. In short, healthy families solve their problems and ineffectively functioning families do not resolve many of theirs.

Families face two kinds of problems: instrumental and affective. Instrumental problems are task oriented and concern issues such as providing

money, clothes, housing, and transportation. Affective problems relate to issues of emotions such as anger and guilt. According to Epstein, if instrumental problems disrupt family functioning, then it will be difficult to resolve affective problems. Affective problems, on the other hand, do not necessarily hinder the resolution of instrumental problems.

Effective families solve most problems efficiently and easily and have few if any problems that go unresolved. Problems that exist are relatively new and are dealt with quickly and systematically. These families identify the problem, discuss it, lay out alternatives, select one course of action, and evaluate its effectiveness. Families that engage in ineffective problem-solving approach problems less systematically and make attempts to avoid, minimize, or discount the importance of the problem. Today's problems are likely to be yesterday's as well because these families either have some need to keep problems alive or they are threatened by addressing the problem's source.

Some problems are of such magnitude that even families with superior problem-solving skills lose their coping abilities. The source of these problems is usually outside the family and affects instrumental functioning. Stressful conditions in the immediate environment, especially those related to income and job security, are the most important predictors of parental stress (Pittman, Wright, & Lloyd 1989).

Communication

The second dimension of family functioning in the McMaster Model of family functioning is communication, the exchange of information. Family communication is also subdivided into instrumental and affective areas, which have the same implications here as they do in the problem-solving dimension.

The model also assesses two other elements of communication: clarity and directness. The clarity aspect of family communication determines whether messages are clearly conveyed or masked, camouflaged, or vague. Directness concerns the degree that messages go to their appropriate targets or are deflected to other people.

Research and clinical data consistently report that healthy families' communication is more effective than families judged to be dysfunctional. Functional families send clear and direct messages in both the instrumental and affective areas. In ineffective families, messages often have double meanings, are indirect, and are ambiguous. In these families, communication is often an expression of an emotional state, rather than a vehicle to transmit an idea or an emotion that leads to solving a problem.

Role Functioning

The third dimension of family functioning involves the performance of roles, which Epstein and associates (1993) define as the repetitive patterns of behaviors by which family members fulfill family tasks. This dimension focuses on those tasks that are necessary for the family to maintain itself as an effective and healthy system. The McMaster Model identifies five necessary family functions, which are the basis of the roles within a family, that should be assessed in order to determine the health of a family system. These tasks include:

1. Provision of resources such as food, clothing, and shelter;
2. Nurturance, reassurance, love, and support;
3. Adult sexual gratification;
4. Personal enhancement through developing skills for personal achievement;
5. Maintenance of the family system through establishing rules for decision-making, maintaining boundary integrity, controlling behavior, dealing with household finances, and providing health care functions.

Role functioning is assessed by considering two factors. First, the concept of *role allocation* is concerned with the ways families assign roles and how satisfied family members are with performing them. Second, *role accountability* refers to the process families use for making sure that roles are fulfilled. Role accountability includes determining family members' sense of responsibility and duty to the family and how they correct inadequacies.

Affective Responsiveness

Affective responsiveness refers to a family's potential range of emotional responses. Well-functioning families react to each other and the social environment with a full spectrum of emotional responses that correspond to the stimulus or situational context. Emotional responsiveness is measured along a continuum. Values along the continuum range from emotional absence, which is the failure of the family to make any kind of emotional response, to reasonable or expected affective response, to overresponsiveness.

Epstein's research finds that healthy families show a full range of emotions and that when an emotion is expressed it is done so in an appropriate context and with the correct intensity and duration. Troubled families, however, have a narrow range of emotional expressions. They rely on a small number of affective states to get them through all kinds of situations. These families show less affective flexibility, essentially using the same emotional response regardless of the context.

Affective Involvement

Affective involvement refers to the degree that family members demonstrate interest in the activities and well-being of each other. This dimension of family behavior is concerned with questions such as: Do family members value each others' activities and "personhood"? To what degree do family members invest themselves in one another? Do family members maintain appropriate separateness from one another?

In devising the McMaster Model, Epstein and associates found that the range of styles of affective involvement extended from no interest or investment in one another at one end of the continuum to *symbiotic involvement* at the other (see Table 12.2). Symbiotic involvement refers to an extreme and pathological interest in others. Where this occurs, it is difficult to separate one person from another. At this extreme, boundaries do not exist and individuation is obscured.

Underinvolved families are those whose internal boundaries are rigid and lack permeability.

Members of these families, known as *disengaged* families, are not accessible to each other because independence is the primary family goal. In disengaged families, rules are very permissive and the parental style is characterized by minimal authority, discipline, and affection. Brown and Christensen summarize these families well:

> Obviously such separateness among family members allows for independence: yet what happens when someone gets lonely or discouraged in his or her daily world? The rigidity of personal boundaries serves as a barrier in such families—a barrier to the benefits of reciprocal support, consolation, and nurturance (1986: 61).

The process of family overinvolvement describes the notion of *enmeshment.* An enmeshed family system is one in which family members are overprotective and subsystem boundaries are diffuse. In enmeshed families, internal family boundaries are too permeable and little differentiation of family members or subsystems occurs. These families routinely demonstrate a low tolerance for personal autonomy, which can hinder individual psychosocial development. When individuals in enmeshed families venture to express their independence, they are perceived as harmful and threatening by others who may attempt to control them (Brown & Christensen 1986).

Epstein considers *empathetic involvement* the optimal functioning type for families. In this style, boundaries are respected and maintained and family members are appropriately interested in each other. Family members preserve their own identity, yet they feel that they belong and are loyal to their family. Research has shown that problems in a family's ability to maintain boundaries predicts difficulty in parenting. Pittman, Wright, and Lloyd's (1989) research found that the lack of privacy is one factor that results in greater parental stress and decreased parental effectiveness.

Behavior Control

This dimension refers to the behavior styles and rules a family uses for handling behavior in three areas: (1) physically dangerous situations, (2) situations that involve the meeting and expressing of psychobiological needs and drives, and (3) situations involving interpersonal behavior among family members and between family and people outside the family.

The McMaster Model identifies four styles of how families control behavior in these areas. The styles are differentiated by variations in family rules and the latitude they allow family members in following those standards.

1. Rigid behavior control: Standards are narrow and specific and there is minimal negotiation or variation across situations.
2. Flexible behavior control: Standards are reasonable, and there is opportunity for negotiation and change, depending on the context.
3. Laissez-faire behavior control: At the extreme, no standards are held, and total latitude is allowed, regardless of the context.
4. Chaotic behavior control: There is unpredictable and random shifting between other styles, so that family members do not know what standards apply at any one time or how much negotiation is possible (Epstein et al. 1993: 152).

Flexible behavior control is the most effective style of controlling behavior in families. In this style, individuals are more likely to understand the rules, know what to expect in a given situation, and believe the rules are fair.

The other styles operate without regard to the emotional and developmental needs of all family members. Rigid control stems from parents' needs to be dominant and to control all aspects of family living. This style emphasizes control over children's needs and stifles their attempts to grow psychologically, express themselves, and explore their environment. In the laissez-faire style, parents may feel threatened by imposing and enforcing rules. They may believe, for example, their children would not love them if they were "too harsh." Other parents may not have wanted children and are not interested in being highly involved in their children's development. Finally, the chaotic style is common in alcoholic families where executive behavior is unpredictable. This style leaves spouses and children confused about what is normal, and there is no firm structure on which to establish attachments.

LIFE CYCLE FAMILY TASKS

Family systems are in a constant state of dynamic tension. As families move through time, they experience different challenges that become the focus of their energy. Both internal and external stressors tug at families, compelling them to adapt and change in order to survive. There are two types of internal stressors. First, there are disruptions to normal functioning and development due to individual misfortune. Examples include illness, death, and developmental disorders such as mental retardation. The second type includes developmental transitions of individual members of the family, e.g., the transition to adolescence. Most of the time, individuals will deal with these developmental imperatives within a family context. Consequently, the family system must adapt to those developmental demands and alter its structure to accommodate them. It is no coincidence that most family problems are paired with developmental transitions.

Family systems must also adapt to external stressors presented by non-family systems. Systems external to the family exert pressure, but also provide resources. Families must deal with macrosystems such as the political–economic system, the forces of culture, and community membership, as well as exosystems, mesosystems, and other microsystems, such as friendships. From these systems, the family not only receives the resources it needs to thrive, e.g., a job for income and a community for identity, but the family is also subject to the fluctuations and destructive forces of these systems, e.g., unemployment, due to a shortage of jobs, and discrimination because of inter-group hostility. Families are the bridges between individuals and all of these dynamics.

As families move through time, they undergo transitions, passing from one family life cycle stage to the next. Transitions are periods of instability, disorganization, stress and potential change (Anderson & Sabatelli 1995). Important family transitions are marked by major individual milestones such as the birth of a baby, the departure of a grown child, or retiring from employment. These individual changes, in turn, force family roles to change as well. For example, the arrival of the first baby creates the parental subsystem and the adults, who previously only played marital subsystem roles in their family unit, now must add parental tasks to their role load, and amend their marital roles. The new parents no longer can relate to each other as they did before the baby arrived. In short, the family structure has changed, not just by adding a new member, but because the internal dynamics have been altered.

Most family theorists and practitioners agree with Carter and McGoldrick's (1980) model that defines six stages in the life cycle of a family. These stages are: the beginning family, the new-parent family, the family with young children, the adolescent family, the launching family, and the postparental family.

The Beginning Family

When two people decide to marry and form a family, a great deal more than simply deciding to live together is occurring. They are forming a system of interaction with each other and uniting the roles, myths, and ideas of family life they bring from their families of origin. Each person further brings their individual level of separation from their own parents to the new family.

The degree to which couples establish their independence is largely based on the extent to which they have developed a separate personal identity within their families of origin. Spouses who have a stable sense of self, make their own decisions, and feel emotionally separated from their parents are likely to be more successful in their marriage. They can be intimate without game-playing, maintain boundaries, and remain instrumentally independent with greater ease and less anxiety if they are appropriately detached from their families.

In many cases, when the spouses have not fully separated from their families of origin, they transfer their dependencies from their parents to their new spouses. This process, known as *fusion,* describes a level of attachment in which individuals lose their identity and sense of selfhood in the relationship. When people are fused, they feel that their happiness is the responsibility of their partners and often blame the other for problems in the relationship. Fused partners have trouble negotiating and problem-solving because they fear that "giving in" means losing one's identity (Brown & Christensen 1986).

People who have achieved emotional autonomy are better able to set family goals and priorities and resolve problems because the inevitable problems in a marriage are not perceived as threats to personal identity. Negotiating who vacuums the floors, for example, is seen as a necessary task and not an attack on the ego. Therefore, devising strategies to solve problems and meet individual needs, an important task in new marriages, is best predicted by the qualities each individual brings to the marriage.

Another important task of beginning families is the decision to have children. The couple needs to talk about how many children to have and how they will raise them. Of course it is impossible to know and predict all parenting decisions in advance. Nonetheless, there are many issues that couples can resolve before the first baby arrives. These issues include such tasks as planning finances, managing stress, and balancing work and parenting roles. Couples that are most stable in their marriages, have developed sound problem-solving techniques, and have maintained a deep level of love and attachment are best equipped to handle the role demands and stressors of parenthood. Unfortunately, many people approach parenthood as carelessly as they approach marriage and other commitments, and they find the level of

care required in having a child a great burden (McGoldrick 1980).

The Family with Young Children

When the first child arrives, the family roles divide into subsystems separated by boundaries. The new parents can no longer continue their previous lifestyle and must reorganize themselves to deal with the new tasks involved in caring for the baby. This reorganization is not a one-time responsibility, for each time the child reaches a developmental milestone, new tasks emerge and demand further role adjustments. For example, changing diapers and accompanying a five-year-old to the bathroom are not necessarily the same. When children become competent walkers, parents must watch over them more carefully. When children begin school, new tasks, such as preparing lunches and helping with homework and other learning activities, must be divided to the parents' and children's satisfaction.

Families with children must be conscious of family boundaries. Parents must allow each other personal "space" from time to time while continuing to nurture their marriage by giving themselves time for intimacy and recreation. The parents must decide how to integrate personal and family goals. Parents must also allow children to have age-appropriate privacy, personal possessions, and friends.

Parents must establish rules concerning tolerable behavior and communication. Setting limits is a task that baffles many parents. Finding the right balance of control, discipline, and permission can be difficult, especially if the parents do not agree on discipline, have no good models of parental functioning themselves, or have irrational ideas or feelings about the nature of disciplining children. Rules of discipline serve several purposes: They must provide safety, teach children to conform to the demands of social living, and provide children a sense of structure and organization. At the same time, family rules must tolerate some degree of flexibility and allow children the space to experiment with new behaviors, practice making decisions, and explore the environment. Children that can safely rehearse autonomy within a structure of rules are more likely to trust the people in their environment and eventually separate from their families of origin in appropriate ways.

Not all adults are prepared to have children. Many parents are too involved in their own narcissistic activities and gratification to spend time nurturing their children. They are focused on their work, social networks, or dependencies, and see their children as burdens and nuisances. The emotional abandonment of children is frequently a replay of the parents' own experience of emotional abandonment. Whatever they are doing instead of paying attention to their children is a compensatory behavior that is fulfilling some need that was unfilled as a child. These parents create family systems that are either overly permissive and without rules, or systems that are authoritarian and loaded down with countless rigid rules.

The Adolescent Family

When the first child in a family reaches puberty, that family system must adjust to accommodate the developmental needs of that adolescent. The parental subsystem is required to renegotiate autonomy and control between adolescents and their parents (Carter & McGoldrick 1980). Parenting styles and rules now must change because the teenager is moving toward adulthood and independence.

Family systems often have difficulty making this adjustment. Parenting a teenager is not easy. Mothers and fathers have to change their parenting styles to give up some measure of the complete control they had when their children were younger. At the same time, adolescents are challenging and testing the rules of the family, especially those concerning control and responsibilities.

As I discussed in Chapter 4, the primary developmental tasks of adolescence are identity formation and independent functioning. Family systems should facilitate those tasks by easing

control and allowing children opportunities to have responsibilities. Finding the right balance between control and tolerance is hard for many families. Many parents, for example, are threatened by their adolescents' quests for autonomy and fail to recognize the children's individual needs to become independent (Brown & Christensen 1986). As teenagers become more assertive, the family rules may become more inflexible or support may be withdrawn. When this happens, teenagers often become depressed and may abandon their own assertions for autonomy in order to regain approval from parents. The family has failed in its task of preparing the adolescent to leave home.

As children reach adolescence, their parents are approaching middle age. Therefore the family system must adjust to the needs of the parents who are reaching developmental milestones themselves. For example, parents of teenagers may be caring for their own elderly parents and may be becoming more involved in their careers.

The Launching Family

Launching is a metaphor that refers to children leaving home. In general, launching styles are dichotomized as appropriate and inappropriate. The qualities of children's family systems determine which way they will leave home.

Appropriate launching occurs when a child departs from home to pursue adult tasks such as attending college, serving in the military, working, or marrying. Children who are appropriately launched do so feeling secure and prepared to separate from their family of origin. These family systems have been successful in rearing children with a secure identity who are capable of emotional differentiation. These children also know that returning home is an option should their plans for independent living fail.

Inappropriate launching occurs when a child leaves home under conditions of maltreatment, guilt, or excessive dependency. They may pursue the same goals as the appropriate group, but they may do so under stressful terms. Inappropriate launching occurs in dysfunctional families that fail to prepare children for adult living and to meet the children's developmental needs. Consciously or unconsciously, children will find some reason to escape the burdens of their families. When family systems identify children as responsible for the family's problems (i.e., scapegoating), abuse or neglect, or otherwise fail the child, children are more likely to engage in dangerous, destructive, or depressive behavior and seek any avenue of departure. Abusing drugs, running away from home, and early pregnancy and marriage, for example, are usually symptomatic of a poorly organized family system.

Sometimes children do not leave home at appropriate times. They continue to live at home well into their twenties and even thirties. Many of these cases may be temporary because the child remains in school or cannot get a job that pays enough for her or him to live independently. The other cases may be consequences of excessive dependency created by dysfunctional family processes. In these situations, family dynamics have caused the child to feel guilty about pursuing individual goals and the child feels obligated to remain at home. These adult children may have left the family on one or more occasions only to return

because they believe that living apart from their parents endangers their sense of self and somehow threatens the parents.

The Postparental Family

The postparental family stage begins when the last child leaves home. Now the parents are alone at home and must renegotiate their relationship. For some marriages, the absence of children is liberating because the parents now have time to enjoy each other's company, engage in activities without concern for the children, and have uncompromised privacy. The dynamics of the family system are now dominated by marital roles, rather than a balance of marital and parental functions.

This can be a threatening undertaking in some family systems, however. In less than optimal families, the children may have been a buffer for stress in the marriage. Rather than relate to each other and confront their complaints and unhappiness, the parents may have diverted their energies to the children and disengaged from one another. Now that the children are gone, their buffer is gone, and the family system may become distressed.

During the postparental stage of the family life cycle, losses are common. The family must

When a family experiences developmental changes, it is important to assess the conditions surrounding the changes. A successful launching occurs when a child leaves home voluntarily, with parental support, and without tension or crisis. This 18-year-old is leaving home to attend college, a normative act, with assistance from her parent and sibling. When transitions go smoothly, it is usually an indication that the family has less conflict, has sound problem-solving skills, and manages stress well.

develop strategies to grieve the death of its members and the loss of roles through retirement or bad health. On each occasion of loss, the family system is changed. People relate to each other differently and tensions may arise.

On the other hand, new roles are also added to the family. Parents and their children must realign their relationships to include in-laws and grandchildren.

A Critique of the Life Cycle Model

Recently, critics have contended that the life cycle approach described above is too linear, meaning that it is one-dimensional, and that it no longer fits what is actually happening in the world today. Despite its apparent utility, this model lacks external validity because it describes the stereotypical "normal" family. It assumes that adults marry in their mid-twenties, have children after a couple of years, and then stay together to the end of their lives. This model fails to consider demographic changes and all the variations in modern family forms. For example, it does not include how divorce (which affects 50 percent of all marriages), cohabitation, remarriage, blended families, single-parent households, and the processes of delaying marriage and childbirth may affect the way a family accomplishes its tasks (Glick 1989). The expectations of each of the stages described above would certainly be altered if the adults began the family life cycle significantly older (or younger, for that matter) than the middle twenties, the average age at first marriage, were previously married, or had children from another relationship.

CONCLUSION

The family is not an isolated, private social system untouched by the outside society. Instead it is an open system, and its boundaries are permeable. Many family practices are enactments of society-wide social processes. What happens inside families is highly influenced by the environmental conditions in which they exist. Those conditions help or hinder families as they move through the life cycle and resolve problems.

The structural model of social work practice provides a useful framework for understanding the diversity in family life. Perhaps the most important interaction between families and their environments concerns the exchange of resources. What often separates families that meet their goals from those that do not are differences in the resources available to them. Most differences in family life are related to the availability of material assets (e.g., income, housing, and security). Emotional assets (e.g., problem-solving skills and parenting styles) are usually associated with the material conditions of the family.

The structural model leads social workers to assess the balance of exchanges between the family and its environment. If a family's environment fails to produce enough resources for the family to meet its needs, then the solution to the problem lies not with internal family processes as much as with the family's relationship to that environment. Effecting change in the surrounding environment or helping families locate and take advantage of the resources they need are the main practice goals in this model.

The model also looks at the family as a structured environment from which resources are drawn to meet human needs. For example, children rely on the family structure for protection and nurturance, qualities they need to thrive. When the family environment fails to provide those resources, then emotional deprivations are likely to occur.

The next two chapters will discuss how variations in the psychosocial environment result in differences in family lifestyles as well as problems such as divorce and domestic violence. Despite the cliché, money can buy love—families that have more material assets are more satisfied with their families and are more likely to accomplish their goals.

CASE STUDY REVIEW QUESTIONS

After reading this chapter, you should be able to answer these questions about the couple described in the case study at the beginning of the chapter.

1. What are the main stressors that are affecting this family?
2. This family has coped well in the past. What is different now that makes them more vulnerable to stress?
3. Use the McMaster Model to assess the level of functionality of this family. Given the information you have, would you say the family is functional or dysfuntional?
4. The social worker and the family worked out an intervention with four objectives. How might each objective be effective? Are there other things this family could do?

KEY TERMS

Affective involvement: The degree to which family members demonstrate interest in each other's activities and well-being.

Disengaged family: Underinvolved families in which internal boundaries are rigid and lack permeability; members of disengaged families are not accessible to each other because independence is the primary family goal; rules are very permissive and the parental style is characterized by minimal authority, discipline, and affection.

Empathetic involvement: The optimal functioning style for families: boundaries are respected and maintained and family members are appropriately interested in each other; family members preserve their own identity, yet they feel that they belong and are loyal to their family.

Enmeshed family: A family system in which family members are overprotective and subsystem boundaries are diffuse; in enmeshed families, internal boundaries are too permeable and little differentiation of family members occurs.

Family rules: Shared cognitive perceptions family members have about each other, the family unit itself, and the world at large.

Fusion: A level of attachment in which individuals lose their identity and sense of selfhood in a relationship; when people are fused, they feel that their happiness is the responsibility of their partners.

Launching: A metaphor that describes children leaving home; qualities of the family system determine if a child leaves home with or without distress.

McMaster model: A well-known measure of family health that assesses families on six dimensions of functioning.

Monogamy: Having one spouse at a time.

Polyandry: A marriage system in which women could take multiple husbands.

Polygyny: A common marital system in which men can legitimately take more than one wife.

Role accountability: The process families use for making sure that roles are fulfilled.

Role allocation: The ways families assign roles and how satisfied family members are with performing them.

Symbiotic involvement: An extreme and pathological interest in others; in these families, it is difficult to separate one person from another; boundaries do not exist and individuation is obscured.

CHAPTER 13

FAMILY DIVERSITY

BARBARA GRISSETT

OBJECTIVES

After reading this chapter, you should be able to answer the following questions:

1. What are the different family forms? and how do they affect family life?
2. How does social class affect family life?
3. How does membership in racial or ethnic minority groups affect family life?

CASE STUDY

Diane had not received a child support check for three months. Her ex-husband, James, kept promising to pay soon, but finally admitted he had lost his job. His employer had downsized and James had been permanently laid off. His unemployment checks were inadequate to support his current family, so he could not afford to support his children from his marriage to Diana. All his attempts to find another job had so far come to nothing. He had told her, "You can't get blood out of a turnip!"

Diane and James had met in college. Excellent students, they had both been awarded academic scholarships. To their families' dismay, they had quickly fallen in love and moved in together. This had really upset their families. Both came from working class African American families, and they had been raised with the parental expectation that they would be college graduates. The parents were afraid marriage would interfere with this goal. This disapproval was very difficult for Diane and James, who had always felt close to and supported by their families.

When an unexpected and unwanted pregnancy brought Diane health problems, she dropped out of school. After their son was born, Diane and James married. For the next three years, Diane worked to support James while he finished college. Early in James's senior year, a daughter was born. Between working part-time and studying, James saw little of his family, and most of the burden of caring for the home and children fell on Diane. Weary and feeling exploited, she had looked forward to the day when James would graduate, get a good job, and she could return to college.

On graduation with a degree in personnel management, James landed a job as a personnel officer with a successful manufacturing company. The potential for advancement was promising. They decided Diane should work until James's student loans were paid, then she could quit work and return to school.

The sudden increase in family income tempted Diane and James to spend beyond their means, and they were soon deeply in debt. They argued over money, and Diane became increasingly resentful as she saw her dream of a college education being pushed farther into the future. James became more distant, and spent little time at home. Finally, he admitted to having an affair with JoAnn, a colleague in the personnel office. JoAnn was pregnant. He said he felt his marriage to Diane had been over for a long time, and he wanted a divorce so he could marry JoAnn. Devastated, Diane resisted the divorce, and their relationship became increasingly hostile. Eventually they separated and divorced.

After the divorce, Diane was stuck with a low-paying job, no marketable skills, several debts, and no assets except an old car. James was ordered to pay child support of $300 per month and provide medical insurance for their two preschoolers. Although her income, plus the child support, was inadequate to pay all the bills, she did not qualify for government assistance.

She turned to her family for support. Her twenty-eight-year-old brother sent her money each month, and her mother, widowed the year before, helped by letting Diane use her washer and dryer, cooking meals, sewing, and baby-sitting. The family's network of church and community friends provided car repairs, used clothing, and vegetables from their gardens.

Six months after the divorce, Diane decided to return to college and pursue an Associate's degree in nursing. She would go part-time for two years, then full-time for one year.

For two years, Diane had been a full-time mother and part-time student, receiving financial aid and working thirty hours per week. She had managed to get out of debt and pay her current bills, and was preparing to go to school full-time and finish her degree.

About that time, James failed to pay his child support. After he had missed three months, Diane called her lawyer. James and his new family moved out of the state and he refused to make any more child support payments. Diane was now in trouble. Her family could provide no further assistance and she could barely pay her rent. Her landlord was threatening to evict her.

INTRODUCTION

There are many kinds of families. They vary in form and composition and they are influenced by social class and ethnicity. Diversity among families means more than differences in family customs. It implies variations in family members' well being, roles performance, needs fulfillment, values, and access to resources. Family form affects how families relate to the society-at-large, and vice versa. For example, minority group families strive to maintain unique cultural traits while coping with and adapting to the majority culture. Sensitivity to diversity in family life helps social workers assess family functioning more accurately, and plan and carry out intervention more effectively.

This chapter reviews three ways in which families are diverse. First, differences in family forms are examined. Then the influences of social class and ethnicity on family life are discussed.

DIVERSITY IN FAMILY STRUCTURE

Family form refers to the organization of family members in a family system. It is determined by their relationships with each other, and the roles they play. Family forms vary in complexity. Two people who live together in one household and consider themselves a family make up the most simple family type, while a stepfamily with resident children of the mother, resident children of the father, and the biological children of the couple makes up one of the more complex family structures. Differences in family form affect family dynamics, which influences how role functions are performed by family members. Family dynamics refers to the ways family members relate to one another and carry out family functions. Each structure of family life has its own unique strengths and vulnerabilities.

Couples with No Children

The simplest type of family consists of two persons in an intimate, committed relationship who live in one household. They may have adult children who live elsewhere, minor children with whom they have little involvement, or no children. Those with no children may be unable to have them, may have chosen not to have them, or may be planning to become parents at a later time. The two individuals may both be employed, or may depend on the earnings of one of them.

Roles in families with no children may follow traditional or egalitarian expectations. Tasks such as cooking, making repairs, cleaning, yard work, and laundry may be divided by sex or according to other, perhaps more fair, criteria. Many younger couples without children maintain an egalitarian division of labor, though they may become more traditional when children arrive. Couples whose children have left home may continue playing roles in the same way as they did when their children were around.

Couples with no children are usually stable with a low stress level. Because they are the only ones in the household, the couples can spend more resources on themselves and have greater freedom to pursue recreational activities, careers, and other interests. These couples enjoy more privacy and a less complex lifestyle.

This type of family is vulnerable to several problems, however. Couples with adult children may be pulled into crises, conflict, and expenses relative to their children. Elderly couples with no children may lack the support and resources children could have provided. Unless couples have adequate social support systems, there is the risk that one or both individuals may become overly dependent on the partner or be too demanding, controlling, or possessive.

Families with Two Parents and Their Biological Children

Although this family type represents the ideal family form, it is becoming less common as single-parent families and stepfamilies become more prevalent. Families with two parents and their biological children accounted for only 18 percent of families in 1992 (Reskin & Padavic 1994).

Conservative policy-makers and commentators call for a return to this model as the normative family type, while liberal policy-makers believe this family type is no longer realistic, given current economic and political realities.

In the traditional family, the father performs instrumental tasks and roles. As the breadwinner, the father occupies an *executive position* within the family; that is, he is the one who makes the major decisions and controls finances and other resources. The father is usually the ultimate disciplinarian of the children, and is dominant in the marital relationship as well. If he performs any home maintenance duties, those are likely to be repairing appliances or cars, caring for the lawn, and other tasks requiring strength or technical skills.

The mother, on the other hand, is expected to perform expressive tasks and roles. She works in the home, providing services such as child care, housekeeping, laundry, and cooking. She may entertain to enhance her husband's career and the family's social standing. She is the parent most likely to see that the children's emotional and social needs are met. She is responsible for nurturing her husband and children. She defers to her husband in major decisions, and is less dominant in their marital relationship. Boundaries between parents and children are somewhat rigid. Children are expected to respect and obey their parents, and accept their decisions with little questioning.

Several trends have contributed to the decline of the traditional family, including the growing appreciation of children's rights and the increase in working mothers. While the number of mothers who choose to work outside the home continues to increase, many women who would prefer to be traditional mothers have been forced to work out of financial necessity.

Families with Two Working Parents. In 1992, families with two employed parents accounted for 42 percent of all families with children (Reskin & Padavic 1994). When both parents work outside the home, adaptations to the traditional model are needed. Due to the hours spent working away from home, mothers have less time and energy for child care and domestic maintenance duties. In such families, husbands and children may take on some of these responsibilities. Sometimes child care and/or household domestic help is purchased. Some families adapt by becoming more relaxed in their expectations for order, cleanliness, and home-cooked meals.

Women in the Workforce. Women joined the workforce in great numbers during World War II. Their numbers decreased after the war, but never again fell to the prewar level. In 1960, 34.8 percent of women worked. By 1988, the percentage was 55.9. In 1986, 53 percent of never-married mothers worked, as did 60 percent of married mothers and 80 percent of divorced mothers. Working married mothers have an employment advantage as compared to those never married, in that only 9 percent of working married mothers are younger than 25, as compared with 43 percent of the never-married working mothers. As for education, 16 percent of working married mothers are high school dropouts and 18 percent have college degrees, while among never-married working mothers 36 percent are high school dropouts and only 5 percent have college degrees (Zimmerman 1992).

As married women, including mothers, have increased their participation in the paid workforce, their husbands have not assumed commensurate duties and responsibilities in the areas of domestic maintenance and child care. This phenomenon has been studied since the 1960s, when Alexander Szalai (1972) concluded that the average working woman spent three hours per day on housework and fifty minutes exclusively with her children, while the average man spent seventeen minutes on housework and twelve minutes with his children. In addition, husbands of working mothers had more leisure time than their wives and averaged one-half hour more sleep at night. Hochschild (1989) estimated, based on major time use studies from the 1960s and 1970s, that women worked about fifteen more hours per week than did men. In a study of fifty two-earner families

What type of custodial arrangement works best? Traditional wisdom and judicial precedents have favored mothers in awarding custody of children following the dissolution of a marriage. However, joint custody, a court order that awards both parents equal participation in child-rearing, has many advantages. In this arrangement fathers are more likely to fulfill their child support obligations, litigation is less common, there is less conflict between former spouses, and children adjust better.

done in the 1980s, wives reported doing 75 percent of the housework. Among men, 18 percent did as much as half of the domestic and child care work, 21 percent did between 30 percent and 45 percent, and 61 percent did less than 30 percent (Hochschild 1989). These researchers used the phrases "double day" and "second shift" to describe the situation in which a working woman must work a full day for her employer, then go home and work another "shift" in order to do the majority of home maintenance and child care tasks. Hochschild (1989) believed that this heavy workload created in working wives both fatigue and resentment toward their less busy mates, which in turn placed strain on marriages.

Studies that compare different family types overwhelmingly report better outcomes for children raised by both biological parents, compared with children raised in stepfamilies or by single parents. Children from intact families are better adjusted than those from other family structures (Bronstein, Clauson, Stoll, & Abrams 1993). Parents in intact families are more involved in their children's extracurricular activities, spend more time with their children, and have a more cooperative parenting style than parents in stepfather households. Parents in single-parent and stepfather families exhibit more ineffective parenting, have more arguments, and are less connected, compared to parents in intact families. The parenting style in intact families is more likely to include appropriate rule setting and enforcement (Bronstein, Clauson, Stoll, & Abrams 1993).

Dawson (1991) also compared intact families with stepfather and single-mother families, and found that children in intact families are less likely to repeat school grades or be expelled from school; children from intact families have higher class standing, and are less likely to be in clinical treatment for such problems as depression, stress, anxiety, and aggression. Children who live with both parents have fewer overall behavior problems and are less vulnerable to health problems. Vosler and Proctor (1991) studied the families of children being seen in a child guidance clinic and found that intact families reported about half as many family problems as did stepfamilies, and half as many *socioenvironmental stressors* as did single-parent families. Socioenvironmental stressors, events in or characteristics of the social environment that create stress for a system, include such things as task overload, too few resources, conflict with extended family members, and problems with social institutions.

On average, intact families have more financial resources than single-parent families. Meyer and Garasky (1993) reported that only 7.3 percent of two-parent families are poor, compared with 18.2 percent of father-only families and 42.6 percent of families headed by single mothers.

This family type carries certain vulnerabilities. In traditional families, rigid adherence to gender roles and to task assignments by gender do not model for children the flexibility they may need to succeed in their future families. Needs and feelings of children and women may not be as respected and valued as in more egalitarian families. Women who spend many years as stay-at-home traditional wives may lack job readiness and skills, and ability to function autonomously, should they experience widowhood or divorce.

Further, women who do unpaid domestic work in their own homes are ineligible for Social Security benefits in their own name and for Worker's Compensation should they be injured.

Single-earner families may have inadequate resources to achieve family goals. In two-earner families, financial resources may be more available but at a cost of task overload, especially for working wives. Such families need to find ways to care for household duties and children that do not unfairly burden some members of the family.

Single-Parent Families

According to the United States Bureau of the Census (Rawlings 1993), over 30 percent of American families with children are headed by a single parent. The major types of single parents are never-married parents, divorced or separated parents, and widowed parents. It is projected that half of young children will spend some of their childhood in a single-parent family, most because of parental divorce. The majority of these children will spend the rest of their childhoods in a single-mother-headed family (Bumpass 1990). Numbers of children living with single parents who were divorced or never married rose between 1960 and 1980. Since 1981, the percentage of children living with divorced single parents has fallen somewhat while the percentage of children living with never-married single parents has risen dramatically. Figure 13.1 shows these trends. Note that, while the gap is closing, there still are more children living with divorced than never-married single parents.

Single parents must perform both instrumental and expressive roles in order to meet their needs and those of their children. They perform tasks such as obtaining housing and other basic necessities, paying bills, making decisions, and bringing resources such as wages, child support, and government benefits into the family. Single parents are expected to establish functional family systems with appropriate boundaries and rules and that nurture themselves and their children,

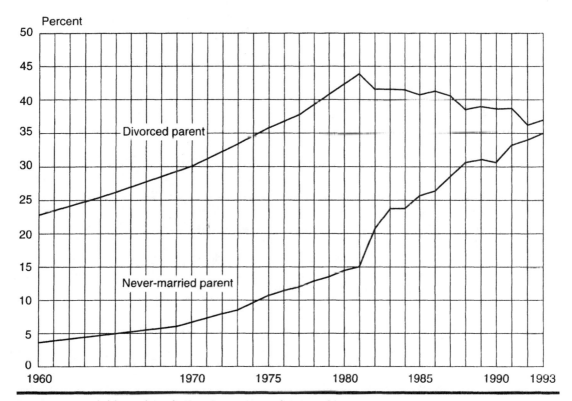

FIGURE 13.1   Children of Single Parents, By Marital Status of Parent: 1960–1993*
*Between 1981 and 1983, changes were made in data collection and processing.
Adapted from: Saluter, A. F. (1994) Marital Status and Living Arrangements: March 1993. U.S. Bureau of the Census, Current Population Reports, Series P20-478. Washington, DC: U.S. Government Printing Office.

meet psychological needs, and make provisions for their children's socialization. Many times they find themselves called upon to be both mother and father. For these reasons, single parents often feel overwhelmed. Role conflict occurs when parents cannot meet the demands of children and of employment. Overburdened single parents sometimes expect children to assume adult responsibilities.

Despite being stigmatized and stereotyped as irresponsible, many single parents form strong, functional families that meet the needs of their members (Green & Crooks 1988; Olson & Haynes 1993). Several strengths were evident in the single parent families studied by Richards and Schmiege (1993). These parents developed en-

hanced skills in parenting, family management, and communication. Many single mothers feel proud of their ability to provide the financial support of their families. A large number of single parents also think their experiences contribute to their personal growth. Successful single-parent families share several qualities (Olson & Haynes 1993). Single parents who fare well share several characteristics:

• They accept responsibility and challenges, and seek solutions;
• They make sacrifices of money, time, and energy, and consider their parenting role primary;
• They use consistent, nonpunitive discipline;

- They emphasize open communication within the family;
- They foster each family member's individuality within a supportive family unit;
- They recognize the need for nurturing themselves;
- They create and maintain family rituals and traditions.

Single parents with these abilities are more likely to experience positive family functioning.

Members of families headed by single parents are vulnerable in a number of ways. Children in single-parent families are less likely to complete high school than children living in two-parent families (McLanahan 1985). Women who lived for a part of their childhood in a family headed by a single mother are at increased risk of early marriage and childbearing, premarital births, and disruption in their own marriages (McLanahan & Bumpass 1988). Parents' problems include being overwhelmed by too many tasks and roles, having inadequate social support networks, money, and other resources, having difficulty with sexual relationships due to their lack of time away from children, and experiencing conflict with their children's absent parents and the extended families of the absent parents (Richards & Schmiege 1993). Vosler and Proctor (1991) found that single-parent family problems and poor child functioning in these families were associated with financial problems, including lack of child support, and the stigma experienced by single parents. Poverty and financial problems are associated with many of the negative outcomes researchers have found in studying single-parent families (McLanahan 1985; Richards & Schmiege 1993).

Types of Single-Parent Families.   Some single parents never marry. Although a small number of never-married fathers are raising their children, there are six times as many never-married mothers heading households as fathers (Rawlings 1993). Many of these mothers had their first child while they were still teenagers, and many live in poverty. They may lack high school educations

and job skills that would enable them to earn more than minimum wage. Never-married mothers are less likely than divorced mothers to be awarded child support by a court. The involvement of the childrens' fathers varies greatly. Sometimes the fathers' identity is unknown, while in other situations child support payments are regularly made by fathers and visitation occurs frequently between the fathers and their children.

Widowed single parents have a clearer role and a more socially accepted status than single divorced parents. As a rule, widows may have more social support, adjust more easily to singlehood, and have more positive views of their former spouses than divorcées (Kitson et al. 1980). Important tasks of widowed parents include managing their own grief processes, helping their children understand and accept the deaths of their other parents, assisting children in forming realistic memories of deceased parents, and dealing with the financial aftermath of death.

Bumpass (1990) projects that 60 percent of first marriages will be disrupted by separation or divorce. Each year, these disruptions affect about one million children (U.S. National Center for Health Statistics 1991). Although divorce has become much more commonplace over the past twenty-five years, it is still traumatic to the families that experience it. In a review of the literature, Hutchinson and Spangler–Hirsch (1989) found that divorce may precipitate such stressors as geographical relocation, children seeing less of both their custodial and absent parent, changes in extended family relationships, especially with the family of the noncustodial parent, more responsibility placed on older children, and less money.

Divorced single parents with custody are still mostly mothers, although the number of fathers being awarded custody is increasing. From 1974 to 1990, the number of father-only families increased by 300 percent (Meyer & Garasky 1993), and these families now make up 15 percent of all single-parent households. Single fathers have nearly twice (187 percent) the mean personal income of single mothers; therefore, children living in single-father families are less than half as likely to be poor as those living with single mothers. Even children living with their fathers, however, are more than twice as likely to be poor as those living in two-parent families (Meyer & Garasky 1993).

Divorced parents of both genders must establish patterns of visitation and other contacts between ex-spouses and their extended families and the children. They have the difficult tasks of managing their own grief processes over the end of the marriage and trying to resolve negative feelings toward their ex-spouses. They must also try to meet the needs of their children by offering realistic, age-appropriate explanations about the reasons for and consequences of their divorces, and attempt to help children have positive regard for and meaningful relationships with their absent parents. They often must establish new households with diminished resources.

Child Support.   The problems of single-parent families are usually tied to inadequate financial resources. Child support can be an important contribution to financial stability and adequacy for single parents. Unfortunately, state child support laws and their enforcement have not served to protect the interests of children living in single-parent families. Problems include the courts' failure to award child support in each case, the courts' failure to ensure that the child support award is adequate, the failure of absent parents to pay child support as ordered, and the difficulty and expense required for custodial parents to have the child support award enforced when the absent parent does not comply with the court order.

Given that children born in the United States have a 50 percent chance of living in a single parent family before age eighteen (Bumpass, 1984), and that one-fourth of American children are living with single parents, the majority of whom are never-married and divorced mothers (Glick 1988), the presence of inadequate, poorly enforced child support awards is of great concern to child advocates. The federal Office of Child Support Enforcement (1988) reported that, nationally, less than half of single mothers receive regular child support.

Single fathers also experience problems with child support. For fathers with custody, a Wisconsin study indicated that only 30 percent were awarded child support from the noncustodial mother, while 80 percent of custodial mothers received child support awards. Of fathers who did receive child support awards, 49 percent were paid nothing, compared with 27 percent of custodial mothers with support awards. The percentage of custodial mothers and fathers who received only partial child support payments was similar (Meyer & Garasky 1993).

Children's Adjustment to Parental Divorce. Wallerstein (1985) studied the consequences for children of parental divorce, and found that divorce often, at least temporarily, results in diminished parenting. In the time following divorce, parents show less emotional sensitivity toward their children. Parents receive less pleasure from parenting and their relationships with children: They are less attentive to children's needs and wishes, interact with them less often, and express anger more inappropriately. Children easily become overburdened following divorce. In many cases, children become responsible for their own upbringing or for the care of a regressed or dysfunctional parent. They are targets of ongoing disputes and court battles between parents. These struggles leave children feeling guilty, angry, helpless, confused, and unwanted. Chapter 14 will present the symptoms of children of divorce in more detail; such symptoms include somatic complaints, sleep disturbances, fear of abandonment or impending disasters, underachievement, suspiciousness, hyperalertness, emotional constriction, poor peer relationships, and depression.

At one time, trauma from divorce was considered a temporary stressor that parents and children would overcome in a year or two. More recently, Wallerstein (1987) challenged that assumption. In a follow-up study of children ten years after a parental divorce, sixteen- to eighteen-year-olds still felt sad, vulnerable, and needy. They felt they were not as close to their fathers. Half of the boys in the study and one-fourth of the girls were considered poorly adjusted or high risk. In an analysis of ninety-two studies on children's adjustment to divorce, Amato (1993) found that divorce is problematic for them in two ways. First, it produces stressors, such as interparental conflict and disruptive life changes. Second, it can interfere with children's use of parental resources in three ways: by reducing the quality of the relationship between children and custodial parents, by lowering the children's contact with the noncustodial parent, and by decreasing children's access to parental income.

Several researchers have recommended ways to reduce the problems of divorce. Fathers who have more physical and decision-making involvement with their children, for example, through shared custody arrangements, are more likely to comply with child support orders (Dudley 1991). Children seem, according to Glover and Steele (1989) and Schnayer and Orr (1989), to prefer custody arrangements that allow continuous, flexible contact with both parents. Wall (1992) found that a central determinant of frequency of contact between noncustodial fathers and their children is the degree of hostility between the ex-spouses. He also reported that younger fathers are at greater risk of reducing contact with their children, and that fathers who remarry have more contact. Hutchinson and Spangler–Hirsch (1989) recommend that ex-spouses lower conflict and increase cooperation, and that divorced families make good use of support systems.

Families Formed by Remarriage

Many people whose first marriages end through divorce or widowhood choose to marry again. The resulting families are called remarried couples or, if there are children of either or both spouses, stepfamilies or blended families. Stepfamilies are among the most complex of all family structures, because they involve primary relationships and vital interactions among family members and persons external to the household.

There are many varieties of stepfamilies. The simplest type is comprised of a noncustodial biological parent whose children visit regularly, and whose spouse has no children. The couple must make accommodations for the visits of the children, not only in terms of household space, but in the planning of suitable family rules, roles, and activities. Sometimes both spouses of remarried couples have noncustodial children, and must decide whether to have all children visit at the same times, or different times, or some combination of the two.

Stepfamilies in which the biological children of one spouse reside in the household are more complex, and require such adaptations as instant parenthood for stepparents and the establishment of workable visitation arrangements between the children and their absent parents. For many of these families, there is the added dimension of *noncustodial children* of the stepparents, who visit regularly and have claim to parental time, energy, and resources. Healthy relationships between resident and nonresident stepsiblings can be difficult to achieve, because of jealousy and competition for parental attention.

When both remarried spouses have custody of children from previous marriages, the resulting stepfamily must cope with many challenges. Family rules, roles, values, and discipline acceptable to all family members must be established. Relationships must be cultivated between stepsiblings, between stepparents and stepchildren, and between the spouses. The spouses must negotiate both their marital relationship and a partnership for effective and consistent parenting of the children. The new family must also achieve workable visitation arrangements for children and their absent parents and the various extended family members. Any of these types of stepfamilies can become more complex if the remarried couples choose to have children together.

Stepfamilies by definition have unique characteristics that create additional tasks necessary for healthy family functioning. In all remarried couples, at least one spouse has experienced the end of a previous marriage through death or divorce, and the resulting losses, changes, and adaptations. The success of the attachment to a new spouse is related to how well the loss of the previous relationship has been handled. When children are involved, they too must grieve losses and adapt to changes.

Stepfamilies are much more likely than intact families to consist of individuals or subsystems at different developmental stages. For example, a divorced woman of twenty-eight with custody of two preschoolers may marry a divorced man of forty-eight with a grown, married child and grandchildren. His interests, emotional needs, and energy level may not be compatible with parenting preschoolers.

The values, lifestyles, and traditions that individuals bring to stepfamilies may be incompatible. The members of the new family must negotiate and develop family rules and traditions that help to achieve a new family identity and meet individual needs of family members.

While in intact families, parents have a chance to form couple bonds prior to the birth of children; in stepfamilies, children are part of the picture from the beginning. Couples must find ways to establish strong marital relationships while not neglecting their parental duties.

Stepparents must find ways to be appropriately involved in parenting stepchildren, while respecting the children's need for (and right to) relationships with absent parents. Stepfamilies are more effective when spouses are partners in the executive and parenting subsystems in the family. They should be consistent in their expectations for children's behavior and in their methods of discipline.

Stepfamilies are likely to contain residential children who visit their absent parents and/or nonresidential children who come to visit from their custodial parents' homes. This constant changing of household composition is stressful for parents, especially if there is disagreement about how or when visits take place. Planning holiday celebrations, arranging family outings, and maintaining household rules are all much more complicated than in nuclear families. Child can feel as if they have two quasi-homes rather

than one stable home, and the effort to sort out and abide by differing rules in multiple households can be stressful.

Another unique feature of blended families is that stepparents rarely have any legal relationship with stepchildren. Without special court action to award stepparents custody or adoption of stepchildren, there are no legal rights of stepparents to involvement with stepchildren in the event of a divorce, or the death of the biological parent. These characteristics of stepfamilies and the resulting tasks they must accomplish help explain why stepfamily life is unique and can be stressful (Visher & Visher 1988).

There are several dynamics that predict the success of stepfamilies. First, when children are familiar with the stepparent prior to the remarriage, they adjust better to stepfamily life and have fewer problems. Second, younger children are more accepting of stepparents than adolescents. Third, children are more accepting of stepparents who proceed gradually and carefully with discipline and demonstrate an open mind and willingness to compromise. Children seem to regard custodial stepparents more positively than their noncustodial stepparents (Knaub & Hanna 1984).

The added complexity of the stepfamily structure can create motivation for family members to enhance their skills in coping, communication, and adaptability. Children have access to additional parent figures, whose perspectives and resources can enrich life experiences and opportunities. Stepfamilies usually have expanded extended family systems, which broadens the possibility of additional social support.

Stepfamilies share with single-parent families difficulties with child support being paid as ordered, but, overall, have more resources than single-parent families (Vosler & Proctor 1991).

Remarried families are at increased risk for marital disruption, in that second marriages are less stable than first marriages (Martin & Bumpass 1989). Remarried families experience nearly twice as many total family problems as biological families, including parental violence, difficulty with extended family members, and child sexual abuse. In remarried families, stress piles up from reactions to many changes in the family systems and family disequilibrium. It generally takes these families two to five years to establish a new homeostasis (Vosler & Proctor 1991).

Compared to children in biological families, children in blended families are at risk as well. Behavioral disruptions and academic problems in school, depression, stress, anxiety, aggression, and bad health are more frequent among stepchildren (Dawson 1991).

Many stepfamilies lack appropriate models for establishing successful remarried families. They may believe some of the common myths about stepfamilies, and judge themselves as inadequate according to these unrealistic expectations. Figure 13.2 compares common myths about stepfamilies with more realistic beliefs.

Multigenerational Families

Families with two or more generations of adults can be made up of couples or single adults caring for aging relatives, families with aging relatives as well as minor children still in the home, or parents with adult children still living at home.

When the executive subsystem of a family includes both parents and older relatives, such as grandparents, children may be confused by conflicting parenting styles and contradictory rules and expectations.

Role strain can occur when aging relatives need care. Many such relatives, regardless of whether they are related to the husband or the wife, become the responsibility of the wives (Reskin & Padavic 1994). Wives who are in the work force and/or have minor children in the home often feel overburdened.

When aging parents become financially or otherwise dependent on their adult children, the shifting and even reversing of roles requires major adjustments for all family members.

Aging relatives can be valuable members of families. They can offer wisdom, advice, financial and other resources, and provide loving child care.

They can contribute time, talent, and energy to the maintenance of the home.

These families are vulnerable to stress in several ways. For example, when adult women care for aging parents, they often experience difficulty in asserting authority with their parents, feeling instead that they are still children and the parents maintain power over them. Problems with boundaries are evident in the difficulty adult daughters experience in saying no to excessive demands of aging parents, especially mothers. Many caretaking adult children experience a great sense of loss as elderly parents deteriorate physically and/or psychologically (Abel 1991). Families who lack the space, financial means, time, or willingness to share their home with aging parents or adult children are at risk of crowding, impoverishment, increased conflict and the abuse or neglect of vulnerable family members. Such families need help with resources to enable them to care for their dependent relatives, or they may seek help with finding suitable alternative living arrangements for such relatives.

Other Types of Family Diversity

Foster Families. Families may provide temporary homes to related or unrelated children informally, through mutual agreement with the children's parents, or formally, through affiliation with a *child placing agency.* Child placing agencies are authorized by the state to find suitable substitute care for children who cannot live with their biological families. Foster families who care for children from agencies are usually licensed, and must conform to rigorous standards and comply with agency rules and procedures. They receive partial reimbursement for expenses, and are paid daily rates based on the number and types of foster children in their homes.

Several unique features of foster family life affect daily living:

- The very close involvement of representatives of the court and child placing agencies;
- Foster children's biological families;

FIGURE 13.2   Common Myths about Stepfamilies

MYTH	REALISTIC BELIEF
• Stepfamilies are just like biological families.	• Stepfamilies are complex in structure, and differ from other family forms in many significant ways.
• Stepfamily members adjust quickly to the new family.	• New homeostasis is only reached after two to five years of hard work.
• Stepfamily members will learn to love each other quickly.	• Although the remarried couple may love one another, there is no certainty that stepparents and stepchildren will ever develop loving relationships with each other.
• Stepmothers who try hard will not be perceived as "wicked."	• Stepparents who push too hard may experience more resistance from stepchildren than parents who are more relaxed in their approach.
• Minimizing a child's relationship with a biological parent helps the child develop a better relationship with the stepparent of the same sex.	• Children who have satisfying relationships with their biological parents are more likely to establish good relationships with stepparents.
• If anything negative happens, it's due to being in a stepfamily.	• There are many reasons for individual and family problems in stepfamilies, most of which are not caused by the family structure per se, but by developmental or interactional problems.
• Love is finite.	• There is always enough love to go around.
• Adequate preparation for stepfamily living will prevent the emergence of uncomfortable feelings such as jealousy and anger.	• Uncomfortable feelings are part of any major life adjustment. Preparation can help stepfamily members deal more appropriately with these feelings.
• Stepfamilies formed after a parental death are easier than those formed after parental divorce.	• Both types of stepfamilies are challenging, but in different ways.
• Being a noncustodial stepparent is easier than being a custodial one.	• Children are more positive toward their custodial stepparents, probably because they have had more opportunity to build strong relationships with the stepparent with whom they live.

Adapted from *Old Loyalties, New Ties: Therapeutic Strategies with Stepfamilies* by E. B. Visher and J. S. Visher (1988)

• The regular comings and goings of foster children, who may differ from foster families in significant ways.

All of this requires flexibility and cooperation on the part of foster family systems, and the skilled training of and consultation with family members by personnel of child placing agencies.

Families who informally foster children may lack the resources, knowledge, skills, and support necessary to properly care for these children. Such families may lack any legal means to protect children from inappropriate actions on the part of their biological families.

The biological children of foster families should be involved in their family's decision to temporarily care for other children. Fostering will impact their lives in many ways, and their attitudes and behaviors will influence the quality of the substitute placement for foster children.

Adoptive Families.   Currently, adoptions of children happen in many ways. They can be the result of private agreements between related or unrelated people, or they can be handled through licensed child placing agencies, either private or public. They can be *open* (i.e., biological parents are allowed some degree of contact with their children following the adoption) or *closed* (i.e., records are sealed, no contact is allowed, and little information is exchanged between adoptive and biological families). While in the past most children placed for adoption were infants, today many children are placed at older ages. Adoption is desirable for many children who cannot be raised by their biological parents due to parental incapacity or child maltreatment. These children are usually placed in foster care while efforts are made to restore the children to their biological families. When these efforts prove unsuccessful, then adoption becomes an option.

Children who are over twelve years old, are part of a sibling group, have disabilities, or are members of racial minority groups are considered *special needs or hard-to-place children,* due to a scarcity of qualified families willing to adopt them. These children are eligible for *subsidized adoption,* in which adoptive parents receive help with medical expenses and/or monthly payments to defray costs of raising the children.

Adoptive parents should be open to the possibility that adoptive children will have differences from them in temperament, ability, and preferences. Adopted children may desire to learn about or find their biological families, especially during teenage and adult years. These needs are most easily met by parents who understand that their adopted children have separate roots and a past that does not include them, and who are accepting of the child's right to an identity that incorporates that past. Adopted children benefit when they know from a very early age that they are adopted. They need factual explanations of the circumstances of their adoptions, and accurate information about their biological families.

Many adoption agencies offer excellent pre-placement training for adoptive families and post-placement support services. These are especially helpful for families who adopt special needs children. These services can prevent *adoption disrup-*

tions, when children are returned to the agency by parents no longer willing to adopt them.

Present-day adoption practice is not concerned with placing children with families they physically resemble, but rather with families who are likely to accept and nurture these children, and who have the skills and resources to effectively parent them over time.

DIVERSITY IN SOCIAL CLASS

A family's social class influences the values of its members with regard to marriage and parenting. A strong relationship exists between social class and values, even when such other variables as national origin, religion, urban or rural residence, and race are statistically controlled (Luster, Rhoades, & Haas 1989). Social class is also related to family access to resources, which in turn is related to stress level and ability to cope with crisis. For these reasons, social class membership is a major determinant of the quality and characteristics of family life.

Upper-Class and Middle-Class Families

Families in the middle and upper classes have many advantages. Their economic well-being has increased in recent years, especially those in the upper class. Husbands and wives in these classes tend to have college or professional education, job security, adequate income for all family necessities as well as for luxuries, and options for handling family tasks, such as child care and household maintenance. Their jobs also offer such fringe benefits as paid sick and vacation leave, health insurance, pension plans, and expense accounts. They are able to provide their children with good education and enrichment activities.

Marriage in the middle and upper classes tends to be more egalitarian, with wives having more status and autonomy within marital relationships than do wives in lower social classes. The division of labor is not heavily influenced by gender role stereotypes. Marriages occur later, and child-bearing is typically postponed, allowing

Female Husbands

LINDA MILLER MATTHEI

Anthropologists sometimes describe marriage as a "cultural universal" because it is found in nearly every known society in the world, but their research also reveals that marriage can take a variety of forms cross-culturally. Although monogamy, the union of a man and woman, is the most common marital pattern around the world, polygyny, marriage between a man and more than one woman, is the *preferred* form in most of the world's societies (Haviland 1993: 220). We tend to think of the United States as strictly monogamous, and, indeed, only monogamous marriages are legally recognized. However, an estimated 50,000 Americans—mostly in the Rocky Mountain states—live in polygynous relationships (Haviland 1993).

In the United States, the decision to marry is by and large an individual one. But in much of the world, marriage is viewed as more than an affirmation of a couple's love for each other. Marriage involves, rather, a significant political and economic alliance between groups, and, as such, is negotiated and contracted carefully by members of both families. Marriage in such societies is considered simply too important to be placed in the hands of inexperienced young men and women.

Although marriage is typically assumed to involve the union of a man and woman, this is not always the case. Marriage may not necessarily involve a sexual relationship between partners. In sub-Saharan Africa, for example, it is not uncommon for a woman to take a wife. Though the specific circumstances which give rise to such marriages vary from group to group, woman/woman marriage is generally undertaken for political or economic reasons.

One of the more recent accounts of woman/woman marriage is provided by Regina Smith Oboler (1980) who describes the practice among the Nandi in western Kenya. The Nandi, who are herders and farmers, are a polygynous society; that is, men commonly have more than one wife. Ownership of cattle, their major form of wealth, is controlled by males, and only sons can inherit their fathers' wealth. On a man's death, then, his cattle

are passed down to the sons of his various wives. A wife who has produced no sons or is barren thus finds herself in a disadvantaged position because she has no one to inherit her proper share of the husband's wealth. For this reason, a woman may choose to take a "wife" to bear the sons that she has been unable to produce. The wife of the now "female husband" enters into a sexual relationship with a man of her own or the female husband's choosing. Any children born of the union are considered to be the social and legal offspring of the woman/woman marriage, thus providing the female husband with heirs to her male husband's estate. The marriage is, therefore, undertaken primarily for economic purposes.

Why would a woman agree to become the wife of another woman? The relationship is not a sexual one. In fact, female husbands are precluded from any sort of sexual relationship once they have undertaken the marriage. According to Oboler, the wives of female husbands are usually young women who are otherwise unlikely to find a male partner because of some mental or physical defect, or, more commonly, because they have already produced illegitimate children. Though most women prefer to marry a man, Oboler points out that some women actually express a preference for woman/woman marriage. Some argue, for example, that female husbands, in their efforts to attract a spouse, are more generous than men. Others enjoy the sexual freedom and greater measure of independence characteristic of such marriages, since female husbands are less likely to display sexual jealousy than males. Finally, some women argue that female husbands are kinder and more sympathetic than male spouses. Because they, themselves, were once wives, these women are more empathetic to a wife's problems and needs.

Woman/woman marriage, is, of course, a rather unique marital form. By becoming familiar with the diversity of marriage patterns found throughout the world, perhaps Americans can better understand the complex social and economic issues that underlie our own marital relationships.

couples to complete education, establish careers, and form strong marital bonds, which remain central even after children join the family.

Parenting styles among the upper and middle classes are less authoritarian than in the working and lower classes. Children are encouraged to develop according to their unique talents, personalities, and interests. Parents are more responsive to children's cries, and emphasize reading to and talking with their children. They place few restrictions on their children's exploratory behaviors, thus encouraging initiative and autonomy (Luster, Rhoades, & Haas 1989). Discipline is less likely to be corporal and is aimed at developing children's internal control and ability to make correct moral decisions. Parents expect schools to offer their children opportunities to develop creativity and social skills, in addition to academic skills. Children are thus prepared to eventually assume their places in the world of university-educated, white-collar workers. They are taught to value such attributes as individuality, being upwardly mobile, having control over their lives and work, and working with their heads rather than their hands.

Working-Class Families

The term "blue-collar worker" was coined to describe factory and other skilled or semi-skilled industrial workers. At one time these workers actually made higher salaries and had better benefits than some white collar workers, due largely to effective collective bargaining by labor unions. As the U.S. economy has changed from an industrial to a service economy over the past few years, blue-collar jobs have become more scarce, and less dependable and lucrative than they once were.

Today's working-class families are often headed by hourly wage workers who may not have such benefits as paid leave, health insurance, and pension plans. Their jobs are vulnerable to economic and seasonal fluctuations. Many of these workers have only a high school education, or less, and no specialized occupational skills.

Working-class couples tend to meet in high school, and marry soon after. First children often are born after only a few months of marriage. These young couples are virtually trapped in a never-ending struggle for survival, and feel helpless and powerless in the face of the demands of daily living.

Marriage in working-class families is seen as the rite of passage to full social adulthood, and is entered into by many young people as an escape from the demands and hardships of their families of origin. Without job skills or education, they all too often find they have exchanged one difficult family life for another. Couples in the working-class are more likely to adhere to gender role stereotypes: men are more dominant and fulfill instrumental roles, and women tend to be more subservient and fulfill expressive roles.

Parents, especially mothers, tend to make the parenting role primary, which can strain already fragile marriages. Children are taught to respect authority, value obedience, and submit to external control. Discipline is more often *corporal punishment,* for example spanking or whipping, and there is less emphasis on helping the child learn to make independent moral decisions. Parents expect schools to teach children obedience, conformity, and job-related knowledge and skills. Parents are hard-pressed to help children succeed in college or be upwardly mobile (Rubin 1976). This socialization prepares children to be compliant with employers' expectations, and to need a certain amount of external structure and direction.

Poor Families

Families who live in poverty are disproportionately minority group members, or headed by single mothers. Most of the poor are employed, but sporadically or in minimum wage jobs that are not secure and offer no benefits. These "working poor" families have increased in numbers over the past several years. Currently, 11.5 million poor families are headed by employed parents who earn too little to meet their families' basic needs (U.S. Bureau of the Census 1994). Child care plans are often unsatisfactory, and these families do not have adequate resources for even basic necessities. Many lack proper food at least some of the time. Growing numbers of families with children are joining the ranks of the homeless. Prenatal and health care are rarely accessible. These conditions contribute to the high rates of poor health and nutrition among the poor. Parents may lack the time or energy to provide proper supervision and guidance to their children. They may also be unable to help and encourage their children with regard to school work. Children from these families are often treated with low regard by school and law enforcement personnel.

Children are expected to be obedient and respectful, and tend to be strictly disciplined. They are taught to value conformity to external authority. Parents are afraid they might spoil their children if they are too permissive. Consequently, they employ more physical punishment. They limit children's exploratory behavior and provide restraints for children rather than encouraging initiative and freedom (Luster, Rhoades, & Haas 1989).

Family stress levels are very high and many poverty-class families are crisis ridden. Reactions to high stress levels and helplessness to improve family situations contribute to symptoms such as substance abuse, family violence, child abuse, divorce, and desertion.

DIVERSITY IN ETHNIC OR RACIAL GROUP MEMBERSHIP

Membership in an ethnic or racial minority group affects family life in several ways. Such families often suffer the effects of institutional or individual racism, which may reduce employment and educational opportunities. Membership in an ethnic or racial group influences values, parenting techniques, and family communication patterns.

African American Families

The African American family has been studied a great deal since the 1960s. Daniel Patrick Moynihan's 1965 report, entitled *The Negro Family: The Case for National Action,* blamed slavery for black family deterioration of African American families (U.S. Department of Labor 1965). He wrote that female-headed or matriarchal African American families were harmful to young children, depriving them of adequate male influence, and that the increase in single-mother-headed households was at the root of many social problems in African American communities. The report, based on theories widely accepted at the time, has since been criticized for its generalizations and failure to address African American family and community strengths. The report did result in a tremendous increase in the study of and published literature on African American families. More recent authors advocate studying African American families with a comprehensive approach that includes consideration of socioeconomic factors, African cultural heritage, and behavioral adaptations, considers African American families as different from European American families, and as functional, not pathological (Taylor 1994).

An important characteristic of African American families is that households are often connected to a large, extended network of other family and non-family households. These households share resources with one another, providing insurance against economic hardships, and increasing the social support available to each individual member. The single-mother-headed family is rarely an isolated unit, but is usually supported by an extended family network (Leigh & Green 1982; Taylor 1994).

Children are valued, and are encouraged to be separate and unique individuals. Children under three receive a great deal of positive attention and cuddling, and are encouraged to interact with people in preference to manipulating and exploring things. Older children are given authority over and some responsibility for younger siblings over three. These childrearing practices prepare children for life in the African American community, where relatedness and connectedness are highly valued. Gender differences in childrearing are evident as children become adolescents. Parents expect more and earlier responsible behavior from teen daughters than from sons (Leigh & Green 1982).

Elderly members of the extended family network are valued. They often provide material resources to younger members, or valued services such as child care. They may have a leadership role within the network.

Over the past two decades, several marriage trends have occurred among African Americans. Young people are postponing marriage until later than people of other races, due to such factors as high unemployment rates among young men, and the practice of cohabitation before legal marriage. First marriages are shorter, and time between marriages is longer. There is also a declining ratio of men to women. At age twenty, the sex ratio is 97 men to 100 women. At age forty however, there are only 94 men to every 100 women. This reduces the likelihood of remarriage for divorced women. Ball and Robbins (1986) found that African American men who were married reported lower life satisfaction than those with other types of marital status. Race and social class interact to make it difficult for African American men to support their families and they also have less education than their wives. For these reasons, African American married men may feel inadequate and less satisfied with their lives. These factors may help explain why African American women spend only a third of their non-widowed adult life in a marriage. This is only half as long as the average duration of married life for European American women (Martin & Bumpass 1989). Yet marriage is predominant among African Americans. In 1988, two-thirds of African American ever-married men and half of African American ever-married women were living with their spouses (Taylor 1994).

Using a national sample, Zill and Nord (1994) found that 29 percent of African American children live with both parents, while 54 percent live with their mothers only, compared with 65 percent and 16 percent, respectively, for European American children. Forty-six percent of African American children live below the poverty line, compared to 13 percent of European American children. The high poverty rate is not due to the single-parent family form per se, but rather to low educational and employment opportunities, both outcomes of institutional racism.

The family is the core of the African American community. The extended family network is a great strength to African American families. Deep spirituality and concern for the welfare of others are strong cultural values (Daly, Jennings, Beckett, & Leashore 1995). Both young and old are valued. Hard work and a good education are seen as desirable and the way to success within the larger society (Aguilas & Williams 1993; Prater, 1992). African American families are flexible with gender roles. In fact, the middle-class African American family is the most egalitarian of all family types (Willis & Greenblatt 1978).

McKenry and Fine (1993) compared the post-divorce parenting behaviors of African American single mothers with those of European American single mothers. African American mothers showed a higher degree of continuity in parenting following divorce and had less trouble establishing authority. They had higher expectations for their children with regard to independence, control of temper, and compliance with parental commands. The African American single mothers also enjoyed a greater amount of community acceptance and support than the European American mothers.

Families in the African American community face many challenges. A major concern is the rising unemployment of African American men. Recent trends in business, such as mergers and plant closings, have resulted in layoffs of factory workers. This reduction of blue-collar jobs with good salaries and benefits has disproportionately affected African American men. During the same time period, European American flight to the suburbs has diminished the resources available to cities and the minority populations who remain in them. African American poverty had been reduced between 1959 and 1979 through such mechanisms as an expanded economy, more educational opportunities, anti-poverty programs, and the enforcement of civil rights and affirmative action legislation. Since 1979, these mechanisms have been reduced, and consequently, by 1985,

African American poverty rates had again become very high. African American male unemployment is associated with substance abuse, family violence, and criminal activity, all of which are social problems of great concern. Ironically, the African American community characteristic that has been most denigrated by the majority culture, i.e., single-mother families, is related to African American male unemployment as well. Since 1960, female-headed African American families have increased from 21 percent to 44 percent, while African American male unemployment rose from 22 percent to 46 percent (Billingsly 1988). The solution to problems of African American families, then, depends upon economic and educational opportunities, especially for African American men.

Hispanic Families

Hispanic families are close-knit and form extensive mutual aid networks. Children are highly valued, as are the elderly. Family roles tend to be gender stereotypical, with women responsible for expressive roles and men for instrumental roles. The family structure is hierarchical, with males and older family members holding power and females and younger members deferring to them.

The practice of incorporating *godparents* into the extended family network provides children with additional supportive adults, and, if needed, resources. Godparents are people, usually unrelated, who are given special responsibilities for children through formal religious rituals or informal understandings. Parents take pains to meet their children's needs, and consider their parenting roles as their most important obligations. Both cultural and religious influences encourage large families. The majority of Hispanics are Roman Catholic, at least in name. Women, especially, are taught that any birth control method other than the rhythm method is sinful, and that sexuality is permissible only within marriage. Divorce is also discouraged by the church, and spouses often stay together, even if unhappy, for the children's sake.

For these reasons, families are important sources of strength and support to their members (de Valdez & Gallegos 1982).

Children are taught cultural values, such as duty to the family, respect for elders, and that the group is more important than the individual. When children are more fluent in English and more acculturated than older family members, they may take on the responsibilities of relating for the family with social institutions and individuals of the majority culture, thereby threatening the traditional lines of power and authority. Older children may drop out of school to help with younger children, or to work to help meet family needs. High school and college dropout rates are high (Delgado 1992).

Hispanic family strengths include a strong commitment to children and marriage, extended family support, the cultural and religious practice of godparenting, and a sense of duty to care for one another within the family and community.

Hispanic families are vulnerable in a number of ways. Areas of concern include the high rate of poverty for Hispanic children, especially those living in mother-only households. Forty percent of Hispanic children live below the poverty line, compared with 13 percent of Anglo children (Zill & Nord 1994).

Hispanic families have a low rate of using health and social services. This may be due to distrust of Anglo-dominated agencies and governmental institutions, lack of bilingual staff, and discriminatory policies and staff behaviors. Unfortunately, this puts a strain on natural helping systems within the Hispanic community (de Valdez & Gallegos 1982), and can create economic problems and intergenerational stress within the family (Purdy & Arguello 1992).

Asian American and Pacific Islander Americans

Kinship is very important in Asian cultures, and the individual's needs are considered secondary to those of the group (Ishisaka & Takagi 1982).

Children are taught to respect and obey their elders. Ancestors are also highly valued. Children are encouraged to succeed in school, and bring honor to the family. Traditional child-rearing methods involve strict enforcement of expectations, little praise, and encouragement of hard work and conformity. Asian Americans, especially Chinese Americans and Japanese Americans, have high average educational attainments, and aspire to white-collar jobs. Acculturation erodes traditional practices such as arranged marriages, and can cause problems between generations within families. Young second or third generation Asian Americans may be more influenced by their peers and the majority culture than by their elders and family cultural traditions. This can create conflict with parents and grandparents, who wish the young to adopt traditional ways.

Members of the majority culture increasingly hold positive views of Asian Americans and Pacific Islander Americans. Family cohesion, mutual concern, and loyalty are important strengths. The willingness to work hard and the encouragement of young people to acquire good educations and pursue desirable occupations have contributed to the success of many families in this group.

Despite the fact that many Asian Americans do well, family problems persist. The "model minority" stereotype can create undue pressure on young people to live up to difficult expectations. Intergenerational conflicts, centering around ac-

Many Asian American families are close, cohesive units. Respect for elders and a strong sense of duty to family are pervasive characteristics. One of the advantages of this family system is that loneliness and isolation of elders is infrequent.

culturation differences between generations, create tension for many families. Gangs are a growing problem among Asian American youth.

Native Americans

As a group, Native American families are more likely to be large and headed by women than are Anglo families. Native American women tend to marry earlier and are more likely to divorce than either Black or Anglo women.

Intermarriage, forced migration and resettlement, and such practices as forcing children to attend boarding schools have caused varying degrees of acculturation and consequent loss of traditional family lifestyles. Tribes differ in family forms, kinship patterns, and values.

Native American families accord special honor to the elders of the family, who are considered wise. Elders also are valued members of the larger community.

Values include a relaxed attitude toward time, being in harmony with nature, demonstrating cooperation and leadership, and being willing to share. Tribal identity is very important (Yellowbird & Snipp 1994). Children are taught to be emotionally controlled and independent. They are highly valued, and accepted as assets to the tribe and family.

Native Americans' values and adaptability have enabled them to survive the invasion of their lands, the destruction of their historic livelihoods, and the attempts of European Americans to destroy their cultures. Strengths include loyalty and dedication to the community, strong family and tribal identity, and values of cooperation and sharing, which make natural helping networks viable within the community. Parents' strong desire and efforts to pass on tribal culture will enable their children to retain knowledge and appreciation of their historical heritage.

Native Americans have high rates of unemployment, substance abuse, and family breakdown. These social problems are thought to be related to past U.S. government policies toward Native American peoples, such as poor social, health, and educational services, and attempts to devalue and eradicate the traditional cultures.

CONCLUSION

Families are the building blocks of both communities and societies, and the link between those communities and societies and individual family members. The functions of the family are vital to the well-being of individuals who live in them, and, ultimately, to the survival of society itself. Family functioning can be impaired by lack of resources, prejudice, and discrimination in the social environment, or by structural characteristics within the family. When this happens, the harm spreads beyond the members of affected families and extends to family networks and friends, organizations, communities, and society. Therefore, communities and society help themselves when they support families by providing the resources they need to ensure healthy family functioning. Communities and societies that fail to support families place themselves at risk.

The structural model of social work practice allows social workers to consider aspects of family diversity in problem assessment. Analysis of how family structure and/or minority group or social class membership relate to family problems is always appropriate. The structural model also provides a basis for intervention with environmental systems as a part of solving family problems. When family problems are related to aspects of diversity, working for change in environmental systems becomes an important part of social work intervention.

American society faces many challenges that must be addressed in order for American families to be more functional. Eradicating prejudice and discrimination directed at members of racial or ethnic minority groups must be very high on the agenda. Public policies and resource availability need improvement in the areas of quality day care for children, child support for children with absent parents, community programs for latchkey children, and supportive services for single parents and people caring for elderly family members. Finally, ways must be explored to ensure that all families have adequate resources so they can provide for the needs of their members. Social workers have the knowledge and skills to be valuable contributors in making these improvements.

CASE STUDY REVIEW QUESTIONS

Now that you have learned about family diversity, refer back to the case study at the beginning of the chapter, and answer the following questions:

1. In what ways did being a single parent make Diane's situation more difficult?
2. What strengths did Diane have from her community and extended family?
3. How might growing up in a working-class family have affected how Diane managed after her divorce?
4. What services and resources would have helped Diane manage her current crisis?
5. What factors in Diane's psychosocial environment may have contributed to her current situation?
6. How did Diane's ex-husband's social class background contribute to the roles he played in the family before the divorce?

KEY TERMS

Adoption disruption: When a family decides they are no longer willing to be responsible for a child placed with them for adoption, and asks to have the child removed from them both physically and legally.

Child placing agencies: States require agencies that place children for foster care or adoption to meet certain standards and to be regulated through licensing.

Closed adoptions: Adoptions in which court and agency records are sealed, at least until the children are adults, and there is no postadoption contact between biological parents and their children.

Corporal punishment: A form of child punishment involving physical force; the most common form is spanking.

Executive position: Position within a system that confers power to make decisions and exert control over other members of the system.

Godparents: People, usually unrelated, who are given special responsibilities for children through formal religious rituals or informal understandings.

Noncustodial children: Children not under the custody of a biological parent.

Open adoptions: Adoptions in which biological parents are allowed varying degrees of involvement in the adoptive placement of their children and/or postadoption contact with their children.

Socioenvironmental stressors: Events in or characteristics of the social environment that create stress for a system.

Special needs children: Children who are available for adoption, but are harder to place because of being part of a sibling group, being twelve years old or over, having disabilities, and/or being members of racial or ethnic minority groups.

Subsidized adoption: Adoptions, usually of hard-to-place children, that are made possible through government financial support given to adoptive families; subsidized adoption makes permanent placement possible for many children at a cost similar to or lower than permanent foster care.

CHAPTER 14

MARITAL VIOLENCE AND DISSOLUTION

OBJECTIVES

After reading this chapter, you should be able to answer the following questions:

1. What is the best approach to understanding spouse abuse? What are the characteristics of battering families, offenders, and victims? How does spouse abuse affect children?
2. What causes divorce?
3. What is the process of divorce and how does divorce affect children and adults?

CASE STUDY

Darias and Shauna dated throughout high school. After graduation, Darias began working as a truck driver making local deliveries for a soft drink company. Shauna attended community college, but in her second semester, she became pregnant and dropped out of school.

The couple married soon thereafter and, at age nineteen, Shauna delivered a healthy baby girl. In the next five years, she had two more children, both girls as well.

Darias maintained close contacts with his friends. He played cards every Thursday night and worked out at a gym two nights and played basketball on Saturdays. When he was at home, he helped with household and parenting chores when asked. He rarely volunteered.

Shauna's mother followed traditional roles. While her father worked outside the home, her mother was responsible for the children, the house, and managing the family finances. At first, Shauna thought this was what she was supposed to do, too. Shauna and her friends from high school and college had gone their separate ways and now most of her current friends were the wives of Darias' married friends.

Shauna decided that when the children began school, she would return to college herself. Darias was opposed to her attending college and tried to undermine her efforts to gain an education. He rarely cleaned the house while she was away and often complained that he and the children were not receiving good meals. He made noise while she was studying and began to accuse her of being selfish.

Eventually Darias and Shauna realized they had grown apart and no longer had anything in common. He moved out and within a few months they divorced. When the divorce was final, the children were seven, eight, and twelve years of age.

Shauna received custody of the girls and Darias received liberal visitation privileges. He was also ordered to pay child support every month. Their house was ordered sold by the judge who re-viewed their divorce proceedings and the assets were divided equally between Darias and Shauna. Shauna and the girls were forced to move to a smaller apartment. Darias made his child support payments, though he was usually late. Sometimes Shauna had to call him to urge him to pay. They argued often over the issue of child support.

Shauna began working outside the home soon after she and Darias separated. Her income was only about 80 percent of what Darias was making in his job. She also continued to take classes in the evenings and on weekends.

INTRODUCTION

All family problems reverberate throughout the entire household. When a problem exists in one area of the family system, all parts of the system must react to that problem and the attempts to resolve it. This final chapter on the family discusses two important problems within the marital subsystem that exert significant pressure on families: spouse abuse and divorce. These two problems, which social workers encounter frequently, are particularly destructive to family functioning, and to both adults' and children's psychosocial development. In addition, divorce and domestic violence are closely associated with the conditions of the psychosocial environment. The environment plays a critical role in causing and maintaining as well as ameliorating these conditions.

SPOUSE ABUSE

How Violent Are Families?

Spouse abuse is an old problem in Western history. Until very recently, wife battering was hardly even considered a problem. As a matter of fact, religious and secular law either looked the other way or actively condoned husbands controlling their wives with violence. The expression "rule of thumb" comes from a British law that prohibited husbands from hitting their wives with an object greater in width than the husband's thumb. By the middle of the 1900s, spouse abuse was widespread, but also denied and minimized by society in general and families in particular. Since the 1970s, a great deal has happened to highlight spouse abuse as a social problem. The shelter movement, education programs, the women's rights movement, and a growing public awareness of wife battering have helped to bring domestic violence into the open.

Violence between partners, however, remains uncomfortably common. According to Gelles and Straus (1988), one in six (16 percent of) wives say that they are struck by their husband during the course of their marriage. About 30 per 1,000 women report being severely beaten by their husbands each year and the average battered wife is attacked three times annually. When violence towards husbands is added, a married person has about a one in four chance of being physically or sexually abused at least once in the marriage. From these statistics, it is easy to see why the family is often portrayed as the most violent institution in this society. To illustrate this point, Gelles and Straus make the following comparison:

> *The American public fears violent crime in the streets—and those odds are measured in terms of one per 100,000 people. Family violence is measured in terms of one per one thousand families. The family is hardly a haven... (1988: 106).*

Why Spouse Abuse Happens

Social work practitioners and researchers agree that wife battering is easy to describe, but difficult to explain (Yegidis 1992). There are many qualities that separate batterers and their wives from nonabusers and nonvictims. Many couples who come to blows, however, do not look alike. Most mental health professionals further contend that no single theory satisfactorily explains spouse abuse. Instead a multilevel ecological approach is perhaps the best way to understand domestic violence. Carlson's research provides a useful outline for approaching spouse abuse ecologically. She contends that it is necessary to analyze spouse abuse at four equal and interacting levels (see

Table 14.1): sociocultural, social structural, family, and individual.

Sociocultural Factors. Carlson (1984) identifies three sociocultural factors that contribute to

TABLE 14.1 Four Levels of Analyzing Spouse Abuse

LEVEL I: SOCIOCULTURAL FACTORS
Sexism
Sex Role Stereotyping
Acceptance of Violence

LEVEL II: SOCIAL STRUCTURAL FACTORS
Economic Stress—Unemployment and Underemployment
Community Denial of Problem
Police Practice and Policies

LEVEL III: FAMILY FACTORS
Traditional Sex Roles
Unequal Decision-Making
Recurrent Marital Stress
Conflicts Over Core Areas of Marital Life
Cycle of Violence
Continuum of Violence
Poor Communication Patterns

LEVEL IV: INDIVIDUAL QUALITIES	
Offender	*Victim*
Self-Esteem Issues	Self-Esteem Issues
Low Stress Tolerance	Low Stress Tolerance
Family History of Violence	Family History of Violence
Alcohol Abuse	Fear and Anxiety
Status Incompatibility	Assumes Responsibility

Adapted from Carlson (1984)

causing and maintaining domestic violence: sexism, sex role stereotyping, and the general acceptance of violence.

Sexism is a pervasive and powerful philosophy that denigrates women and legitimates violence against them. In all historical examples of systematic victimization of a less powerful group, oppressors develop an ideology to justify their actions. In the case of wife battering, sexism serves that function by promoting sexual inequality, passivity in women, aggression in men, and a sexual division of labor. Violent men use these beliefs to justify their so-called right to be the head of their households.

Sex role stereotyping, an outcropping of sexism, is a cultural belief that channels women into one set of characteristics and behaviors and men into another. Traditional expectations of women foster passivity and dependence, while men's expectations are of power, control, and independence. Violent men usually believe that they are entitled to the services of women.

Last, violence is largely accepted in this culture. The general approval of violence in almost all areas of social life sends the message to potential and current offenders that violence is a legitimate strategy for solving problems and expressing certain needs. The general approval of violence "establishes a context for the toleration and the acceptance of violence in intimate situations" (Carlson 1984: 578).

Social Structural Factors.   Several aspects of social organization contribute to causing and maintaining domestic violence: unequal resources, community norms and values, and organizational responses (Carlson 1984). First, although spouse abuse occurs in all social classes, it is more prevalent among families that are economically deprived. The contribution economic stress makes toward causing violence is uncertain because most poor families are not violent and many well-to-do families are. Most likely, economic stress has an indirect effect on family violence. Economic deprivation is subjective in many ways. If resources and needs are not well matched, then people may feel frustrated regardless of their assets. Or if a person feels underutilized, frustration and anger are likely outcomes. The subjective side of employment combined with violent beliefs and a low tolerance for stress may cause some spouse abuse.

Second, community norms and values play a part in domestic violence. Many communities deny that spouse abuse is a significant problem. Local prosecutors may hesitate to follow through on abuse complaints and judges may give light sentences if a defendant is convicted. Communities may choose not to promote education programs on violence in families or support shelters and other programs for victims. Similarly, police departments, as well as other professionals, do not always enforce spouse abuse laws or protect women effectively. Many police officers prefer not to get involved in domestic disturbances because they do not see marital assault as a crime or because it is a "low-status" arrest in police culture. Mandatory arrest policies, which have been enacted in many jurisdictions throughout the United States, have reduced officer discretion when answering domestic violence calls and thereby have empowered women by forcing the state to respond on their behalf.

Spouse abuse is found among all cultural groups, though many researchers have found it more prevalent among minority groups, especially African Americans (Straus, Gelles, & Steinmetz 1980; Neff, Holamon, & Schluter 1995; Hamptom & Gelles 1994). The rate of wife battering among Mexican Americans born in Mexico is about the same as Anglos. Among Mexican Americans born in the United States, however, rates of spouse abuse are higher (O'Keefe 1994).

For all three groups, economic stress is a strong predictor of domestic violence. Alcohol abuse, however, may account for ethnic differences between Mexican Americans and European Americans (Neff, Holamon, & Schluter 1995). Hamptom and Gelles (1994) contend that higher rates of domestic violence among African Americans and ethnic minorities are rooted in structural pressures from the social environment. Unemployment, underemployment, and discrimination undermine the ability of minority men to fulfill traditional family roles. Role failures accumulate and threaten men's sense of self, which in turn leads to ineffective coping and increased tension.

Not a great deal has been written on domestic violence among Asian Americans, though it is believed to be high, especially among recent immigrants. Chin (1994) believes that "out-of-town" brides, those who use marriage to flee China, are particularly at risk. Severe and public emotional abuse, forced isolation, economic exploitation, and physical assaults are apparently common among this group. Economic stress is a significant predictor of abuse among Chinese Americans, too, though Chin argues that other sociocultural factors are at work as well. These factors include value conflicts between traditional Chinese and American cultures, values supporting male dominance, males' expectations after spending money to help wives immigrate, the economic and cultural vulnerability of women (e.g., not speaking English and having little knowledge of American support systems), and the absence of women's families for protection.

Family Factors. As a social unit, several characteristics predispose a family to conflict and tension:

> *People spend a great deal of time interacting in the context of the family. The range of activities and events occurring there is quite broad, and family members differ in terms of sex, age, ability, and access to resources.*

All of these factors contribute to a high potential for disagreement and conflict . . .

> *The inherently unstable and ever-changing nature of family structure also results in chronic, high levels of change and stress. In addition, beliefs about the sanctity of family privacy tend to discourage many from taking problems outside the family when they cannot be adequately resolved using internal family resources (Carlson & Davis 1977: 43–44).*

Of course, this description applies to all families. What is different about those that are violent?

First, violent families believe in and practice traditional sex roles. Family roles are rigid, and gender largely decides who does what and when. Second, these families have recurring stress. Power issues are constant themes in family relations because the violent husband has a strong need to assert his dominance, which, in his thinking, is justified simply by the fact that he is male. Communication is very poor, thus violence becomes the husband's means of expressing a multitude of feelings and thoughts. Third, violent families are laden with conflict. These couples argue over the basic or core features of married and family living. Arguments that are most likely to lead to violence are over the children, sex, money, housekeeping, and social activities (Carlson 1984).

Violent couples follow a fairly predictable process over the course of their marriage. Figure 14.1 shows two aspects of the violent marriage: the cycle of violence and the continuum of violence.

Battering marriages follow a *cycle of violence* (Walker 1979), which includes three cyclical stages: tension building, violence, and the "honeymoon." In the tension-building phase, there may be no serious outbreaks of violence, but the husband is beginning to feel anxious and uptight. As the tension mounts, abused wives often make an extra effort to please their husbands in hopes of fending off stress. Some women who have become familiar with the pattern manipulate others not to anger the husband in an effort to keep him from losing his temper. Eventually peacekeeping efforts become less effective and the husband's behavior is less predictable.

Husbands advance the cycle when they assault their wives. The second phase, the actual violence, is usually triggered by some trivial event, called the *precipitating event,* that pushes already frustrated offenders past their ability to cope. The victim may have cooked the wrong vegetable for dinner or the baby may have cried at the wrong time. Whatever it is, the precipitating event is literally the "last straw" for a person with low tolerance for stress. Just because batterers have lost their ability to cope with stress, as they become

The Spiral of Violence

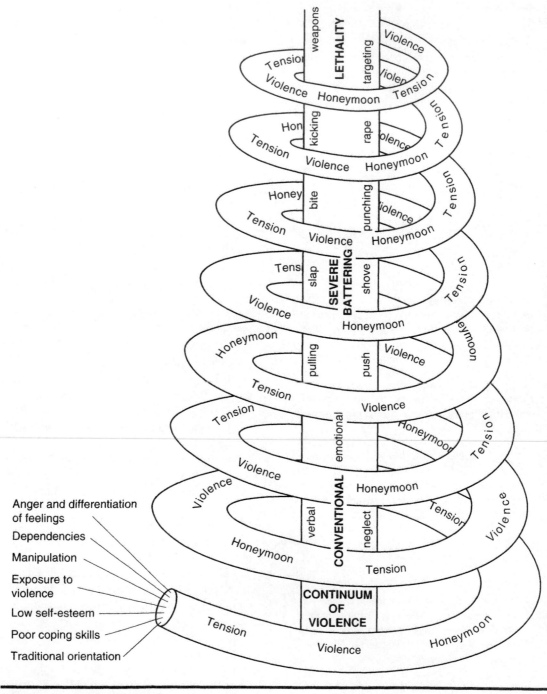

FIGURE 14.1 The Spiral of Violence
From: Lenore E. Walker
Prepared by: A. Furr

violent, it does not mean that they are out of control, which is how many women describe their husbands during phase two. To the contrary, when men batter their wives, there are many indications that they are in full command of themselves. When men batter, for example, they often practice what is called "targeting." This term describes how men target their attacks on particular areas of women's bodies. For instance, if the victim is pregnant, she is likely to be hit, punched, or kicked in the belly. If she takes pride in her facial appearance, then she is likely to be hit or cut there. Targeting requires a great deal of control.

In the third phase, the "honeymoon," the offender is usually contrite and filled with remorse. He offers to attend church, counseling, or AA meetings, and promises to quit drinking and stop hitting. He usually showers his partner with gifts and may make an effort to keep his promises. For a short time, family life improves and the wife is satisfied that the husband will not repeat his violence. The honeymoon phase of the wife battering process performs two functions. First, it allows the marriage to continue. The husband makes his wife believe that love and affection are alive and well in the relationship and that he is truly sorry for his behavior. Second, it becomes a reward for the wife for staying in the marriage. In a sense, he is paying her off.

Some men feel guilty over their violence and stop hitting on their own. For most, however, the conflicts eventually return and the tension-building is renewed. Notice in Figure 14.1 that the cycle of violence changes over time. Early in the relationship, the cycle takes longer to complete. Both the tension-building and honeymoon phases shorten as time goes by, however. This is a result of several factors. The more often that a woman is hit and then stays with the offender, the more likely the husband believes that he can get away with being violent. The more comfortable he feels with violence, the more liberties he will take and fewer barriers will exist to prevent his being violent. If the couple stays together long enough, the honeymoon phase eventually disappears altogether.

The second process found in violent couples is what Walker calls the *continuum of violence*. This concept describes how abuse advances from less destructive to severe. Offenders do not begin their abuse by hitting or kicking. These forms of violence are too severe for a new relationship to deal with. Rather, offenders begin with emotional abuse. They will humiliate or denigrate their partners, neglect their needs, follow them around, question them about their activities, and move to cut them off from their friends and relatives. After a relationship is established, abusers begin light violence against women. They may push their partners against a wall, pull their hair, and hit them with an open hand. If they get away with this, they will progress to more dangerous types of violence. Most offenders do not continue to lethal forms of violence. Offenders eventually reach their own plateau of severity and do not go beyond it.

The cycle of violence and the continuum of violence progress together over time. As the cycle gets shorter, the violence becomes more severe.

Individual Factors. Several psychological factors have been associated with spouse abuse. Individual qualities have been used to understand the violent behavior of the offender as well as why many women stay in violent marriages. It is hard to imagine these characteristics, however, outside their sociocultural context. Therefore, they must not be understood as unilateral causal agents, but as the way that social and cultural factors are expressed in everyday life.

First, let's look at the characteristics that abusers and battered women share: self-esteem issues, dependency, common defenses, and a family history of violence. Self-esteem issues play a large role in causing and maintaining domestic violence. Wife batterers and their victims typically have strong feelings of inadequacy, insecurity, powerlessness, fear, and helplessness. These qualities are usually more visible in women because abusers readily deny, repress, or project negative feelings (Okun 1986).

Some researchers have used the term *learned helplessness* to describe battered women (Walker 1979). Learned helplessness occurs when people are not in control, or perceive themselves to have no control, over events in their lives because they have been repeatedly punished for trying to change a negative situation or condition. Eventually they give up trying to escape and helplessly stay in a no-win situation. The concept was developed to describe abused wives who stayed in their marriages and believed that they had no control over what happened to them and no longer thought about leaving their husbands. Learned helplessness is learned hopelessness and despair; no matter what they try, they are trapped.

Not all battered women fit the learned helplessness profile, however. According to Gelles and Straus (1988), only about 13 percent of battered women can be characterized as compliant, passive, and submissive and actually feel that things are completely hopeless.

Abusers and their victims also possess dependent qualities. These men and women are particularly dependent on others to fulfill psychological needs. They rely on their partners for self-validation and to reaffirm their self-identity. In short, they are "other-driven," which means that they are beholden to others for their self-esteem. Inner- or self-directed people validate their own value and reward themselves for a job well done. Low self-esteem and dependency clearly go together. Feeling unworthy and inadequate, other-driven people turn to others for comfort and eventually rely on relationships to feel good about themselves. Without a relationship, the sense of self suffers. This is one reason why many violent husbands are more dangerous when the wife threatens to leave. Not only are they afraid of being exposed and consequently "caught," but the abusers are threatened by what their wife takes with her: knowledge of their feelings of inadequacy and the sole emotional comfort and relief they have achieved. The love within violent couples is not based on genuine intimacy, but on neediness and the gratification the partner provides.

Offenders and victims share common defense mechanisms as well. Both deny and minimize the scope and severity of the violence. These defenses are key strategies for protecting the self-esteem and public image of the "brutal" husband and the shamed and humiliated wife (Okun 1986). Neither batterers nor victims cope well with stress.

The final quality that batterers and their victims share is that both are likely to have experienced violence in their families of origin. There are several direct and indirect paths in which childhood violence can contribute to violence during adulthood (Carlson 1984). Numerous studies have learned that as many as 60 percent of the victims of spouse abuse were physically and/or sexually abused as children. Abusers also have high rates of physical abuse and neglect as children. In addition, abusers were likely to have been excessively physically disciplined as children and adolescents. Both victims and abusers are more likely to have seen violence between their parents than nonabusers and nonvictims (Carlson 1984). These associations show that violence is a learned behavior and that it is perceived as an acceptable way to solve problems in intimate relationships.

It is easy to rely on simple learning theory to explain wife abuse by saying that it is learned in childhood. Gelles and Straus (1988), however, are quick to point out that many abusers are first generation batterers and that this group is growing.

Abusive husbands have several characteristics distinct from their wives. Batterers are usually possessive and jealous and isolate their wives to prevent them from consorting with another person, especially other men. Jealousy and possessiveness are related to self-esteem needs. These men believe that they are undesirable, unworthy, and unlovable and that their wives know this as well. (This is a good example of the projection defense mechanism.) In batterers' reckoning, because their wives know how "bad" they are, the wives must surely be looking for a way out of the relationship. Therefore, these men make great efforts to prevent that from happening.

Men who hit often bring fewer resources to their marriage than their wives. Men who strongly believe in the ideology of male dominance, but whose wives have more education, earn more income, or have better expressive skills, may feel the need to legitimate their position of dominance in the family by resorting to violence (Allen & Straus 1980). Though spouse abuse occurs in all social classes, it is more prevalent among the working class and poor in part because these men have fewer economic resources and lower job prestige.

Abusive men have internalized cultural messages about violence. They believe that violence is a legitimate strategy for enforcing their power and solving problems. The belief that violence is acceptable is a strong feature of virtually all abusers.

Alcohol abuse is associated with domestic violence. Alcohol abuse precedes wife battering in about 25 percent of reported instances (Kantor & Straus 1987). Alcohol acts as a depressant and a disinhibitor. When alcohol is abused, a drinker is less likely to resist violating norms and taking responsibility for negative acts (Gelles & Straus 1979). Alcohol abuse, however, is neither a necessary nor a sufficient explanation for family violence (Yegidis 1992): Excessive alcohol abuse does not correlate with domestic violence, most episodes of violence do not include alcohol abuse, and many people abuse alcohol without hitting their spouses. Alcohol, nonetheless, plays an important role in wife battering. It may reduce the inhibitions of some men who already have a tendency to be violent.

Women who are victims of domestic violence have certain characteristics that attract men who will eventually abuse them. These qualities help keep them in their relationships once the violence commences. In addition to the qualities they share with batterers, victims are fearful and anxious individuals. Victims live in agonizing terror of their partners' violence. This fear can be so intense that victims are paralyzed to the point that they are unable to resist an assault, retaliate, or leave the abusive relationship (Okun 1987).

Many battered women assume responsibility for their partners' abusive behavior, especially early in the relationship (Okun 1986). The relationship between self-blame and low self-esteem is clearly evident. When women feel they are responsible for the violence done to them, they also believe that they can end the violence by changing their own behavior in order to please their husbands. These women sometimes take extraordinary measures to insure that their husbands get everything they need to be happy. It is often too late when they realize that they do not have any control over the violence and that there is nothing they can do to keep it from happening.

Several factors distinguish women who stay in abusive marriages from those women who get out (Gelles and Straus 1988: 143). The wife's personal resources and family history are the most significant.

- Women who leave violent marriages experienced more severe abuse;
- Women who grow up with violent families are more likely to stay with abusive husbands;
- Compared to women who leave, those who remain are less educated, have fewer job skills, and are likely to be unemployed;
- Women with young children are more likely to stay.

The Impact of Spouse Abuse on Children

Spouse abuse reverberates throughout the family system. When parents hit each other, a "pecking order" emerges in the family. Very often, after husbands abuse their wives, the wives vent their anger and frustration on the oldest children, who, in turn, take out their tension on the next oldest child. Often the family pet is last to bear the brunt of the family's problems.

Children are usually forced to keep the abuse a secret. Keeping secrets teaches children that lying is appropriate, not to seek help from others, and that what goes on in the home is sanctioned. Secret-keeping essentially teaches children that the world is a very unsafe place and that people should not be trusted.

In a study of eight- to twelve-year-old children, Sternberg and her associates (1993) found that those who witnessed domestic violence suffered more emotional and behavioral problems than children not exposed to violence. These children develop depressive symptoms, such as feeling sad and unwanted. They also externalize the family secret by engaging in behavior that gets them into trouble with parents, teachers, and other adults.

Spouse abuse creates tension that ripples throughout the family system. Children in these

---

Exploring the Issues **14.1**

Children's Roles in Alcoholic Families

In her famous book, *It Will Never Happen to Me!*, Claudia Black describes children in families in which at least one parent is an alcoholic. She believes that children in these families never learn about open communication or how to define family roles. Because of their parents' alcoholism, these children have a difficult time learning how to be responsible, to organize, to develop realistic goals, and to enjoy themselves. A majority of children of alcoholics, according to Black, do not learn how to be flexible, autonomous, and spontaneous. Consequently they seldom learn to adapt their behavior to different situations. Instead they tend to act the same way all of the time, regardless of the social context. Black believes that children of alcoholics "become locked into roles based on their perception of what they need to do to 'survive' and to bring some stability to their lives" (6). Alcoholics' children tend to adopt four roles, or combinations of the four: the responsible one, the adjuster, the placater, and the scapegoat.

The responsible one is usually the oldest or only child who becomes the dependable, responsible person in the absence of consistent parenting. These children develop their own family structure and take charge of their immediate family environment. The responsible child cares for younger siblings, takes over household chores, and may even care for the parents themselves. As Black states, these children assume responsibility because they feel the need for structure.

Performing this role brings comfort to responsible children. They are very organized, adept at planning, and skilled at completing goals. They have learned to rely on themselves for stability, organization, and satisfaction in life. Doing so relieves them of the pain their family brings them and helps them make sense of the world.

The adjusters are usually younger children who need not be responsible for themselves, since someone else is doing that for them. These children, according to Black, adapt to chaotic family situations "by simply adjusting to whatever happens... This child doesn't think about the situation, or experience any emotions as a result of it. Whatever happens...is simply handled" (14). The adjuster is less visible in the family than the responsible child and is likely to retreat to private places at home or spend more time with friends. The adjuster appears oblivious to family conflicts and seems to be "lost." Whereas responsible children do well in school, adjusters are usually average students and are somewhat detached from classmates.

The placater role is played by the overly sensitive child who shows emotions more easily and demonstrably. This child tries to feel better and handles family chaos by attempting to make others feel better. The placater tries to lessen tension by mediating problems or being a "clown," that is, by trying to be funny all the time. Others perceive placaters as nice people, mainly because they are always trying to make others feel better. Placaters rarely argue or are disagreeable and are quick to apologize, especially if doing so protects another person.

The scapegoat is usually the child that acts out the family turmoil. These children deal with their family problems by getting into trouble and calling negative attention to themselves. As Black says, the scapegoat is the stereotypical child of an alcoholic. These children disrupt their own families, cause trouble at school, and have difficulty with peers. However, they play an important role in the alcoholic family, because they call attention to themselves and away from the alcohol abuse. Parents can focus on, and blame, delinquent children and avoid dealing with their own problems.

families are particularly anxious. Life from day-to-day is a roller-coaster; no one is certain what will happen next.

DIVORCE

The divorce rate has not always been as high as it is today. Prior to the 1960s, divorce was a fairly uncommon event. Getting a divorce then required going to trial and proving that one partner committed an act that the state specified as sufficient grounds for divorce. Divorce *could* (not necessarily *would*) be granted on such grounds as adultery, failure to support, or abandonment. Physical abuse was usually not listed as legal grounds for divorce.

Because divorce assumed the violation of a code of conduct, those who legally ended their marriages were usually stigmatized by the community and treated as outcasts. Divorcées were seen as people who could not fulfill the community's

expectations of supporting their families, living up to traditional sex roles, and raising children.

What is the difference between the "old days" when divorce was infrequent and contemporary times when over half of first marriages fail? Is this trend simply the unfortunate outcome of a large number of individuals making poor choices in mates, or is something happening *to* families to cause them to break up?

Divorce is best understood when studied at three interacting levels of analysis: (1) sociocultural dynamics, (2) dyadic factors, and (3) individual qualities. Sociocultural forces are those processes that occur at the society and cultural levels. These dynamics are the defining qualities of the society and affect everyone to varying degrees. As shall be seen, several historical changes in the social order correlate with the rising incidence of divorce. Dyadic factors are dynamics of the marital relationship itself that predict divorce. Individual qualities are personal characteristics that are asso-

The leading cause of death and injury among women in the United States is domestic violence. Wife battering is a strategy of terror violent men use to maintain control of women and their households. In societies where the social, economic, and political gap between men and women is relatively narrow, marital assaults are far less common.

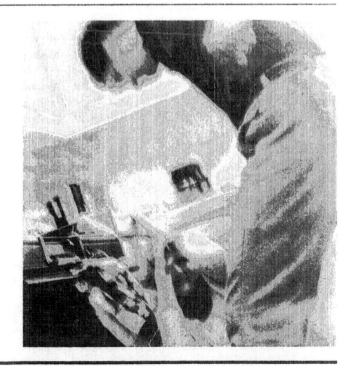

ciated with high rates of divorce. Though it is not a certainty, it is likely that dyadic and individual problems that negatively affect marriages have always been present. Changes in society, however, have made these marital conditions intolerable and escape possible.

Sociocultural Factors

There are two general ways to see how social and cultural factors contribute to the rate of divorce. One, divorce in Western cultures began to rise historically as certain social changes emerged, changes which differentiated the Western world from other cultures. Second, a comparison between Western cultures and non-Western, traditional cultures reveals that divorce is either absent or occurs rarely when Western influence is minimal. As non-Western cultures "westernize," however, their divorce rates go up.

There are four social changes that are associated with high divorce rates in modern industrial and postindustrial nations: a shift in values from sacred to secular, individualism, egalitarianism and women's rights, and an emphasis on economic status.

One, the Western world has changed the emphasis of its values from a sacred orientation to a secular one. *Sacred values* are aspects of social life that are rooted in higher meanings and inspire people to feel and act with respect, awe, and reverence. *Secular values* are shared ideas that concern ordinary or commonplace activities that people take for granted in their everyday lives (Thompson & Hickey 1994). For example, marital vows used to represent sacred values of commitment and obligation. Now wedding vows are largely ceremonial and wind up secondary to the secular values of personal gratification and economic advancement. This shift in cultural focus means that people are more willing to forgo their marriage and family commitments to pursue other activities. There are, in short, fewer moral constraints to bind people to their marriages.

Two, morality within modern culture is oriented toward protecting the sanctity of individualism. Individualism raises people's expectations of emotional gratification in relationships and leads people to think and act more in terms of personal happiness and gratification and less in terms of social responsibility. Individualism's credo, "If it feels good, do it!" fails to prepare individuals for the hard work and self-sacrifice that marriage and parenting require. When one is focused on the self too much, there is little energy remaining to attend to the needs of others. As the emphases of marriage shifted from economic survival and child-rearing to the emotional fulfillment of adults, the divorce rate soared.

Three, social and cultural changes with respect to egalitarianism and women's rights have led to higher divorce rates. When men were the *de jure* and *de facto* heads of households, divorce was far less common. Women had few economic opportunities, therefore they were less likely to leave a distressing marriage because they could not survive on their own. Now that women have access to education and jobs, they can live independently without being financially dependent on men. Furthermore, egalitarianism makes divorce more accessible because the law assumes that individuals should have the right to dissolve a marriage just as they have the right to enter one.

Four, industrial and postindustrial economies are associated with divorce. These economic systems emphasize social and geographical mobility, personal achievement, materialism, and competition. Many scholars argue that these processes contradict family life and commitment. When people spend a large amount of energy enhancing personal accomplishments, gaining social power, and being competitive, they must borrow time from their families and hence neglect their familial responsibilities.

Divorce among many ethnic minorities differs slightly from the Anglo majority (see Figure 14.2). Until recently Hispanics have enjoyed a "stability advantage" despite the rapid rise of divorce rates in the society-at-large (Frisbie, Ortiz, & Kelly 1985). Rates of divorce among Latinos is now about the same as Anglos. As Figure 14.2 shows, African Americans experience a high divorce rate. Oppressive economic and social conditions, declining employment opportunities for African American men, and violence create substantial and often irreconcilable hardship on marriages.

Dyadic Factors

Stresses within the marital subsystem can lead to divorce. Income, for example, plays a role in divorce risk. Up to a point, higher family income is a barrier to divorce (Raschke 1987). Marriages that do not have sufficient resources to meet family needs and realize the expectations they had for marriage have a higher probability of divorce (White 1990). Low-income groups also tend to marry at younger ages, another high-risk divorce behavior. A decline in socioeconomic status is also associated with divorce. Divorce among high income groups is somewhat higher than middle-income earners. The pursuit of wealth and success can wear away marital closeness and economic independence makes the necessity of economic cooperation unnecessary (Lamanna & Riedmann 1994).

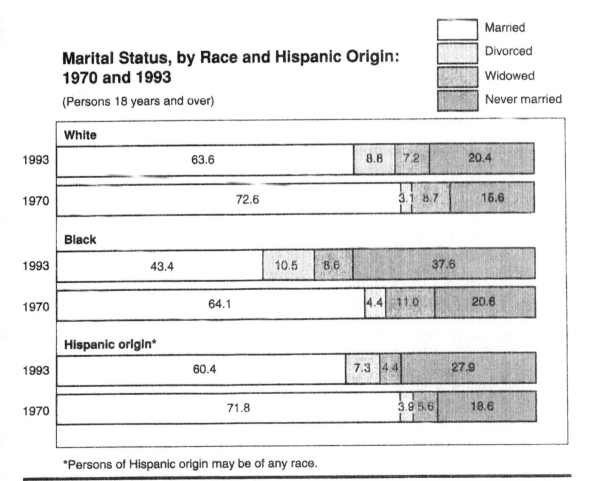

FIGURE 14.2 Marital Status by Race and Hispanic Origin: 1970 and 1993
Source: Saluter (1994)

Time is another marital dynamic that affects divorce rates. First, a short time of acquaintance before marriage is associated with divorce. When couples know each other for only a few weeks or months before marrying, they are probably still in the passionate stage of their relationship. They have not yet learned all there is to know about their partners, organized their roles, and developed a strong sense of attachment. The couple has not learned to solve problems together, nor to see each other at their worst. Second, most divorces occur early in the marriage. According to government statistics, about 9 percent of couples married three years divorced. Over one-third of divorces occurred among couples married less than five years. About 66 percent of all divorces go to couples married less than ten years (U.S. National Center for Health Statistics 1991). Older marriages are more stable because the couple has developed effective coping skills, maintained deep levels of affection, are satisfied with their family roles, have common economic interests, and a shared friendship network. However, divorce among older couples is rising.

Children can affect the likelihood of a couple divorcing. Though firstborn children increase marital stability during their preschool years, older children and children born before the marriage have a destabilizing effect on marriages (Waite & Lillard 1991). Young children's demands for parental attention can stabilize a marriage because the costs of single parenting are high. When children are older, according to Waite and Lillard, they require less care and their presence reduces their parents' marital happiness. Couples with sons are less likely to divorce than couples with daughters. Presumably this is due to fathers being more involved with sons (Bird & Melville 1994).

Couples who divorce usually have trouble making interpersonal adjustments to married life. They perhaps continued to think of themselves as single people and therefore did not develop a high degree of *familism*, which means feeling attached to or embedded in family life.

When couples cite specific problems that they believe caused their marriages to split up, they mention communication, unequal roles, alcohol and drugs, work situations, and abuse (Parker & Drummond–Reeves 1993). Communication is the cause most often reported. Without question, if a couple does not communicate well they cannot do the things they need to strengthen their relationship. Problem-solving, conflict management, negotiating boundaries, and showing affection do not come easy if people cannot talk with each other. Many in the helping professions reframe communication problems as symptoms rather than as causal factors, however. Communicating frankly and directly is impaired when people place their family commitment in a secondary position or have emotional troubles of their own. Communication patterns such as holding things in, being passive–aggressive, or being domineering reflect conflicts in other areas of life.

Finally, couples who have a high degree of social heterogeneity are a high risk for divorce. When two people from very different social backgrounds marry, they have a great deal to negotiate. Couples whose social class, religious, or ethnic differences are broad, face a high risk of divorce. Pressure from their families of origin and peers as well as opposing orientations to family life may be too strong to overcome.

Individual Factors

Numerous characteristics that individuals bring to a marriage may contribute to marital failure. One of the highest risk categories is young age at marriage. The younger one's age, the more likely a person does not have the personal resources to build a strong marriage. In this society, adolescence is extended well into the late teenage years and early twenties and young men and women are not expected to have the economic and interpersonal skills necessary to be competent husbands and wives. Unfortunately, most young people live up to these expectations and have an extremely high divorce rate.

Another individual factor that affects the likelihood of divorce is emotional stability. Depression, anxiety, narcissism, and other psychiatric complaints make gratifying marital life difficult. These conditions force individuals to focus on themselves and to relieve their problems by being dependent, dominant, passive, or game players. One example of how emotional qualities affect marriage success is that people whose own parents divorced have a high divorce rate. In fact, marriages in which both partners experienced a family breakup have the highest divorce rates (Bumpass, Martin, & Sweet 1991). Parental divorce can have a destabilizing effect on children that often emerges when children begin contemplating marriage for themselves. When they do marry, anxieties concerning their childhood, fears of abandonment, and apprehensions about intimacy make getting close and attachment anxiety-producing tasks. Other individual qualities associated with divorce include: second marriages, a high motivation for achievement, and unrealistic expectations of marriage.

THE PROCESS AND CONSEQUENCES OF DIVORCE

Divorce as Process

Though some separations take friends and relatives (as well as some spouses) by surprise, divorce is rarely an impulsive act. Couples who divorce experience a fairly predictable sequence of events. For the initiator of the separation, the process is usually longer. Not all couples go through the process of divorce exactly the same way, but most will follow a similar pattern.

The Stations of Divorce. Anthropologist Paul Bohannan (1970) concluded that divorce involves six "stations," or facets (see Table 14.2). Bohannan's model not only illustrates the complexity of divorce, but the progression of emotions, behaviors, and tasks that ending a marriage entails. Bohannan's model does not necessarily imply a sequencing of events; rather the six facets suggest different aspects of divorce. Nonetheless, there is a loose order in which the stations are usually ex-

perienced: (1) the emotional divorce, (2) the legal divorce, (3) the economic divorce, (4) the coparental divorce, (5) the community divorce, and (6) the psychic divorce.

The *emotional divorce* is the aspect of divorce in which spouses come to question the marriage. Arguments, feelings of emptiness, and uncertainty about the future seem ever-present to the couple. At least one of the partners is dissatisfied with the marriage and that spouse focuses on negative evaluations of the partner. Initiating partners, the "dumpers," privately begin to total up the shortcomings of the mate, the "dumpee," and start building an argument to justify their discontent with the marriage. The initiator often feels a heightened sense of remorse and guilt, compared to the dumpee who may be completely unprepared for the announcement (Wallerstein & Kelly 1980). This period is typically very stressful and conflicted. As the family begins to realize that the marriage is disintegrating, the family system starts to change (Anderson & Sabatelli 1995). Old roles are no longer performed, and in the absence of new roles, there is a certain degree of family chaos. Many couples seek marital therapy and other interventions during this aspect of divorcing.

The *legal divorce* is the facet of divorce in which the state intervenes to dissolve the legal marriage. The legal divorce is often very painful as the partners must accept the intrusion of outsiders such as attorneys and judges. Partners may feel somewhat out of control of their affairs if attorneys play a large role in dissolving the marriage. Once the marriage has legally ended, each partner is economically and legally free of the other. The legal divorce phase usually creates the need to grieve the loss of the marriage. Now that a court has officially ruled the marriage terminated, the process of gaining closure begins.

The *economic divorce* often invokes great bitterness and hostility. During this time, partners are dividing their assets and planning other financial arrangements. Many couples' conflicts come to a head during this phase of the divorce process, especially if their assets are extensive. Contests over the couple's wealth may produce vindictive

TABLE 14.2 Bohannon's Six Stations of Divorce

THE EMOTIONAL DIVORCE

Common Emotions

Disillusionment	Despair
Anxiety	Emptiness
Depression and Loss	Anger at Self and Partner
Inadequacy	Shock
Betrayal	

Common Behaviors

Disorganization	Denial
Avoidance	Withdrawal
Sulking and Crying	Seek Advice
Argumentative	Bargaining

Tasks

Acceptance
Express Emotions
Seek Support
Communicate Openly

THE LEGAL DIVORCE

Common Emotions

Anger	Confusion
Frustration	Hopeless
Helpless	Defeated
Threatened	

Common Behaviors

Self-Defeating Behavior
Seeking Counsel from Attorney or Mediator
Physical Separation

Tasks

Set Up New Household
Adjust to Living without Partner
Accepting Intrusion of Attorneys and Other
   Professionals
File for Legal Divorce

THE ECONOMIC DIVORCE

Common Emotions

Anger
Sadness and Grief

Common Behaviors

Lifestyle Changes
Relocation
Employment Changes, Especially
   for Women

Tasks

Divide Property and Other Assets
Settle Tax Issues

THE COPARENTAL DIVORCE

Common Emotions

Loneliness	Grief
Anger	Shame and Guilt
Vindictiveness	Fear

Common Behaviors

Game-Playing over Custody and Visitation
Power Struggles

Tasks

Explaining Divorce to Children
Helping Children Express Emotions
Planning Custody Arrangements and Child Support
Maintaining Family Rituals and Roles
Organize Lifestyle around Single Parenting

THE COMMUNITY DIVORCE

Common Emotions

Guilt and Shame	Sadness
Resignation	Regret
Excitement	Optimism

Common Behaviors

Reach Out to Friends and/or Make New Friends
Begin New Activities
Become Focused on Work, Self-Improvement,
   or Parenting

Tasks

Stabilize New Lifestyle
Change Relationships with Relatives and Friends
Finalizing Divorce

THE PSYCHIC DIVORCE

Common Emotions

Confidence	Independent and
Exhilaration	Capable
	Wholeness

Common Behaviors

Seek New Love Relationship
Become Comfortable with New Lifestyle

Tasks

Gaining Closure on Failed Marriage
Help Children Accept End of Marriage
Support Children
Regain Self-Identity

Adapted from: Bohannon (1970) and Kaslow and Schwartz (1987) behavior, especially if one spouse feels unjustly wronged. Mediation services, often provided by social workers, are successful in many such cases.

Divorce is not always a good economic deal for women and their children. In the early 1970s, laws were changed to usher in a new era of legal divorce proceedings. Called *No-Fault Divorce Laws,* these laws treat men and women equally in divorce court and assume that neither spouse is solely responsible for the failure of a marriage. Under these laws, spouses are not punished by an unfavorable financial settlement, nor can they receive more than their fair share. Women, for example, could no longer expect to stay in the family's house and receive financial support from their ex-husbands. The problem with no-fault laws is that men and women are not equal economically. In a landmark book, *The Divorce Revolution* (1985), Lenore Weitzman discovered that the quality of living for men and women after divorce was strikingly different. The standard of living for men improves substantially within a year after divorce while the quality of life for women with minor children declines (Weitzman 1985). Weitzman attributes these findings to differences in earning capacities between men and women. Despite receiving half of the family's assets at the time of divorce, women no longer benefit from men's higher present and future earnings.

A more recent study followed over 1,000 families for three years after they separated (Maccoby & Mnookin 1992). The authors found that, while both women's and men's income increased during the three years they were studied, the median annual earnings for women three years after divorce were still only 60 percent of those of the men. When child support was paid in full, it accounted for only 15 percent of family income. Fathers in this study remained significantly better off than they had been before the divorce. Women's finances improved dramatically only when they remarried.

The *coparental divorce* only applies to couples with children. During this phase, parents have to negotiate custody, child support, and visitation arrangements. Many emotions, such as anger,

loss, fear, and guilt, surface during this time. Fighting over the children can sometimes be bitter because of the emotions involved. Children can become pawns in the ongoing battles between parents who have yet to accept the end of their emotional attachment to each other. In some cases, children lose contact with the noncustodial parent, leaving them to feel additional loss and abandonment. Families who maintain family rituals and roles reduce the impact of separation.

The *community divorce* "station" concerns the announcement to others that the marriage has ended and the realignment of roles to accommodate being single again. Although being divorced no longer carries a negative stigma, it is a new social identity and status. Defining oneself as divorced may invoke feelings of loss or shame, especially after having to tell "the story" over and over to friends and relatives. Attending family of origin functions such as holidays as a single adult may cause sadness and loneliness. Friendship patterns often change, as newly divorced people also lose their relationships with married friends. In time, however, feelings of excitement surface as singlehood presents new social and sometimes employment opportunities.

The *psychic divorce* involves gaining closure on the failed marriage. Divorces should help children accept the end of the marriage as well. Most children fantasize about their parents getting back together; in some cases, such wishful thinking may interfere with normal functioning. Parents should be supportive of children and allow them to express their ideas and emotions, but also assure them of the finality of the divorce. During the psychic phase, adults usually gain a new self-identity and adjust to being single. For most divorced people, it takes about two years to grieve the loss of the marriage, deal with anger at the ex-spouse, and reorganize their daily lives. Some, however, continue to struggle with the hardships of post-divorce living and fail to reach closure. Even years after the divorce, many report high rates of depression, unhappiness, loss, anger, and sexual dissatisfaction (Garvin, Kalter, & Hansell 1993). They continue to fight or play manipulative games with their ex-partners because they have yet to resolve their feelings of attachment.

Not everyone is negatively affected by divorce. Albrecht found that 13 percent of women and 20 percent of men depict the divorce experience as "relatively painless" (1980: 61). Another 20 percent of men and women describe their divorce as unsettling but easier than expected. A large majority of divorces, even those who characterized their divorce as traumatic, believe they are better off after divorce than they were during their marriage or during the divorce process (Veevers 1991).

Children and Divorce

Divorce reverberates throughout all aspects of family functioning and is especially catastrophic for children. The loss of a parent and parental support, being stigmatized by peers, the fear of what will happen in the future, and the change in lifestyle, all create hardships and stressful emotions among children. The relationship between divorce and children is particularly troublesome because (a) the number of children involved in divorce is large, and (b) divorce affects virtually all aspects of children's lives. Table 14.3 illustrates the effects of divorce in several areas of psychosocial functioning.

Though there is no question that the dissolution of their parents' marriage is harmful for children, some researchers have found that parental conflict is the main source of adjustment problems, rather than divorce itself (Brown et al. 1991). When parents are angry and in conflict, children are unable to obtain support for themselves. The more severe the conflict, the greater the impact on children's adjustment.

The impact of divorce on children varies. Children are not all affected in the same ways, nor with the same intensity. Several factors mediate the effect of divorce on children. First, pre-divorce adjustment has significant influence on psychosocial responses to divorce. Children who had already achieved a stable identity, developed strong coping and problem-solving skills, and had ample social support were better able to withstand the divorce and the changes that came with it.

Second, how parents handle the divorce affects outcomes. Stress is reduced if parents explain the divorce and make sure that children realize they are not at fault for their parents' separation. When parents continue their parental roles and provide nurturance and social support after the divorce, children's adjustment and academic problems are reduced (Portes et al. 1992; Dubow & Tisak 1989). If parents separate without lingering attachments, conflict, and game-playing, children's adjustment is better as well.

Third, divorce affects children differently according to their sex and age. Boys experience far more severe and longer-lasting problems from parental divorce than girls (Wallerstein & Kelly 1980). Compared to girls, boys experience more adjustment problems, demonstrate more maladaptive behaviors, and commit more deviant acts after their parents' divorce. Boys' greater rate of adjustment problems may be explained by differences in what happens to boys and girls after the divorce. Custody of children is awarded to mothers in nearly all divorce settlements. For boys, this means learning to live without a same-sex parent (Demo & Acock 1988). Research has found that both boys and girls who live with opposite-sex parents are not as well-adjusted as children who live with a custodial parent of the same sex. Consequently, boys may have more problems because they have less access to their fathers.

Wallerstein (1987) offers another explanation of why girls cope better than boys. She suggests that girls are better able to gain psychosocial support and thus cope with stress better than boys. Boys, on the other hand, tend to act out their problems. Though boys have more problems with aggression, peer relationships, and handling schoolwork, sex differences in adjustment eventually dissipate (Wallerstein & Blakeslee 1989).

Children respond differently according to their age at the time their parents uncouple. How infants directly respond to parental separation is not completely understood. It can be deduced, however, that a negative impact is likely. When

TABLE 14.3 Impact of Parental Divorce on Children

IMPACT ON PERSONAL ADJUSTMENT

All Children

Stress, insecurity, and anxiety
Play is less socially and cognitively mature
Attention problems in school
Withdrawal and dependency

Boys

Maladaptive symptoms
Inappropriate behavior
Unhappiness
Effects of divorce last longer
Less psychosocial development
Judged by teachers to have lower levels of
  social conscience

Girls

Higher internal locus of control

IMPACT ON SELF-CONCEPT

All Children

Children in conflicted families with little support
  have lower self-esteem
Children from divorced families have lower self-
  esteem (some studies do not find these
  differences, however)
Lower perceived cognitive competence

Girls

Lower self-esteem among third-graders; no
  differences by sixth grade
Self-esteem related to parental happiness

IMPACT ON COGNITIVE FUNCTIONING

All Children

Less productive in school
Lower scores on language and total achievement
Lower SAT scores among males

IMPACT ON INTERPERSONAL RELATIONSHIPS

All Children

More immature, ineffective, and negative social
  behaviors
Fewer close friends
Participation in fewer activities

Boys

More contact with friends
More unpopularity

Less sociable

Girls

Problems with friends less long-lasting

IMPACT ON ANTI-SOCIAL BEHAVIOR

All Children

Deviant behavior
Make more decisions without parental input
Hostility and aggressiveness
More overcontrolled and undercontrolled behavior

Boys

More social deviance

Girls

Girls from divorced parents commit more
  delinquent acts such as drug use, larceny,
  and skipping school

Adapted from Demo & Acock (1988)

couples separate, their attention to parenting usually wanes and they experience a wide array of intense emotions such as depression, anger, and sadness. If it takes adults two years to recover from divorce, then the parent–infant relationship is likely to be disturbed during a critical period in the child's development (Hetherington, Cox, & Cox 1978). Consequently, infants' emotional and cognitive growth could be affected if the parent is unusually absent, depressed, or distracted.

A wide array of emotional responses is common to preschoolers when their immediate psychosocial environment is disrupted by divorce. Nightmares, irritability, self-blame, aggression, and guilt are common. Several behavioral changes occur as well. Depressed play, changes in eating patterns, bed-wetting, fighting, and less participation in group activities are typical reactions. Preschoolers are likely to blame themselves for "daddy leaving home." Cognitively young children are very self-oriented. Consequently they internalize family distress and believe that something wrong with them caused their parents to fight and separate. They may believe that had they been better children, nothing bad would have happened. Therefore it is necessary to talk with

Divorce is usually experienced as an overwhelming loss in which all aspects of life are affected. Many divorced people think of themselves as failures, especially immediately following the actual separation. What may be underlying this feeling is the perception that they have failed to achieve the ideal, perfect family.

preschoolers about their role, or lack of it, in their parents' problems.

School-age children may suffer the most dramatic consequences of parental divorce. Depression, withdrawal, grief, anger, feelings of rejection and abandonment, and shame are often experienced by school-age children. In addition, their school performance declines and they may feel a need to show loyalty to one parent over the other. Several factors have been shown to increase social competence among elementary school children. Support from parents, a high but appropriate de-

gree of household responsibility, and parental control help children cope with divorce stress (Amato 1989).

When parents divorce, children have little control over their daily lives and their own future. Because the divorce experience disrupts important aspects of the child's world, most notably the relationship between the children and their parents, divorce events may cause children to feel powerless. Many children may generalize their feelings of helplessness to other areas of life such as peer associations and school work. Feeling out of control can lead to depression and anxiety (Fogas et al. 1992). As a result, this diminished perception of control may interfere with coping with negative divorce-related events and lead to passive coping strategies such as blaming, avoiding, or wishful thinking, rather than active techniques such as problem-solving and seeking social support (Fogas et al. 1992). When children feel more in control, they are better equipped to handle the anxieties and pain of divorce.

For adolescents, adjustment problems appear in their relationships and in their quests for identity and independence. Teenagers may feel embarrassed and ashamed because of their parents' behavior and may worry about the future. Most adolescents in single-parent households have to assume additional domestic, child care, and financial responsibilities. Compared to children from intact families, these hardships result in more absenteeism, tardiness, truancy, fatigue, and conflicts for adolescents in one-adult families (Demo & Acock 1989). Adolescents in divorced families also engage in higher rates of delinquent and deviant behavior. When only one adult is present teenagers are more likely to behave in deviant ways, partly because they tend to make decisions independent of parental input and control. Anti-social behavior, for most teens, is temporary, occurring usually during periods of disruption. Some strengths, such as a heightened sense of responsibility and more androgynous behavior, emerge for adolescents living in single-parent families (Demo & Acock 1989).

CONCLUSION

As an institution, the family is fairly weak. Contrary to politicians who blame the family for all that is wrong with the world, it is quite a far-fetched idea to believe that the family institution is powerful enough to cause corporate layoffs and low wages that place enormous strains on households. It is unreasonable to conclude that families cause racial and sexual discrimination in the workplace or affect public policies that deny civil

rights for gays and lesbians. Do families cause secular values such as consumerism and materialism? It is important to think about the temporal ordering of events and conditions. The family, in many ways, is a pawn to social and cultural changes. For example, families have been slow to adapt to the cultural values of individualism and are trapped between two opposing forces:

> *the traditional values of interpersonal responsibility and commitment and the developmental needs of children*

> *versus*

> *individual gratification and achievement*

Most scholars as well as public orators decry domestic violence and divorce as social problems. It may be more useful, however, to reframe these conditions as symptoms, rather than as problems unto themselves. Both violence against women and divorce, though separate phenomena, are consequences of problems outside the family. The social environment in which families exist creates stresses and tensions that make harmonious family life unlikely for a significantly large number of people. Competitive values, individualism, economic stress, a lack of social support for families, sexism, and the acceptance of violence in daily life are features of Western culture that produce high rates of divorce and violence in families. Peaceful and long-lasting families may contradict this environmental context. Therefore, the real problem is not necessarily divorce and violence, but the conditions of society that produce them.

Adequate resources reduce the likelihood and impact of family stress and dissolution. The structural model of social work practice is particularly useful in working with families. Developing strategies to ensure that adults in families have access to the resources they require to maintain emotional gratification and reach their fullest human potential, while at the same time fulfilling their supportive and nurturance obligations to their children, is the task of all families. To accomplish these goals, families need support at all levels. Social workers should strive to find ways to help families access those resources or develop them if they are nonexistent.

CASE STUDY REVIEW QUESTIONS

Refer to the case of Darias and Shauna at the beginning of Chapter 14. From reading this chapter, how might you answer the following questions?

1. What factors may have made this couple a high risk for divorce?
2. What is the process that Shauna and Darias are likely to experience as they separate and eventually divorce?
3. How might the children's experience be affected by their parents' divorce. What will each parent need to do to minimize the impact of the divorce on them?
4. In what ways has Shauna's quality of living declined since the divorce?

KEY TERMS

Community divorce: The "station" of divorce that concerns the announcement to others that the marriage has ended and the realignment of roles to accommodate being single again.

Continuum of violence: A term that describes how abuse advances in violent couples from less destructive to severe.

Coparental divorce: A facet of divorce when parents have to negotiate custody, child support, and visitation arrangements.

Cycle of violence: The three cyclical stages found in battered marriages, i.e., tension-building, violence, and the "honeymoon."

Economic divorce: Aspect of divorce when partners divide their assets and plan other financial arrangements.

Emotional divorce: The aspect of divorce in which spouses question the marriage.

Familism: Feeling attached to or embedded in family life.

Learned helplessness: A term that describes some battered women; learned helplessness occurs when people are not in control, or perceive themselves to have no control, over events in their lives.

Legal divorce: The facet of divorce in which the state intervenes to dissolve the legal marriage.

No-fault divorce laws: Laws that allow divorce for virtually any reason; laws treat men and women equally, especially compared to grounds-based divorce laws which awarded economic advantages to women with children.

Precipitating event: Some trivial event that triggers domestic violence.

Psychic divorce: The last station of divorce when individuals gain closure on the failed marriage.

Sacred values: Aspects of social life that are rooted in higher meanings and inspire people to feel and act with respect, awe, and reverence.

Secular values: Shared ideas that concern ordinary or commonplace activities that people take for granted in their everyday lives.

REFERENCES

Abel, E. K. 1991 *Who Cares for the Elderly? Public Policy and the Experiences of Adult Daughters.* Philadelphia: Temply University Press.

Adelmann, P. K., Antonucci, T. C., & Crohan, S. E. 1989 A causal analysis of employment and health in mid-life women. *Women and Health,* 16(1):5–20.

Adorno, T. et al. 1950 *The Authoritarian Personality.* New York: Harper & Row.

Aguilar, M. A. & Williams, L. P. 1993 Factors contributing to the success and achievement of minority women. *Affilia: Journal of Women and Social Work,* 8(4):410–424.

Ainsworth, M. D. S., Bell, S. M., & Stayton, D. J. 1974 Infant–mother attachment and social development: Socialization as a product of reciprocal responsiveness to signals. In M. Richards (Ed.), *The Integration of a Child into a Social World.* Cambridge: Cambridge University Press, pp. 99–135.

Ainsworth, M. D. S., Blehar, M. C., Waters, E., & Wall, S. 1978 *Patterns of Attachment.* Hillsdale, NJ: Erlbaum.

Ainsworth, M. D. S. & Wittig, B. A. 1969 Attachment and exploratory behavior of one-year-olds in a strange situation. In B. M. Foss (Ed.), *Determinants of Infant Behavior—IV.* London: Methuen, pp. 113–136.

Albrecht, S. L. 1980 Reactions and adjustments to divorce: Differences in experiences of males and females. *Family Relations,* 29:59–68.

Alexander, F. G. & Selesnick, S. T. 1966 *The History of Psychiatry: An Evaluation of Psychiatric Thought and Practice from Prehistoric Times to the Present.* New York: Harper Row.

Allen, C. & Straus, M. A. 1980 Resources, power, and husband–wife violence. In M. A. Straus & G. T. Hotaling (Eds.), *The Social Causes of Husband–Wife Violence.* Minneapolis: University of Minnesota Press, 188–208.

Allen, L. S. & Gorski, R. A. 1992 Sexual orientation and the size of the anterior commissure in the human brain. *Proceedings of the National Academy of Sciences USA,* 89:7199–7202.

Allen–Mears, P. 1987 Depression in childhood and adolescence. *Social Work,* 32(6):512–518.

Amaro, H. & Russo, N. F. 1987 Hispanic women and mental health. *Psychology of Women Quarterly,* 11(4):393–407.

Amato, P. R. 1989 Family processes and the competence of adolescents and primary school children. *Journal of Youth and Adolescence,* 18(1):39–53.

Amato, P. R. 1993 Children's adjustment to divorce: Theories, hypotheses, and empirical support. *Journal of Marriage and the Family,* 55(1):23–38.

American Humane Association 1985 *Highlights of Official Child Abuse and Neglect Reporting, 1983.* Denver: Author.

American Psychiatric Association 1994 *The Diagnostic and Statistical Manual of Mental Disorders,* 4th Ed. Washington, DC: American Psychiatric Association.

Anderson, C. & Stark, C. 1988 Psychosocial problems of job relocation: Preventive roles in industry. *Social Work,* 33(1):38–41.

Anderson, R. M. et al. 1986 Access of Hispanics to health care and cuts in services: A state-of-the-art overview. *Public Health Reports,* 101(May/June):238–252.

Anderson, S. A. & Sabatelli, R. M. 1995 *Family Interactions: A Multigenerational Developmental Perspective.* Boston: Allyn and Bacon.

Angel, R. J. & Worobey, J. L. 1991 Intragroup differences in the health of Hispanic children. *Social Science Quarterly,* 72(2):361–378.

Anselmo, S. 1987 *Early Childhood Development: Prenatal through Age Eight.* Columbus: Merrill Publishing.

Anson, O. et al. 1993 Gender differences in health perceptions and their predictors. *Social Science and Medicine,* 36(4):419–427.

Anthony, E. J. 1970 Two contrasting types of adolescent depression and their treatment. *Journal of the American Psychoanalytic Association,* 1:841–859.

Antonosky, A. 1967 Social class, life expectancy and overall mortality. *Milbank Quarterly,* 45:31–73.

Arguelles, L. & Rich, B. R. 1984 Homosexuality, homophobia, and revolution: Notes toward an understanding of the Cuban lesbian and gay male experience, part 1. *Signs,* 9(4):683–699.

Aries, E. 1973 Interaction patterns and themes of male, female and mixed groups. Unpublished doctoral dissertation, Harvard University, Cambridge, MA. Cited in Reid (1991).

Arling, G. 1976 The elderly widow and her famly, neighbors, and friends. *Journal of Marriage and the Family,* 38:757–768.

Atchley, R. C. 1976 *The Sociology of Retirement.* New York: Halsted Press.

Atchley, R. C. 1989 A continuity theory of normal aging. *The Gerontologist,* 29(2):183–190.

Bailey, J. M. & Pillard, A. C. 1991 A genetic study of male homosexuality. *Archives of General Psychiatry,* 48:1089–1096.

Bailey, J. M., Willerman, L., & Parks, C. 1991 A test of the maternal stress theory of human male homosexuality. *Archives of Sexual Behavior,* 20(June): 277–293.

Ball, R. E. & Robbins, L. 1986 Marital status and life satisfaction among Black Americans. *Journal of Marriage and the Family,* 48:389–394.

Baltes, M. M. 1994 Aging well and institutional living: A paradox?. In Abeles, R. P., Gift, H. C., & Ory, M. G. (Eds.), *Aging and Quality of Life.* New York: Springer, pp. 185–202.

Bandura, A. 1977 *Social Learning Theory.* Englewood Cliffs, NJ: Prentice-Hall.

Bane, M. J. 1986 Household composition and poverty. In Danziger, S. H. & Weinberg, D. H., (Eds.). *Fighting Poverty.* Cambridge: Harvard University Press.

Banfield, E. 1974 *The Unheavenly City Revisited.* Boston: Little, Brown.

Barglow, P., Vaughn, B. E., & Molitor, N. 1987 Effects of maternal absence due to employment on the quality of infant–mother attachment in a low risk sample. *Child Development,* 58:945–954.

Barnet, J. K., Papini, D. R., & Gbur, R. 1991 Familial correlates of sexually active pregnant and nonpregnant adolescents. *Adolescence,* 26(102): 457–473.

Bartz, K. V. & Levine, E. S. 1978 Child rearing by black parents: A description and comparison to Anglo and Chicano parents. *Journal of Marriage and the Family,* 40(4):709–719.

Bassuk, E. L. 1990 Who are the homeless families? Characteristics of sheltered mothers and children. *Community Mental Health Journal,* 26(5):425–434.

Bavolek, S. 1984 *Handbook for the Adult–Adolescent Parenting Inventory (AAPI).* Park City, Utah: Family Development Resources.

Baydar, N. & Brooks–Gunn, J. 1991 Effects of maternal employment and child-care arrangements on preschoolers' cognitive and behavioral outcomes: Evidence from the children of the national longitudinal survey of youth. *Developmental Psychology,* 27:932–945.

Beaver, M. L. & Miller, D. A. 1992 *Clinical Social Work Practice with the Elderly: Primary, Secondary, and Tertiary Intervention.* Belmont, CA: Wadsworth.

Beavers, W. R. & Hampson, R. B. 1993 Measuring family competence: The Beavers systems model. In F. Walsh (Ed.). *Normal Family Processes,* 2nd ed. New York: Guilford Press, pp. 73–103.

Becerra, J. E. et al. 1991 Infant mortality among Hispanics. *Journal of the American Medical Association,* 265(2):217–220.

Beckwith, L. & Cohen, S. E. 1984 Home environment and cognitive competence in preterm children during the first five years. In A. Gottfried (Ed.), *Home Environment and Early Cognitive Development.* New York: Academic Press, pp. 235–269.

Beckwith, L. 1988 Intervention with disadvantaged parents of sick preterm infants. *Psychiatry,* 51: 242–247.

Belden, J. N. 1993 Housing for America's rural elderly. In C. N. Bull (Ed.), *Aging in Rural America.* Newbury Park: Sage, pp. 71–82.

Belgrave, F. Z., Cherry, V. R., & Cunningham, D. 1994 The influence of Africentric values, self-esteem, and black identity on drug attitudes among African American fifth graders: A preliminary study. *Journal of Black Psychology,* 20(May):143–156.

Bell, A. P. & Weinberg, M. S. 1978 *Homosexualities: A Study of Diversity among Men and Women.* Melbourne: Macmillan.

Bell, A. P., Weinberg, M. S., & Hammersmith, S. K. 1981 *Sexual Preference: Its Development in Men and Women.* Bloomington: Indiana University Press.

Belsky, J. & Vondra, J. 1989 Lessons from child abuse: The determinants of parenting. In D. Cicchetti & V. Carson (Eds.), *Child Maltreatment: Theory and Research on the Causes and Consequences of Child Abuse and Neglect.* Cambridge: Cambridge University Press.

Belsky, J. et al. 1984 The Pennsylvania infant and family development project, I: Stability and change in mother–infant and father–infant interaction in a family setting at 1-to-3 to 9 months. *Child Development,* 59:157–166.

Bem, S. 1981 Gender schema theory: A cognitive account of sex typing. *Psychological Review,* 88: 354–364.

Benn, R. 1986 Factors promoting secure attachment relationships between employed mothers and their sons. *Child Development,* 57:1224–1231.

Beran, N. J., Claybaker, C., Dillion, C., & Haverkamp, R. J. 1992 Attitudes towards minorities: A comparison of homosexuals and the general population. *Journal of Homosexuality,* 23(3):65–84.

Berg, I. K. & Miller, S. D. 1992 Working with Asian American clients: One person at a time. *Families in Society,* 73(6):356–363.

Berger, C. S. et al. 1990 Cocaine and pregnancy: A challenge for health care providers. *Health and Social Work,* 15(4):310–318.

Berger, K. S. 1994 *The Developing Person through the Life Span.* New York: Worth Publishers.

Berger, R. M. 1984 Realities of gay and lesbian aging. *Social Work,* 29:57–62.

Beril, R. A. 1994 Dementia. In Bonder, B. R. & Wagner, M. B. (Eds.) *Functional Performance in Older Adults.* Philadelphia: F. A. Davis, pp. 240–255.

Berk, M. L., Cunningham, P., & Beauregard, K. 1991 The health care of poor persons living in wealthy areas. *Social Science and Medicine,* 32(10): 1097–1103.

Berkman, L. F. et al. 1986 Depressive symptoms in relaton to physical health and functioning in the elderly. *American Journal of Epidemiology,* 124: 372–388.

Bernard, J. 1973 *The Sociology of Communities.* Glenview, IL: Scott, Foresman & Co.

Bieber, I. et al. 1962 *Homosexuality: A Scientific Study.* New York: Basic Books.

Biegel, D. E., Shore, B. K., & Silverman, M. 1989 Overcoming barriers to serving the aging/mental health client: A state initiative. *Journal of Gerontological Social Work,* 13(3/4):147–166.

Billingsley, A. 1988 The impact of technology on African American families. *Family Relations,* 37: 420–425.

Binder, A., Geis, G., & Bruce, D. 1988 *Juvenile Delinquency: Historical, Cultural and Legal Perspectives.* New York: Macmillan.

Bingham, C. R., Miller, B. C., & Adams, G. R. 1990 Correlates of age at first sexual intercourse in a national sample of young women. *Journal of Adolescent Research,* 5:7–17.

Bird, G. & Melville, K. 1994 *Families and Intimate Relationships.* New York: McGraw-Hill.

Black, C. 1981 *It Will Never Happen to Me!* New York: Ballantine Books.

Blackwell, J. E. 1991 *The Black Community: Diversity and Unity.* New York: Harper Collins.

Blau, F. D. & Graham, J. W. 1990 Black–white differences in wealth and asset composition. *Quarterly Journal of Economics,* 105(May):321–339.

Blau, P. M. 1977 *Inequality & Heterogeneity: A Primitive Theory of Social Structure.* New York: Free Press.

Blendon, R. J. et al. 1987 Access to medical care for black and white Americans. *Journal of the American Medical Association,* 261(2):278–281.

Block, M. R. 1979 Exiled Americans: The plight of the Indian aged in the United States. In D. E. Gelfand & A. J. Kutzik (Eds.), *Ethnicity and Aging: Theory, Research, and Policy.* New York: Springer, pp. 184–192.

Blumenfeld, W. J. & Raymond, D. 1988 *Looking at Gay and Lesbian Life.* Boston: Beacon Press.

Blumstein, P., & Schwartz, P. 1983 *American Couples: Money, Work, and Sex.* New York: William Morrow.

Bohannan, P. 1970 The six stations of divorce. In P. Bohannan (Ed.), *Divorce and After.* New York: Doubleday, pp. 113–123.

Bortner, M. A. 1988 *Delinquency and Justice: An Age of Crisis.* New York: McGraw-Hill.

Bosse, R., Aldwin, C. M., & Levenson, M. R. 1993 Change in social support after retirement; longitudinal findings from the Normative Aging Study. *Journal of Gerontology,* 48:210–217.

Bosse, R., Aldwin, C. M., Levenson, M. R., & Workman–Daniels, K. 1991 How stressful is retirement? Findings from the Normative Aging Study. *Journal of Gerontology,* 46:9–14.

Boswell, J. 1980 *Christianity, Social Tolerance, and Homosexuality.* Chicago: University of Chicago Press.

Bousha, D. M. & Twentyman, C. T. 1984 Mother–child interactional style in abuse, neglect, and control groups: Naturalistic observations in the home. *Journal of Abnormal Psychology,* 93:106–114.

Bowlby, J. 1969 *Attachment*. New York: Basic Books.

Bowler, R., Rauch, S., & Schwarzer, R. 1986 Self-esteem and interracial attitudes in black high school students. *Urban Education,* 21(1):3–19.

Bradford, J. & Ryan, C. 1991 Who we are: Health concerns of middle-aged lesbians. In Sang, B., Warshow, J., & Smith, A. J. (Eds.), *Lesbians at Midlife: The Creative Transition*. San Francisco: Spinsters Book Company, pp. 147–163.

Brannock, J. C. & Chapman, B. E. 1990 Negative sexual experiences with men among heterosexual women and lesbians. *Journal of Homosexuality,* 19(1):105–110.

Braverman, S. & Paris, J. 1993 The male mid-life crisis in the grown-up resilient child. *Psychotherapy,* 30(4):651–657.

Brody, E. M., Dempsey, N. P., & Pruchno, R. A. 1990 Mental health of sons and daughters of the institutionalized aged. *The Gerontologist,* 30:212–219.

Broken Nose, M. A. 1992 Working with the Oglala Lakota: An outsider's perspective. *Families in Society,* 73(June):380–384.

Bronfenbrenner, U. 1979 *The Ecology of Human Development: Experiments by Nature and Design*. Cambridge: Harvard University Press.

Bronfenbrenner, U. 1986 Ecology of the family as a context for human development: Research perspectives. *Developmental Psychology,* 22(6):723–742.

Bronstein, P., Clauson, J., Stoll, M. F., & Abrams, C. L. 1993 Parenting behavior and children's social, psychological, and academic adjustment in diverse family structures. *Family Relations,* 42:268–276.

Brook, J. S. et al. 1992 Sequences of drug involvement in African American and Puerto Rican adolescents. *Psychological Reports,* 71(1):179–182.

Brooks–Gunn, J. 1987 Pubertal processes: Their relevance for developmental research. In Van Hasselt, V. B. & Hersen, M. (Eds.), *Handbook of Adolescent Psychology*. New York: Pergamon.

Brown, J. H. & Cristensen, D. N. 1986 *Family Therapy: Theory and Practice*. Monterey, CA: Brooks–Cole Publishing Co.

Brown, J. H., Eichenberger, S. H., Portes, P. R., & Christiansen, D. N. 1991 Family functioning and children's divorce adjustment. *Journal of Divorce and Remarriage,* 17(1/2):81–97.

Bulterys, M. 1990 High incidence of sudden infant death syndrome among northern Indians and Alaska natives compared with southwestern Indians: Possible role of smoking. *Journal of Community Health,* 15(June):185–194.

Bumpass, L., Martin, T., & Sweet, J. 1991 The impact of family background and early marital factors on marital disruption. *Journal of Family Issues,* 12:22–42.

Bumpass, L. L. 1984 Children and marital disruption: A replication and update. *Demography,* 21:71–82.

Bumpass, L. L. 1990 What's happening to the family? Interactions between demographic and institutional change. *Demography,* 27(4):483–498.

Burman, M. A. et al. 1987 Acculturation and lifetime prevalence of psychiatric disorders among Mexican Americans in Los Angeles. *Journal of Health and Social Behavior,* 28:89–102.

Byne, W. & Parsons, B. 1993 Human sexual orientation: The biologic theories reappraised. *Archives of General Psychiatry,* 50(March):228–239.

Caldwell, M. A. & Peplau, L. A. 1984 The balance of power in lesbian relationships. *Sex Roles,* 10(April):587–599.

Cameron, P. et al. 1989 Effect of homosexuality upon public health and social order. *Psychological Reports,* 64(June):1167–1179.

Carlson, B. E. & Davis, L. V. 1977 Prevention of domestic violence. In R. H. Price, et al. (Eds.), *Prevention in Mental Health*. Beverly Hills, CA: Sage Publications.

Carlson, B. E. 1984 Causes and maintenance of domestic violence: An ecological analysis. *Social Service Review,* 58:568–587.

Carrasquillo, A. L. 1991 *Hispanic Children and Youth in the United States*. New York: Garland Publishing.

Carter, E. A. & McGoldrick, M. 1980 *The Family Life Cycle: A Framework for Family Therapy*. New York: Gardner Press.

Carter, J. H. 1983 Vision or sight: Health concerns for Afro-American children. In G. Johnson–Powell (Ed.), *The Psychosocial Development of Minority Group Children*. New York: Brunner/Mazel, pp. 13–25.

Cass, V. C. 1979 Homosexual identity formation: A theoretical model. *Journal of Homosexuality,* 4(3):219–236.

Cass, V. C. 1990 The implications of homosexual identity formation for the Kinsey model and scale of sexual preference. In McWhirter, D. P. et al. (Eds.). *Homosexuality/Heterosexuality: Concepts of Sexual Orientation.* New York: Oxford University Press, pp. 239–266.

Cassidy, J. & Ashur, S. R. 1992 Loneliness and peer relations in young children. *Child Development,* 63(April):350–365.

Cefalo, R. & Moos, M. 1988 *Preconceptional Health Promotion: A Practical Guide.* Rockville, MD: Aspen Publishing Co.

Centers for Disease Control. 1987 *Morbidity and Mortality Weekly Report.* 36(15).

Centers for Disease Control. 1989 *HIV/AIDS Surveillance Report.* (November).

Chambliss, W. J. 1973 The saints and the roughnecks. *Society,* 11(1):341–355.

Chasnoff, I. J., Burns, K. A., & Burns, W. J. 1987 Cocaine use in pregnancy: Perinatal morbidity and mortality. *Neurotoxicology and Teratology,* 9: 291–293.

Chi, I., Lubben, J. E., & Kitano, H. K. 1988 Heavy drinking among young adult Asian males. *International Social Work Journal,* 31(3):219–229.

Children's Defense Fund. 1990 Washington, DC: Children's Defense Fund.

Chin, Ko-Lin. 1994 Out-of-town brides: International marriage and wife abuse among Chinese immigrants. *Journal of Divorce and Remarriage,* 25(1):53–69.

Chodzko-Zajko, W. J., Schuler, P., & Solomon, J. 1992 The influence of physical fitness on automatic and effortful memory changes in aging. *International Journal of Aging and Human Development,* 35(4):265–285.

Christie, D. & Young, M. 1986 Self-concept of lesbian and heterosexual women. *Psychological Reports,* 59:1279–1282.

Christie, N. 1978 Youth as a crime-generating phenomenon. In C. E. Reasons and R. M. Rich (Eds.), *The Children of Ishmael: Critical Perspectives on Juvenile Justice.* Palo Alto: Mayfield, pp. 220–230.

Cicchetti, D. & Aber, J. L. 1986 Early precursors of later depression: An organizational perspective. In L. P. Lipsitt & C. Povee-Collier (Eds.), *Advances in Infancy Research* (Vol. 4). Norwood, NJ: Ablex, pp. 87–131.

Cicchetti, D. 1989 How research on child maltreatment has informed the study of child development: Perspectives from developmental psychopathology. In D. Cicchetti and V. Carlson (Eds.), *Child Maltreatment: Theory and Research on the Causes and Consequences of Child Abuse and Neglect.* Cambridge: Cambridge University Press, pp. 377–431.

Clark, C. M. 1992 Deviant adolescent subcultures: Assessment strategies and clinical interventions. *Adolescence,* 27(106):283–294.

Clebert, J. P. 1963 *The Gypsies.* London: Vista.

Cochran, S. D., Mays, V. M., & Leung, L. 1991 Sexual practices of heterosexual Asian American young adults: Implications for risk of HIV infection. *Archives of Sexual Behavior,* 20(4).381–391.

Cockerham, W. C. 1989 *Sociology of Mental Disorder,* 2nd ed. Englewood Cliffs, NJ: Prentice–Hall.

Cohen, S. & Edwards, J. R. 1986 Personality characteristics as moderators of the relationship between stress and disorder. In Neufeld, R. W. J. (Ed.), *Advances in the Investigation of Psychological Stress.* New York: Wiley.

Cohn, W. 1969 Some comparisons between Gypsy (North American Rom) and American English kinship terms. *American Anthropologist,* 71: 477–478.

Collins, N. L. et al. 1993 Social support in pregnancy: Psycho–social correlates of birth outcome and postpartum depression. *Journal of Personality and Social Psychology,* 65(6):1243–1258.

Colsher, P. L. & Wallace, R. B. 1990 Elderly men with histories of heavy drinking: Correlates and consequences. *Journal of Studies on Alcohol,* 51: 528–535.

Comer, J. P. 1985 The Yale–New Haven primary prevention project: A follow-up study. *Journal of the American Academy of Child Psychiatry,* 24(2): 154–160.

Constantino, G., Malgady, R. G., and Rogler, L. H. 1986 Cuento therapy: A culturally sensitive modality for Puerto Rican children. *Journal of Consulting and Clinical Psychology,* 54(October): 639–645.

Coontz, S. 1992 *The Way We Never Were: American Families and the Nostalgia Trap.* New York: Basic Books.

Cotterel, J. L. 1986 Work and community influences on the quality of child rearing. *Child Development,* 57:362–374

Coutts, J. S. 1987 Masculinity–femininity of self-concept: Its effect on the achievement behavior of women. *Sex Roles,* 16(January):9–17.

Cox, H. 1984 *Later Life: The Realities of Aging.* Englewood Cliffs, NJ: Prentice–Hall.

Cozby, P. C. 1973 Self-disclosure: A literature review. *Psychological Bulletin,* 79:73–91.

Creecy, R. F., Berg, W. C., & Wright, R. 1985 Loneliness among the elderly: A causal approach. *Journal of Gerontology,* 40(4):487–493.

Crittenden, P. M. 1992 Children's strategies for coping with adverse home environments: An interpretation using attachment theory. *Child Abuse and Neglect,* 16:329–343.

Crohan, S. E. & Antonucci, T. C. 1989 Friends as a source of social support in old age. In Adams, R. G. & Blieszner, R. (Eds.), *Older Adult Friendship: Structure and Process.* Newbury Park: Sage, pp. 129–146.

Cross, S. E. & Markus, H. R. 1993 Gender in thought, belief, and action: A cognitive approach. In Bealle, A. E. & Sternberg, R. J. (Eds.). *The Psychology of Gender.* New York: Guilford Press, pp. 55–98.

Cross, W. E., Jr. 1971 Negro to black conversion experience: Toward a psychology of black liberation. *Black World,* 20:13–27.

Crouch, J. L. & Milner, L. S. 1993 Effects of child neglect on children. *Criminal Justice and Behavior,* 20(1):49–65.

Crystal, D. 1989 Asian Americans and the myth of model minority. *Social Casework,* 70(6):405–413.

Cummings, E. M. & Davies, P. T. 1994 Maternal depression and child development. *Journal of Child Psychology and Psychiatry and Allied Disciplines,* 35(January):73–112.

Curran, D. K. 1987 *Adolescent Suicidal Behavior.* Washington, DC: Hemisphere Publishing.

Curry, J., Miller, J., Waugh, S., Anderson, W. B. 1992 Coping responses in depressed, socially maladjusted, and suicidal adolescents. *Psychological Reports,* 71(1):80–83.

Daly, A., Jennings, J., Beckett, J. O., & Leashore, B. R. 1995 Effective coping strategies of African Americans. *Social Work,* 40(2):240–248.

Dan, A. J., Wilbur, J., & Hedricks, C. 1990 Lifelong physical activity in mid-life and older women. *Psychology of Women Quarterly,* 14:531–542.

Dancy, C. P. 1990 The influence of familial and personality variables on sexual orientation in women. *Psychological Record,* 40(Summer):437–449.

Danieli, Y. 1988 Treating survivors and children of survivors of the Nazi Holocaust. In Ochberg, F. M. (Ed.), *Post-Traumatic Therapy and Victims of Violence.* New York: Brunner/Mazel, pp. 278–294.

Davis, J. 1982 *Help Me, I'm Hurt.* Dubuque, Iowa: Kendall/Hunt.

Davis, K. & Moore, W. 1945 Some principles of stratification. *American Sociological Review,* 10(2): 242–249.

Davis, L. E. & Proctor, E. K. 1989 *Race, Gender, and Class: Guidelines for Practice with Individuals, Families, and Groups.* Englewood Cliffs, NJ: Prentice-Hall.

Davis, L. V. 1986 Role theory. In F. J. Turner (Ed.), *Social Work Treatment: Interlocking Theoretical Approaches.* New York: Free Press, pp. 541–563.

Davis, R. L., Helgerson, S. D., & Waller, P. 1992 Smoking during pregnancy among Northwest Native Americans. *Public Health Reports,* 107(Jan/Feb):66–69.

Dawson, D. A. 1991 Family structure and children's health and well-being: Data from the 1988 National Health Interview Survey on Child Health. *Journal of Marriage and the Family,* 53(3):573–584.

DeJong, G., Batavia, A. I., & Griss, R. 1989 America's neglected health minority: Working-age persons with disabilities. *Milbank Quarterly,* 67(supp 2, pt 2):311–351.

deValdez, T. A. & Gallegos, J. 1982 The Chicano familia in social work. In Green, J. W. (Ed.), *Cultural Awareness in the Human Services.* Englewood Cliffs, NJ: Prentice-Hall, pp. 184–210.

DeVita, V., Jr. et al. (Eds.) 1988 *AIDS: Etiology, Diagnosis, Treatment, and Prevention.* Second Edition. Philadelphia: Lippincott.

Dean, E. 1994 Cardiopulmonary development. In Bonder, B. R. & Wagner, M. B. (Eds.), *Functional Performance in Older Adults.* Philadelphia: F. A. Davis, pp. 62–92.

Deaux, K. 1976 *The Behavior of Women and Men.* Monterey, CA: Brooks/Cole.

Delgado, R. 1992 Generalist child welfare and Hispanic families. In Cohen, N. A. (Ed.), *Child Welfare: A Multicultural Focus.* Boston: Allyn and Bacon, pp. 130–156.

Delgado–Gaitan, C. & Truebor, H. 1991 *Crossing Cultural Borders: Education for Immigrant Families in America.* London: Falmer Press.

Demo, D. H. & Acock, A. C. 1988 The impact of divorce on children. *Journal of Marriage and the Family,* 50:619–648.

Denny, N. & Quadango, D. 1992 *Human Sexuality.* St. Louis: Moseby.

Denzin, N. K. 1984 *On Understanding Emotion.* San Francisco: Josey Bass.

Devine, C. M. & Olsen, C. M. 1992 Women's perceptions about the way social roles promote or constrain personal nutrition care. *Women and Health,* 19(1):79–95.

DiLeonardi, J. W. 1993 Families in poverty and chronic neglect of children. *Families in Society,* 74(9): 557–562.

Dietrich, K. N., Starr, R. H., & Weisfeld, G. E. 1983 Infant maltreatment: Caretaker–infants interaction and developmental consequences at different levels of parenting failure. *Pediatrics,* 72:32–540.

Dobson, J. E. & Dobson, R. L. 1985 The sandwich generation: Dealing with aging parents. *Journal of Counseling and Development,* 63(9):572–574.

Doell, R. G. & Longino, H. E. 1988 Sex hormones and human behavior: A critique of the linear model. *Journal of Homosexuality,* 15(3/4):55–78.

Dohrenwend, B. P. & Dohrenwend, B. S. 1976 Sex differences and psychiatric disorders. *American Journal of Sociology,* 81:1447–1454.

Domino, G. 1981 Attitudes toward suicide among Mexican-American youth. *Hispanic Journal of Behavioral Sciences,* 3:385–395.

Doob, A. N. & Gross, A. E. 1968 Status of frustrator as an inhibitor of horn-honking responses. *Journal of Social Psychology,* 76:213–218.

Dowling, C. 1981 *The Cinderella Complex.* New York: Pocket Books.

Doyle, J. A. 1983 *The Male Experience.* Dubuque, IA: William C. Brown.

Drebing, C. E. & Gooden, W. E. 1991 The impact of the dream on mental health functioning in the male mid-life transition. *International Journal of Aging and Human Development,* 32(4):277–287.

Dubow, E. F. & Tisak, J. 1989 The relation between stressful life events and adjustment in elementary school children: The role of social support and social problem-solving skills. *Child Development,* 60:1412–1423.

Dubowitz, H., Black, M., Starr, R. H., & Zaravin, S. 1993 A conceptual definition of child neglect. *Criminal Justice and Behavior,* 20(1):8–26.

Dudley, J. R. 1991 Exploring ways to get divorced fathers to comply willingly with child support agreements. *Journal of Divorce and Remarriage,* 14(3/4):121–135.

Duimstra, C. et al. 1993 A fetal alcohol syndrome surveillence pilot project in American Indian communities in the Northern Plains. *Public Health Reports,* 180(2):225–230.

Durkheim, E. (1964; originally published 1893) *The Division of Labor in Society,* G. Simpson (trans.). Glencoe, IL: Free Press.

Durrett, M. E., O'Bryant, S., & Pennebaker, J. W. 1975 Childrearing report of white, black, and Mexican American families. *Developmental Psychology,* 2:871.

Early, T. J. & Poertner, J. 1993 Families with children with emotional disorders: A review of the literature. *Social Work,* 38(6):743–751.

Eccles, J. S. & Midgley, C. 1990 Changes in academic motivation and self-perception during early adolescence. In R. Montemayor, G. R. Adams, & T. P. Gullota (Eds.). *From Childhood to Adolescence: A Transitional Period?* Newbury Park, CA: Sage.

Egeland, B. & Sroufe, A. 1981 Developmental sequelae of maltreatment in infancy. *New Directions for Child Development,* 11:77–92.

Ehrhardt, A. A. et al. 1984 Sex-dimorphic behavior in childhood subsequent to prenatal exposure of exogenous progestogens and estrogens. *Archives of Sexual Behavior,* 13:457–477.

Eitzen, D. S. 1986 *Social Problems,* 3rd ed. Boston: Allyn and Bacon.

Ekerdt, D. J., Bosse, R., & Levkoff, S. 1985 An empirical test for phases of retirement: Findings from the Normative Aging Study. *Journal of Gerontology,* 40:95–101.

Ellicott, A. 1985 Psychosocial changes as a function of family-cycle phase. *Human Development,* 28(5): 270–274.

Elliot, D. S. & Ageton, S. S. 1980 Reconciling race and class differences in self-reported and official estimates of delinquency. *American Sociological Review,* 45(1):95–110.

Ellis, L. et al. 1987 Sexual orientation as a continuous variable: A comparison between the sexes. *Archives of Sexual Behavior,* 16 (December): 523–529.

Ellis, L. et al. 1988 Sexual orientation of human offspring may be altered by severe maternal stress during pregnancy. *Journal of Sex Research,* 25(February):152–157.

Enkin, M. et al. 1989 *A Guide to Effective Care in Pregnancy and Childbirth.* Oxford: Oxford University Press.

Epstein, N. B., Bishop, D., Ryan, C., Miller, I., & Keitner, G. 1993 The McMaster model: View of healthy family functioning. In F. Walsh (Ed.), *Normal Family Processes,* 2nd ed. New York: Guilford Press, pp. 138–160.

Erikson, E. H. 1963 *Childhood and Society.* W. W. Norton and Co.

Eron, L. D. 1980 Prescription for reduction of aggression. *American Psychologist,* 35:244–252.

Evans, L., Ekerdt, D. J., & Bosse, R. 1985 Proximity to retirement and anticipatory involvement: Findings from the Normative Aging Study. *Journal of Gerontology,* 40:368–374.

Fagot, B. 1978 The influence of sex of child on parental reactions to toddler children. *Child Development,* 49:459–465.

Fagot, B. 1984a Teacher and peer reactions to boys' and girls' play styles. *Sex Roles,* 11:691–702.

Fagot, B. 1984b The consequence of problem behavior in toddler children. *Journal of Abnormal Child Psychology,* 12:385–396.

Fagot, B. 1985 Changes in thinking about early sex role development. *Developmental Review,* 5:83–98.

Farley, J. E. 1990 Family developmental task assessment: A prerequisite to family treatment. *Clinical Social Work Journal,* 18:85–98.

Fasteau, M. F. 1974 *The Male Machine.* New York: McGraw–Hill.

Faulkner, A. O. & Micchelli, M. 1988 The aging, the aged, and the very old: Women the policy makers forgot. *Women and Health,* 14(3–4):5–19.

Faust, M. S. 1983 Alternative constructions of adolescent growth. In J. Brooks–Gunn and A. C. Peterson (Eds.), *Girls at Puberty: Biological and Psychosocial Aspects.* New York: Plenum, 105–126.

Fay, R. E. et al. 1989 Prevalence and patterns of same-gender sexual contact among men. *Science,* 243(January 20):338–348.

Feagin, J. R. 1989 *Racial and Ethnic Relations.* Englewood Cliffs, NJ: Prentice–Hall.

Feinson, M. C. 1987 Mental health and aging: Are there gender differences? *The Gerontologist,* 27:703–11.

Feldman, P. 1985 Smoking and healthy pregnancy; now is the time to quit. *Maryland State Medical Journal,* (October):982–986.

Fellin, P. 1987 *The Community and the Social Worker.* Itasca, IL: F. E. Peacock Publishers.

Field, T. M. & Widmayer, S. M. 1981 Mother–infant interactions among lower SES black, Cuban, Puerto Rican, and South American immigrants. In T. M. Field, A. M. Sostek, P. Vietze, & P. H. Leiderman (Eds.), *Culture and Early Interactions.* Hillsdale, NJ: Erlbaum, pp. 41–60.

Field, T. M. et al. 1980 Teenage, lower class, black mothers and their pre-term infants: An intervention and developmental follow-up. *Child Development,* 51:426–436.

Finkelhor, D. 1984 *Child Sexual Abuse: New Theory and Research.* New York: Free Press.

Finkelhor, D. 1986 *A Sourcebook on Child Sexual Abuse.* Beverly Hills, CA: Sage.

Finkelstein, N. 1994 Treatment issues for alcohol- and drug-dependent pregnant and parenting women. *Health and Social Work,* 19(1):7–15.

Fiorentine, R. 1988 Increasing similarity in the value and life plans of male and female college students? Evidence and implications. *Sex Roles,* 18(3/4): 143–158.

Fisch. L. 1978 Special senses: The aging auditory system. In J. C. Brocklehurst (Ed.), *Textbook of Geriatric Medicine and Gerontology.* New York: Churchill Livingstone, p. 283.

Fish, B. & Condon, S. 1994 A discussion of current attachment research and its clinical applications. *Child and Adolescent Social Work Journal,* 11(2): 93–105.

Fitzpatrick, J. 1982 Transition to the mainland. In E. Cordasco and E. Buchioni (Eds.), *The Puerto Rican Community and Its Children on the Mainland.* Metuchen, NJ: The Scarecrow Press, pp. 59–67.

Flint, G. A., Gayton, W. F., & Ozmon, K. L. 1983 Relationship between life satisfaction and acceptance of death by elderly persons. *Psychological Reports,* 53:290.

Fogas, B. S. et al. 1992 Locus of control as a mediator of negative divorce-related events and adjustment problems in children. *American Journal of Orthopsychiatry,* 62(4):589–598.

Foley, D. 1992 Being black is dangerous to your health. In Rothenberg, P. S. (Ed.). *Race, Class, and Gender in the United States: An Integrated Study.* New York: St. Martin's Press, pp. 209–214.

Fordham, S. 1988 Racelessness as a factor in black students' school success: Pragmatic strategy or Pyrrhic victory? *Harvard Educational Review,* 58(1):54–84.

Fordney, D. S. 1986 Female sexuality during and following menopause. In L. Mastroianni, Jr. & C. A. Paulsen (Eds.), *Aging, Reproduction, and the Climacteric.* New York: Plenum Press, pp. 229–242.

Fox, G. L. 1980 The mother–daughter relationship as a sexual socialization structure: A research review. *Family Relations,* 29:21–28.

Fox, L., Long, S. H., & Langlois, A. 1988 Patterns of language comprehension deficit in abused and neglected children. *Journal of Speech and Hearing Disorders,* 53:239–244.

Frank, D. A. et al. 1988 Cocaine use during pregnancy: Prevalence and correlates. *Pediatrics,* 82:888–895.

Franz, C. E., McClelland, D.C., & Weinberger, J. 1991 Childhood antecedents of conventional social accomplishment in mid-life adults: A 36-year prospective study. *Journal of Personality and Social Psychology,* 60:586–595.

Fredrich, W., Tyler, J., & Clark, J. 1985 Personality and psychophysiological variables in abusive, neglectful, and low-income control mothers. *Journal of Nervous and Mental Disease,* 173:449–460.

Fried, P. A. 1989 Postnatal consequences of maternal marijuana use in humans. In D. E. Hutchings (Ed.), Prenatal abuse of licit and illicit drugs. *Annals of the New York Academy of Sciences,* 562:123–132.

Fried, P. A. & Makin, J. E. 1987 Neonatal behavioral correlates of prenatal exposure to marijuana, cigarettes and alcohol in a low risk population. *Neurotoxicology and Teratology,* 9:1–7.

Friend, R. A. 1987 The individual and social psychology of aging: Clinical implications for lesbians and gay men. *Journal of Homosexuality,* 14(1–2): 307–331.

Frisbie, W. P., Ortiz, W., & Kelly, W. R. 1985 Marital instability trends among Mexican Americans as compared to blacks and Anglos: New evidence. *Social Science Quarterly,* 66:586–601.

Frisch, H. L. 1977 Sex stereotypes in adult–infant play. *Child Development* 48:1671–1675.

Frost, A. K. & Pakiz, B. 1990 Effects of marital disruption on adolescents: Time as a dynamic. *American Journal of Orthopsychiatry,* 60(4):544–555.

Fry, P. S. 1986 *Depression, Stress and Adaptations in the Elderly.* Rockville, MD: Aspen Publishers.

Fry, P. S. 1992 Major social theories of aging and their implications for counseling concepts and practice: A critical review. *The Counseling Psychologist,* 20(2):246–329.

Fujita, F., Diener, E., & Sandvik, E. 1991 Gender differences in negative affect and well-being: The case for emotional intensity. *Journal of Personality and Social Psychology,* 61(3):427–434.

Furino, A. & Muñoz, E. 1991 Health status among Hispanics: Major themes and new priorities. *Journal of the American Medical Association,* 265(2): 255–257.

Furr, L. A. 1992 The impact of sudden inflation on social service agencies: A rural–urban comparison. *Human Services in the Rural Environment,* 16(1): 25–28.

Garbarino, J., Guttman, E., & Seeley, J. 1986 *The Psychologically Battered Child.* San Francisco: Jossey-Bass.

Garcia Coll, C. 1990 Developmental outcome of minority infants: A process-oriented look into our beginnings. *Child Development,* 61:270–289.

Garfinkle, B. D., Froese, A., & Hood, J. 1982 Suicide attempts in children and adolescence. *American Journal of Psychiatry,* 139:1257–1261.

Garfinkle, H. 1956 Conditions of successful degradation ceremonies. *American Journal of Sociology,* 61(March):420–424.

Garvin, V., Kalter, N., & Hansell, J. 1993 Divorced women: Individual differences in stressors, mediating factors, and adjustment outcome. *American Journal of Orthopsychiatry,* 63(2):232–240.

Gelles, R. J. & Straus 1986 Societal change and change in family violence from 1975–1985 as revealed by two national surveys. *Journal of Marriage and the Family,* 48:465–479.

Gelles, R. J. & Straus, M. A. 1979 Determinants of violence in the family: Toward a theoretical integration. In W. R. Burr et al. (Eds.), *Contemporary Theories about the Family.* New York: Free Press, pp. 549–579.

Gelles, R. J. & Straus, M. A. 1988 *Intimate Violence: The Definitive Study of the Causes and Consequences of Abuse in the American Family.* New York: Simon & Schuster.

Gentry, C. S. 1987 Social distance regarding male and female homosexuals. *Journal of Social Psychology,* 127(April):199–208.

George, L. K. & Maddox, G. L. 1977 Subjective adaptation to loss of the work role: A longitudinal study. *Journal of Gerontology,* 32:456–462.

Germain, C. B. & Gitterman, A. 1986 The life model approach to social work practice revisited. In F. J. Turner (Ed.), *Social Work Treatment: Interlocking Theoretical Approaches,* pp. 618–643.

Gibson, R. C. 1994 The age-by-race gap in health and mortality in the older population: A social science research agenda. *The Gerontologist,* 34(4): 454–462.

Gillberg, C., Rasmussen, P., & Wahlstrom, J. 1982 Minor neurodevelopment disorders in children born to older mothers. *Developmental Medicine and Child Neurology,* 24:437–447.

Gilligan, C. 1982 *In a Different Voice: Psychological Theory and Women's Development.* Cambridge, MA: Harvard University Press.

Giunta, C. T. & Streissguth, A. P. 1988 Patients with fetal alcohol syndrome and their caretakers. *Social Casework,* 69(September):452–459.

Given, C. W., Collins, C. E., & Given, B. A. 1988 Sources of stress among families caring for relatives with Alzheimer's Disease. *Nursing Clinics of North America,* 23(1):69–82.

Gladding, S. T. 1991 *Group Work: A Counseling Specialty.* New York: Merrill.

Glick, P. C. 1988 Fifty years of family demography: A record of social change. *Journal of Marriage & the Family,* 50:861–873.

Glick, P. C. 1989 The family life cycle and social change. *Family Relations,* 38:123–129.

Glover, R. J. & Steele, C. 1989 Comparing the effects on the child of post-divorce parenting arrangements. *Journal of Divorce,* 12(2/3):185–201.

Godkin, M. A., Wolf, R. S., & Pillemer, K. A. 1989 A case-comparison analysis of elder abuse and neglect. *International Journal of Aging and Human Development,* 28(3):207–225.

Goffman, E. 1963 *Stigma: Notes on the Management of Spoiled Identity.* Englewood Cliffs, NJ: Prentice–Hall.

Gomez, M. R. 1990 Biculturalism and subjective mental health among Cuban Americans. *Social Service Review,* 64(3):375–389.

Gooren, L. 1990 Biomedical theories of sexual orientation: A critical examination. In McWhirter, D. P. et al. (Eds.), *Homosexuality/Heterosexuality: Concepts of Sexual Orientation.* New York: Oxford University Press, pp. 71–87.

Gordon, M. 1964 *Assimilation in American Life.* New York: Oxford University Press.

Gordon, M. M. 1978 *Human Nature, Class, and Ethnicity.* New York: Oxford University Press.

Gould, S. J. 1978 Morton's ranking of races by cranial capacity. *Science,* 200(May 5):503–509.

Gove, W. R. & Herb, T. R. 1974 Stress and mental illness among the youth: A comparison of the sexes. *Social Forces,* 53:256–265.

Gove, W. R. & Tudor, J. 1973 Adult sex roles and mental illness. *American Journal of Sociology,* 77: 812–835.

Goy, R. W. & McEwen, B. S. 1980 *Sexual Differentiation of the Brain.* Cambridge, MA: M.I.T. Press.

Green, R. G. & Crooks, P. D. 1988 Family member adjustment and family dynamics in established single-parent and two-parent families. *Social Service Review,* 62:600–613.

Greif, G. L. & Lynch, A. A. 1983 The eco-systems perspective. In C. H. Meyer (Ed.), *Clinical Social Work in the Eco-Systems Perspective.* New York: Columbia University Press, pp. 35–74.

Grissett, B. & Furr, L. A. 1994 Effects of parental divorce on children's financial support for college. *Journal of Divorce and Remarriage,* 22(½): 155–166.

Gropper, R. C. 1975 *Gypsies in the City.* Princeton: Darwin.

Grotevant, H. D. & Cooper, L. R. 1986 Individuation in family relationships. *Human Development,* 29: 82–100.

Guidubaldi, J., Cleminshaw, H. K., Perry, J. D., & McLoughlin, C. S. 1983 The impact of parental divorce on children: Report of the nationwide NASP study. *School Psychology Review,* 12.300–323.

Gutierrez, J. & Sameroff, A. 1990 Determinents of complexity in Mexican-American and Anglo-American mothers' conceptions of child development. *Child Development,* 61(2):384–394.

Gwinn, M. et al. 1991 Prevalence of HIV infection in childrearing women in the United States: Surveillance using newborn blood samples. *Journal of the American Medical Association,* 265(13):1704–1708.

Hall, G. C. N. & Hirschman, R. 1992 Sexual aggression against children: A conceptual perspective of etiology. *Criminal Justice and Behavior,* 19(1): 8–23.

Hall, G. R. 1988 Care of the patient with Alzheimer's Disease living at home. *Nursing Clinics of North America,* 23(1):31–46.

Hamm, M. S. 1993 *American Skinheads.* Westport, CT: Praeger.

Hamptom, R. L. & Gelles, R. J. 1994 Violence toward black women in a nationally representative sample of black families. *Journal of Divorce and Remarriage,* 25(1):105–119.

Hans, S. L. 1989 Developmental consequences of prenatal exposure to methadone. In D. E. Hutchings (Ed.), Prenatal abuse of licit and illicit drugs. *Annals of the New York Academy of Sciences* 562:195–207.

Hans, V. P. & Fironburg, N. 1985 The effects of sex-role attitudes and group composition on men and women in groups. *Sex Roles,* 12(March):477–490.

Harel, Z. 1988 Coping with extreme stress and aging. *Social Casework,* 69:575–583.

Hargreaves, D. J. 1987 Psychological theories of sex-role stereotyping. In Hargreaves, D. J. & Colley, A. M. (Eds.), *The Psychology of Sex Roles.* Cambridge, MA: Hemisphere Publishing, pp. 27–41.

Harman, S. M. & Talbert, G. B. 1985 Reproductive aging. In Finch, C. E. & Schneider, E. L. (Eds.), *Handbook of the Biology of Aging.* New York: Van Nostrand Reinhold Co., pp. 457–510.

Harris, M. B. 1974 Mediators between frustration and aggression in a field experiment. *Journal of Experimental Social Psychology,* 10:561–571.

Harris, M. B. 1994 Growing old gracefully: Age concealment and gender. *Journal of Gerontology,* 49(4):149–158.

Harris, R. L., Ellicott, A. M., & Holmes, D. S. 1986 The timing of psychosocial transitions and changes in women's lives: An examination of women aged 45 to 60. *Journal of Personality and Social Psychology,* 51(2):409–416.

Harrison, W. D. 1989 Social work and the search for postindustrial community. *Social Work,* 34:73–75.

Harry, J. 1984 *Gay Couples.* New York: Praeger.

Harry, J. 1990 A probability sample of gay males. *Journal of Homosexuality,* 19(1):89–104.

Hartup, W. W. 1970 Peer relations. In T. D. Spencer & N. Kass (Eds.), *Perspectives in Child Psychology: Research and Review.* New York: McGraw-Hill, 261–294.

Hartup, W. W. 1983 Peer relations. In P. H. Mussen (Ed.), *Handbook of Child Psychology, Vol. 4. Socialization, Personality and Social Development.* New York: Wiley.

Hatch, E. E. & Bracken, M. B. 1986 Effects of marijuana use in pregnancy on fetal growth. *American Journal of Epidemiology,* 124:986–993.

Hausman, B. & Hammen, C. 1993 Parenting in homeless families: The double crisis. *American Journal of Orthopsychiatry,* 63(3):358–369.

Hausman, P. B. & Weksler, M. E. 1985 Changes in the immune response with age. In Finch, C. E. & Schneider, E. L. (Eds.), *Handbook of the Biology of Aging.* New York: Van Nostrand Reinhold Co., pp. 414–432.

Haviland, W. A. 1993 *Cultural Anthropology.* 7th Ed. Fort Worth: Harcourt Brace College Publishers.

Hawkins, W. E., Hawkins, M. J., & Seeley, J. 1992 Stress, health-related behaviors and quality of life on depressive symptomatology in a sample of adolescents. *Psychological Reports,* 71(1):183–186.

Helsel, D., Petitti, D. B., & Kunstadter, P. 1992 Pregnancy among the Hmong: Birthweight, age, and parity. *American Journal of Public Health,* 82(October):1361–1364.

Helson, R. & Picano, J. 1990 Is the traditional role bad for women? *Journal of Personality and Social Psychology,* 59(August):311–320.

Hendrey, L. B. et al. 1992 Adolescent perceptions of significant individuals in their lives. *Journal of Adolescence,* 15:255–270.

Henry, W. A. 1994 Pride and Prejudice. *Time,* 143(June 27):54–59.

Hepworth, D. H. & Larsen, J. A. 1993 *Direct Social Work Practice: Theory and Skills.* Pacific Grove, CA: Brooks/Cole.

Herdt, G. H. 1984 Semen transactions in Sambia culture. In Herdt, G. H. (Ed.), *Ritualized Homosexuality in Melanesia.* Berkeley: University of California Press.

Herek, G. M. 1987 Religious orientation and prejudice: A comparison of racial and sexual attitudes. *Personality and Social Psychology Bulletin,* 13(March):34–44.

Herek, G. M. 1988 Heterosexuals' attitudes toward lesbians and gay men: Correlates and gender differences. *The Journal of Sex Research,* 25: 451–477.

Herrenkohl, R. C & Herrenkohl, E. C. 1981 Some antecedents and developmental consequences of child maltreatment. In R. Rizley & D. Cicchetti (Eds.), *Developmental Perspectives on Child Maltreatment. New Directions for Child Development, No. 11.* San Francisco: Jossey–Bass.

Herrenkohl, R. C., Herrenkohl, E. C., & Egolf, B. P. 1983 Circumstances surrounding the occurrence of child maltreatment. *Journal of Consulting and Clinical Psychology,* 51:424–431.

Herrnstein, R. J. & Murray, C. 1994 *The Bell Curve.* New York: Free Press.

Herrnstein, R. J. 1973 *IQ in the Meritocracy.* Boston: Little, Brown.

Hetherington, E. M., Cox, M., & Cox, R. 1978 Effects of divorce on parents and children. In M. E. Lamb (Ed.), *Nontraditional Families: Parenting and Child Development.* Hillsdale, NJ: Erlbaum, pp. 233–288.

Hightower, E. 1990 Adolescent interpersonal and familial precursors of positive mental health at mid-life. *Journal of Youth and Adolescence,* 19:257–275.

Hill, J. & Holmbeck, G. N. 1987 Familial adaptation to biological change during adolescence. In R. M. Lerner and T. T. Foch (Eds.), *Biological–*

psychological interactions in early adolescence. Hillsdale, NJ: Erlbaum, 207–223.

Hillary, G. A. 1968 *Communal Organizations: A Study of Local Societies.* Chicago: University of Chicago Press.

Hilliard, A. 1985 Parameters affecting the African American child. Paper presented at the Black Psychology Seminar, Duke University, Durham, NC. Cited in V. S. Thompson (1992).

Hirsch, K. 1986 Childhood without a home: A new report on the youngest victims. *The Boston Phoenix.*

Hirschi, T. 1969 *Causes of Delinquency.* Berkeley: University of California Press.

Hochschild, A. 1989 *Second Shift.* New York: Viking.

Hockenberry, S. L. & Billingham, R. E. 1987 Sexual orientation and boyhood gender conformity: Development of the boyhood gender conformity scale (BGCS). *Archives of Sexual Behavior,* 16(60): 475–492.

Hoebel, E. A. 1972 *Anthropology: The Study of Man,* 4th ed. New York: McGraw–Hill.

Hoelter, J. W. 1982 Race differences in selective credulity and self-esteem. *Sociological Quarterly,* 23, 4:527–539.

Hogg, M. A. & McGarty, C. 1990 Self-categorization and social identity. In Abrams, D. and Hogg, M. A. (Eds.), *Social Identity Theory: Constructive and Critical Advances.* New York: Springer, pp. 10–27.

Hogge, W., Schonberg, S., & Golbus, M. 1986 Chorionic Villus Sampling: Experience of the first 1,000 cases. *American Journal of Obstetrics and Gynecology,* 154:1249–1252.

Hooper, C. R. 1994 Sensory and sensory integrative development. In Bonder, B. R. & Wagner, M. B. (Eds.), *Functional Performance in Older Adults.* Philadelphia: F. A. Davis Co., pp. 93–106.

Hops, H., Sherman, L., & Briglan, A. 1990 Maternal depression, marital discord and children's behavior. In G. R. Patterson (Ed.), *Depression and Aggression in Family Interaction.* Hillsdale, NJ: Erlbaum, pp. 185–208.

House, J. S. et al. 1994 The social stratification of aging and health. *Journal of Health and Social Behavior,* 35:213–234.

Howard, J. et al. 1989 The development of young children of substance-abusing parents: Insights from seven years of intervention and research. *Zero to Three: Bulletin of the National Center for Clinical Infant Programs, 9* (June).

Howes, C., Hamilton, C. E., & Matheson, C. C. 1994 Children's relationships with peers: Differential associations with aspects of the teacher–child relationship. *Child Development,* 65(February): 253–263.

Huang, L. J. 1976 The Chinese American family. In C. H. Mindel & R. W. Habenstein (Eds.), *Ethnic Families in America.* New York: Elsevier, pp. 124–145.

Hughes, M. & Demo, D. H. 1989 Self-perceptions of black Americans: Self-esteem and personal efficacy. *American Journal of Sociology,* 95, July: 132–159.

Hultsch, D. F. & Deutsch, F. 1981 *Adult Development and Aging: A Life Span Perspective.* New York: McGraw–Hill.

Hunt, M. 1974 *Sexual Behavior in the 1970s.* Chicago: Playboy Press.

Hunter, S. & Sundel, M. 1989 *Mid-life Myths: Issues, Findings, Practice, and Implications.* Newbury Park, CA: Sage.

Huston, A. C. 1985 The development of sex-typing: Themes from recent research. *Developmental Review,* 5:1–17.

Hutchinson, R. L. & Spangler–Hirsch, S. L. 1989 Children of divorce and single-parent lifestyles: Facilitating well-being. *Journal of Divorce,* 12(2/3): 5–24.

Hymel, S., Bowker, A., & Woody, E. 1993 Aggressive versus withdrawn unpopular children: Multiple domains. *Child Development,* 64(June):879–896.

Iannetti, P. et al. 1989 Acquired immune deficiency syndrome in childhood: Neurological aspects. *Child's Nervous System,* 5:281–287.

Icard, L. 1986 Black gay men and conflicting social identities: Sexual orientation versus racial identity. *Journal of Social Work and Human Sexuality,* 4:83–93.

Indian Health Service 1994 *Regional Differences in Indian Health.* Washington, DC: Department of Health and Human Services.

Ishisaka, H. A. & Takagi, C. Y. 1982 Social work with Asian- and Pacific-Americans. In Green, J. W. (Ed.), *Cultural Awareness in the Human Services.* Englewood Cliffs, NJ: Prentice-Hall, pp. 122–156.

Izard, C. et al. 1991 Infant cardiac activity: Developmental changes and relations with attachment. *Developmental Psychology,* 27 (May):432–439.

Izzard, C. 1991 *The Psychology of Emotions.* New York: Plenum.

Jackson, J. 1980 *Minorities and Aging*. Belmont, CA: Wadsworth.

Jacobson, S. W., Jacobson, J. L., & Sokol, R. J. 1993 Prenatal alcohol exposure and infant information processing ability. *Child Development*, 64(December):1706–1721.

Jaeger, A. & Greenstein, R. 1989 *Poverty Rate and Household Income Stagnate as Rich–Poor Gap Hits Post-War High*. Washington, DC: Center on Budget and Policy Priorities.

Jencks, C. et al. 1979 *Who Gets Ahead? The Determinants of Economic Success in America*. New York: Basic Books.

Jensen, A. R. 1969 How much can we boost IQ and scholastic achievement? *Harvard Education Review*, 39:1–123.

Johnson, H. L. & Rosen, T. S. 1990 Mother–infant interaction in a multirisk population. *American Journal of Orthopsychiatry*, 60(2):281–288.

Johnson, J. E., Waldo, M., & Johnson, R. G. 1993 Stress and perceived health status in the rural elderly. *Journal of Gerontological Nursing*, 19(10):24–29.

Johnson, S. R. & Palermo, J. L. 1984 Gynecologic care for the lesbian. *Clinical Obstetrics and Gynecology*, 27(3):724–734.

Johnston, L. D., O'Malley, P. M., & Bachman, J. G. 1991 Drug use among American high school seniors, college students and young adults, 1975– 1990. Rockville, MD: National Institute on Drug Abuse, U.S. Department of Health and Human Services.

Jones, E. W. 1986 Black managers: the dream deferred. *Harvard Business Review*, 64(May/June):84–93.

Jones, W. S. & Man, E. B. 1969 Thyroid function in human pregnancy: VI. Premature deliveries and reproductive failures of pregnant women with low serum butanol extractable iodines. *American Journal of Obstetrics and Gynecology*, 104:909–914.

Jones–Webb, R. J. et al. 1993 Symptoms of depression among blacks and whites. *American Journal of Public Health*, 83(February):240–244.

Julian, T. W., McKenry, P. C., & Arnold, K. 1990 Psychosocial predictors of stress associated with the male mid-life transition. *Sex Roles*, 22(11–12):707–718.

Jung, C. G. 1933 *Modern Man in Search of a Soul*. New York: Harcourt, Brace, World.

Kagan, J. 1983 Social orientation among Mexican-American children: A challenge to traditional classroom structure. In E. E. Garcia (Ed.), *The Mexican-American Child: Language, Cognition, and Social Development*. Tempe, Ariz.: Center for Bilingual Education.

Kahn, M. J. 1991 Factors affecting the coming out process for lesbians. *Journal of Homosexuality*, 21(4):1–15.

Kallen, J. E. 1993 Race, intervening variables, and two components of low birth weight. *Demography*, 30(August):489–506.

Kalter, N., Kloner, A., Schreier, S., & Okla, K. 1989 Predictors of children's postdivorce adjustment. *American Journal of Orthopsychiatry*, 59(4):605–618.

Kameny, F. E. 1971 Homosexuals as a minority group. In E. Sagarin (Ed.), *The Other Minorities: Nonethnic Collectivities Conceptualized as Minority Groups*. Waltham, MA: Xerox College Publishing, pp. 50–64.

Kannel, W. B. 1985 Hypertension and aging. In Finch, C. E. & Schneider, E. L. (Eds.), *Handbook of the Biology of Aging*. New York: Van Nostrand Reinhold Co., pp. 859–877.

Kantor, G. K. & Straus, M. A. 1987 The "drunken bum" theory of wife beating. *Social Problems*, 34(3):213–231.

Kantrowitz, B. et al. 1992 Sociology's lonely crowd. *Newsweek*, February 3:55.

Kaplan, K. M. et al. 1990 A profile of mothers giving birth to infants with congenital rubella syndrome: An assessment of risk factors. *American Journal of Diseases of Children*, 144:118–123.

Karmel, B. Z., Gardner, J. M., & Magnano, C. L. 1990 Neurofunctional consequences of in utero cocaine exposure. In *Problems of Drug Dependence: Proceedings of the 52nd Annual Scientific Meeting*. (NIDA Research Monograph) Richmond, Va.: Committee on Problems of Drug Dependence, pp. 535–536.

Kaslow, F. & Schwartz, L. 1987 *The Dynamics of Divorce*. New York: Brunner/Mazel.

Katz, L. F. & Gottman, J. M. 1993 Patterns of marital conflict predict children's internalizing and externalizing behaviors. *Developmental Psychology*, 29(6):940–950.

Kaufman, J. & Zigler, E. 1987. Do abused children become abusive parents? *American Journal of Orthopsychiatry*, 57:186–93.

Kaufman, P., Harrison, E., & Hyde, M. 1984 Distancing for intimacy in lesbian relationships. *American Journal of Psychiatry*, 14:530–533.

Kaufmann, T. 1994 Mobility. In Bonder, B. R. & Wagner, M. B. (Eds.), *Functional Performance in Older Adults.* Philadelphia: F. A. Davis Co., pp. 42–60.

Kaye, S. H. 1989 The impact of divorce on children's academic performance. *Journal of Divorce,* 12(2/3):283–298.

Kehoe, M. 1990 Loneliness and the aging homosexual: Is pet therapy an answer? *Journal of Homosexuality,* 20(3–4):137–143.

Keil, J. E. et al. 1992 Does equal socioeconomic status in black and white men mean equal risk of mortality? *American Journal of Public Health,* 82(8):1133–1136.

Keith, V. M. & Smith, D. P. 1988 The current differentials in black and white life expectancy. *Demography,* 25(4):625–632.

Kelly, J. A. 1983 *Treating Child-Abuse Families.* New York: Plenum.

Keniston, K. 1965 *The Uncommitted: Alienated Youth in American Society.* New York: Harcourt, Brace.

Kenney, R. A. 1989 *Physiology of Aging: A Synopsis.* Chicago: Year Book Medical Publishers.

Kephart, W. M. 1987 *Extraordinary Groups: An Examination of Unconventional Life-Styles.* New York: St. Martin's Press.

Kercher, G. & McShane, M. 1984 The prevalence of child sexual abuse victimization in an adult sample of Texas residents. *Child Abuse and Neglect,* 8:495–502.

Kerns, V. 1989 *Women and the Ancestors.* Chicago: University of Chicago Press.

Kessler, R. D. & Cleary, P. D. 1980 Social class and psychological distress. *American Sociological Review,* 45(3):463–478.

Kiefer, C. W. et al. 1985 Adjustment problems of Korean American elderly. *The Gerontologist,* 25(5):477–482.

Kihl, M. R. 1993 The need for transportation alternatives for the rural elderly. In C. N. Bull (Ed.), *Aging in Rural America.* Newbury Park: Sage, pp. 84–100.

Kimble, C. E. et al. 1981 Vocal and verbal assertiveness in same-sex and mixed-sex groups. *Journal of Personality and Social Psychology,* 40:1049–1054.

Kimbrough, V. D. & Salomone, P. R. 1993 African Americans: Diverse people, diverse career needs. *Journal of Career Development,* 19(4):265–279.

Kimmel, D. C. 1978 Adult development and aging: A gay perspective. *Journal of Social Issues,* 34:113–130.

Kinsey, A. C., Pomeroy, W. B., & Martin, C. E. 1948 *Sexual Behavior in the Human Male.* Philadelphia: W. B. Saunders.

Kinsey, A. C., Pomeroy, W. B., Martin, C. E., & Gebhard, P. H. 1953 *Sexual Behavior in the Human Female.* Philadelphia: W. B. Saunders.

Kitano, H. H. L. 1991 *Race Relations.* Englewood Cliffs, NJ: Prentice–Hall.

Kitano, H. H. L. 1992 *Race Relations,* 4th ed. Englewood Cliffs, NJ: Prentice-Hall.

Kitson, C. G., Lopatata, H. Z., Holmes, W. M., & Meyering, S. M. 1980 Divorcees and widows: Similarities and differences. *American Journal of Orthopsychiatry,* 50(2):291–301.

Klein, B. W. & Rones, P. L. 1989 *A Profile of the Working Poor.* Bulletin 2345. Washington, DC: U.S. Department of Labor.

Klitzmiller, J. et al. 1981 Diabetic nephropathy in perinatal outcome. *American Journal of Obstetrics and Gynecology,* 141:741–751.

Knaub, P. K. & Hanna, S. L. 1984 Children of remarriage: Perceptions of family strengths. *Journal of Divorce,* 7(4):73–90.

Kohn, M. L. & Schooler, C. 1983 *Work and Personality: An Inquiry into the Impact of Social Stratification.* Norwood, NJ: Ablex Publishing.

Kollock, P. L., Blumstein, P., & Schwartz, P. 1985 Sex and power in interaction: Conversational privileges and duties. *American Sociological Review,* 50:34–46.

Koski, K. J. & Steinberg, L. 1990 Parenting satisfaction of mothers during mid-life. *Journal of Youth and Adolescence,* 19(October):465–474.

Kozol, J. 1991 *Savage Inequalities: Children in America.* New York: Crown.

Krause, N. & Markides, K. S. 1985 Employment and psychological well-being in Mexican–American women. *Journal of Health and Social Behavior,* 26:15–26.

Krause, N. 1983 The racial context of black self-esteem. *Social Psychological Quarterly,* 46, 2:98–107.

Kriegal, L. 1971 Uncle Tom and Tiny Tim: Some reflections on the cripple as Negro. In E. Sagarin (Ed.), *The Other Minorities: Nonethnic Collectivities Conceptualized as Minority Groups.* Waltham, MA: Xerox College Publishing, pp. 165–183.

Kuehn, W. C. 1971 Ex-convicts conceptualized as a minority group. In E. Sagarin (Ed.), *The Other Minorities: Nonethnic Collectivities Conceptualized as Minority Groups.* Waltham, MA: Xerox College Publishing, pp. 275–287.

Kurdek, L. A. & Schmitt, J. P. 1986 Relationship quality of partners in heterosexual married, heterosexual cohabiting, and gay and lesbian relationships. *Journal of Personality and Social Psychology,* 5(October):711–720.

Kurdek, L. A. & Schmitt, J. P. 1987 Partner homogamy in married, heterosexual cohabiting, gay, and lesbian couples. *Journal of Sex Research,* 23(May): 212–232.

Kurdek, L. A. 1988 Correlates of negative attitudes toward homosexuals in heterosexual college students. *Sex Roles,* 18(June).727–738.

Lamanna, M. A. & Riedmann 1994 *Marriage and Families: Making Choices and Facing Change.* Belmont, CA: Wadsworth.

Lamb, M. E. 1977 The development of mother–infant and father–infant attachments in the second year of life. *Developmental Psychology,* 12:435–443.

Lamb, M. E. 1987 *The Father's Role: Cross-Cultural Perspectives,* Hillsdale, NJ: Lawrence Erlbaum Associates.

Lamb, M. E. et al. 1985 The effects of child maltreatment on security of infant–adult attachment. *Infant Behavior and Development,* 8:35–45.

Lamb, M. E., Easterbrooks, M. A., & Holden, G. W. 1980 Reinforcement and punishment among preschoolers: Characteristics, effects, and correlates. *Child Development,* 51:1230–1236.

Lamison–White, L. 1992 *Income, Poverty, and Wealth in the United States: A Chart Book.* Current Population Reports. Washington, DC: Bureau of the Census.

Lamke, L. K. 1982 Adjustment and sex-role orientation in adolescence. *Journal of Youth and Adolescence,* 11:247–259.

Land, H. & Levy, A. 1992 A school-based prevention model for depressed Asian adolescents. *Social Work in Education,* 14(3):165–176.

Langman, L. 1981 *Medical Embryology.* Baltimore: Williams & Wilkins.

Lasch, C. 1978 *The Culture of Narcissism.* New York: Norton.

Last, C. G. & Perrin, S. 1993 Anxiety disorders in African-American and white children. *Journal of Abnormal Child Psychology,* 21(April):153–164.

Latting, J. E. & Zundel, C. 1986 World view differences between clients and counselors. *Social Casework,* 67:533–541.

Lauver, P. J. & Jones, R. M. 19 factors associated with perceived career options in American Indian, White, and Hispanic rural high school students. *Journal of Counseling Psychology,* 38(2): 159–166.

Laveist, T. A. 1993 Segregation, poverty, and empowerment. Health consequences for African Americans. *Milbank Quarterly,* 71(1).41–64.

Lawler, K. A. & Schmeid, L. A. 1992 A prospective study of women's health: The effects of stress, hardiness, locus of control, Type A behavior, and physiological reactivity. *Women and Health,* 19(1):27–41.

Lazarus, P. J. 1982 Counseling the native American child: A question of values. *Elementary School Guidance and Counseling,* 17(2):83–88.

LeCroy, C. W. & Ashford, J. B. 1992 Children's mental health: Current findings and research directions. *Social Work Research and Abstracts,* 28(1):13–20.

LeCroy, C. W. 1986 An analysis of the effects of gender on outcome in group treatment with young adolescents. *Journal of Youth and Adolescence,* 15: 497–508.

LeVay, S. 1991 A difference in hypothalamic structure between heterosexual and homosexual men. *Science,* 253:1034–1037.

Lee, J. J. 1986 Asian American elderly: A neglected minority group. *Journal of Gerontological Social Work,* 9(4): 103–116.

Leigh, G. K. & Peterson, G. W. 1986 *Adolescents in Families.* Cincinnati: Southwestern Publishers.

Leigh, J. W. & Green, J. W. 1982 The structure of the Black community: The knowledge base for social services. In Green, J. W. (Ed.), *Cultural Awareness in the Human Services.* Englewood Cliffs, NJ: Prentice-Hall, pp. 94–121.

Lengermann, P. M. & Wallace, R. A. 1985 *Gender in America: Social Control and Social Change.* Englewood Cliffs, NJ: Prentice–Hall.

Lennon, M. C. & Rosenfield, S. 1992 Women and mental health: The interaction of job and family conditions. *Journal of Health and Social Behavior,* 33:316–327.

Leonard, P., Dolbeare, C., & Lazere, E. 1989 *A Place to Call Home: The Crisis in Housing for the Poor.* Washington, DC: Center on Budget and Policy Priorities.

Leong, F. T. L. & Tata, S. P. 1990 Sex and acculturation differences in occupational values among Chinese

American children. *Journal of Counseling Psychology,* 37(2):208–212.

Lerner, H. E. 1983 Female dependency in context: Some theoretical and technical considerations. *American Journal of Orthopsychiatry,* 53: 697–705.

Lester, B. M. & Tronick, E. Z. 1994 The effects of prenatal cocaine exposure and child outcome. *Infant Mental Health Journal,* 15(2):107–121.

Lester, B. M. et al. 1991 Neurobehavioral syndrome in cocaine-exposed newborn infants. *Child Development,* 62:694–705.

Levinson, D. J. 1986 A conception of adult development. *American Psychologist,* 41(1):3–13.

Levinson, D. J., with Darrow, C. N., Klein, E. B., Levinson, M. H. & McKee, B. 1978 *The Seasons of a Man's Life.* New York: Alfred A. Knopf.

Levy, E. F. 1992 Strengthening the coping resources of lesbian families. *Families in Society,* 73(January):23–31.

Lewis, C. 1987 Early sex-role socialization. In Hargreaves, D. J. & Colley, A. M. (Eds.), *The Psychology of Sex Roles.* Cambridge, MA: Hemisphere Publishing, pp. 95–117.

Lewis, O. 1959 *Five Families.* New York: Basic Books.

Lewittes, H. J. 1988 Just being friendly means a lot: Women, friendship, and aging. *Women and Health,* 14(3–4):139–159.

Lia–Hoagberg, B. et al. 1989 Barriers and motivators to prenatal care among low income women. *Social Science and Medicine,* 30(4):487–495.

Liebow, E. 1967 *Tally's Corner.* Boston: Little, Brown.

Lin, N. & Ensel, W. M. 1989 Life stress and health: Stressors and resources. *American Sociological Review,* 54(3):382–400.

Lincoln, R. 1986 Smoking and reproduction. *Family Planning Perspectives,* 18:79–84.

Lipman, A. 1986 Homosexual relationships. *Generations,* 10(4):51–54.

Lobl, M., Welcher, D. W., & Mellits, E. D. 1971 Maternal age and intellectual functioning of offspring. *Hopkins Medical Journal,* 128:347–357.

Logsdon, M. C. 1990 The relationship between social support and postpartum depression. D. N. S. diss., Indiana University School of Nursing.

Long, J. E. & Caudill, S. B. 1992 Racial differences in homeownership and housing wealth, 1970–1986. *Economic Inquiry,* 30(January):83–100.

Longres, J. 1990 *Human Behavior in the Social Environment.* Itasca, IL: F. E. Peacock Publishers.

Lott, B. & Maluso, D. 1993 The social learning of gender. In Bealle, A. E. & Sternberg, R. J. (Eds.), *The Psychology of Gender.* New York: Guilford Press, pp. 99–125.

Lum, D. 1986 *Social Work Practice and People of Color: A Process–Stage Approach.* Monterey, CA: Brooks/Cole Publishing.

Luster, T., Rhoades, K., & Haas, B. 1989 The relation between parental values and parenting behavior: A test of the Kohn Hypothesis. *Journal of Marriage and the Family,* 51:139–147.

Lyons, C. H. 1975 *To Wash an Aethiop White.* New York: Teachers College Press.

McGauhey, P. J. & Starfield, B. 1993 Child health and the social environment of white and black children. *Social Science and Medicine,* 36(7): 867–874.

McGoldrick, M. 1980 The joining of families through marriage: The new couple. In Carter, E. A. & M. McGoldrick (Eds.), *The Family Life Cycle: A Framework for Family Therapy.* New York: Gardiner, pp. 93–120.

McGoldrick, M., Heiman, M., & Carter, B. 1993 The changing family life cycle. In F. Walsh (Ed.), *Normal Family Processes,* 2nd ed. New York: Guilford Press, pp. 405–443.

McInnis, K. 1991 Ethnic-sensitive work with Hmong refugee children. *Child Welfare,* 70(Sept/Oct): 571–580.

McIntosh, K. 1984 Viral infections of the fetus and newborn. In M. E. Avery & H. W. Taeusch, Jr. (Eds.), *Schaffer's Diseases of the Newborn,* 5th ed. Philadelphia: W. B. Saunders.

McKenry, P. C. & Fine, M. A. 1993 Parenting following a divorce: A comparison of black and white single mothers. *Journal of Comparative Family Studies,* 24:99–111.

McKinlay, S. M. & McKinlay, J. B. 1986 Health status and health care utilization by menopausal women. In L. Mastroianni, Jr. & C. A. Paulsen (Eds.), *Aging, Reproduction, and the Climacteric.* New York: Plenum Press, pp. 243–262.

McLanahan, S. & Bumpass, L. 1988 Intergenerational consequences of family disruption. *American Journal of Sociology,* 94(1):130–152.

McLanahan, S. & Glass, J. L. 1985 A note on the trend in sex differences in psychological distress. *Journal of Health and Social Behavior,* 26:328–336.

McLanahan, S. 1985 Family structure and the reproduction of poverty. *American Journal of Sociology,* 90(4):873–901.

McLaughlin, D. K. & Jensen, L. 1991 Poverty among older Americans: The problem of the nonmetropolitan elderly. Working Paper No. 1991-22. University Park, PA: Population Issues Research Center, Pennsylvania State University.

McLemore, D. S. 1982 *Racial and Ethnic Relations in America.* Boston: Allyn & Bacon.

McQuaide, S. 1989 Working with southeast Asian refugees. *Clinical Social Work Journal,* 17(2): 164–176.

McRae, J. A. & Brody, C. J. 1989 The differential importance of marital experiences for the well-being of women and men: A research note. *Social Science Research,* 18:237–248.

McWhirter, D. P. & Mattison, A. M. 1984 *The Male Couple: How Relationships Develop.* Englewood Cliffs, NJ: Prentice-Hall.

MacDonald, A. P. et al. 1973 Attitudes toward homosexuals: Preservation of sex morality or the double standard. *Journal of Consulting and Clinical Psychology,* 40(1):161.

Maccoby, E. & Jacklin, C. N. 1974 *The Psychology of Sex Differences.* Stanford, CA: Stanford University Press.

Maccoby, E. E. & Mnookin, R. H. 1992 *Dividing the Child: Social and Legal Dilemmas of Custody.* Cambridge: Harvard University Press.

Mace, N. & Rabins, P. V. 1981 *The 36-Hour Day: A Family Guide to Caring for Persons with Alzheimer's Disease, Related Illnesses, and Memory Loss in Later Life.* New York: Warner Books.

Macionis, J. J. 1993 *Sociology,* 4th ed. Englewood Cliffs, NJ: Prentice–Hall.

Mack, R. W. 1968 *Race, Class, and Power,* 2nd ed. New York: Van Nostrand.

Mahler, M. S. 1974 On the first three subphases of the separation–individuation process. *Psychoanalysis and Contemporary Science,* Vol. 3:295–307.

Mahler, M. S., Pine, F., & Bergman, A. 1975 *The Psychological Birth of the Human Infant.* New York: Basic Books.

Mahran, M. 1981 Medical dangers of female circumcision. *International Planned Parenthood Federation Medical Bulletin,* 2:1–2.

Main, M. & Hesse, E. 1990 Parents' unresolved traumatic experiences are related to infant disorganized attachment status: Is frightened and/or frightening parental behavior the linking mechanism? In M. Greenberg, D. Cicchetti, & E. M. Cummings (Eds.), *Attachment in the Preschool Years: Theory, Research and Intervention.* Chicago: University of Chicago Press, pp. 161–182.

Main, M. & Weston, D. R. 1982 Avoidance of the attachment figure in infancy: Descriptions and interpretations. In C. M. Parke & J. Stevenson-Hinde (Eds.), *The Place of Attachment in Human Behavior.* New York: Basic Books, pp. 31–59.

Malatesta, C. Z., Culver, C., Tesman, J. R., & Shepard, B. 1989 The development of emotional expression during the first two years of life. *Monographs of the Society for Research in Child Development.* 54(1/2):1–104.

Maldonado, D., Jr. 1979 Aging in the Chicano context. In D. E. Gelfand & A. J. Kutzik (Eds.), *Ethnicity and Aging: Theory, Research, and Policy.* New York: Springer.

Malmquist, C. P. 1971 Depressions in childhood and adolescence. *New England Journal of Medicine,* 284:887–893, 955–961.

Man, E. B., Holden, R. H., & Jones, W. S. 1971 Thyroid function in human pregnancy: VII. Development and retardation of 4-year-old progeny of euthyroid and of hupothyroxinemic women. *American Journal of Obstetrics and Gynecology,* 109: 12–19.

Mansfield, P. K. 1988 Mid-life childbearing: Strategies for informed decision-making. *Psychology of Women Quarterly,* 12:445–460.

Mantsios, G. 1992 Rewards and opportunities: The politics and economics of class in the U.S. In Rothenberg, P. S. (Ed.), *Race, Class, and Gender in the United States: An Integrated Study.* New York: St. Martin's Press, pp. 96–110.

Marcenko, M. O., Spence, M., & Rohweder, C. 1994 Psycho–social characteristics of pregnant women with and without a history of substance abuse. *Health and Social Work,* 19(1):17–22.

Marger, M. N. 1994 *Race and Ethnic Relations: American and Global Perspectives,* 3rd ed. Belmont, CA: Wadsworth.

Markides, K. S. & Coreil, J. 1986 The health of Hispanics in the southwestern United States: An epidemiologic paradox. *Public Health Reports,* 101(3): 253–265.

Markides, K. S. & Krause, N. 1985 Intergenerational solidarity and psychological well-being among older Mexican Americans: A three generations study. *Journal of Gerontology,* 40:390–392.

Markides, K. S. & Mindel, C. H. 1987 *Aging and Ethnicity.* Newbury Park, CA: Sage.

Markides, K. S. 1986 Minority status, aging, and mental health. *International Journal of Aging and Human Devleopment,* 23(4):285–300.

Markson, E. W. 1979 Ethnicity as a factor in the institutionalization of the ethnic elderly. In D. E. Gelfand & A. J. Kutzik (Eds.), *Ethnicity and Aging: Theory, Research and Policy.* New York: Springer, pp. 341–356.

Marmor, J. 1980 (Ed.), *Homosexual Behavior.* New York: Basic Books.

Marshall, J. & Cooper, C. L. 1979 *Executives Under Pressure.* New York: Macmillian Co.

Martin, H. P. & Beezley, P. 1976 Personality of abused children. In H. P. Martin (Ed.), *The Abused Child,* Cambridge: Cambridge University Press, pp. 105–111.

Martin, T. C. & Bumpass, L. 1989 Recent trends in marital dissolution. *Demography,* 26:37–51.

Masis, K. B. & May, P. A. 1991 A comprehensive local program for the prevention of fetal alcohol syndrome. *Public Health Reports,* 106(Sept/Oct): 484–489.

Maslow, A. H. 1968 *Toward a Psychology of Being.* Princeton: Van Nostrand.

Maslow, A. H. 1970 *Motivation and Personality.* New York: Harper & Row.

Masters, W. H. & Johnson, V. E. 1979 *Homosexuality in Perspective.* Boston: Little, Brown.

Masters, W. H., Johnson, V. E., & Kolodny, R. C. 1992 *Human Sexuality,* 4th ed. New York: HarperCollins.

Maton, K. I. 1989 Community settings as buffers of life stress? Highly supportive churches, mutual help groups, and senior centers. *American Journal of Community Psychology,* 17:203–232.

Merriam, S. B. & Clark, M. C. 1993 Work and love: Their relationship in adulthood. *International Journal of Behavioral Development,* 16(4):609–627.

Meyer, C. H. 1983 *Clinical Social Work in the Eco-Systems Perspective.* New York: Columbia University Press.

Meyer, D. R. & Garasky, S. 1993 Custodial fathers: Myths, realities, and child support policy. *Journal of Marriage and the Family,* 55(1):73–89.

Miller, D. A. 1981 The "sandwich" generation: Adult children of the aging. *Social Work,* 26:419–423.

Miller, P. 1983 *Theories of Developmental Psychology.* San Francisco: Freeman.

Millis, J. B. & Kornblith, P. R. 1992 Fragile beginnings: Identification and treatment of postpartum disorders. *Health and Social Work,* 17(3):192–199.

Miodovnik, M. et al. 1990 Spontaneous abortions in repeat diabetic pregnancies: A relationship with glycemic control. *Obstetrics and Gynecology,* 75:75–78.

Mirande, A. 1986 Adolescence and chicano families. In G. K. Leigh & G. W. Peterson (Eds.), *Adolescents in Families,* Cincinnati: Southwestern Publishers.

Mirowsky, J. & Ross, C. E. 1984 Mexican culture and its emotional contradictions. *Journal of Health and Social Behavior* 25:2–13.

Mirowsky, J. & Ross, C. E. 1989 *Social Causes of Psychological Distress.* New York: Aldine de Gruyter.

Mischel, W. 1979 On the interface of cognition and personality: Beyond the person–situation debate. *American Psychologist,* 32:246–254.

Mitchum, N. T. 1989 Increasing self-esteem in Native American children. Elementary School Guidance and Counseling, 23(4):266–271.

Moen, P., Dempster–McLain, D., Williams, R. M. 1992 Successful aging: A new life-course perspective on women's multiple roles and health. *American Journal of Sociology,* 97:1612–1638.

Money, J. 1987 Sin, sickness, or status? Homosexual gender identity and psychoneuroendocrinology. *American Psychologist,* 42(April):384–399.

Moore, J. & Pachon, H. 1985 *Hispanics in the United States.* Englewood Cliffs, NJ: Prentice–Hall.

Morrison, G. C. 1988 *Early Childhood Education Today,* 4th ed. Columbus, OH: Merrill.

Moss, S. Z. & Moss, M. S. 1989 The impact of the death of an elderly sibling: Some considerations of a normative loss. *The American Behavioral Scientist,* 33:94–106.

Mundal, L. D. et al. 1991 Maternal–infant separation at birth among substance using pregnant women: Implications for attachment. *Social Work in Health Care,* 16(1):133–143.

Munroe, R. L. & Munroe, R. H. 1971 Male pregnancy symptoms and cross-sex identity in three societies. *The Journal of Social Psychology,* 84:11–25.

Murdock, G. P. 1934 *Our Primitive Contemporaries.* New York: MacMillan.

Mutran, E. 1985 Intergenerational family support among blacks and whites: Response to culture and socioeconomic differences. *Journal of Gerontology,* 40:382–389.

Myers, H. F. et al. 1992 Parental and family predictors of behavior problems in inner-city black children. *American Journal of Community Psychology,* 20(5):557–576.

National Commission to Prevent Infant Mortality 1987 *Perinatal AIDS.*

National Indian Council on Aging 1981 1981 White House Conference on Aging: The Indian issues. *National Indian Council on Aging Quarterly,* 4(1).

National Institute of Mental Health. 1986 Use of inpatient psychiatric services by children and youth under age 18, United States, 1980. Mental Health Statistical Note No. 175. Washington, DC: U.S. Department of Health and Human Services.

Neff, J. A., Holamon, B., & Schluter, T. D. 1995 Spousal violence among Anglos, Blacks, and Mexican Americans: The role of demographic variables, psychosocial predictors, and alcohol consumption. *Journal of Family Violence,* 10(1):13–24.

Nelson, K. E., Saunders, E. J., & Landsman, M. J. 1993 Chronic child neglect in perspective. *Social Work,* 38(6):661–671.

Nelson, M. D. 1992 Socioeconomic status and childhood mortality in North Carolina. *American Journal of Public Health,* 82(8):1131–1133.

Newman, B. M. & Newman, P. R. 1975 *Development Through Life: A Psychosocial Approach.* Homewood, IL: Dorsey Press.

Newman, B. S. 1989 The relative importance of gender role attitudes to male and female attitudes toward lesbians. *Sex Roles,* 21(October):451–465.

Newman, J. L., Roberts, L. R., & Syre, C. R. 1993 Concepts of family among children and adolescents: Effect of cognitive level, gender, and family structure. *Developmental Psychology,* 29(November): 951–962.

Nichols, M. 1990 Lesbian relationships: Implications for the study of sexuality and gender. In McWhirter, D. P. et al. (Eds.), *Homosexuality/Heterosexuality: Concepts of Sexual Orientation.* New York: Oxford University Press, pp. 350–367.

Nolen–Hoeksema, S. 1987 Sex differences in unipolar depression: Evidence and theory. *Psychological Bulletin,* 101:259–282.

Notelovitz, M. 1987 Climacteric medicine: Cornerstone for mid-life health and wellness. *Public Health Reports,* (supp.):116–123.

Novello, A. C. et al. 1991 Hispanic health: Time for data, time for action. *Journal of the American Medical Association,* 265(2):253–255.

O'Connor, D. & Wolfe, D. M. 1991 From crisis to growth at mid-life: Changes in personal paradigm. *Journal of Organizational Behavior,* 12(4):323–340.

O'Keefe, M. 1994 Racial/ethnic differences among battered women and their children. *Journal of Child and Family Studies,* 3(3):283–305.

Oboler, R. S. 1980 Is the female husband a man? Woman/woman marriage among the Nandi of Kenya. *Ethnology,* 19(1):69–88.

Office of Child Support Enforcement. 1988 *Twelfth Annual Report to Congress for the Period Ending September 30, 1987.* Washington, DC: U.S. Government Printing Office.

Okun, L. 1986 *Woman Abuse: Facts Replacing Myths.* Albany: State University of New York Press.

Olson, M. K. & Haynes, J. A. 1993 Successful single parents. *Families in Society,* 74(5):259–267.

Olvera–Ezzell, N., Power, T. G., & Cousins, J. H. 1994 The development of health knowledge in low-income Mexican-American children. *Child Development,* 65(April):416–427.

Ortega, S. T., Metroka, M. J., & Johnson, D. R. 1993 In sickness and in health: Age, social support, and psychological consequences of physical health among rural and urban residents. In C. N. Bull (Ed.), *Aging in Rural America.* Newbury Park: Sage, pp. 101–116.

Otten, M. W. et al. 1990 The effect of known risk factors on the excess mortality of black adults in the United States. *Journal of the American Medical Association,* 263(6):845–850.

Oyen, E. 1992 Some basic issues in comparative poverty research. *International Social Science Journal,* 44:615–626.

Padgett, D. 1988 Aging minority women: Issues in research and health policy. *Women and Health,* 14(3–4):213–225.

Padilla, Y. C. 1990 Social science theory on the Mexican American experience. *Social Service Review,* 64(3):261–275.

Parillo, V. N. 1994 *Strangers to These Shores.* New York: Macmillan Publishing.

Parish, T. S. & Wigle, S. 1985 A longitudinal study of the impact of parental divorce on adolescents' evaluation of self and parents. *Adolescence,* 20: 239–244.

Parish, T. S. 1987 Family and Environment. In V. B. Van Hasselt and M. Hersen (Eds.), *Handbook of Adolescent Psychology.* New York: Pergamon.

Parker, B. L. & Drummond–Reeves, S. J. 1993 Death of a dyad: Relational autopsy, analysis and aftermath. *Journal of Divorce and Remarriage,* 21(1/2):95–120.

Paton, R. N., Huber, R., & Netting, F. E. 1994 The long-term care ombudsman program and complaints of abuse and neglect: What have we learned? *Journal of Elder Abuse and Neglect*, 6(1):97–115.

Patterson, G. 1982 *Coercive Family Process*. Eugene, OR: Castalia Publishing Co.

Penning, M. J. & Chappell, N. L. 1993 Health promotion and disadvantaged elderly: Rural–urban differences. In C. N. Bull (Ed.), *Aging in Rural America*. Newbury Park: Sage, pp. 117–133.

Peplau, L. A. & Cochran, S. D. 1990 A relational perspective on homosexuality. In McWhirter, D. P. et al. (Eds.), *Homosexuality/Heterosexuality: Concepts of Sexual Orientation*. New York: Oxford University Press, pp. 321–349.

Peters, D. F., Wilson, S. M. & Peterson, G. W. 1986 Adolescents and rural Appalachian Families. In G. K. Leigh & G. W. Peterson (Eds), *Adolescents in Families*. Cincinnati: Southwestern Publishers, pp. 456–471.

Peters, D. K. & Cantrell, P. J. 1991 Factors distinguishing samples of lesbian and heterosexual women. *Journal of Homosexuality*, 21(4):1–15.

Peterson, A. C., Sargiani, P. A., & Kennedy, R. E. 1991 Adolescent depression: Why more girls? *Journal of Youth and Adolescence*, 20(2):247–256.

Petti, T. A. & Larson, C. N. 1987 Depression and suicide. In V. B. Van Hasselt & M. Hersen (Eds.), *Handbook of Adolescent Psychology*. New York: Pergamon.

Piechowski, L. D. 1992 Mental health and women's multiple roles. *Families in Society*, 73(3):131–141.

Pillemer, K. & Finkelhor, D. 1989 Causes of elder abuse: Caregiver stress versus problem relatives. *American Journal of Orthopsychiatry*, 59(2):179–187.

Pittman, J. F., Wright, C. A., & Lloyd, S. A. 1989 Predicting parenting difficulty. *Journal of Family Issues*, 10:267–286.

Pitts, K. S. & Weinstein, L. 1990 Cocaine and pregnancy: A lethal combination. *Journal of Perinatology*, 10:180–182.

Porter, J. R. & Washington, R. E. 1993 Minority identity and self-esteem. *Annual Review of Sociology*, 19:139–161.

Portes, P. R. et al. 1992 Family functions and children's postdivorce adjustment. *American Journal of Orthopsychiatry*, 62(4):613–617.

Potter, L. B. 1991 Socioeconomic determinants of white and black males' life expectancy differentials, 1980. *Demography*, 28(2):303–321.

Prater, G. S. 1992 Child welfare and African-American families. In Cohen, N. A. (Ed.), *Child Welfare: A Multicultural Focus*. Boston: Allyn and Bacon, pp. 84–106.

Pruzinsky, E. W. 1987 Alcohol and the elderly: An overview of problems in the elderly and implications for social work practice. *Journal of Gerontological Social Work:* 11(½):81–93.

Purdy, J. K. & Arguello, D. 1992 Hispanic familism and caretaking of elder adults. *Journal of Gerontological Social Work*, 19(2):29–43.

Pyant, C. T. & Yanico, B. J. 1991 Relationship of racial identity and gender–role attitudes to black women's psychological well-being. *Journal of Counseling Psychology*, 38(3):315–322.

Quinn, P. K. & Reznikoff, M. 1985 The relationship between death anxiety and the subjective experience of time in the elderly. *International Journal of Aging and Human Development*, 21(3):197–210.

Rafferty, Y. & Rollins, N. 1989 *Learning to Limbo*. New York: Advocates for Children.

Rakowski, W. & Hickey, T. 1992 Mortality and the attribution of health problems to aging among older adults. *American Journal of Public Health*, 82:1139–1141.

Rappaport, J. 1977 *Community Psychology: Values, Research, and Action*. New York: Holt, Rinehart and Winston.

Raschke, H. C. 1987 Divorce. In M. B. Sussman & S. K. Steinmetz (Eds.), *Handbook of Marriage and the Family*. New York: Plenum, pp. 597–624.

Rawlings, S. W. 1993 Household and family characteristics: March 1993. U.S. Bureau of the Census. Current Population Reports, Series P-20–477. Washington, DC: U.S. Government Printing Office.

Rawlins, W. K. 1992 *Friendship Matters: Communication, Dialectics, and the Life Course*. New York: Aldine de Gruyter.

Red Horse, J. 1982 American Indian and Alaskan Native elders: A policy critique. In E. P. Stanford & S. A. Lockery (Eds.), *Trends and Status of Minority Aging*. San Diego: San Diego State University, pp. 15–26.

Redick, L. T. & Wood, B. 1982 Cross-cultural problems for Southeast Asian refugee minors. *Child Welfare*, 61(June):365–373.

Reid, K. E. 1991 *Social Work Practice with Groups: A Clinical Perspective*. Pacific Grove, CA: Brooks/Cole.

Reinke, B. J. 1985 Psychosocial changes as a function of chronological age. *Human Development*, 28(5): 266–269.

Reisberg et al. 1989 The stage of specific temporal course of Alzheimer's disease: Functional and behavioral concomitants based upon cross-sectional and longitudinal observation. *Progress in Clinical and Biological Research*, 317:23–41.

Reiter, L. 1989 Sexual orientation, sexual identity, and the question of choice. *Clinical Social Work Journal*, 17:139–150.

Rendely, J. G., Holmstrom, R. M., & Karp, S. A. 1984 The relationship of sex-role identity, life style, and mental health in suburban American homemakers: Sex role, employment, and adjustment. *Sex Roles*, 11:839–848.

Repetti, R. L. et al. 1989 Employment and women's health: Effects of paid employment on women's mental and physical health. *American Psychologist*, 44(November):1394–1401.

Reskin, B. & Padavic, I. 1994 *Men and Women at Work.* Thousand Oaks, CA: Pine Forge Press.

Resnick, R. 1986 Age related changes in gestation and pregnancy outcome. In L. Mastroianni, Jr. & C. A. Paulsen (Eds.), *Aging, Reproduction, and the Climacteric.* New York: Plenum Press, pp. 167–177.

Ricci, J. M., Fojaco, R. M., & O'Sullivan, J. J. 1989 Congenital syphilis: The University of Miami/Jackson Memorial Medical Center experience, 1986–1988. *Obstetrics and Gynecology*, 74:687–693.

Rich, B. R. & Arguelles, L. 1985 Homosexuality, homophobia, and revolution: Notes toward an understanding of the Cuban lesbian and gay male experience, part 2. *Signs*, 11(1):120–136.

Richards, L. N. & Schmiege, C. J. 1993 Problems and strengths of single parent families: Implications for practice and policy. *Family Relations*, 42: 277–285.

Ricks, M. H. 1985 The social transmission of parenting: attachment across generations. In I. Bretherton & E. Waters (Eds.), *Growing Points of Attachment: Theory and Research. Monographs of the Society for Research in Child Development*, 50(No. 209), pp. 211–227.

Riley, K. P. 1994 Depression. In Bonder, B. R. & Wagner, M. B. (Eds.), *Functional Performance in Older Adults.* Philadelphia: F. A. Davis Co., pp. 256–268.

Robertson, I. 1987 *Sociology*, 3rd ed. New York: Worth.

Rodriguez, C. E. & Cordero–Guzman, H. 1992 Placing race in context. *Ethnic and Racial Studies*, 15(October):523–542.

Rodway, M. R. 1986 Systems theory. In F. J. Turner (Ed.), *Social Work Treatment: Interlocking Theoretical Approaches.* New York: Free Press, pp. 514–540.

Roff, J. D. & Wirt, R. D. 1984 Childhood social adjustment, adolescent status, and young adult mental health. *American Journal of Orthopsychiatry*, 54: 595–602.

Rogeness, G. A. et al. 1986 Psychopathology in abused and neglected children. *Journal of the American Academy of Child Psychiatry*, 25:659–665.

Rogers, D. 1986 *The Adult Years: An Introduction to Aging.* Englewood Cliffs, NJ: Prentice–Hall.

Rogers, R. G. 1992 Living and dying in the U.S.A.: Sociodemographic determinants of death among blacks and whites. *Demography*, 29(May): 287–303.

Rogers, S. M. & Turner, C. F. 1991 Male–male sexual contact in the U.S.A.: Findings from five sample surveys, 1970–1990. *Journal of Sex Research*, 28(November):491–519.

Rogot, E. et al. 1992 *A Mortality Study of 1.3 Million Persons by Demographic, Social, and Economic Factors: U.S. National Longitudinal Mortality Study.* Bethesda, MD: National Institutes of Health.

Rose, J. H. 1991 A life course perspective on health threats in aging. *Journal of Gerontological Social Work*, 17(3–4):85–97.

Rosenblith, J. F. 1992 *In the Beginning: Development from Conception to Age Two*, 2nd ed. Newbury Park: Sage Publications.

Rosenzweig, J. M. & Lebow, W. C. 1992 Femme on the streets, butch in the sheets? Lesbian sex-roles, dyadic adjustment, and sexual satisfaction. *Journal of Homosexuality*, 23(3):1–20.

Ross, M. W. & Arrindell, W. A. 1988 Perceived parental rearing patterns of homosexual and heterosexual men. *Journal of Sex Research*, 24:275–281.

Ross, M. W. 1989 Married homosexual men: Prevalence and background. *Marriage & Family Review*, 14(¾):35–57.

Ross, M. W. 1992 Understanding the homosexual patient. In Dynes, W. R. & Malden, D. (Eds.), *Homosexuality and Medicine.* New York: Garland.

Ross, M. W., Paulsen, J. A., & Stalström, O. W. 1988 Homosexuality and mental health: A cross-cultural review. *Journal of Homosexuality,* 15(1–2): 131–152.

Rotheram–Borus, M. J. & Phinney, J. S. 1990 Patterns of social expectations among black and Mexican-American children. *Child Development,* 61(April): 542–556.

Rotnem, D. 1989 An examination of the association between maternal depression and the behavioral functioning of school-aged children. *Smith College Studies in Social Work,* 59:55–66.

Rowe, J. W. & Minaker, K. L. 1985 Geriatric medicine. In Finch, C. E. & Schneider, E. L. (Eds.), *Handbook of the Biology of Aging.* New York: Van Nostrand Reinhold Co., pp. 932–960.

Rubin, C. et al. 1992 Depressive affect in "normal" adolescents: Relationship to life stress, family, and friends. *American Journal of Orthopsychiatry,* 62(3):430–441.

Rubin, J. L., Provenzano, F. J., & Luria, Z. 1974 The eye of the beholder: Parents' views on sex of newborns. *American Journal of Orthopsychiatry,* 4:512–519.

Rubin, L. B. 1976 *Worlds of Pain: Life in the Working-Class Family.* New York: Basic Books.

St. Clair, M. 1986 *Object Relations and Self Psychology: An Introduction.* Monterey: Brooks/Cole.

Sagarin, E., (Ed.) 1971 *The Other Minorities: Nonethnic Collectivities Conceptualized as Minority Groups.* Waltham, MA: Xerox College Publishing.

Sakauye, K. 1992 The elderly Asian patient. *Journal of Geriatric Psychiatry,* 25(1):85–104.

Salholz, E. et al. 1990 The future of gay America. *Newsweek,* 115(11):20–26.

Saluter, A. F. 1994 Marital Status and Living Arrangements: March, 1993. U.S. Bureau of the Census, Current Population Reports, Series P20–478. Washington, DC: U.S. Government Printing Office.

Salzinger, S., Feldman, R. S., & Hammer, M. 1993 The effects of physical abuse on children's social relationships. *Child Development,* 64(February): 169–187.

Sameroff, A. J. 1986 Environmental context of child development. *Journal of Pediatrics,* 109:192–200.

Sanchez, C. D. 1992 Mental health issues: The elderly Hispanic. *Journal of Geriatric Psychiatry,* 25(2): 69–84.

Sandberg, D. E., Brook, A. E., & Campos, S. P. 1994 Short stature: A psychosocial burden requiring growth hormone therapy? *Pediatrics,* 94(6): 832–840.

Sanderson, S. K. 1988 *Macrosociology.* New York: Harper & Row.

Sands, R. G. 1991 *Clinical Social Work Practice in Community Mental Health.* New York: Merrill.

Sang, B. 1991 Moving toward balance and integration. In Sang, B., Warshow, J., & Smith, A. J. (Eds.), *Lesbians at Mid-life: The Creative Transition.* San Francisco: Spinsters Book Company, pp. 206–214.

Sang, B., Warshow, J., & Smith, A. J. (Eds.) 1991 *Lesbians at Mid-life: The Creative Transition.* San Francisco: Spinsters Book Company.

Schachere, K. 1990 Attachment between working mothers and their infants: The influence of family processes. *American Journal of Orthopsychiatry,* 60(1):19–34.

Schaefer, R. T. 1993 *Racial and Ethnic Groups.* New York: Harper Collins.

Scharlach, A. E. & Fredrikson, K. I. 1993 Reactions to the death of a parent during mid-life. *Omega,* 27(4):307–319.

Schlesinger, B. 1989 The "sandwich generation:" Middle-aged families under stress. *Canada's Mental Health,* 37(3):11–14.

Schnayer, R. & Orr, R. R. 1989 A comparison of children living in single-mother and single-father families. *Journal of Divorce,* 12(2/3):171–184.

Schoenfeld, D. E. et al. 1994 Self-rated health and mortality in the high functioning elderly—a closer look at healthy individuals: MacArthur field study of successful aging. *Journal of Gerontology,* 49:109–115.

Schonfeld, L. & Dupree, L. W. 1991 Antecedents of drinking for early- and late-onset elderly alcohol abusers. *Journal of Studies on Alcohol,* 52: 587–592.

Schor, J. B. 1991 *The Overworked American: The Unexpected Decline of Leisure.* New York: Basic Books.

Sebald, H. 1977. *Adolescence: A Social Psychological Analysis.* Englewood Cliffs, NJ: Prentice–Hall.

Segal, E. A. 1991 The juvenilization of poverty in the 1980s. *Social Work,* 36(5):454–457.

Segroi, S. M. 1982 *Handbook of Clinical Intervention in Child Sexual Abuse.* Lexington, MA: D.C. Heath.

Seltzer, V. C. 1989 *The Psychological Worlds of the Adolescent: Public and Private.* New York: John Wiley & Sons.

Sena–Rivera, C. 1980 La familia Hispana as a natural support system: Strategies for prevention in mental health. In R. Valle & W. Vega (Eds.), *Hispanic Natural Support Systems*. Sacramento: State of California Department of Mental Health.

Sennett, R. & Cobb, J. 1973 *The Hidden Injuries of Class*. New York: Vintage Books.

Shafii, M., Carrigan, S., Whittinghill, J. R., & Derrick, A. 1985 Psychological autopsy of completed suicide in children and adolescents: A comparative study. *American Journal of Psychiatry*, 142: 1061–1064.

Shinn, M. 1978 Father absence and children's cognitive development. *Psychological Bulletin*, 85:295–324.

Shon, S. P. & Ja, D. Y. 1982 Asian families. In M. McGoldrick, J. K. Pearce, & J. Giordano, (Eds.), *Ethnicity and Family Therapy*. New York: Guilford Press.

Siegel, J. M. & Kuykendall, D. H. 1990 Loss, widowhood, and psychological distress among the elderly. *Journal of Consulting and Clinical Psychology*, 58:519–524.

Simmons, R. G., Blyth, D. A., & McKinney, K. L. 1983 The social and psychological effects of puberty on white females. In J. Brooks–Gunn & A. C. Peterson (Eds.), *Girls at Puberty: Biological and Psychosocial Aspects*. New York: Plenum, 229–272.

Sinclair, D. C. 1989 *Human Growth After Birth*. Oxford: Oxford University Press.

Singleton, C. 1987 Sex roles in cognition. In Hargreaves, D. J. & Colley, A. M. (Eds.), *The Psychology of Sex Roles*. Cambridge, MA: Hemisphere Publishing, pp. 60–93.

Singleton, E. G., Harrell, J. P., & Kelly, L. M. 1986 Racial differentials in the impact of maternal cigarette smoking during pregnancy on fetal development and mortality: Concerns for black psychologists. *Journal of Black Psychology*, 12:71–83.

Small, S A., Eastman, G., & Cornelius, S. 1988 Adolescent autonomy and parental stress. *Journal of Youth and Adolescence*, 17:377–391.

Smetana, J. G., Yau, J., Restrepo, A., & Braeges, J. L. 1991 Adolescent–parent conflict in married and divorced families. *Developmental Psychology*, 27: 1000–1010.

Smith, C. & Lloyd, B. 1978 Maternal behavior and perceived sex of infant: Revisited. *Child Development*, 49:1263–1265.

Smith, D. F. & Allred, G. H. 1990 Adjustment of women divorced from homosexual men: An exploratory study. *American Journal of Family Therapy*, 18(Fall):273–284.

Smith, J. M. 1996 *AIDS and Society*. Upper Saddle River, NJ: Prentice Hall.

Smith, K. R. & Moen, P. 1988 Passage through midlife: Women's changing family roles and economic well-being. *The Sociological Quarterly*, 29: 503–524.

Smith, L. A. 1988 Black adolescent fathers: Issues for service provision. *Social Work*, 33(3):269–271.

Snow, L. J. & Parsons, J. L. 1983 Sex role orientation and female sexual functioning. *Psychology of Women Quarterly*, 8(Winter):133–143.

Sorenson, S. B., Richardson, B. A., & Peterson, J. G. 1993 Race/ethnicity patterns in the homicide of children in Los Angeles, 1980 through 1989. *American Journal of Public Health*, 83(5): 725–727.

Specht, R. & Craig, G. J. 1987 *Human Development: A Social Work Perspective*. Englewood Cliff, NJ: Prentice Hall.

Spence, A. P. 1989 *Biology of Human Aging*. Englewood Cliffs, NJ: Prentice–Hall.

Spence, J. T. & Helmreich, R. L. 1978 *Masculinity and Femininity: Their Psychological Dimensions, Correlates, and Antecedents*. Austin: University of Texas Press.

Sroufe, L. A. 1985 Attachment classification from perspective of infant–caregiver relationships and infant temperament. *Child Development*, 56:1–14.

Sroufe, L. A., Fox, N. E., & Pancake, V. R. 1983 Attachment and dependency in developmental perspective. *Child Development*, 54:317–325.

Stafford, I. P. 1984 Relation of attitudes toward women's roles and occupational behavior to women's self-esteem. *Journal of Counseling Psychology*, 31(July):332–338.

Statistical Abstract of the United States. 1992 Washington, DC: U.S. Bureau of the Census.

Stein, J. A et al. 1991 The influence of ethnicity, socioeconomic status, and psychological barriers on use of mammography. *Journal of Health and Social Behavior*, 32(June):101–113.

Steinberg, K. K. 1987 Women's health: Osteoporosis. *Public Health Reports*, (supp.):125–127.

Steinberg, L. 1990 Autonomy, conflict and harmony in the family relationship. In S. S. Feldman & G. R. Elliod (Eds.), *At the Threshold: The Developing Adolescent*. Cambridge, MA: Harvard University Press, 255–276.

Steinberg, L., Elmen, J. D., & Mount, N. S. 1989 Authoritative parenting, psycho-social maturity, and academic success among adolescents. *Child Development,* 60:1424–1436.

Steinberg, S. 1981 *The Ethnic Myth: Race, Ethnicity, and Class in America.* New York: Atheneum.

Stern, D. N. 1985 *The Interpersonal World of the Infant.* New York: Basic Books.

Sternberg, K. J. et al. 1993 Effects of domestic violence on children's behavior problems and depression. *Developmental Psychology,* 29(1):44–52.

Stewart, W. A. 1977 A psychosocial study of early adult life structures in women. Unpublished doctoral dissertation, Columbia University.

Stolar, G. E., MacEntee, M. I., & Hill, P. 1993 The elderly: Their perceived supports and reciprocal behaviors. *Journal of Gerontological Social Work,* 19(3–4):15–33.

Storms, M. D. 1981 A theory of erotic orientation development. *Psychological Review,* 88:340–353.

Straus, M., Gelles, R. & Steinmetz, S. 1980 *Behind Closed Doors: Violence in the American Family.* Garden City, NY: Doubleday.

Sue, D. W. 1981 *Counseling the Culturally Different.* New York: John Wiley & Sons.

Sue, S. & McKinney, H. 1980 Asian Americans in the community mental health care system. In R. Endo, S. Sue, and N. N. Wagner, (Eds.), *Asian Americans: Social and Psychological Perspectives,* 2. Palo Alto: Science and Behavior Books.

Sumner, W. G. 1906 *Folkways.* Boston: Ginn.

Sutherland, A. 1975 *Gypsies: The Hidden Americans.* New York: Free Press.

Szalai, A. (Ed.) 1972 *The Use of Time: Daily Activities of Urban and Suburban Populations in Twelve Countries.* The Hague: Mouton.

Tajfel, H. 1978 *Differentiation between Social Groups.* London: Academic Press.

Tajfel, H. 1981 *Human Groups and Social Categories.* Cambridge: Cambridge University Press.

Tamir, L. M. 1989 Modern myths about men at midlife: An assessment. In Hunter, S. and Sundel, M. (Eds.), *Mid-life Myths: Issues, Findings, and Practice Implications.* Newbury Park, CA: Sage, pp. 157–179.

Tannen, D. 1990 *You Just Don't Understand: Women and Men in Conversation.* New York: Morrow.

Taylor, R. L. 1994 Black American families. In Taylor, R. L. (Ed.), *Minority Families in the United States: A Multicultural Perspective.* Englewood Cliffs, NJ: Prentice-Hall, pp. 19–46.

Terkel, S. 1972 *Working: People Talk About What They Do All Day and How They Feel About What They Do.* New York: Pantheon Books.

Thomas, R. M. 1985 *Comparing Theories of Child Development,* 2nd ed. Belmont, CA: Wadsworth.

Thomas, V. G. & Shields, L. C. 1987 Gender influences on work values of black adolescents. *Adolescence,* 22:37–43.

Thompson, L. W., Breckenridge, J. N., Gallagher, D., & Peterson, J. 1984 Effects of bereavement on self-perceptions of physical health in elderly widows and widowers. *Journal of Gerontology,* 39(3): 309–314.

Thompson, M. S. & Peebles–Wilkins, W. 1992 The impact of formal, informal, and societal support networks on the psychologial well-being of black adolescent mothers. *Social Work,* 37(4):322–329.

Thompson, R. A., Lamb, M., & Estes, D. 1982 Stability of infant–mother attachment and its relationship to changing life circumstances in an unselected middle class sample. *Child Development,* 53:144–148.

Thompson, V. S. 1992 A multifaceted approach to the conceptualization of African American identification. *Journal of Black Studies,* 23(1):75–85.

Thompson, W. E. & Hickey, J. V. 1994 *Society in Focus.* New York: HarperCollins.

Thornberg, H. D. 1982 *Development in Adolescence.* Monterrey: Brooks/Cole.

Tiedje, L. B., Wortman, C. B., & Downey, G. 1990 Women with multiple roles: Role-compatibility perceptions, satisfaction, and mental health. *Journal of Marriage and Family,* 52:63–72.

Tobin, S. S. & Lieberman, M. A. 1976 *Last Home for the Aged.* San Francisco: Jossey–Bass.

Tonnies, F. (1957; originally published 1887) *Community and Society.* East Lansing, MI: Michigan State University Press.

Tower, C. C. 1993 *Understanding Child Abuse and Neglect.* Allyn and Bacon: Boston.

Tung, M. 1991 Insight-oriented psychotherapy and the Chinese patient. *American Journal of Orthopsychiatry,* 61(2):186–94.

Turner, J. C. 1982 Towards a cognitive redefinition of the social group. In *Social Identity and Intergroup Relations,* H. Tajfel (Ed.), Cambridge: Cambridge University Press, pp. 17–40.

Turner, J. H. 1982 *The Structure of Sociological Theory.* Homewood, Ill.: Dorsey Press.

Turner, J. S. & Rubinson, L. 1993 *Contemporary Human Sexuality.* Englewood Cliffs, NJ: Prentice-Hall.

U.S. Bureau of the Census 1990 *Census of the Population.* Washington, DC: Government Printing Office.

U.S. Bureau of the Census 1992 Current Population Reports, Special Studies, P23–178RV, *Sixty-five Plus in America.* Washington, DC: U.S. Government Printing Office.

U.S. Bureau of the Census. 1994 *Statistical Abstract of the United States.* Washington, DC: U.S. Government Printing Office.

U.S. Census. 1991 *Census of the Population.* Washington, DC: U.S. Bureau of the Census.

U.S. Census. 1991 Measuring the effects of benefits and taxes on income on poverty:1990. Current population reports, Series P-60, No. 176-RD. Washington, DC: U.S. Government Printing Office.

U.S. Department of Health & Human Services. 1987 *Report of the Surgeon General's Workshop on Children with HIV Infection and Their Families.*

U.S. Department of Health & Human Services. 1988 Special report: Pediatric HIV infections. *Children Today,* 17(3).

U.S. Department of Health and Human Services 1992 *Health United States and Healthy People 2000 Review.* Publication No. 93–1232. Hyattsville, MD: Department of Health and Human Services.

U.S. Department of Health and Human Services 1990 Study findings: Study of national incidence and prevalence of child abuse and neglect. (DHHS Publication No. (OHDS) 20–01099). Washington, DC: Author.

U.S. Department of Labor 1965 *The Negro Family: The Case for National Action,* Washington, D.C.: U.S. Government Printing Office.

U.S. National Center for Health Statistics 1991 *Advance Report of Final Divorce Statistics 1988.* Washington, DC: U.S. Government Printing Office.

Ulbrich, P. M., Warheit, G. J., & Zimmerman, R. S. 1989 Race, socioeconomic status, and psychological distress: An examination of differential vulnerability. *Journal of Health and Social Behavior,* 30(1):131–147.

United Nations 1995 *Demographic Yearbook.* New York: United Nations.

Valdiserri, E. V. 1986 Fear of AIDS: Implications for mental health practice with reference to ego-dys-tonic homosexuality. *American Journal of Orthopsychiatry,* 56(October):634–638.

Valentine, D. P. 1982 The experience of pregnancy: A developmental process. *Family Relations,* 31: 243–248.

Valliant, G. E. & Valliant, C. O. 1990 Natural history of male psychological health, a 45-year study of predictors of successful aging at age 65. *The American Journal of Psychiatry,* 147:31–37.

Van den Berghe, P. 1967 *Race and Racism.* New York: John Wiley & Sons.

Van der Geest, H. 1993 Homosexuality and marriage. *Journal of Homosexuality,* 24(3/4):115–123.

Veevers, J. E. 1991 Traumas vs. stress: A paradigm of positive versus negative divorce outcomes. *Journal of Divorce and Remarriage,* 15(1/2):99–126.

Verbrugge, L. M. & Madans, J. H. 1985 Social roles and health trends of American women. *Milbank Fund Quarterly/Health and Society,* 63:691–735.

Verbrugge, L. M. 1985 Gender and health: an update on hypotheses and evidence. *Journal of Health and Social Behavior,* 26:156–82.

Verbrugge, L. M. 1989 The twain meet: Empirical explanations of sex differences in health and mortality. *Journal of Health and Social Behavior,* 30: 282–304.

Vincent, C. E. 1966 Familia Spongia: The adaptive family. *Journal of Marriage and the Family,* 28:29–36.

Virgil, D. 1979 Adaptation strategies and cultural life styles in Mexican-American adolescents. *Hispanic Journal of Behavioral Sciences,* 1:375–392.

Visher, E. B. & Visher, J. S. 1988 *Old Loyalties, New Ties: Therapeutic Strategies with Stepfamilies.* New York: Brunner/Mazel.

Vital & Health Statistics 1990 Health of black and white Americans: 1985–1987. Washington, DC: U.S. Department of Health and Human Services.

Vital Statistics of the United States 1992 National Center for Health Statistics. Washington, DC: Public Health Service, U.S. Government Printing Office.

Vital Statistics, Monthly Report. 1992 Vol. 40, No. 8(S)2. January 7.

Vondra, J. I., Barnett, D., & Cicchetti, D. 1990 Self-concept, motivation and competence among preschoolers from maltreating and comparison families. *Child Abuse and Neglect,* 14:535–540.

Vosler, N. R. & Proctor, E. K. 1991 Family structure and stressors in a child guidance clinic population.

Families in Society: The Journal of Contemporary Human Services, 72(3):164–173.

Wagner, K. D. & Lorion, R. P. 1984 Correlates of death anxiety in elderly persons. *Journal of Clinical Psychology,* 40:1235–1241.

Waite, L. J. & Lillard, L. A. 1991 Children and marital disruption. *American Journal of Sociology,* 96(4): 930–953.

Walker, C. E., Bonner, B. L., & Kaufman, K. L. 1988 *The Physically and Sexually Abused Child: Evaluation and Treatment.* New York: Pergamon Press.

Walker, L. E. 1979 *The Battered Woman.* New York: Harper & Row.

Wall, J. C. 1992 Maintaining the connection: Parenting as a noncustodial father. *Child and Adolescent Social Work Journal,* 9(5):441–456.

Wallerstein, J. & Kelly, J. 1980 *Surviving the Break-up: How Children Actually Cope with Divorce.* New York: Basic Books.

Wallerstein, J. S. & Blakeslee, S. 1989 *Second Chances: Men, Women, and Children a Decade after Divorce.* New York: Ticknor & Fields.

Wallerstein, J. S. 1985 The overburdened child: Some long-term consequences of divorce. *Social Work,* 30(2):116–123.

Wallerstein, J. S. 1987 Children of divorce: Report of a ten-year follow-up of early latency-age children. *American Journal of Orthopsychiatry,* 57(2): 199–211.

Walster, E. & Walster, G. W. 1978 *A New Look at Love.* Reading, MA: Addison–Wesley.

Warren, K. R. & Bast, R. J. 1988 Alcohol-related birth defects: An update. *Public Health Reports,* 103 (Nov/Dec):638–642.

Warren, R. L. 1978 *The Community in America.* Chicago: Rand McNally.

Warriner, C. K. 1970 *The Emergence of Society.* Homewood, IL: Dorsey Press.

Waters, E. 1978 The reliability and stability of individual differences in infant–mother attachment. *Child Development,* 49:483–494.

Weinstein, E. & Rosen, E. 1991 The development of adolescent sexual intimacy: Implications for counseling. *Adolescence,* 26(102):331–339.

Weitzman, L. J. 1985 *The Divorce Revolution: The Unexpected Social and Economic Consequences for Women and Children in America.* New York: Free Press.

Weller, R. H. & Bouvier, L. F. 1981 *Population: Demography and Policy.* New York: St. Martin's Press.

Wertlieb, E. C. 1985 Minority group status of the disabled. *Human Relations,* 38:1047–1063.

Westman, A. S., Canter, F. M., & Boitos, T. M. 1984 Denial of fear of dying or of death in young and elderly populations. *Psychological Reports,* 55: 413–414.

Whitbourne, S. K. 1985 *The Aging Book.* New York: Springer-Verlag.

White, J. L. 1984 *The Psychology of Blacks: An Afro-American Perspective.* Englewood Cliffs, NJ: Prentice-Hall.

White, L. K. 1990 Determinants of divorce: A review of research in the eighties. *Journal of Marriage and the Family,* 52:904–912.

Whiting, L. 1976 Defining emotional neglect. *Children Today,* 5:2–5.

Whitley, B. E. 1990 The relationship of heterosexuals' attributions for the causes of homosexuality to attitudes toward lesbians and gay men. *Personality and Social Psychology Bulletin,* 16(June): 369–377.

Whitley, R. J. et al. 1980 The natural history of herpes simplex virus infection of mother and newborn. *Pedatrics,* 66:489–494.

Whittler, T. E., Calantone, R. J., & Young, M. R. 1991 Strength of ethnic affiliation: Examining black identification with black culture. *Journal of Social Psychology,* 131:461–467.

Widmayer, S. M., Peterson, L. M., & Larner, M. 1990 Predictors of Haitian–American infant development at twelve months. *Child Development,* 61(April):410–415.

Widom, C. S. 1989 Does violence beget violence? A critical examination of the literature. *Psychological Bulletin,* 106:449–457.

Wiehe, V. R. 1992 *Working with Child Abuse and Neglect.* Itasca, IL: F. E. Peacock.

Wilkerson, I. 1992 Middle class blacks try to grip a ladder while lending a hand. In Rothenberg, P. S. (Ed.), *Race, Class, and Gender in the United States: An Integrated Study.* New York: St. Martin's Press, 113–119.

Wilkinson, R. G. 1992 National mortality rates: The impact of inequality? *American Journal of Public Health,* 82(8):1082–1084.

Williamson, J. M., Borduin, C. M., & Howe, B. A. 1991 The ecology of adolescent maltreatment: A multilevel examination of adolescent physical abuse, sexual abuse, and neglect. *Journal of Consulting and Clinical Psychology,* 59:449–457.

Willis, C. V. & Greenblatt, S. L. 1978 Four "classic" studies of power relationships in black families: A review and a look to the future. *Journal of Marriage and the Family,* 40(4):691–697.

Wilson, M. & Daly, M. 1987 Risk of maltreatment of children living with stepparents. In R. J. Gelles & J. B. Lancaster (Eds.), *Child Abuse and Neglect.* New York: Aldine de Gruyter.

Wilson, M. L. 1984 Female homosexuals' need for dominance and endurance. *Psychological Reports,* 55(August):79–82.

Wilson, M. R. 1989 Glaucoma in blacks: Where do we go from here? *JAMA,* 261(2):281–282.

Wilson, P. M. 1986 Black culture and sexuality. *Journal of Social Work and Human Sexuality,* 4(3): 29–46.

Winkelstein, M. L. & Carson, V. J. 1987 Adolescents and rooming-in. *Maternal–Child Nursing Journal,* 16(1):765–788.

Wirth, L. 1945 The problem of minority groups. In R. Linton (Ed.), *The Science of Man in the World Crisis.* New York: Columbia University Press, pp. 347–372.

Wiswell, T. 1990 Routine neonatal circumcision: A reappraisal. *American Family Practice,* 41:859–863.

Wodarski, J. S. et al. 1990 Maltreatment and the school-aged child: Major academic, socioemotional and adaptive outcomes. *Social Work,* 35:460–467.

Wolf, J. H., Breslau, N., Ford, A. B., Ziegler, H. D., & Ward, A. (1983) Distance and contacts: Interactions of Black urban elderly adults with family and friends. *Journal of Gerontology,* 38:465–471.

Wolfe, D., O'Conner, D., & Crary, M. 1990 Transformations of life structure and personal paradigm during the middle transition. *Human Relations,* 43(10):957–973.

Wolff, C. 1971 *Love Between Women.* New York: Harper & Row.

Wolock, I. & Horowitz, B. 1984 Child maltreatment as a social problem: The neglect of neglect. *American Journal of Orthopsychiatry,* 54:530–543.

Wood, G. G. & Middleman, R. R. 1989 *The Structural Approach to Direct Practice in Social Work.* New York: Columbia University Press.

Wood, V. & Robertson, J. F. 1978 Friendship and kinship interaction: Differential effect on the morale of the elderly. *Journal of Marriage and the Family,* 40:367–375.

Woodward, J. C. & Frank, B. D. 1988 Rural adolescent loneliness and coping strategies. *Adolescence,* 23(91):559–565.

Woodward, J. C. & Kalyan-Masih, V. 1990 Loneliness, coping strategies, and cognitive styles of the gifted rural adolescent. *Adolescence,* 25(100): 977–988.

Wright, E. O. & Cho D. 1992 State employment, class location, and ideological orientation: A comparative analysis of the United States and Sweden, *Politics and Society,* 20(2):167–197.

Wrightsman, L. S. 1994 *Adult Personality Development: Theories and Concepts.* Volume 1. Thousand Oaks, CA: Sage.

Yankelovich, D. 1981 *New Rules: Searching for Self-Fulfillment in a World Turned Upside Down.* New York: Random House.

Yegidis, B. L. 1992 Family violence: Contemporary research findings and practice issues. *Community Mental Health Journal,* 28(6):519–530.

Yellowbird, M. & Snipp, C. M. 1994 American Indian families. In Taylor, R. L. (Ed.), *Minority Families in the United States: A Multicultural Perspective.* Englewood Cliffs, NJ: Prentice-Hall, pp. 179–201.

Zahn, I. S. et al. 1992 Dependency in urban black families following the birth of an adolescent's child. *Journal of Marriage and Family,* 54(3): 496–507.

Zellner, W. W. 1995 *Countercultures: A Sociological Analysis.* New York: St. Martin's Press.

Zeskind, P. S. 1983 Cross-cultural differences in maternal perceptions of cries of low- and high-risk infants. *Child Development,* 54:1119–1128.

Zilboorg, G. & Henry, G. W. 1941 *A History of Medical Psychology.* New York: W. W. Norton.

Zill, N. & Nord, C. W. 1994 *Running in Place: How American Families are Faring in a Changing Economy and an Individualistic Society.* Washington, DC: Child Trends.

Zimmerman, S. L. 1992 Family trends: What implications for family policy? *Family Relations,* 41(4): 423–429.

Zintz, M. V. 1969 *Education across Cultures.* Dubuque, IA: Kendall/Hunt Publishing.

Zuger, B. 1987 Childhood cross-gender behavior and adult homosexuality. *Archives of Sexual Behavior,* 16(February):85–87.

Zuger, B. 1989 Homosexuality in families of boys with early effeminate behavior: An epidemiological study. *Archives of Sexual Behavior,* 18:155–166.

Zuravin, S. J. & Greif, J. L. 1989 Normative and child maltreating AFDC mothers. *Social Casework,* 70:76–84.

Zuravin, S. J. 1991. Research definitions of child physical abuse and neglect: Current problems. In R. H. Starr, Jr. & D. A. Wolfe (Eds.), *The Effects of Child Abuse and Neglect: Research Issues.* New York: Guilford.

Zweigenhaft, R. L. & Domhoff, G. W. 1991 *Blacks in the White Establishment?: A Study of Race and Class in America.* New Haven: Yale University Press.

INDEX

413

PHOTO CREDITS

Chapter 1: p. 1, ©NASA/The Image Works; p. 6, ©Susan Lapides/Woodfin Camp & Associates; p. 21, ©Robert Harbison. **Chapter 2:** p. 27, ©David Witbeck/The Picture Cube, Inc.; p. 33, ©Vincent Zuber/Custom Medical Stock Photo; p. 53, ©Robert Harbison. **Chapter 3:** p. 61, ©Robert Harbison; p. 67, ©Bob Daemmrich/The Image Works; p. 73, ©John Lei/Stock, Boston. **Chapter 4:** p. 89, ©Mary Ellen Lepionka; p. 95, ©Robert Harbison; p. 112, ©Billy E. Barnes/ Stock, Boston. **Chapter 5:** p. 117, ©David Young-Wolff/PhotoEdit; p. 135, ©Alan Carey/The Image Works; p. 141, ©Elizabeth Crews/Stock, Boston. **Chapter 6:** p. 147, ©Robert Harbison; p. 158, ©Mary Ellen Lepionka; p. 165, ©Robert Harbison. **Chapter 7:** p. 183, ©Robert Harbison; p. 192, The Bettmann Archive; p. 204, ©P. Werner/The Image Works. **Chapter 8:** p. 207, ©Spencer Grant/The Picture Cube, Inc.; p. 210, ©Robert Harbison; p. 225 (a,b) ©J. H. Rieger/University of Louisville. **Chapter 9:** p. 231, ©Daniel Sheehan/The Image Works; p. 242, ©Margot Granitsas/The Image Works; p. 246, ©Mark Harmel/FPG International. **Chapter 10:** p. 261, David Jule Giraudon/Art Resource; p. 269, ©Michael Siluk/The Image Works; p. 278, ©Robert Harbison. **Chapter 11:** p. 287, ©Steve Baratz/The Picture Cube, Inc.; p. 294, AP/Wide World; p. 312, ©Bob Daemmrich/The Image Works. **Chapter 12:** p. 315, ©Mary Ellen Lepionka; p. 317, ©Tony Howarth/Woodfin Camp & Associates; p. 332, ©McLaughlin/The Image Works. **Chapter 13:** p. 335, ©Robert Harbison; p. 339, ©Robert Harbison; p. 354, ©Bob Cramer/The Picture Cube, Inc. **Chapter 14:** p. 357, ©Michael A. Schwarz/The Image Works; p. 367, ©Ron Chapple/FPG International; p. 376, ©Jim Whitmer/Stock, Boston.